CHURCHES UNDER SIEGE
OF PERSECUTION AND ASSIMILATION

Churches under Siege of Persecution and Assimilation

The General Epistles and Revelation

B. J. OROPEZA

Apostasy in the New Testament Communities
VOLUME 3

CASCADE Books • Eugene, Oregon

Churches under Siege of Persecution and Assimilation
The General Epistles and Revelation

Apostasy in the New Testament Communities, vol. 3

Copyright © 2012 B. J. Oropeza. All rights reserved. Except for brief quotations in critical publications or reviews, no part of this book may be reproduced in any manner without prior written permission from the publisher. Write: Permissions, Wipf and Stock Publishers, 199 W. 8th Ave., Suite 3, Eugene, OR 97401.

Cascade Books
An Imprint of Wipf and Stock Publishers
199 W. 8th Ave., Suite 3
Eugene, OR 97401

www.wipfandstock.com

ISBN 13: 978-1-61097-291-8

Cataloging-in-Publication data for series:

Oropeza, B. J., 1961–

    Apostasy in the New Testament Communities / B. J. Oropeza.

    xviii + 326 p. ; 25.4 cm. Includes bibliographical references and indexes.
    Contents:
    v. 1, In the Footsteps of Judas and Other Defectors: The Gospels, Acts, and Johannine Letters.
    v. 2, Jews, Gentiles, and the Opponents of Paul: The Pauline Letters.
    v. 3, Churches under Siege of Persecution and Assimilation: The General Epistles and Revelation.

    ISBN 13: 978-1-61097-289-5 (v. 1); 978-1-61097-290-1 (v. 2); 978-1-61097-291-8 (v. 3); 978-1-61097-206-2 (vols. 1–3)

    1. Apostasy—Biblical teaching. 2. Apostasy—Christianity. 3. Bible N.T.—Theology. I. Title. II. Series.

BS2395 O55 V.3 2012

Manufactured in the U.S.A.

To Jared and Justin

μειζοτέραν οὐκ ἔχω χαρά

Contents

Preface ix

Abbreviations xi

Introduction 1

1. Hebrews: Warnings of Apostasy with No Restoration 3
2. James: Perseverance through Suffering and the Restoration of Jewish-Christian Apostates 71
3. 1 Peter: Identity, Perseverance, and Persecution of Marginalized Christians 105
4. 2 Peter: Denying the *Parousia* and Distorting Paul—Apostate Teachers in the Christian Community 132
5. Jude: Antinomianism and the Vilification of Apostate Church Intruders 154
6. Revelation: Overcoming Assimilation and the Imperial Cult in Asia Minor 175

Conclusion 234

Bibliography 249

Ancient Sources Index 267

Author Index 313

Subjects Index 318

Preface

As in the previous volumes, which cover the Gospels, Acts, and Johannine writings (vol. 1) and Pauline letters (vol. 2), this third and final volume of my work completes a thorough study on the subject of apostasy in the New Testament. In this volume I examine the communities of the General Epistles and Revelation. The communities in Hebrews, James, 1 and 2 Peter, Jude, and the seven churches in Asia Minor are the focus. The letters of John are included with my chapter on the Johannine community in volume one.

In the process of producing this work many have assisted along the way. I wish to thank Shirley Decker Lucke, formerly of Hendrickson Publishers, and Chris Spinks of Cascade Books, for their assistance as my editors. Also a very special thanks goes out to my colleagues, friends, and academic readers who have taken time to provide me with feedback and criticisms on various prepublished versions of chapters and selections in this book. These individuals include Paul Anderson, Richard Ascough, Bart Buhler, Scott Caulley, David deSilva, Don Garlington, Robert Hall, David Horrell, Roy Jeal, Fred Long, Lynn Losie, James McGrath, Mark Nanos, C. K. Robertson, Kenneth Schenck, Kay Smith, Jerry Sumney, Kenneth Waters, Robert Webb, Adam Winn, and Karen Winslow.

At Azusa Pacific University I was able to participate at the Center for Research on Ethics and Values (CREV), headed by Carol Lambert, which allowed me time off my teaching load and the ability to present drafts of some of my chapters to fellow colleagues for their feedback. The CREV participants in fall 2006 included Ruth Anna Abigail, Mark Eaton, Carole Lambert, Daniel Park, Carrie Peirce, Karla Richmond, and Kay Smith; and in fall 2008 the participants were Mark Eaton, Randy Fall, Emily Griesinger, Craig Keen, Carole Lambert, Annie Tsai, and Steven Wentland. I would like to thank also Dr. Mark Eaton for chairing the award committee and choosing me to receive the Beverly Stanford Hardcastle Fellowship (2009–2010), which allowed me time off my teaching duties for a semester. A very special thanks goes out also to my research assistant, Maranatha Wall.

I would also like to thank at APU the School of Theology, headed by David Wright, Russell Duke, and now Scott Daniels (deans), Bill Yarchin and Kenneth Waters (assistant deans), and Kay Smith (chair of biblical studies), for their support and providing me with various types of assistance, time for research, and great colleagues. Colleagues that I have not mentioned already that deserve special mention for helping me with ideas and resources to this book are Ralph Martin, Roger Oakland, and Don Thorsen. I also give a warm thanks to administrative assistants Sheryl Lindsay, Pat Losie, Marilyn Moore, and Laura Smith Webb.

Finally, at APU I also wish to thank Kimberly Battle-Waters and again Carol Lambert for providing me with opportunities to get away to the beautiful Franciscan monastery in Malibu, California, for the annual Faculty Writer's Retreat. Friends, students, and assistants that have helped directly or indirectly with this book and deserve honorable mention include Joel Fowler, Amanda Rudd, Sybil Schlegel, Eric Ciampa, Breonna Wharton, Garret Granitz, Claire Moellenberndt, and Jessica Chessum.

For my sabbatical at the University of Tübingen, I wish to thank Professor Dr. Michael Theobald of the Katholisch-Theologischen Fakultät for graciously inviting me to do research and use the facilities of the Bibliothek des Theologicums, Dr. Thomas Schmeller of the Universität Frankfurt for helping arrange this connection; and Dr. Thomas Scott Caulley, director of the Institut zur Erforschung des Urchristentums, and Dr. Hermann Lichtenberger of the Evangelisch-Theologischen Fakultät, who were kind enough to invite me to present a paper on my research at their seminar. In Tübingen, Timothy Sailors and Petra Keller also deserve special mention for their friendship and assisting me with daily living protocols and use of the university housing and facilities.

Abbreviations

MODERN SOURCES

AB	Anchor Bible
ABD	*Anchor Bible Dictionary*, edited by D. N. Freedman, 6 vols. (New York: Doubleday, 1992)
AcBib	Academia Biblica
ACCS	Ancient Christian Commentary on Scripture
AGJU	Arbeiten zur Geschichte des antiken Judentums und des Urchristentums
ALGHJ	*Arbeiten zur Literatur und Geschichte des hellenistischen Judentums*
AnBib	Analecta biblica
*ANRW*2	*Aufstieg und Niedergang der römischen Welt, Principat* (part 2)
ANTC	Abingdon New Testament Commentary
APOT	*Apocrypha and Pseudepigrapha of the Old Testament*
AUSS	*Andrews University Seminary Studies*
BBR	*Bulletin of Biblical Research*
BCBC	Believers Church Bible Commentary
BDAG	Danker, F. W., W. Bauer, W. F. Arndt, and F. W. Gingrich, *A Greek-English Lexicon of the New Testament and Other Early Christian Literature*, 3rd. ed. (Chicago: University of Chicago Press, 2000)
BDB	Brow, F. S. R. Driver, and C. A. Briggs, *A Hebrew and English Lexicon of the Old Testament* (Oxford: Clarendon, 1907)
BDF	Blass, F. A. Debrunner, and R. W. Funk, *A Greek Grammar of the New Testament and Other Early Christian Literature* (Chicago: University of Chicago Press, 1961)
BECNT	Baker Exegetical Commentary on the New Testament
BFCT	Beiträge zur Förderung christlicher Theologie
BIS	Biblical Interpretation Series
BibInt	*Biblical Interpretation*
BJRL	*Bulletin of the John Rylands University of Manchester*
BNTC	Black's New Testament Commentaries
BRS	Biblical Resource Series

Abbreviations

BSac	*Bibliotheca sacra*
BST	The Bible Speaks Today
BTB	*Biblical Theology Bulletin*
BZNW	Beihefte zur Zeitschrift für die neutestamentliche Wissenschaft
CBQ	*Catholic Biblical Quarterly*
CBR	*Currents in Biblical Research*
CC	Continental Commentary
CEB	Commentaires évangéliques de la Bible
CNT	Commentaire du Nouveau Testament
CNTOT	*Commentary on the New Testament use of the Old Testament*, edited by G. K. Beale and D. A. Carson (Grand Rapids: Baker Academic, 2007)
ConBNT	Coniectanea biblica, New Testament Series
ConJ	*Concordia Journal*
CTJ	*Calvin Theological Journal*
DLNT	*Dictionary of the Later New Testament and Its Developments*, edited by R. P. Martin and P. H. Davids (Downers Grove, IL: InterVarsity, 1997)
EBib	Etudes bibliques
EpC	Epworth Commentaries
EDNT	*Exegetical Dictionary of the New Testament*, edited by H. Balz, G. Schneider, 3 vols. (Grand Rapids: Eerdmans, 1990–93)
EKKNT	Evangelisch-katholischer Kommentar zum Neuen Testament
ErFor	Erträge der Forschung
ETR	*Evangelical Theological Review*
EvQ	*Evangelical Quarterly*
ExpTim	*Expository Times*
F&M	*Faith & Mission*
FRLANT	Forschungen zur Religion und Literatur des Alten und Neuen Testaments
GNTE	Guides to New Testament Exegesis
HCS	Hellenistic Culture and Society
HNT	Handbuch zum Neuen Testament
HTR	*Harvard Theological Review*
ICC	International Critical Commentary
IVPNTC	InterVarsity Press New Testament Commentary Series
JBL	*Journal of Biblical Literature*
JETS	*Journal of the Evangelical Theological Society*
JNES	*Journal of Near Eastern Studies*
JSNT	*Journal for the Study of the New Testament*
JSNTSup	Journal for the Study of the New Testament Supplement Series
JSOT	*Journal for the Study of the Old Testament*
KEK	Kritisch-exegetischer Kommentar über das Neue Testament
LEH	Lust, Johan, Erik Eynikel, and Katrin Hauspie, *Greek-English Lexicon of the Septuagint*, rev. ed. (Stuttgart: Deutsche Bibelgesellschaft, 2003)

Abbreviations

LES	Library of Ecumenical Studies
LNTS	Library of New Testament Studies
LQ	*Lutheran Quarterly*
Mus	*Mus Muséon: Revue d'études orientales*
NABPRDS	National Association of Baptist Professors of Religion Dissertation Series
NABPRSS	National Association of Baptist Professors of Religion Special Studies
NAC	New American Commentary
NCB	New Century Bible
NCBC	New Cambridge Bible Commentary
NEchtB	Neue Echter Bibel
	New Testament Guides
NHS	Nag Hammadi Studies
NIBC	New International Biblical Commentary
NICNT	New International Commentary on the New Testament
NIDNTT	*New International Dictionary of New Testament Theology*, edited by C. Brown, 4 vols. (Grand Rapids: Regency Reference Library, 1975–85)
NIGTC	New International Greek Testament Commentary
NIVAC	NIV Application Commentary
NovT	*Novum Testamentum*
NovTSup	Supplements to Novum Testamentum
NTC	New Testament Commentary
NTL	New Testament Library
NTM	New Testament Monographs
NTS	*New Testament Studies*
NTTh	New Testament Theology
OBO	Orbis biblicus et orientalis
ÖTKNT	Ökumenischer Taschenbuch-Kommentar zum Neuen Testament
OTL	Old Testament Library
PFES	Publication of the Finnish Exegetical Society
PNTC	Pillar New Testament Commentary
PTMS	Paternoster Biblical Monograph Series
RBL	*Review of Biblical Literature*
ResQ	*Restoration Quarterly*
RevExp	*Review and Expositor*
RNT	Regensburger Neues Testament
RSR	*Recherches de science religieuse*
SB	Sources bibliques
SBEC	Studies in the Bible and Early Christianity
SBG	Studies in Biblical Greek
SBibL	Studies in Biblical Literature
SBibTh	*Studia Biblica et Theologica*
SBLDS	Society of Biblical Literature Dissertation Series

Abbreviations

SBLSymS	Society of Biblical Literature Symposium Series
SBT	Studies in Biblical Theology
ScrBul	*Scripture Bulletin*
SNTSMS	Society of New Testament Studies Monograph Series
SP	Sacra pagina
SPhiloA	*Studia Philonica Annual*
SPSH	Scholars Press Studies in the Humanities
Str.B.	Strack, Hermann Leberecht, and Paul Billerbeck, *Kommentar zum Neuen Testament aus Talmud und Midrasch*, 6 vols. (Munich: C. H. Beck, 1922–61)
SVTP	Studia in Veteris Testamenti pseudepigrapha
TANZ	Texte und Arbeiten zum neutestamentlichen Zeitalter
TDNT	*Theological Dictionary of the New Testament*, edited by G. Kittel and G. Friedrich, translated by G. W. Bromiley, 10 vols. (Grand Rapids: Eerdmans, 1964–76)
TDOT	*Theological Dictionary of the Old Testament*, edited by Johannes Botterweck, Helmer Ringgren, and Heinz-Josef Fabry, rev. ed. translated by John T. Willis, 15 vols. (Grand Rapids: Eerdmans, 1974–2006)
	The Bible and Its Modern Interpreters
ThHist	Théologie Historique
THKNT	Theologischer Handkommentar zum Neuen Testament
THNTC	Two Horizons New Testament Commentary
TNTC	Tyndale New Testament Commentaries
TNTL	Tyndale New Testament Lecture
Trans	*Transformation*
TynBul	*Tyndale Bulletin*
TZ	*Theologische Zeitschrift*
UBSHB	United Bible Society Handbook Series
VT	*Vetus Testamentum*
WBC	Word Biblical Commentary
WC	Westminster Commentaries
WMANT	Wissenschaftliche Monographien zum Alten und Neuen Testament
WPC	Westminster Pelican Commentaries
WTJ	*Westminster Theological Journal*
WUNT	Wissenschaftliche Untersuchungen zum Neuen Testament
ZNW	*Zeitschrift für die neutestamentliche Wissenschaft und die Kunde der älteren Kirche*

SCRIPTURES AND ANCIENT SOURCES

1/2 Clem.	*1/2 Clement*
1/3 En.	*1/3 Enoch*
2 Apoc. Jas.	Second Apocalypse of James

Abbreviations

2 Bar.	2 Baruch
Abot R. Nat.	Avot of Rabbi Nathan
Acts. Thom.	Acts of Thomas
Ambrose, *Paen.*	De Paenitentia
Apoc. El.	Apocalypse of Elijah
Apoc. Ezra	Apocalypse of Ezra
Apoc. Pet.	Apocalypse of Peter
APOT	*Apocrypha and Pseudepigrapha of the Old Testament*, edited by R. H. Charles, 2 vols. (Oxford: Clarendon, 1913)
Aristeas	Letter of Aristeas
Aristotle, *Part. an.*	Parts of Animals
As. Mos.	Assumption of Moses
Ascen. Isa.	Martyrdom and Ascension of Isaiah (6–11)
Aulus Gellius, *Att.*	Attic Nights
Cicero, *Ros. Amer.*	Pro Sexto Roscio Amerino
Clement of Alexandria, *Paed.*	Paedagogus (Christ the Educator)
Clement, *Salvation*	Salvation of the Rich
Cyprian, *Laps.*	On the Lapsed
Demosthenes, *Macart.*	Against Macartatus
Did.	Didache
Dio Chrysostom, *Or.*	Orations (Discourses)
Diog. Laer. *Lives*	Diogenes Laertius, *Lives and Opinions of Eminent Philosophers*
Ep. Diog.	Epistle to Diognetus
Epiphanius, *Pan.*	Refutation of All Heresies
Eusebius, *Hist. eccl.*	Ecclesiastical History
Gos. Phil.	Gospel of Philip
Gos. Thom.	Gospel of Thomas
Hel. Syn. Pr.	Hellenistic Synagogal Prayers
Herm. Mand.	Shepherd of Hermas, Mandates
Herm. Sim.	Shepherd of Hermas, Similitudes
Herm. Vis.	Shepherd of Hermas, Visions
Hippolytus, *Haer.*	Refutation of All Heresies
Hippolytus, *Trad. ap.*	The Apostolic Tradition
Ign. *Eph.*	Ignatius, *To the Ephesians*
Ign. *Magn.*	Ignatius, *To the Magnesians*
Ign. *Phil.*	Ignatius, *To the Philadelphians*
Ign. *Poly.*	Ingatius, *To Polycarp*
Ign. *Rom.*	Ignatius, *To the Romans*
Ign. *Smyrn.*	Ingatius, *To the Smyrnaeans*
Ign. *Trall.*	Ignatius, *To the Trallians*
Irenaeus, *Haer.*	Against Heresies
Jdt	Judith
Jerome, *Vir. ill.*	De Viris Illustribus
Jos. Asen.	Joseph and Aseneth
Josephus, *Ag. Ap.*	Against Apion

Abbreviations

Josephus, *Ant.*	*Jewish Antiquities*
Josephus, *J.W.*	*Jewish War*
Jub.	*Jubilees*
Justin, *Dial.*	*Dialogue with Trypho*
Justin, *Hort.*	*Hortatory Address to the Greeks*
L.A.B.	*Liber antiquitatum biblicarum*
Liv. Pro.	*Lives of the Prophets*
Lucian, *Merc. cond.*	*Salaried Posts in Great Houses*
Mart. Pol.	*Martyrdom of Polycarp*
Martial, *Spec.*	*Liber spectaculorum*
Odes Sol.	*Odes of Solomon*
Origen, *Cels.*	*Against Celsus*
Philo *Sacr.*	*On the Sacrifices of Cain and Abel*
Philo, *Abr.*	*On the Life of Abraham*
Philo, *Alleg. Interp.*	*Allegorical Interpretation*
Philo, *Cher.*	*On the Cherubim*
Philo, *Embassy*	*On the Embassy to Gaius*
Philo, *Flight*	*On Flight and Finding*
Philo, *Good Person*	*That Every Good Person Is Free*
Philo, *Migr.*	*On the Migration of Abraham*
Philo, *Mos.*	*On the Life of Moses*
Philo, *Post.*	*On the Posterity of Cain*
Philo, *Prelim.*	*On the Preliminary Studies*
Philo, *QG*	*Questions and Answers on Genesis*
Philo, *Rewards*	*On Rewards and Punishments*
Philo, *Sacrifices*	*On the Sacrifices of Cain and Abel*
Philo, *Spec.*	*On the Special Laws*
Philo, *Unchangeable*	*That God Is Unchangeable*
Philo, *Virt.*	*On the Virtues*
Philo, *Worse*	*That the Worse Attacks the Better*
Plutarch, *Cat. Min.*	*Cato the Younger*
Pol. Phil.	Polycarp, *To the Philippians*
Pr. Jos.	*Prayer of Joseph*
Ps.-Philo	Pseudo-Philo
Pss. Sol.	*Psalms of Solomon*
Rhet. Her.	*Rhetorica ad Herennium*
Seneca, *Clem.*	*De Clementia*
Seneca, *Ep.*	*Epistulae morales*
Sib. Or.	*Sibylline Oracles*
Suetonius, *Cal.*	*Gaius Caligula*
Suetonius, *Dom.*	*Domitian*
T. 12 Patr.	*Testament of the Twelve Patriarchs*
T. Ash.	*Testament of Asher*
T. Benj.	*Testament of Benjamin*
T. Dan	*Testament of Dan*
T. Gad	*Testament of Gad*

Abbreviations

T. Iss.	*Testament of Issachar*
T. Jac.	*Testament of Jacob*
T. Job	*Testament of Job*
T. Jos.	*Testament of Joseph*
T. Jud.	*Testament of Judah*
T. Levi	*Testament of Levi*
T. Mos.	*Testament of Moses*
T. Naph.	*Testament of Naphtali*
T. Reub.	*Testament of Reuben*
T. Sim.	*Testament of Simeon*
T. Zeb.	*Testament of Zebulun*
Tertullian, *Marc.*	*Against Marcion*
Tertullian, *Ux.*	*To His Wife*
Tg. Neof.	*Targum Neofiti*
Tg. Onq.	*Targum Onqelos*
Tg. Ps.-J.	*Targum Pseudo-Jonathan*

Introduction

This third and final volume of *Apostasy in the New Testament Communities* covers the writings known as the General Epistles (Hebrews, James, 1 and 2 Peter, Jude)[1] and the communities of the Book of Revelation: Ephesus, Smyrna, Pergamum, Thyatira, Sardis, Philadelphia, and Laodicea from Asia Minor. This work and its two predecessors provide a thorough examination of the scriptures aiming at clarity on how the subject of apostasy is understood among the various New Testament communities. We understand apostasy as the phenomenon of religious followers or groups repudiating or turning away from the core beliefs and practices they once embraced in a spiritual community.[2]

This study completes our endeavor to cover all the Christ-communities of the New Testament. My approach to the subject is the same as the previous volumes. First, I *identify the communities* from which apostasy occurs or from which the warnings against falling away originate. In this step we pursue the identity of the author, audience, and apostates or opponents. Second, I examine the *perceived nature of apostasy within the respective communities*. The adversities the communities face in this third volume frequently include assimilation and persecution. Third, I point out the perceived *consequences of apostasy*. The authors of these writings may reserve vituperative language against those who lead others astray, and they express dire warnings of divine judgment awaiting defectors. The consequences of falling away are thus explored and whether apostates can be restored back to faith.

Finally, on the subject of apostasy I will *compare the various views of the New Testament writers and their communities*. This final volume has the advantage of examining this issue in a thorough manner after all the communities have been

---

1. The Johannine Letters are covered under the chapter on Johaninne literature in volume 1 of this work.

2. See the more thorough treatment of this term in the Introduction of volume 1.

Introduction

explored. The conclusion of this study will distill the similarities and differences between these communities, taking into consideration all the New Testament writings.

1

Hebrews

Warnings of Apostasy with No Restoration

The early traditional viewpoint considered Hebrews to be authored by Paul even though his name does not appear in the text. The work was accepted with reservations as Pauline in the Eastern churches, but the Western churches were more reluctant to follow this view until after the fourth century.[1] Contemporary scholarship, however, rejects Paul's authorship of this work. Distinctions between Paul's writings and Hebrews outweigh the similarities, and there are numerous linguistic dissimilarities.[2] Among the differences is that the author writes as though the audience and himself are a later group of believers who received the word of salvation from earlier leaders (Heb 2:3–4), which is not the way Paul thought about his own reception of the gospel (e.g., Gal 1:11–12). The author of Hebrews appears to be male given that he uses the masculine singular participle διηγούμενον when referring to himself (Heb 11:32).[3] He personally knew his audience if he requests prayer that he be restored to them (13:19). Possibly this restoration suggests his imprisonment

---

1. Cf. Eusebius, *Hist. eccl.* 3.3.5; 6.14.2–4; 6.20.3; 6.25.11–14. For a survey of ancient sources see Lünemann, *Hebrews*, 335–43. The Chester Beatty papyrus (P⁴⁶), along with some later manuscripts, place Hebrews immediately after Paul's letter to the Romans, and witnesses such as ℵ, B, C placed it after 2 Thessalonians; cf. Metzger, *Textual Commentary*, 591–92. The late minuscule 81 includes the prescript: "To the Hebrews written from Rome by Paul to those in Jerusalem." See also the Clementine Vulgate. Other late manuscripts belonging to the majority text (e.g., KJV) have Timothy's name at the end of the work.

2. See, e.g., Spicq, *Hébreux*, 1.145–55; for similarities see 155–60.

3. This observation would seem to discredit views that propose the author as Mary (the mother of Jesus) or Pricilla (the wife of Aquila and teacher of Apollos in Acts 18). For the former option see Ford, "Mother of Jesus," 49–56; for the latter, Hoppin, *Priscilla's Letter*.

(cf. 13:3). Given that Timothy's name appears in the work (13:23), a colleague of Paul or someone affiliated with the Pauline tradition may be its writer.[4] His gifted knowledge of the scriptures and eloquent Greek style suggest he is a Hellenistic Jew. Speculations on the identity of the author have run the gamut over the centuries, but in the end we are probably no closer to identifying him than were the church fathers many centuries ago.[5]

The historical location of the author and the recipients of Hebrews are likewise perplexing. Those "from Italy" who greet the recipients may suggest the work originated from Italy (13:24), but this could refer to some individuals who happen to be with the author as he wrote the work and are simply greeting fellow members of their congregation back home in Italy. Italy, then, might be either the home of the author or the recipients. Our guess favors the former.[6] A second option for the place of destination is Palestine or Jerusalem, which complements the traditional view that the work was written to "Hebrews" or Jews.[7]

A third location for the destination is a community in Asia Minor.[8] This location seems to explain more consistently the combination of dangers related to apostasy that involves both persecution and loss of zeal arising from within the same community. Such phenomena resemble to some extent the communities of Asia Minor in Rev 2–3. As well, the recipients in Hebrews are "on the move" (cf. Heb 3–4), and their problems with alienation caused by outsiders[9] bears an interesting similarity with 1 Peter, another work directed at Christian communities in Asia Minor. The key criterion for the heroes of faith in Heb 11 seems to be their marginalization. The author portrays these heroes as having the value of faithfulness through marginalization "of whom the world was not worthy" (cf. 11:38).[10] The recipients of Asia Minor in 1 Peter are likewise experiencing hardships as resident aliens (cf. 1 Pet 1:1, 17; 2:11). The author in Hebrews also stresses Christ as preeminent over angels and cultic aspects of the old covenant (Heb 1; 8–9), which resonates with the high Christology promoted in Colossians, another city in Asia Minor (Col 1:15–18; 2:8–10; 2:16–23).[11] Similarities between Hebrews, Revelation, 1 Peter,

---

4. As suggested by Hurst, *Epistle of Hebrews*, 124.

5. On options for authorship see Lünemann, *Hebrews*, 351–67; Gräßer, *Hebräer*, 1.19–22.

6. Perhaps Rome is more precisely meant (cf. Acts 18:2; 27:1 6; 28:14). This viewpoint, according to Mitchell, *Hebrews*, 7, is now held by the majority of scholars.

7. E.g., Gleason, "Eschatology of the Warning in Hebrews," 97–120. For criticisms see Mackie, *Eschatological and Exhortation*, 129–32.

8. E.g., Dunnill, *Covenant and Sacrifice*, 22–24.

9. Heb 10: 32–34; 13:3, 7, 11–14; cf. 11:8, 9, 13–16, 26, 38; 12:3.

10. Cf. Eisenbaum, *Jewish Heroes*.

11. See, e.g., Manson, "Problem of the Epistle to the Hebrews," esp. 11–13.

and Colossians may give some credence to repetitive problems caused by outsiders against the Christians of Asia Minor. We can only surmise, however, that Hebrews was written in the latter part of the first century with the author somewhere in Italy and the recipients in Asia Minor.[12]

Some interpreters insist that Hebrews was written to a Gentile audience informed by formative Judaism.[13] Others posit variations of a mixed congregation of Jews and Gentiles.[14] Still others opt for the traditional view that the recipients are Jewish.[15] An oddity with this perspective is that the author assumes that Jewish laws and customs related to Sabbath, food, and drink would be understood by the recipients as things of the past.[16] Such a view seems to be more in keeping with either a mixed group or a Jewish Hellenistic church heavily influenced by Pauline teachings on such issues. Prolific expectations of the audience's knowledge of Israel's scriptures, the use *Gezerah sawah* (Heb 4:4f; 7:3), mention of the Sabbath (though reconfigured), Levitical priesthood, aspects of the tabernacle (chs. 8–10), mention of the Maccabee family and other Israelites (e.g., 11:36–38), all fit well with the assumption that this groups is predominantly Jewish. The use of the Septuagint in this work, wisdom Christology, and the topic of angelic mediation (ch. 1), might suggest them as Hellenistic Jewish-Christians. However, one problem with our adducing an ethnicity based on the topics in the text is that these believers are not new converts. They have been Christ-followers for a long time (e.g., 5:12—6:3; 10:32–34), certainly long enough for a Gentile audience to be well informed about the Jewish heritage behind their faith. Nevertheless, if "to the Hebrews," in P^{46} is to be followed (c. 200 CE), this would suggest the recipients are in fact Jewish.[17] The author, in any case, designates the recipients with language and titles that assume they are bona fide Christ-followers who have faith in Christ. They are called "beloved" (6:9), "saints" (13:24), holy partners (3:1), and called "brothers and sisters" in faith[18] just as Timothy is a "brother" (13:23). We therefore suggest that the recipients are Christians with a significant amount of Hellenistic-Jewish believers among them.

---

12. For discussion on the date of Hebrews see Feld, *Hebräerbrief*, 14–18. The homily may have been circulated among various congregations.

13. E.g., Hvalvik, "Jewish Believers," 208; Weiss, *Hebräerbrief*, 70–72.

14. E.g., deSilva, *Perseverance in Gratitude*, 6; Schnelle, *Einleitung*, 369.

15. E.g., Guthrie, "Hebrews in Its First-Century Context," 427; Witherington, *Jewish Christians*, 24–26.

16. See Koester, *Hebrews*, 77.

17. See further on the Jewish Christian view, e.g., Salevao, *Legitimation*, 109–17.

18. Heb 3:1, 12; 10:19; 13:22; cf. 2:11–12, 17.

Churches under Siege of Persecution and Assimilation

SITUATIONS OF POTENTIAL APOSTASY

We are able to suggest some possible situations for Hebrews. The author repeatedly warns against apostasy (2:1–4; 3:7–4:13; 5:11–6:12; 10:19–39; 12:1–29). He also repeatedly exalts the person and work of Christ above all other persons, institutes, and works related to Israel's covenant[19] and frequently cites or alludes to Israel's scriptures to support his expositions on Christ and exhortations to persevere.[20] *The obstacles that attempt to hinder the recipients' faith would seem to include persecution*, which involved the confiscation of their property in the past (10:32–34), and *in the present it includes apparent imprisonment and verbal abuse* (13:3, 13, 23). The miracles performed by their Spirit-filled leaders seems to be a thing of the past (2:4; cf. 13:7), and *their initial fervency seems to have cooled down to the point of spiritual despondency and neglecting congregational fellowship* (2:1–3; 4:1; 5:11–12; 6:11–12; 10:25). *This phenomenon possibly included their loss of zeal, lack of confidence, and failing hope.*[21] Perhaps a good number of the church members were relatively affluent—they had property that was once confiscated, and they could presently entertain guests at their homes and share their material possessions with others (13:2, 16). Consequently they are warned against the love of money (13:5).[22]

No doubt the expositions in Hebrews aim to encourage perseverance by showing, among other things, the superiority of Christ over all competitors and how his sacrificial death provides a salvation leading to everlasting life. The author shows that the prior institutes of Israel, such as the old covenant, tabernacle, Aaronic priesthood, are inferior and incomplete in comparison to Christ. These expositions would not seem to be irrelevant to the situation in Hebrews, and a number of scholars have suggested the recipients were in danger of some sort of relapse back to emergent Judaism.[23] Along these lines, the Christology we find in chapter 1, Christ's unique sonship, deity, and the aspect of his sitting at God's right hand and thus participating in God's cosmic rule (Heb 1:13/Ps 109[110]:1) are the kinds of statements that might be considered blasphemy to Jewish opponents. The last of these claims is sometimes presented as the incentive for the executions of Jesus (Mark 14:61–64), Stephen (Acts 7:55–60), and James, brother of Jesus (Eusebius, *Hist. eccl.* 2.23.3–20).[24] The

---

19. 1:1–14; 2:5—3:6; 4:14—5:10; 6:13—10:18.

20. E.g., 1:5–13; 2:12–13; 3:7–11; 8:7–12; 10:5–8; 11:7–38; 12:26, 29.

21. So Peterson, *Hebrews and Perfection*, 186; Harrington, *Letter to the Hebrews*, 77.

22. We notice similar problems related to wealth and lethargy as venues for apostasy in the churches of Asia Minor (1 Tim 6:6–10; Rev 2:4–5; 3:16–19).

23. E.g., Salevao, *Ligitimation*, 108–18; Johnson, *Going outside the Camp*, 129; Rhee, *Faith in Hebrews*, 155.

24. Although exalted figures may be found in other early Jewish writings (e.g., *1 En.* 48.2–7; *Pr. Jos.*

author's warning for his audience not to be carried away by strange teachings associated with foods may be referring to Jewish cultic meals (Heb 13:9–10).[25] The food does not need to be located in the temple in Jerusalem; it possibly refers to meals at festive occasions in a local synagogue that show some solidarity with the sacrificial system related to the temple.[26] The congregation's enticement with such foods is not necessarily an indication of a proselytizing effort on the part of perceived opponents, however. The community of believers may have been simply fascinated with their Jewish origins.

The status of formative Judaism as a *religio licita* in the Roman Empire is sometimes mentioned as an incentive why Christ-followers would be tempted to find safety under this religion's wing.[27] It is certainly conceivable that the members of the community in Hebrews grew weary of being socially marginalized as Christians by outsiders. Relief could be found by stepping under the umbrella of the local synagogue. This hypothetical situation works under the assumption that the Christians of this community had *already* parted company with the local synagogue. Whether their persecution came from non-believing Gentiles, Jewish opponents, Christian sectarians, or a combination of these, it is not difficult to imagine that their rivals could make up false charges against them before officials and magistrates. It is also quite possible that opponents could incite some sort of mob action against the believers independent of any legal system, as is sometimes portrayed in Acts (e.g., Acts 14:19; 19:23–34).

Such scenarios are admittedly speculative, and at best we should consider the relapse to emergent Judaism as only one possible situation behind Hebrews.[28] The temptation for them to follow strange teachings related to foods might well refer to the influence of some other Jewish, Christian, or Hellenistic sect similar to the problems faced in the Pauline churches of Ephesus and the Lycus Valley (1 Tim

---

A 1–3; cf. *3 En.* 10.3–6; 12:5; 16:1), the early Christians in the sources we mentioned above apparently believed their opponents considered such status for Jesus to be blasphemy. Perhaps the exalted aspect of Jesus was correlated with the Son of Man (Dan 7) to portray him as an eschatological judge who will in fact judge the Christians' accusers. This seems to add to the grounds for why opponents might have considered Jesus' status as blasphemy. See further Bauckham, "For What Offense," 199–232. On the possibility of Stephen's speech in Acts 7 as a source for Hebrews, see Manson, *Epistle to the Hebrews*, 25–46.

25. Cf. Lane, *Hebrews*, 2.530-36. These foods seem to be understood literally as Attridge, *Hebrews*, 393-95, affirms. On the meaning of erring or being lead astray for παραφέρω (13:9) see LSJ, 1329.

26. So Lindars, *Theology of the Letter*, 10.

27. Bénétreau, *Hebreux*, 1.28–29.

28. More speculative is the suggestion that these Jewish Christians belonged to the company of priests who believe (cf. Acts 6:7) and were in danger of falling away: e.g., Rissi, *Theologie des Hebräerbriefs*, 5–25; Tongue, "Concept of Apostasy," 19–27; Grelot, *Une lecture de l'épitre*, 191.

4:1–5; Col 2:13–23). In fact, since Timothy is mentioned as an apparent colleague of the author (Heb 13:23), Hebrews might be addressing a community of Pauline churches that reaches these areas. It is perhaps best to remain tentative about a detailed reconstruction behind the situation in Hebrews, and there is no reason that we have to choose between options—in our view Hebrews may be opposing more than one means to apostasy.

More helpful for our study is that this community continues to experience persecution from outsiders, and they may be tempted to commit apostasy because of external pressures and malaise (e.g., 10:32–34; 13:3, 13).[29] Another relevant condition may include a lack of commitment and zeal (2:1; 10:35).[30] Perhaps we could understand this condition as a spiritual struggle or indifference that was brought on by the congregation members' despondency over being marginalized.

A HOMILY OF WARNINGS, ENCOURAGEMENTS, CHRISTOLOGY, AND ESCHATOLOGICAL TENSION (5:2; 6:18–19; 7:25; 8:12; 10:14–17; 13:5)

Many scholars have recognized Hebrews as primarily a homily.[31] The author claims his work is an "exhortation" (παράκλησις: 13:22), and this is perhaps similar to what would be declared in a synagogue (cf. Acts 13:15). Various structural approaches to Hebrews will not detain us other than our conceding with George Guthrie that this writing requires a distinction be made between expositional and hortatory sections.[32] We will focus our attention on the hortatory sections of the homily because they present us with the warnings related to apostasy.[33]

Nevertheless, the expositional texts use inferential terms such as "therefore" that connect these sections with the warnings (Heb. 2:1; 3:1; 6:1; 10:19; 12:1). These sections have the agenda of encouraging the recipients with confidence and salvific assurances by reminding them of Christ's priestly intercession for them,[34] the for-

---

29. Koester, *Hebrews*, 64–72, describes the social situation in three phases: 1) proclamation/conversion, 2) persecution/solidarity, and 3) ongoing friction between Christians and outsiders, along with malaise.

30. See, e.g., Osborne, "Christ of Hebrews," 249–67. See discussion on community problems in Mackie, *Eschatology and Exhortation*, 9–17.

31. E.g., Thyen, *Stil des jüdisch-hellenistischen Homilie*; Koester, *Hebrews*, 80–82; and for older sources see Sqicq, *Hébreux*, 1.19–20.

32. Guthrie, *Structure of Hebrews*; albeit, Guthrie places the positive examples of heroes in Heb 11 in the exhortation section (144).

33. These sections include Heb 1:1–14; 2:5–18; 4:14—5:10; 6:13—10:18; and 11:1–40.

34. Heb 4:14–16; 5:2; 7:25.

giveness of sins via the new covenant,[35] their assurance of hope and faith,[36] and God's faithfulness to them (13:5). There is also a prayer wish that God graciously equip them to do God's will (13:20–21). While it remains possible for us to accept such words as salvific guarantees of the final perseverance of those who truly have saving faith, despite the warnings of apostasy,[37] a better explanation is that these assurances do not invalidate the audience's potential to commit apostasy. Several examples from Hebrews suggest that both confidence in salvation and the potential for apostasy are maintained by the author.

In 5:2 it is affirmed that Christ as the high priest can deal gently with those who are ignorant and "go astray" (πλανάω), a phenomenon that happens to apostates earlier in the homily (3:12).[38] The context of 5:2, however, relates to Christ's compassion and ability to relate to human weaknesses (cf. 2:17; 4:15; 7:16–28; 9:7); the passage focuses on a human condition rather than apostasy.[39] As well, 5:2 is probably understood as a hendiadys: those who "ignorantly go astray."[40] It is possible that our author may be informed by the idea that God's people commit both intentional or witting sins (Num 15:32–36; Deut 17:12) and unintentional or unwitting sins (Num 15:24–29; Lev 4:2, 13, 22, 27; Ezek 45:20; cf. Rom 10:3; 1 Tim 1:13). If so, the idea of straying in ignorance would seem to fall under the category of unintentional sins; whereas the various types of apostasy in Hebrews would probably register in the author's mind as witting sins.

Possibly, the notion of witting sin may also be helpful for understanding a limit to God's promise, "their sins will I remember no more" (cf. Heb 8:12; 10:16–17/Jer 31:33–34). These passages are bound up with the disposition of the new covenant in which Christ's death has become the final, unrepeatable sacrifice for sin that was unattainable through the old covenant (cf. Heb 9:14, 26, 28; 10:10). The sins that are "forgotten" by God under the new covenant are presumably ignorant sins and transgressions that are not equated with willful sinning that is a post-conversion phenomenon tantamount with apostasy in 10:26. It seems that the promise of God forgetting sins is actualized on a personal level when one repents and converts to the new covenant. When a person apostatizes, however, that individual is said to

---

35. 8:10–12; 10:14, 17–18.

36. 6:9–11, 18–19; 10:22; 11:1.

37. Another option is that we have run into an irresolvable tension between these words of comfort and the warnings against apostasy: e.g., Borchert, *Assurance and Warning*, 151–214. For various scholarly viewpoints on the warnings see Oropeza, "Warning Passages in Hebrews," 1–21.

38. On πλανάω and restoration see Jas 5:19–20; Titus 3:3; 1 Pet 2:25; Matt 18:12.

39. See Löhr, *Umkehr und Sünde*, 40.

40. Cf. Attridge, *Hebrews*, 144.

repudiate Christ and his sacrificial death, the very basis for the new covenant and its divine claim to remember sins no more (cf. 10:26–31).

Passages on confidence and assurance that encourage the readers by speaking of a steadfast and secure hope related to the promised inheritance of rest and salvation (6:18–20), and of Christ's intercession and ability to save completely those who draw near to God through him (7:25), must be tempered with passages warning that this *same confidence* can be thrown away by committing apostasy (cf. 3:6, 12–14; 10:35).[41] Christians have the responsibility of drawing near to God in faith and confidence (4:16; 7:25; 10:22), and they must not turn away from him in unbelief and disobedience (3:12; 4:1, 11). Moreover, the assurances found in such passages as 7:23–25 and 10:14–17 are grounded in Christ's work and the new covenant (e.g., 7:22; 10:16), both of which can be rejected by a believer so as to cut off that person from the benefits of Christ's work and the new covenant (cf. 10:29).[42] God is not under obligation to save congregation members who reject Christ and his saving work in the new covenant, and yet their apostasy by no means diminishes the value of Christ's sacrificial death or ability to save. The author's words of assurance and confidence have the rhetorical aim of getting the audience to realize that by virtue of Christ and his saving work they can boldly approach God in faith, worship, and prayer without being afraid of what outsiders might do or think. They do not need to be ashamed about their Christian confession.

The assurance that God never abandons nor forsakes his people in 13:5 does not preclude that they can forsake him. In the original context of this saying God's people in fact forsake God, and as a result God forsakes them (Deut 31: 6, 8; cf. 31:16–17; cf. 32:18–20; Isa 8:17; Mic. 3:4; 2 Chr 12:5; *Barn.* 4.14).[43] The assumption of our author in Hebrews 13:5 seems to be that this promise pertains only to faithful believers, not unfaithful ones who repudiate Christ. A parallel passage in *1 Clem.*

---

41. Koester, *Hebrews*, 334, astutely writes regarding Heb 6:19: "Hebrews' imagery suggests that the listener's hope has already been secured at their port of destination. To be sure, they have not disembarked at God's place of rest (Heb 4:1–11) in the heavenly Jerusalem (12:22–24), but the anchor has been planted, and they are no longer at the mercy of the winds on the open sea. The trouble is that they seem to be in danger of drifting from their Christian moorings (2:1b) and must therefore hold fast (2:1a)."

42. Even though his agenda defends a theological dogma, Cockerill, "Wesleyan Arminian View," 237–42, correctly recognizes this aspect.

43. This should not be viewed as though God double-crossed Israel with his promise. His forsaking them is temporal and does not include every individual Israelite. The unconditional aspect of the promise seems to rest on the language of a surviving remnant. In terms of a corporate community God will restore his people after they commit apostasy, as the blessing/curses section and song of Moses demonstrate (Deut 28–32). Apostates in Hebrews, however, are denied restoration partly on the basis of Ps 94[95] and Num 14. On Heb 13:5 in relation to the blessing/curse motif and its Deuteronomic background, see further Allen, *Deuteronomy and Exhortation*, 67–71.

11.1 is instructive by claiming that God does not forsake those who hope in him, but he appoints to punishment those who turn away from him. Be that as it may, the author of Hebrews does not directly associate 13:5 with final salvation. He communicates instead that because God is reliable and will not abandon his care for the believing community, its members should not trust in money, material possessions, or be frightened by outsiders who might confiscate their property—God is faithful to supply all their needs (cf. Heb 13:6/Ps 117[118]:6f).

Again, these assurances do not contradict or nullify the audience's possibility of committing apostasy if the assurances themselves can be abandoned by the congregation members (e.g., Heb 10:35; cf. 3:6, 14). The words of encouragement in the homily function as incentives for the audience to persevere in their present salvation, and the ultimate exemplar of perseverance and reception of final salvation is Jesus.

Christology intersects with perseverance throughout the homily. First, God is speaking through his Son at the end of time, providing a great salvation, and the Son's followers should not neglect these words. The proclamation of Jesus as an exalted individual sitting at the right hand of God not only conveys that the Christian message is greater than previous ones of earlier eras, but it also suggests that the message ought to induce a confession of allegiance for Christ-followers (1:1—2:4). Next, Jesus stands in solidarity with his faithful followers. He is not ashamed of them but calls them "brother and sisters," and they belong to his "house." As Christ was faithful to God, so those who share in Christ are to remain faithful and not fall away as did the wilderness generation (2:5–4:13). Jesus is then viewed as a high priest and provides a once-for-all sacrifice for sin, ratifying a new covenant in which believers can be cleansed of their sins. Through Jesus' supplications and obedience he is perfected and becomes the source of everlasting salvation, which both encourages believers to have full confidence in approaching God and provides hope in relation to their salvific inheritance. The author wishes to show his audience from such portraits that there is no good reason for them to be reluctant hearers and fall away. Even though their confession of Christ has marginalized them from society, they are to live by faith and fear God rather than outsiders (4:14–10:39). Finally, as the righteous heroes of old lived by faith despite marginality and suffering, so believers are to endure their salvific contest, follow on Jesus as their ultimate exemplar of faithfulness and suffering, and make sure not to give up the contest, fall from grace, or reject God's voice before arriving at their ultimate destination of the heavenly Jerusalem (11:1—12:29). They must therefore fix their eyes on Christ who is the author and completer of faith (12:1-2).

A stress on Christ's preeminence throughout Hebrews is buttressed by an eschatological theme—the old age has been eclipsed by a new one, and the pivotal moment was marked by God speaking and revealing his word through Christ (1:2). In the "now" the believers benefit from Christ's atoning death and exalted status in the era of the new covenant (7:11, 19; 8:7–13; 9:11, 26; 10:1; cf. 1:5f; 2:5–8). Although the present age provides them with glimpses of the heavenly world to come, where Christ presently reigns,[44] the recipients have not yet experienced final salvation. Final deliverance has not yet taken place but will happen at Christ's return and when the heavenly city appears (9:28; 11:10, 16; 13:14). At that time blessings and a great inheritance will be given to the faithful,[45] but the wicked will be punished, including the apostates (2:1–3; 3:16–19; 6:4–8; 10:26–31; 12:25–29).[46] Spatial and temporal dimensions collide in Hebrews with the heavenly reality being superior to the present visible cosmos, which will not persist after the eschatological "shaking" occurs (12:26–28).[47]

As with a number of early Christian writings, the author of Hebrews thus works within an eschatological timeframe of "now" and "not yet" in which salvation is presently being experienced by God's people even though it has not reached its finality. Similar to Paul, one of the ways this author warns his audience against falling away is by comparing his audience with Israel's wilderness generation, who were judged by God before entering into the final rest or "not yet" culmination of their journey (3:7–4:11; cf. 1 Cor 10:1–12). From the author's point of view, *the recipients face the danger of failing to persevere until the culmination of the eschaton when Christ returns, and both the encouragements and warnings in Hebrews function as rhetorical strategies—one to encourage them to continue their faith in Christ until he returns; the other to dissuade them from committing apostasy.*

NEGLECTING A GREAT SALVATION (2:1–4)

The central thesis of the homilies may be 2:1–4.[48] It is the first warning and possesses in a concise manner the form that the following warnings adopt. The pattern follows an admonition against committing apostasy and then mentions a severe

---

44. 1:2, 5f; 2:3–5; 6:4–5.

45. 1:14; 6:7, 10–12, 17; 10:35–36; 11:26.

46. Synopses of eschatology in Hebrews are given by Mackie, *Eschatological and Exhortation*, 35–37; and Koester, *Hebrews*, 100–104.

47. On creation and apocalypticism in Hebrews see deSilva, *Perseverance in Gratitude*, 27–32.

48. Rice, "Apostasy as a Motif," 33, goes further, arguing that a concern over the danger of apostasy rests behind the entire work, even in the expositions of Hebrews.

consequence of divine judgment that will take place if the apostasy is committed. The first warning in Hebrews is shorter than the following ones but has in a succinct manner the basic structure for the rest.[49] The introduction of the pericope on warning is marked by a transitional cue (2:1a: διὰ τοῦτο), the warning involves some form of apostasy (2:1b, 3) and a punishment comparable to, but more severe than, a judgment on violators from among God's people in Israel's scriptures (2:2–4).

The author opens in 2:1–4 with the exhortation, "we must pay even closer attention" to the things heard (2:1). The comparative aspect in this verse suggests that the audience's attention should be greater than the Israelites' when hearing God's commandments (cf. 2:2).[50] Although the first-person plurals in the passage may have some rhetorical effect of joining the preacher with his audience, *the repetitive use of "we" and "us" throughout Hebrews gives us the strong impression that the author does not consider himself exempt from the danger of these warnings* (2:1, 3; cf. 3:6, 14; 4: 11, 13; 12:1f, 25).[51] Sometimes "we" is even emphatic, as in 2:1–4.[52] Moffat encapsulates the idea well when he writes regarding 2:1, "ἡμᾶς = we Christians . . . you and I, as in v. 3."[53] In this way not only is the author building rapport with his audience by their sharing a common identity, but he is also implying that "I, too, am susceptible to these dangers of apostasy," and perhaps even that "if I as a leader am susceptible to them, how much more are all of you?" The solidarity shared between the author and the audience is bound up with their filial relationship to Christ as his children (cf. 2:5–13).

The concept of paying attention (προσέχειν: 2:1) has a range of meanings including to be on guard, to devote oneself to something, and significantly "to bring to port" a ship (e. g, Herodotus *Histories* 1.2; 3.48; 2.182; 9.99; Euripedes, *Orestes*

---

49. However, 5:11—6:12 deviates from the pattern somewhat, as we will notice below.

50. With Ellingworth, *Hebrews*, 135. Contrast Hughes, *Hebrews*, 73, who reads the phrase as a superlative: "We must pay the *closest* attention."

51. Notice also the hortatory subjunctive "let us" in 4:1, 11, 14, 16; 6:1; 10:22–24; 12:28; 13:13, 15, which connects the speaker with his audience. Contrast Thomas, *Case for Mixed-Audience*, 235–36, who though at one point admits that the author is not exempt from the danger of his warnings "in a general sense," claims that "the use of the first person plural in such warnings as we find in Hebrews does not necessarily mean the author is implicating himself" (235). However, the ancient recipients of Hebrews no doubt would have considered the dangers of these warnings as applicable to both themselves *and* the author when the author uses first person plurals. The author, who has real faith, admits his own susceptibility to committing apostasy, and this undermines Thomas's view that "failure to persevere (to heed the warnings) is indicative of a spurious faith . . . the warnings serve as a test of one's profession since the criterion of a genuine faith is that it perseveres" (15–16).

52. Cf. Ellingworth, *Hebrews*, 136. Wallace, *Grammar*, 396, on "we" in Hebrews says, "The author clearly and often associates himself with the audience."

53. Moffat, *Hebrews*, 17.

362).⁵⁴ In Hebrews it is perhaps comparable to "hold fast" (cf. κατέχω: Heb 3:6, 14; 10:23).⁵⁵ The word's connection with the thought of drifting away (παραρρέω) may suggest a nautical coloring behind Heb 2:1.⁵⁶ If so, προσέχειν envisages the necessity of a boat being brought to or kept at port; it must not lose its moorings and drift off to sea (cf. 6:19). Interestingly, the Pauline author in 1 Tim 1:19, when addressing Timothy (cf. Heb 13:23!), uses nautical imagery to depict the apostasy of Hymenaeus and Alexander as a shipwreck of their faith. Unlike 1 Timothy, however, the author in Hebrews is not communicating a defection from the past. *The danger of drifting away is a potential one for his audience, which, if not corrected, may lead to their being spiritually lost at sea or shipwrecked.* The believers must remain fastened to the hope set before them that begins with their salvific relationship with Christ and ends in the full realization of promised blessings related to the heavenly Jerusalem.

If the warning in 2:1 is multilayered, another tack understands προσέχειν in the nuance of someone guarding or keeping watch. It has this meaning in a number of passages that warn against apostasy and deception (Deut 4:9; 32:46; Sir 13:8; Matt 7:15; Acts 20:28; Luke 21:34; cf. Neh 9:34–36). Perhaps 2:1 echoes a thought from Prov 3:21 LXX, where guarding (τηρέω) is used with drifting away (παραρρέω).⁵⁷ The "son" is not to drift away but keep/guard the counsel and understanding of his father's wisdom so that his soul may live and he may walk confidently in peace without his foot stumbling. The notion of not being able to escape a greater judgment of God than old covenant predecessors (Heb 2:3) reappears in 12:25, and within the latter context the author cites Prov 3:11–12 (Heb 12:5–6). Our author, it seems, knows the content of Proverbs 3. Perhaps he noticed a commonality between this wisdom source and what he was attempting to communicate in Hebrews, especially in reference to filial relationships, keeping godly instruction, and fearing God (Prov 3:7, 25/Heb 12:20–21, 28; cf. 2:1–3; 4:1; 12:5–6, 28).

The peril of falling away is also understood as *neglecting* salvation (Heb 2:3).⁵⁸ The author of Hebrews warns his audience against a lack of concern for God's mes-

54. See LSJ, 1512.

55. So Lane, *Hebrews*, 1.37.

56. On "drift away" (παραρρέω) as nautical see Herodotus, *Histories* 2.150; Strabo, *Geography* 9.2.31; LSJ, 1322. Spicq, *Hébreux*, 2.24, rejects nautical implications in Heb 2:1 and opts for a sense of slipping ("nous ne glissions à côtè"). Alternative renderings would then be "slip away" or "break away." Bateman, *Four Views*, 32, translates 2:1 as "slip away" in the sense of forgetting teachings about the Son. Examples from classic literature include, a ring slipping off a finger (Plutarch, *Moralia* 754a) and a morsel going down the wrong windpipe (Aristotle, *Part. an.* 3.3; cf. Hughes, *Hebrews*, 73n73). Παραρρέω appears only in the NT in Heb 2:1 and twice in the LXX (Prov 3:21; Isa 44:4: "flowing" water).

57. Even in Prov 3:21, however, nautical influence might be surmised from the mention of the sea (abyss) and clouds streaming dew in Prov 3:20.

58. In other contexts relevant to apostasy ἀμελέω conveys a disregard for the righteous (Wis 3:10),

sage spoken through the Son. Such negligence becomes a rejection of what they are supposed to be doing—hearing and obeying God's word that brings about salvation. Its nuance seems closer to spiritual indifference than a deliberate repudiation of God or Christ. In any case the consequence that would result from this apostasy is the loss of their great "salvation" that assumes a prior purification through Christ's atoning death (1:3; 2:9, 17) and freedom from the fallen world and devil's dominion (2:14–15; 11:38).[59] Salvation in Hebrews is eschatologically oriented, having antipodes in the "now" and "not yet"—the believers experience present salvation (2:3; 7:25; cf. 6:5), but final salvation is up ahead and will be fully realized when Christ's dominion over his enemies comes to completion (2:5–9; cf. 1:14b; 6:9; 9:26–28; 11:20).[60] It is precisely this futuristic element to salvation that makes apostasy possible for both the author and audience who presently benefit from it. In this present tension the believers' sanctification is not yet complete. They are presently saved and holy (10:10, 29; 12:10; cf. 12:28), and yet they are still being made holy (2:11; 10:14).[61]

This great salvation was spoken to the audience, suggesting their earlier reception of the gospel message that brought about their spiritual deliverance (2:3 cf. Acts 2:19, 22, 43; Rom 15:19; Gal 3:5). The author wants his audience to remember their legacy and how in their spiritual infancy they came to inherit the message of salvation, presumably by faith (cf. Heb 4:2, 12; Rom 10:17). Their experience with signs and wonders in the past suggests this congregation had cooled down significantly from their earlier charismatic enthusiasm. The older members probably still recalled how God's Spirit worked through miracles when their early leaders preached to them, confirming their message and witness as coming truly from God (2:4; cf. 13:7). Such memories would have been passed on to newer members, but the same fervency had not been maintained. It seems that *the congregation now suffers from spiritual decrepitude.* We are not told in the passage the cause of this condition. Our best guess is that, based on a comparative reading with the other warning passages, they had become discouraged on account of long-term marginalization. They grew weary of enduring persecution for the sake of Christ and perhaps started neglecting

a neglecting of priestly duties (2 Macc 4:14; cf. Josephus, *Ant.* 4.67), or God's commands (*Apoc. Pet.* 15:30), or by inference God's call (Matt 22:5). Conversely, the word is used in Hebrews to convey that God disregards apostates among his people (Heb 8:9/Jer 31:32).

59. On σωτηρία see further 1:14; 2:10; 5:9; 6:9; 9:27; cf. 7:25; Gräßer, *Hebräer*, 1.96. In 5:9 "eternal salvation" probably does not mean "without beginning or end" as in 9:14 but "without end" or lasting forever, as in 6:2 (cf. 9:12; 13:20; Ellingworth, *Hebrews*, 295). It seems derived from Isa 45:17, which, like Hebrews, follows up this phrase with stern warnings; cf. Isa 48.

60. On the interface between soteriology and the two ages in Hebrews, see further Mackie, *Eschatology and Exhortation*, 100–101. Μέλλω in Hebrews (1:14; 2:5; 6:5; 8:5; 10:1, 27; 11:8, 20; 13:14) often involves "eschatological realities promised but not yet fully realized" (Ellingworth, *Hebrews*, 133).

61. Cf. Bateman, *Four Views*, 25.

spiritual devotion, fellowship, and being a visible witness. Similar to the churches in Ephesus, Sardis, and Laodicea in Rev 2–3, it seems that these Christ-followers had lost their original love for the things of God, their spiritual life was ebbing away, and they needed to be zealous once again. *They were becoming unresponsive toward the messages of their leaders and were in danger of gradual defection.* Nothing in the text would seem to suggest that they had succumbed to false teachings, destructive vices, or idolatry.

The audience's potential neglect of salvation would result in a punishment more severe than those who transgressed and disobeyed the valid message of angels, that is, the Mosaic Law (Heb 2:2; cf. Gal 3:19; Acts 7:53).[62] Deuteronomy 33:2 speaks of the message from Sinai that was delivered by angels. This verse stands in proximity to the Song of Moses, which delineates Israel's future apostasy and warns them to keep (προσέχειν) the words of the Law (Deut 32:46; cf. 32:8, 43/Heb 1:6; 2:5). Tremors from the Deuteronomic blessings and curses may be felt here and elsewhere in the warning passages of Heb 6:4–8 and 12:15–17.[63] But this background for Heb 2:2 is not entirely clear. That angels administrated the covenant of Moses seems to be common knowledge among Hellenistic Jews.[64] Our author might have no specific text in mind here. The believers' judgment would be more severe because the message of salvation that was spoken to them came through the Son who is superior to angels (Heb 2:3f; cf. ch. 1).[65] The Law prescribed a death penalty for various transgressions, including sins of neglect and ignorance (Exod 21:29–34; Num 15:27),[66] but a greater penalty would await the audience if they fell away. They would not be able to "escape" God's retribution at the eschaton (cf. 1 Thess 5:3; Rom 2:3; Luke 21:36).[67] *What Christian apostates stand to lose, then, is eternal salvation.*

Clear citations from Israel's scripture in Heb 2 highlight the importance of solidarity between Christ and his followers as "brothers and sisters" sharing a common humanity (Heb 2:5–13/Ps 8:5–7; Ps 21[22]:22–23; Isa 8:17). Psalm 8 may be used to capture an Adamic commission over creation that culminates with messiah as the

---

62. On the author's use of *qal wahomer* (or *a fortiori*) see also 9:13–14; 10:28–29; 12:9, 25. The term "valid" (βέβαιος) is a legal one stressing the seriousness of keeping the delivered word, making more explicit the punishments for sins of commission (transgression) and omission (disobedience); so Attridge, *Hebrews*, 65.

63. See especially Allen, *Deuteronomy and Exhortation*, 104–8, 141–43, 244–45.

64. *Jub.* 1:27–29; 5:1–13; Josephus, *Ant.* 15.136; Acts 7:30, 35, 38, 53; *Pesiq Rabbati* 21; *Mekilta Exod.* 20.18; cf. CD 5.18

65. Cf. Mitchell, *Hebrews*, 62.

66. Cf. Koester, *Hebrews*, 209.

67. The concept of recompense (μισθαποδοσία) is used negatively for apostasy in Heb 2:3 but positively for faithfulness in 10:35 and 11:26.

second Adam (Heb 2:5–9/Ps 8:4–6).[68] More than this, solidarity seems to include several important aspects in Heb 2:10–13.

First, there is a perfection/completion through the suffering of Christ that leads his followers to complete sanctification (2:10).[69] The "glory" that the "sons and daughters" experience appears to be eschatological salvation, which is made possible by the suffering and priestly work of Christ[70] who is already exalted and leads the way for their own perfection in glory (Heb 2:5–8 cf. 1:14; 11:40; 12:2–3). This solidarity implies a movement in which Christ brings the believers to their final destination in the heavenly realm by paving the way for them.

Second, Christ is not ashamed of the solidarity he has with these children (Heb 2:11–12). The author has in mind Ps 21[22]:5, 23 LXX, where the psalmist claims that "our fathers" (cf. Heb 1:1) were "not ashamed" to hope in God. Hebrews transfigures this language to mean that Christ is not ashamed of his followers, but a faint implication may arise for the audience if they are to be one with Christ in this area. The author may be suggesting on another level that believers should neither be ashamed about expressing their faith before others nor be shy about associating with Christians in public on account of fearing reprisals from outsiders. More specifically, however, it is *Christ* who is not ashamed of his followers (cf. 11:16), and this thought points to Jesus' warning for his disciples not to be ashamed of him or else he would be ashamed of them at his second coming (Mark 8:38; Luke 9:26). If his followers continue towards complete sanctification and salvation, and they endure suffering through persecution, he will not be ashamed to maintain his solidarity with them before his God. A reciprocal assumption underlies the text: Jesus is not ashamed of those who are not ashamed of him.

Third, their names will be proclaimed in the midst of the congregation (Heb 2:12). Our author refers to Ps 21[22]:23, a messianic passage used by early Christians to speak of Jesus' suffering and crucifixion (cf. Ps 21[22]:1). Originally the lowly psalmist suffers mistreatment (Ps 21[22]:6–18) but will declare the Lord's name in the midst of the assembly. Here thoughts may have been filtered into Hebrews with a hint that the followers' solidarity with Christ involves not just partaking in the frailties and temptations of human suffering (cf. Heb 2:18), but also speaking and encouraging one another in church settings (cf. 10:25). If the solidarity between Christ and his followers holds true on this point, then there may also be a hint that Christ will confess their name before God and the angels at the eschaton.

---

68. See Leschert, *Hermeneutical Foundations of Hebrews*, 119–21; Guthrie, "Hebrews," 946.

69. A helpful understanding of perfection in Hebrews is "having been brought to the final goal" (deSilva, *Perseverance in Gratitude*, 199; cf. 194–204).

70. 5:9; 7:28; 9:11; 10:14.

Fourth and finally, "I will put my trust in him" (Isa 8:17/Heb 2:13a) refers to Christ and his followers' faithfulness and obedience to God,[71] and "Here am I, and the children God whom God has given me" (Isa 8:18/Heb 2:13b) adds further depth to the notions of trust, obedience, filial relationships, and perhaps also an affirmation of service and commission to proclaim God's message, if we assume that "here I am" is a phrase used in the author's Isaianic source for accepting God's prophetic call (Isa 6:8). In Isa 8:11–18, there is a refusal to go down the path of the apostate Israelites (cf. Isa 6:9–10), and trusting in God is seen as more important than fearing what the apostates fear, for God will be a sanctuary (ἁγίασμα) for the person who fears him. In the Isaiah text an anonymous person proclaims his trust in God (Isa 8:17 cf. v. 14), and he and the children whom God has blessed him with will be for "signs and wonders" (σημεῖα καὶ τέρατα) to the house of Israel.[72] In the Masoretic version the identity of the person in 8:17–18 refers to Isaiah and his sons as signs for the house of Ahaz (cf. Isa 7:3, 8:3; cf. 7:14), but in the LXX this person is kept anonymous ("And he/one will say": καὶ ἐρεῖ). From the latter text the author of Hebrews is able to identify this person as Christ, and his "children" are identified as the Christ-followers. Several touchstones from the passage become relevant for our author in Hebrews: 1) similar to Isaiah, the audience of Hebrews is to avoid the path of apostasy (e.g., Heb 2:1–4; 4:1; 6:4–6; 10:25–30); 2) they are to fear God rather than conform to the values and fears of outsiders (12:28–29); 3) they are to trust God (ch. 11) and perceive their place of worship in light of a heavenly sanctuary rather than an earthly one (3:2–6; 8:1–5); 4) they are to view their child-parent solidarity with Christ as a work of divine grace (2:9; cf. 2:4c) much the same way the prophetic person acknowledges that it was God who gave him his children; and 5) as the children become a proclamation of "signs and wonders" in the Isaianic text, so the audience in Hebrews are to remember the infant stage of their great salvation when signs and wonders were performed in their community through the Spirit and the proclamation of the gospel was emphasized.

The implications of this solidarity between Christ and his followers for the warning in Heb 2:1–4 would seem be at least threefold. First, the author assumes that *those in danger of drifting away are identified as Christ's "children" who fully belong to him (2:11–13; 3:1).* He considers them to be in every way Christian believers, just as he is. Second, if these children drift away from the spoken word, they would sever their relationship with Christ; *apostasy breaks the binding rope of a tight-knit,*

---

71. The confusion over "I" being Christ and yet also referring to his followers may be alleviated by the author's stress on the latter's solidarity with Christ (2:11a). Christ's faithful attitude may be seen as representing their attitude.

72. Hebrews follows the LXX, but not an extant version; so McCullough, "Isaiah in Hebrews," 161.

filial relationship between Christ and his followers. Third, the author wants his audience to realize that *to follow Christ is to share in his sufferings* (2:10-13; cf. 13:13), *an outlook that further equips them to persevere on the metaphoric path to perfected salvation and not be ashamed of their Christian identity before others.* If they endure in the present, then at the end of their journey when the eschaton takes place, Christ will maintain his solidarity with them and not be ashamed to identify them as his own family members. The author unpackages more of their journey in chapters 3-4 and stresses its culmination in chapter 12.

ISRAEL'S APOSTASY IN THE WILDERNESS AND WARNINGS TO THE AUDIENCE (3:7—4:13)

As in 2:1-4 we see another warning beginning in 3:7, this time in the imagery of the wilderness wanderings rather than a drifting off to sea. In 3:7—4:13 our author uses Israel's apostasy in the wilderness as an example to warn his audience not to fall away. Our author reconfigures a narrative that shares a negative attitude toward the wilderness generation in common with early Jewish and Christian traditions (Ps 77[78]; 80[81]; 105[106]; Isa 63:7-14: Ezek 20:1-22; Amos 5:21-27; Wis 18:20-25; Acts 7:38-42; 1 Cor 10:1-11). The wilderness is typically viewed as a place of testing, and it frequently assumes connotations related to barrenness, perishing, and endangerment to the body.[73] In cultural-anthropological models, the wilderness becomes archetypical for a state of liminality.[74] The liminar's "betwixt and between" status may be comparable with the "now and not yet" eschatological status of the Christian who faces an ongoing ordeal in an effort to survive the present overlap of two ages and come to final rest when Christ returns. Our author views the present state of the believer as temporal and transitional, a metaphoric place of preparation between the poles of repentance and rest in which spiritual dangers might overtake the people of God. In this section the author gives warnings using second-person plural imperatives ("beware": 3:12; "exhort": 3:13), second-person prohibitive subjunctives ("harden not your hearts": 3:8, 15; 4:7), and hortatory subjunctives that include himself ("let us fear": 4:1; "let us make every effort": 4:11).

The author of Hebrews expounds primarily on Ps 94[95] (cf. Heb 3:7-11, 15; 4:3, 7). His first exhortation cites Ps 94[95]:7-11 LXX and urges the audience not to harden their hearts as their ancestors did in the wilderness during the time of

---

73. Cf. Deut 1:19, 31; 8:15; 32:10; Ps 106[107]:40; Isa 13:21-22; *1 En.* 10.4; Mark 1:12-14; Luke 8:29; 2 Cor 11:26

74. See further Oropeza, *Paul and Apostasy*, 120-22.

Churches under Siege of Persecution and Assimilation

"rebellion" (Heb 3:8).[75] Their spiritual obduracy in the psalm does not include a divine hardening; here the people harden themselves.[76] This involves a refusal to obey God's will.[77] The event in the psalm recalls the Israelites testing God at Massah and Meribah[78] and at Kadesh Barnea;[79] in the latter location the people murmur against Moses, rebel against God, and want to return to Egypt after Israel's spies gave a bad report of the land of Canaan.[80] Moses warns the people against becoming deserters by abandoning the Lord as a result of their fearing the land's inhabitants (Num 14:9 LXX).

According to the voice of the Spirit, the people constantly went astray (πλανάω) in their hearts and did not know God's ways (Ps 94[95]:10/Heb 3:10).[81] Πλανάω characteristically depicts a deception or going astray from a specific course, and it frequently refers to apostasy in early Jewish and Christian sources.[82] In Ps 94[95] the obdurate hearts of the people have led them astray from the way God intended for them, a way of living in a manner pleasing to God and that would lead them to final rest. That they had not known God's "ways" reaffirms this meaning (cf. Heb 3:10c). The wilderness people's lack of knowledge perhaps centers on their failure to keep the instructions and commandments God gave them (cf. Deut 10:12–13; 26:17; 28:9; 30:16; 32:4; Ps 118[119]:15, 33, 151). They ignored God's precepts and were not willing to hear his voice.

---

75. The "provocation" or "rebellion" (παραπικρασμός) in Heb 3:8 and LXX may have been originally derived from *Meribah*, the Hebrew place of rebellion (Ps 94[95]:8). The location known as *Massah* ("testing" in Hebrew) also seems to have been reduced to the concept of testing in Ps 94[95]:9. Both locations are mentioned together in Exod 17:7 and Deut 33:8.

76. Cf. Exod 32:9; 33:5; 34:9; Deut 9:6, 13; 10:16; 31:27.

77. Cf. Koester, *Hebrews*, 255, and see also 2 Kgs 17:14; Jer 17:23; Zech 7:12.

78. Exod 17:7; Deut 6:16; 9:22; 33:8; Num 20:2–13.

79. Num 14:11, 21–23.

80. In this context the provocation, tempting, and testing are done by Israel towards God (Exod 17:2; Deut 33:8; Ps 105:14); that is, they push "the limits of his tolerance" (Johnson, *Hebrews*, 115). God is not testing his people here (cf. Deut 4:34; 8:2; 13:3).

81. The adverbial ἀεί in Heb 3:10 is understood as "constantly" (BDAG, 22). This term may presuppose a repetitive pattern of behavior during Israel's forty-year journey. The word does not suggest that the wilderness generation was never truly God's people. In Ps 94[95]:7 God's election is presupposed for Israel and the psalmist: "he is our God . . . we are the people of his pasture and the sheep of his hand" (cf. Exod 29:45; Deut 7:6–9; Jer 32:38). The psalmist, no doubt, took for granted the Israelites as God's chosen people via their deliverance from Egypt (cf. Exod 4:22–23). The author of Hebrews shares a similar view, reckoning both the Christians and Israelites of old as God's people (Heb 4:9).

82. E.g., Deut 13:6; Hos 8:6; Amos 2:4; Isa 41:9; Wis 14:12; 2 *Bar.* 4.8; Matt 24:4, 11, 24; Luke 21:8; Jas 5:19; 2 Pet 2:15; 1 John 2:26; Rev 2:20; *1 Clem.* 16.6; *Herm. Vis.* 3.7.1. See further Braun, "πλανάω," 6.228–53.

The author in essence summarizes the first exhortation for his audience to avoid hardening their hearts (Heb 3:7-11) by warning them to "beware" (βλέπετε) lest there be in any of them a wicked heart of unbelief that falls away from the living God (3:12). If they harden their hearts, this would mean that they are operating with wickedness and unbelief at the core of their beings, an action identified as apostasy. When coupled with a negative particle and subjunctive, βλέπετε is often used in early Christian sources as a warning against deception, sin, and falling away (3:11; 12:25).[83] This warning extends to every one of the congregation members and is linked with apostatizing from God (3:12). In early Jewish and Christian sources the verb ἀφίστημι used here normally means to withdraw, go away, or revolt, and it frequently refers to religious apostasy, a falling away from God.[84] The Septuagint more precisely uses the aorist active infinitive ἀποστῆναι (as does 3:12) almost categorically to connote a defection from the Lord/God[85] or from the Law.[86]

We find two warnings similar to 3:12 in 4:1 and 4:11. In 4:1 the audience is to fear, lest they should be judged to have failed to reach the promised rest.[87] This aspect of failing (ὑστερέω) is elsewhere used to connote their potential inability to attain the grace of God (cf. 12:15).[88] In 4:11 the believers are to make every effort to enter into the promised rest, lest any of them fall away through the same pattern of disobedience as the wilderness generation. "Lest . . . fall away" (ἵνα μὴ . . . πέσῃ) resembles the use of πίπτω in 1 Cor 10:12, another passage that uses the example of the wilderness generation's defection to warn believers. In both cases the meaning for πίπτω is virtually the same: the audience is warned against committing apostasy and

---

83. Cf. Matt 24:4; Mark 13:5; Acts 13:40-41; 1 Cor 8:9; 10:12; Gal 5:15; 2 John 8; BDAG, 179.

84. Cf. ἀφίστημι: Deut 7:4; 32:15; Jer 2:5; 3:14; Ezek 20:8, 38; Dan 9:9 [Theodotian]; Bar 3.8; Wis 3:10; 1 En. 5.4; Josephus, Ant. 1.14; Luke 8:13; 1 Tim 4:1; Herm. Sim. 8.8.2, 5; 8.9.1; Herm. Vis. 2.32; 3.7.2. See also the conceptual equivalent in 1QS 7.18-23, and further examples in Schlier, "ἀφίστημι," 1.512-14; Bauder, "Fall, Fall Away," 1.606-8.

85. Josh 22:22-23, 29; 2 Chr 28:22; Sg Three 1:6; Pss. Sol. 1.9; Odes Sol. 7.29; cf. 1 Macc 2:19-20; Jer 39:40.

86. Cf. 2 Macc 2:3. Two exceptions are 2 Sam 2:23 and Sir 35:3. The latter mentions a departure from evil and unrighteousness.

87. The negative μή (μήποτε δοκῇ) functions as an expression of apprehension (BDF, 188 §370), and here δοκέω ("to think," or "to seem") probably has a forensic meaning: to be "found" or "judged" as failing (cf. Prov 27:14; Josephus, Ant. 8.2.2; Philo, Planting 176; Plato, Statesman 299C; Attridge, Hebrews, 124). A less wooden translation would be, "so that God will not judge any of you as not having received": Ellingworth and Nida, Hebrews, 73. It probably does not mean that they merely had wrong beliefs about the promise of rest being open to them or that they only appeared to fail but really did not. Such ideas would be extremely awkward when combined with the strong words "let us fear," and similar warnings in 3:12 and 4:11.

88. For the wilderness generation, failing to keep the Passover would result in being cut off from God's people (Num 9:13; cf. v. 7).

falling into eschatological ruin.[89] The combined ramification of these verses makes clear that the apostasy threatening the audience follows after the rebellion of Israel in the wilderness. *The Christ-followers in Hebrews are identified as God's people in the last days, and they are in danger of rejecting God and failing to enter the promised eschatological rest.*

It is sometimes suggested from 3:12 that apostasy from "the living God" makes better sense if the audience were Gentiles. They would be in danger of turning back to dead idols. If Jewish Christians were reverting back to some type of formative Judaism, this would not constitute idolatry—they would still be serving the living God.[90] But it may suffice to explain that our author is echoing God's solemn oath at Kadesh Barnea to the wilderness generation. God would not let them enter the land of rest because of their provocations and not listening to his voice. The oath begins twice with the LORD saying, "As I live" (Num 14:21–23, 28–35). Moreover, the "living God" is sometimes used to refer to God in his wrath (Deut 5:26; Josh. 3:10; Jer 10:10),[91] and this would certainly fit the phrase's meaning in Heb 3:12; 10:31; and 12:22.[92] It is quite possible that our author has combined the oath by God from Num 14 with the psalmist's pronouncement against the wilderness rebels that they would never enter into God's "rest" (Heb 3:11; 4:3). This intertextual blend may provide a ground for our author's rigorous stand of claiming that apostates in his day are not able to be restored (Heb 6:6; 10:26; 12:17). Hence, the author's designation "living God" does not necessarily suggest that those being warned in 3:12 were in danger of reverting back to idolatry. Our author does not specify if the apostates would be turning away to a Hellenistic or Jewish sect, the imperial cult, or simply no longer trusting and obeying God similar to the wilderness generation's apostasy. If the audience is a mixture of Jews and Gentiles, then all these venues are possible options. The author's concern, at any rate, does not rest on what they would be joining but what they would be forsaking.[93] They are in danger of abandoning God and the final salvation that comes at the end of their journey.

---

89. See πίπτω in Rom 14:4; Sir 28:22–26; cf. Sir 1:30; *Pss. Sol.* 3:9–12; Prov 16:18; 18:12. We notice a similar thought for falling (πταίω) in 2 Pet 1:10.

90. Cf. Isa 37:4, 17; 2 Kgs 19:4; *Jub.* 21:4–5; 1 Thess 1:9; Acts 14:15. See also Weiss, *Hebräer*, 262.

91. Cf. Buchanan, *Hebrews*, 222.

92. Alternatively, the "living God" may center on the notion that God is the source and giver of life—he is the God of the living (cf. Ps 36:10; Jer 2:13; 17:13; Mark 12:27): cf. Gräßer, *Hebräer*, 186–87. He is the one who speaks the "living word" that delivers people from "dead works" (cf. Heb 4:12; 9:14).

93. In agreement with Isaacs, *Reading Hebrews*, 59. This is not too different than many people today in Western societies who celebrate Christmas and attend church whenever someone they know is married or buried. They are not atheists, they are not religionists, they are not necessarily driven by secular ideologies, but they do not practice their own religion or any devotion to God.

Their potential rejection of God would happen through disobedience and unbelief.⁹⁴ These terms stand out prominently throughout the author's comparative description of the wilderness generation's rebellion and his warnings to his audience (3:17–19; 4:2–3, 6, 11). The thought of hearing God's voice also suggests obeying and believing his words (3:7, 15; 4:2, 7). Deuteronomy 9:23 speaks of the Kadesh Barnea rebellion and combines these aspects.⁹⁵ Perhaps our author was informed by this verse: "And when the Lord sent you forth from Kadesh Barnea saying, 'Go up and inherit the land which I am giving you,' then you disobeyed the word of the Lord your God and did not believe him and did not listen to his voice" (LXX). The event in Numbers likewise informs the meaning of the sin mentioned in Heb 3:17 (ἁμαρτάνω: cf. Num 14:9, 29–33, 40). The incident at this location recalls the people's unbelief (Num 14:11 cf. vv. 1–5), murmuring (14:27, 29, 36), provoking God (14:11, 22), and disobedience (14:33).⁹⁶ Again, *unbelief and disobedience toward God seem to be at the heart of this rebellion.* We could only guess that that the author of Hebrews may have perceived disobedience towards Christian leaders as disobedience towards God (cf. Heb 13:7, 17). Equally, failure to respond to the leaders' messages and godly exhortations from fellow believers, as well as attend fellowship meetings, may have been interpreted as signs of unbelief towards God (cf. 2:1; 10:25).

PREVENTATIVES AGAINST APOSTASY: FAITH, EXHORTATION, AND PERSEVERANCE (3:13–14; 4:2–3; CF. 3:6)

Faith is contrasted with the wilderness generation's unbelief in 4:2–3, and the audience's task of exhorting one another and holding fast to their confidence in 3:13–14 (cf. 10:25; 12:15) is contrasted with warnings against unbelief and apostasy in 3:12. These may be regarded as preventatives against falling away.⁹⁷ The wilderness generation in 4:2 did not benefit from the good news of entering God's rest. They were not united in faith with those who listened (i.e., those who obeyed the good news).⁹⁸

---

94. The thought of disobedience resurfaces again in 11:31 as a descriptor for the inhabitants of Jericho who are destroyed as a result of their disobedience. On obedience see 5:8–9; 11:8; 13:17.

95. See Löhr, *Umkehr und Sünde*, 94.

96. In Numbers 14:33 πορνεία is probably to be understood as spiritual unfaithfulness (cf. Exod 34:16), not literal fornication. Sexual immorality does not take place until Numbers 25.

97. Other preventatives in Heb 3–4 include spiritual alertness and diligence (3:12; 4:11), fearing God (4:1), obedience to God's word (e.g. 4:7 [implied]), and prayer/worship (4:16; cf. 10:19–22).

98. Text variations of 4:2 are legion and confuse the understanding of συγκεράννυμι. The accusative perfect passive participle plural συγκεκερασμένους is preferred; cf. Metzger, *Textual Commentary*, 595. Zerwick, *Grammatical Analysis*, 660–61, translates the relevant portion of 4:2 as "those not intimately united with the ones who heard with faith." The alternative reading, which uses a nominative perfect passive participle singular (א, Vulgate, Peshitta, etc.), reads: "the word not being blended with faith."

The identity of the second, faithful group might refer to the faithful remnant that survived the wilderness—Joshua, Caleb, and the younger generation—but the author is more likely referring to the Christians ("we") who believe the gospel/good news and are in the process of entering God's rest (4:3).[99]

Faith, then, is considered a preventative against apostasy. For our author, this faith is grounded in the work of Christ whose sacrificial death for sin made him the pioneer of the faithful (2:10; 10:19–23; 12:2). Hebrews does not center on the content of beliefs; rather, it is bent on a moral quality embracing the idea of fidelity and confidence towards the unseen future (3:14; 4:14–16; 11:1, 6).[100] As such, faith requires obedience and perseverance, and so it combines the elements of trust and faithfulness.[101] The heroes of Israel's past, culminating with Jesus, become exemplars of those who live by this kind of faith (11:4—12:2).

A second preventative against apostasy is for the congregation members to *exhort one another on a daily basis* so that they do not become hardened by the "deceit of sin" (3:13). If the author's warning against the audience committing ἁμαρτία in 3:13 anticipates the wilderness generation's sin in 3:17, then to "sin" in this context may be synonymous for unbelief and disobedience towards God. They could be deceived in the sense of having their hearts hardened and so be led away from their trust and obedience (cf. 3:10).[102] The antidote would be for them continually to exhort one another much the same way the author is exhorting them through his homily (cf. 13:19, 22).[103] If such warnings and encouragements are to take place on a routine basis, then opportunities for Christian fellowship and gatherings must have been available on a regular basis. The author is adamant about the audience assembling together as a congregation because failure to participate in Christian fellowship is one of the first steps towards apostasy (cf. 10:24–26). The exhortations, of course, would not prevent defection if the hearers who attend church reject the exhortations. The author no doubt assumes that such words of encouragement must

---

See further discussion in Löhr, *Umkehr und Sünde*, 95–96.

99. The present middle εἰσερχόμεθα in 4:3 suggests the entrance into rest is taking place, and yet believers are to make every effort to enter into the rest (4:10–11), which reads as though the "rest" is not already taking place. Some have interpreted 4:3 as indicating the believers already have entered this rest (Lane, *Hebrews*, 1.99), or they will enter in the futuristic (Koester, *Hebrews*, 270), or the verse stands in tension with 4:11, suggesting present and future aspects of entering into rest (Mackie, *Eschatology and Exhorthation*, 49–54). Perhaps a better option is to see εἰσερχόμεθα in 4:3 as a true present tense demarcating the believers at the threshold of entering (deSilva, *Perseverance in Gratitude*, 153–56).

100. See Lindars, *Theology of the Letter*, 103–13.

101. McKnight, "Warning Passages of Hebrews," 32, rightly suggests the author holds to the "obedience of faith."

102. Koester, *Hebrews*, 259, adds that deception has the false "appearance of being good."

103. Cf. Attridge, *Hebrews*, 117.

be received by faith, and faith itself grows by the hearer responding positively to such words (cf. Rom 10:17).

Perseverance is a third preventative (Heb 3:14; cf. 3:6).[104] The intensive "if" of Hebrews 3:14 (ἐάνπερ) stresses a provisional aspect to being partakers or sharers in Christ (cf. μέτοχος: 3:1; 6:4; 12:8). The concept of sharing in Christ is comparable with Paul's thought of participating "in Christ" in which believers as a community share in a relational-mystical solidarity with Christ (Gal 3:27–28; 2 Cor 5:17; cf. Heb 2:11–17; 3:1, 6; 6:4).[105] In Hebrews the relationship in Christ is maintained by the author and audience *holding fast* (κατέχω) to this reality[106] of being in Christ from the beginning of their faith-based relationship with him until the culmination of the eschaton or the end of their mortal lives (Heb 6:11; cf. 10:25, 37–38). Κατέχω here suggests an active holding on to one's boldness and hope (3:6)[107] and one's relationship with Christ (cf. 3:14). It thus involves perseverance (cf. Heb 10:23; Luke 8:15; 1 Cor 15:2). In Pauline conditional sentences relevant to perseverance, apostasy likewise remains a danger that threatens those who share in Christ (e.g., Col 1:22–23; Rom 11:22).

Sometimes the perfect tense γεγόναμεν in Heb 3:14 ("we have/are become" sharers . . .) is used to imply that only genuine believers from the Christian community persevere to the end; spurious or superficial believers do not.[108] But this may be reading too much meaning into this tense.[109] The parallel passage in 3:6b uses the present tense ἐσμεν: "We are [God's] house if we hold fast our confidence and boasting of hope." Both passages intend to stress a sharing with Christ as something that is a present reality the audience already experiences. It is likely that they once were *not* in this state.[110] And if they do not persevere, they will not *remain* in this state.

---

104. Both Hofius, *Katapausis*, 133, and Lane, *Hebrews*, 1.88, affirm 3:14 as the antithesis to apostasy.

105. Unlike Paul, this picture of Christ includes his priestly role and partaking in humanity (e.g., Heb 2:14–18).

106. We understand ὑπόστασις here as "reality" (cf. 11:1) loosely. It could also include or alternatively mean "confidence" given παρρησία in the parallel passage of 3:6.

107. Παρρησία in 3:6 probably refers to an outward confidence or boldness that confesses Christ before others and is not ashamed to be a Christ-follower and belong to his household (cf. 2:11–13; 3:1–5). It also involves "the right to full access before God" and drawing near to him; cf. 4:16; 10:19; Thompson, *Hebrews*, 91. See further Ellingworth, *Hebrews*, 211.

108. See Carson, *Exegetical Fallacies*, 84–85.

109. Wallace, *Greek Grammar*, 575; cf. 574, 576, lists Heb 3:14 as an intensive perfect, which stresses a resultant state: "Consequently, *stative* verbs are especially used in this way. Often the best translation of the intensive perfect is as a *present* tense." Alternatively, Porter, *Verbal Aspect*, 269–70, says that the perfect tense γεγόναμεν is a timeless perfect: "we are become partakers of Christ if we might hold firmly to our beginning confidence until the end." Also see Schreiner and Caneday, *Race*, 200–202.

110. Cf. Johnson, *Hebrews*, 118.

Churches under Siege of Persecution and Assimilation

Paul Ellingworth notices that γέγονα frequently appears in the homily (5:11–12; 7:16, 20, 23; 12:8), and it "may well mean no more than ἐσμεν. The logic of such translations as [Revised English Bible] '. . . we have become partners with Christ, if only we keep our initial confidence firm to the end,' which appears to make a past condition dependent on a future, is perhaps unnecessarily difficult. The implication is rather: 'We have become, and are now, partners with Christ; and we shall remain such if we hold fast to the end.'"[111] In this manner *the audience have become sharers in Christ and belong to his house (with present beneficial results), and they will continue to benefit from this relationship provided that they continue to hold fast to the end.* This meaning is confirmed in view of the larger context of Heb 3–4: the audience is being warned against apostasy, and a similar defection took place in the past among God's people in the wilderness. Hebrews 3:6 and 14, then, should be read in light of this larger context and subject matter that is confirmed repetitively by the multiple warnings throughout the homily. Conversely, there is no reason for us to read the multiple warnings throughout this homily in light of a highly debatable interpretation of 3:6 and 14.[112]

In sum, *the sharers in Christ are still susceptible to apostasy, and this is why they must hold fast to their relationship with Christ to the end.* The author is also a sharer in Christ and considers himself susceptible to falling away (cf. "we" 3:14 and "us" in 4:1).[113] An interesting parallel to 3:14 is the warning of Jesus to his followers, "the one who perseveres to the end will be saved" (Matt 10:22; 24:13; Mark 13:13). But

---

111. Ellingworth, *Hebrews*, 227.

112. *Pace* Thomas, *Case for a Mixed-Audience*, 187–89, 272–80, who inverts this order by having 3:6 and 14 as his interpretative centerpiece. He opts against a cause/effect relation for the conditional clause and chooses instead an "evidence/inference" sense in 3:6 and 3:14 in which the believers have been shown to be the "house" and "partners of Christ" (i.e., they are genuine believers) if indeed they persevere to the end (see also Fanning, "Classical Reformed View," 172–219). However, in view of the repeated warnings in the context above, 3:6 and 14 seem to be cause-effect or consequential conditions. There is no compelling basis for why these verses should be the foundation for interpreting the warnings in Hebrews when they neither function as the thesis nor the first, last, or most extensive argument of the homily and/or its warnings. See scholarly examples of theses in Hebrews in Joslin, "Can Hebrews be Structured?," 99–129.

113. See Heb 2:1 above. The use of plurals in relation to apostasy does not mean that a corporate apostasy alone is in view. Not only do we find "we" (e.g., 3:19; 4:2–3, 11), and "you" (pl.) (3:7f, 12, 13, 15; 4:7), but also "anyone/someone" (3:12, 13; 4:1; 4:11; cf. Löhr, *Umkehr und Sünde*, 103–06). The author of Hebrews recognizes that apostates could be individuals (3:12; 4:1; 12:15–17); *contra* Verbrugge, "Towards a New Interpretation," 61–73. Πάντες in 3:16 perhaps in some sense is corporate, but its inclusion in Hebrews may be primarily lifted from Num 14, which often uses "all" (Num 14:2, 5, 7, 10, 22) even though the tradition recognizes a remnant that did not apostatize (i.e., Caleb, Joshua, and the younger generation). Alternatively, the first of the rhetorical questions in 3:16–18 may not be a question but a statement: "some (τίνες) heard and rebelled but not all who came out of Egypt" (3:16; cf. Isaacs, *Reading Hebrews*, 60).

closer to home, the believers can look to Jesus as the ultimate model of perseverance. He is the forerunner of the faithful who remained steadfast from beginning to the end throughout his sufferings, and he has now entered into his rest (e.g., Heb 2:10; 12:1–2).

THE CONSEQUENCE OF APOSTASY: FAILURE TO ENTER INTO REST (3:11, 18; 4:1, 3–11)

Using subtexts from the wilderness generation and especially Ps 94[95], the author warns that if the audience turns away from God they would fail to enter a final place of rest (κατάπαυσιν: Heb 3:11, 18; 4:1, 3, 5, 8–11). The εἰ in Heb 3:11; 4:3, 5 is not conditional but a Hebraism related to solemn assertions: i.e, "they *certainly* will *not* enter into my rest."[114] Given that God does not change his oaths, and the fact that in Israel's traditions the wilderness generation died before entering the land of rest, we are safe in saying that this oath can be interpreted as "they will *never* enter into my rest."[115] This punishment is graphically portrayed in 3:17 when the author alludes to the ancient Israelites' bodies dropping dead in the desert (cf. Num 14:16, 29–32). The portrait lends to the author's rhetoric of "fear" (cf. Heb 4:1). The dead corpses remain unburied in the wilderness, open to the elements and wild beasts. Such a death connotes the shameful brand of curse that comes on those who violate God's covenant and abandon him (Deut 28:26; Lev 26:27–30; cf. 1 Kgs 14:7–11; 21:20–26; 2 Kgs 9:34–37; Isa 66:24). Later Jewish traditions would claim that the wilderness generation has no share in the world to come (*m. Sanhedrin* 10.3; *b. Sanhedrin* 110b). The author of Hebrews is more concerned about his audience's own fate, suggesting through the wilderness story that if God did not spare his own people from judgment when they rejected him, neither would he spare hardened and disobedient Christians.

Similar to the macrostructure of Hebrews, which segues from the exalted Christ to warnings against apostasy, Ps 94[95] moves from an invitation to exult the Lord (vv. 1–7) to an exhortation against the people of God hardening their hearts (vv. 8–11). The psalm is festal belonging to the corpus of Ps 93–100, which emphasize the Lord's royal reign. Psalm 94[95] addresses a complication that might hinder that reign.[116] The word "today" (Ps 94[95]:7–8) perhaps recalls σήμερον and similar words that introduce the Deuteronomic formula of keeping God's commands in

---

114. Cf. BDF 189[§ 372.4]; BDAG, 278. On the rest motif in early Jewish and Christian literature see Wray, *Rest*, 9–46.

115. On this translation see, e.g., Ellingworth and Nida, *Hebrews*, 64.

116. Cf. Hossfeld and Zenger, *Psalms*, 2.459, 462.

relation to the covenant of blessings and curses (cf. Deut 27:11; 28:1; 30:18–19; cf. 4:26, 39f; 6:6, 24; 8:11; 32:46). The people are to hear God's "voice," that is, obey his message and commands (Deut 9:23; 30:20).[117] The "rest" in Ps 94[95]:11 recalls Israel's wilderness travels, but the original auditors of Ps 94[95] may have applied it to the LORD dwelling in Jerusalem and their living in a state of peace amidst surrounding enemies (cf. 1 Chr 22:9, 18; 23:25–26). The Septuagint translators may have interpreted the psalm as "penitential liturgy," a song delineating grief over the endangerment of the people's covenant relationship with God.[118] If the people do not obey God's voice, then covenant curses will come upon them that include defeat at the hands of their enemies and expulsion from their land. In this sense they would fail to experience God's rest.

Our author in Hebrews transforms Ps 94[95] by primarily focusing on the concept of rest, which together with the idea of God resting on the seventh day (Heb 4:4, 10/Gen 2:2–3; Exod 20:11), expands on the concept "today" from the psalm to claim that God's people still await a Sabbath rest.[119] It remains available for his people[120] but not in terms of their finding rest in the earthly land of Canaan. Rather, the place of rest is a transcendent "space" where God himself rested after he finished his work of creation.[121] And as God rested from his works, so God's people will be able to desist from their "works," which probably means that they rest from their diligent toiling to resist sin and persevere to the end (Heb 4:10; cf. v. 11; 12:4, 15).[122] The new "today" in Hebrews is the eschatological present in which the believers are sanctified by the death and priestly work of Christ (e.g., 2:14–17); they have embarked on their wilderness journey to the place of final rest which will be fully realized when Christ returns.[123] Until then they must adhere to God's word spoken through Christ in the present era. The motif of the wandering people in Hebrews draws our attention to a perspective of "rest" (κατάπαυσις) as the culmination of the wilderness journey. The perception of movement complements the homily's way of showing Christians either moving towards their destination (e.g., Heb 12:1–2) or away from it by backsliding

---

117. Cf. Deut 4:30–36; 5:20–26; 8:20; Exod 3:18; 4:1, 9; Gen 3:17.

118. Cf. Hossfeld and Zenger, *Psalms*, 2.462.

119. Mackie, *Eschatology and Exhortation*, 53, associates "today" with "eschatological time," which certainly seems relevant for this verse.

120. Cf. Wray, *Rest*, 83.

121. See Attridge, "Psalms in Hebrews," 207.

122. Alternatively it could mean good works (6:10; 10:24), such as performing virtues and love, which will be done until the *parousia*.

123. Jesus will give his people rest at the culmination of all things, something the "Jesus" of the old covenant (Joshua LXX) was unable to accomplish (Heb 4:3–10).

(e.g., 2:1; 3:10; 13:9).[124] Notably, παρα-prefixed words frequently indicate movement away from God (3:8, 15–16; cf. 2:1; 6:6; 12:12; 13:9).[125] *The concept of rest implies the final culmination of movement towards God.*

Jon Laansma seems correct by understanding "rest" in terms of the author's concern with salvation that presently exists but is not yet "entered *qua* κατάπαυσις." It is thus futuristic, bound up with the second coming of Christ, and until that time "the believers are on probation."[126] If "rest" is essentially the state of completion at the end of the believers' metaphoric journey when they experience glorification and inheritance in the presence of God and when heavenly "Zion" is fully realized (cf. 12:22–28; 13:14), then *failure to enter rest would thus be equated with the loss of final inheritance.* The depiction of God's people being destroyed in the wilderness is perhaps set as some sort of precursor to the eschatological destruction that will happen to Christian apostates (3:17; cf. 6:7–8; 12:28–29). In typical lesser to greater fashion, the author implies that the disobedient Christians' destruction will be more severe than the destruction of their predecessors who fell in the wilderness. The recipients must pay attention to this word of warning.[127]

In hindsight, Heb 3–4 is the second of five major warnings to the recipients. Through the story of the wilderness generation, primarily from Ps 94[95] and secondarily from Num 13–14, the author warns the recipients that they must not exemplify the same pattern of disobedience and unbelief as the hardened Israelites who fell away from God. If they do so, they will fall away from the living God who once swore that his rebellious people would never enter into his rest. The concept of rest suggests for the believers the culmination of the eschaton when Christ returns. Their defection would constitute the loss of their final inheritance, and they would suffer destruction worse than the wilderness generation who died in the desert. The believers are to exercise faith, perseverance, and exhort one another on a regular basis as preventatives against apostasy. They will continue to partake of solidarity in Christ if they endure to the end of their eschatological journey.

---

124. On the concept of movement see Klauck, "Moving in and Moving out," 427–28; Löhr, *Umkehr und Sünde*, 250–74.

125. Cf. Proulx, and Schökel, "Heb 6,4–6," 198.

126. Laansma, *Rest Motif*, 314. Differently, Wray, *Rest*, 91, considers entering into rest as a participation that is to be maintained "in the completed cosmic work of God" (cf. 163).

127. In 4:12–13, for our author, this "word" or message about the wilderness generation is powerful enough to affect its promises, including judgment upon the disobedient, since nothing is hid from God's sight. See further on the "word" in Pfitzner, *Hebrews*, 83–85, who considers these final verses as climactic for the entire pericope.

RELUCTANT LISTENERS AND FOUNDATIONAL INSTRUCTION (5:11—6:12)

The author's message on the high priesthood of Christ is interrupted to address the audience's spiritual dullness in an *inclusio* from 5:11 to 6:12.[128] In these verses he uses the term νωθρός negatively associating it with the audience's lack of maturity when it comes to moral and spiritual instruction (5:11–14). Preisker understands νωθρός here as "a lack of receptivity for Christian *gnosis*, and a stale, exhausted spirit instead of the glowing joy of hope. When Christian life shows exhaustion both in breathing in (hearing and receiving) and in breathing out (believing confidence in the future), the author of Hb. calls his readers νωθροί."[129] Although spiritual sluggishness may generally define the meaning of the term, this could be easily misunderstood in our context. Its nuance is more the sense of mental dullness[130] than laziness. Their condition fails to make use of what they have been taught. Johnson is on target by adding a volitional element to the term. They are *reluctant listeners*: "Obedience, as we have seen, is a form of responsive *hearing*. The listeners' reluctance to learn more about such a messiah, therefore, may have much to do with their perception that such learning leads them into the same path of suffering. The difficulty faced by the author is not simply mental laziness, but spiritual resistance."[131]

Their reluctance towards listening to instruction might seem close to the Isaianic perspective of apostate Israel being heavy of hearing (Isa 6:9–11), a thought often repeated in the gospels when Jesus exhorts his audiences to take heed how they hear (Matt 13:9, 12–15; Mark 4:9, 23–25; Luke 8:4–10; 14:23). A crucial distinction is that in some of these gospel texts God is the one who dulls their hearing as form of judgment. We find no support for this idea in Hebrews. More relevant is the earlier warning that the recipients should not neglect the spoken word related to salvation (Heb 2:1–4). The audience's spiritual dullness functions as a way of shaming them. They do not live up to appropriate standards for the Christ community, and they have not grown to maturity but still lack discernment between good and base things. Society at large shames them for being candidly Christian, and the author counters by shaming them for their lack of proactivity in society and encouraging one an-

---

128. The perfect νωθροὶ γεγόνατε in 5:11 suggests the audience is already in this state of mental dullness. On its tension with the aorist subjunctive ἵνα μὴ νωθροὶ γένησθε in 6:12, and its alleviation see Koester, *Hebrews*, 300.

129. Preisker, "νωθρός," 4.1126. In a negative sense the term can be used for someone lacking deeds (Sir 4:29) and in contrast to someone who is skillful (Prov 22:29 LXX). See also various uses in Philo, *Dreams* 1.237; Plutarch, *Cat. Min.* 1.6; Epictetus, *Discourses* 1.7.30; Polybius, *Histories* 3.63.7; 4.8.5; 4.60.2; Bateman, *Four Views*, 75–76n57.

130. See Attridge, *Hebrews*, 156–57.

131. Johnson, *Hebrews*, 155.

other.¹³² The rhetorical strategy of such language beginning in 5:11 aims to get them to change their reluctant hearing. We are not able to determine what the recipients thought about their own behavior.

Despite their apparent longevity as Christians, assumed by the fact that they ought to be teachers by now (5:12a), the audience needs to be taught again the "elementary principles" (τὰ στοιχεῖα τῆς ἀρχῆς) of the words of God. They must be fed "milk" as baby Christians rather than "solid food" as mature adults (Heb 5:12b–14; cf. 1 Cor 3:1–3).¹³³ The author's thoughts recollect levels of education similar to Hellenistic moral philosophical training;¹³⁴ the believers need further training in moral reasoning.¹³⁵ The author then lists six basic teachings that are foundational (Heb 6:1–3).

Repentance (μετάνοια) from "dead works" heads the list and relates to conversion (Heb 6:1; cf. Matt 3:8, 11; Mark 1:4; Luke 3:3; 24:47; Acts 13:24; 19:4). It involves a movement away from something else, and in this case the neophyte turns away from "dead works," which refers either to rituals related to the Levitical priesthood,¹³⁶ devotion to lifeless idols,¹³⁷ or works that lead to death.¹³⁸ The third option makes sense of the pre-converted status as lacking spiritual life. This view is complementary to all audiences regardless of whether they are Jewish or Gentile.¹³⁹ For our author it seems that repentance is unrepeatable or at least ineffectual the second time around (Heb 6:6; 12:17).

Faith towards God is next on the list. If repentance involves a turning from dead works, then faith in God is the natural corollary—it may refer here to an initial turning to God in trust. It could be argued that the Jewish sector of the congregation would have already trusted in God prior to their Christian commitment, and so the reference targets Gentile converts. Our author, however, seems to believe that anyone who does not have faith in God can displease him, and this would not be limited to Gentiles (11:6; cf. 4:2). Moreover, the concept of placing faith in God may involve

---

132. See deSilva, *Perseverance in Gratitude*, 210–14.

133. See similar uses of food and learning in Philo, *Agriculture* 9; *Prelim.* 19; *Good Person* 160; Epictetus, *Discourses* 2.16.39.

134. Plato, *Republic* 433A; Aristotle, *Politics* 1291A; Seneca, *Ep.* 88.20 cf. Philo, *Planting* 160.

135. Cf. Johnson, *Hebrews*, 156.

136. Cf. 9:10–14; 10:3–4; Lane, *Hebrews*, 1.140.

137. Cf. Wis 15:5, 17; Acts 14:15; 1 Thess 1:9; DeSilva, *Perseverance in Gratitude*, 216–17.

138. Cf. Deut 30:15; Jer 21:8; Rom 6:23; Eph 2:5; Löhr, *Umkehr und Sünde*, 148–52.

139. For the former, e.g., Matt 4:17; Mark 1:4–5; Acts 3:19; 5:31; for the latter, e.g., Acts 11:18; 17:30; 20:20; 2 Pet 3:9.

a Jewish call to repentance (cf. Isa 7:9; Hab 2:4).[140] Early Christian kerygma involves both Jews and Gentiles turning not only to Christ but "God" (cf. Acts 20:21; 26:20).

The next pair of foundational instructions are "baptisms" and the "laying on of hands." The masculine βαπτισμός in 6:2 has been understood sometimes as "washings" (Heb 9:10 cf. Mark 7:4, 8), whereas the neuter βάπτισμα often means baptism (Matt 3:7; Mark 11:30; Acts 1:22). Even so, βαπτισμός sometimes may refer to baptism also (cf. Col 2:12; Josephus, *Ant.* 18.5.2). But the plural is strange in 6:2 and perhaps anticipates the washing in 10:22 in which both ablution of the outer body with water and cleansing of the inward conscience by the blood of Christ are meant (cf. Heb 9:11–10:18; 12:24; Ezek 36:25). Hence, the plural "baptisms" can refer to both inward and outward cleansing. Another alternative is that the thought conveys both water baptism and Spirit baptism. The latter of these, however, makes more sense with the next phrase, "laying on of hands," which served several different functions in the early church,[141] but one of its most significant uses involved the reception of God's Spirit at conversion (cf. Acts 8:17–19; 9:17–18; 19:6).

The final pair pertain to the coming age: resurrection of the dead and eternal judgment (Heb 6:2b cf. John 5:28–29; Rev 20:12–13; 1 Cor 15; Matt 25:31–46). The last point is mentioned again in this pericope when the author uses agricultural imagery to describe the final judgment of apostates (Heb 6:7–8). Why is it not considered an elementary teaching in the latter verses? Perhaps in 6:2b this pair is mentioned in relation to basic instruction given before baptism and possibly confessed during conversion-initiation.[142] In this sense the basics of eschatology are foundational.

Our author assumes his audience already knows the foundational instructions prior to listing them in 6:1–2. *Since all the teachings may be related to conversion-initiation, he seems to be reminding them of their earliest instruction that led to their confession when they were baptized.* His reminder provides confirmation of the audience's identity as Christian converts. Even if the author claims them babes in Christ, they are still bona fide believers. They are holy brothers and sisters who share in Christ (3:1, 6), have already repented, placed initial faith in God, experienced baptism in water and Spirit, and placed their hope in the resurrection of the dead and day of recompense. Moreover, *it seems they have been believers for a long time* (5:12), *and so their potential to fall away is probably not precipitate but a gradual drifting*

---

140. Attridge, *Hebrews*, 263–64, notices the similarities with 6:1–2 and a Jewish catechesis. For discussion see Löhr, *Umkehr und Sünde*, 181–87.

141. Laying on of hands also included commissioning (Acts 6:6; 13:3), healing (5:12; Mark 6:5), blessing (Mark 10:16), and imparting spiritual gifts (1 Tim 4:14).

142. Christian catechetical instruction prior to baptism became more prominent in the second century, but a rudimentary form of it might be suggested for Hebrews. See Attridge, *Hebrews*, 163–64. We notice that the Apostles' Creed contains such elements.

away (cf. 2:1). The author's reaffirmation of their Christian identity may function as an implicit means of discouraging them from returning to their pre-converted status prior to their having a spiritual life in Christ. Even though they are to press on towards maturity, they must not forget how they first became Christ-followers. Our author may also believe that anything short of advancing forward to maturity would be a step backward, which eventually leads to backsliding. *An important preventative against falling away, then, is for the audience to move forward.*[143] This reiteration of the foundational teachings sets up our author for his next warning.

THE APOSTASY OF THOSE WHO WERE ONCE CONVERTED (6:4-6)

The author turns from directly addressing his audience to speak primarily in aorist masculine plural participles about others in 6:4–6. The string of participles describing these people prior to their failing away would seem to imply that they had also experienced conversion and understood the elementary teachings in 6:1–2. *The audience would have doubtless thought that these apostates were also once Christians.* Our author mentions them vaguely as "those" (τοὺς . . . ἑαυτοῖς). When speaking about others in the context of his warnings, and whether they are anonymous (e.g., 10:38–39) or not (e.g., 3:16–19; 12:16–17), the author uses their example as a springboard to directly challenge his recipients not to behave in a like manner. Here he mentions apostates (6:6), but he implies through the larger context that the recipients' reluctant hearing might become the cause of their own defection. Unlike the wilderness generation (chs. 3–4) or Esau (12:16–17), the defectors in this case are Christian: they are associated with crucifying Christ again and putting him to an open shame (6:6). Our author might even have in mind an actual event in the audience's past in which certain members of the community fell away. Another possibility is that, if this document is written late enough, the author from Italy is recalling Nero's persecution of Christians in Rome (c. 64 CE). In our view certain believers defected at that time, as can be adduced from Mark's gospel (see volume 1).

With the immediate context of 6:1–3 fresh in the author's mind, the thought of those who "were once enlightened" (ἅπαξ φωτισθέντας) probably refers to conversion or "saving illumination" as in 10:32 where the word φωτίζω refers to the audiences' actual conversion in the past.[144] In 6:4 the word assumes conversion as a

---

143. Marshall, *Kept by the Power*, 141, seems to agree and adds that the author wants them to advance "with the proviso of God's permission [Heb 6:3] since there may be among his readers those who have in fact slipped so far back that it is impossible for them to profit even by a repetition of elementary doctrine."

144. The word in Heb 10:32 is reasonably understood by Lane, *Hebrews*, 2.298, as the "saving illumination of heart mediated through preaching the gospel," but in 6:4 he is somewhat vague: "renewal

one-time event with the adverb "once" (cf. 9:7, 26–29; 10:2; 12:26f).[145] This conversion, it seems, takes place through repentance, faith, water and Spirit baptism, and perhaps a confession made during the initiation process (cf. 6:1–2). Other passages in early Christian traditions likewise portray conversion as coming out of darkness into "light" in which the neophyte belongs to God's people and kingdom (Col 1:13; Eph 5:8; 2 Cor 4:4–6; Acts 26:18; 1 Pet 2:9–12).[146] The alternative meaning is that the enlightenment refers to Christian baptism, which is once-for-all (Justin, *Apology* 1.62.12; 65.1; *Dial.* 22.5; *Syriac Peshitta*).[147] The connection between enlightenment and baptism in the first century, however, is not clear. Even so, the early church regarded baptism to be an important part of the conversion-initiation process, and our author agrees (Heb 6:1–2; cf. Acts 2:38; 1 Pet 3:21). Enlightenment then, most likely refers to conversion or at least an essential aspect of it.

An association between φωτισθέντας with Israel under the wilderness cloud makes for a reading that is not clearly present in 6:4.[148] The concept of "once" seems to have no correlation with the wilderness generation being under the cloud; that is, unless it awkwardly stands for their entire forty-year journey in which the cloud was apparently present (cf. Exod 40:38; Ps 94[95]:10; Neh 9:21; Heb 3:10, 17). It is probable that our author does not have any specific scripture consciously in mind by using the word φωτίζω.[149] But even if an allusion hides behind the text, it would not seem to nullify the word's more obvious meaning related to the audience's own initial experiences as believers (cf. Heb 10:32).[150] *The text is referring to their conversion and this is the primary meaning of φωτίζω in 6:4.*

---

of mind and life" (1.141). Contrast Grudem, "Perseverance," 1.144, who understands the meaning as "heard and understood the gospel." The enlightenment here goes beyond mere Christian instruction that is certainly repeatable, unlike conversion. See "once" in 6:4 and further study on the concept of enlightenment in Gräßer, *Hebräer*, 1.349–50.

145. The ἅπαξ in 6:4 does not need to be distributed to all four participles that follow (cf. Ellingworth *Hebrews*, 319); it would seem difficult to maintain in 6:5. The "once" also steers us away from thinking this is some sort of later enlightenment related to Christian living, unless such an event would be commonly understood by the recipients.

146. In Jewish traditions see similar ideas in *Jos. Asen.* 8.9–10; Philo, *Virtues* 164.

147. On this view see Salevao, *Legitimation*, 272–77; Conzelmann, *TDNT*, 9.355–58.

148. E.g., Exod 13:21; Ps 105:39; Neh 9:12, 19. See Mathewson, "Reading Heb 6:4–6," 215–16.

149. If so, it may be unhelpful and possibly distracting in certain cases to bring to the foreground a scriptural subtext for every word of the author.

150. Interestingly, in the context of a warning against apostasy, Paul uses the wilderness cloud for the express purpose of affirming the notion of conversion (1 Cor 10:2; Oropeza, *Paul and Apostasy*, 95–97, 115–16), but he does not use φωτίζω in the context.

An echo from the wilderness generation's eating of manna possibly appears through the next phrase, "had tasted of the heavenly gift" (6:4b).[151] If so, the allusion might point to the Lord's Supper.[152] Some weaknesses with this interpretation are that the Eucharist is not directly mentioned elsewhere in Hebrews, and it is not associated with δωρεά or the phrase "heavenly gift" elsewhere in earliest Christian literature.[153] Another interpretation suggests the heavenly gift refers to the Spirit, which is seen as God's agent of grace (Heb 6:2; 10:29; cf. Acts 2:38; 8:20; 10:45; Luke 11:13; John 4:10, 23; *Barn.* 1; Justin, *Hort.* 32). The idea of tasting in 6:4 might correspond to the notion of drinking in the Spirit (cf. 1 Cor 12:13; John 7:37–39). But if the next line in 6:4c refers to the Spirit, then the gift in 6:4b probably refers to something else. Other alternatives include grace or salvation as the heavenly gift.[154] Attridge understands the meaning of this gift to be more eclectic: it is "the gracious bestowal of salvation, with all that entails—the spirit, forgiveness, and sanctification."[155] This is perhaps the best interpretation of the phrase. Important for our purposes is that the "tasting" of this gift does not mean a mere sip or sampling[156] but the reality of experiencing something related to personal salvation.[157] The author uses the term earlier to refer to Christ "tasting" death (Heb 2:9; cf. Matt 16:28). *Whatever else the author means in 6:4, he is conveying that the apostates were at one time converted and experienced the grace of God.*

They also "shared in the holy Spirit" (6:4c: μετόχους γενηθέντας πνεύματος ἁγίου), a thought that comes close to the mystical union of sharing in a relationship with Christ (cf. 3:1, 14). Here the focus may be on the Spirit's relationship, communion, and solidarity with the believers,[158] an early Christian hallmark for determining conversion-initiation, new life, and sanctification (Acts 11:15–18; Rom 8:9–14; 2 Thess 2:13; Titus 3:5; Eph 1:13–14; John 3:3–7). *There is in fact no passage in the New Testament that affirms unbelievers or fake Christians having a share in the Holy*

---

151. Cf. Exod 16:4, 15; Ps 77[78]:24; 104[105]:40; Neh 9:15; John 6:31–58

152. Mathewson, "Reading Heb 6:4–6," 216. On the Eucharist interpretation see Bruce, *Hebrews*, 120–21.

153. Passages such as Heb 9:15 and 10:29, at best, indirectly assume the Lord's Supper.

154. For the former see Rom 5:15; 2 Cor 9:14f; Eph 3:7; 4:7; Hughes, *Hebrews*, 209. For the latter, 1 Pet 2:2–3/Ps 33[34]:9; Williamson, "Eucharist and the Epistle," 300–312.

155. Attridge, *Hebrews*, 171.

156. For the diminutive view of "tasting" see, e.g., Montefoire, *Hebrews*, 108–9.

157. See Weiss, *Hebräer*, 343; Behm, *TDNT* 1.675–77. The reason why our author did not simply say they were once "saved" is probably because he did not share the same soteriological perspective of the modern theologians who would want him to say exactly this. As we have already noted, the author of Hebrews considers salvation to be a futuristic enterprise, not just a present one.

158. Cf. 1 Cor 12:13; 2 Cor 13:13–14; Phil 2:1.

Spirit.¹⁵⁹ Even Matt 7:21–23 does not affirm that the miracles done by false prophets in Jesus' name were performed by the power of the Spirit. On the other hand, as we have noticed in Galatians and 1 Corinthians, authentic Christians who are Spirit-filled can fall away. The same appears to hold true for our author, who recalls earlier days of the Spirit's activity in the congregation (Heb 2:3–4) but now warns them that outraging the Spirit of grace is tantamount to apostasy (10:29).

They had also "tasted of the good word of God and the powers of the age to come" (6:5). This refers back to the theme of God speaking through his Son in the final days (1:3). The apostates were taught the spoken word, the gospel message of salvation and life (2:3; 4:1; 5:9; 6:12). The powers of the coming age likely points to the signs and wonders experienced by early Christian communities (Heb 2:2–4; cf. 1 Cor 12:4–11). By way of comparison we recall persons such as Ananias and Sapphira, who probably experienced miraculous events, fellowship with the Spirit, the gift of salvation, and were probably among the three thousand who had repented and were baptized on the Day of Pentecost (Acts 2; cf. 4:31). Yet they sinned greatly by lying to the Spirit and were struck dead (Acts 5:1–11).

The upshot in Heb 6:4–6 is that *despite all these salvific blessings these individuals experienced, they fell away (καί παραπεσόντας)*. In 6:6 καί may connote temporal succession "and then" highlighting a nuance of unexpectancy.¹⁶⁰ There is no conditional "if" in the Greek text and none should be imported.¹⁶¹ The warning does not express what hypothetically happens to apostates even though Christians cannot really become apostates.¹⁶² The danger of apostasy is a real threat for the community. The severity of language and repeated warnings attest to this regardless of whether the apostates in 6:4–6 are anonymous or people the author and audience once knew. Παραπίπτω appears nowhere else in the New Testament, but in the LXX it normally conveys some form apostasy from God, righteousness, or wisdom (Ezek 14:13; 15:8; 18:24; 20:27; Wis 6:9; 12:2).¹⁶³ The meaning in 6:6 is quite similar to πίπτω in 4:11: both words refer to committing apostasy.

---

159. A point raised by Marshall, *Kept by the Power*, 143. Contrast Grudem, "Perseverance," 148, who claims without proper support that they were partakers of *some* benefits of the Holy Spirit.

160. Cf. Ellingworth, *Hebrews*, 322.

161. Contrast KJV; Cockerill, "Wesleyan-Arminian Viewpoint," 276. See further on the Greek of this point in Wallace, *Greek Grammar*, 633.

162. *Contra* Hewitt, *Hebrews*, 108 cf. 111. For criticisms of the hypothetical view see Bruce, *Hebrews*, 122–23. On the reality of the danger see Hughes, *Hebrews*, 206.

163. In Esther 6:10 it means to leave or neglect (referring to Haman's inadvertent words of rewarding Mordecai). Johnson, *Hebrews*, 161, claims that it can vary elsewhere from: missing something as literal as a road (Polybius 12.12.2), to missing the truth (8.11.8).

We are not told specifically in 6:6 what they fall away *from*, but we can adduce from the immediate context that it would be a turning away from conversion and salvific benefits described in 6:1–5.[164] The author, in any case, refers to Christians who were once converted, sharers in God's Spirit, and experienced gracious salvation, God's word, and the miracles of the coming age. At very least, then, they commit apostasy by rejecting God's grace and God's Spirit (cf. 10:29c). *There is little reason for the author to bother compiling an entire list of salvific blessings described in 6:1–4 if he were intending to communicate to his audience that these people were inauthentic believers.*[165] We might assume that both the author and audience would have known people who had left their congregations who were never truly committed, or doubted their beliefs, or perhaps were compromised with immoral conduct. Perhaps the author wants to affirm by the compilation of these participles in 6:4–6 that he is *not* referring to this type of half-hearted churchgoer, but to those who had been unmistakably converted. The surprise of their apostasy is implied in 6:6: they experienced all the gifts and blessings a normal Christian experiences, and yet they fell away. *Our author presents this passage, then, as part of his effort to shake the audience free from their spiritual dullness.* His rhetorical strategy for them comes through loud and clear: "if these other Christians fell away who had experienced conversion and spiritual blessings just like you experience, watch out lest the same thing happen to you!"

THE IMPOSSIBILITY OF THE APOSTATES' RESTORATION (6:4–6)

The author of Hebrews not only affirms that Christ-followers can fall away, but that once they do they cannot be renewed again to repentance (6:4–6).[166] The mean-

---

164. Some other options or additional reasons are that they fell away from God through unbelief and disobedience (cf. Heb 3–4), they repudiated Christ (cf. 10:29a), or, if Nero's persecution is in view, they may have denied being Christian and possibly betrayed other Christians to authorities. A combination of these is also possible.

165. This point is not sufficiently explained by those who would suggest the author refers to "ungenuine" Christians; e.g., Guthrie, *Hebrews*, 229–30.

166. "ἀδύνατον . . . πάλιν ἀνακαινίζειν εἰς μετάνοιαν." An alternative meaning is to move repentance to the back of the sentence and claim it is impossible to renew them again, "crucifying a second time for one's own ends the Son of God" with a view to repentance (εἰς μετάνοιαν); or as Zerwick, *Grammatical Analysis*, 665, translates it: "For it is impossible to crucify a second time the Son of God for one's own repentance, so making a mock of him, in order to renew again those who have once [been enlightened . . .]." See also Sabourin, "Crucifying Afresh," 264–71; Proulx and Schökel, "Heb 6,4–6," 193–209. The impossibility would then rest on crucifying the Son a second time rather than repentance. Attractive as this translation may appear to be, there is no good reason for rearranging repentance as the last aspect of this already long and complicated sentence, and the translation does not ultimately nullify the impossibility of repentance in the homily anyway (see above).

ing of the adjectival neuter αδύνατον means an unqualified "impossible," as it does elsewhere in the homily (6:18; 10:4; 11:6; cf. 9:9; 10:1, 11).[167] If the author wanted to say "difficult" instead of "impossible" he probably would have used δύσκολος to distinguish the meaning from impossible.[168] For our author, it is impossible to bring the apostate again to repentance and conversion. The reason why it is impossible is not specified. Perhaps God will not allow it to happen. It is God who declares that the wilderness generation will never enter into his rest after they reject his ways (3:11).[169] Then again, if an apostate repudiates Christ, he or she rejects the very basis upon which atonement and forgiveness is made possible (cf. 10:26–29). The author might assume both ideas.

Some take the present participles "re-crucifying the Son of God and putting him to an open shame" as an adverb of time, i.e., "*while* those who fall away are continuing in this state, it is impossible for them to repent . . ." (cf. NIV footnote).[170] Apart from being a truism, this translation does not take into account other places in Hebrews where there are similar thoughts about no second chance after apostasy (cf. 10:26; 12:17). The participles appear to be causal: "because" or "since" they are recrucifying the Son . . ."[171] By doing so they act as Christ's enemies did when he was exposed and shamed on the cross. The act of recrucifying the Son of God contrasts the one-time sacrifice of Christ on the cross which is the bedrock of salvation (7:27; 9:12, 26, 28; 10:10, 14, 26). In this manner those who apostatize cut off their means to salvific reconciliation.[172] In 10:29 the thoughts of trampling underfoot the Son of God and profaning the "blood of the covenant" may be somewhat synonymous with the idea of crucifying Christ again in 6:6.[173] Although it is clear that there is no

---

167. Hence, to mitigate this meaning or claim that with God it is still possible (e.g., Mark 10:27) introduces thoughts foreign to text at hand. For those who mitigate the meaning see, e.g., Spicq, *Hébreux*, 2.167–78; Oberholtzer, "Thorn-Infested Ground," 323; Mitchell, *Hebrews*, 128.

168. We notice that Philo distinguishes the two words, but they are close in meaning: "it is difficult (δύσκολον), and rather impossible (ἀδύνατον)" to train up someone who distrusts his teacher (*Rewards* 49). Although parallels on apostasy in Philo and Hebrews may be found (*Rewards* 165–67/ Heb. 12:16–17; *Mos.* 1.29–38; 2.31–32/Heb. 3–4; *Spec. Leg.* 2.243–56; cf. Williamson, *Philo and the Epistle*, 302–303), unlike Hebrews, Philo thinks restoration is possible after apostasy (cf. *Rewards*, 152–63).

169. McCullough, "Impossibility of a Second Repentance," 2, considers renewing impossible because "God wills it."

170. E.g., Elliott, "Post-Baptismal Sin," 330–32.

171. The present tense also describes a continuous repudiation of the Son (cf. Attridge, *Hebrews*, 172), and "to themselves" (ἑαυτοῖς) is a dative of (dis)advantage.

172. Alternatively, the ἀνα- in ἀνασταυροῦντας could mean "up" rather than "again," so as to lift *up* the Son again in crucifixion, a meaning that can be found in exposure to shame by public hanging (so Johnson, *Hebrews*, 161).

173. So Klauck, "Moving in, Moving out," 422. Fanning, "Classical Reformed View," 185, correctly

repentance for the defector, the author does not explain clearly why a single act of atonement necessitates that repentance must also be a once-for-all act for humans.[174] Some options for understanding this difficult thought are as follows:

Some of the church fathers distinguished between apostasy as restorable but baptism as unrepeatable,[175] which was the traditional interpretation of this passage prior to the Reformation.[176] It is questionable, however, that repentance in 6:4-6 should be understood specifically as baptism.

More intriguing is the idea that the author of Hebrews considers the eschaton as so immanently present (1:3; 3:13; 4:10; 6:8; 9:26-28; 10:24-25) that there would be no time to repent in a genuine way after repudiation takes place. His warning would be similar to apocalyptic traditions that warn of the end being so near that there will be no time to repent (cf. Rev 22:11; *2 Bar.* 85.12; *Sib. Or.* 1.165-70). Nevertheless, the imminent consummation is not the reason given by our author for the impossibility of repentance.[177]

We might be tempted to suggest 6:4-6 is highly rhetorical, with the author writing as though apostasy were non-restorative for the sake of generating a fear in his audience that would discourage them from falling away. Barnabas Lindars writes in this vein by saying that the author "exaggerates the impossibility of the renewal after apostasy because he knows that the readers have not actually committed it, but then immediately assures them that he knows that they would never do such at thing because he is terrified that this is what they will do!"[178] Perhaps our author thinks the end justifies the means even though he really does not believe that restoration is categorically impossible. But this explanation is weakened when we compare 6:4-6 with similar thoughts in 10:26 and 12:17. Are we to suggest that all three passages are purely rhetorical on this point? The combination of these passages may suggest that the impossibility of restoration is something the author actually believed.

---

states: "one who insolently rejects the sacrifice of the great Priest over the house of God will find that no further provision for sin is available" (cf. Heb 10:26, 29 with 10:19-21). One alternative is Mitchell, *Hebrews*, 130, who turns the passage on the idea of the apostate going back to rituals of purification and cleansing, thus making the accomplishment of Christ's self-sacrifice insufficient. This view fits well with a relapse to emergent Judaism perspective.

174. On this thought see further Löhr, *Umkehr und Sünde*, 242-49; Koester, *Hebrews*, 320.
175. E.g. Ambrose, *Penance* 2.2.
176. See further examples in Heen and Kray, *Hebrews*, 84-85; Koester, *Hebrews*, 25, 40.
177. On this view see also the criticisms of Löhr, *Umkehr und Sünde*, 229-33.
178. Lindars, *Theology of the Letter*, 135. Language on assurance follows on the heels of the warning in 6:9-12. Lindars writes further that such a warning "cannot be taken as a reliable guide" to Hebrews' moral position. Witherington, *Jewish Christians*, 218, considers the language here to be "hyperbolic."

Churches under Siege of Persecution and Assimilation

The Johannine distinction between sins "not unto death" and the "sin unto death" may also be compared with the idea of no restoration for apostates in Hebrews (cf. 1 John 5:16–18). In John's case the "sin unto death" is associated with apostates who abandon the Johannine community for rival teachings denying Jesus as the Christ and in league with the spirit of Antichrist (cf. 1 John 2:18–24; 4:1–6). The nature of this apostasy, then, seems different than what is described in Hebrews. Moreover, the Elder does not encourage that his congregants pray for those whose sin leads to death,[179] but it is not clear from this that those who commit such a sin can never be restored to God or the Christ community.

Along these lines sometimes Heb 6:4–6 and 1 John 5:16–18 are explained as equivalent to the unpardonable sin of blaspheming of the Holy Spirit in the Synoptic Gospels (Mark 3:29; Matt 12:31; Luke 12:10). In Hebrews the act is clearly apostasy, and it is committed by Christians. In Matthew and Mark, the scribes and Pharisees blaspheme the Spirit by attributing the miracles of Jesus to demonic powers. Only Luke's version allows for the possibility of Christians committing the unpardonable sin; this gospel seems to connect the term with denying Christ when being persecuted. Although the apostasy that is warned against in Heb 6 involves the recipients' spiritual dullness, it is possible that the apostates whom the author mentions in 6:4–6 denied Christ when being persecuted. Moreover, the defection in Heb 10:19–31 may be related to repudiating Christ because of persecution. The notion of insulting the Spirit of grace in 10:29 comes close to the Lukan idea of blaspheming the Spirit. A clear connection between Heb 6:4–6 and Luke 12:10, however, evades us. Luke's unpardonable sin is committed when the Spirit is manifested in a unique way,[180] and other types of defectors and failed Christ-followers can be restored in the Lukan narrative (e.g., Luke 12:9; 15:11–32; 22:54–62).

At best, then, we can affirm that the impossibility of repentance in Hebrews describes a phenomenon somewhat similar to Luke's unpardonable sin and the Elder's sin that leads to death. Unique to Hebrews is that it offers no restoration for apostasy regardless of whether it comes through malaise, unbelief, disobedience, or persecution.

Ultimately, *the author probably found his ground for rigorism on this issue from Israel's scriptures and other ancient Jewish thoughts that support similar ideas.*[181] Some examples include a distinction made between unintentional/forgivable sins and

---

179. See on the Johannine writings in volume 1.

180. Other types of defectors and failed Christ-followers, however, can be restored (e.g., Luke 12:9; 15:11–32; 22:54–62).

181. See further sources in Buchanan, *Hebrews*, 109–10; Attridge, *Hebrews*, 168–69; Koester, *Hebrews*, 319; Str.B. 4.230.

intentional/unforgivable sins (e.g., Num 15:26–31) and presumptuous sin as unpardonable (Deut 29:18–20). Likewise, there is no repentance available for breaking vows (2 *En.* 62.2–3[J]), for causing the community to sin (*m. Aboth* 5.18), for blaspheming (Philo, *Flight* 84), or for committing apostasy and persistent wicked deeds (Jub 35.14; Philo, *Alleg. Interp.* 3.213; *Shemoneh Esreh* Benediction 12; *t. Sanhedrin* 13.5).[182] In the Qumran community, unlike other wrongdoings in which members could be restored after discipline, certain sins were more heinous, such as a person swearing by the Name or betraying the community. Such members would be expelled from the community and not able to return again (1QS 6.27–7.2; 7.16–24). The author of Hebrews was not unique in his declaration that apostates could not be restored. *The verdict for the apostates in Hebrews is similar to God's verdict for the wilderness generation who are rejected because of their persistent unbelief and disobedience when he swears "they will never enter into my rest"* (Heb 3:11; 4:3, 5). This divine oath from Ps 94[95]:11 and Num 14:21–35 provides a strong undercurrent for the author's ultimate rejection of apostates who reject God in the final "today" of salvific history. What remains a mystery is how the author or community would determine when a person has committed apostasy as opposed to unintentional sins. Presumably, some of the factors would seem to be that they no longer want to attend church meetings and listen to exhortations and messages (e.g., Heb 10:25).

RESTORATION IN THE NEW TESTAMENT AND NO RESTORATION IN HEBREWS (6:4–6; CF. 10:26; 12:17)

The impossibility of restoration in Hebrews teaches something quite different than many of the other New Testament writings. Paul argues that apostate Israel will be restored before Christ's return (Rom 11), and hope is held out for the restoration of defectors and sinners among his congregations (1 Cor 5:5; 2 Cor 2:5–7; Gal 6:1; cf. 2 Tim 2:24–26). Beyond these examples, Jas 5:19–20 and Jude 22–23 encourage their communities to restore apostates, and Peter finds repentance after denying Christ and is reinstated as a disciple and leader (John 21). The nature of the apostasy varies: Israel fell through unbelief, the Corinthian offender commits sexual immorality with his stepmother, Timothy attempts to restore those led astray by false teachings, James involves the restoration of those who succumbed to trials and temptations, and Jude reaches out to the immoral false teachers and their followers. If the author of Hebrews has in mind the apostasies that occurred during Nero's persecution in 6:4–6, then this opens up the strong possibility of conflicting perspectives about the

---

182. A different type of rigorism is found in Jer 7:12–16 in which God determines judgment on his rebellious people with no other recourse available.

defectors who live in Rome—the Markan community grants them restoration; the author of Hebrews does not.

One attempt to resolve the competing views on restoration for apostates in the New Testament is given by Grant Osborne, who distinguishes between *passive* apostasy, in which Jas 5:19–20 denotes sin that "crowds Christ out of a person's life" and is restorable, and *active* apostasy in which a person commits the unpardonable sin, as in Heb 6:4–6.[183] The distinction does not hold up well under scrutiny. Even if one wishes to maintain a passive apostasy in James, Jude's apostates would definitely be active defectors, and yet they could be restored also (Jude 22–23). On the other hand, in Hebrews both aggressive (10:26–29) and passive (10:35–39) forms of apostasy seem depicted, though perhaps under a different set of parameters than defined by Osborne. It can be argued, at any rate, that there are examples of restoration for both active and passive apostates in the New Testament, while at the same time Hebrews denies the restoration of both.

If it could be demonstrated that Hebrews lacks restoration after apostasy because it refers to the unpardonable sin, akin with Luke's gospel, then the content of the unpardonable sin would seem to include (via Hebrews) apostasy through malaise and repudiating Christ. Elsewhere in the New Testament, however, repentance seems possible for apostates who sin in ways similar to what we find in Hebrews. Those who deny Christ can be forgiven (e.g., Peter's denials; Markan community), and so could congregations that suffer from a lack of zeal (Rev 2:4–5; 3:1–3, 16–19). It is also not clear how long a person must be in a particular state of sin before it is considered unpardonable. We see examples of unpardonable sins in the Christian scriptures but no uniform way of defining them and determining which sins allow for restoration.

The two differentiating tracks on the restoration of apostates may be seen together in the *Shepherd of Hermas*, the author of which is probably familiar with Hebrews. This early church writing allows for a second repentance (*Vis.* 2.2.1–5; *Sim.* 9.26.5–6), but repentance would not seem to be profitable if a person who was restored fell away again (*Mand.* 4.1.8; 4.3.1–7; cf. *Sim.* 8.6.4–6; 9.19.1–3). In the context of persecutions under Rome, the Novatians refused the readmittance of apostates who had denied Christ,[184] but the Donatist allowed for their restoration.[185] Ambrose allowed for restoration, but not for a second baptism (*Penance* 2.2).[186] The

---

183. Osborne, "Classical Arminian View," 87, 115.

184. Epiphanius, *Pan.*, 59.1.1–59.3.5.

185. Cf. Cyprian, *Epistles* 50–52[47–48]; *Laps.*; Eusebius, *Hist. eccl.* 5.1–2; 5.2.8; 6.43.

186. See further references in the early church fathers in Oropeza, *Paul and Apostasy*, 4–5, 8–12; Buchanan, *Hebrews*, 108–9; Strecker, *Johannine Letters*, 203–8.

diversity of Christian opinion on apostates and their restoration may have been set in motion from the first century as a result of diversity in the New Testament on this issue. The earliest Christians did not consider all sins and apostasies to be alike. Perhaps the early leaders of the local Christian communities, guided by apostolic teachings, scripture, and the Spirit, had to determine if apostasy had been committed on a case-by-case basis, and some appear to be more tolerant than others depending on the nature of the sin committed.

One corollary point that remains difficult for us to understand is that the New Testament apostles and authors claim their messages to be authoritative for their churches,[187] often based on the authority of Israel's scriptures,[188] and yet in their messages they determine those who are "in" and those who are "out" of God's community quite differently. Paul, for example, considers his Christian opponents in Galatians and 2 Corinthians to be false teachers and apostles. He warns his congregations against committing apostasy by following these leaders, and yet it is almost certainly the case that his opponents would *not* have perceived themselves the way Paul perceives them. Paul himself, at least according to Luke, is perceived as an apostate by much of the Jewish-Christian population of his time (Acts 21:20–21).[189] Similar observations might be gleaned in reference to the Christian opponents in the Johannine writings, Pastoral Letters, Matthew, Jude, and so forth. Likewise, even the apostles themselves do not agree on what observances derived from the Mosaic Law the Gentile-Christians must keep (e.g., Gal 2:1–16).[190]

What the New Testament canon might teach *us* from these observations is at least two-fold.

First, however we may wish to define the authority of the New Testament today, that definition should take into consideration the inherent diversity of viewpoints in these writings in reference to apostasy, restoration, Christian identity, Torah, Jewish and Gentile relationships, and so on. Ultimately, it seems that New Testament authority must rest on God's authority,[191] and perhaps we are reminded by diversity in the scriptures that only God can determine in a final sense who is "in" and who is "out" of God's community.

---

187. E.g., 1 Thess 2:13; 2 Pet 3:2; Rev 22:18–19.
188. E.g., Matt 4:4; John 10:35b; Rom 3:1–2; 2 Tim 3:16.
189. See further in volume 1 of this work.
190. See volume 2.
191. Exploring biblical authority from this perspective are, e.g., Bauckham, "Scripture and Authority," 5–11; idem, "Tradition in relation to Scripture," 117–45; Wright, *Last Word*; idem, "How Can the Bible Be Authoritative?," 7–32.

Second, amidst the diversity we have noticed, there appears to be a couple of universal truths or assumptions held in common by all the New Testament authors. Namely, *if a person renounces Jesus Christ, that person is an apostate.* Technically speaking, they are "out" of the community in Christ. It may be sufficient to say that the New Testament authors and their communities confessed Jesus as the risen Lord and promised Messiah/Christ from Israel's scriptures.[192] The confession or denial of *Jesus* as the Christ, however, meant more in a Jewish context than in a Gentile world. Belief in a Jewish Messiah meant little to uninformed Gentiles and Romans unless such a belief posed a perceived threat to local Gentile communities and Rome. Of course, quite often it was perceived as a threat to the social and political stability of society. To such outsiders who were more interested in the prospect that Christians stop being Christians, a believer's public denial of *Christ*, whoever this person might be, would seem to suffice. Alternatively, the Christ-follower's denial might involve an allegiance to Caesar rather than Jesus as Lord. This kind of external pressure on the Christian may be seen in the communities of 1 Peter and Revelation who suffer for the sake of Christ's *name*. In relation to denying Christ, the Johannine community's definition of Christ seems to include his preexistence and deity;[193] hence, they would consider as apostates those who affirm Jesus as Messiah but deny his preexistence and deity. Such specificity no doubt betrays a developing definition of Christ among the emerging Christians, and it is not clear that the other authors in the New Testament would perceive the Johannine opponents as apostates also. A final aspect related to this denial is that such a person might retract his or her renunciation of Christ, and here the question of restoration might generate different responses among the New Testament authors.

Another universal point related to apostasy is this: *all the New Testament authors seem to believe that one's conduct could become so contrary to the central teachings of Christ, or so immoral, that such behavior constitutes a denial of Christ even if that person does not verbally or otherwise renounce Christ.* Hence, one's keeping the teachings of Jesus, especially the command to love God and one's neighbor, becomes essential for emergent Christian identity and behavior. Whether or not other Christian leaders of the first century, for example the opponents of the New Testament authors, would hold to this truth is unknown to us. Also, the notions of loving God and neighbor might be nuanced differently by the New Testament authors. Loving God, for example, would no doubt include shunning idolatry, but what constitutes idolatry may be understood differently by the authors. Tension between James and Paul on whether Gentile Christians should eat idol meats, for example, is a classic

---

192. In terms of unity in the New Testament, along these lines see Dunn, *Unity and Diversity*.
193. See volume 1.

case of this (cf. Acts 15:19–29; 1 Cor 8–10). Be that as it may, these truths in general appear to be held in common by the authors of the New Testament. Related to this is Christ's golden rule (Matt 7:12), but this may be seen perhaps as another variant of loving one's neighbor as oneself. Immoral behavior, whether understood in terms of lawlessness (Matthew) or committing vices (Paul), characterizes the behavior of apostates and outsiders.

JUDGMENT ON THE APOSTATES AND ENCOURAGEMENT TO THE AUDIENCE (6:7–12)

The punishment of the apostates is described through a comparison between well-watered and fruitful ground blessed by God, and useless ground that produces thorns and thistles and "is about to be cursed; its end is for burning" (6:7–8).[194] The blessing and curse distinction may recall the Deuteronmic tradition's divine blessing on covenant keepers and curses on violators (Deut 11:11, 26–28; 30:1, 19).[195] In this tradition fire is related to divine judgment (Deut 32:22; cf. 2 Sam. 23:6; Isa 33:12). More specifically, however, the burning in Heb 6:8 recalls eschatological judgment comparable to Jewish apocalyptic and early Christian traditions (Matt 13:31–32; 1 Cor 3:10–15; Rev 20; cf. Isa 66:24; *1 En.* 102.1; *4 Ezra* 16.78).[196] The metaphor of burning useless thorns and thistles is also evident in the gospels that depict the imagery of fire related to a judgment on the wicked at the end of the age (e.g., Matt 13:30, 36–43; cf. Matt 7:16–26; John 15:6).[197] In Hebrews final judgment will take place when Christ returns, and the apostates will be punished with fiery destruction at that time (Heb 10:30–31; 12:29). Most likely, a similar thought about *the apostates' final destruction is being conveyed in Heb 6:8.*

---

194. On ἀδόκιμος (useless) see especially 1 Cor 9:27; 2 Tim 3:8; Titus 1:16; Ign. *Trall.* 12.3. On κατάρα (cursed) see Gal 3:10; 2 Pet 2:14.

195. On this source in Hebrews 6:7–8 see Allen, *Deuteronomy and Exhortation*, 130–31. DeSilva, *Perseverance in Gratitude*, 232, makes the interesting case that Ps 94[95]:7–11 itself has recontextualized Deut 11:26–28.

196. Nongbri, "Touch of Condemnation," 272–73, likewise views the influence of apocalyptic literature on Heb 6:7–8, which has as one of its purposes to instill fear (cf. Dan 9:11; *4 Ezra* 9.10–12; *Jub.* 15.34; 33.13–16).

197. In the last days, according to Isaiah, when God establishes his coming ruler only the holy will live in Jerusalem and a spirit of "burning" (καῦσις) will cleanse away the filth of Zion (Isa 4:2–6), which sounds similar to the temporary things being destroyed and excluded from heavenly Zion in Heb 12:22, 25–29. These ideas from Isaiah are followed by the parable of the Israel as an apostate vineyard (Isa 5:1–7), which is often suggested as an allusion in Heb 6:7–8. On the final point see, e.g., McCullough, "Isaiah in Hebrews," 166–67.

The third major warning in Hebrews ends where it began—the audience is not to be reluctant hearers (Heb 6:9-12; cf. 5:11). More than this, however, the author ends by comforting the audience and affirming better things for them than divine punishment. Their reward will be salvation and God has not forgotten their services to the saints. Our author encourages them to be zealous.[198] By contrasting the apostates in 6:4-8 and his recipients, he is not claiming that the latter are immune to falling away but is rhetorically distancing them from any thoughts they might have about defection. This strategy adds to his approach by encouraging good will rather than accusing them (cf. *Rhet. Her.* 4.37.49-50; Dio Chrysostom, *Or.* 32.11; Aristotle, *Rhetoric* 2.5.1, 16).[199] It was also common in ancient Mediterranean societies that in frank speech directed at friends, praise should be given after disseminating harsh language. Paul makes similar rhetorical maneuvers in Gal 5:10 and 1 Cor 10:13 after severe warnings to his congregations.

CONFESSION WITHOUT WAVERING (10:19-23)

After a discussion on the all-sufficient sacrifice of Christ for sin, the author makes a hortatory appeal for those who have been cleansed as a result of the accomplishment of Christ to draw near to the presence of God (10:19-22; cf. 4:16). The believers are encouraged to have confidence (παρρησία) and full assurance (πληροφορία) of faith when approaching God.[200] The appeal has the function of deterring the recipients from wandering in the direction of doubt and uncertainty (cf. Heb 11:1, 6; Rom 14:4, 23). It will turn out, however, that this type of confidence can be thrown away by the audience (Heb 10:35). We notice the spatial movements in 10:19-39: the recipients are to draw near to God (10:19-22) and gather together in fellowship as the eschaton approaches (10:25), and they are not to "draw back" (10:38-39) but hold fast their confession of hope "without wavering" (10:23).

Perhaps 4 Macc 6:7 is significant for the final thought because this verse arises from a milieu of Israel suffering persecution under the Seleucid dynasty during the Maccabean revolt,[201] and the persecution of the church is mentioned in our passage in Hebrews. The Jewish martyr Eleazar keeps his reasoning upright and "unwaver-

---

198. See Attridge, *Hebrews*, 175.

199. On the topic of rhetorical fear and comfort in this passage see further Nongbri, "Touch of Condemnation," 274-78.

200. On the former term see 3:6; 10:19, 35; Balz, "παρρησία," 3.45-47; on the latter see Heb 6:11; 1 Thess 1:5; Col 2:2; Hübner, "πληροφορία," 3.107. On God's faithfulness in Heb 10:23b, see 1 Thess 5:24; 2 Thess 3:3; 1 Cor 1:9; 10:13; 2 Cor 1:18; Rev 1:5. That the promise can be abandoned by some believers does not make God any less faithful; see Heb 13:5.

201. Our author evidently knows the Maccabean tradition (cf. Heb 11:34-40).

ing" (ἀκλινής) when being tortured for refusing to eat foods prohibited by the Law. Using a nautical metaphor, the author of 4 Maccabees describes Eleazar as steering a straight course into eternity after suffering tortures. It is said of the faithful hero that he allowed reason to rule his mind, he held on to virtues, and he did not give in to emotions that would cause him to profane himself by eating defiled foods (cf. 4 Macc 7:1–3). In a way Eleazar resembles Christ—as he was being burned he asks God to be merciful to his people and substitutes his life for theirs that his blood might become their purification (4 Macc 6:27–29). The narrator mentions afterward that Eleazar "despised" (περιφρονέω) the tortures at the cost of his life (4 Macc 7:16; cf. 6:9; 14:1; Heb 12:2).[202] His trust in God and refusal to waver became safeguards preventing him from abandoning the Law as he endured suffering and death. This story highlights a stand against wavering similar to Heb 10:23, which anticipates the believers' experience of persecution in 10:32–34. One major distinction between the texts is that the threat of apostasy in Heb 10:23 would not be an abandonment from the Law but from the "confession of hope." *The believers must hold fast and not waver in this confession, that is, their confession of Jesus as the Son of God and anticipation of sharing an eternal inheritance with him* (cf. Heb 1:2, 14; 3:1; 4:14).[203]

FORSAKING THE ASSEMBLY (10:24–25)

The community is to provoke one another to love and good works (10:24) and exhort one another when assembled together, not forsaking fellowship in the Christ community (10:24–25; cf. 6:10). The idea of assembling together probably refers to their gathering in a local setting, most likely in house churches (cf. Phlm 2; Acts 18:7). The importance of attending worship gatherings is often stressed in early Jewish and Christian communities.[204] Some members, it seems, would not attend the church homes and have fellowship with other believers; they had fallen into the custom or "habit" (ἔθος) of not coming to church (10:25a). The author describes this problem as abandoning (ἐγκαταλείπω) the assembly, a word sometimes used of God's people forsaking God and his commandments (Jer 2:13; *Barn.* 11.2; 19.2; *Did.* 4.13; cf.. 2 Tim 4:10).[205] It is quite possible that our author thought those who were not attend-

---

202. Here περιφρονέω probably conveys a sense of defying as a remedy (cf. LSJ, 1393). Hebrews 12:2 uses καταφρονέω: "to despise" or "look down on."

203. Cf. Koester, *Hebrews*, 450.

204. Cf. Philo, *Migr.* 90–92; *m. Abot* 2.4; *1 Clem.* 46.2; *Did.* 16.2; Ign. *Eph.* 5.3; *Barn.* 4.10; *Herm. Vis.* 3.6.2; *Herm. Sim.* 9.26.3.

205. See further Ellingworth, *Hebrews*, 528.

ing the gatherings anymore had fallen away; at the very least he regarded them to be on the brink of apostasy and evidence of wavering in their confession.

The reason for their not attending local congregations may be related to their negligence and dullness of hearing, which elsewhere in the homily places them in spiritual jeopardy (cf. Heb 2:1–3; 5:11; 6:12). Their lack of motivation to hear spiritual messages, in part, might have been due to a sense of disillusionment caused by a delayed *parousia* (cf. 10:36–39). They were not new converts; they probably heard sermons on the imminence of Christ's return numerous times, and this message might have begun to wear thin on their patience. But if so, the author does not shy away from proclaiming an imminent *parousia* and attempting to motivate his audience by it.[206] They are to participate in fellowship and be aware that the "day" is quickly approaching them, a reference to the second coming and final judgment (Heb 3:14; 6:8, 11; 10:35f; 13:14; cf. Joel 1:15; 4:14; Ezek 7:7; Matt 4:17; Rom 13:12). For the faithful this will be a time of blessing, reward, and rest from societal harassment; for the unfaithful it will be a time of severe punishment (cf. 10:27–31, 38–39). The coming day suggests for the audience both positive and negative outcomes, depending on whether they continue in fellowship or contemplate leaving the church.

A more immediate cause for the recipients not attending the meetings, however, may due to the external pressures they faced. The community's persecution is not only something that took place in their past (10:32–34), but it seems to be a present reality that would flare up from time to time (cf. 10:38–39; 13:3, 13), but not to the point of martyrdom (12:2–4). Perhaps some were fed up with the continual harassment by outsiders and did not want to be seen anymore in company with other Christians, whether at house meetings, open gatherings, or visiting Christians in prison (13:3; cf. 11:24–27). In order to avoid potential conflicts with outsiders, they would keep their Christian beliefs secret and not attend fellowship gatherings. If some of them maintained a private belief in the Christian way, by neglecting fellowship these downtrodden believers were unable to receive the encouragement and exhortations community members gave to one another (10:24–25 cf. 3:13). A drop in attendance at the local gatherings would have no doubt discouraged even some of the faithful members, and so our author promotes congregational participation.

SINNING WILLFULLY (10:26–31)

In the opposite direction of receiving the forgiveness of sins, maintaining confidence, and exhorting one another the author writes: "For if we continue sinning willingly (ἑκουσίως) after receiving the knowledge (ἐπίγνωσις) of the truth, there no

206. It is not impossible that a form of cognitive dissonance is at play here.

longer remains a sacrifice for sins" (10:26).²⁰⁷ The present tense participle for "continue sinning" (ἁμαρτανόντων) may suggest a state of sin rather than a single act of sin.²⁰⁸ The "knowledge of the truth" refers to the proclamation of the gospel and Christ's atoning sacrifice that brings forgiveness of sin. Here it may imply the notion of conversion similar to the Pastoral Letters (1 Tim 2:4; 4:3; 2 Tim 2:25; 3:7).²⁰⁹ "We" includes both the author and audience (cf. Heb 2:1). Their spiritual transformation is implied in 10:22 (cf. 9:13), where repentance and the removal of sin is contrasted with the old covenant that could not deliver from the consciousness of sin (cf. 9:9; 10:2). The body washed in water is probably referring to baptism. In light of 10:22, the sin in 10:26 is committed after conversion.²¹⁰ *This verse refers to the danger of believers who after being converted and fully accepting and understanding the gospel message then reject it.*

Alcimus the high priest, vilified as a competitor against Judas Maccabaeus, was said to have "willingly" (ἑκουσίως) defiled himself as a priest when the Israelites were threatened by persecution and assimilation to Hellenism. Knowing that he would not remain safe but soon be barred from further access to the Holy Place after his defilement, Alcimus secured his position through a political alliance with King Demetrius of Syria and started to speak against Judas before the king (2 Macc 14:3; cf. 14:4–26; 1 Macc 7:5–25; 9:54–57).²¹¹ From the point of view of the Hasmoneans and their sympathizers, Alcimus turned into an apostate and treacherous opponent. The story, if not present in the thoughts of our author in Heb 10:26, attests closely to the way ἑκουσίως is used in this verse. It exemplifies a treacherous person who becomes the enemy of God and his people after falling away (cf. Heb 10:27, 29–30).

Perhaps the most celebrated parallel to Heb 10:26 comes from Numbers and distinguishes intentional and unintentional sins (Num 15:22–31; cf. Lev 4:1–2; 5:18; Deut 19:4; Heb 5:2; 9:7). An Israelite's commitment to witting sin showed contempt for God and barred forgiveness, excluding the violator from God's people.²¹² It is clear that our author was familiar with this source; he echoes it earlier in the homily when speaking about the wilderness generation's rebellion and punishment (Heb 3–4/Num 14). In Hebrews the sinning believers cannot claim ignorance; they know

207. Here "for" (γάρ) connects with not only the previous pericope of 10:19–25 but also 10:1–18, especially when we compare 10:18 with 10:26. Although no "if" appears in the text, the force of the genitive absolute conveys a condition or "if" (cf. 2:2; Ellingworth, *Hebrews*, 532).

208. Cf. Mitchell, *Hebrews*, 219–20.

209. See Hackenberg, "ἐπιγινώσκω," 2.25. See also John 8:32; 17:3; 1 John 2:21; 2 John 1. On this thought as stressing the intellectual side of faith see Gräβer, *Glaube im Hebräerbrief*, 136.

210. Cf. Michel, *Hebräer*, 350.

211. See Rappaport, "Alcimus," 1.145.

212. See Forkman, *Limits of Religious Community*, 153.

fully the message of salvation in Christ and yet reject it (Heb 10:26, 29). This is akin with committing witting or intentional sin, and it is virtually synonymous with committing apostasy, as 10:29, 35 and 38–39 suggest (cf. also 3:13). Hebrews 10:29 gives three descriptions of the apostate: 1) he[213] tramples underfoot the Son of God (10:29a); 2) he profanes the blood of the new covenant by which he was sanctified (10:29b); and 3) he has insulted/outraged the Spirit of grace (10:29c).

Regarding the first description (Heb 10:29a), καταπατέω is used of trampling something underfoot (cf. Matt 5:13; Luke 8:5; 12:1). In Matt 7:6 the "pigs" that trample on pearls probably identify apostates and false teachers as unclean persons who reject the gospel message, perhaps violently (cf. 2 Pet 2:22). At its most basic level the notion of trampling in Hebrews refers to the apostate rejecting the Son of God. More specifically the thought may connote breaking an oath (cf. Homer, *Iliad* 4.157),[214] or it conveys a "cosmic reversal of fortune" when compared with Christ placing his enemies under his feet (Heb 1:13; 10:13).[215] Another alternative relates the trampling to πατέω, which is associated with the profanation of that which is holy, such as Jerusalem or its temple being trampled underfoot.[216] If so, then to trample on the Son of God conveys for our author a profanation similar to the enemies of God defiling God's holy places. In any case the author's use of the term "Son of God" implies a repudiation of Jesus as the Son of God and eschatological ruler of the cosmos (Heb 1), *a reversal of the Christian confession* that was considered a brash challenge to Caesar according to Roman opponents and blasphemy according to Jewish opponents.

Regarding the second description (10:29b), the thought of reckoning unclean the blood of the covenant refers to a repudiation of the new covenant work of Christ involving his sacrificial death that provides the forgiveness of sin (cf. Heb 9:12, 13–14, 20; 10:19; Acts 21:28; Rev 21:17). Here the atoning death of Christ related to the new covenant is being denied. Johnson astutely writes, "The apostasy, in effect, reverses the effect of Christ's priestly work."[217] Also significant in 10:29b is that *the*

---

213. Since 10:29 uses the masculine singular article ὁ to describe this person, we will address the apostate as "he."

214. Cf. Moffat, *Hebrews*, 151.

215. Gray, *Godly Fear*, 151. See a similar reversal of fortune in Deut 32:35. The footstool of Christ, however, seems stagnate and intimates subjugation, whereas trampling assumes movement and often connotes oppression, violence, or defilement. Interestingly, Gray brings out the historic persecution of Christians in seventeenth-century Japan, in which suspected Christians would be forced to tread on a copper plate with the engraved image of Christ on it (cf. Endo, *Silence*, 1969).

216. Zech. 12:3; *Pss. Sol.* 8.12; cf. Isa 63:18; Dan 8:13; 1 Macc 3:45, 51; 3 Macc 2:18; 2 *Bar.* 67.2; Josephus, *J.W.* 4.171; Luke 21:24; Rev 11:2. Notice also that the bottom of the foot may be considered impure (cf. Exod 3:5). See further sources in Aune, *Revelation*, 2.608.

217. Johnson, *Hebrews*, 265.

apostate was at one time "sanctified" (ἐν ᾧ ἡγιάσθη) through Christ's sacrifice. There is no doubt that the author considers the apostate as being once a genuine Christ-follower thoroughly converted and cleansed from sin before his repudiation of the new covenant.[218]

The third description (10:29c) asserts that the apostate outrages or insults (ἐνυβρίζω) the Spirit of grace, implying insolence of the arrogant sort.[219] Some interpreters associate the thought with blaspheming the Holy Spirit.[220] This is certainly possible, but the author probably intends to convey something more than this. The "Spirit of grace" relates to the arrival of the eschatological era and may echo Zech 12:10, a passage that our author would probably interpret as Christ's death on the cross (cf. John 19:34–37; Rev. 1:7). The idea, then, may refer to a *repudiation of the baptism and outpouring of the Spirit during the end times*, which was considered a gift (i.e., "grace") associated with miraculous signs, conversion, and the believers' new life in Christ (cf. Heb 2:4; 6:4; Acts 2:4, 38–39; 11:15–18; 1 Cor 12:13; Rom 8:9; John 3:5).

The person in Heb 10:26–29 commits the sin of apostasy: he repudiates the confession of Jesus as Son of God, reverses his atoning death, and arrogantly rejects the gift of God's Spirit.[221] This apostate seems antagonistic towards his former faith.[222] There no longer remains a sacrifice that could bring this person back to right standing with God. Since Christ's once-for-all sacrifice is considered unrepeatable, and this person has rejected this sacrifice, he cannot be renewed, nor can he turn to the old covenant priestly sacrifices that were offered yearly to cover sins, because

---

218. Contrast Guthrie, *Hebrews*, 230, who translates the phrase ἐν ᾧ ἡγιάσθη as impersonal: "by which one is sanctified." However, all the other singular verbs in 10:29 refer to the apostate (i.e., ἀξιωθήσεται, καταπατήσας, ἡγησάμενος, ἐνυβρίσας). Also, if the author wanted to express that he was not referring to the apostate, he could have easily used a first or second person plural instead of a third person singular for ἁγιάζω in order to clarify this, similar to what he does by using οἴδαμεν in 10:30 and δοκεῖτε in 10:29. More on target is Lane, *Hebrews*, 2.294, who writes: "This phrase ['by means of which he was consecrated'] in v 29 corroborates that 10:26–31 is descriptive of the Christian who has experienced the action of Christ upon his life."

219. Cf. ὑβρίζω: 2 Macc 14:42; 3 Macc 3:9; Matt 22:6; Acts 14:5; 1 Thess 2:2; Ellingworth, *Hebrews*, 541. The rare ἐνυβρίζω occurs nowhere else in the New Testament. Spicq, *Hébreux*, 2.325 considers ὑβρίζω to be a very appropriate antonym for grace.

220. E.g., Marshall, *Kept by the Power*, 148.

221. Weiss, *Hebräer*, 537, views the sin in Heb 10:29 generally as a fall from faith and God. More specifically, Thomas, *Case for Mixed-Audience*, 140, 143–79, perceives a Trinitarian-like rejection of God who speaks through his Son (1:1–4; 12:25; cf. 3:12), a contempt for the Son (6:6; 10:29), and a despising of the Spirit of grace (10:29c). Based largely on Heb 10:26–29, apostasy means a final and willful repudiation of the gospel. Further, it involves "open denial of the salvific value of the death of Christ by which alone access to God is possible" (179).

222. See sociological classifications for defectors in Wilson, *Leaving the Fold*, 122–25.

according to our author such things were rendered obsolete by Christ's sacrificial death (cf. 10:9, 18).²²³ *In essence 10:26, similar to 6:4–6, teaches that it is impossible for the apostate to be restored,*²²⁴ *and 10:29, similar to 6:4–6, teaches that the apostate was once an authentic believer.*

FEAR OF JUDGMENT (10:27–31)

What remains for the apostate, according to our author, is judgment in the form of a fearful, impending punishment from God (10:27–31).²²⁵ The judgment is described in at least three significant contours.

First, the apostate is to expect a "fiery zeal" (πυρὸς ζῆλος) from God that will consume God's enemies (10:27). A natural inference is that the defecting Christian has now become an enemy of God deserving punishment. This form of retribution uses the Isaianic tradition in which God sends fiery judgment against his adversaries on the appointed "day" that is fast approaching (Heb 10:27/Isa 26:11 cf. Isa 26:1, 20/ Heb 10:37a).²²⁶ Hebrews relates this judgment to eschatological destruction on the "day" Christ returns (10:25), in other words, the day after "today" (cf. 4:7–11).

Second, using *qal wahomer*, our author affirms a punishment (τιμωρία) worse than the penalty of physical death prescribed under Mosaic Law (Heb 10:28–29).²²⁷ We notice similar *qal wahomer* punishments in Philo, who offers no pardon for the blasphemer (*Flight* 84) and severe punishment on the person who denies God (*Spec.* 2.255). According to the Law, no pity should be given to heinous violators of God's covenant, and by the testimony of two or three witness the punishment was prescribed (Heb 10:28/Deut 17:2–6; cf. Deut 13:5–11; 19:11–13, 21; 25:12). Hebrews, in turn, presents three greater witnesses against the apostate who repudiates the new covenant; these are the Son of God (10:29a), the "blood of the covenant" (10:29b),

---

223. On the atonement aspects of Christ's death, see further Löhr, *Umkehr und Sünde*, 22–68; Lindars, *Theology of the Letter*, 107; cf. 84–98. The change of covenants should not be confused with a supersessionism of Christian or Gentile over Jew. Hebrews is addressed, at least in part, to a Jewish Christian audience that find continuity with the Jewish heroes of faith.

224. Lane, *Hebrews*, 2.291, adds some interesting parallels between 6:4–6 and 10:26–29, including: past experiences (6:4–5; 10:26), the apostasy (6:6; 10:29), impossibility of renewal (6:4, 6; 10:26), and covenantal curse due to the apostasy (6:8; 10:27). The main distinction for Lane is the cultic formulation of the last passage.

225. Similar to the transition in 10:26–27, the idea of insulting or outraging virtue, according to Aristotle, *Rhetoric* 2.5.5, results in fear for the person committing the act, especially if it is against a benefactor who will require justice; cf. Gray, *Godly Fear*, 152; DeSilva, *Perseverance in Gratitude*, 353.

226. See also Zeph 1:18.

227. The noun τιμωρία in Heb 10:29 does not refer to corrective punishment, but punishment related to vengeance; see Johnson, *Hebrews*, 264.

and the Spirit of grace (10:29c).²²⁸ The living God then executes the judgment (10:30–31).

Third, the Song of Moses is cited twice by the author in Heb 10:30-31(Deut 32:35–36; cf. 17:6): "vengeance is mine, I will repay," and "the Lord will judge his people." The song testifies of God's people breaking their covenant with God and thus incurring covenant curses as a result. Our author used this song earlier as background for first warning in Heb 2:1–4.²²⁹ In this song the day of vengeance and destruction draws "near" when God will punish his enemies. God will avenge the blood of his "sons," recompense the opponents, and the land will be purged (Deut 32:35f, 41–43). The song affirms that God makes alive and none can deliver from his "hands"; he lives forever (32:37–39). The song may have influenced the passage in Hebrews several ways. It reinforces that our author has in mind the concepts of apostasy, covenant breaking, and God's judgment against his people at an impending time.²³⁰ The Deuteronomic day of vengeance is reconfigured into the day of Christ's return and final judgment. The enemy judged by God is the apostate.²³¹ At the same time, God's faithful servants will be delivered, which may be seen in light of the Deuteronomic benefit of covenant blessings (cf. Heb 10:39). The cleansing of the land in the song perhaps anticipates the final "shakedown" presented in 12:26–29 (albeit, the passage in chapter 12 relies primarily on Haggai 2). Moreover, the song's stress on God as living and making alive, as well as his hands bringing judgment, probably influenced 10:31: "it is a terrifying thing to fall into the hands of the living God."

This all plays into the *author's rhetorical strategy of portraying God's judgment on covenant violators in a graphic manner in order to instill the audience with fear of falling away* (Heb 10:27, 30–31; cf. 4:1; 12:21). The author's concept of fearfulness (10:27, 30–31), in fact, reflects the characterization of covenant curses (Deut 28:66–67; cf. Deut 10:17).²³² The recipients must choose between fearing God (Heb 4:1; 10:30–31) or fearing humans who harass and marginalize them (10:32–34;

228. The "blood of covenant" (10:29b), however, may not count as a person, unless God or Christ is assumed as its maker.

229. On the Song of Moses in Hebrews, see further Allen, *Deuteronomy and Exhortation*, 19–42. For the motif of apostasy in the song, see Oropeza, "Laying to Rest the Midrash," 60–62.

230. Given the seriousness of the context, our author probably uses the verb κρίνω (Heb 10:30/Deut 32:36) as "to judge" rather than "to vindicate." Originally the Deuteronomic text leaned more towards the idea of vindication of God's people. See Mackie, *Eschatology and Exhortation*, 128–29; *pace* Proctor, "Judgment or Vindication?," 65–80.

231. Interestingly, the enemy's foot stumbles on the day God avenges (Deut 32:35). It is just possible that this thought is set in contrast with the apostates treading underfoot the Son of God (Heb 10:29).

232. So Allen, *Deuteronomy and Exhortation*, 141. On the fear of God see also Neh 4:14; Ps 46[47]:3; 2 Macc 1:24.

11:23–28; 13:6). Such a decision was repeatedly made by the emerging Christians (Matt 10:28; Luke 12:4–5; cf. 1 Pet 3:14–15/Isa 8:12–13). They could backslide and not come to Christian gatherings as a result of intimidation caused by outsiders, but it would be far better for them to fear God rather than be punished by him as apostates on judgment day. Even so, their fear is not supposed to be the same thing as being traumatized with anxiety attacks because of God; they are to have "godly fear" involving moral response to submit to God's will (cf. 5:7; 12:28).[233] This requires their possessing both a sense of awesomeness about God as well as a deep realization that God will punish the wicked at the end of time, and for our author this includes any Christians who reject God.

PERSECUTION IN THE PAST AND SHRINKING BACK IN THE PRESENT (10:32–39)

The author then challenges the audience to recall their early days as believers (10:32–34). After they had been "enlightened," that is, converted (cf. 6:4), they endured a severe contest of sufferings related to public "insults," unnamed afflictions, and a sharing with others who experienced mistreatment.[234] They were sympathetic towards prisoners, and they experienced the confiscation of their property but joyfully accepted it knowing that salvific reward awaited them at the eschaton. The recipients experienced persecution through verbal abuse and the ransacking of their property. The prisoners most likely were Christians, and hence some sort of legal action was taken against them.[235] Perhaps the outsiders instigated magistrates to oppose them by trumping up false accusations. To our frustration, our author does not identify the persecutors—he is more concerned about warning the insiders than discussing the outsiders. The author brings up the past as a way to stir up members to renew the attitude and fervency they once had in earlier days. Likewise, he reminds them that their endurance will be rewarded if they persevere until the end.

He continues that they must not "throw away" their confidence (Heb 10:35). Among other meanings, the word ἀποβάλλω can refer to literally casting aside a

---

233. See Gray, *Godly Fear*, 214, who also highlights Christ's example of εὐλάβεια in Heb 5:7 (cf. 188–205), and says, "Fear of God as both Hebrews and critics of superstition like Plutarch usually perceive, is not anxiety directed at a fickle, sadistic, and totally unpredictable deity. More accurately, the gods elicit fear because they are thorough to punish wrongdoing, whether in this world or in the next" (217).

234. On "insults" (ὀνειδισμός) cf. 11:26; 13:13; Rom 15:3.

235. On the seizure as official or unofficial see Koester, *Hebrews*, 460. The confiscation was probably a unique situation experienced by the congregation. Contrast Gräßer, *Hebräer*, 3.58–65, who thinks it was typical.

garment (Mark 10:50), or metaphorically taking off vices or evil works (Rom 13:12), and in a negative sense it can refer to the sin of rejecting one's parents (Prov 28:24 LXX). It is also used of divine rejection (2 *Clem.* 4.5; *Herm. Sim.* 9.18.3–4).[236] In 10:35 it conveys a throwing away of confidence as though it were a virtue with which believers clothe themselves.[237] A discarding of this confidence (παρρησία) would mean the negation of eschatological hope (cf. 3:6). This passage suggests that *whatever salvific promises are attached to παρρησία, it could still be rejected by believers so that they are excluded from salvation.* The believers are to maintain perseverance and follow God's will, and God's will for them is to imitate Christ by remaining faithful and obedient to God, endure sufferings, and so finally experience the promise of final salvation (10:35–36; cf. 10:7–10; 12:1–3; 13:21).[238]

Habakkuk 2:3–4 is then used to encourage the audience to wait for a very brief time (cf. Isa 26:20) until the "coming one" arrives. Our author adds from Habakkuk that "my righteous one will live by faith, and if he shrinks back, my soul takes no pleasure in him" (Heb 10:37–38).[239] For the author of Hebrews the "coming one" is Christ, whose second advent is to appear shortly (cf. 9:26–28). His understanding of the "righteous one," however, is not messianic but designates the Christian believers.[240] In this manner he reads the "righteous one" similar to the way Paul does (Gal 3:11; Rom 1:17/Hab 2:4) and encourages his audience to live by faith. He will continue encouraging them through Heb 11 to follow the ancient examples of faithful heroes from the past.

Our author adds from the Septuagint version of Habakkuk that if the righteous one "shrinks back" God will not be pleased with this person. The word ὑποστέλλω often distils a nuance of someone drawing or shrinking back in fear or intimidation of others, frequently in relation to withholding speech.[241] In Paul's farewell discourse

---

236. Differently, it is also used of apostates (2 *Clem.* 4.5; *Herm. Sim.* 9.18.3–4).

237. See a similar meaning in Dio Chrysostom, *Or.* 34.39.

238. On the *imitatio Christi* theme see Attrdige, *Hebrews*, 301. On perseverance (ὑπομονή) see also Luke 8:15; 21:19; 2 Thess 1:4; Rom 5:3; Rev 3:10; 14:12; Gräßer, *Hebräer*, 3.73.

239. The passage seems to follow the LXX, but on the distinctive alterations in Hebrews see Fitzmyer, "Habakkuk 2:3–4," 243; Gheorghis, *Septuagint in Hebrews*, 218–23. Some witnesses (e.g., D, Old Latin, Peshitta) place the μου after πίστεως ("my faithfulness"); others (e.g., P¹³, Majority text) omit μου. Strong witnesses, however, favor the inclusion of μου after δίκαιος (e.g., P⁴⁶, ℵ, A, Vulgate, Coptic, Armenian) to read "my righteous one." See further Koch, "Hab 2⁴ᴮ in der Septuaginta," 75–78; Metzger, *Textual Commentary*, 601.

240. In agreement with Gheorghis, *Septuagint in Hebrews*, 223–24.

241. Cf. Philo, *Mos.* 1.[14].83; Josephus, *Ant.* 6.86; *J.W.* 1.387; *Life* 278; Euripedes, *Orestes* 607; Demosthenes, *1 Olynthiac* 1.16. On ὑποστέλλω as a drawing back in fear and intimation see also Demonsthenes, *1 Philippic* 4.51; Isocrates, *De Pace* 41; Diodorus Siculus 13.70.3; Deut 1:17; Wis 6:7; Gal 2:12; cf. Rengstorf, "ὑποστέλλω," 7.597–98; LSJ, 1895; BDAG, 1041. On the meaning as a fear-

to the elders of Ephesus, he claims that he did not "shrink back" from speaking about what was profitable for them or from declaring the purpose of God to them (Acts 20:20, 27). In Hebrews the word may convey timidity in the face of persecution and probably hints at believers refraining from the public confession of Christ. *The concept of shrinking back may be viewed as the antipode of the righteous person finding life through fidelity to God, and as such it is another expression of falling away.*[242] The very next pericope is instructive here: it is impossible to please God without faith (Heb 11:6).

The result of God taking displeasure in the person who shrinks back connotes rejection of that person (10:38). It frequently has this meaning in the Septuagint where it is used in cultic settings and associated with rejecting those who sin or fall away (cf. Jer 2:19; 14:10–12; Sir 34:19).[243] Significantly it is used of God's rejection of Korah and his followers in the wilderness (Sir 45:18–19), and Paul relates it to God's rejection of the wilderness generation in order to warn the Corinthians against apostasy (1 Cor 10:5). *God's displeasure* with the person who shrinks back does not communicate a mild discontentment but an *absolute rejection* of that individual (Heb 10:38; cf. Heb 12:17).

Our author's understanding of righteous individuals shrinking back, then, provides us with one more example of committing apostasy that has eschatological destruction as its end result (cf. ἀπώλεια: 10:39).[244] Nevertheless, a silver lining of encouragement ends the pericope at 10:39. Our author claims that "we" are not of those who shrink back to destruction but are of those who have faith to the preserving of the soul. This sudden confidence in the audience's capabilities is rhetorically charged, offsetting the harsh language the author has been using since 10:26. This maneuver is commonly done in frank speeches of the time, and is similar to the one he uses in 6:9–11.

One distinctive feature stands out between the apostasy in 10:26–29 and the one in 10:35–39: the former is mentioned as willful sinning and the latter is described

---

ful retreat from battle see Josephus, *Life* 215; Diogenes Laertius, *Lives* 4.6; Polybius, *Histories* 6.40.14; 10.32.3. Other translations of the word include, "to draw in," "contract," "reduce," "subordinate," and "avoid."

242. The idea of shrinking back in the sense of withdrawing to hide (cf. Isa 26:20), as proposed by Lewis, "If He Shrinks Back," 88–94, mitigates the idea of apostasy in this verse. This view is weakened by the fact that this person is rejected by God (10:38: "no pleasure in him") and eschatological destruction is the outcome of shrinking back (10:39). This seems to be a rather severe punishment for merely withdrawing to hide. See further criticisms of Lewis's position in Gray, *Godly Fear*, 158n152.

243. See also Ps 146:10; 49[50]:18–19; Add Ps 151:5; *Pss. Sol.* 2:4 [variant]; Heb 10:6, 8/Ps 39[40]:6.

244. Elsewhere in the New Testament such destruction (ἀπώλεια: 10:39) awaits both God's enemies (Phil 1:28; 2 Thess 2:3; 2 Pet 3:7; Rev 17:8, 11) and apostates (John 17:12; 2 Pet 2:1–3; 3:16; Rom 9:22; Phil 3:18–19; cf. *Pss. Sol.* 3.10–12).

as casting away confidence and shrinking back. The first case is more arrogant and deliberate than the second. The author's introduction of the community's past experiences with persecution in 10:32-34 seems to have toned down the mood and added an element of compassion for the audience that appears to be missing in the earlier warning. His language is most personal in 10:35-36, where he uses second-person plurals to address the audience. We can suggest from this distinction that our author does not consider all defections to be alike. *Both arrogance (10:26-29) and intimidation (10:35-39) are culprits leading to apostasy. The latter seems to be stressed by the experience of persecution; the former seems more generalized and may stress an attitude of disobedience and unbelief conveyed earlier in chapters 3-4.*

ENDURING THE RACE AS DISCIPLINED CHILDREN OF GOD (12:1-13)

Since the believers have so many previous examples of faith who stand as a cluster of spectators or "cloud of witnesses," they are encouraged to run their metaphoric footrace of life with endurance (Heb 12:1; cf. ch. 11; 1 Cor 9:24-27).[245] Hebrews uses the imagery of a footrace as one more example of God's people "moving" towards the goal of eschatological completion, similar to the wilderness generation journeying to the place of "rest" (Heb 3-4). The race metaphor, in any case, eventually breaks down when we realize that our author is not concerned about who gets first prize but just that all the contestants run until reaching the finish line. Once that has been achieved, the location is transformed from a stadium to the heavenly Jerusalem (12:22). Hence, the footrace concerns the participants' endurance, and apostasy would seem to be the outcome for those who do not finish the race. The runners are to mimic the attitude of the faithful champions who are now watching them in the stadium as the runners participate in the contest. In this race they must not return once they have gone out (cf. 11:15-16a). If they continue the race God will not be ashamed of them but will grant them entrance into the heavenly city (cf. Heb 11:16b; contrast Mark 8:38). *The point for our author is not that some in the congregation will not start the race, but that some will not finish it.*

To run this race appropriately they should lay aside every impediment and easily obstructing sin, similar to a runner who loses excess body weight and sets aside heavy clothes or anything else that would hinder the athlete's speed (cf. Philostratus, *Gymnasticus* 48; Philo, *Sacrifices* 63). The sin is unspecified, and some exegetes surmise it as the sin of apostasy (cf. Heb 3:13; 10:26).[246] The closest prior mention of sin

245. The language of this passage is hortatory including the author ("we"): 12:1-2, 25b, 28; cf. vv. 9, 10, 29. Second person plurals are emphasized in 12:3-8, 12-25, and individuals among them in 12:14-16.

246. E.g., Käsemann, *Wandering People of God*, 45-48.

is in 11:25, which speaks of Moses choosing mistreatment with God's people over the temporary pleasures of sin. That sin also has been understood as apostasy.[247] But its connection with pleasure (ἀπόλαυσις/cf. ἀπολαύω), when used in a negative sense, often refers to enticements related to forbidden foods and sensual vices,[248] and this comes close to the meaning of sin in 12:16. The imagery of laying aside excess impediments in 12:1 is something normally done before the race starts, which tend to make the "sin" relevant to pre-conversion impediments that would hinder the participants during their new course of life if they are not discarded.[249] The sin in 12:1 therefore refers to pre-converted sins or sin in general (cf. 9:26). It is not referring to apostasy per se.[250]

Interestingly, disrobing before baptism was practiced in Christian circles in the second century, and a similar practice may be operating in Asia Minor in the first century, which uses the same word in 12:1 (ἀποτίθημι) to describe disrobing.[251] In any event, post-baptismal sins could always resemble pre-baptismal ones that do lead to apostasy, and sin would seem to ensnare easily any runner (cf. 12:1, 14–16).

As runners focus their eyes down the track at a person "seated in the place of honor," so the believers are to keep their eyes on Jesus.[252] He has already run the race of faith and finished his course having endured great suffering to the shedding of blood, something the believers have not yet experienced (12:2–4). Jesus is thus the ultimate exemplar of faithfulness as well as the object of faith for the runners. He endured crucifixion and despised "shame," affirming the societal honor system and public opinion as unreliable regarding its evaluation of crucifixion as dishonorable. Our author deems Jesus' death to be noble, voluntarily allowed in obedience to God, dedicated to virtue, and for the benefit of others (cf. 2:9–10, 14f; 4:14–16; 5:7–10; chs. 7–10).[253] By setting their eyes on Jesus and his accomplishment on the cross, the believers will be encouraged not to grow fatigued and "give up" on the race (ἐκλύω: 12:3, 5).[254]

---

247. E.g., Moffat, *Hebrews*, 180.

248. Cf. Prov 7:18; 4 Macc 5:8; Philo, *Embassy* 3.80; *T. Jos.* 5.4; 2 *Clem.* 10.3.

249. Notice that ἀποθέμενοι is an aorist participle in this verse and may be understood in antecedent time to the present tense hortatory subjunctive τρέχωμεν ("let us run") that functions as the governing verb in the sentence (see grammar points in Wallace, *Greek Grammar*, 640, 642). The sentence may be translated thusly: "after laying aside [ἀποθέμενοι] every impediment . . . let us run . . ."

250. Cf. Montefoire, *Hebrews*, 214.

251. See Eph 4:20–24; Col 3:8–10; cf. *Gos. Thom.* 37; *Gos. Phil.* 101; Hippolytus, *Trad. ap.*

252. Quote from Koester, *Hebrews*, 523.

253. Cf. deSilva, *Despising Shame*, 170–73. Compare the despising of suffering related to martyrdom in 4 Macc 6:9; 8:28; 13:1.

254. The NET is lucid on 12:3: "Think of him who endured such opposition against himself by

The believers, as good athletes, are to endure "discipline" (παιδεία), rigorous training conducive for running a good race (12:5–11). The author reconfigures the idea of παιδεία from a loving yet punitive and correcting discipline the LORD gives to children in Prov 3:11–12 to a non-punitive discipline in Heb 12. The discipline and suffering the believers experience, in other words, are not the result of divine punishment. Rather, the training and suffering fosters virtuous living with the special qualities of holiness and righteousness (12:10–11).[255]

Children who are without this training from the Father, something all God's children participate in, are "illegitimate and not sons" (Heb 12:8; cf. Wis 4:3). These words do not accuse some of the audience as false believers. The author gives us no clear indication of such a problem within this community.[256] The homily suggests instead that the members have in fact experienced suffering and are currently enduring the struggle of salvation, and this is why he encourages them to press on— they *are* legitimate children belonging to Christ (Heb 2:13; 3:1; cf. 10:32–34). Their training and suffering should be considered as badges of honor; being illegitimate is a mark of dishonor. The argument probably aims to counter their supposing that discipline and suffering brings shame. David deSilva rightly argues in 12:8: "The author thus makes the experience of reproach and loss suffered for the sake of Christ a sign of favor and honor, and, more astounding, the lack of such hardship a sign of disfavor and dishonor! Those who shrink back so as to avoid these experiences find themselves shamed because they no longer experience what all children of God share in common."[257]

Moreover, *the thought of illegitimacy also stresses the reality of a person being denied the right of inheritance as a legal child* (cf. Gen 21:10; 25:5–6; Gal 4:30).[258] In this homily such an inheritance ends with everlasting salvation (Heb 1:14; 6:12; 9:15; 11:8), and *if one is without discipline, one could anticipate a fate similar to Esau who*

---

sinners, so that you may not grow weary in your souls and give up."

255. See Croy, *Endurance in Suffering*, 158, 210–14, 218. For examples of training for virtuous living see especially Seneca, *De Providentia*, and 4 Maccabees. On suffering as non-punitive see further Deut 8:2–5; Wis 3:1–12; 4 Macc 10:10; 11:20; 4Q504, 3; and Croy, 160–61.

256. Rightly Ellingworth, *Hebrews*, 651, who brings up the example of false brothers in Gal 2:4, a problem that is not the case in Hebrews. Ellingworth thinks that illegitimate children may refer to apostates in 10:39 and the party of Korah, which may be echoed in 12:3 (651). If so, it is not that their inability to persevere until the end proved them to be illegitimate children all along even while they appeared to be faithful Christians; rather, they were once legitimate children who became illegitimate because of their apostasy (cf. 6:4–6; 10:29; 12:16–17).

257. deSilva, *Perseverance in Gratitude*, 451.

258. Cf. Koester, *Hebrews*, 528; Lane, *Hebrews*, 2.243, and further examples of illegitimate children being excluded from family lineage in Aristophanes, *Birds* 1649–50. Demosthenes, *Macart.* 51; Plutarch, *Pericles* 37.2–5; *Agesilaus* 3.1–5.

sold his birthright and lost his rightful inheritance (Heb 12:16-17; cf. v. 23). Esau's profane act nullified his rightful privileges as the firstborn son; and if the believers fall away from their spiritual footrace they will become illegitimate children by losing their place in the family of God and Christ (cf. 2:13b; 3:1, 6; 12:23).

The imagery turns to a fatigued or crippled runner who needs reviving so as to continue advancing: "Therefore strengthen your drooping hands and your feeble knees and make straight paths for your feet so that what is crippled may not be dislocated [ἐκτρέπω] but rather be healed" (Heb 12:12-13/Prov 4:26).[259] In this passage ἐκτρέπω is sometimes interpreted as a turning aside from the course, suggesting apostasy.[260] Or it may have a medical meaning, referring to the dislocation of a joint.[261] A dislocation would cause the runner to fall or not be able to continue the race, so in either case it seems that the runner would not be able to make it to the finish line. Thus committing *apostasy is implied as a negative outcome of what might happen if the runner is not healed and strengthened once again.* The author's exhortation intends to bring about the audience's strengthening and renewing; the congregants are presumed to be *spiritually fatigued* and about to give up the metaphoric race that leads to eternal inheritance.

FAILING TO ATTAIN THE GRACE OF GOD AND SELLING ONE'S BIRTHRIGHT (12:14-17)

The recipients are given an imperative to follow in 12:14—they must pursue sanctification and peace with everyone. Perhaps this kind of peace involves non-violence and non-retaliation, especially in relation to their hostile persecutors (cf. Rom 12:14, 17-21; Matt 5:39-44).[262] The sanctification they should pursue may involve the prevention of activities leading to assimilation with outsiders, such as participating in social events that encourage sexually immoral activities or the extravagance of wealth (cf. Heb 13:4-5). Some of the congregants may have thought that assimilation would deflect harassment. Without holiness, the author claims that no one will see the Lord (12:14b). Profane individuals will not enjoy the presence of Christ and God in the heavenly city (Heb 12:22-24; cf. Rev 22:4; Matt 5:8; 1 John 3:2).

---

259. The echo of making straight paths for the feet comes from Prov 4:26, which contrasts two ways or modes of living—the righteous and evil ways.

260. See, e.g., Pfitzner, *Hebrews*, 179; Michel, *Hebräer*, 450.

261. See, e.g., Mitchell, *Hebrews*, 274.

262. The verb "to pursue" (διώκω) frequently means "to persecute" in other contexts (cf. Matt 5:12-13; Acts 7:52; Rom 12:14; Gal 1:13; Phil 3:6; *1 Clem.* 4.9, 13; 5:2; 6:2; 45:4; *Barn.* 5.11). Its use might be some sort of converse of how hostile outsiders treat them.

They must watch carefully lest any among them fails from the grace of God (12:15: ὑστερέω ἀπὸ τῆς χάριτος). *This failure no doubt refers to apostasy* (cf. 4:1), which involves their departure from the grace they presently experience.[263] The one who falls away from grace misses out on the salvation that has been given by God through his Son and the eschatological inheritance of the unshakable kingdom of God (12:28; cf. 2:9; 10:29). This failure resembles Gal 5:4. Ultimately, however, what may have influenced our author is an exhortation in Deut 29:14-21, which warns that none among the Israelites should "turn away" (ἐκκλίνω: 29:18) in their thoughts from God to serve the gods of the nations and that there be no "root of gall and bitterness springing up" among them. The Lord will not forgive individuals who presumptuously go astray in their hearts (29:19-20a). Such might be said to have hardened their hearts with a false perspective of security.[264] God's anger will burn against them and the curses of the covenant will pertain to them. Moreover, their names will be blotted out from under heaven (29:20b-21) and their exclusion from the community helps preserve the innocent from being destroyed because of them (29:20e).

Several touchstones from this tradition may be present in our text. First, both Hebrews and Deuteronomy address apostasy in terms of rejecting God; albeit, Deuteronomy is concerned about idolatry. Second, both passages posses a similar structure built on μή τις ("lest any . . ."/"that no one . . ."), suggesting the author of Hebrews may have adopted language from the Deuteronomic text. Third, the person who goes astray in Deuteronomy will not be pardoned, much like Esau in Heb 12:16-17 and other apostates throughout Hebrews. Next, both passages are concerned about maintaining holiness in the assembly of God's covenant people, recognizing that individual rebellions may affect the larger community. Deuteronomy is more elaborative, mentioning that turning away from God may happen first with a man, a woman, a family, or tribe (Deut 29:18). For Hebrews, "many" in the congregation could be defiled by the unholy conduct of individual apostates.[265] The "root of gall and bitterness" in Deuteronomy may have originally suggested a poison herb (ראש/רוש MT: cf. 32:32-33) that was then translated in Greek texts as πικρία ("bit-

---

263. Cf. ἀποστῆναι + ἀπὸ in Heb 3:12; ὑστερέω + ἀπὸ in Sir 7:34; Allen, *Deuteronomy and Exhortation*, 103-4, who rightly opines for the meaning of ὑστερέω as a volitional turning back akin with Deut 29:18. The falling away in Heb 12:15 is "to show contempt for and actively reject life under YHWH's (new) covenantal dispensation and community . . . it may represent a more gradual drifting away [than 10:29] . . . but it remains nonetheless the attitude of an apostate member of the community" (104).

264. So Katz, "Quotations from Deuteronomy," 214.

265. On the notion of defiling (μιαίνω) as a spreading contamination see Josephus, *J.W.* 4.311; *Herm. Sim* 5.7.2; and more generally see Jude 8; Titus 1:15; *Herm. Mand* 4.1.9; *Aristeas* 166.

terness"), the word our author uses.²⁶⁶ For our author, this "bitterness" is perhaps recontextualized to refer to the resentment some congregants may have felt as a result of their marginalization from the society on account of their Christian confession.²⁶⁷ It may be more correct, however, to connect πικρία with the similar forms of παραπικρασμός (Heb 3:8, 15) and παραπικραίνω (3:16) to suggest an affinity with the wilderness generation's provocation and rebellion.²⁶⁸ *The root of bitterness, in essence, may be another way of identifying a budding rebellion within the community that might lead to the apostasy of many members.*

Finally, in both Deuteronomy and Hebrews, God will punish apostates with destruction (Deut 29:19b–21/Heb 10:39). In relation to divine judgment, the apostate's name is blotted out from under heaven (Deut 29:20), which may be similar to the notion of giving up one's "birthright" (τὰ πρωτοτόκια) and thus being excluded from the firstborn children who are "enrolled in heaven" with Christ the Son (Heb 12:23; 12:16; 1:6; 2:9–13).²⁶⁹ In Israel's scriptures the "firstborn" belong specially to God and receive a double portion of the family inheritance (cf. Gen 25:32–33; 27:36; Exod 13:13; Num 18:15).²⁷⁰ In Hebrews it relates to those favored and blessed by God to be his children through Christ. The Deuteronomic judgment is bound up with the blessing/curse motif (cf. Deut 11, 28–30). The author of Hebrews adopts the motif in 6:7–8, and it may be implied also in 12:15–17.²⁷¹ But if so, the connection is faint because our author is more concerned about discussing the concept of blessing in terms of an inheritance, which is a theme derived from the story of Esau in Gen 27.

Examples of persons who could defile the congregation in Heb 12:16 include the fornicator (cf. 13:4) and the profane person (βέβηλος) as the violator of sanctification.²⁷² An example of an unholy person who loses his birthright is Esau, a story

---

266. Cf. BDB, 912.2. There are variant Greek texts of Deuteronomy, but the closest to the author of Hebrews seems to be Alexandrinus, which may have some resemblances to the MT. See further Allen, *Deuteronomy and Exhortation*, 83–85.

267. Attridge, *Hebrews*, 368, is similar but also associates the bitterness with the possibility of loss of eschatological hope. Differently, Witherington, *Jewish Christians*, 334, attributes the bitterness to "false thinking and practice" related to a relapse back to another sect of emergent Judaism. Buchanan, *Hebrews*, 217–18, thinks it involves marriage (cf. 13:4)! More plausibly the bitterness can recall Esau's crying out in bitterness over his lost blessing (Gen 27:34). But it seems more likely the "root of bitterness" from Heb 12:15 prompted the idea of bitterness related to Esau's birthright in 12:16–17 rather than vice/verse.

268. Along these lines see Allen, *Deuteronomy and Exhortation*, 86–87.

269. Cf. Exod 4:22; 32:32; Rev 3:5; 20:12; Luke 10:20; Phil 3:20.

270. See further sources in Gräßer, *Hebräer*, 3.295; Attridge, *Hebrews*, 369.

271. On this point see especially, Allen, *Deuteronomy and Exhortation*, 135–40.

272. cf. βέβηλος: 1 Tim 1:9; 3 Macc 2:14; Philo, *Spec*. 1.102. See also the verb form (βεβηλόω) in Acts 24:6; Lev 18:21; 2 Macc 8.2; *Herm. Sim* 8.6.2. Attridge, *Hebrews*, 368, divides βέβηλος into the cultic sphere (Lev 10:10; Ezek 4:14; 22:26; 1 Sam 21:4f; 2 Macc 5:16) and moral sphere (1 Tim 1:9; 4:7;

originating from Genesis (Heb 12:16/Gen 25:29-34; 27:30-40). *Esau also seems to be associated with the fornicator.*²⁷³ In Genesis he marries two foreign women (Hittites) and in later traditions he is vilified and associated with wickedness, vice, sensual activities, or having an illegitimate marriage (Gen 26:34-35).²⁷⁴ There is a strong possibility that our author is concerned about sexual immorality in the congregation even though this is not regarded as the major threat to perseverance in the community (13:4; cf. 11:25). A community mixed with Jews and Gentiles could be tempted by fornication if strongly influenced by Hellenism, which seems to be the case for the recipients of Hebrews. Given that New Testament communities are perpetually vexed with sexual immorality (e.g., Mark 7:21; Acts 15:20, 29; 1 Thess 4:1-8; 1 Cor 6:9-20; Col 3:5-7), there is no need to claim the vice in 12:16 as spiritual rather than physical fornication.²⁷⁵

Even so, Esau is mentioned here most of all not for committing fornication but for failing to inherit the blessing intended for him (Heb 12:17); he sold his birthright for a bowl of stew in order to satisfy his temporary hunger. Later on he missed out on Isaac's blessing, which was given to Jacob instead (Gen 25:29-34; 27:30-40). The author of Hebrews highlights Esau being rejected from his inheritance, but he does not indicate who it is that enacts the rejection. The audience must fill in the blank with either Isaac or God. Perhaps both are intended, but contextually it seems that the author wants the audience to insert the missing subject with God.²⁷⁶ It is said that Esau was not given an opportunity for repentance after selling his birthright,²⁷⁷ and he could not gain back his birthright and blessing pertaining to it, though he sought the blessing with tears (Heb 12:17; cf. Gen 27:34, 38). The feminine "it" (αὐτήν) in

---

6:20; 2 Tim 2:16; 3 Macc 2.2, 14; 4.16; Philo, *Alleg. Interp.* 1.62; *Spec.* 4.40).

273. Both the fornicator and profane person may refer to Esau because ἤ might take on the flavor of a copulative conjunction: cf. Acts 1:7; John 8:14; 1 Thess 2:19; BDF, 231 §446

274. Cf. *Jub.* 25:1-8; Philo *Sacr.* 81, 120, 135; *Alleg. Interp.* 3.2; *Migr.* 153; *Flight* 39; *Gen. Rabbah* 65. See further the excursus on Esau and *Haggada* in Löhr, *Umkehr und Sünde*, 123-29.

275. Contrast Attridge, *Hebrews*, 369; Allen, *Deuteronomy and Exhortation*, 136.

276. Compare Esau being rejected (ἀποδοκιμάζω) with the rejection (ἀδόκιμος) in Heb 6:8. Both passages deal with the "metaphor of plant-growth" (Moffat, *Hebrews*, 212). On God rejecting his people (ἀποδοκιμάζω) see Jer 6:30; 7:29; 14:19.

277. On the combination of repentance (μετάνοια) and "place" as its "opportunity" (τόπος), see Wis 12:10; *1 Clem.* 7.4-5; *Herm. Vis* 3.7.5 (cf. also Rev 2:21; *4 Ezra* 9.11-12; *2 Bar.* 85.12; Livy, *History of Rome* 44.10.2; Pliny, *Letters* 10.96.2. Another alternative is that μετανοίας should be translated more literally here as "to change the mind" in which Esau tried to change the mind of his father for the blessing (see NRSV note: "no chance to change his father's mind"). This view is shot down by Ellingworth, *Hebrews*, 668: "To understand μετανοίας . . . εὗρεν of Esau being unable to make Isaac change his mind (Héring) does violence to the grammatical structure of the passage, in which there is no explicit mention of Isaac, and also to its meaning." Koester, *Hebrews*, 533, adds that the terminology for repentance characteristically involves the change of one's own mind, not another's mind.

Heb 12:17 may refer back to either the repentance or blessing as the object sought by Esau.[278] The advantage of the interpretation that Esau is seeking the blessing rather than repentance is twofold: 1) in Gen 27:38, after losing his birthright, Esau cries and begs his father to bless him; 2) there is no mention of Esau seeking repentance in the story.[279] Even so, αὐτήν is ambiguous enough in this verse to suggest that even if the author understood its reference to be "blessing," some of his readers would be led to think it refers to "repentance."[280] No doubt his rhetorical agenda would be served if some of his audience would think that Esau sought diligently to repent but could not do so, even when he cried about it! The author, in any case, seems to have added the thought about repentance in keeping with his conviction that it is impossible for apostates to be renewed to repentance a second time (cf. Heb 6:6; 10:26). *God would not allow Esau to repent.* Using *qal wahomer*, our author uses the lesser punishment of Esau losing an earthly "blessing" to point to a greater punishment of Christian apostates losing a heavenly inheritance: *losing one's "blessing" involves losing one's "birthright" as a firstborn child of God and Christ with the eternal inheritance pertaining to it; all that is left for that person is final judgment* (12:17, 23, 28–29; cf. 1:14; 6:12; 9:15; 11:7–8).[281]

HEAVENLY ZION AND FINAL JUDGMENT (12:18–29)

In 12:18–29 thoughts about divine judgment merge with the finishing line of the runner and the place of "rest" for the moving people of God portrayed in the earlier portion of the homily (Heb 3–4). The end of the race is met with a festival gathering

---

278. On the close connection between the two see Hagner, *Hebrews*, 223; and see Allen, *Deuteronomy and Exhortation*, 136–37, for a brief discussion and supporters on both sides of this debate.

279. Hence, the NET is correct: ". . . he found no opportunity for repentance, although he sought the blessing with tears."

280. In the standard Greek sentence of Heb 12:17, μετάνοια is placed closer to αὐτήν (eight words before αὐτήν; εὐλογία is 10 words before αὐτήν).

281. Since the author's strategy is rhetorical and from lesser to greater, he is concerned about the eschatological fate of his audience; he is not literally concerned about the spiritual destiny of the historic patriarch named Esau. Gleason, "Moderate Reformed View," 169–70, notices Isaac blessing both Jacob and Esau in Heb 11:20 and then concludes that "Esau is not an example of an apostate who is forever excluded from the life to come." To be sure, Esau's own fate after death is not explicated in Hebrews (nor in Genesis), but Hebrews does affirm from a lesser to greater argument that Esau's loss points to the greater loss of heavenly blessings for apostates (see main text). The blessing in 11:20 is inconsequential for 12:16 because the point of the former verse centers neither on the nature of the blessing nor the eternal destinies of Jacob and Esau. It stresses Isaac's faith and his own openness toward the future. Esau's faith is not mentioned; in fact his selling of his birthright for immediate gratification is the antithesis of those who have faith and shun instant gratification in hope of a better future (cf. Heb 11:25–26). Along these lines see further Hagner, *Hebrews*, 222.

(πανήγυρις) appropriate for the end of a competition.[282] The scene in Hebrews is primarily eschatological with the believers having arrived in Zion, and the heavenly Jerusalem (12:22).[283] The city is paradoxically yet "to come" (13:14; cf. 11:10). In 12:18–24 our author seems to be stripping away the curtain that hides the presently unseen reality so that the audience could get a magnificent glimpse or sneak preview of the heavenly city awaiting them at the culmination of the race. The scene depicts a location where the blessings of God's promises are fully realized: the faithful enter into a final state of rest and receive their reward of inheritance.

In heavenly Zion, God is the judge, Jesus is enthroned, the firstborn assembly is registered as its citizens,[284] and both angels and perfected "spirits" reside there. If our author is primarily fast-forwarding the recipient community's race so that they could see in advance the final scene, then the "church" and firstborn in Zion might include the recipients who have persevered. If so, then the "spirits" of the righteous ones are probably those who had already died by the time the author presented this homily.[285] This group might be identified as the heroes of faith in chapter 11 (cf. 10:38a) or early Christian leaders and martyrs (cf. 13:7), or both. 11:39–40 claims that the people of faith from bygone eras could not be perfected "without us," that is, they could not be completed without believers who presently live in the new covenant era (cf. 7:19; 10:10, 14). This group, it seems, will be perfected when Zion is fully realized to all the firstborn at the end of time.[286]

A final comparison from lesser to greater is given in 12:18–29. God speaking in the past from Mount Sinai is compared with God speaking in the present from the heavenly city. At Sinai when the old covenant was established Moses trembled exceedingly and the people were terrified at God's voice. Even beasts were to be destroyed if they touched the mountain of divine presence (cf. 12:18–21).[287] Fearful as Israel's past experience with the divine presence might have been, the future heav-

---

282. Cf. Isocrates, *Panegyricus*, 43, 46; Philo, *Gaius* 12; cf. Amos 5:21; Hos 2:13; Ezek 46:11; Josephus, *Ant.* 2.45; *J.W.* 5.230. See also Koester, *Hebrews*, 544–45.

283. Cf. Isa 2:3; 8:18; 28:16; 46:13; 51:11 16 66:8–18; *4 Ezra* 10.44; 13:35–39; Rev 14:1. On heavenly Jerusalem see, e.g., cf. *4 Ezra* 7.26; *2 Bar.* 4.2; Rev 21:1–2.

284. Presumably God or the angels may be seen as registering them. Hebrews does not give us enough information to determine whether this enrollment takes place in prehistory or at the start or finish of the race. In all events, we have argued in 12:15–17 that the claim as firstborn does not guarantee or secure one's enrollment while the eschatological race is still going on.

285. On the dead as present with God already see Wis 3:1; *4 Ezra* 7.99; *1 En.* 22.3–9; *2 Bar.* 3.20; Rev 6:9–11.

286. We can also speculate that the perfection in 12:23 might involve the future resurrection of the dead (Heb 11:35; cf. 1 Cor 15). The incomplete spirits of the righteous dead are finally "perfected" with a body when heavenly Zion is fully realized.

287. Cf. Deut 4:11–12; 5:22–25; Exod 10:21–22; 19:12–19.

enly Zion is intended to be even more fearful and operates on the new covenant of Jesus with God as judge (12:22–24). God's voice shook the earth when his presence was manifest at Sinai, but now a promise remains that at the end of the age God will also shake "the heaven" (12:25–26). The shaking of heaven and earth resembles apocalyptic imagery and destruction that must take place before the end (Rev 6:12–14; 16:18–21; 21:1–2; 2 Pet 3:5–7; Isa 59:3; Joel 2:10–11; cf. Isa 33:20). Such shaking communicates the fearful presence and intervention of God (cf. Nah 1:5; Joel 3:16; Isa 13:13; Jer 10:10; Ezek 39:20).[288] In Israel's scriptures, the shaking motif prevailed in theophanies (Exod 19:19; 1 Kgs 19:11), warrior imagery (Judg 5:2–31), and eschatological scenes.[289]

An echo from Hag 2:6–7 (cf. 2:21) is felt here which was originally addressed to Zerubbabel of Judah and "Jesus the high priest." In the prophetic book the day of the Lord was soon approaching, and at that time everything would be affected by it. A shaking would take place horizontally on sea and dry land and vertically on earth and in the heaven. Then all the nations would surrender their treasures and submit to Jerusalem and its temple so that that latter house of God would be greater than the former temple (Hag 2:6–9). Our author in Hebrews relates the shaking from Haggai to the final eschatological visitation in which the temporal and unholy things will be removed and only that which is permanent and holy will remain for the coming kingdom of God.[290]

The implication for believers seems clear enough. The author essentially warns that if the fearful presence and voice of God from the heavenly city is greater than the theophany at Sinai, then how much greater and terrifying will be the judgment of God on those who reject God's voice in the new covenant era? The author's final warning resembles the first one in Heb 2:1–4. The audience is to take heed (βλέπετε) and not to refuse God who now speaks from heaven.[291] The author and the community to whom he writes ("we") will not be able to escape the final judgment if they *turn away* (ἀποστρέφω) from the one who warns from heaven (12:25, 29).[292] God is viewed as a consuming fire, a thought that alludes to his judgment against

---

288. Cf. Kessler, *Book of Haggai*, 175–76.

289. See further Kessler, *Book of Haggai*, 176–77. In essence "when 'the divine warrior' arrives, both humans and nature tremble" (176).

290. On μετάθεσις in Heb 12:27 as removal rather than transformation (*contra* BDAG, 639) see Schenck, "Philo and the Epistle to the Hebrews," 120–21; also Heb 7:12; 11:15.

291. This exhortation to listen to God's voice at the end of Heb 12 becomes all the more relevant if, as claimed in Koester, *Hebrews*, 552, the audience had already been listening to this homily for about 45 minutes! Weiss, *Hebräer*, 684, associates the warning (βλέπετε) in Heb 12:25 with 1 Cor 10:12. See also βλέπετε in Heb 3:12.

292. Cf. Jer 15:6; Ezek 3:18–20; Hos 8:3; Acts 7:39; 2 Tim 1:15; 4:4; *2 Clem.* 15.1

enemies and those who violate his covenant (cf. Deut 4:23–24; 9:3; Isa 33:14). Our author has in mind a burning judgment and picture of final destruction akin with early apocalyptic traditions (Isa 66:16, 24; Zeph 1:18; *1 En.* 91.9; *4 Ezra* 7.38; *2 Bar.* 44.15).[293] Put differently, *if the malaise Christian community that suffers from dullness of hearing commit apostasy by rejecting God's message, then God will consume them with a fiery punishment at the eschaton.*

Given that the audience is in the process of inheriting an unshakable kingdom, the appropriate way to worship God, then, is for all believers to show gratitude (Heb 12:28), which is the proper response beneficiaries are to show to the benefactor who gives them a gift. In this case the benefactor is God.[294] They are also to offer service pleasing to God with "godly fear" (εὐλάβεια) and "dread" (δέος).[295] Again the author uses fear as a strategy in his warning (4:1; 10:27, 31; 12:21; cf. 11:7). The believers are exhorted to worship God acceptably and not commit apostasy but inherit instead the promised blessing of rest in heavenly Zion.

CONCLUSION

The author of Hebrews is unknown but probably writing from Italy in the latter part of the first century, and the community to whom he writes appears to be comprised of both Jewish and Gentile followers of Christ, possibly somewhere in Asia Minor. A large number of the recipients may be Hellenistic Jews. They seem to have been Christ-followers for quite some time (5:12; 10:32–34), and the content of the warnings suggest their potential to commit apostasy on at least two fronts. The community faced persecution in the past and this is still a problem when the author writes to them (e.g., 10:32–39; cf. 12:2–4; 13:3, 13). Their mistreatment by outsiders probably included insults, occasional imprisonments, and at one time the confiscation of their property. Members of the community are in danger of defecting by shrinking back in fear and intimidation as a result of being harassed. Some had stopped attending church meetings. The second danger perhaps developed from the first. The believers

---

293. See further *T. Zeb.* 10.3; *Jub.* 16.5; 4 Macc 12:12; Jdt 16:17; *Sib. Or.* 2.286–95; 1QS 2.8; 4.13; 1QH 17.13; Rev 20:10, 15; *Herm. Vis* 4.3.3; Lichtenberger, "πῦρ, ός, τό *pyr* fire," 3.200. The judgment is more severe than mere forfeiture of future rewards; it is the forfeiture of final salvation and eternal life. *Contra* Oberholtzer, "Failure to Heed," 67–75.

294. See deSilva, *Perseverance in Gratitude*, 473–76.

295. On the former word ("godly fear") see Heb 5:7; on the latter ("dread") see Gray, *Godly Fear*, 210, who lists 2 Macc 3:17; 12:22; Herodotus, *Histories* 4.115; Plato, *Euthyphro* 12B–C; *Protagoras* 358D; Epictetus, *Discourses* 2.23.38. The meaning of "dread" frequently conveys the idea of "terror." Gray notes that most translations downplay that aspect of fear, translating the words as "reverence and awe" (cf. NASB, NRSV, NIV, etc.). He suggests that "godly fear" has religious nuance, and "dread" stresses emotion.

seem to be suffering from malaise, manifested in a loss of zeal and reluctance to hear the spiritual messages from leaders and receive exhortation from fellow believers (e.g., 2:1–4; 5:11; 6:12; 10:25). The warnings mostly follow a pattern of stating the nature of the apostasy and then describing a corollary judgment that would be greater than divine judgment on apostate Israelites in the past. Traditions that our author draws upon include the rebellion of the wilderness generation (Heb 3–4), apostasy and curse motifs from Deuteronomy and the Song of Moses (6:4–8; 12:15–17), the righteous person who lives by faithfulness or shrinks back in Habakkuk (10:36–39), and God's judgment to shake heaven and earth in Haggai (12:25–29). Likewise Esau from Genesis is used as an example of apostasy by selling his birthright (12:15–17).

Hebrews 2:1–4 describes the problem of apostasy in a blueprint manner for the rest of the homily. The author addresses his warning using "we," which fosters solidarity between the author and audience. In the warnings it also serves a rhetorical function implying that if their orator is susceptible to apostasy, how much more they? They also are viewed as family members in Christ, who is not ashamed of those who are not ashamed of him (cf. 2:5–13). Using nautical and filial imagery, our author warns his audience against drifting away from the message that was spoken to them. The nautical implication of being spiritually shipwrecked is used to depict their potential apostasy. They are in danger of defection on account of their negligence and reluctance to hear spiritual messages.

In Heb 3–4 they must not fall away by hardening their hearts through disobedience and unbelief as the wilderness generation did, especially at Kadesh Barnea when God swore in his wrath that they would not enter into his rest (Ps 94[95]; Num 13–14). The believers face a greater judgment of not entering into the eschatological rest God has prepared for them if they apostatize from God. As God swore that the wilderness generation would not enter into rest, preventatives against falling away include faith (4:2–3), exhorting one another in fellowship (3:13), and persevering by holding fast to their relationship in Christ until the completion of the current era (3:14). The Israelites' defection results in God declaring by oath that they would never enter into his rest, and this thought seems to inform in part our author's view that apostates cannot be restored.

In Heb 5:12—6:12 the audience is reminded of their conversion experience, and yet they must move on from elementary teachings to spiritual maturity and refrain from reluctant hearing that may lead to apostasy. The author mentions Christian apostates whom he affirms as having been once converted, saved by grace, having fellowship with the Spirit, understanding the gospel message, and experiencing signs and wonders. And yet they fell away with no repentance possible (6:4–6).

What remains for them is a fiery judgment of destruction at the end of time (6:7–8). The author may be reflecting on an incident in his community's past in Italy or Rome, such as the Christian defections that took place during Nero's persecutions. By addressing the apostates in such harsh language the author attempts to stir up his audience with godly fear and steer them away from contemplating apostasy. Among the multitude of explanations for the rigorism in Hebrews, this tradition seems most influenced by texts from Israel's scriptures that suggest no forgiveness is available for the apostate or witting sinner (e.g., Num 15:26–31; Deut 29:18–20; 1QS 6.27–7.2; 7.16–24; *Jub.* 35.14). As well, God's oath to apostate Israel in the wilderness that they would not enter his rest has informed the author.

In Heb 10:19–39 the believers are not to waver in their confession but be faithful to the end, and the Jewish martyr-hero Eleazar (cf. 4 Macc 6–7) may be an exemplar here. Failure to assemble together and encourage fellow believers can result in apostasy. Members of the Christ community, it seems, were not attending church gatherings out of malaise and fear of harassment. The author stirs them to exemplify the fervency they once had in their earlier years. The person who commits the willful sin of apostasy reverses his or her confession of Jesus as Son of God, despises the atoning death of Christ that is the basis for the new covenant, and rejects God's Spirit. For our author, there is no other sacrifice for sin apart from Christ's once-for-all sacrifice, and hence the apostate who rejects Christ and his atoning death cannot be brought back to restoration again even though such an individual was once sanctified. Apostasy is viewed as violating a greater covenant than that of Moses, and the defector can only expect a fearful retribution from God. Through such teachings the believers are warned not to throw away their confidence of eschatological hope. They must remain faithful and not shrink back through intimidation by outsiders; otherwise, they will bring upon themselves divine rejection. Hebrews 10 highlights the despondent and arrogant behavior of the apostate in 10:26–29, and yet there is a timid apostate who fears persecution in 10:35–39.

Finally, 12:1–28 depicts a salvific track course in which believers are runners who must endure discipline to make it to the finishing line of the race, as did Jesus their forerunner and example of faithfulness. At the end of the contest those who persevered will join in the blessing of eschatological inheritance in the heavenly city of Jerusalem where Christ resides, his firstborn children live, and God is judge. Failure to finish the race constitutes apostasy. Until the race is over the community members must not exchange their place of enrollment as children of God through profanity, as did Esau who sold his birthright as a firstborn son and was unable to get it back. The author's reconfiguration of this story in Genesis provides a third example in which it is impossible for an apostate to repent (Heb 12:17). Esau is also seen as a fornicator in this homily, which suggests that the author is aware that certain vices could also undermine the faith of believers (cf. 13:4). The believers must fear God and obey his voice because a great judgment will soon shake heaven and earth, and apostates and God's enemies will be destroyed.

The nature of apostasy in Hebrews shares some similarities with warnings against lacking zeal that we find in some of the churches of Asia Minor (Rev 2–3). Both documents seem to be addressed to Christian communities that had existed for quite some time. These churches are called to repent of their backslidden ways, but in Hebrews there is no repentance for backsliders. The homily also resembles warnings from the gospels against falling away in the end times as a result of persecution. Luke's version of the unpardonable sin in this regard (Luke 12:10) is perhaps the closest New Testament parallel to Hebrews. The homily's "no second chance" policy for apostates stands in contrast to other New Testament traditions such as Jas 5:19–20, Jude 21–22; Gal 6:1; 1 Cor 5:5; and Mark's community that allowed for restoration of apostates and heinous sinners. This evidence shows that the early Christian communities were not uniform in their beliefs about whether apostates could be restored. Amidst the diversity of viewpoints in the New Testament writings, we have stated that two points are universal regarding apostasy: first, all the writers seem to agree that if a person repudiates Christ, then that person is an apostate; second, they also agree that one's lifestyle as a Christ-follower could violate the central commands of Jesus or be so immoral that this invalidates one's confession of Christ.

2

James

*Perseverance through Suffering and the Restoration
of Jewish-Christian Apostates*

James, the person whose name is attached to the beginning of this letter, is supposed to be the brother (or step-brother) of Jesus and early leader of the church in Jerusalem (Jas 1:1; cf. Mark 6:3; Matt 13:55; Gal 1:18–19; 2:9; Acts 21:17–18).[1] There is no scholarly consensus, however, on whether or not he is the actual author of the letter.[2] This author seems to be quite familiar with Hellenism and among other things uses the Septuagint,[3] diatribe,[4] rhetorical questioning,[5] and a polished Greek style.[6] Such proclivities do not rule out that a Galilean Jew from the first century could have written the letter,[7] especially if Hellenized Jews belonged to the early

---

1. For sources and evaluation on James as the son of Joseph but not Mary, see Painter, *Just James*, 182–223.

2. Brosend, *James and Jude*, 5, conveniently lists a number of scholars who hold to the traditional view and those who deny it. A mediating position is held by, e.g., Davids, "Palestinian Traditions," 54–55; Hartin, *James*, 24–25. See further sources on the authorship and dating in Penner, *James and Eschatology*, 28–30.

3. E.g., Jas 2:8/Lev 19:18; Jas 2:11/Exod 20:13–14 and Deut 5:17–18; Jas 2:23/Gen 15:6; Jas 4:6/Prov 3:34.

4. E.g., Jas 3:13; 4:14; 5:13–14.

5. E.g., Jas 2:4–7, 14, 16, 20; 3:11–12; 4:1, 4–5; 5:6.

6. On these points, see Johnson, *James*, 8–10. Ropes, *James*, 50, is one author who argues against the traditional authorship because of the letter's Hellenistic cues.

7. Archaeological and literary evidence indicate that Hellenism pervaded first-century Palestine, and many Jews from the area may have known Greek fluently. See Hengel, *Judaism and Hellenism*, 1.58–106; Sevenster, *Do You Know Greek?*, esp. 4–21; 190–91. Contrast Feldman, *Jew and Gentile*, 3–44.

group of Christ-followers in Jerusalem (Acts 6). The crucial question is whether James would have known enough Greek to write this document as a firsthand letter. Generalizations about Hellenistic influence in Palestine do not provide us with compelling answers.[8]

The letter maintains a history of problems related to its authenticity. It is not listed in the Muratorian Canon (second century CE), and Eusebius claims it as one of the disputed books or *antilegomena* (*Hist. eccl.* 2.23.25). Also one Gnostic text attributes dual authorship to the letter (2 *Apoc. Jas.* 44.13–17). Jerome mentions that it may have been edited by someone other than James; the letter was only gradually recognized by the church (*Vir. ill.* 2). The letter's slow acceptance into the New Testament canon may have been related to early questions about its authorship, possibly even some fears of it being written by someone other than James. Perhaps another reason for its slow acceptance centered on the fact that the church became increasingly Gentile in the second and third centuries, and the letter was intended for Jewish readers (Jas 1:1).

If the pseudonymous view is accepted, the date of the letter normally ranges between 75–110 CE.[9] Those who hold to James as the author date it from before his death in 62 CE to as early as the late 40s CE.[10] We will surmise the position that either the brother of Jesus is the original author of this letter or a collection of his sayings are included in this letter even though compiled and edited by a later editor who remains unknown. A date in the late 50s or early 60s CE can be maintained by textual implications supporting a problem with poverty in Palestine (1:9–11, 26–27; 2:1–14; 5:1–6),[11] simplicity in the congregation's structure (3:1–2; 5:13–19), low Christology (1:1: 2:1), and imminent eschatology (5:3, 5, 7–9; cf. 1:12; 2:12; 3:1). The letter also might suggest that Jewish Christians were still meeting in the synagogue (2:2).[12]

---

8. See further the discussion on this issue in Frankemölle, "Semantische Netz des Jakobusbriefes," 166–67; Penner, *James and Eschatology*, 35–47.

9. E.g., Frankemölle, *Jakobusbrief*, 1.60.

10. E.g., Geyser, "James and the Social Condition," 25–33.

11. Cf. Acts 11:28; 24:17; Gal 2:10; Rom 15:26.

12. Cf. Acts 13:5, 14f, 43; 18:26; 19:8; 22:19; 26:11. Other possibilities include that the meeting in Jas 2:2 was judicial: cf. Ward, "Partiality in the Assembly," 87–97. Or the term "synagogue" (συναγωγή) is simply being used to describe church meetings (cf. Jas 5:14). Against the judicial view, see Witherington, *Jewish Christians*, 454–55. There is evidence, in any case, that some Christians were still using this term in the second century even though they were not meeting in Jewish synagogues: cf. Ign. *Poly.* 4.2; Ign. *Trall.* 3; *Herm. Mand.* 11.9, 13, 14; Schrage, "συναγωγή." 7.840–41.

JAMES: LAW-KEEPER, MARTYR, AND APOSTATE

New Testament sources present James and his brother Jude as leaders among the early Christians.[13] It is not clear that James became the leader of the Christ-followers in Jerusalem immediately after Jesus' ascension. Acts implies Peter as the first leader (Acts 1:15–16; 2:14; 5:3–5; cf. 3:1, 11; 4:1, 13, 23; 8:14). James apparently takes over once Peter departs from Jerusalem due to persecution (12:17). Paul calls James, Peter, and John "pillars" of the church in Jerusalem (Gal 2:1, 9). The relatives of James reportedly become leaders among the Jewish Christians in Palestine (cf. Eusebius, *Hist. eccl.* 3.19.1–3.20.7 [Hegesippus]; 4.5.1).

Mark's gospel portrays Jesus' immediate family members as outsiders, James included (Mark 3:20–21; cf. 6:3). All of Jesus' close contacts are obdurate, whether family or disciples, in keeping with the gospel's motivation to highlight spiritual blindness and apostasy as vivid dangers for the Christian community (see gospel of Mark in volume one). John's gospel portrays Jesus' brothers as unbelievers (John 7:2–5). John may be insinuating that true kinship ties involve faith in Jesus as the deified savior, and spiritual relationships go deeper than blood relations (cf. John 1:10–12). It is possible that these authors meant only to convey the pre-Easter attitudes of James and his brothers prior to their believing in Jesus as the Christ. Then again, such passages betray possible conflicts between the communities of these authors and the community of Jesus' relatives. If so, these authors may be criticizing the beliefs of Jewish Christians in Palestine who are being represented by James and his siblings.[14] We are not told what these beliefs are, but in John's gospel a conflict centers on the nature of Christ's deity, and in Mark 7:1–23 Pharisaic customs related to eating and table fellowship are criticized. These issues may or may not be related to the Jerusalem Christians; nonetheless it is interesting that both Paul and Luke depict James as a devout keeper of Jewish customs and Mosaic Law (Gal 2:1–16; Acts 21:18–24).

Apart from the New Testament, Josephus says that James, the brother of Jesus, was stoned at the instigation of Ananus II, the high priest (Josephus, *Ant.* 20.9.1[199–203]). Later sources consider James the first bishop of Jerusalem who was cast down from the parapet and beaten to death after the procurator Festus had died but before a new governor could be established over the province (62 CE). He was reportedly killed for refusing to deny his faith in Jesus Christ (Eusebius, *Hist. eccl.* [Clement of Alexandria] 2.1.2–4; 2.23.1–3; cf. *Gos. Thom.* 12). Hegesippus calls him the just one. James adheres to a Nazarite kind of lifestyle and develops calloused

---

13. Jude 1; 1 Cor 9:1–2; 15:7; Acts 12:17; 15:13–21; 21:17–18; Gal 1:19; 2:9, 12.
14. Along these lines see Bernheim, *James, Brother of Jesus*, 85–86.

knees as a result of praying for forgiveness on behalf of his people. The scribes and Pharisees interrogated him because the people were reportedly going astray after Jesus on account of him. They asked him, "Who is the gate of Jesus?," and James proclaimed Jesus as the Son of Man who sits in heaven at the right hand of power and will come again on the clouds of heaven. They claimed James had gone astray, and after throwing him down they stoned him as he prayed for them. Finally, a fuller beat him on the head with his club (Eusebius, *Hist. eccl.* 2.23.3–20).[15]

The historical reliability of these accounts is beyond the scope of this chapter. More relevant for our purposes is that early Christian traditions considered James to be the leader of the Jerusalem church. He died as a martyr according to the Christians, but *he was considered an apostate who led the Jewish people astray according to his opponents*. Stoning would be prescribed for blasphemy (cf. Lev 24:10–23; *m. Sanhedrin* 7.5) and for being a *maddiah*, a person who leads astray others; a prime example of the latter is one who leads God's people astray to follow other deities (cf. Deut 13:6–18). For Richard Bauckham, "in either case, James must have been condemned for making exalted Christological claims about Jesus."[16] Bauckham notices similarities between the basis for James's death (in Hegesippus) and for Jesus (Mark 14:55–62) and Stephen (Acts 7:51–57). All three make a claim that the Son of Man is exalted at the right hand of God, and thus Jesus participates in God's cosmic rule (cf. Ps 110:1; Acts 2:32–36).

THE COMMUNITY AND SITUATION OF JEWISH CHRISTIANS (1:1)

The recipients are identified as the twelve tribes of the Diaspora (διασπορά: Jas 1:1), which frequently refers to Jews living outside of ancient Palestine and dispersed among the nations. In this letter the term does not appear to be symbolic for the church universal, comprising of Jews and Gentiles, nor does it imply for the audience that God has punished them in exile from Palestine.[17] The term resonates with the hope of restoration for God's elect people in the messianic age,[18] and the "twelve

15. Contrast the Pseudo-Clementine *Recognitions* 1.66–71, a source that opposes Pauline Christianity and has him as the enemy who kills James. For early sources on James see Painter, *Just James*, 159–223.

16. Bauckham, "James and the Jerusalem Community," 75–77 (quote from 77); idem, "For What Offense Was James Put to Death?" 199–232. In these sources, Bauckham interprets "Who is the gate of Jesus?" from Ps 118:20: "This is the gate of YHWH; the righteous shall enter through it." The divine name may have been understood as Jesus, "the gate through which the righteous enter the eschatological temple" (77).

17. Contrast 1 Pet 1:1 in which the dispersion takes on a nuance of marginalization that is predominantly Gentile.

18. E.g., *4 Ezra* 13; *Pss. Sol.* 17; Ezek 34; cf. Sir 36:13–14.

tribes" makes specific that James is addressing all Jewish believers in Jesus as the Christ (cf. Jas 2:1; 5:14) who live in various communities outside of Palestine or Jerusalem.[19] A valid case could be made for the faithful community in Jerusalem as the letter's originator, thus complementing traditions purporting James as head of the Jerusalem church. Internal evidence could be rallied to support a Palestinian center, such as the hot wind on vegetation (1:11), use of the place-name *Gehenna* (3:6), mention of figs, olives, and grapes that grow in the area (3:12), day laborers in the fields (5:4), and so on.[20] Another prominent option is to place the letter's matrix in Antioch of Syria, another Christian center familiar with the community of James (cf. Gal 2:1–15). This location works well with a post-66 CE date for the letter of James, when Jerusalem was under siege by Rome and its temple eventually destroyed.

A Jewish audience seems confirmed by such things as the letter's emphasis on the Law (Jas 1:25; 2:8–12; 4:11), concern for works related to faith (2:14–26; cf. 3:13), almsgiving related to the poor (2:15–16), and an assumption that the audience knows stories about Abraham, Rahab, Job, and Elijah (2:21–25; 5:11, 17).[21] We do not know from this letter how James felt about Gentile believers. Perhaps he took seriously his mission to the circumcision and let others care for the uncircumcision (cf. Gal 2:1–9). He may have considered the separation of Jewish and Gentile Christians to be necessary given that the Jewish believers he influenced held to ancestral customs and the Law more fully than the minimal mandates prescribed to the Gentile Christians (cf. Acts 15:19–29).[22] With hardly any mention of Jesus,[23] the letter resembles a Jewish rather than Christian document, perhaps what one might expect from a community that considered itself Jewish and upheld the Law. On the other hand, as many scholars have observed, the epistle mimics phrases from Matthew, Q, and the Sermon on the Mount,[24] suggesting that James may have possessed proto-texts of certain gospels or knew by memory a number of sayings attributed to Jesus or both.[25] More importantly, his use of such sayings shows that James' view of Mosaic Law is grounded in the teachings of Jesus, and in this regard

19. Bauckham, *Wisdom of James*, 15. Differently, on 1:1 as Gentile God-fearers see Laws, "James," 3.623–24.

20. See further Davids, "Palestinian Traditions," 33–57.

21. The meetings in the synagogue (2:2) may also be used as support if worship or judicial meetings are being held at the Jewish synagogue.

22. See on Gal 2 above. For discussions on James' relationship with Gentile Christians, see Myllykoski, "James the Just," 73–122.

23. See exceptions in 1:1; 2:1.

24. E.g. Jas 1:22–25/Matt 7:24–27; Luke 6:47–49; Jas 5:9/Matt 7:1; Jas 5:12/Matt 5:34.

25. See further, Kloppenborg, "Jesus Tradition," 121–50; Hartin, *James and the Sayings of Jesus*.

he probably adheres to Jesus' interpretation of the Law similar to what is found in the Sermon on the Mount (Matt 5:17–20; 7:12).

Some possible scenarios behind the content of James are worth noting. Certain scholars believe the letter responds to Paul or a misrepresentation of Paul (or later Paulinists) or the letter itself misrepresents the Pauline position regarding faith (Jas 2:14–26).[26] Tensions between Paul and James go as far back as Gal 2 and the Jerusalem meeting in Acts 15 (c. 49–50 CE). A very early date for the letter of James (c. 47–49 CE) may reflect this tension from James' point of view. A moderately early date (c. 50–61 CE) allows for tensions to brew between James and Paul, and it assumes the Jerusalem meeting did not resolve all the differences between the two. Problematic for this view might be the way no conflict exists between James and Paul when they meet in Acts 21 and discuss issues related to the Law and the Gentiles (c. 59–60 CE). But it is quite possible, of course, that Luke ignores or waters down the tensions. A later date for James, after the death of both James and Paul (70 CE onward), works well with a reaction against distorted post-Paulinism comparable with what is found in 2 Pet 3:15–16. There is certainly a strong possibility that the letter reacts against some variant of Paul's teaching (see below). However, this does not appear to be the *leitmotif* of the entire letter. Issues related to works and faith are subsumed under the more weighty topics of the Law of love and helping the poor.

Another possible situation locates the letter in two stages, first originating with James in Jerusalem and then edited by someone else in Antioch after James' death in 62 CE.[27] On this view some of the Jewish Christians from Jerusalem may have fled as refugees to Antioch during the time of the Jewish War (66–70 CE). They brought with them a collection of James' sayings that were later embellished and arranged by a Hellenistic writer. This background to the letter has the advantage of working with both an early and late date for the writing, and Jas 4:1–4 may reflect zealot imagery relevant to the Jewish War. The audience would be encouraged to persevere through various trials they might face during the uncertain crises related to Roman/Jewish and Roman/Christian conflicts of the 60s. Likewise, similarities between the writings of James and Matthew make good sense if they arose from the same community, and it is quite possible that Matthew's community lived in Antioch.[28]

---

26. On the author of James as refuting Paul see, e.g., Hengel, "Jakobusbrief als antipaulinische Polemik," 248–78; Tsuji, *Glaube*, esp. 199. On James misrepresenting Paul see Popkes, "Two Interpretations of Justification," 129–46; Painter, *Just James*, 265–69. For a list of options, see Mitchell, "Letter of James," 77–79.

27. See Martin, *James*, lxxiv–lxxvii.

28. Martin, lxxiv–lxxvii; Sandt, *Matthew and the Didache*.

Some observations about the Antioch hypotheses are in order. First, a number of scholars suggest Galilee rather than Antioch as the home of the Matthean community, but the point is certainly debatable. Our assumption is that Matthew's community may have expanded beyond one location, but it certainly could have included Antioch (see the gospel of Matthew in volume one). Second, we may wish to question if there is still any compelling reason why the letter could not have been written by James or under James' authority prior to his death. Third, although the concept of suffering trials is a major motif of the letter, if not the *leitmotif*, there is no clear mention of suffering related to religious persecution. This is rather peculiar if James' martyrdom and conflicts related to Sadducees, Zealots, and/or Romans are supposed to be part of the situational background behind the writing of this letter. Despite its limitations, a two-stage hypothesis for the letter's origin remains a valid option. If the letter is to be read by a large audience of Jewish believers abroad who may be facing numerous issues and problems within their respective communities, then we are perhaps safe to suggest some general rather than specific issues behind the letter. The letter is perhaps best described as a paraentic encyclical that resembles Jewish wisdom literature.[29] The internal purpose of letter seems to be threefold: it addresses perseverance through various trials, wisdom related to conduct (including speech and prayer), and issues related to wealth and poverty. At best, then, *we can surmise that Jewish Christ-followers needed to be reminded through practical wisdom how to behave morally within their communities, and they were probably quite familiar with suffering* (1:2–4).

PERSEVERANCE THROUGH DIVERSE TRIALS (1:2–4)

The nature of the trials/temptations (πειρασμός) are manifold in James, and 1:2–11 perhaps functions as a prolonged thesis for the letter, anticipating the themes and cycles to come. Πειρασμός carries with it the possibility of committing apostasy, and that is why people rather than objects are so tested (cf. Mark 14:38; Matt 26:41; Luke 4:13; 8:13; 22:28; Acts 20:29; 1 Tim 6:9; 1 Pet 1:6; 4:12).[30] The sufferings in James appear to include: 1) enduring the temptation to commit sin at the prompting of one's own covetousness (1:12–15); 2) resisting internal and congregational strife prompted by the Devil (4:1–10); 3) suffering exploitation and oppression at the hand of the rich and powerful (2:6; cf. 5:1–6); 4) being patient and enduring general suf-

---

29. In agreement with Bauckham, *Wisdom of James*, 12–13, 29. It contains various literary wisdom forms such as prudent sayings (2:13), didactic wisdom (1:5–8), beatitudes (1:12, 25), and comparisons or two ways (Jas 1:9–11; 1:12, 15, 22–24; 3:14–18; 4:4).

30. So Davids, "Why Do We Suffer?," 436–37.

ferings until the *parousia* (5:7–11, 13); 5) putting up with others (5:9, 16, 19f); and 6) experiencing illnesses (5:14). *Diverse sufferings leave the testing open to more than one venue.*

Those who experience trials that test their faith are to rejoice, knowing that affliction works perseverance (ὑπομονή) thus building moral character (Jas 1:3–4; cf. Rom 5:3–5). James' ὑπομονή may be understood as "staying power" or an "unswerving constancy to faith and piety in spite of adversity and suffering"; a notion held in common with this virtue's frequent use elsewhere in the New Testament (e.g., Luke 8:15; 21:19; Rom 15:4–5; 2 Pet 1:6; Heb 10:36; 12:1; Rev 2:2, 3, 19).[31] The ultimate goal of such perseverance is for the recipients to be mature and complete, lacking nothing (1:4; cf. 1 Cor 2:16; Eph 4:13).[32] Similar to Paul, James considers these trials to be generally a good thing. They produce virtue, lead to maturity, and are reminders of the eschatological blessings up ahead for the person who endures patiently. Unlike Paul, however, James does not equate trials with religious persecution.

In James, the testing leads to "perfection." This concept (τέλειος), repeated several times in the letter (3:2 cf. 1:17, 25; 2:22), refers to moral maturity or "wholeness," an idea that originates from cultic worship (cf. Exod 12:5 LXX). As Patrick Hartin maintains, it involves in Israel's scriptures a person remaining true to his or her original makeup, single-hearted and unconditional devotion to God (relationship), and obedience to the Torah and will of God.[33] These three dimensions are apparent in James, for τέλειος "embraces a search for wholeness as an individual and as a community in relationship to the one God who guides them through the Torah."[34] The word for being complete (ὁλόκληρος: Jas 1:4) appears significantly in Paul's prayer-wish for believers to be sanctified completely and be blameless at the second coming (1 Thess 5:23).[35] The meaning in James suggests freedom from defect and lacking no virtue (cf. Stobaeus, *Eclogae* 2.7.11; Philo, *Abr.* 34).[36]

James 1:2–4 stresses the corporate community's perseverance and moral perfection.[37] It encourages Jewish Christians of the Diaspora to persevere through their

---

31. Cf. Ropes, *James*, 135–36.

32. On the aspect of faith related to trials, Moo, *James*, 54–55, perceptively writes, "The 'testing of faith' here, then is not intended to determine whether a person has faith or not; it is intended to purify faith that already exists."

33. See Hartin, *Spirituality of Perfection*, 57–92; idem, *James*, 71–74.

34. Hartin, *James*, 73.

35. See also the combination of τέλειος and ὁλόκληρος in Philo, *Abr.* 47: cf. Popkes, *Jakobus*, 85.

36. "Lacking nothing" (ἐν μηδενὶ λειπόμενοι) functions as an expansion of ὁλοτελής; so Davids, *James*, 70.

37. In agreement with Johnson, *James*, 82–83, who asserts that James is not teaching individual perfectionism nor individual virtue apart from the community. Individual identities will come to the

various sufferings and to proceed on to moral completion. When combined with 1:5–11 this message implies that moral completion is attained by wisdom and a proper attitude towards the poor. The letter will unpack these ideas later on. Moral maturity in any case is not automatically attained whenever the faithful successfully endure suffering. Testing is a lifelong process culminating at the *parousia*, and the hope of these Jewish Christians is that their trials produce the necessary moral character for them to be declared blameless on judgment day and given eschatological reward (Jas 1:12; 5:11; cf. 1 Cor 1:8; Phil 1:10). Till then, they must persevere through all trials.[38] *At the core of this letter's message, then, the community is instructed on how to endure trials and move on to moral completion until the eschaton. The necessity for such instruction was self-evident for James and his audience: they knew that Christ-followers do not always endure but sometimes fall away, and such individuals jeopardize their eschatological life* (cf. Jas 5:19–20).

WRONGFUL DESIRES THAT BIRTH DEATH (1:12–18; CF. 4:1–5)

There may be a subtle shift in the author's language from diverse testings in 1:2 to temptations in 1:12–15 even though πειρασμός is used for both.[39] James affirms that eschatological reward awaits the person who overcomes temptation, and no one is to consider themselves tempted by God. Several explanations have been given as background for this final thought: 1) it may be sparked by a misunderstanding from the Lord's Prayer that God the Father is directly responsible for leading his earthly children into temptation (Matt 6:13; Luke 11:4); 2) James is responding to a general tendency among his audience to place blame for their temptations on uncontrollable circumstances, hence, God's will; 3) the passage responds to the idea that God created human propensity for desire; or 4) it responds to a view that God himself directly tests individuals (e.g., Abraham in Gen 22). Whichever nuance is preferred, the idea avoids personal responsibility by blaming temptation on God. It generally parallels the problem in Sir 15:11–20.[40] Both Sirach and James claim that God cannot be blamed for individuals who are led astray. They are led astray by their own decisions to choose death over life and thus commit apostasy (Sirach) or by their own desires that tempt them to commit sins eventually leading to death (James).

---

foreground beginning in 1:5.

38. Similarly Penner, *James and Eschatology*, 199–201, stresses the eschatological connection of ὑπομονή and compares the term with Revelation 1:9; 2:2, 19; 3:10; 13:10; 14:12. He also contrasts the notions of continuation in steadfastness with the idea of "drawing back" (cf. Heb 10:36–39). Note also Matt 24:13. The perseverance here is not automatic; cf. Moo, *James*, 55.

39. See BAGD, 793.

40. For more parallels see Frankmölle, *Jakobus*, 1.192–94, 284.

Churches under Siege of Persecution and Assimilation

Sirach's rebuttal is that God does not do what he hates, and he abhors abominations; James says that God is "without temptation" (ἀπείραστος), which probably means that God has nothing to do with tempting humans to commit sinful deeds.[41] Similar to Sirach, James also sets before his audience the way of life and death in relation to apostasy (Jas 5:19–20; cf. 1:15/Sir 15:17), and both authors exhort their readers to be steadfast and trust in God when tested (Jas 1:2–4, 12–16/Sir 2:1–11). James may be informed by Sirach on these issues. If so, this tends to fortify the notion that when James refers to sin that leads to *death* (1:14–15), he has apostasy in mind.

For James temptation arises from within. A person is dragged away and enticed (δελεάζω) by his or her own desire (ἐπιθυμία). The language in 1:14 may convey the metaphor of a fish being drawn out the water and hooked by its desire for the bait.[42] Although temptation is sometimes instigated by demonic powers (cf. 4:7) in 1:13–15 it seems related more to an evil inclination belonging to humans (cf. 4:5). Perhaps James, akin with other early Jewish sources, believes that God created this inclination or *yetzer* for human procreation and preservation. It may not be intrinsically evil but can either be affected by evil or offset by a good inclination (cf. 1QS 3.25–4.26; CD 2:14–16; *T. Ash.* 1–4).[43] At all events, for James, humans have the ability to resist evil urges and receive divine grace to defeat them. They can also fail to resist, and so allow for the enablement of more temptation, sin, and demonic influence (Jas 4:5–7; cf. 1:13–18).

On the surface James' presuppositions about human sin appear to be quite different than Paul's hereditary view that sin is passed on from Adam, the first transgressor, to humanity (Rom 5:12–20).[44] Their differences, in part, may be due to their approaching the topic of sin's origin from different angles. James focuses on sin anthropologically in terms of an individual's propensity to succumb to temptation. Paul in Rom 5 looks at sin corporately and christologically. He is more concerned about sin's entrance in the world, its effect on humanity, and its defeat that was brought about through the death of Christ. In the letter of James the remedy for sin is personal perseverance, self-control, dependency on the word of truth, and knowl-

---

41. It could mean alternatively that God should not be tested by evil persons this way; cf. Deut 6:16; Cargal, *Restoring the Diaspora*, 80–81. Davids, "Meaning of ἀπείραστος," 386–92, writes that the person who is tempted internally "cannot blame either the external divine or the external demonic" (392).

42. See sources in LSJ, 377.

43. On the *yetzer haraʿ* in James, see further Marcus, "Evil Inclination," 606–21; Davids, "Why Do We Suffer?," 454–59. In later Jewish traditions God creates the evil impulse (*yetzer haraʿ*) and good impulse (*yetzer tob*). The *yetzer tob*, as well as Torah, become preventatives against the destructive impulse (cf. b. *Berakot* 5a; *Abot R. Nat.* 20; cf. *Gen. Rabbah* 9:7; b. *Yoma* 69b; Schechter, *Aspects of Rabbinic Theology*, 242–92).

44. See also 2 *Bar.* 48.42–43; 4 *Ezra* 7.116–31; cf. Sir 25:4.

edge that resisting temptation will be rewarded at the eschaton. Paul's solution to sin is that God has given the gift of Christ, the second Adam, who makes the sinners righteous. Even so, Paul's familiarity with something similar to the evil inclination that James mentions may be evident in Rom 7:14–25 when he addresses good and evil tendencies that war within the human person.[45]

A dominant undercurrent in 1:13–16 is sexual in nature: when desire/lust has conceived (συλλαμβάνω) and then is brought to the full term (ἀποτελέω) of its pregnancy, it gives birth to death instead of life. Walter Wilson examines thoughts from Philo to address sexual imagery in common with the anthropology of James and highlights desire (ἐπιθυμία) as the personification of a female temptress (cf. Philo, *Cher.* 71; *Rewards* 117; cf. *QG* 1.47).[46] In Philo the soul, vexed with vices and passions, "has for its children [τέκνα] pleasures and desires, which render it feeble and deathly weak" (*Rewards* 159; cf. *Spec.* 4.80–82).[47] Wilson adduces from Greco-Roman and Hellenistic-Jewish thought that female weakness and passivity are associated with an individual giving in to sexual temptation, whereas endurance/perseverance (ὑπομονή) is associated with the heroic male (e.g., 4 Macc 15:30; *T. Jos.* 2:6–7; 3:8). It is through submission to God who is symbolized in masculine terms such as "father" that the dominant and submissive roles find harmony (cf. Jas 4:7–10; cf. 1:17–19). Humans are to accept a passive role of dependence on God, and hence, "the development of the active, 'virile' self, the self defined vis-à-vis feminized desire, finds its completion in the realization of the passive, receptive self, the self defined vis-à-vis a masculinized God."[48]

To be sure, such imagery smacks of a male-biased patriarchal society,[49] but an important value of Wilson's study is its stress on the sexually-based language in Jas 1:12–19. With this approach in mind, a person's giving in to desire is like a man submitting to the seductions of a harlot. The bastard conceived through this relationship is "sin" that leads to "death." And here death does not primarily refer to a macro-enemy coming into the world (cf. 1 Cor 15:25–26), nor is it merely physical death as the outcome of sinful behavior (cf. 11:29–30), nor yet is it referring to death by murder (cf. Jas 4:1–4; 5:6). *This death refers to the person's apostasy and the eschatological judgment that ensues because of it.* At this point the metaphor of

---

45. On this possibility see Davids, "Why Do We Suffer," 460–62, who also compares Paul and James and thinks the main difference between their views when it comes to the origin of sin is that Paul centers his solution on Christ, and James on the Torah.

46. Wilson, "Sin as Sex," 147–68.

47. Ibid., 152.

48. Cf. ibid., 164–68; quote from 168.

49. Not all weakness and sin in James are feminized (cf. masculine 4:1–4).

begetting becomes blurred. The character of the offspring is now projected back on its father so that the father misses out on salvation and will suffer eternal death on judgment day (1:15; 5:19–20; cf. 2:12; 4:12).[50] The failed father becomes the antipode of the courageous man who receives eschatological blessing by persevering against temptation and the temptress of desire (1:12). The warning in 1:15–16 is reminiscent of those who take the path of destruction down to the home of the adulteress (Prov 7:25–27). The auditors in James are thus exhorted against being led astray; they must not walk down the detour route where the brothel of desire is located.

The audience is therefore left with a choice between acting like one of two masculine subjects: the courageous man who endures the temptress ἐπιθυμία and is blessed at the eschaton, or the weak man who submits to her and begins walking along the path that leads to apostasy and destruction. This defection involves a process—first comes the desire, then enticement, then the sinful act that leads to apostasy and divine punishment (1:13–15). Later on it will turn out that one's confession of sin provides forgiveness, and restoration is possible (5:15–20), but here James colors his language with graphic metaphors of sin's inevitable outcome in an attempt to dissuade his audience from succumbing to temptation. James runs with the sexual metaphor a bit further by insinuating that a holy union is one in which the audience, now feminine, receives the "word of truth" that comes from God, the father of creation and originator of redemption who is in the business of giving good things to his followers. God's having willed to give birth (βουληθεὶς ἀπεκύησεν: 1:18) demonstrates God's initiative and good pleasure in producing the original creation of humankind as well as his further plan to give new life. The passage affirms that God gives physical and spiritual life rather than being the cause of temptation and death. This union between the physical and spiritual gives birth to Christ-followers—the "firstfruits" perhaps identifies the Jewish remnant of believers in the new creation (cf. Rom 11:16; Rev 14:4), and they are being led to eschatological salvation (Jas 1:17–18, 21).[51]

Later on in the letter, lustful desire is combined with envy and murder to create an inner battle within the human person (4:1–5).[52] The passage alludes to Matt 5:21–26 in which murder is seen as the logical outcome of an inward disposition of anger

50. Similarly, Burchard, *Jakobusbrief*, 74.

51. On the feminine role of salvation in this passage, see Baker, "Gendered Birth Images," 195–207.

52. The warring, fighting, and killing beginning in 4:1 might also betray a situation comparable with the zealots during the Jewish war with Rome (cf. 2;11; 4:2; 5:6); Townsend, "James 4:1–14," 211–13; Martin, *James*, 144. The struggle, however, seems best identified as an inward disposition (4:1 cf. 3:6) recalling the Sermon on the Mount. Johnson, *James*, 277, rightly affirms a logical connection between envy and murder: "competition moves in the direction of elimination" (cf. Gen 4: 1–8; Matt 27:18; Acts 5:17; 13:45; Wis 2:24; *T. Sim.* 3.2f; Plato, *Laws* 869E–870A).

and strife towards a fellow brother or sister. In diatribe form James calls these lustful individuals "adulteresses" and advances the polarity that one's friendship with the world makes one an enemy of God (Jas 4:4; cf. 1 John 2:15; 2 Tim 3:4).[53] Perhaps the author's label "adulteress" is sparked from the progression of thought in the Sermon on the Mount that moves from the topic of murder (Matt 5:21–26) to adultery (Matt 5:27). Or possibly the label is informed by the order of sins listed in the Decalogue (cf. Jas 2:11/Exod 20:13–14). The unfaithful spouse is feminine, however, and more pointedly alludes to Israel's spiritual unfaithfulness to God's covenant (cf. Isa 57:3; Jer 3:9; Ezek 16:38; 23:45; Hos 3:1; Prov 2:16; 30:20).[54] In Prov 7:6–27 lady wisdom contrasts the adulteress, and only senseless individuals are lured to death by the latter. *Intertextual tremors of lust, adultery, and covenant breaking intimate for James in 4:4 that friendship with the world may be equivalent to apostasy.* The words of Sophie Laws ring true along these lines. For James the world "denotes in general the values of human society as against those of God, and hence the man who pursues pleasure aligns himself with the world and compromises or *actually denies* his relationship with God."[55]

To be an enemy of God in Jas 4:4 would then be to oppose God and risk being condemned with the fallen world at the *parousia* when Christ returns and God judges the world (5:7).[56] In this letter the world or cosmos is perceived as a sphere that values selfish desires and indulgences, wealth, and arrogance (cf. 1:27; 3:13–16; 4:4–10).[57] It is also the realm where Satan apparently resides (4:7; cf. 3:15), and it pollutes believers from wholeness and moral maturity (cf. 1:27). James addresses separation from the world in terms of purity, stressing boundaries of 'in" and "out" with the friends of God as insiders and those who belong to the world as outsiders. The two groups have oppositional lifestyles "between a way of life that is informed by the values of wholeness, purity, and harmony as opposed to a way of life that

---

53. The added male "adulterers" (KJV) is found only in some later and inferior manuscripts of 4:4 (e.g., K, L, P).

54. On covenant breaking see Popkes, *Jakobus*, 267; Frankemölle, *Jakobusbrief*, 2.597.

55. Laws, *James*, 174; emphasis added. Notice Davids, *James*, 161: "That this self-seeking is tantamount to apostasy appears in the following parallel clauses, introduced by the typical reference to parenesis, οὐκ οἴδατε ὅτι (e.g. Rom 6:16; 1 Cor 3:16; 5:6; 6:2–19; 9:13–24; cf. 1 Thess 3:3, 4; 1 Thess 4:2; 2 Thess 2:6)."

56. On 4:4, deSilva, *Introduction*, 829, writes, "Walking in line with the convictions and values we have learned from God is seen to be essential for salvation itself; and in this way we will not be found to be God's 'enemy' on the day of judgment (Jas 2:12–13; 5:20)."

57. The sexual imagery in 1:13–15 and 4:4 might lead us to surmise a literal problem with sexual immorality in the communities, but this is not clearly specified in James. Some other implications may be that the world values unrighteousness (3:6) and is associated with the old creation (as opposed to new creation in 1:18).

is incomplete, divided, and polluted."[58] In such thinking "wholeness as exclusion" reinforces the identity of the insiders.[59] If the sinners and the double-minded among James' readers are to be insiders, they need to cleanse and purify themselves from the values of the world (4:8). The danger in 4:4 is that the attitude of outsiders is infiltrating God's faithful people as a result of their wrong-headed desires. These desires, it seems, are related to envy, selfish ambition, arrogance, wealth, and judging others, which are causing divisions in the Jewish-Christian communities (4:1–2; cf. 3:14–16; 4:11–17). In this regard the author views acculturation with Hellenistic society negatively. More specifically, to break ties with attitudes that resemble the outsiders, the "adulteresses" need to submit to the will of God, draw near to him in prayer, purify their external conduct and inner attitude, and humble themselves (4:6–10).

WISDOM, DOUBLE-MINDEDNESS, AND THE TWO WAYS (1:5–8, 19–27; 3:1–18; 4:8, 11–12; 5:12)

The idea of the audience asking God for wisdom in 1:5–8 is relevant to what precedes: their persevering through trials and continuing on to moral completion requires godly wisdom. For James wisdom comes from God and involves praying in faith and exercising righteous conduct promoting virtues, similar to the fruit of the Spirit in Paul's writings (cf. 3:13–17). Richard Bauckham's definition is on target: "It seems that wisdom is the God-given ability of the transformed heart to discern and to practice God's will. It is the way in which Torah is internalized, so that outward obedience to Torah flows from an inner understanding and embracing of God's will expressed in Torah."[60]

James 1:5–8 also introduces the two ways motif that pervades the rest of the letter. The person who asks God in faith for wisdom is contrasted with the one who is double-minded (δίψυχος), a concept associated with doubting (cf. Sir 1:28; *1 Clem.* 23.3; *Herm. Mand.* 9.1–11; *Herm. Vis.* 4.2.6). The double-minded person is presumably a Christ-follower who prays but is unable to trust God fully and perhaps thinks that God is not entirely good (cf. 1:13; contrast 1:17). More than this, such an individual is "unstable in all his ways" (1:8), suggesting that double-mindedness extends beyond mere doubt and distrust. The term is picked up again in 4:8 where sinners are to cleanse their "hands" (change external behavior) and the double-minded are to purify their hearts. Namely, they must alter their inner attitude that desires the

---

58. Hartin, *James*, 74.
59. Phrase from Bauckham, *James*, 180.
60. Ibid., 152.

contaminated world which is allied with the devil and pursue instead an untainted love for God (cf. Jas 4:4–8; cf. 1:27; 3:6; Ps 23[24]:4). *The double-minded believers, then, seem to possess a dual allegiance to the world and God; and they must let go of the world and draw closer to God if they are to continue on the path to moral perfection.*

Similar to James, the two ways of good and evil in the *Testament of Asher* 1–6 brings together insights about contrasting human dispositions (*T. Ash.* 1.5–9; 3.1–7) and being "two-faced" in contrast to being "single-minded" (3.1; 4.1; cf. 6.2).[61] The two-faced person looks down both the right and wrong path. The Shepherd of Hermas is possibly dependent on James for the term; this source considers the double-minded to be neither dead nor alive (*Sim.* 8.7.1; 9.21.2, 4). Todd Penner maintains in James that the double-minded not only lack faith and wisdom but also steadfastness, and so "such a person will not endure until the end and consequently stands under judgment (they will receive nothing from God) . . . The double-minded person, lacking wisdom, can therefore be regarded as being on the same level as the unrighteous and proud/rich."[62] Luke Timothy Johnson does not hesitate to make double-minded individuals the "most obvious target" of James' exhortation regarding "friendship with the world" against "friendship with God" (Jas 4:4). Hence, such a person is an adulteress—the double-minded "wants to be friends with everyone!"[63]

If the double-minded person is at least indirectly associated with the adulteress (4:4) and the sinner (4:8), these connections may suggest a link between the thought of double-mindedness and apostasy. Such a person is seen as an enemy of God by aligning with the world's values (4:4b). The term "sinner," which is mentioned alongside the double-minded in 4:8, appears again in 5:20 to refer to apostates on their way to eschatological death and needing restoration. The double-minded must purify their hearts or they might end up undergoing the same fate as the apostates. Then again, if some of them lacked only faith and prayer (1:5–7), this could simply mean that their petitions might remain unanswered and their level of spirituality might never reach complete maturity. In later decades the concept of double-mindedness will become more firmly entrenched with Christian apostasy as the term begins to convey the changing of one's mind and the cowardly behavior associated with those who succumb to worshipping idols because they are too ashamed to take a stand for Christ (cf. *1 Clem.* 11.2; *Herm. Sim.* 9.21.3; *Herm. Mand.* 10.2.2). Even so, if Jas 1:5–7 centers on doubting when in prayer, the double-mindedness in 4:8 seems to be more severe.

---

61. See translation in *OTP* 1.816–18. On the possibility of double-mindedness referring to the Jewish *yetzer*, see Seitz, "Term *Dipsychos*," 211–19.

62. Penner, *James and Eschatology*, 203.

63. Johnson, *James*, 87.

The contrast between maturity and praying by faith over against double-mindedness and praying in doubt establish the first of many contrasts in the letter (1:4-8). This polarization, common in wisdom literature, continues with contrasts between poor and rich (1:9-11), enduring temptation and succumbing to desire (1:12-14), sin begetting death and God begetting life (1:15-18), wrongful anger/speech and righteousness (1:19-21), hearing the word and doing the word (1:22-25), true religion and vain religion (1:26-27), showing favoritism and showing love (2:1-13), faith without works and faith with works (2:14-26), heavenly wisdom and earthly wisdom (3:13-18), friendship with the world and friendship with God (4:1-10), judging others and letting God do the judging (4:11-12), boastful ambition and submitting to God's will (4:13-17), the rich exploiter and oppressed laborer (5:1-6), patience and complaining (5:7-11), taking oaths and speaking truthfully (5:12), and the way of death and the way of life (5:19-20).[64] The various antithetical ideas intimate a motif of two ways that eventually ends with the presentation of the way of life or death in 5:19-20.[65] If we bring the metaphor into sharper relief, James encourages his recipients to persevere in trials and press on to moral completion as they walk on the path that leads to eschatological salvation.[66] Sinners and apostates walk on a different path that leads to eschatological death (5:19-20). Binary positions throughout the text may be viewed as metaphoric road markers helping the traveler stay on course with exhortations such as, "be a doer of the word, not merely a hearer," "practice pure instead of vain religion," "let works show that you have faith," and so on.

In the following wisdom pericope (1:19-27) the recipients are to put away vices and receive with humility God's "word" if their moral righteousness is to be approved by God (1:19-21).[67] The basic meaning of λόγος here seems to be the message of wise instruction that brings about salvation (1:18, 21-22). More specifically, the "implanted word" (1:21) probably refers to the Torah as interpreted by Jesus and lodges within the hearts of those who participate in the new creation (cf. Pet 1:23-25; Mark 4:10-12; *Hel. Syn. Pr.* 11.2-3). Λόγος overlaps in meaning with the "law" (νόμος: 1:25), and the latter in James is probably to be understood in a similar way to the gospel of Matthew—νόμος refers to the Mosaic Law filtered through the teachings of Jesus, and the "royal law" refers to the command to love your neighbor as yourself (Jas 2:8-12; 4:11; cf. Matt 7:11; 22:37-41; Lev 19:18). If the Law is ob-

64. See a similar scheme in the argumentative structure proposed by Lockett, *Purity and Worldview*, 79-92.

65. Cf. Deut 30:15; Josh 24:15; Sir 15:11-17; Prov 4:10-27; 14:12; 16:25; Ps 86:11; Jer 21:8-14; *T. Ash* 1-6; *T. Jos.* 1.3; *2 En.* 30:15; *Sib. Or.* 8.399-400; Matt 7:13-14; *Did.* 6; *Barn.* 18.

66. Notice that "walking with God" in Israel's traditions involves ethical obedience that combines faith and works (cf. Gen 5:22-24; 6:9; Mic 6:8; Mal 2:6; Hartin, *Spirituality of Perfection*, 26).

67. On δικαιοσύνην θεοῦ (1:20) as an objective genitive, see Ropes, *James*, 169-70.

served it brings about moral completion and liberation from the spiritual contamination coming from the polluted world (1:25, 27).[68] To be a "doer" of the word, then, is to obey the message of Jesus and proceed to moral completion with the Law as the community's guide.

Misuse of the tongue is said to make a person's piety worthless (1:26-27). The religious activities mentioned in this context presumably involve such things as prayer, fasting, and religious customs associated with Jewish communities.[69] The words may reflect Jesus' warning to his hearers not to make an outward show of their religious acts (Matt 6:1-18; cf. Matt 23:23-27). Such persons are hypocrites, self-deceived, and having an impure admixture of religious piety without self-control over their words. Their piety is as worthless as worshipping dumb idols (Jas 1:26; cf. Jer 2:5; 8:19; 10:3; Acts 14:15). The person addressed in 1:26 is an inclusive "anyone" (τις), including Christ-followers. In a rhetorical sense James considers this person to be an inauthentic worshipper of God. Conversely, true piety consists of being unstained by the world and helping orphans and widows (1:27).

The misuse of the tongue is addressed again in 3:1-12, which begins with a warning: not too many in the audience should become teachers because such vocation warrants receiving a "greater judgment" (μεῖζον κρίμα λημψόμεθα). The teachers could hardly be referring to Pauline extremists here[70] if James includes himself among the teachers ("we"). Here the problem involves control of the tongue, not necessarily Pauline faith set in opposition to works.[71] In view of the repeated verses on eschatological judgment in this letter (cf. 1:10-11; 2:12-13; 4:12; 5:1, 9, 12), the passage refers to the accountability of teachers or rabbis as they stand before God on judgment day. They will either be judged by stricter standards than those they teach, or they will be punished with a greater condemnation than others if they teach amiss (cf. Matt 23:13; Mark 12:40; Luke 12:48; 20:47; 23:40; John 19:11). The issue, however, is more likely both/and rather than either/or. *Teachers of the emerging Christian movement will be judged by stricter standards on judgment day, and condemnation rather than reward remains a possibility for those who abuse their position or lead astray others by promoting immoral conduct.*[72] There may be a faint echo in James

---

68. See Hartin, *James*, 108, who adds that "just as the mirror shows how to improve one's appearance, so reflection on the law can lead to moral improvement."

69. So Davids, *James*, 30.

70. On this view see Vouga, *Saint Jacques*, 94-95.

71. Again in 3:2 James uses the first-person plural, this time to say that everyone "stumbles" (πταίω: 3:2 cf. 2:10; Rom 11:11). The idea does not seem to convey apostasy here but an ancient maxim similar to the modern adage, "nobody's perfect"; see Johnson, *James*, 256.

72. Johnson, *James*, 263, lists some failures of teachers as "arrogance and domination over students; anger and pettiness at contradiction or inattention; slander and meanness toward absent opponents;

3:1–2 of Jesus' saying that every careless word that people speak they will have to give an account for on judgment day (Matt 12:36–37).

If the "we" in Jas 3:1 is not entirely rhetorical, then a provocative possibility comes to the foreground. Even the main leader of the entire Jewish-Christian community is susceptible to eschatological punishment if he does not control his tongue, and so how much more other teachers who may be less qualified? If this understanding is implied, James would agree with Paul that *even great Christian leaders are not guaranteed final salvation if they fail to be self-controlled at the present time* (cf. 1 Cor 9:27). This negative view of teachers probably takes on the rhetorical strategy of the author attempting to weed out unqualified instructors from the faithful communities, especially because such persons influence many and are considered models of moral conduct. More than this, leaders of this sort normally do not tolerate anyone perceived as a rival, and they could easily cause divisions in the communities.[73]

In vivid but perplexing language, the harmful use of the tongue is depicted as an untamed evil, lethal poison, and a polluting source filled with curses (Jas 3:7–12). It contaminates the entire body, is a "world of unrighteousness," and sets on fire the "circle of nature" (i.e., destroys from the beginning to the end of creation)[74] with the "fires of *Gehenna*" (3:3–6). A questionable interpretation of this passage associates *Gehenna* as a codename for the devil or the evil he causes.[75] The devil is not mentioned in this passage, however, and the thought of him living in "hell" was not popular in the first century. New Testament writers rarely make this association, and when they do, a fiery place is connected only with the devil's *future* punishment (e.g., Matt 25:41; Rev 20:10). James locates Satan in the realm of "the world," not hell (4:7 cf. 4:4). *Gehenna* is imagined as a destructive fire originating from a filthy garbage dump in Jerusalem that oversteps its boundaries and has now gone wild. The rhetoric turns on the littleness of the tongue and the widespread, incalculable damage it could cause. Nevertheless, the recipients familiar with Jesus' teachings may have associated *Gehenna* with a place of punishment after death (cf. Matt 5:29; 18:9; Mark 9:47). *If final judgment is still in view from Jas 3:1, then Gehenna might imply for them that misuse of the tongue has the ability to send many people to hell, including individuals from among Jewish-Christian community* (cf. "our" and "we"; 3:1–2, 6, 9).[76] The tongue is a pollutant that prevents moral purity and wholeness, and as such it has the power to destroy the spiritual life of the faithful.

---

flattery of students for the sake of vainglory."

73. See Wall, *Community of the Wise*, 162.

74. Cf. Brosend, *James and Jude*, 91.

75. E.g., Dibelius and Greeven, *James*, 198; Hartin, *James*, 186–87.

76. In our view, 3:3–11 is particularly relevant to the teachers in 3:1–2, but in a secondary sense the

The importance of speech likewise touches on the issues of slandering and judging others (4:11–12), which are violations of the law of love (Lev 19:18; Matt 7:1–5). The faithful must speak with sincerity (5:12; cf. Matt 5:34–37). Wholeness in Jas 5:12 excludes the dangerous mixture of truth and deceit (cf. 1:16, 22, 26; 3:13),[77] *and the judgment that oath-breakers might face is probably the same as 5:9: on judgment day they would be punished by God for their conduct and destroyed* (cf. Jas 4:12; Matt 10:28; Rom 14:4). In a cogent sense James believes that the tongue, when wrongfully used by Christ-followers, can lead to their potential condemnation. Harmful speech is therefore another temptation that must be overcome by the faithful, and like other sins it has the potential to lead them to apostasy and spiritual death. Their showing mercy and confessing personal sin, however, provides salvation and offsets final judgment (2:13; 5:15–16).

POVERTY, WEALTH, AND FINAL JUDGMENT
(1:9–11; 2:1–13; 4:13–17; 5:1–6)

Another major topic centers on the poor and rich. For James the poor are seen as God's chosen and, echoing Jesus' words, they are heirs of God' kingdom (Jas 2:5; cf. Luke 6:20; Matt 5:3; *Gos. Thom.* 54). The poor are assumed to be Christ-followers: they meet at the synagogue (Jas 2:2–3), exercise faith (2:5), and are identified as the fellow brothers and sisters of the Jewish believers being addressed in the letter (Jas 1:9; 2:15; cf. Matt 12:46–50). The rich on other hand will perish. Unlike the poor they have no future reward or salvific status (Jas 1:10–11; cf. v. 12).[78] An inference we might draw from their disposition is that they will be punished at the *parousia*. Similarly, landowners who oppress day-laborers will suffer the wrath of God on judgment day (Jas 5:1–6; cf. Ps 37:2; 129:6; Isa 40:6). The rich in Jas 1:10–11 do not appear to be Christ-followers, and in 2:6–7 they are outsiders, which also appears to be the case in 5:1–6.[79]

Differently, the wealthy merchants in 4:13–17 may be Christ-followers if they are expected to follow God's will (4:15) and know what is morally good (4:17). The maxim in 4:17 is reminiscent of early instructions about faith without works and believers hearing but not doing the word, subjects directed at the letter's recipients (cf. 1:22–27; 2:14–26). The merchants' boastful attitude is considered evil and sin

---

passage would have been understood as pertaining to all the recipients.

77. Cf. Bauckham, *James*, 180.

78. See further, Witherington, *Jewish Christians*, 432.

79. If so, then neither rich nor poor are to be always associated with the readers. Popkes, *Jakobus*, 18, suggests the addressees as a socioeconomically intermediate class.

(4:15–17). It specifically relates to arrogance, which is contrasted with submitting to God's will. Their preoccupation with business endeavors agrees with a lifestyle that neglects the recognition that one's life ultimately belongs to God. *The merchant needs to submit to divine guidance. Failure to do so amounts to sin, and if sin leads to eschatological death (1:15), a further implication may be that the preoccupied merchant may suffer a fate similar to the rich landowner in 5:1–6* (cf. 4:2, 6). And, comparable with the rich who "wither away" (1:10–11), the merchants' life is like a vapor that vanishes (Jas 4:13–14; cf. Prov. 27:1). Whether believer or non-believer, then, the rich seem to be vilified in James. Even so, both the author and audience probably recognized that some wealthy people could in fact please God. Job and Abraham would be two examples of this (e.g., Gen 24:35; Job 42:10–17). Job's great wealth at the end of his trial, however, is refocused by James on God's compassion and mercy for Job (Jas 5:11).

James' recipients are challenged against favoring the rich at their meetings (2:1–13). The person who shows such favoritism violates the royal law of loving one's neighbor as oneself (Lev 19:18) and is thus a violator (παραβάτης) of the Torah. *This passage suggests the person who shows such favoritism against the poor has defected from God's Law.* Some manuscripts of 2:11 in fact confirm this idea by identifying the offender as a "deserter" or apostate (ἀποστάτης) from the Law.[80] Liability to the whole Law, in any case, is charged against the person who violates a single command from the Decalogue (2:10–13).[81] For James, the lawgiver is God and to obey him is to follow his will entirely (2:11–12; cf. 4:11–12). The communities James writes to must be mindful that they will have to give account of their actions on judgment day, and so they should be merciful to the poor and exemplify love. By doing so, they will experience God's mercy at the eschaton (Jas 2:13; cf. Matt 5:7; Luke 6:36). Job would also be a model of helping the poor and not placing trust in his own riches (Job 29:11–12; 31:16–25; cf. 5:11, 16f; 15:29f; *T. Job* 9–15).

---

80. Cf. Alexandrinus, P74 texts; Kilpatrick, "Übertreter des Gesetzes," 433. On other commands in Lev 19 as representative of the law of love, see Johnson, "Use of Leviticus," 391–401.

81. To follow the whole law and yet offend at one point and thus become "guilty of all" (πάντων ἔνοχος: 2:10) is not quite the same thing as saying that if a person breaks one commandment he/she has broken every commandment. "All" here is a rhetorical way of referring to the "whole law" (cf. Ropes, *James*, 200). It conveys that when a person shows partiality he/she becomes a violator of the "whole law," having violated its essence by breaking the commandment to love one's neighbor. See the enthymemes in Witherington, *Jewish Christians*, 460–61, and parallels in Matt 5:19; *T. Ash* 2.5–10; Mayor, *James*, 92–93.

ON FAITH AND WORKS: A RESPONSE TO PAUL? (2:14-26)

James addresses the subject of helping the poor in relation to his discussion that faith without works is useless (2:14-26). Is he responding to Paul's view of faith and works? It would be rather naïve for us to assume that no conflict existed between Paul and James. Paul admits tensions between his view and the party of James over Jewish and Gentile relationships and the Law (Gal 2:1-16), despite the settlement on such issues described in Acts 15. As well, Paul does not adhere to the Jerusalem meeting's decisions in Acts 15 very well, as we maintain in 1 Cor 8-10 (see Acts in volume 1 and Galatians and 1 Corinthians in volume 2). We can suggest that some tensions may have lingered between Paul and James beyond Gal 2 and Acts 15.

What is harder to determine is whether their differences persisted even after Paul's visit to Jerusalem and subsequent arrest in Acts 21. Luke has James commending Paul's Gentile mission and reaffirming the earlier decision of the Jerusalem meeting in Acts 15, suggesting that James still only required Gentile Christians to keep the Mosaic mandates of abstaining from idol meats, fornication, blood, and things strangled. Luke's portrait in Acts suggest the tension was not with Paul and the followers of James but with other Jewish Christians who considered Paul to be teaching apostasy from the Mosaic Law (Acts 21:20-24). To be sure, Luke presents an idealistic meeting between James and Paul, but his account cannot be easily dismissed as *entirely* an invention or his way of subverting deep hostilities between the two leaders. Luke definitely has his agendas, but one of them does not seem to be a complete denial of conflicts existing between Paul and other early Christian leaders (cf. Acts 15:36-39). Luke Timothy Johnson suggests that neither Luke nor Paul should be accepted uncritically, but "beneath the rhetoric of the separate writings, Paul and the Jerusalem church were in the first generation of the Christian movement more in a cooperative than competitive relationship."[82] In the end, however, it is perhaps best to suggest that neither Luke nor Paul should determine our interpretation of the letter of James, or vice versa for that matter. A thorough comparison between James and Paul on faith and works is beyond the scope and subject of this book. It will have to suffice to bring out some of the highlights only.

First, the "works of the Law" that Paul argues against foster boasting and division among his congregations, which does not seem to be the same kind of works James is discussing. For James, works are required on the ethical ground of loving one's neighbor including the poor. He places faith and works in the larger rubrics of assisting the poor and aligning one's conduct with the law of love. Paul would agree with this ethic (e.g., Gal 2:10; 6:1-5). The interpretation of faith and works in Jas

---

82. Johnson, *James*, 98.

2:14–26 pays homage to 2:1–13 where believers must put to practice the law of love. The works James refers to, then, are moral, and to neglect them is to violate the command to love one's neighbor as oneself. The rhetorical question he poses in 2:14 is answered in the immediate context: "faith cannot save a person without works; faith without works is useless." In this letter, then, to practice works is to put faith and love in action. This is strikingly similar to Paul's own language about believers practicing works of faith and love (e.g., 1 Thess 1:3; Gal 5:6).

Second, a Christ-follower who does not work in this way is violating the Law and will give an account for this on judgment day (Jas 2:12). Without stating it, the author places into sharper relief what Paul and other ancient Jewish writers mean by saying that everyone, including the faithful, will be judged according to their works (cf. Rom 2:6; 14:14; 2 Cor 5:10; Rev 20:12–13; Matt 25:31–46; 4 *Ezra* 8.33; 1 *En.* 100.7). Here again on works James and Paul seem to agree.

Third, James never mentions the term "works of the Law," and he does not discuss explicitly circumcision, food laws, and calendar observances, which are among the main points of contention between Paul and his Jewish-Christian opponents. Implicitly, however, Jewish customs related to the Torah are mentioned (e.g., Jas 1:26–27). At any rate, if there was still a conflict between the followers of James and Paul over such issues when this letter was written, they do not seem to have surfaced in the letter unless here in a general way regarding faith and works.

Fourth, James is not interpreting "faith" with the same pair of eyes as Paul. The former stresses a dead or false faith removed from the matrix of believing in Jesus; the latter characteristically discusses faith in terms of faithfulness to Christ (e.g., Gal 2:16; Rom 1:17). A point of common ground for James and Paul is that faith is ongoing and requiring obedience and perseverance, without which the faithful would fall away (cf. volume 2 of this work). Yet James is concerned about faith as "staying in" a saving relationship with God through obedience to God's will and keeping the Torah as interpreted by Jesus. Such faith must move on to completion or maturity through action (Jas 2:22). Paul, as a missionary to Gentiles, is concerned with both "getting in" and "staying in" saving faith even though his letters are primarily aimed at those who are already "in." James attacks a faith void of ethical obedience and commitment to God that even demons could accept (2:19). Typical of the many antithetical statements in this letter, there seems to be two kinds of faith, though not always named as such—genuine faith (1:3, 6; 2:1, 5, 22, 24; 5:15) and false, dead, or useless faith (2:17, 18–20, 26).[83]

---

83. On true and false faith see Chester and Martin, *James, Peter, and Jude*, 25; Jeremias, "Paul and James," 368–71.

Fifth, one distinction between James and Paul on the Law is that, whereas Paul interprets the Law as fulfilled through the eschatological advent, death, and resurrection of Christ, and that being "in Christ" begins a new creation, James maintains the importance of keeping the Mosaic Law as interpreted by Jesus, and it is through this word that God gives life and a new creation (cf. 1:18, 21; 2:8–12). This distinction over the Law, however, does not center on faith and righteousness but on their views of Christ and his relationship with the righteous community.

Sixth and finally, a more complex problem is that both authors happen to refer to Abraham in Genesis when discussing faith in relation to works (Gal 2:6; Rom 4:3/Gen 15:6; Jas 2:23/Gen 15:6; cf. Jas 2:21/Gen 22). Indeed, using wording similar to Paul's, James makes a very different point that righteousness does *not* come by faith alone (Jas 2:24). If isolated from its context, this verse appears to stand either in contradiction of, or in pointed tension with, the Pauline passages that seem to argue just the opposite (Rom 3:28; 4:2–3, 6). Similar wording between James and Paul on this point may be due to their sharing in a similar stream of thought for the time. Abraham was frequently used in Second Temple sources as an example of faithfulness and righteousness, especially in relation to his offering up of Isaac (e.g., 1 Macc 2:52; Sir 19–21; *Jub.* 17.15–18; *m. Abot* 5.3). Paul, however, stresses faith alone by referring to Abraham's pre-circumcised, pre-Isaac trust in God's gracious promise to him of fatherhood (cf. Gen 12).[84] Abraham is reckoned as righteous (Gen 15:6) prior to the work of circumcision (Gen 17) or his offering up of Isaac (Gen 22). Differently, James, in keeping with his theme of testing, presents Abraham's test of faith in offering up Isaac as a "work" of obedience to God that confirms or makes "complete" his faith (Jas 2:21–23). In sum James interprets Abraham's faith and righteousness in Gen 15:6 in view of Abraham's subsequent act of obedience, whereas Paul interprets the same verse in view of Abraham's antecedent calling and trust in God's promise. These nuances complement the authors' agendas: Paul emphasizes initial and ongoing faith for his Gentile audiences; James discusses the ongoing and completion of faith for his Jewish recipients.

These observations show both similarities and differences between James and Paul on the subject of faith and works. Whatever the case might be in Jas 2, Paul did not teach that faith can save independent of obedience or moral behavior. *Both James and Paul taught that Christ-followers must persevere in faith if they are to be saved, and both affirm that believers could become apostates or live in a way so riddled with immoral behavior that it brings divine judgment on them at the* parousia.

---

84. See Dunn, *Theology of Paul*, 374–79.

Be that as it may, there remains a strong possibility that James is in some sense responding to Paul's teaching, especially if we consider that the Diaspora to which James writes (1:1) are perhaps the same people that think Paul teaches apostasy from the Law (cf. Acts 21:20–21). If he is writing to correct Paul's teachings or clarify his own view, it is not entirely clear which Pauline sources, if any, James (or his editor) might have possessed or known.[85] *The author may have been aware through conversations and continual hearsay that differences existed between the teachings of the two leaders. Hence, apart from the author instructing his audience to demonstrate their love by works, this section may have a secondary, roundabout agenda of clarifying faith and works for the sake of his Jewish-Christian audience from the Diaspora, who also probably heard or knew about some differences between James and Paul.* Other possibilities include that James is correcting an extreme form of Paulinism in his day, perhaps with libertine tendencies similar to the Corinthian congregation, or he misunderstood Paul, or that a later editor has in mind teachers that distorted Paul's view into antinomianism similar to 2 Pet 3:15–16. At all events, given that Jas 2 emphasizes faith working itself out in love and obedience to God, we find little to suggest that Paul would have vehemently opposed James' teaching on this matter. And certainly the hypothetical objector in 2:18, 20 does not sound anything like Paul.

THE RESTORATION OF APOSTATES (5:19–20)

The letter of James ends with the topic of restoration from apostasy: "My brothers, if any person among you strays from the truth and someone turns him back; let him know that the one who turns a sinner from the error of his path will save his soul from death and will cover a multitude of sins."[86] Some ambiguities persist about the person being saved from death and the one having his sins covered. Possibly, the restorer saves his own soul and it is his own sins that are covered by the act of restoring the sinner. Or the sinner is saved and the restorer has his own sins covered (cf. Ezek 3:21; 1 Tim 4:16).[87] More plausibly, however, the sinner is saved and it is his sins that are being covered.[88] In these verses he is identified by αὐτός. The fallen state of those who need restoration in 5:19–20 belong(ed) to the Jewish-Christian community ("among you"). Possibly their fallen state is related to the prescriptions in 5:12–16—

---

85. See Popkes, "Two Interpretations," 138.

86. On text variations see Metzger, *Textual Commentary*, 615.

87. Cf. Adamson, *James*, 202–4, for the former, and Mussner, *Jakobusbrief*, 233, for the latter. On the passive aorist πλανηθῇ used with middle force, see Deut 22:1; Ezek 34.4; Mayor, *James*, 181–82. Contrast Rev 18:23.

88. On this position see Hartin, *James*, 286–87; Davids, *James*, 201; Martin, *James*, 220.

the one who does not call the elders for prayer and healing, here associated with sin (5:15c), and the one who does not confess his or her sins to others (5:16a) are susceptible to the backslidden state in 5:19–20.[89] But more likely the nature of sin in these verses is broader and points back to the thesis of believers persevering through various tests (1:2–4). *The person who needs restoration is the one who has given in to temptations and fails to endure tests of sufferings* (cf. 1:2–4, 13–16).

Timothy Cargal posits an inverted structure in James so that 1:1 and 5:19–20 together refer to the need for the readers' restoration as the Diaspora, which is understood both in terms of their being "scattered" and persecuted in an antagonistic world, and their being "led away" from the truth: "by the end of the book James challenges them to accept the view that they are (also) the 'Diaspora' because they have 'wandered from the truth.' But James has brought them back to the 'truth' through the course of the letter," and thus covered their sins and saved them from death (5:20).[90] Cargal identifies the problem in 5:19–20 as apostasy, which is to be understood as rejecting or failing to do God's will (cf. 4:11–17).[91]

His view rightly reveals that the passage deals with apostasy. The concept of being led astray in 5:19 (πλανάω) is frequently found in contexts portraying a falling away to deception (Matt 24:4–11, 24; John 7:12; 1 John 2:26; 3:7; Rev 2:20; cf. 2 Tim 3:13; 1 Pet 2:25). In James it marks the conduct of yielding to temptation and perhaps blaming God for the moral failure (1:16). In light of the two-ways motif, it involves someone who strays from the path of righteousness to the way of lawlessness, destructions, and curse.[92] The man in 5:19–20 is already an apostate with the clear implication that if he does not turn back to the right path he will not be saved at the eschaton. Nevertheless, a rejection of God's will would only seem to be one facet of falling away in James. The more obvious significance for apostasy centers on a failure for members of the Christ community to persevere through trials and temptations. A chief setback for Cargal's view is the notion that this apostasy is to be associated with the Diaspora of 1:1, and if the "twelve tribes" represent all Christians or all Jewish Christians in a collective sense[93] then the entire Christian community,

---

89. We notice Marshall, *Kept by the Power*, 159: "What happens, however, if the sick man does not call the elders and seek their prayers? May it be that a failure to admit the possibility of sin and to seek healing from the Lord will lead to death? We should then have a situation similar to that in 1 Corinthians 5."

90. Cargal, *Restoring the Diaspora*, 49; cf. 45–56, 198, 201–2, 212–13. For criticisms on Cargal's inverted structure see Watson, Review of *Restoring the Diaspora*, 348–51.

91. Cargal, *Restoring the Diaspora*, 194 cf. 179.

92. Cf. Wis 5:6–7; 12:24; Deut 11:28; *Did.* 6; *Herm. Vis* 3.7.1.

93. Cargal, *Restoring the Diaspora*, 47–48, leaves open the ethnic identity of this community, and yet he seems to think the "twelve tribes of the Diaspora" in 1:1 would be understood by Jewish and

at least the one James is writing to, would seem to have become apostate.[94] Contrary to this perspective, those who stray in 5:19–20 are identified as individuals rather than the entire community of believers, as the masculine singulars of αὐτός in this passage imply. The backslidden believer has strayed from the beliefs and practices of Jewish Christians, and the members are encouraged to win such a person back to a right standing with God and the community.

Moreover, James speaks of the restorer in the third person and gives no clear signals to his readers that he is referring to himself, especially when he charges his readers with the imperative "let him [i.e., the restorer] know . . ." (5:20). It is far more likely that the author is addressing those who are faithful and mature in the Jewish-Christian communities to restore others who have fallen away. The language of Paul in Gal 6:1–6 is similar: those who are spiritual in the community should attempt to restore those who have sinned, and this restoration is to be sought as way to bear one another's burdens and love one's neighbor. The task of restoring those who have fallen into sin is to be done by the faithful congregants.[95] In James it is not clear whether the apostate still attends community functions or not. Given the multitude of recipients he addresses in various locations, perhaps his instruction is intended to be broad enough to cover both possibilities.

One way to interpret the "truth" from which they have strayed in 5:19 is for us to view it as the belief that God is purely good, in contrast to double-minded thinking that claims that God is both good and bad. Loss of trust in God as purely good can lead to ethical failure (cf. Jas 1:17).[96] The meaning of this word, however, seems to connect better with the "word of truth" or Law as interpreted by Jesus and related to wise instruction for moral completion (cf. 1:18; 3:14). It keeps a person on the path of life (cf. Pss 24[25]:5; 25[26]:3).[97] The defectors no longer keep the moral instruction of the community; they have turned from the path of life to walk down the metaphoric road that ends in eschatological death (cf. Jas 1:13–15; 5:20). James stresses the two ways in terms of the ultimatums of truth and error, life and death. Even so, with the help of the restorer the sinners are able to "turn" (ἐπιστρέφω: 5:20) once again to the way of life and return to the truth. The ASV uses "convert" for ἐπιστρέφω, but since these individuals had already been converted or

---

Gentile readers alike as a reference to Christians as a new "people of God" and "spiritual Israel."

94. Notice how such a reading is difficult to reconcile with passages such as Jas 1:2–4, 9; 2:5, 3:1, 13–18; and 5:7–11, 14, which make better sense if we assume the readers are not already backslidden (even so, Cargal, *Restoring the Diaspora*, 206, on 5:13–16 admits that some believers had not strayed).

95. We also find similar language in 1 John 5:16 and Jude 22–23, which leads us to suspect that the topic of restoration is a conventional way to end an ancient letter.

96. So Cargal, *Restoring the Diaspora*, 206; cf. 83–85.

97. See Hartin, *James*, 283.

may have always been part of the community, this is probably not the best way to translate the word. To be sure, the term is used for conversion (1 Thess 5:19; 12 Cor 3:16) and in certain contexts it could also identify a turning *to* apostasy (Gal 4:9; cf. ὑποστρέφω in 2 Pet 2:21), but here it marks a restoration or turning away from apostasy.[98] The result of the sinner returning cancels this person's spiritual death and appointment with destruction and "hides a multitude of sins" (Jas 5:20b). The hiding of sin conveys forgiveness and probably reflects Jewish thought about God blotting out personal sin (cf. Ps 32:1; 51:9).[99] The offenses covered are not only those the apostate committed while living in that condition but those the apostate *would have* committed had he or she not been restored.[100]

This recovery of the sinner in James may recall Jesus' stories about the restoration of lost Israelites intimated in the Parables of the Lost Sheep and the Prodigal Son (Matt 18:10–14; Luke 15:1–17) and the attempted reconciliation of an offending brother or sister (Matt 18:15). A major distinction in Matthew, however, is that the offending person is recalcitrant, refusing to be brought back to right standing with the religious community and is thus finally shunned (18:16–17).

Excursus: The Covenant Pattern of Apostasy, Punishment, and Restoration in Select Passages from Israel's Ancient Traditions

In Israel's scriptures,[101] after God's people commit apostasy their restoration is made possible due to their covenant relationship with the LORD. The Deuteronomic tradition emphasizes warnings to ancient Israel against turning away from God and the Mosaic covenant. When Israel obeys the covenant, this brings blessings; when the people reject it, this brings curse and punishment. If Israel returns (ἐπιστρέφω/שׁוב) to the LORD and obeys the covenant commands, this brings restoration from curses (Deut 30:2; cf. chs. 27–30). The Israelites must not turn aside from God's commandments if they wish to live long and prosper in the land of promise (e.g., Deut 5:32–33; 17:11,

---

98. Cf. Luke 22:32; Mark 4:12; John 12:40; *Herm. Mand* 12.6.2; Isa 6:10; Mal 2:6; Ezek 18:30 cf. ἀποστρέφω: 18:21, 24; 33:11.

99. Cf. Adamson, *James*, 203-4. The phrase in James was a common one for early Christians, but it was used in different contexts (cf. 1 Pet 4:8; *1 Clem.* 49.5; *2 Clem.* 16.4; cf. *T. Jos.* 17.2; Prov 10:12).

100. So Johnson, *James*, 339.

101. This excursus merely provides samplings of the pattern from Israel's ancient traditions. See further examples of Israel's apostasy and restoration in, e.g., Gileadi, *Israel's Apostasy and Restoration*; Holladay, *Root Sûbh*; Thiel, "Bundbrechen im AT," 214–29; Dov, "Apostasy," 3.201–16; Kaufmann and Gottheil, "Apostasy and Apostates from Judaism," 2.12–18; Snaith, *Distinctive Ideas*, 131–42; Forkman, *Limits of Religious Community*; Brown, "Concept of Apostasy," Urbrock, "Blessings and Curses," 1.755–61; Hasel, *Remnant*; Marshall, *Kept by the Power*, 29–50; Wilson, *Leaving the Fold*, 23–65.

20). If they forget the covenant stipulations and follow other deities, God will expel them from the land and cause them to perish, but if they repent God will remember his covenant with their forefathers and they will be restored (4:23–31; 11:16–17; 13:1–18; 17:12; 19:11–13; 29:17). The LORD promises to never leave nor forsake Israel, and yet in almost the same breath God affirms that he *will* forsake them if they forsake him (Deut 31:6, 8, 16–17). Knowing beforehand that Israel will turn away from God, God commands Moses to write a song the Israelites are to remember while in a state of apostasy and expulsion (31:19–22, 29–32:43). The purpose of the song is to testify of God's justice and mercy before Israel in hope of their repentance and restoration.[102] The pattern of apostasy, punishment, and restoration found in the Deuteronomic covenant provides the backdrop for similar patterns in Israel's ancient traditions.[103]

In Judges six cycles of Israel's defections and restorations are recorded. The people's apostasy is described in terms of turning from the ways of their fathers and from obeying God's commands (Judg 2:17). They turn to other gods (Judg 2:19; 8:13), and forget and forsake the LORD to serve Baal (Judg 3:7 cf. 10:10; 1 Sam 12:9). They "do evil in the eyes of the LORD" (e.g., Judg 2:11; 3:7, 12; 4:1), and so God hands them over to their enemies (Judg 2:14; 3:8; 4:2; 6:1; 10:7; 13:1 cf. Neh 9:27; Ps 106:41).[104] The cycles of backsliding thus result in God permitting the surrounding nations to oppress Israel. In the midst of such punishments, the Israelites turn to God who then remembers his covenant relationship with his people and raises up deliverers to restore them (Judg 2:10–23; 3:7–11; 3:12; 4:3; 6:6–7; 10:6–16). The epoch is epitomized by lawlessness in

---

102. Cf. Christensen, *Deuteronomy 21:10—34:12*, 776: "the hope is that when disaster comes the song will prevent the people from thinking it is accidental, so they may see that it is caused by their own behavior. In short, the intention of the song is to elicit true repentance." See relevant contours of apostasy in this song in Oropeza, "Laying to Rest the Midrash," 60–64.

103. The genre of blessings and curses has predecessors in other law codes of the ancient Middle East such as the Code of Hammurabi. See sources in Hartley, *Leviticus*, 459. Also Deuteronomy is not the only Mosaic writing to possess the covenantal blessing/curse motif. At the end of the Holiness Code in Leviticus, the text has similar promises of blessings for covenantal faithfulness (Lev 26:1–13) and warnings of covenantal curses that will come upon Israel if they worship idols and refuse to hear the LORD's voice (Lev 26:14–39). The curses are arranged with increasing severity: if they continue to rebel and refuse to receive God's correction, God will multiply their curses until they are taken captive by their enemies. Nevertheless, if Israel confesses that they have acted unfaithfully against God after he curses them, God will remember his covenant and not reject them so as to destroy them completely (Lev 26:40–44). There is some interplay between Leviticus and Deuteronomy in relation to this subject, but the two may have originated independently even though drawing upon the same general tradition: cf. Noth, *Pentateuchal Traditions*, 195; Hartley, *Leviticus*, 459. The Deuteronomic version is our focus because it is more influential for the NT and is the more elaborate of the two.

104. Even some of the judges and religious figures abandon the ways of God. Micah, for example, owns a shrine full of idols and hires a Levite to be his personal priest (Judg 17). Eli's sons Hophni and Phineas suffer premature deaths for treating God's offering with contempt. God raises another priest (1 Sam 2:17, 29, 34–35).

which everyone did what they saw fit, evidently because no king was in the land (17:6; 18:1; 19:1; 21:25).

Judges perhaps originally functioned as an apologetic for Israel's monarchy and was written between the turbulent times of 722–586 BCE when Israel was repeatedly warned by prophets about their idolatry and liaisons with foreign nations.[105] During these times divine punishment would come by way of other nations, especially the Assyrians and Babylonians, but restoration would also take place (e.g., 1 Kgs 8:46–50; 2 Chr 6:36–39; 36:1–23). The sins of Manasseh during this period are remarkably similar to the book of Judges in which everyone did what was right in their own eyes (2 Kgs 21:2).[106] God's prophets proclaim that since Manasseh committed more evil than the Amorites before him, God would wipe Jerusalem as one wipes a dish. He would forsake the remnant of his inheritance and hand them over to their enemies (2 Kgs 21:13–14, 27). In another rendition of Manasseh's apostasy found in 2 Chr 33:10–13, however, Manasseh rather than Jerusalem is punished, and he humbles himself before God after being captured by the Assyrians; thus God restores him back to his kingdom.[107]

Hosea provides another example of apostasy, punishment, and restoration. Northern Israel's defection is portrayed in terms of being an unfaithful wife and adulteress (Hos 1–2). The children of Hosea's wife are named "not loved" and "not my people," implying God's rejection of Israel (1:6, 9) as a result of Israel forsaking and forgetting his covenant by consulting other deities and engaging in prostitution and drunkenness (Hos 4:10-13 cf. 5:4–7; 6:7; 7:2; 9:10). The people of Israel are destroyed for lack of knowledge because the priests practice fertility rituals and fail to give proper religious instruction (4:6–19; cf. 2:8–10; 8:4–6; 10:1–8; 13:1–3). Israel's punishment includes natural and military calamities (1:5; 2:9–12; 4:3; 5:7; 10:14–15)[108] and also exile described as going back to "Egypt" (8:13; 9:3–17; 11:5). This turn of events not only recalls one of the curses of the Deuteronomic covenant (Deut 28:68), but in Hosea Egypt seems to be a codename for Assyria. God nonetheless calls Israel to turn back to him (Hos 5:4; 6:1; 7:10; 14:2–3). God would heal the waywardness of Israel's adultery if the people return to him (Hos 2:15; 4:4–5; 8:14; 13:6), and he would also bring them back to their original relationship with him in the wilderness so that they could be his people once again (2:14–23).[109] In the imagery of fertile vegetation they will once again

---

105. See further, Noth, *Deuteronomic History*; Bolling, "Judges," 3.1107–14. "By historical examples he [the author of Judges] would warn his contemporaries against a like apostasy" (Moore, *Judges*, xvi.)

106. Cf. Block, *Judges, Ruth*, 56–59, 66–67, who finds a number variant parallels to the phrase in 1–2 Kgs (484n42).

107. On the theme of rewards and retribution in 2 Chronicles, see Dillard, *2 Chronicles*, 76–81.

108. See Wolff, *Hosea*, xxvii–xxix.

109. Cf. Mays, *Hosea*, 13; and see further elaboration on the covenantal/wilderness themes in Hosea based on Deut 4:20–31 in Stuart, *Hosea-Jonah*, 7.

be restored to their land and abide in covenant blessings (14:1–7; cf. 2:25; 3:5; 6:1, 11; 11:10–11).

In the Isaianic tradition, the children of Israel have turned from the LORD to serve other gods, have despised the Holy One of Israel, and have rebelled against him, and so it is predicted that their country would be left desolate (Isa 1:4–9; 5:24; 6:1–10; 57:17–18; 59:13 cf. 53:3; 65:11).[110] The LORD's rejection of Israel is depicted in the imagery of a creditor who sells a slave, and a husband who divorces his wife (45:13; 50:1; 52:3 cf. 54:6–7; 62:4). Israel will also suffer from spiritual blindness and dullness of hearing (6:9–10). But God only temporarily forsakes them (49:14; 54:7; cf. 42:14–16). As a woman cannot forget her children, so the LORD cannot forget Israel (49:14–15). A remnant will survive the impending disasters (Isa 1:9; 4:2–3; 10:20–23; 46:3 cf. Mic 2:12), the blind will once age see and the deaf hear (e.g., Isa 29:18–19; 35:5), and God will establish a new era depicted in the imagery of water in the desert and a new exodus plight (35; 40–44; 51; 63).

Jeremiah prophesies that Israel's enemies will rule over them because they forsake the LORD. The people will know that it is an evil thing to desert God (Jer 2:13–19 cf. 1:16; 17:13). They forget God[111] and turn to serve idols and Baal (2:11; 5:7, 19; 9:12–14; 18:15; 19:4–6; 22:9). Judah is called an apostate who refuses to return to the LORD (3:6–12 cf. vv. 14, 22; 2:19; 4:1; 5:1–6). God claims that since the days he led their fathers out of Egypt they have been a stiffed-necked people. The generation of Jeremiah is under divine wrath (7:24–29; 12:7–13; 15:6; 16:11; 23:33–40). God's abandonment of Israel is most graphically portrayed in terms of the destruction of Solomon's temple in Jerusalem and the captivity of its people by the Babylonians (Jer 39–45; Lam 1–5). Despite their exile, God assures the Israelites that they have not been utterly forsaken; God will eventually destroy their captors (Jer 51:5). God will once again restore the Israelites even though he had rejected Israel and Judah, and he will establish a new covenant with them (31:36–37; 33:24–26).

God permits Ezekiel to see a vision of idolatry in the very temple of God. The idolaters are killed by divine judgment, and the glory of God departs from the temple area (Ezek 8–10). Israel did not forsake the idolatry and prostitution that it started in Egypt (20:30–32; 23:3, 8), and so God will pour out his wrath against them and they will be scattered abroad (20:33–34). The LORD will bring them into the desert of the nations to execute judgment on them just as he had judged their fathers in the wilderness. After God has purged them of their rebels, he will bring them again into a covenant relationship with him (20:35–38). In the valley of dry bones, God declares that he will save the people of Israel from their backsliding so that they will not defile themselves

110. See also Isa 1:28; 43:27; 46:8; 48:8; 53:12; 59:13; 66:24; cf. BDB, 833.

111. Jer 2:32; 3:21–22; 13:25; 18:15; 23:27, 33–40.

with idols any more (37:23). They will forget their unfaithfulness (39:26), and the glory of God will return and dwell in the prophetic new temple (Ezek 40–48).

We can glean a few relevant observations regarding the pattern of apostasy, punishment, and restoration found in Israel's scriptures. First, Israel's defections are frequently described in terms of breaking the covenant (Lev 26:15, 44; Deut 31:16, 20; Judg 2:1; Isa 24:5; Jer 11:10; 31:32; Ezek 17:15–19), transgressing the covenant (Deut 17:2; Josh 7:11–15; 23:16; Judg 2:20; Hos 6:7), or forsaking the covenant (Deut 29:24–25; 1 Kgs 19:10; Jer 22:9).[112] Covenant language thus provides an established foundation for God's reciprocating nature in relation to Israel's obedience and disobedience. When Israel forsakes God, God forsakes Israel (cf. Deut 7:6–7; 31:6–16; Judg 2).[113] Second, Israel's apostasy characteristically leads to punishment or exile or both, in keeping with the Deuteronomic covenant of curses that include, among other things, disease and natural catastrophe (e.g., Deut 28:20–24), captivity by foreigners (28:36–37), and culminating with a return back to Egypt and slavery (28:68).[114] We notice such punishments of exile primarily in relation Israel's captivity by Assyria (e.g., Hosea) and Babylon (e.g., Jeremiah). Third, when Israel repents of its rebellions, God remembers his covenant and restores them (Deut 4:23–31; 2 Kgs 17:36–41; Jer 14:21; cf. Pss 77[78]; 80[81]; 105[106]:44–48; Zech 3; Mal 2:10–12 with 4:5–6). The promise of restoration is normally given to a remnant who are purified and restored through repentance or who do not fall away (Deut 4:28–31; Judg 2–6; 1 Kgs 19:14–18; Ezek 20:35–38). The nation of Israel may suffer corporate judgment—such as a military slaughter (2 Chr 28:6) or a generation that goes into captivity (Jer 7:24–29)—but because of God's promises with Israel's forefathers God does not forsake all the Israelites (Jer 5:10, 18; 31:36–37; cf. Mic 7:18–20).[115]

The pattern of apostasy, punishment, and restoration carries over into early Jewish writings (e.g., Tob 14:4–6; CD 20.1–8; 4Q393 3.3; 4Q504 4.7; *2 Bar.* 85.1–9; *Jub.* 1.5–25; Ps.-Philo 12.4; Philo, *Rewards* 152–63, 172; *t. Demai* 2.9; *b. Bekhorot* 31A). One

---

112. Cf. Weinfeld, "בְּרִית," 2.261–62.

113. Sometimes God forsakes Israel and its people by using the very language he does to describe their election (1 Sam 2:27–36; Ezek 20:5–31; 2 Kgs 21:13-15; Hos 1–5; Amos 3:1–2; cf. Jer 22:24; Ezek 18:5–9, 21–32). Such cases demonstrate in the narratives that God is not necessarily obligated to keep his promises to individuals who rebel against him.

114. See Mayes, *Deuteronomy*, 358.

115. It should be noted here that remnant language is not exclusively in relation to the restoration of Israel from captivity or from its enemies. In early traditions, a faithful remnant can be seen in Noah's family escaping the flood (Gen 6–9), Lot's family escaping Sodom (Gen 19), Joseph preserving life in Egypt (Gen 37–50 esp. 45:7), and Caleb surviving the wilderness generation (Num 14:23–24). See Meyer, "Remnant," 5.670.

prominent example is found in the *Testament of the Twelve Patriarchs*.[116] The various tribes of Israel are predicted to fall away in the last days and suffer divine punishment through their captivity and being scattered abroad, but their restoration to God is also normally predicted if they repent (cf. *T. Naph.* 4–7; *T. Ash.* 7; *T. Gad* 8). The people of tribe of Issachar will align themselves with Beliar and evil desires, and so they will be scattered among the nations. But their children will be restored to the land if they return to the LORD (*T. Iss.* 6). The tribe of Zebulon will abandon the LORD to worship idols. They will be taken captive until the time of the end, but their repentance and deliverance from Beliar is also predicted (*T. Zeb.* 9; cf. *T. Jud.* 23.5; *T. Dan* 5.9; *T. Naph.* 4.3). The tribe of Dan will commit apostasy and follow the deeds of the Gentiles such as committing sexual promiscuity. Their prince will be Satan. They will suffer captivity and the plagues of Egypt, but God will have mercy on them if they turn back to him (*T. Dan* 5).

Distinct from its predecessors in Israel's scriptures, and reminiscent of New Testament and Hellenistic Jewish authors, apostasy in the *Testament of the Twelve* centers on committing vices, and there is a preponderance of sexual sins (e.g., *T. Reu.* 3; *T. Iss.* 4; *T. Ash.* 5; *T. Benj.* 6).[117] *The Twelve* not only reflects the language of responsibilities of Jacob's heirs from Gen 49 but also the covenant of blessing and curses in Deuteronomy.[118] A well-noticed pattern in *The Twelve* centers on the theme identified as sin–exile–return.[119] This pattern is often introduced with a remark about the tribe's apostasy in the last days (*T. Levi* 10.2; 14.1; *T. Iss.* 6.1; *T. Zeb.* 9.5), and restoration involves a return from captivity with God's intervention on account of the tribe's forefathers or the tribe's repentance (*T. Jud.* 23.5; *T. Iss.* 6.3; *T. Zeb.* 9.7; *T. Dan* 5.9; *T. Naph.* 4.3).[120]

Some of the emergent Christian writers who were familiar with Israel's scriptures and Jewish traditions seem to be informed by this repetitive pattern of apostasy,

---

116. This writing was originally Jewish, but later Christian interpolations were added. On the document's Jewish origin (close to the Maccabean period), see Becker, *Untersuchungen zur Entstehungsgeschichte*; Ulrichsen, *Grundschrift der Testament der zwölf*. Differently, De Jonge, *Testament of the Twelve Patriarchs*; Hollander and De Jonge, *Testament of the Twelve Patriarchs*, think the document comes from a Christian person or group. For discussion on the document's development and Christian interpolations, see Elgvin, "Jewish Christian Editing," 286–92; Collins, "Testamentary Literature in Recent Scholarship," 268–76.

117. See Kee in *OTP* 1.779 for a convenient list of virtues and vices in *T. 12 Patr.* Other culprits to apostasy include Beliar (e.g., *T. Reu.* 4.8–10; *T. Iss.* 6.1) and the Watchers (*T. Reu.* 5.6).

118. Cf., e.g., Baltzer, *Covenant Formulary*, 146.

119. See De Jonge, *Testament of the Twelve Patriarchs*, 83–86.

120. Cf. De Jonge, 84–85. Given the interpolation view, another possible distinction is that punishment by exile may reflect Jerusalem's capture by the Romans in the 70 CE (*T. Naph.* 4.4–5; cf. *T. Levi* 15; 16.5).

punishment, and restoration, but they reconfigure it to embrace the punishment and recovery of apostate Christ-followers. Both Matt 18 and 1 Cor 5 seem to adopt the idea of expulsion from the Deuteronomic tradition, but the apostate's "exile" in such cases is from the Christ community rather than from Jerusalem or the promised land. Paul, who considers Israel of his day to be apostate, interprets from the scriptures a hope of Israel's complete restoration, grounding it at the culmination of the ages when Christ returns (Rom 9–11). Frequently the New Testament authors switch the order of punishment and restoration. As we have seen repeatedly, final condemnation of the apostate is reserved for judgment day. Until then, the Christ-followers attempt to restore fallen comrades regardless of whether they are Jewish Christians (Jas 5:19–20; Jude 22–23; cf. Matt 18:15; Luke 22:31–32) or Gentile Christians (Gal 6:1; 2 Cor 2:5–8; 2 Tim 2:24–26).[121] In a significant way, their motivation to recover fallen comrades seems rooted in Jesus' command for all believers to love their neighbors as themselves (cf. Jas 2:8; 4:11 Gal 6:1–5; cf. Jude 21–23).

CONCLUSION

The epistle of James is said to be a letter written by James, the brother of Jesus and leader of the church in Jerusalem, who was martyred by his opponents who thought him an apostate leading the Jewish people astray. There is some evidence to support that the letter may have been written from Jerusalem or Palestine to address the needs of Jewish-Christian communities of the Diaspora (1:1). The purpose of the letter is to foster wise and moral behavior among these communities. The author structures his message in a threefold manner, stressing perseverance through various trials, the encouragement of wisdom related to speaking, and proper attitudes regarding wealth and poverty. The primary goals of perseverance through testing are for members of the communities to become morally mature and be finally saved at the *parousia* (e.g., 1:2–4; 5:7–11). The antipode of endurance is apostasy. Temptations seek to undermine the spiritual life of the Christ-followers, which come by way of human desire (ἐπιθυμία). Allurement to temptation is depicted as a temptress who eventually draws the believer to beget sin and death (1:13–16). James understands death in this context as apostasy, with the end result of Christ-followers missing out on final salvation. Other temptations come by way of the devil and friendship with the fallen world (4:1–10; cf. 3:14–17); the double-minded have an allegiance to both God and the world, but to embrace the latter is tantamount to committing apostasy. The author affirms that companionship with the world makes one an enemy of God.

---

121. Obviously not all the authors do this: contrast the impossibility of restoration for apostates in 1 John 5:16; Heb 6:4–6; and similarly, the unpardonable sin in Mark 3:28–30; Matt 12:31–32; Luke 12:10.

For James the faithful community is adopting Hellenistic society's attitudes of envy, arrogance, self-ambition, and mishandling of wealth, and such problems create divisions in the churches (3:14—4:6; 4:11–17). A negative form of acculturation has thus crept into the gatherings. Two ways are presented to the recipients: the way of life and the way of death (5:19–20; cf. 1:15–18); to walk in wisdom, perseverance, and abiding by the Law of love leads to salvific life. For the faithful to fall into sin, misuse the tongue (especially leaders), refuse to submit to God, and defect from the law of love leads to death and final judgment (e.g., 2:9–11; 3:1–6; 4:12; 5:12). At the end of his message James encourages the Jewish Christian community to restore the apostate, that is, those individuals who have failed to persevere through suffering and temptation, to a renewed salvation (5:19–20). Their restoration would prevent them from spiritual death and destruction.

Some similarities and differences between Paul and James in this letter are worth observing. Both James and Paul affirm that trials are a good thing because they lead to spiritual maturity (Jas 1:2–4; Rom 5:3–5; 2 Cor 1:3–7). But whereas Paul views suffering as coming primarily by persecution (e.g., 1 Thess 2:14; Rom 8:18–39), James sees it coming in diverse ways, including temptation, strife among community members, illness, and exploitation by the wealthy and powerful (Jas 1:12–15; 2:6; 4:7; 5:1–6). Persecution does not appear to play a major factor on his interpretation of suffering. James' use of πειρασμός seems to include both general testing of faith and temptation to sin (1:2–4; 1:12–16). Both authors affirm the possibility that Christian leaders, including themselves, could fall away from faith (Jas 3:1–2; 1 Cor 9:24–27). On the issue of faith and works, for James faith is ongoing, requiring works that manifest themselves through love and obedience (Jas 2). There is a strong possibility concerning this point that the author responds to a teaching of Paul through the use of Abraham's righteousness in relation to faith and works, but James is not defining works in this letter in terms of Paul's "works of the Law" as described significantly in Galatians. Rather, he advances works as epitomized by loving one's neighbor as oneself, and adherence to the Mosaic Law as filtered through the teachings of Jesus. Both James and Paul affirm that faith must be accompanied by obedience and that everyone, including believers, will be judged according to their works on judgment day. The author shares in common with Matthew a stress on keeping Jesus' interpretation of the Torah, and the Sermon on the Mount has informed James' ethics. Both the letters of Jude and James are written to Jewish Christians audiences, and their messages end with a call for believers to restore the apostates. A major distinction between them is that Jude's apostates include false teachers.

3

1 Peter

*Identity, Perseverance, and the Persecution
of Marginalized Christians*

The apostle Peter is the traditional author of 1 Peter (1 Pet 1:1),[1] but contemporary scholars often suggest the letter to be a pseudonym.[2] One of the reasons for this is that the Greek is said to be too sophisticated for a non-native speaker, especially when tradition claims the author was once a simple fisherman from Galilee.[3] But if Peter presumably grew up as an Aramaic speaker, this does not mean that he could not have known Greek.[4] Karen Jobes raises some doubts about the letter originating from a Greek-speaker. Her study develops various syntactical criteria that help her to detect Semitic influence in the letter.[5] The author could be Jewish.[6] But even if her recent study begins to swing the pendulum of scholarship on the letter's original

---

1. For ancient attestation of the author as Peter, see in Skaggs, *1 Peter, 2 Peter*, 6.

2. See, e.g., Feldmeier, *Petrus*, 23–26; Elliott, *1 Peter*, 118–30; Achtemeier, *1 Peter*, 1–43. The authorship of Peter is supported by, e.g., Miller, *First Peter*, 57–75; Schreiner, *1, 2 Peter, Jude*, 20–35; Bauckham, "Pseudo-Apostolic Letters," 490–92. A convenient summary of pros and cons related to the authorship of 1 Peter is found in deSilva, *Introduction*, 845–46.

3. Peter may have been uneducated (cf. ἀγράμματος: Acts 4:13), which could mean that he was illiterate, uneducated, or less likely, he was not formally schooled in Jewish law (cf. Newman and Nida, *Acts*, 99; BDAG, 15). For vocabulary and style elements see Elliot, *1 Peter*, 41–80.

4. Cf. Hengel, *Judaism and Hellenism*, 1.58–106.

5. Jobes, "Syntax of 1 Peter," 159–73.

6. Notice also Schutter, *Hermeneutic and Composition*, 83–84, who, observing Semitic "tendencies" in the text such as a redundant personal pronoun (1 Pet 2:24c) and "imperative participles and adjectives," suggests someone with "extended contact with Jewish culture" and "a Jew by birth and education" may have written 1 Peter.

Churches under Siege of Persecution and Assimilation

language, this would not necessarily prove that Peter was the firsthand author of the letter.[7] As the debate over authorship continues to unfold, we currently do not know with any confidence who actually wrote it.

The author claims to be writing from "Babylon" (5:13),[8] which may be cryptic for Rome,[9] and early church traditions locate Peter and Mark in this city (Ign. *Rom.* 4.3; Irenaeus, *Haer.* 3.1.5; Eusebius, *Hist. eccl.* 2.14.6; 2.15.2; 2.25.1–8; 3.39.15).[10] Another possibility is that "Babylon" is chosen as our author's point of departure for the "diaspora" to which he writes (διασπορά: 1 Pet 1:1). If so, he may have in mind the exile and restoration of God's remnant people from Babylon, as depicted in the second exodus-wilderness travels of passages such as those found in Deutero-Isaiah (e.g., Isa 35:8–10; 40:1–11; 43:5–7; 49:6; cf. 11:1–12; 56:8).[11] However, those from "Babylon," along with Mark, send greetings to the recipients (1 Pet 5:13), which seems to suggest the author actually knows those who are sending the greeting from "Babylon." In all probability the author is saying that both Mark and other believers from Rome are sending greetings to the letter's recipients. The combination of traditions associating this letter with Peter and the location of "Babylon" as a codename for Rome make it safe for us to suggest the author as "Petrine."

The letter may have been written any time between 65 and 100 CE.[12] The letter's primary purpose is to encourage the recipients to stand firm in God's grace (5:12b).[13]

---

7. Another suggestion that the letter may reflect the work of Peter's colleague Silvanus is answered by the specific wording "διὰ Σιλουανοῦ" (1 Pet 5:12), which probably indentifies the letter's courier rather than its amanuensis (cf. Ign. *Smyrn.* 12.1; Ign. *Phil.* 11.2; Ign. *Poly.* 8.1; Polycarp, *Phil.* 14.1). For the amanuensis view see, e.g., Davids, *1 Peter*, 6–7, 198. Against the amanuensis view see Brox, *Petrusbrief*, 241–43; Elliott, *1 Peter*, 123–24. Eusebius, *Hist. eccl.* 4.23.11, provides us with a similar example in which διά does refer to the author. However, Richards, "Silvanus," 417–32, presents many examples of διά referring to the courier. Even so, this does not preclude that Silvanus might be both amanuensis and courier or that another secretary is responsible for the work.

8. It is not impossible that the provenance of the letter was the ancient capitol of Babylon in Mesopotamia, given that Judeans lived there in the first century and Mesopotamians are listed among the hearers of Peter's first message on the Day of Pentecost (Acts 2:9; cf. Philo, *Embassy* 282; Josephus, *Ant.* 11.131–33; 15.14, 39; 18.310–73). But evidence for Mark, Silvanus, Peter, or a Petrine community residing in this city is lacking. The city was practically desolate by about 115 CE; cf. Elliott, *1 Peter*, 882–83.

9. Cf. Rev 14:8; 16:9; 17:3, 5, 9; 4 *Ezra* 3–5; 10:19–48, 15:43–16:34; 2 *Bar* 11.1; *Sib Or* 5.137–78.

10. See further Bauckham, "Martyrdom of Peter," 539–95.

11. Similarly, Brox, *Petrusbrief*, 247.

12. Thinking this letter was known in *1 Clement* (c. 95 CE), Elliott, *1 Peter*, 134–38, narrows the *terminus ad quem* to 92 CE and the *terminus ad quo* at 73 CE. But the first clear allusions from 1 Peter are in Polycarp, *Phil.* (c. 110–135 CE): see Bigg, *Peter and Jude*, 9.

13. On 5:12 as the thesis see, e.g., Brox, *Petrusbrief*, 16–17; Elliott, *1 Peter*, 103. For discussions of the letter's purpose and genre, see Bechtler, *Following in His Steps*, 1–22; Elliott, "1 Peter in Recent Research," 243–54. On its structure see Martin, *Metaphor and Composition*, 161–267.

Presumably, it was intended to be read as an encyclical by recipients north of the Taurus mountains in Asia Minor—the area spans well over 100,000 square miles, with Galatia, Cappadocia, Asia (e.g., Sardis), Pontus, and Bithynia listed as regions (1:1).[14] The recipients are Gentiles, formerly unbelievers (1:14, 18, 23; 2:10; 4:2-4).[15] An assumption might be that they are relatively new believers; their compatriots are surprised that they no longer participate in the vices they once did (4:3-4). The author identifies them with language reminiscent of that which is used to identify the children of Israel (e.g., 1:1, 15-16, 2:5, 9; 3:6). Even so, Jewish Christians may have formed a minority in some of these churches.[16] The ones who harass the Christians in this letter are outsiders among the Gentiles (4:2-4). J. Ramsey Michaels writes, "the absence of any mention of real Jews suggests the possibility that there may have been a tacit alliance between (Gentile) Christian and Jewish communities either in Rome or Asia Minor or both in the face of a common enemy—the enemy being not the Roman Empire as such, but hostile public opinion among the pagan citizenry."[17]

THE PERSECUTION OF RESIDENT ALIENS IN A HOSTILE SOCIETY (1:1, 17; 2:11; 3:16-17; 4:2-4)

The people of the community in 1 Peter are considered "resident aliens" (παρεπιδήμους: 2:11; cf. 1:1, 17), and the household codes identify some as slaves (2:18-20). Designations of the Christians as foreigners and the διασπορά (1:1; cf. 2:11) are intended as central identity markers in this letter. John Elliott opines that the congregations are a socially marginalized people that come from rural backgrounds, live as "strangers" (παροίκους), are deprived of privileges such as landholding, and suffer discrimination from local non-Christian outsiders. Contrary to views that situate the community's persecution under the reign of Nero (54-68 CE), Domitian (81-96 CE), or Trajan (98-117), Elliott argues that their maltreatment is not related to official Roman pogroms; there is no evidence in the letter that their trouble comes directly from Rome. The Christians in fact should honor the emperor and respect civil authority (2:13, 17). Although persecution seems worldwide in-

---

14. See further Achtemeier, *1 Peter*, 83-85. Michaels, *1 Peter*, 4, claims over 300,000 square miles, but Elliott, *1 Peter*, 84, has the figure at about 129,000, with approximately 8,500,000 people living there by 17 CE.

15. Contrast the *diaspora* of Jewish Christians in James 1:1.

16. In agreement with Brown, *Churches the Apostles Left Behind*, 75-83; Achtemeier, *1 Peter*, 50-51. Contrast Lapham, *Peter*, 117-48, who argues for a Jewish audience, a view also taken by Stewart-Sykes, "Function of Peter," 8-21; Jobes, *1 Peter*, 23-27, 267-68; and certain church fathers (e.g., Eusebius, *Hist. eccl.* 3.1.1-2; cf. "forefathers" 1 Pet 1:18).

17. Michaels, *1 Peter*, liv.

stead of localized (1 Pet 5:9), outsiders verbally malign the Christians. In the letter there is no use of "physical aggression, trials, torture, or execution of the believers" (cf. 2:12; 3:16; 4:4, 14).[18] Elliott also believes that the Christians' status as resident aliens is actual rather than metaphorical, comparable to how παροικία is used in Israel's scriptures to refer to Abraham, Israel, Moses, and others (e.g., Gen 23:4; Lev 19:34). The audience of 1 Peter lived as resident aliens in Asia Minor even before their conversion.[19] However, some qualifications and alterations of these perspectives seem to be in order.

First, regarding the lack of evidence for physical persecution, Christian slaves suffer physical beatings from their masters (1 Pet 2:19–20), and Christian wives are probably physically abused at times by their unbelieving husbands (3:1). The idea of the Christian being harmed in 3:13 (κακόω) may be physical (cf. Acts 12:1; 18:10) and reflects abuse experienced by slaves and spouses.[20] Contextually their abusers are non-believers. This, however, is more a suffering related to domestic violence than persecution as such. Even so, beyond such violence it is questionable that the community's persecution is entirely non-physical. If the Christians are being slandered, this probably includes accusations of criminal activities before magistrates (cf. 1 Pet 3:16–17; 4:15), and so *physical punishments or imprisonments would seem to be the logical consequence experienced for at least some of the faithful in Asia Minor and elsewhere.*[21] The believers in Asia Minor are informed by the author that the persecutions they experience are likewise the lot of other believers throughout the Mediterranean world (5:9).

In the early second century Pliny the Younger (c. 110–116), the emperor's personal legate, writes to Trajan about the Christians in this part of Asia Minor (Bithynia-Pontus) that are being accused of political factions against Rome. Pliny says that when he interrogates them, if they confess to being Christian he has them executed. He also tortured two female deacons who were slaves. Some claimed before Pliny that they ceased being Christian long ago, as much as twenty years earlier (*Letters* 10.96.1–10). In other words, some of those who were interrogated commit-

18. Elliott, *Home for the Homeless*, 62–64; idem, *1 Peter*, 97–103, quote from 101. Contrast Revelation, which was also written to persecuted Christians in Asia Minor; unlike 1 Peter 2:13, 17, it squarely condemns the empire and its institution.

19. Elliott, *Home for the Homeless*, 21–58, 67–84.

20. Elliott, *1 Peter*, 619–20, on the other hand, argues that the harm in 3:13 comes closer to the mistreatment of God's people as aliens (cf. Acts 7:6). The verse affirms confidence in the Lord's help (cf. Isa 50:9).

21. Cf. Acts 13:50; 14:5–6, 19; 19:29–31; cf. Acts 12:1–5; 16:19–24; 2 Cor 11:25–26; Tacitus, *Annals* 15.44; Suetonius, *Nero* 16, 38; Eusebius, *Hist. eccl.* 2.25.1–8. On outsider accusations against Christians, see Eusebius, *Hist. eccl.* 4.7.11; 5.1.14–26; 9.5.2; Justin, *Apology* 1.26; Tertullian, *Apology* 2.6–7; Wilken, *Christians as the Romans Saw Them*, 15–24; Benko, "Pagan Criticism of Christianity," 1081–89.

ted apostasy. *The earliest defections Pliny mentions would seem to have taken place in the early 90s CE during the reign of Domitian, a time that might reflect a period close to 1 Peter.*[22] If so, then however we may interpret the persecution in this letter, it would need to be severe enough to cause believers in Asia Minor to abandon their faith.

Second, Elliott's perspective on the community as resident aliens is commendable, but there remain valid reasons for suggesting the author of 1 Peter does not preclude metaphoric meaning for transient terms.[23] Torrey Seland argues lucidly from the Septuagint and Philo that such terms function "as metaphors drawn from the social world of proselytes (source domain), characterizing the social situation of the Petrine Christians (target domain)," in which their social situation as aliens is similar to the social conditions of Jewish proselytes of the Diaspora (e.g., Exod 22:21 LXX; Lev 19:34; 25:23; Deut 10:19; Philo, *Virt.* 212-20; *Abr.* 60-67).[24] Likewise, similar language related to early Christian conversions may be found in Eph 2:12, 19 and Phil 3:20. In view of Philo and *Joseph and Aseneth*, some central aspects shared in common regarding proselytism include: 1) changing from polytheism to monotheism, 2) departing from one's family and country, 3) enmity with friends and family, and 4) joining a new community of "fictive kinship and brotherly love."[25]

The Christians experienced disenfranchisement on account of their conversion (1 Pet 4:2-4). Their departure from a lifestyle that conformed to societal beliefs and practices, no doubt, was perceived as threatening the breakdown of ancestral customs and undermining the economy of those who sold idols. Among other things, Gentiles feared that if the gods were not properly respected these deities might indiscriminately strike with wrath against their citizens (cf. Tertullian, *Apology* 40.2; Horace, *Odes* 3.6.5-8).[26]

---

22. For comparison on Pliny and 1 Peter, see further Horrell, "Label Χριστιανός," 370-76. Horrell explains a possible scenario behind 1 Peter (375-76): "It is likely that the popular slander included some of the typical kinds of criminal accusation—that the Christians committed incest, were murderers, cannibals . . . ([cf. 1 Pet] 4:15)." Horrell continues that the most pointed accusation would be the confession of being Christian, which would lead to death similar to Christ's own suffering.

23. On the metaphorical view of foreigner terms, see Feldmeier, *Christen als Fremde*, esp. 45-51; Seland, "Proselyte Characterizations," 239-68.

24. Seland, "Proselyte Characterizations," 239-68, quote from 240. See metaphorical meanings also in Lev 25:23; 1 Chr 29:15; Ps 38[39]:12; 118[119]:19. Another point worth noting is Achtemeier, *1 Peter*, 56: "The fact that the phrase in 2:11 is introduced with ὡς, a particle regularly used in 1 Peter to identify a metaphorical word or phrase, points rather to a metaphorical than a literal intention of the two concepts" (e.g., 1 Pet 2:2, 5).

25. Seland, "Proselyte Characterizations," 268.

26. Cf. Talbert, "Plan of 1 Peter," 145. For examples of cultural hostility towards those who broke with traditional Greco-Roman religions, see Cicero, *Laws* 2.7.19-27; Plutarch, *Dialogues on Love*, 756 A-B, D; Origen, *Cels.* 2.3; 5.35; 8.69; Eusebius, *Hist. eccl.* 8.17.6-9; 9.1-3; 9.9.1.

Even so, there is no compelling reason to suggest these Christians were resident aliens even prior to conversion. In fact it is doubtful that the author would have known the social status of his many readers well enough to be making such a claim. Some of his audience may have been wealthy (cf. 1 Pet 3:3), and Pliny's description of Christians from the area includes both sexes, all ages, every class, and not only those from rural districts but also from the towns and villages (Pliny, *Letters* 10.96).[27] The people who housed the congregations in this region likely come from diverse backgrounds and statuses. *It appears that their identification as foreigners has more to do with their Christian conversion than their socioeconomic upbringing.* Their alienation from society happened as a result of their peculiar status before God. Reinhard Feldmeier rightly determines that the alienation of the Christians corresponds to their belonging to God's new society via their spiritual rebirth (1 Pet 1:3, 23; 2:2). This new status has brought about conflicts with the secular society, and yet the conflicts do not indicate that God has abandoned them; rather, the conflicts confirm the author's recipients as belonging to God.[28]

STANDING FIRM AND MAKING A SOFT DIFFERENCE IN A HOSTILE SOCIETY (1:6–7; 2:9–11; 4:12; 5:12)

The question of whether these believers are conformists or non-conformists to the larger society[29] is perhaps best explained by a mediating position. Much like the Christian community described in the *Epistle to Diognetus* (c. 150 CE), the language of which seems dependant of 1 Peter, they are considered aliens and yet generally "participate in all things as citizens" (*Diognetus* 5.5; cf. 5.1–17).[30] They are sectarian in exclusivity of membership and breaking with their former lifestyles of vicedoing (1 Pet 1:3, 14, 18, 23; 4:3–4), but they are supportive of societal conventions when those conventions do not infringe on their central beliefs and ethical behavior (2:13–14, 17–18; 3:1–9). As Charles Talbert affirms, the author is interested in two goals: 1) the "social cohesion" of the Christian community, and 2) the "social adaptation" of the

---

27. Cf. Dubis, "Research on 1 Peter," 205.

28. Feldmeier, *Christen als Fremde*, 97–98.

29. Elliott, "1 Peter, Its Situation," 61–78, compares early Christians with sect typologies and argues that the community in 1 Peter fosters inner cohesion and group identity with strong boundaries against conforming to society. Conversely, Balch, "Hellenization/ Acculturation," 79–102, considers the household codes (1 Pet 3:1–7; cf. 2:18–20) as an indication of Christian acculturation of societal structures that alleviate the tensions between the Christians and non-Christian society. In these codes Christian wives are to be submissive to their non-Christian husbands.

30. The connection between Diognetus and 1 Peter was first drawn to my attention by Winter, "Seek the Welfare of the City," 91–94.

Christians with their culture: "Without the first, Christian identity would have been lost. Without the second, Christians would have had no social acceptability, which is also necessary for survival and outreach."[31]

They do not vilify their oppressors; their testimony to outsiders includes what Miroslav Volf calls a "soft difference" that assumes fearlessness, security in God, and winning others through invitation and witness rather than manipulation, pressure, or condemnation (3:1, 6, 14).[32] The Christians are called to seek the peace and well-being of the society (cf. 3:11), declare the virtues of their deliverer (2:9–10), follow the example of the suffering Christ (2:21), and "bestow the blessing of doing good" to others (3:9).[33] Their good works are not set at distance from the culture, nor are their benefactions done in order to be assimilated into it; rather, their works are for the well-being of outsiders and to quell the voice of opposition (2:12–15; 3:9).[34]

Hence, their being named as aliens and strangers by the author is a way to confirm their common identity as a holy people of God who do good to outsiders but do not participate in their moral excesses (2:9–11; cf. 1:15–17). Even in 2:11 the accent is not placed on an attitude that supports "us Christians" against "them pagans." Volf rightly posits, "The force of the injunction is not 'Do not be as your neighbors are!' but 'Do not be as *you were!*'"[35] It is through the Christians' new identity of being set apart for God's purposes that makes them resident aliens and distinguishes their conduct from their pre-converted lifestyle. Dryden writes that because of the temptation for these Christians to "revert back" to their former lifestyles, the author stresses their identity as παροίκους and παρεπιδήμους, which "reinforces their *difference* from the surrounding culture and thus weakens the lure of assimilation. Their estrangement then is not simply an unfortunate reality to be coped with, but something to be *fostered*."[36] *Their designation as societal aliens is meant to reinforce their Christian identity so that they will not succumb to trials and temptations and thus fall away* (cf. 1:6–7; 4:12; 5:8–9).[37]

The purpose of the letter seems to be conceptualized in 5:12b: "I have written briefly to you, exhorting and testifying this to be the true grace of God; stand firm in it." Namely, the content of the author's message which is rooted in the gospel con-

31. Talbert, "Plan of 1 Peter," 141–51, quote from 148.

32. Volf, "Theological Reflections," 24. On the middle position between acculturation and distinctiveness, see also Brown, "Just a Busybody?," 567–68.

33. Cf. Winter, "Seek the Welfare of the City," 92–93.

34. See Dubis, "Research on 1 Peter," 213; Winter, "Public Honouring of Christian Benefactors," 96–97.

35. Volf, "Theological Reflections," 21.

36. Dryden, *Theology and Ethics in 1 Peter*, 130 cf. 138.

37. On temptation/πειρασμός as a threat to faith, see also Feldmeier, *Petrus*, 54–55.

cerns the grace of God—the kind of favor God gives to Christians by calling them, strengthening them through sufferings, and leading them to final salvation (e.g., 1:10-12, 13; 3:7; 5:10).[38] This grace therefore involves past, present, and future.[39] It does not exclude human responsibility, for Christians are to persevere ("stand firm") in this grace. Failure to do so would constitute apostasy that leads to divine judgment at the appearance of Christ (cf. 1:17; 4:17; cf. 5:4).[40] *At the heart of this letter, then, is a call for Christians to persevere as resident aliens in the midst of a hostile environment.* It has a deliberative emphasis, with exhortations intending to persuade the audience to take a future action of doing good works despite their personal sufferings.[41]

THE NEW EXODUS-WILDERNESS PEOPLE OF GOD AND THE DANGER OF ASSIMILATION (1:1-5, 10-19; 2:5-9)

At their conversion Christians begin a metaphorical pilgrimage as God's chosen people (ἐκλεκτός: 1:1) concomitant with Israel's exodus and wilderness travels. God's elect people receive redemption (1 Pet 1:18/ Exod 6:5-6; 32:1-4)[42] related to the Passover lamb (1 Pet 1:19/Exod 12:5-7); they are to gird up their loins for the journey as wanderers (1 Pet 1:13; cf. 2:11/Exod 12:11); they are not to commit apostasy by going back to their former ways of desiring (1 Pet 1:14/Exod 16:2-3); they are commanded to be holy (1 Pet 1:15-16/Lev 19:12); they are promised a future inheritance that reflects the "promised land" hope of the Exodus generation (1 Pet 1:4, 17); and their worship is associated with Israel's priesthood and sanctuary (1 Pet 2:5-9, 12/Exod 19:6 LXX).[43]

The imagery of Israel's exile into Babylon and the return of a remnant to Jerusalem likewise provides a backdrop for 1 Peter.[44] In essence the Christians are fulfilling the prophetic return as exiles from the dispersion (cf. 1:1, 10-12). Their

---

38. Alternatively, 2:19, 20 uses the demonstrative pronoun with grace (as does 5:12) and turns on the idea of humans doing something well pleasing before God; so Brox, *Petrusbrief*, 244. On this interpretation 5:12 concerns how to live in a truly praiseworthy manner before God, and the readers are to persevere in pleasing God.

39. Cf. Bénétreau, *Pierre*, 280.

40. With Schreiner, *1, 2 Peter, Jude*, 249.

41. Differently, Thurén, *Rhetorical Strategy of 1 Peter*, 95-98, views the letter as epideictic rhetoric intending to reinforce values they already have. On 1 Peter as deliberative rhetoric, see Thompson, "Rhetoric of 1 Peter," 237-50, esp. 243; Campbell, *Honor, Shame*, 30-31.

42. Cf. Deut 7:8/Isa 52:3.

43. See further parallels in Deterding, "Exodus Motifs in First Peter," 58-65; Nixon, *Exodus in the New Testament*, 27-28.

44. E.g. Isa 49:6; Jer 29:4-23; Deut 30:4; Ps 146:2; 2 Macc 1:27; Jdt 5:9-19; 2 Bar. 78:1-7; 84-85; *Pss. Sol.* 8.28-30; 9.2.

yearning is for the completion of the eschaton when Christ finally returns to deliver and vindicate them (1:5, 7, 9, 13; 2:12; 4:5; 5:4),[45] and the community is presently living in a liminal place, metaphorically speaking. They are not integrated into society but not completely outside it, and they will live this way in between the eschatological events of Christ's first coming and the consummation of all things.[46] On a similar note Troy Martin argues the importance of Diaspora as the controlling metaphor of the letter (1:1) and interprets it in relation to Israel's temporary wanderings until it reaches the homeland. This idea has been attributed to the Christians: "They have embarked upon an eschatological journey that takes them from their new birth to the eschaton," and their present eschatological situation is expressed in terms of now and not yet, highlighting their sojourning as aliens (1:1, 3–12).[47] The present time of suffering and testing will finish for them with joy and glory (1:7–11). Preparations for the journey include girding up one's loins, being attentive, being armed, and leaving behind unneeded baggage (1:13; 2:1; 4:1; 5:8).[48] Regardless of whether the Diaspora is the controlling metaphor or not,[49] Martin's stress on the eschatological journey of God's people in 1 Peter is no doubt correct.

In a manner resembling the danger facing Diaspora Jews being assimilated into their pagan surroundings, one of 1 Peter's primary purposes is to encourage Christians to stand firm as a holy people and dissuade them from defection to the host society and the practices of their unbelieving compatriots. The author, however, only infrequently uses words referring to apostasy (e.g., πειρασμός: 1:6; σκάνδαλον: 2:8), but another way he may address the problem is by what Martin calls a "rhetorical strategy of suppression," in which antonyms are used to move the Christian audience away from (i.e., suppress) contemplations about apostasy to thoughts about sober living (1:13, 18; 4:7, 12; 5:6, 8), hope (1:3, 13, 21; 3:15), and remaining steadfast (1:21; 5:9–10, 12).[50] In this manner *the strong language of assurance related to their future salvation in 1:1–5 may be rhetorical strategy the author uses to help them realize all their benefits in Christ and thus steer them far away from apostasy.*[51] There

---

45. See Michaels, "1 Peter," 921, who considers 1 Peter as a "preapocalyptic letter" with a decisive revelation in the future.

46. In agreement with Bechtler, *Following in His Steps*, 109–78, 207–8.

47. Martin, *Metaphor and Composition*, 144–61, quote from 153.

48. Ibid., 154.

49. Prasad, *Foundations of the Christian Way*, 391, believes that a controlling metaphor may do injustice to the letter as whole.

50. Martin, *Metaphor and Composition*, 156–58, 266.

51. Positive language is to be expected in the beginning or *exordium* of a letter that is rhetorically motivated, which is normally reassuring irrespective of potential threats to faith that are addressed later on in the letter (e.g., 1 Cor 1:1–9; Phil 1:1–11).

is "a salvation and inheritance kept in heaven" for them (1:4–5),[52] which is seen in relation to Christ's second coming (cf. 1:9, 13, 21; 2:2, 6; 3:7, 9; 4:13; 5:4–6). They have a "living hope" (1:3) that is "still capable of realization."[53] By raising the hope of future salvation, the author wishes to rouse the audience to obedience and an incentive to either receive this salvation or fear losing it.[54] Nevertheless, an emphasis is placed on receiving it. Our author reinforces *who they presently are*, the elect in Christ, *with the incentive that they do not return to who they once were*. Here the salvation and protection of God's elect is reminiscent of the assurance given to the Isaianic remnant who make their journey to Zion (Isa 12:2; 31:5; 33:22; 35:4; 43:1–7; 45:17; 49:8, 25; 52:12; 58:8).

THE "CHRISTIANS" AS ELECT IN CHRIST
(1:1; 2:4–9; 3:16; 4:14, 16; 5:13–14)

The Christian community's identity as God's elect was according to the foreknowledge (κατὰ πρόγνωσιν) of God the Father, through (ἐν) the Spirit's sanctifying work (conversion), and for (εἰς) obedience to Christ (1:2). Obedience is related to human obligation similar to Paul's "obedience of faith" (Rom 1:5). Paul Achtemeier may be correct regarding 1 Pet 1:2: "its force will be that Christians have become elect sojourners in accordance with God's plan empowered by the sanctifying action of the Spirit to the end that they be the people of a new covenant, which like the covenant with Israel entails obedience and sacrifice, in this case the sacrifice of Christ."[55] God's "foreknowledge" (πρόγνωσις) and election is Christologically bent, and probably should be read with 1:20 where Christ is foreknown before the foundation of the world. It comes close to Acts 2:23 in which the plan of God is to bring about salvation via the Christ, and this salvation, predicted by the prophets of old, has now been

---

52. By God's power the Christians are "protected through faith" (1 Pet 1:5a: φρουρουμένους διὰ πίστεως). This could mean either their own faith(fulness) or God's faithfulness in guarding them. The phrase is left ambiguous perhaps to imply both, but in 1:7–9 the faith of the believers comes foremost in view. Horrell, *Peter and Jude*, 150–51, is noteworthy: "Either way the readers are assured that God is at work not only guarding their inheritance in heaven, but also, despite appearances to the contrary—the harsh realities of hardship and suffering—protecting them by his power."

53. So Martin, *Metaphor and Composition*, 54.

54. Cf. Thurén, *Argument and Theology of 1 Peter*, 202–3, 216, 224–25, who holds in tension the language of certain and uncertain salvation of this letter. Differently, Dryden, *Theology and Ethics in 1 Peter*, 34, 102, 115, speaks of antithesis between old and new life as a paraenetic strategy to show the believers their conversion is "irreversible." The new birth (1:3, 23) is a new existence, irreversible because "one cannot be unborn" (115). Even so, Dryden does not seem to deny the danger of believers reverting back to their pre-conversion state (130). If "irreversibility" is seen as something more than a strategy, it would run into difficulties where the potential for Christian apostasy is implied (e.g., 2:11; 5:8).

55. Achtemeier, *1 Peter*, 89.

revealed in its proper time to the Christians. God's foreknowledge of them would seem to be "in Christ" (cf. 1 Pet 5:10, 14). This foreknowledge stresses solidarity with Christ as a corporate body of believers who are foreknown and kept safe as they remain in Christ. God had determined ages ago that he would save people through Christ, and this is perhaps made possible in the author's cosmology because Christ is preexistent (1 Pet 1:11, 20; cf. John 17:5, 24; Eph 1:4); he was loved before his incarnation not merely as a divine thought but relationally. The election and foreknowledge of Christians rest on a corporate dimension that seems to be grounded in the believers' participation in *the elect one*, Christ (cf. vol. 2 on Eph 1:1–14).

What is attributed to Israel in the scriptures has now been inherited by the recipients of 1 Peter. Second exodus and exilic imagery is seen clearly through the concept of elect dispersion in 1:1. Here ἐκλεκτός is pregnant with Isaianic thoughts relevant to 1 Peter.[56] The same word is used to identify the elect cornerstone in 1 Pet 2:4, 6, citing Isa 28:16 (cf. Isa 8:14). The stone represents Christ,[57] and a stress is laid on Christ as the elect individual who is the founder or preeminent one in God's house. No doubt he is being associated with God's elect servant (Isa 42:1; cf. 1 Pet 2:9/Isa 43:20–21; 1 Pet 2:21–25/Isa 53; 1 Pet 4:14/Isa 11:2).[58] It is via Christ, the elect one, that the Christian community belongs to God's house and is named an elect race and chosen people (1 Pet 2:8–9; cf. Isa 43:20–21, 44:1–2; 65:9, 15, 23).

In Isa 43:14—44:5 Babylon's demise is anticipated and will be accomplished through God's anointed king (43:14–15).[59] Recalling the imagery of parting the Red Sea in the exodus narrative, the text predicts that the Lord will do a new thing by creating rivers in dry land and making a way in the wilderness (43:16–20; 44:3–4) for his people, who are a chosen race (Isa 43:20/1 Pet 2:9a), his personal possession (Isa 43:21/1 Pet 2:9d), called (Isa 43:22/1 Pet 2:9e), and who declare his praiseworthy deeds (Isa 43:21/1 Pet 2:9e).[60] The Isaianic background to 1 Peter likewise implies the Lord's dissatisfaction with sacrifices such as sheep and silver, and Jacob's inability to present such items before God. In the era of new things, the Lord himself will blot out their sins (Isa 43:23–25). These thoughts resonate well with 1 Pet 1:18–19,

---

56. Elliott, *1 Peter*, 315, associates election here with the first exodus (Exod 19:3–8). But given the prominence of the Isaianic tradition in 1 Peter, as well as diaspora/exile language in the tradition, it seems more relevant to connect election also with the second exodus.

57. Cf. Rom 9:33; Eph 2:20; Mark 12:10; Matt 21:42; Luke 20:17; Acts 4:11. First Peter 2:6 does not precisely follow the MT or LXX but may be a loose adaptation of the latter: see Carson, "1 Peter," 1025–26.

58. See further Dubis, *Messianic Woes*, esp. 186–87. Consistent with the stress on Deutero-Isaiah is Pearson, *Christological and Rhetorical Properties*.

59. Here there is an allusion to Cyrus: cf. Baltzer, *Deutero-Isaiah*, 168–69.

60. Other echoes in 1 Pet 2:9–10 include Exod 19:5–6 and Hos 2:23–25.

which presents Christ's sacrificial death as the spotless lamb of God ransoming God's people. In Isaiah, moreover, the Lord will put his spirit upon Jacob's "seed" and blessings will be on his children (Isa 44:3b), which seems to recall the audience of 1 Peter as infants who are sanctified by the Spirit and born anew with an imperishable seed (1 Pet 1:2–3, 23a; 2:2–3). On this point, however, 1 Pet 1:23–25 follows more closely Isa 40:6–8, which refers to the word of God and is another passage about God's people travelling in the way of the wilderness, this time with the "glory" of the Lord making an appearance and all people seeing the salvation God provides (Isa 40:1–5; cf. 11:1–2). Our author relates such thoughts to Christ (1 Pet 1:5b–9; 4:14; 5:1, 4). Through the language of election, the author of 1 Peter associates the remnant sojourners passing through the "wilderness" in Isaiah with the believers to whom he is writing—they are considered the Diaspora who have been delivered by the blood of Christ and journey through a metaphorical second exodus-wilderness until Christ returns.

That the author of 1 Peter is borrowing the language of election from Isaiah is neither coincidental nor insignificant. His choice of the word ἐκλεκτός provides an *inclusio* with the content of this letter between 1:1 and 5:13–14, the latter passage identifying the Christians in Babylon as the συνεκλεκτή ("co-elect") who together with all believers are the people of God "in Christ" (5:14; cf. 5:10). The author's phrase "in Christ" may be similar to Paul's use in having a locative or "sphere" in which the followers share a union with Christ through his Spirit. Yet 1 Peter stresses that those "in Christ" are to have Christ-like behavior and be identified as "Christian" (3:16; cf. 4:14, 16).[61] The beloved are thus called by the very name of Christ as "Christians" (cf. χριστιανός: 4:16). This designation for the believers likewise finds echoes with the restoration of God's elect people in Isaiah. The pericope of Isa 44:24—45:7 highlights the Lord laying the foundation to his holy house (Isa 44:28/1 Pet 2:4–9), addressing his elect people (Isa 45:4/1 Pet 2:8f; 5:13), and acquiring the nations/Gentiles and treasures of darkness (Isa 45:1, 7/1 Pet 2:9–10). He calls Cyprus by name, who happens to be God's χριστός (Isa 45:1, 3–4). The Isaianic text has probably informed the author's thoughts even though the origin of the name "Christian" may not have been derived from Isaiah but from outsiders and enemies of the Christians as a derogatory term that the early followers of Christ then adopted and wore proudly.[62]

61. Similarly, Howe, *Because You Bear this Name*, 234–35; Achtemeier, *1 Peter*, 236–37. Horrell, "Label Χριστιανός," 365–66, notices Paul leaning toward Christian identification by the phrase in 2 Cor 12:2.

62. This would be similar to the origins of names given to the Pharisees and Cynics: cf. Horrell, "Label Χριστιανός," 379–80. Apart from 1 Pet 4:16, the word "Christian" appears in Acts 11:26; 26:28; Tacitus, *Annals* 15.44; Seutonius, *Nero* 16.2; Pliny, *Letters* 10.96.1–3; *Did.* 12.5; Ign. *Eph.* 11.2; Ign. *Rom.* 3.2; Ign. *Poly.* 7.3.

1 Peter

As in other early Christian writings, this identity of election stresses God's people as a community; *individuals benefit from God's grace not via their independent election as individuals but as members of the community "in Christ"* (e.g., 1 Pet 2:4–10; 5:14).[63] Collective terms are used to identify them as a chosen and "holy people" of God (1:1, 13–15; 2:4–10; 5:13), a "brotherhood" (2:17; 5:9), the "flock of God" (5:2; cf. 2:25), the "household of God" (2:5; 4:17), being "in Christ" (3:16; 5:10, 14), a "holy priestly community," "elect stock," "royal residence," and God's "possession" and "people" (2:9).[64] The Christians become the building of Zion that God constructs, so that what God was doing in Isaiah becomes a type for what he is doing for those who are in Christ (1 Pet 2:4–10/Isa 28:16; Ps 117[118]:22; Isa 8:14; 43:20; Exod 19:6).[65]

The disobedient, on the other hand, are "set" or "appointed" (ἐτέθησαν) by God for their role of unbelief in 1 Pet 2:8. The interpretation turns on the neuter relative pronoun "which" (ὅ), possibly referring back to their being appointed to stumble as a result of their choice of disobedience, or suggesting that they were appointed to disobedience and stumbling, i.e., they were predestined for reprobation.[66] The interpretation can go either way, but what seems more decisive for its meaning is what else 1 Peter says about unbelievers. The unbelievers in 2:8 "stumble" (προσκόπτω) over the rock of stumbling (σκάνδαλον), which is derived from the language of Jewish apostasy in other early Christian texts.[67] In 2:4–9, however, Israel or the Jewish people are not mentioned even though this pericope is filled with citations and allusions from Israel's scriptures.[68] The Christians' conduct before Gentile unbelievers is the focus of 1 Peter, and disobedient Gentiles are the most obvious group that would come to mind for the early Christian readers of 2:8.

Still, it is possible that the unbelievers in 2:8 refer to *all* unbelievers, whether Jew or Gentile. In favor of this view is that the author alludes to unbelievers in Isa 8

---

63. See especially Elliott, *Elect and the Holy*; idem, *1 Peter*, 112–15, 449–55.

64. Elliott, *1 Peter*, 113, 452, rightly argues against emphasizing 2:4–10 as a priesthood of individual believers; instead, the passage stresses their unity with Christ and "their distinction from non-believers, and their consolidation as the elect and holy people of God, the household of the Spirit" (453).

65. See Marshall, *1 Peter*, 71–72. We do not need to choose a solo meaning between family or temple behind the metaphor "spiritual house" (1 Pet 2:5). As Truex, "God's Spiritual House," 185–93, shows through early Christian and Jewish literature in the face of the temple's destruction in 70 CE, "Both sets of images disclosed new realities for understanding the traumatic historical and social crises they [the community] faced" (190).

66. For the former see Panning, "Exegetical Brief," 48–52; Klein, *New Chosen People*, 241–43; Green, *1 Peter*, 58; Elliot, *1 Peter*, 433–34. For the latter see Dryden, *Theology and Ethics in 1 Peter*, 125; Schreiner, *1, 2 Peter, Jude*, 112–13; Achtemeier, *1 Peter*, 162–63; Kelly, *Peter and Jude*, 94.

67. Mark 12:10–12; Matt 21:42–44; Luke 20:17–19; Rom 9:32–33; cf. 1 Cor 1:23; Gal 5:11.

68. For a summary of these sources see, e.g., Schutter, *Hermeneutic and Composition*, 137.

not only here (1 Pet 2:8a/Isa 8:14) but again in 3:14-15 (cf. Isa 8:12-13), where the Christians are to not to fear outsiders but be ready to give an answer to "everyone" who asks them the reason of hope in them.[69] Nowhere else in this letter (unless in 2:8) does the author think that unbelievers are destined for disobedience, let alone locked into this condition for life.[70] Perhaps the unbelievers' "fall" in 2:8 was destined as a result of God's plan to bring Christ into the world; from the author's point of view their fall was predicted by the prophets of earlier times (Isa 8:14; Ps 117[118]:22; cf. 1 Pet 1:10-12; 2:4-10). Christ's coming into the world had to happen, and the event of his coming made the stumbling of the disobedient inevitable. Essentially, all people are now destined either to believe and obey Christ or to disbelieve and stumble on account of him (cf. Luke 2:34).[71] Thus, God's appointing (τίθημι) of both Christ (the stone in 1 Pet 2:6) and unbelievers to stumble (2:8) is essentially the same appointment with two results.[72]

We do not, in any case, find in 1 Peter an arbitrary double predestination for individuals; we encounter instead human obligation to believe the gospel message (1:21; 2:7)[73] and be obedient to God and Christ (1:2, 14, 22; 2:8). If unbelievers were appointed to stumble because of the advent of Christ, this does not mean that they are inevitably locked up, as it were, in their unbelief until judgment day. In fact, similar to the Gentile Christians who were once *not* God's people (and hence, non-elect; 2:9-10), the author hopes that more unbelievers might become Christian converts and so belong to the elect community (cf. 1 Pet 2:12; 3:1, 15).

HOLY LIVING AND PERSEVERANCE IN THE NEW EXODUS-WILDERNESS (1:13-21; 2:11; 3:9-12)

The way the Christians are to conduct their lives until the eschaton recalls God's words to Israel after the exodus—they are to be holy as God is holy and do what is good (1 Pet 1:15-16/Lev 11:44; 19:2; cf. 1 Pet. 2:14-15, 20; 3:6, 17; 4:19).[74] This would

69. Cf. Elliott, *1 Peter*, 432-33.

70. Selwyn, *1 Peter*, 165, while holding to predestination in this passage, nevertheless rightly qualifies it by affirming it as neither final nor irretrievable.

71. Notice Panning, "Exegetical Brief," 49: "Neutrality over against Christ is impossible. Hence it has rightly been observed that Christ's gospel invitation never leaves the hearer the same. The invitation either creates or strengthens faith in the hearer, or it hardens him [sic] and increases his antipathy to the message. Thus it can be said that in a real sense Christ and his gospel can 'cause' a person to stumble."

72. So also Michaels, *1 Peter*, 107; Jobes, *1 Peter*, 155.

73. On πιστοὺς in 1:21 (A, B, vg) as an active trust, see Achtemeier, *1 Peter*, 132. The alternative reading is πιστεύοντας (p^{72}, ℵ, C, TR). While having strong witnesses, it is more common and hence less likely to be original: Metzger, *Textual Commentary*, 617.

74. See also 1 Pet 1:2, 19, 22; 2:5, 9; 3:5, 15.

mean that their behavior or walk of life during their journey must be exemplary, a point stressed throughout the letter.[75] Whereas God keeps the community safe for final salvation (1:5), this is not guaranteed on an individualistic level apart from faith and obedience (1:2, 3, 5, 7, 8, 9, 14, 21, 22; 2:6, 7; 4:19; 5:9). The believers must live ethically, and there may be hints that some who do not do so or succumb to external pressures might defect from the Christian community (1:17; 3:9, 17; 4:16–18; 5:8). In this regard, the letter functions as paraenesis involving transformation of lifestyle. It teaches the wanderers how to live uprightly, shun their former ways, and survive the second exodus-wilderness journey.[76] The author wants them to embrace the ancient story so that it is reaffirmed as *their* story—so that these "resident aliens" who are called "Christian" (1:1; 2:12; 4:16) might have their identity reinforced as God's people by adopting the exodus narrative. In this manner, the author is getting the recipients to recontextualize their existence, reshape their moral values, and draw closer to God.[77]

The recipients are to be "girding up the loins" of their minds, be sober, and set their hope completely on the grace that will be brought to them at the imminent return of Christ (1:13; cf. 1:5, 7, 10–13; 4:5, 7, 17; 5:1, 4). This girding up depicts tucking one's robe in one's belt for better mobility, as did Jeremiah at the beginning of his prophetic ministry (Jer 1:17), and as did Elijah in order to outrun Ahab (1 Kgs 18:46). In 1 Pet 1:13 the believers' embark on a long journey reminiscent of the preparation involved for the original exodus-wilderness trek (Exod 12:11).[78] Their being "sober" recalls the warnings in the gospels for Jesus' followers to keep alert until his second coming (Luke 12:35; Matt 24:13; cf. 1 Pet 4:17; 5:8). The necessity for attentiveness is at least twofold: 1) it encourages believers to stay faithful and not commit vices during the interim before Christ's return (Matt 24–25); and 2) their patience will be needed to endure the sufferings, trials, and persecutions up ahead (Matt 24:8–13). Ignatius uses similar language by urging Christians to watchfulness and sobriety as God's athletes. The prize to be won is incorruptibility and eternal life (Ign. *Poly.* 2.1–3). In 1 Peter the prize for Christians after the journey is their

---

75. Cf. ἀναστροφή 1 Pet 1:15, 18, 2:12; 3:1–2, 16; ἀναστρέφω 1:17; συνοικέω 3:7; βιόω 4:2; συντρέχω 4:4.

76. Dryden, *Theology and Ethics in 1 Peter*, 27, divides moral instructions into four types: maxims, exhortations, virtue/vice lists, and "moral exemplars."

77. Cf. Dryden, *Theology and Ethics in 1 Peter*, 88, who rightly points out that the author is weaving two stories: "the grand 'meta-narrative' of God's plan of redemption and the story of the readers, i.e., their election and resulting estrangement from society" (68).

78. With Goppelt, *Commentary on 1 Peter*, 105. Prasad, *Christian Way of Life*, 174, supports the exodus tradition of this text but considers the girding up in terms of preparedness for action "in a situation of suffering" (155).

reception of final salvation (1:9). As well, a crown will be given to faithful leaders (5:4), which depicts a victory prize at the end of a race or a reward for public duty as a benefactor or statesman.[79]

The elect believers must conduct themselves in an ethical manner and not conform to their former lustful passions during their pre-converted days (1 Pet 1:14; cf. Rom 12:2). As Moses proclaimed during their wilderness travels, God's people are called to be holy (1 Pet 1:15–16/Lev 11:44). In Asia Minor they are to live in a way set apart for God's purposes during their sojourning (1 Pet 1:17), and their godly living will become a testimony before outsiders. The community must also conduct themselves "with fear" (1:17; 2:17). God would seem to be the object of this fear,[80] and possibly the thought reflects a judgment similar to Matt 10:28, in which Jesus tells his followers not to fear their persecutors but God who is able to sentence them to hell. More likely, however, the concept of fearing the Lord reflects Isa 8:11–15 LXX (cf. 1 Pet 2:8), in which God's faithful are to turn away from the course of apostate Israel and not fear what they fear but rather fear the Lord and be set apart for him. If they place their trust and obedience in the Lord, he will be for them a sanctuary and they will not come against him as against a stumbling stone (λίθου προσκόμματι) or falling rock. *The perspective of fearing God is seen as a preventative against apostasy and divine punishment.* The Christians must be conscious of the fact that everything they do is subject to divine scrutiny.[81] The author of 1 Peter believes that God will be the judge of everyone, and God's judgment will be impartial (1:17; 4:5, 17–18).[82]

Liberation in 1:18–21 (cf. 2:9) is also tied into the exodus with the idea of Israel being freed from Egyptian slavery as a purchased possession of God (Exod 19:5–6).[83] As aliens and sojourners, the Petrine community enjoys God's protection and sustenance in the new wilderness, finding life and feeding off of "milk" rather than manna (1 Pet 1:22—2:3). The letter moves from new birth (1:23–25) to the sustaining of this new life in troublesome times (2:1–3). Jobes distills from 2:1–3 that God is the one who both conceives and sustains the new babes, opening the metaphor of milk wider than the word of God to a divine "life-sustaining grace in Christ."[84] When

79. See other examples in 2 Macc 8:33; *1 En.* 100.7; 2 Pet 2:13; Col 3:25; Eph 6:8; 2 Cor 5:10; Heb 10:36; Achtemeier, *1 Peter*, 329.

80. Cf. Exod 19:12–16; Deut 9:19; Heb 12:20–21.

81. With McKnight, *1 Peter*, 89, who adds, "This fear is neither dread nor anxiety; rather it is the healthy response of a human being before an altogether different kind of Being, God, and is a sign of spiritual health and gratitude."

82. Cf. Rom 2:6; 14:10, 12; 1 Cor 3:10–17; 4:4; 2 Cor 5:10; Rev 22:12. On God as an impartial judge, see Acts 10:34; Rom 2:11; Eph 6:9; Col 3:25; and Witherington, *Hellenized Christians*, 2.104, who writes, "if we who know and believe do not do right, we may be held more accountable than nonbelievers."

83. Cf. Prasad, *Christian Way of Life*, 396–97.

84. Jobes, *1 Peter*, 141.

comparing this passage with Ps 33[34] (esp. vv. 5–15), Jobes observes that ethical behavior consistent with the new birth involves growing up and putting off evil, deceit, hypocrisies, jealousies, and backbiting. This is an exhortation consistent with Ps 33[34], in which those who expect the Lord's deliverance must pursue peace, turn from evil, and stop speaking deceitfully (cf. Ps 33[34]:13–15).[85]

Holy living requires that the believers shun the vices of their pre-converted status (cf. 1 Pet 1:14; 2:1, 11–12; 4:1–4, 15). The Christians are being reminded of their conversion and turning away from their former practices. The futility of their former lifestyle as unbelieving Gentiles is placed in antithesis to the present benefits of their new life.[86] The desires of the fleshly or sinful nature "war against the soul" and are opposed to the believer's spiritual life (2:11).[87] Whether "soul" in this verse refers to the inner nature or the entire person (cf. 1:9, 22; 2:25; 4:19), *losing this battle with the sinful nature would ultimately amount to the same thing: spiritual death.*[88] If they do not put away vices they will be cut off from their spiritual sustenance altogether, much like many of God's elect during the original wilderness travels were destroyed because of murmuring, unbelief, and other vices (e.g., Num 13–20). This would amount to apostasy involving forfeiture of their place in the family of God and his household with all the entailing protection and privileges.[89]

The letter at any rate does not indicate that Christians stand condemned before God every time they commit a sin.[90] Salvation is inherited rather than earned, and the author seems more concerned about a lifestyle characteristic of unethical behavior and vicedoing than whether a Christian commits tit-for-tat sins. *The primary emphasis for abstaining from vices nonetheless centers on the Christians' ethical conduct being a positive testimony before the watchful eyes of their accusing neighbors.* Their holy living might win more converts to the faith and prevent them from slandering the church (2:12; 3:1, 16–17; 4:4, 14–16). They are called to bless and love their

---

85. Ibid., 135–41.

86. On these strategies see Dryden, *Theology and Ethics*, 94–113.

87. Cf. Jas 4:1; Gal 5:17; Rom 7:23; 8:4–13; Polycarp, *Phil.* 5.3.

88. We notice Schreiner, *1, 2 Peter, Jude*, 121: "The whole person is in view, showing that sinful desires, if they are allowed to triumph, ultimately destroy human beings." See also Kelly, *Peter and Jude*, 105.

89. In agreement with Martin, *Metpahor and Composition*, 188, 208, 275.

90. As various commentators correctly note, e.g., Jobes, *1 Peter*, 219; Witherington, *Hellenized Christians*, 2.169.

enemies (1 Pet 3:9; cf. Luke 6:27–28),[91] and by living morally they themselves will inherit final salvation (1 Pet 1:4; 3:7, 9b cf. Heb. 1:14; 6:12; 12:17).[92]

The converse of godly behavior in 3:9–12b would be to do evil (3:12c), that is, practice the methods and vices the believers used to practice before their conversion (1 Pet cf. 2:1, 16; 3:10–12/Ps 33[34]:13–17). Negatively, God's face is against evildoers, which, when contrasted with his attentiveness to the prayers of the righteous, alludes back to the dishonorable Christian husband in 1 Pet 3:7 whose prayers are hindered. Those who do evil in 3:12c would therefore seem to be referring to Christians who behave unethically. Positively, God's blessing is upon those who do righteous. For those who endure unjust hostility, 3:9–12 is a source of encouragement, anticipating their future benefits and recalling Jesus' words to the marginalized: "Blessed are you when men hate you and when they exclude and revile you and cast out your name as evil on account of the Son of Man. Rejoice in that day and leap for joy! For behold, your reward is great in heaven" (Luke 6:22–23a).

GENTILE APOSTATES AND RESTORATION? (2:22–25)

The message in 1 Pet 2:22–25 alludes to the suffering Servant in Isa 53, and the audience are viewed as straying sheep who have returned to their shepherd, Christ. While it is possible that going astray and returning in 2:25 hints at Peter's desertion of Jesus the night he was betrayed (cf. Mark 14:27–29, 50),[93] this verse more clearly alludes to Isa 53:5–6, which originally refers to apostate Israel going astray as sheep without a shepherd, and the Servant bearing their iniquities.[94] Since the author of 1 Peter makes the passage applicable to his readers who are primarily Gentile, in what sense were they apostate if prior to their conversion they were never considered God's elect people? One option is that the author of 1 Peter believes the Gentiles once knew God in primordial times but fell away because of sin and spiritual obduracy, similar to Paul's view of the Gentiles in Rom 1 or their inheriting Adam's sin in Rom 5. In 1 Peter they are presumed to be rebels as far back as the time of Noah (1 Pet 3:18–20; 4:6). Problematic with this view is that our author never claims from the primeval era that they once knew or were in right standing with God.

91. The εἰς τοῦτο in 3:9b can refer either to what came before or after it. In favor of the former is its use in a similar thought in 2:20–21. However, I am inclined to think it looks both ways. Green, *1 Peter*, 105–6, referring to Piper, *Love Your Enemies*, 122–29, speaks of the love command working in terms of the ethic of "enemy-love."

92. Cf. Michaels, *1 Peter*, 179.

93. So Michaels, "1 Peter," 921–22.

94. For comparison see Moyise, "Isaiah in 1 Peter," 182–84, who also notices similarities with 1 Pet 2:25 and Isa 6:10 and Ezek 34:4, 16.

Another option, perhaps more plausible, is that their straying and returning is to be understood somewhat conventionally. The image of straying or shepherdless sheep representing God's people is not uncommon in the scriptures,[95] and so the Gentile audience's "turn" (ἐπιστρέφω) in 2:25 might simply be adopting such language because they have now become God's people, the exiles of prophetic literature who are being restored and heading for Zion. If so, then perhaps a prior apostasy should not be read into this verse—it merely refers to their conversion.[96] Interestingly, a present participle for going astray is used in 1 Pet 2:25 (πλανώμενοι). Isaiah 53:6 (LXX) uses an aorist passive indicative (ἐπλανήθημεν). The nuance in 1 Peter might imply a continual going astray and thus suggest that these Gentiles were never right with God prior to their conversion. *They were like sheep that perpetually went astray*; that is, until they turned away from the wrong path to follow Christ, the shepherd of their souls (2:25; cf. 5:4).

SUFFERING AS CONFIRMATION FOR CHRISTIANS (4:12–19; CF. 1:6–7, 11, 2:20; 3:17)

Various words are used to convey suffering in 1 Peter.[97] The concept of suffering that prevails in this book comes specifically from persecution the Christians experience from outsiders and the devil (1:6–7; 2:19–20; 3:14, 17; 4:1, 12–13, 15, 19; 5:8–10). Indeed most references to suffering in the New Testament center on persecution and believers' conflicts with the fallen world.[98] Through afflictions the Christians participate in the experiences of Jesus, and their trials are viewed in eschatological light as part of the messianic woes that will cease when Christ returns (1 Pet 1:11; 2:21, 23; 3:18; 4:1, 13; 5:1; cf. Phil 3:10). In the present time hardships must be endured as part of God's will (1 Pet 1:6; 3:17; 4:19).[99] The time of testing ends permanently when believers receive final salvation (1:6–7, 9; 2:2; 5:4). It is through their suffering that they will be able to rejoice when Christ returns (4:12–14).[100] Those who presently suffer and are reviled for Christ's sake are blessed, and the Spirit of "glory" rests on

---

95. E.g., Isa 53; Ezek 34; Zech 13:7; Isa 13:14; Jer 27:6 LXX; Jdt 11:19; Num 27:17.

96. Elliott, *1 Peter*, 538, compares ἐπιστρέφω with Gentile conversion in Acts 14:15; 15:19; 26:18, 29; 1 Thess 1:9, and suggests this return is general.

97. E.g., πειρασμός: temptation/trial (1:6; 4:12); δοκίμιον: testing (1:7); λύπη/ λυπέω: sorrow, distress (1:6; 2:19; 4:9); πάσχω: to suffer (2:19–20, 23; 3:14, 17; 4:1, 15f, 19; 5:10); πάθημα: suffering (4:13; 5:9); πύρωσις: burning ordeal (4:12).

98. See Davids, *1 Peter*, 30–44, esp. 37, 38, 40.

99. Cf. Webb, "Intertexture and Rhetorical Strategy," 97.

100. This thought adopts the joy of deliverance for the exilic sufferers (Isa 25:6–11; 26:7–10; 35:10; 51:11; 52:7–12; 61:7).

them. Isaiah 11:2 might be echoed here, but the author has apparently altered the future tense "will rest" (ἀναπαύσεται) in that verse to the present/near future "rests" (ἀναπαύεται) in 1 Pet 4:14, perhaps implying a fulfillment of the Isaianic text by the recipients of his letter.[101] This transference from the messianic individual in Isa 11 to the community in 1 Peter is perhaps best explained by the former tradition's anticipation of God's spirit resting not only on the Davidic ruler but also on God's people (Isa 32:14–15; 44:2–3; 59:21). God's "glory" relates to the cloud of Presence that is with the restored exilic people in the exodus-wilderness prophecies (Isa 35:2; 52:1; 60:1–13; 66–12).[102] Our author in 1 Peter adopts the idea of the Spirit and spiritual gifts coming from the messianic ruler in Isa 11:2–3 and being imparted to the messianic community that he calls Christians (1 Pet 4:10–11; cf. 1 Cor 12:8–13). The saints in 1 Pet 4:14 are assured that God's holy presence is with them in a very special way through their trials. He has not abandoned them.

Suffering, however, should not be caused by the Christians' own wrongdoing (1 Pet 4:15). Their claim to being Christian is sufficient to incite persecutions, whether verbal or physical. In a reversal of what might be expected socially, they should *not* be ashamed (μὴ αἰσχυνέσθω) of suffering for being a Christian but boldly confess this name before others (4:14, 16).[103] The reversal is all the more pointed given the probable backdrop to the concept of being ashamed. It is not merely a subjective feeling of timidity about openly confessing Christ, but it reflects the words of Jesus who warned his followers not to deny him before others when persecution comes their way (cf. Mark. 8:38; Luke 9:26; cf. 12:9; Matt 10:33).[104] In all probability *the Petrine writer equates the idea of not being ashamed of the name "Christian" with not committing apostasy by denying Christ before outsiders.*

Our author considers suffering as a means to soul-building and purification from sin (1:6–7; 4:1–2), a view he shares in common with Paul (cf. Rom 5:3; 12:12). The converse remains an undercurrent, however—there is always the potential to commit apostasy if one is overwhelmed by affliction caused by persecution (1 Pet 5:8; cf. 1 Thess 3:5). Two aspects related to perseverance are relevant for such ordeals:

101. Cf. Moyise, "Isaiah in 1 Peter," 186. Perfect tense developments of ἀναπαύεται in some Greek manuscripts of 4:14 appear to be secondary, according to Metzger, *Textual Commentary*, 624.

102. See further Dubis, *Messianic Woes*, 118–29, 187.

103. See Horrell, "Label Χριστιανός," 379–80.

104. See also Rom 1:16; 2 Tim 1:8, 12, 16; 2:15; and further, Brox, *Petrusbrief*, 221–22. Notice Achetemeier, *1 Peter*, 314: "the verb αἰσχύνω can be used in Christian tradition to mean to be ashamed of and hence to deny one's faith... The contrast here to feeling shame, namely, to 'glorify God' (δοξαζέτω τὸν θεόν), confirms that such a denial is meant, since glorifying God in early Christian tradition can be used, in addition to signifying praise for God's mighty acts, to describe an appropriate confession of faith" (cf. 2 Cor 9:13; Rom 15:6).

both God's power (1 Pet 1:5) and human faith (1:7–9) are at work in the believers as they endure suffering. Since God is involved with the process of salvation, they may be assured that his grace will be sufficient for them to receive a heavenly inheritance at the eschaton (1 Pet 1:4). But because humans are responsible for exercising faith, there is still room for failure and committing apostasy. Troy Martin brings to light this inference, maintaining that it is "through the agency of their faith" that believers remain under God's protection; without believing they would lose God's guardianship.[105] Even so, their testing anticipates a positive salvific outcome. The rhetorical strategy of the author is to comfort the persecuted congregations rather than unsettle them by stressing the dangers of their potential to defect.

Another mishap is implied when the author communicates a *Tobspruch* that it is better for the recipients to suffer now for doing right than for doing wrong (3:17; cf. 2:20), which means more than the obvious "better to do good than evil." *In 3:17 the notion of doing wrong probably means to betray the faith under persecution and thus suffer divine judgment in the future.*[106] In this manner suffering and persecution become incentives for exercising perseverance. It is only by the Christians enduring and remaining steadfast in hope during the eschatological present that future salvation is to be received (1:3, 8, 13, 21; 3:6, 15; 4:7, 13; 5:6, 10, 12).[107] A similar implication related to perseverance is found in 4:12–18. Here the testing by a fiery ordeal may reflect Satan's attempt to get the Christian to fall away from faith (cf. 5:8).[108] Moreover, 4:17–18 mentions judgment beginning with the "house of God." This likely refers to the household of God in which believers are all family members, and the eschatological time of testing is presently upon them (καιρός: 4:17; cf. 1:11). Mark Dubis interprets "the sufferings of Christ" in 4:13 (cf. 1:11; 5:1) not merely as a subjective genitive involving the sufferings experienced by Christ, but also as a genitive of description: "the messianic sufferings" or woes described in early Jewish and Christian apocalyptic traditions that point to the inception of the final period of judgment (Rev 6–16; *4 Ezra* 8.50–9.13; *2 Bar.* 48.30–41; *Apoc. Abr.* 30.4–31.3; *T. Levi*

---

105. Martin, *Metaphor and Composition*, 55. Conversely, Schreiner, *1, 2 Peter, Jude*, 65, writes, "God's power protects us because his power is the means by which our faith is sustained." Even so, there seems to be human responsibility implied by the believer's obedience (1:2) and faith (1:7–9). It is also assumed by the author that believers are responsible to persevere until the eschaton (e.g., 1:13–17; 4:16–19; 5:8–10, 13), which no doubt requires the human must respond by faith.

106. See Michaels, *1 Peter*, 191–92. Contrast Horrell, *Peter and Jude*, 68–69.

107. In agreement with Webb, "Intertertexture and Rhetorical Strategy," 97. Schreiner, *1, 2 Peter, Jude*, 157–58, rightly views the participles of doing good and not being afraid in 1 Peter 3:6 as conditional, suggesting perseverance is necessary for eternal life. Contrast Achtemeier, *1 Peter*, 216, who sees these participles as attendant circumstance of the past.

108. So Achtemeier, *1 Peter*, 305–6.

4.1; *T. Mos.* 8–9).[109] From this vantage point, judgment begins with God's people,[110] who will survive the "woes" of the tribulation period, but only with difficulty (Mark 13:20; Matt 24:22; *4 Ezra* 13.16–20; *2 Bar.* 75.5). They persevere and survive because God protects them (Matt 24:22; Rev 7:14; *4 Ezra* 6.26; 13.16–23; *2 Bar.* 28.3; 75.5; *Apoc. Abr.* 29.3, 17; cf. 1 Pet 1:5). The ungodly also face end-time woes, but they will be destroyed.[111] Our author's reference from Prov 11:31 (1 Pet 4:18) would seem to suggest that if the righteous suffer even in their own land and in the "best of circumstances," how much more will outsiders who mistreat them suffer divine retribution?[112] Behind such language is perhaps also the ethic that believers must not take vengeance or retaliation into their own hands; they must instead rely on God who will repay their tormentors accordingly (cf. Rom 12:17–21).

This passage is helpful for explaining that God's elect are not exempt from eschatological calamities. The judgment in 1 Pet 4:17 is related to messianic woes, and its purpose is to provide the believers with inner purification so that when they stand before God on judgment day they will be able to inherit salvation rather than be rejected (cf. 1:17; 4:5).[113] In this sense the woes may be understood as the present sufferings and persecutions the audience currently face.[114] And such tribulations are the first installment of the final judgment.[115] The balance is seen in 4:19: Christians should entrust themselves to the faithful God (cf. 1 Cor 1:8–9; 10:13), which emphasizes God's relentless consistency to keep believers spiritually safe and never abandon them. Those who continually entrust themselves to their Creator have this assurance.[116] To sum up, 1 Pet 4:17–19 affirms that Christians must persevere through the present hardships brought about by their persecutors, knowing that such godless individuals will not escape God's judgment at the end of the eschaton. They should not think of alleviating their persecutions by denying Christ; to do so will invite greater suffering on judgment day (cf. 1 Pet 1:17; Matt 10:28).[117] As the Christians

---

109. Dubis, *Messianic Woes*, 189–90.

110. Ezek 9:6; 11:9–11; Jer 25[32]:29; Amos 3:2; Mal 3:1–6; 1QH 11.3–18; 1QS 3.13–4:26; *2 Bar.* 13.9–11; *Jub.* 23; *T. Benj.* 10.8–9; *T. Mos.* 9.1–7; *Apoc. El.* 4.2.

111. 2 Thess 1:4–10; 2 Macc 6:12–16; Wis 12:20–26; *4 Ezra* 5.41; 6.25; 7.27; 13:48–50; *1 En.* 38.2; 45.4–5; *2 Bar.* 9.2; 13.8–11; *Sib. Or.* 3.601–615. See also Dubis, *Messianic Woes*, 139–71, 190.

112. So Dubis, *Messianic Woes*, 164–66.

113. Similarly is McKnight, *1 Peter*, 251–52.

114. See Selwyn, *1 Peter*, 301, 399; Dubis, *Messianic Woes*, 141.

115. Cf. Selwyn, *1 Peter*, 300. This early "judgment" on believers therefore may not be intended as a punishment but helps them avoid final punishment. On the possibility of judgment as non-punishment, see Jobes, *1 Peter*, 293–94.

116. Here παρατιθέσθωσαν is a present imperative, suggesting continuity; cf. Michaels, *1 Peter*, 273.

117. In agreement with Goppelt, *Commentary on 1 Peter*, 332–33; Achtemeier, *1 Peter*, 316.

travel through their eschatological wilderness a remnant will indeed survive to the end, as did Israel through the original trek. This will happen despite the possibility of some of them falling away, a phenomenon the author seems to assume as a present reality due to the persecutions.

SATAN AND THE DANGER OF WILD BEASTS IN THE WILDERNESS (5:8-10)

The Christians are charged to be sober and watchful because their adversary the devil as a roaring lion seeks someone to devour. They must resist him being steadfast in faith (1 Pet 5:8-9).[118] The "lion" is often understood as a metaphor representing those who persecute the faithful (cf. Ps 21[22]:14-15; Ezek 22:25; *Jos. Asen.* 12.9-11; 2 Tim 4:17).[119] Jobes suggests it refers to the imperial sociopolitical system of Rome influenced by Satan.[120] Differently, Boris Paschke argues that the lion in 5:8 can be understood quite literally. He adduces from ancient sources pertaining to the Roman Empire that executions *ad bestias*, in which victims were thrown to wild beasts, was practiced from the time of Caligula onward (e.g., Suetonius, *Caligula* 27.3; *Nero* 29.1; *Domitian* 10.1; Dio Chrysostom, *Or.* 60.13.4; Aulus Gellius, *Att.* 5.14.7-11; Martial, *Spec.* 5, 7, 8, 21). Not only were criminals condemned to face the beasts, but sometimes those showing impiety or refusing emperor worship, as well as innocent spectators, became victims (Suetonius, *Cal.* 27.3; Dio Chrysostom, *Or.* 59.10.3). Lions may even be viewed as "the *ad bestias* animal par excellence" (cf. Seneca, *Clem.* 1.25.1).[121] The roaring lion in 1 Pet 5:8, according to Paschke, "refers to the lion that walked in the arena hungry and . . . then literally swallowed its . . . victims . . . [the devil] then would be seen as responsible for what was going on in the arena at the *ad bestias* executions of Christians."[122]

Some potential shortcomings with this view are that the examples given by Paschke for *ad bestias* in the first century mostly take place in Rome, not Asia Minor, and the clear reference to Christians (via Nero's persecution) involves wild dogs rather than lions (Tacitus, *Annals* 15.44).[123] It should be noticed here that other

---

118. Τινα ("someone") is in certain reliable manuscripts of 5:8, but it is omitted in others (e.g., B, Origen). The word does not seem to change the meaning much. For discussion, see Metzger, *Textual Commentary*, 624.

119. Feldmeier, *Petrus*, 166, notices the contrast between a lion who brings death to preserve its own life and Christ as the Lamb who gives life (eternal) through his death (cf. 1 Pet 1:18).

120. Jobes, *1 Peter*, 313-14.

121. Paschke, "Roman *ad bestias*," 489-500, quote from 494.

122. Ibid., 498.

123. Ibid., 495 admits the former point but adds that it may have been practiced elsewhere in

Churches under Siege of Persecution and Assimilation

Christians throughout the empire face similar trials (1 Pet 5:9), which makes the view of *ad bestias* less plausible without further evidence. Still, it is always possible that the Petrine author had such imagery in mind in 5:8, especially if he lived in Rome (i.e., "Babylon"). It is more plausible, however, that the lion is mentioned metaphorically as characteristic of the devil. Several aspects in 5:8 suggest this.

First, the lion in 5:8 "walks about" (περιπατέω), which probably means that the animal roams around being on the prowl, an idea that makes more sense of a free predator seeking to capture its prey than a captured beast that is thrown into the Roman arena.[124] In this case the prey are Christians as God's "flock" of sheep (1 Pet 5:2; cf. Amos 3:2), and the appropriate location would seem to convey a pasture or wilderness where wild animals attempt to devour the sheep. The thought of Satan perhaps blends with this imagery by recalling his role as the accuser who travels "to and fro on the earth, and . . . walking up and down on it" (cf. Job 1:7 RSV) looking for opportunities to undermine God's children (cf. 2 Cor 2:11; 1 Thess 3:5; Eph 4:27).

Second, the lion devours or "swallows up" (καταπίνω) its Christian victim. This suggests something more than physical death. Unless the believers expected a deliverance from lions similar to Dan 6:16–27, their resisting the enemy in *faith* (1 Pet 5:9) seems awkward if referring to *ad bestias*. The passage probably refers to Christians resisting the schemes and temptations of Satan and then being spiritually strengthened as a result of the trial (5:10). If they were to be devoured by the lion represented by Satan, this would likely mean that they denied faith and committed apostasy.[125] The thought may be confirmed by the imperatival necessity for Christians to be sober and watch out (νήψατε, γρηγορήσατε: 5:8; cf. 1:13; 4:17). Both terms are related to Thief in the Night sayings in which Christ's followers are to watch for his return and resist immoral behavior. Those who fail to do so will suffer divine judgment at the *parousia*.[126] The purpose of being watchful in 5:8, then, may be based on a similar assumption: *Christians who are not spiritually alert might become the devil's victim and lose their spiritual life*. Whereas the author's call for the recipients to be alert in 5:8 stresses moral preparation in an effort to keep them from practicing their former vices (cf. 4:4–6), πάθημα in 5:9 suggests that suffering related to persecution is also in view. While persecution is inevitable, spiritual sobriety and

---

the empire, and mosaics and other art from the first century related to *ad bestias* attest to this: cf. Wiedermann, *Emperors and Gladiators*, 26–27, 86–90.

124. Arichea and Nida, *Peter*, 168, translate περιπατεῖ in 5:8 as "roams around," which can be expressed as "goes from place to place," "walks here and there," or "walks about."

125. In agreement with many scholars: e.g., Bénétreau, *Pierre*, 277; Schreiner, *1, 2 Peter*, 242; Horrell, *Peter and Jude*, 97.

126. Mark 13:35–37; Matt 24:42; 25:13; 1 Thess 5:6–8; cf. Acts 20:31; Polycarp, *Phil.* 7.2; 2 Clem. 13.1.

godly living is needed in order for the recipients to alleviate some of the harassment. They must not provoke incidents but submit to human institutes whenever possible and walk blamelessly before their unbelieving neighbors and household members (cf. 2:12–18, 3:1). Satan's temptations through vice and persecution come together via his instigation of outsiders who pressure the believers to renounce their faith and conform to immoral behavior.

This leads to the third point. If the devil can tempt the unwatchful Christian to turn away from faith through vices and persecution, this would amount to the believer's failure to finish the eschatological journey. That person would be devoured in the metaphorical wilderness. Again the lion imagery is pertinent here. Not only was it common knowledge that shepherds in rural areas needed to watch out for their sheep lest they be eaten by wild beasts, but many people throughout the empire would know about the dangers of travelling through wilderness areas where wild creatures might attack them. Likewise, imagery of the devil as a dangerous predator trying to tempt or consume God's elect in the wilderness seems well known among early Christians (Rev 12:13–17; Matt 4:1–11; Mark 1:12–13; Luke 4:1–13). *In 1 Peter the new exodus-wilderness pilgrimage of God's people identifies them as aliens and sojourners who must endure trials, sufferings, and dangers from satanic attacks, described in the imagery of a lion hunting down its prey.* As they make their way through this journey to the consummation of the eschaton, they must stay alert and persevere until the culmination of the present era if they are to share in the glory to be revealed.

CONCLUSION

The letter of 1 Peter addresses a large cluster of predominantly Gentile congregations in Asia Minor. By and large their suffering was brought about by Gentile outsiders who persecuted them (4:1–6, 14–19). A minor theme in this letter is that suffering is brought on by domestic violence (2:18–21; 3:1; cf. v. 13). More prominently, the Christians were being slandered and perhaps physically harmed if Pliny's record is relevant for the time and region. The author identifies the converts as resident aliens and Diaspora, not because they all come from a similar disenfranchised socioeconomic status but because through their rebirth as "Christians" they have joined the elect people of God. They are likewise a holy people set apart from their pre-coverted lifestyles of vicedoing that typifies the behavior of their compatriots. The author stresses their identity as transients in the present society so as to reinforce a distinction between themselves and their surrounding culture (1:1–5; 2:1–9; cf. 4:16; 5:14b). Although the author opposes their assimilation with the larger society, he admonishes them to live a "soft" difference that loves and does not vilify their enemies and attempts to win them over through blessing them and exemplifying a holy lifestyle (e.g., 2:12–3:6). In the imagery of the exodus-wilderness plight of God's people, the author views them as the prophetic Diaspora and sojourners making their way through a metaphorical desert to the final eschaton (cf. 1:1, 13–19; 2:11).

On their dangerous journey they are encouraged by the assurance that God is at work in them and has blessed them with the hope of final salvation. The aim of their suffering is viewed as something positive; it purifies their being and prepares them for final salvation (1:6–9; 4:12–16; 5:9–10). Nevertheless, they must also conduct themselves in the fear of God, knowing that judgment day is coming and they must resist their sinful nature that wars against their person—to lose this war may result in loss of spiritual life with the consequence of divine judgment (1:17; 2:17; cf. 2:11; 3:17). They must therefore be spiritually alert and persevere, not falling away by renouncing their faith on account of persecution or succumbing to vices (5:8–10, 12b). The devil, as a roaring lion, instigates outsiders to pressure the Christians to give up their faith. In this manner he seeks to "devour" them. The letter only infrequently addresses apostasy, mostly by way of inference. It is silent about restoration after apostasy, unless the author implies an ancient falling away of Gentiles whom God is calling to return (2:22–25), similar to Paul in Romans. The author is more concerned about comforting the congregations through their afflictions and reinforcing their identity as Christians. It has been suggested that his positive affirmations suppress negative thoughts the recipients might have about falling away.

Unlike 2 Peter, Jude, Paul, and other authors in the New Testament, the author of 1 Peter does not vilify the opponents. Part of the reason would seem to be that his audience's persecutors are Gentile unbelievers, rather than apostates and false teachers as in many of the other New Testament writings. He instructs the congregations to exemplify upright living in order to win their unbelieving neighbors to faith. His attitude stands in contrast to Revelation, another early writing addressed to Christians in Asia Minor, which depicts the church's persecutors—the unbelieving Roman economic system and imperial cult—in villainous roles. Be that as it may, the Petrine author still affirms that outsiders, especially the church's persecutors, will suffer divine retribution at the second coming (4:17–18). This view he holds in common not only with John in Revelation but also Paul in the Thessalonian and Philippian correspondences, which deal with a similar opposition. The Petrine author's stress on Christian identity reflects the Pauline letter to the Ephesians, which similarly reinforces the boundary between believers and Gentile outsiders by affirming the community's election in Christ. Both letters seem to suppress thoughts of apostasy by advancing positive assurances to the recipients of Asia Minor. But whereas the threat in 1 Peter centers on conformity with the sinful practices of outsiders as a result of persecution, the threat in Ephesians is more complex, coming not only by way of conformity with Gentile vices but also false teachings from diverse sources, from Jewish religious customs to pagan magic to the imperial cult. As well, virtually nothing is said about this community's suffering through persecution, and unlike the disenfranchised Asians in 1 Peter, those addressed in the Pauline churches of Asia Minor must be warned against committing apostasy as a result of wealth and greed.

The churches in 1 Peter, however, span a larger geographic area than the Pauline network in western Asia Minor, and it is not at all clear that these two letters were written at parallel times. They might be written at different times and in different sociopolitical climates. It is not even clear that the cluster of churches in "Asia" to whom the Petrine author writes, even if he writes at the same time as the Pauline letters and to the same cities, should be identified as the same churches addressed by Paul. There is evidence, however, that some of the Pauline churches accepted Petrine authority (1 Cor 1:12; 9:5; cf. 2 Pet 3:15). On a rather tentative note, it is possible that the authors of 1 Peter and Revelation are addressing some of the same congregation members in Asia Minor. One could surmise that the epilogue in John 21 conveys the merging of the Johannine and Petrine communities. This speculation works if 1 Peter reflects Petrine churches, Revelation addresses Johannine churches, and both sources were written after the merge. The condition of the churches in 1 Peter, however, does not resemble that of John's churches in Revelation. Most of the congregations in the latter are called to repent due to complacency, materialism, or compromising with the Roman economic system and imperial cult. Differently, the churches in 1 Peter do not appear to be in a backslidden condition. They seem to be fairly recent converts (1 Pet 4:3–4), unlike the Christians in Revelation, who appear to have been Christians for a long time but are gradually defecting.

4

2 Peter

Denying the Parousia and Distorting Paul—
Apostate Teachers in the Christian Community

The letter of 2 Peter appears to be written as a final testament or farewell discourse.[1] The majority of scholars maintain that 2 Pet 2:1—3:4 borrows from Jude.[2] The author of 2 Peter reconfigures information from Jude to address the specific situation of his recipients, using the Septuagint text but not relying on Pseudepigrapha writings such as *1 Enoch* and the *Assumption of Moses*, as does Jude.[3] The letter exhibits noticeable dissimilarities with 1 Peter, including its style,[4] Hellenistic language, classification of Paul's letters as "scripture" (3:15–16), post-apostolic senti-

---

1. This would be similar to *Testament of the Twelve*, *2 Bar.* 78–86, 2 Timothy, and Acts 20. On this view, see e.g., Fuchs & Reymond, *Saint Pierre, Saint Jude*, 25–26; Davids, *2 Peter and Jude*, 143, 148. Bauckham, *Jude, 2 Peter*, 134, views the work as "transparent fiction" in which "readers familiar with the genre must have expected it to be fictional." On the other hand, if the readers assumed the letter was authentically written by Peter, then we may have a "noble" forgery in the canon. For simplicity's sake, we will call 2 Peter a letter.

2. E.g., Jude 4/2 Pet 2:1–3; Jude 6–7/2 Pet 2:4, 6; Jude 8–10/2 Pet 2:10–12; Jude 11–13/2 Pet 2:13, 15, 17; Jude 16/2 Pet 2:18; Jude 17–18/2 Pet 3:1–3. See further, Callan, "Use of the Letter of Jude," 42–64; Gilmour, *Significance of Parallels*; Paulsen, *Zweite Petrusbrief und der Judasbrief*, 97–100. Other views include: 1) these letters as mutually dependent on one another (Lapham, *Peter*, 152–71); 2) they are mutually dependent on an earlier source or oral tradition (Green, *2 Peter and Jude*, 50–55); 3) an unknown author wrote both Jude and 2 Peter, and so Jude is the letter of 2 Pet 3:1 (Smith, *Petrine Controversies*, 74–78); and 4) Jude was dependant on 2 Peter (Bigg, *St. Peter and St. Jude*, 216–24).

3. See Bauckham, *Jude, 2 Peter*, 138–40.

4. Kraus, *Sprache*, 318–20, lists 56 *hapax legomena*.

ment of a delayed *parousia* (3:3-4), and the oddity of mentioning "your apostles"[5] as if from a previous generation (3:2).[6] These provide some formidable reasons why the scholarly consensus rejects the author as the Apostle Peter who was martyred in the 60s CE. Even some church fathers expressed doubts about the letter's authorship (Eusebius, *Hist. eccl.* 3.31, 4; 3.25.3-4; 6.25.11; Jerome, *Letters* 120.11). The book seems to be written by a Jewish-Hellenistic Christian.[7]

Its content reflects a time when Christians may have questioned the delay of the second coming of Christ, and so some date it after 70 to about 100 CE.[8] The author would appear to be a disciple or colleague of Peter to write in the similitude of Peter's voice and attach Peter's name to the work (1:1).[9] The letter reflects a community of recipients acculturated with Hellenistic thought and language as well as having some knowledge of Jewish traditions.[10] We can assume that early on the letter was associated with the Petrine tradition (3:1; cf. 1:16-18).[11] If so, the audience might be the same as addressed in 1 Pet 1:1—Gentile Christians living in Asia Minor.[12] They also seem to be a church or network of congregations familiar with the Pauline mission: Paul had previously corresponded with them (2 Pet 3:15). Even so, it is safer to say that we do not know the exact location of the recipients. Possibly 2 Pet 1:1 compares Gentile Christians ("those") with the Jewish believers including the author ("us"). Then again, the recipients in this verse may be compared with the apostles or an earlier generation or both.

---

5. Some manuscripts have ἡμῶν (e.g., Ψ, 614), but the witnesses for ὑμῶν are older and many.

6. Supporters of 2 Peter as a pseudonym are legion, e.g., Bauckham, *Jude, 2 Peter*, 151-58; Chester and Martin, *James, Peter, and Jude*, 137-46; Senior and Harrington, *1 Peter, Jude and 2 Peter*, 235-36; Vögtle, *Judasbrief, 2 Petrusbrief*, 125-27; Kümmel, *Introduction*, 430-34. Scholars against the pseudonym include, e.g., Kruger, "Authenticity of 2 Peter," 645-71; Green, *2 Peter Reconsidered*; Schreiner, *1,2 Peter, Jude*, 259-76; Moo, *2 Peter, Jude*, 21-26.

7. Cf. Elliott, "Peter," 5.284-85.

8. E.g., Spicq, *Saint Pierre*, 194-96 (90 CE). There is no reason to date the work towards the mid-second century as an example of early catholicism, *pace* Käsemann, "Apologia for Primitive Christian Eschatology," 169-95.

9. Parallels with the writings of Clement and Hermas might suggest a leader from Rome such as Silvanus or Linus the bishop wrote the book: cf. 1 Pet 5:12; 2 Tim 4:21; Irenaeus, *Haer.* 3.3.3; Eusebius, *Hist. eccl.* 3.13, 21; 5.6.1; Bauckham, *Jude, 2 Peter*, 158-62; Witherington, *Hellenized Christians*, 2. 282-83.

10. Cf. Fornberg, *Early Church*, 111-48.

11. On 2 Pet 3:1 as referring to 1 Peter, see Vögtle, *Judasbrief, 2 Petrusbrief*, 211-12.

12. Differently, Witherington, *Hellenized Christians*, 2.283-85, thinks it an encyclical addressed to the entire existing church of the postapostolic era. On the letter's Hellenistic milieu, see Fornberg, *Early Church*.

THE THREAT OF ASSIMILATION

The opponents in 2 Peter, similar to Jude's opponents, are said to deny Christ, revile angels, and practice immorality related to greed and sexual promiscuity.[13] The opponents in both letters speak against the eschaton. In Jude they seem to deny the coming judgment related to the *parousia*; in 2 Peter they not only deny this (2:3–10) but also the imminence of the second coming (3:1–4).[14] In fact they seem to doubt that the event will ever take place (cf. 1:16–21). The evidence is too slim for us to equate the opponents of both letters, especially given the vituperative stereotypes both texts articulate against them. Jerome Neyrey and others suggest the opponents share similarities with the Epicureans; others suggest, less plausibly, that Gnostic-like opponents are in view.[15] The author's use of lawless terms to describe the opponents may suggest this group is antinomian.[16] They turn from the holy "commandment" to commit apostasy (2:21). Then again, it was conventional for writers to describe end-time opponents of God's people as lawless (e.g., 2 Thess 2:3, 8; *Barn.* 15.5; *T. Dan* 6.16).

There may be some credibility to the author's unique claim that they have distorted Paul's teaching (2 Pet 3:15–16). Given the descriptions of the opponents' conduct in this letter and the immediate context in which the author encourages righteous and blameless living (cf. 3:13–14), the false teachers may have abused Paul's instructions related to grace in order to support their immoral behavior.[17] More than this, it is possible that they twisted Pauline teachings related to the delay of the *parousia* (3:1–4, 9; cf. 2 Thess 2:1–3), again perhaps to justify their lax moral conduct. Similar to the wicked servant in Jesus' story of the Thief in the Night, they think they could live immorally because the lord is delaying his coming (Luke 12:41–46; Matt 24:45–51; cf. 1 Thess 5:1–9). The Petrine author may be familiar with both Jesus and Pauline traditions regarding the necessity of moral preparation in view of Christ's return as a thief in the night (cf. 2 Pet 3:10–11). *We can therefore suggest that the opponents are perceived by the author as immoral, and abuse Pauline teachings to justify their behavior.* The author considers them false teachers and apostate Christians (2:1,

---

13. The angels in 2 Pet 2:10–11 are possibly demonic, but more likely they are benevolent angels who do not bring judgment against "them," i.e., the revilers. Contrast Bauckham, *Jude, 2 Peter*, 155.

14. We equate the opponents in 2 Pet 2 with the ones in 2 Pet 3.

15. On the former view see, e.g., Neyrey, "Form and Background," 407–31; Kraftchick, *Jude, 2 Peter*, 77–78. On the latter see, e.g., Smith, *Petrine Controversies*, 92–100; Kelly, *Peter and Jude*, 231. For more views see Caulley, "False Teachers," 27–42; Bauckham, "II Peter," 3713–52.

16. E.g., ἄθεσμος: 3:17; cf. 2:7; ἄνομος: 2:8; παρανομία: 2:16. See further Kraus, *Sprache*, 327, 329 (cf. 355).

17. We notice also, for example, that the aspects of freedom and enslavement in relation one's behavior in 2 Pet 2:19 sounds similar to Paul in Rom 6:16–23.

20–22); *the threat they pose for the audience is assimilation with "pagan," Hellenistic ideas.*[18] Not only have they brought into the churches their immoral behavior but possibly an eclectic blend of teachings from several sects, philosophies, or streams of thought.[19]

The letter is primarily deliberative rhetoric, intending to persuade the recipients through reminder, teaching, and exhortation to think properly or take action, mainly in the future, in relation to spiritual growth and eschatology.[20]

GROWING IN VIRTUES AND AVOIDING APOSTASY (1:1–10; CF. 3:18)

The letter opens by affirming the community as those who have received a faith as precious as the apostles (1:1). This faith is freely given through Christ's righteousness,[21] and it is subjective yet based on the objective gospel.[22] The context implies personal faith related to virtues (1:5–10). Although faith is God-given and unearned in 1:1 (cf. Rom 12:3 1 Cor 12:9),[23] it is seen as the starting point of the Christians' personal responsibility to grow in ethical conduct. They must practice moral living and virtues in a way worthy of their calling (1:5–10).[24] They also must add to their faith moral excellence (ἀρετή), knowledge (cf. 3:18), self-control (contrast 2:2, 18; 3:3; 2 Tim 3:1–3), perseverance (contrast 2:16, 19–22; 3:17), godliness (contrast 2:5–6; 3:7), filial affection, and love. The list resembles virtues mentioned by Hellenistic moral philosophers,[25] but dissimilar to these, faith is set as the foundation of Christian

---

18. See Caulley, "They Promise Them Freedom," 129–38, who interprets their promise of "freedom" in 2 Pet 2:19 with assimilation, which for him finds parallels in Balaam and Num 25, where Israelites slept with Moabite women and Zimri becomes the spokesperson for apostates by arguing for self-determination and freedom from Moses and the Law (cf. Josephus, *Ant.* 4.140–49).

19. Davids, *Second Peter and Jude*, 220–21, presents a similar view. Differently, Bauckham, *2 Peter, Jude*, 239–40, raises the possibility that the plural derives from a saying of Jesus in the *Agraphon*: "there will be divisions and heresies" (cf. Justin, *Dial.* 35.3; 51.2; *Ascen. Isa.* 3.2).

20. On the letter's arrangement, see Watson, *Invention, Arrangement, and Style*, 14–42, 85–86.

21. In 2 Peter righteousness has an ethical flavor (e.g., 2 Pet 2:5–8, 21). In 1:1 it may connote justice—Christ/God is impartial to apostles and ordinary believers, Jew and Gentile alike: cf. Arichea and Hatton, *Jude and Second Peter*, 67–68.

22. Cf. Bauckham, *Jude, 2 Peter*, 167.

23. See Hanse, "λαγχάνω," 4.2.

24. In agreement with Charles, *Virtue amidst Vice*, 157–58; cf. 159–74.This perspective also informs the notion of Christians partaking of the "divine nature," which is not a reference to deification or assimilation into God but their sharing in the knowledge of God that leads to godly moral conduct; see Starr, *Sharers in the Divine Nature*.

25. E.g., Seneca, *Ep.* 85.2; Maximus of Tyre 16.3b; Cicero, *Ros. Amer.* 27.75; Charles, *Virtue amidst Vice*, 99–111.

ethics, displacing ἀρετή or "moral excellence" as the centerpiece. Faith becomes the prerequisite for appropriate virtue, and love is its goal.[26]

The benefit of the Christians pursuing moral conduct results in the productivity of their knowledge of Christ (1:8), their personal relationship of knowing the Lord that started at conversion. Knowledge in 1:2–3, 8, and 2:20–21 (ἐπίγνωσις) may be nuanced differently than the virtue of knowledge in 1:5 (γνῶσις). The former, ἐπίγνωσις, connotes knowledge arising from conversion, as a number of scholars suggest.[27] It implies a relational knowledge in the opening verses of 2 Peter. The latter, γνῶσις, may be acquired and developed involving practical wisdom or comprehension of apostolic teaching. Nevertheless, the two words at times overlap in meaning, and it is possible that they do with γνῶσις mentioned in 2 Pet 3:18. In this verse the believers' growth in the knowledge of Jesus Christ seems to be both relational and intellectual. They are to advance both in knowing Christ personally and knowing about Christ through apostolic teaching.

The person who lacks these virtues is said to be so shortsighted that he or she becomes blind, forgetful of once being cleansed of sins at conversion (1:9).[28] This myopic individual may be similar to the false teachers who use their eyes for adulterous purposes (2:14). In contrast, righteous Lot was tormented by *seeing* on a daily basis the immorality of Sodom's residents (2:7–8). If the opposite of virtue is vice, then defective eyesight in this case suggests spiritual insensitivity and obduracy towards ethical living. Such individuals fail to remember and appreciate how Christ cleansed them from the sins of their pre-conversion lives. The thought might assume that some of the recipients have been Christians for quite a long time, complimentary with the notion that some Christian communities, particularly in Asia Minor, were becoming complacent at the end of the first century (cf. Rev 2:4–5; 3:1–2, 14–15). In a similar way, the author of 2 Peter arouses the recipients as though from sleep (διεγείρω) to remind them of apostolic instruction (2 Pet 1:12–13; 3:1). Some of the members who had been part of the congregation for quite some time may be in danger of a gradual defection from spiritual dullness to spiritual death. The new and unstable members are also in spiritual danger (cf. 2:14, 18; 3:16).[29]

---

26. Cf. Charles and Waltner, *1–2 Peter, Jude*, 214–16.

27. Cf. Heb 10:26; Eph 1:17; 1 Tim 2:4; Titus 1:1; *1 Clem.* 59.2; *Mart. Pol.* 14.1. For further options on the term see in Picirelli, "Meaning of 'Epignosis,'" 85–93.

28. Cf. Titus 3:5; Eph 5:26; 1 Cor 6:11; Acts 22:16; 1 Pet 1:14, 18; 4:3. In 1:9 blindness (τυφλός) and short-sightedness (μυωπάζω) clash. "If a person is blind, that person cannot be shortsighted at the same time" (Arichea and Hatton, *Handbook on Jude*, 82). The ESV tries to capture the distinction: "he is so near-sighted that he is blind."

29. Alternatively, the different condition of members in the opening of 2 Pet 1 might betray that a portion of this chapter comes from a different source or time than 2 Pet 2.

The congregation members must be diligent to make their calling and election firm (1:10a). Here their calling and election are virtually synonymous,[30] and the aspect of making "firm" (βέβαιος) conveys a sense of ratification, reliability, or guarantee. Bauckham rightly affirms regarding this passage: "Christ has called the Christian into his kingdom (v 3), promising him [sic] immortality (v 4), but an appropriate moral response is required if his final salvation is to be guaranteed . . . This passage [1:10] does not mean that moral progress provides the Christian with a subjective assurance of his election . . . but that the ethical fruits of Christian faith are objectively necessary for the attainment of final salvation."[31] To this we add that the present tense participle ποιοῦντες might suggest a conditional and continual doing. If they maintain the practice of virtues and confirm their election, they will never fall (1:10b). In view of the way the apostates did not practice virtues (2 Pet 2), this type of "fall" (πταίω) refers not merely to one's stumbling or falling into sin, but committing apostasy (cf. Deut 7:25 LXX).[32] The idea of a person practicing virtues so that he or she will never sin is a tautology.[33] The meaning of apostasy in 1:10 makes more sense and is confirmed in the context—*if the Christians persevere in faith and virtuous conduct, they will never fall away but participate in Christ's eternal kingdom when he returns* (1:11; cf. 3:10–15). The converse of this thought would seem to be that if they apostatized they would be punished on judgment day just like those who had already fallen away (cf. 2:1, 9, 20–22). The author exhorts the beloved recipients because he wants them to grow in their knowledge and not become defectors or spiritually stagnate (cf. 2:18–22; 3:17).

"HERESIES" AND THE DESTRUCTION OF FALSE TEACHERS (2:1–3)

After the author answers accusations against the *parousia* as a contrived tale (1:16–19) and prophecy related to it as coming from human origin or on the basis of one's own whimsical interpretation (1:20–21),[34] he begins counteraccusations against the

30. See parallel combination in Rev 17:14.

31. Bauckham, *Jude, 2 Peter*, 190. Cf. Wis 6:17–20; 2 *Clem.* 5.5–6; 11.6–7; *Barn.* 4.13.

32. The word can be understood in certain contexts as a fall in battle (Josephus, *Ant.* 7.4.1[75]; Herodotus, *Histories* 9.101; Diodorus Siculus 15.33.1). "Stumble" (HCSB) and "stumble into sin" (NET) are not forceful enough. The ESV captures the sense better by simply translating πταίω as "fall." The GNB "abandon your faith" and LVB "fall away" are on track even though paraphrased.

33. Cf. Davids, *Second Peter and Jude*, 188–89. Bauckham, *Jude, 2 Peter*, 191: "The metaphor must rather be given the same sense as in Jude 24 . . . it refers to the disaster of not reaching final salvation."

34. On 2:20–21 see Skaggs, *1 Peter, 2 Peter, Jude*, 109–12. Differently, Caulley, "They Promise Them Freedom," suggests the opponents thought themselves prophets in an era when prophecy centered on interpretation of Scripture rather than preaching or prediction. They were involved in "the prophetic task of interpreting Scripture" (137). The prophetic function, however, may be understood as some-

opponents. As there were false prophets among God's people in previous eras, so there will be false teachers among the Christians (2 Pet 2:1; cf. Jer 6:13; 33[26]:7–16 LXX; Zech 13:12; Deut 13:1–5; 18:20–22).[35] These are not outsiders but those who attend churches and bring into congregations what is from the outside—ideologies and immoral behavior from the non-Christian world.[36] The false teachers are mentioned at this point in the letter to show how Jesus' predictions about the rise of false prophets, false christs, and apostates would be a sign of the coming eschaton (Matt 7:15, 21–23; 24:11, 24; Mark 13:22).[37] In ironic fashion those who mock prophecies in 2 Pet 3:1–4 are fulfilling the sign predicted by Jesus. The prophecies of old about false teachers and prophets were already coming to pass by the time the Petrine writer sends this letter.[38]

Several accusations that are raised against the false teachers here are noteworthy. First, they secretively bring in from the outside "heresies of destruction" (2:1: αἱρέσεις ἀπωλείας). The church fathers often use the term αἵρεσις to label false doctrine (Ign. *Eph.* 6.2; Ign. *Trall.* 6.1; Justin, *Apology* 36; *Dial.* 35.3; Irenaeus, *Haer,* 2.19.8). It typically means "sect," "faction," or "discrimination" by the New Testament authors (Acts 5:17; 24:5; 26:5; Gal 5:20; 1 Cor 11:19; cf. Titus 3:10).[39] In 2:1 the meaning is beginning to reflect a technical use of conveying an embodiment of false teachings—the "heresies" are brought into the church by false teachers (ψευδοδιδάσκαλοι). Nevertheless, 2 Peter was written too prematurely to be contrasting heresy against a defined set of "orthodox" beliefs or rules that were universally accepted by the Christian church. The opponents' errors are related to both false doctrine and immorality—they deny the *parousia* along with prophetic inspiration, *and* they embrace a lawless and lustful lifestyle (cf. 2:1–22). The Petrine author's use of "heresy," then, is transitional. He combines elements of factional and immoral be-

---

thing communicated and interpreted by Jesus and the apostles (1:15–19; 3:1–9).

35. Ψευδοπροφήτης pertains to the false prophets of past eras, and ψευδοδιδάσκαλος is used to describe future false teachers that are already present by the time the recipients hear the letter. The author will compare the false teachers with Balaam the false prophet (2:15–16).

36. Παρεισάγω in 2:1 means something coming in from the outside (cf. Gal 2:4): Louw-Nida, *Greek-English Lexicon*, 1.162§13.132; Kraus, *Sprache*, 327.

37. Cf. Acts 20:28–32; 1 Tim 4:1; 2 Tim 3:1–5; 1John 4:1; Rev 16:13; *Apoc. Pet.* 1.1; *Did.* 11.5–10; 16.3.

38. The future tense in 2:1 does not mean that the false teachers are not already influencing the congregations. This is supposed to be the final testament of Peter, and it was read postmortem, when such teachers were already influencing the church. See 1 Tim 4:1–4 and 2 Tim 3:1–5 where future and present collide in relation to the coming of false teachers and apostasy. Contrast aorist and present tenses in Jude 4. Also see qualification in Bauckham, *Jude, 2 Peter*, 239.

39. On the development of the term in the ancient world see, e.g., Simon, "Greek Hairesis to Christian Heresy," 101–16.

havior associated with first-century Christian uses of the term, but he adds to these an element that would eventually epitomize the word's meaning in later centuries of Christianity: he affirms heresy as false doctrine. The αἱρέσεις are destructive because they will bring condemnation on both the teachers and adherents on judgment day (cf. 2 Pet 2:3, 6, 9, 12–13a; 3:7, 9; Jude 5). At least three more aspects in relation to the "heresies" seem crucial for our author and the congregations: the false teachers 1) deny Christ as master (2:1), 2) have wandered off the way of truth (2:2), and 3) abandon righteous living (2:15). *What is central to Christian belief at the writing of 2 Peter are the affirmations of Christ as Lord, belief in the gospel message of the apostles and prophets, and an ethical way of living in obedience to Christ and the gospel. To teach in a way that strays from or contradicts these pillars is to introduce destructive heresies.*

Second, the false teachers deny their master, Jesus (2 Pet 2:1; cf. Jude 4), who bought them.[40] As in Jude, the claim is made by the author, not the opponents, and so we are left at the mercy of the author to describe the opponent's disposition. The opponents probably still confess Christ, at least outwardly, if they are able to influence unstable believers and new converts (2 Pet 2:14, 18). From the *author's* perspective, they have denied Christ and will face divine judgment if remaining in this state. In the imagery of bondservice, their former master was Christ and they belonged to his spiritual household.[41] Moreover, the thought of Christ as master perhaps insinuates that because of their immoral lifestyle, they do not really serve him or surrender to his lordship. Here the notion of buying (ἀγοράζω) might have evoked for some readers the thought of manumission from slavery, but the term is absorbed into a salvific metaphor for early Christians.[42] They were "bought" with Christ's redemptive death on the cross (cf. 1 Cor 6:20; 7:23; Rev 5:9; 14:3–4; cf. Acts 20:28; Gal 3:13).[43] Hence, *2 Pet 2:1 claims that the false teachers were once redeemed Christians, but through their immoral living and denial of the* parousia (cf. 3:1–13), *they have become apostates.* As a result they are enslaved once again to the corruption that their sinful vices bring (2 Pet 2:19 cf. 1:3–4; Rom 6:16, 20–23). *These thoughts clearly*

40. On the concept of denial, see further on Jude 4 below.

41. See further Neyrey, *2 Peter, Jude*, 191–92.

42. Cf. Green, *Jude and 2 Peter*, 240–41.

43. It is doubtful that the author had in mind in 2:1 the concept of what certain systematic theologians understand as "universal atonement": that Christ's death paid the price for all humanity (rather than only the elect), but the lost among humanity must believe in Christ in order to benefit from the purchase. In the New Testament ἀγοράζω, when it focuses on Christ doing the purchasing, always has in mind the believers rather than potential believers (see references in the main text). In 2:1 it refers specifically to *them* (αὐτοὺς): i.e., the false teachers prior to their apostasy (cf. 2:20–22). From the author's point of view, they were once redeemed believers, not merely potential believers of the same lot as rest of lost humanity.

demonstrate that the author of 2 Peter believes that authentic Christians can fall away and lose their redemption.

Third, many will follow these false teachers (2 Pet 2:2). Those who are especially susceptible to their teachings, greed, deceptive exploitation, and sexual enticement are unstable Christians and new converts (2:3, 14, 18; 3:16). This is one reason why the author must stress that his audience grow in their knowledge of Christ and apostolic teachings (1:5–10; 3:18). Maturity in knowledge and spirituality will help them resist the influence of false teachers.[44] Through their pompous and vain speaking, these teachers, as though fishing, entice or "catch by a bait" (δελεάζω: 2 Pet 2:18; cf. Jas 1:14)[45] those who have scarcely escaped the unbelieving society that lives in error.[46] The new converts they reach are examples of what Stephen Wilson calls precipitate defectors. Differently, the false teachers, with their eclectic beliefs and philosophies that have led to their mockery of prophecies related to the *parousia* (3:1–4), may be compared with contemporary defectors who fall away from faith on account of intellectual doubts and losing a sense of urgency related to the end times.[47]

Fourth, the way of truth will be blasphemed because of these teachers (2 Pet 2:2; cf. Isa 52:5). They will present themselves as Christians, but their immoral living and false teachings will contradict their claim. When outsiders see the hypocrisy, they will not make a distinction between the false teachers and apostolic leaders who proclaim the true gospel. Hence, in their minds the "Christians" commit licentious and greedy acts that exploit their followers (cf. Jude 4). The upshot of this is that the churches will suffer a loss of reputation and outsiders will not want to become Christian converts. This fourth point also lends some credibility to the notion that our author is not *merely* stereotyping these opponents as bad apples. He seems genu-

---

44. Although this passage is more relevant for the new converts in the congregations, even some of the members who have been attending the gatherings for a long time could be spirituality immature, similar to the congregation addressed in Hebrews 5:12–6:3.

45. Cf. LSJ, 377. On 2:18, Bigg, *Peter and Jude*, 285, is still worth repeating: "There is great passion in the words. Grandiose sophistry is the hook, filthy lust is the bait, with which these men catch those whom the Lord had delivered or was delivering."

46. The alternative text variant of 2:18 reads "really" or "certainly" (ὄντως: ℵ, C, *Byz*) rather than "scarcely" (ὀλίγως: P^{72}, A, B, Vg, Syr, etc.). In this case the ones who are enticed would not seem to be new converts but more stable Christians who have *certainly* escaped those who live in error. But ὀλίγως has better textual support: cf. Metzger, *Textual Commentary*, 635.

47. On these aspects as a means of defection in contemporary sociological studies of religion, see Wilson, *Leaving the Fold*, 122–24. Concerning defection through intellectual doubt Wilson (29–33, 89–91, 95–99) claims examples from the ancient Jewish and Christian world including, among others, Philo's nephew Tiberius Julius Alexander, the Bar Kokhba Christians, Ammonius, and Julian the Apostate (cf. Josephus, *Ant.* 20.100; Justin, *Apology* 1.31.6; Eusebius, *Hist. eccl.* 4.6.2; 6.19.9).

inely concerned about what outsiders might think regarding the unethical conduct that takes place within the congregations.

Finally, the false teachers will bring swift destruction (ἀπώλεια) upon themselves (2:1, 3). Their condemnation and destruction is repeated or implied throughout the text (2:4–6, 9, 12–13, 17; 2:21; 3:7, 9, 16).[48] The author compares their judgment with the sinning angels who are held captive in the subterranean underworld (*Tartarus*), the ungodly of the ancient world who died in the flood of Noah, and the cities of Sodom and Gomorrah that were condemned while Lot was rescued (2 Pet 2:4–7; cf. Jude 6–7). Another great destruction will take place on the earth at the *parousia* in which the ungodly, including the false teachers, will perish (cf. 3:7, 10–13). *God will separate and protect the righteous but bring condemnation on the unrighteous* (2:9). This verse assumes final salvation for the former and final condemnation for the latter. The idea that God keeps the unrighteous under punishment for judgment day may be understood as either taking place in the present—i.e., they are being punished now and will be punished at the eschaton also—or it could be understood as taking place in the future—i.e., they will be punished at the eschaton. The meaning of the passage probably turns on whether the author thinks a future judgment still awaits the unrighteous who died and are already being punished (2:4–7), or if he has the unrighteous who are still alive in mind. As far as the false teachers are concerned, they are included with the unrighteous that are still alive, and they are not presently being punished. It is not clear whether the apostates' condemnation is fixed. The author's repetitive condemnations of them in chapter 2 would certainly lead us to believe this, but even so, predictions of their destruction do not necessarily mean that every individual apostate must perish; it is possible that God is still giving them opportunity to repent (cf. 3:9). In this case perhaps the sense in 2:9 is that they are being held under *the prospect of punishment* on judgment day.[49]

If final punishment is already present in 2:9, then the passage may assume that once the unrighteous are dead (e.g., the examples from the primordial world of Genesis) there are no more opportunities for them to repent. In other words, both the phenomena of death and the eschaton mark the end of opportunities to repent. For the unrighteous, it seems that punishment begins after death and will reach it full confirmation on judgment day. Conversely, the author reminds the recipients that God will ultimately deliver and vindicate the righteous who persevere through their trials (2 Pet 2:4–10a; cf. Jude 24).[50]

---

48. Cf. Jude 5, 10; Matt 7:13; Rom 9:22; Phil 3:19; 2 Thess 2:3; Heb 10:39.

49. Cf. Witherington, *Hellenized Christians*, 2.354.

50. Πειρασμός in 2:9 may refer to either a trial or temptation (cf. Matt 6:13). Whichever nuance is used, the πειρασμός these recipients faced is probably brought about by their interaction with immoral

BALAAM AND THE TWO WAYS (2:15)

The author then delivers a torrent of accusations denouncing the opponents in 2:11–19. As the passage unfolds, the false teachers' apostasy is discerned through the intertext of Balaam's error. They abandon (καταλείπω) the "straight way" and have gone astray (πλανάω) after the "way of Balaam," who loved the gain of unrighteousness (2:15). Καταλείπω has multiple meanings, but here it is related to apostasy (cf. Sir 28:23; Heb 4:1; *Mart. Pol.* 17.2). Likewise, πλανάω conveys the idea of deception that leads to apostasy (cf. Matt 24:4, 11, 24; Mark 13:5; 2 Tim 3:13; Heb 3:10; Rev 2:20; 13:14; 1 John 1:8). *The false teachers have forsaken the straight path (2:15a)— they have committed apostasy.* Their abandonment engages the motif of two ways commonly found in early Jewish and Christian writings (2 Pet 2:21; cf. Eph. 4:1, 17; 1 Thess 4:1, 5).[51] In particular it interacts with Matt 7:12-19 (cf. 21:32), where Jesus teaches his followers to beware of false prophets whose immoral conduct or "fruit" will always give them away. His followers are to walk the straight path of righteousness over against the path of lawlessness that leads to the false prophets' destruction.[52] As in Matthew and other traditions, the two paths in 2 Pet 2:15 exemplify moral and immoral conduct. In 2 Peter the godly and faithful followers of the Lord are described with terms related to righteousness (1:1, 13; 2:5, 7, 8, 15, 21; 3:13), whereas the ungodly and lawless are considered unrighteous (2:9, 13, 15).[53] The way of truth is likewise understood in terms of righteous conduct (2 Pet 2:2; cf. Ps 118:30 LXX; Tob 1:3; Wis 5:6; CD 3:15; 1QS 4:2; *1 Clem.* 35.5) and here perhaps denotes the Christian message that results in ethical living.[54]

The two ways are the straight way of righteousness (2 Pet 2:15a, 21) and the way of Balaam (2:15b), a venue the false teachers take, and this path leads to destruction.[55] Interestingly the author replaces the way of Cain in Jude 11 with the way of Balaam, perhaps to highlight Balaam's role as a prophet comparable with the false prophets and teachers (cf. 2 Pet 2:1a), and to allude to Israel's turning away (ἀφίστημι: Num

---

people. Notice that Lot's distress is mentioned in the milieu of his compatriots' lawless conduct (2 Pet 2:7-8).

51. See also *Did.* 1–6; *Barn.* 18–20; 1QS 3.18–4.26; Wis 1–6; *1 En.* 91–105; *Sib. Or.* 8.399-401; *Orphica* 5-8; cf. Deut 30:15, 19; Jer. 21:8 and further sources in Niederwimmer, *Didache*, 58–63.

52. Other similarities between 2 Peter and Matthew have been distilled by Dschulnigg, "Theologische Ort," 168–76.

53. The former verses use δικαιοσύνη/δίκαιος; the latter verses use ἄδικος/ἀδικία/ἀδικέω.

54. Cf. Bauckham, *Jude, 2 Peter*, 242.

55. That 2 Peter omits Jude's mention of Cain when the Targums and Hellenistic Jewish sources associate him with Epicurean-like godlessness and denial of afterlife (e.g., *Tg. Neof.* Gen 4:8; *Tg. Ps.-J.* Gen 4:8; Philo, *Worse* 50; 103; 119), weakens the view of Neyrey, *2 Peter, Jude*, 72–73, 124–25. See Caulley, "They Promise Them Freedom," 132n16.

31:16 LXX) from the word of God by sinning with the Moabite women so as to make a connection between apostasy, sexual vice, and false teachers (Num 25; cf. Josephus, *Ant.* 4.140–49; Philo, *Mos.* 1.294–304). Balaam himself is not an apostate; there is no clear evidence that he was on the right path at one time and then turned away from it (see on Jude below). Rather, as a false prophet his disposition typifies the wrong path and he seduces others to join him on that path. The Christians who defected in 2 Pet 2:1 have joined him on the road to destruction. By way of this negative example the Christians are warned against following these deceivers into sexual license (2:14, 18). In short they are warned against assimilation.[56]

DOGS, PIGS, AND DEFECTION FROM THE HOLY COMMANDMENT (2:20–22)

The author ends chapter 2 by saying that if the apostates had escaped the defilements of the world by their knowledge of Christ (i.e., their conversion) and again become entangled and overcome by these defilements, then their last state has become worse than the first. It would have been better for them not to have known the way of righteousness than to turn back from the holy commandment after knowing it (2:20–22). Here again two ways are implied—the way of righteousness would be set in contrast to the way of unrighteousness that Balaam and the false teachers follow, and the author stresses righteousness as an ethical quality.

It is clear that these verses are not speaking about issues that have no correlation with reality. The conversion of these individuals in 2:20a and 21a is assumed and is no less real than their apostasy in 2:20b, 21b, and 22. The "if" (εἰ) in 2:20 is combined with an indicative making it a first-class or "simple" conditional sentence and conveying logical assertions for argument's sake. It can even be translated "since" in some cases (cf. John 1:12; Mark 4:23).[57] Arichea and Hatton rightly affirm regarding 2:20: "The word *if* is used here not to mark a condition that is contrary to fact, but rather to mark a conditional statement that is true. In other words Peter is not questioning or doubting the initial faith of the false teachers (or, recent converts) but is asserting the fact that they had at one time left their heathen loyalties and become members of the Christian community."[58] The proverbial illustration of apostasy "has happened to them" (συμβέβηκεν αὐτοῖς); they have already fallen away.[59] Less clear

---

56. Cf. Caulley, "They Promise Them Freedom," 133–37.
57. See Porter, *Idioms*, 256–57.
58. Arichea and Hatton, *Jude*, 136.
59. If one were to argue from 2:1 that the entire pericope is futuristic (which is difficult to maintain from vv. 10 onward) or that 2:20–22 reflects only the unstable Christians in 2:18–19 who have not yet

is whether the author has in mind the new converts from 2:18b or the false teachers from 2:19a. Conceptual parallels between 2:20-22 and 2:18-19 can be used to support either case.[60] It is probably correct to affirm that both are in view but with an emphasis on the false teachers. They are the ones highlighted in the pericope, and it has already been determined that they were once Christians who turned away from Christ (cf. 2:1, 15).

Several words and phrases underscore this defection. Duane Watson rightly argues that the *exordium* in 1:3-4 is echoed in 2:18-20, where apostasy in the latter text presents the antithesis to the imagery in former. Both passages speak of having knowledge and escaping from the world's corruption. In the first case the promises of God enable the way to escape from corruption in the world that is caused by "passion," but the antithesis has the ones who had escaped the world lured back to corruption by promises made by the false teachers "because of licentious passions of the flesh."[61] The impact of the word "escape" (ἀποφεύγω) in 2:20 mirrors 1:4 and refers to Christian conversion.[62] Both passages convey an escape from the world's immoral influence, whether through corruption (1:4) or defilements (2:20).[63] The word in 1:4, at least, not only suggests ethical corruption but also alludes to spiritual death that leads to final destruction (cf. 2:12).[64] *The author affirms that his faithful recipients have presently escaped the world's immorality (1:4), whereas the apostates had once escaped it but are no longer in this position (2:20-21; cf. 2:1). The clear implication is that the defectors were once as much believing Christians as are the present recipients of the letter.* The recipients are identified by salvific and election terms such as "called," "beloved," partakers of the divine nature, and sharing a common faith with the author (1:1-5; 3:17). If the author would have written this epistle

---

fallen away, then the remark of Kelly, *Peter and Jude*, 344, on v. 22 would seem to be apropos: "what has happened" is "a dramatic perfect which treats what is certain to befall as already accomplished" (350). More correctly, though, as we have argued in 2:1, the apostate teachers were already influencing congregations when this letter was written, and 2:20-22 certainly does not *preclude* them. Hence, v. 22 conveys apostasy as having already happened.

60. E.g., the notions of slavery to and being overpowered by corruption can be applied to the false teachers; the notions of being overpowered and escaping can be applied to the new converts. On the false teachers being in view here, see Fornberg, *Early Church*, 106; Vögtle, *Judasbriefe, 2 Petrusbrief*, 207; etc. Rightly holding to both is Schreiner, *1, 2 Peter, Jude*, 360.

61. Watson, *Invention, Arrangement, and Style*, 122.

62. Rightly, Bauckham, *Jude, 2 Peter*, 277. On the term as escape from error and vice, see Green, *Jude and 2 Peter*, 301.

63. On possible distinctions between corruption (φθορά) and defilement (μίασμα) in these verses, see Davids, *2 Peter and Jude*, 248-49. The latter does not merely refer to cultic defilement but can also relate to vices and criminal offenses: cf. Ezek 33:31; 1 Macc 13:50; Jdt 13:16; *1 En.* 10.22; Josephus, *J.W.* 2.17.10[455].

64. See Kelly, *Peter and Jude*, 346-47.

years earlier when the apostates were still in good standing, he would have no doubt addressed them in a similar way.

After escaping the defilements of the world, "they are again entangled in them" and are defeated or "overpowered" (2:20). The apostates are again entangled (ἐμπλέκω) in the world's defilements, similar to sheep's wool that gets caught in thorns (cf. 2 Tim 2:4; *Herm. Sim.* 6.2.6-7).[65] Although our author uses ἐμπλέκω, the thought drifts close to the idea of ensnarement similar to σκάνδαλον in the Septuagint, which often refers to the apostasy of God's people or their destruction or both (e.g., Josh 23:13; Judg 2:3; Pss 105[106]:35-42; 139[140]:5-6; 140[141]:9; Wis 14:11). The idea of the backslider in 2 Pet 2:20 being overpowered (ἡττάομαι) conveys the thought of succumbing or yielding to the type of corruption that enslaves vicedoers and leads them to eschatological destruction (cf. 2:19; Rom 6:12-19; 2 Tim 2:26; Heb 12:1; *T. Reu.* 5.3; *Barn.* 4.1; 2 *Clem.* 10.1).

They "turn" (ὑποστρέψαι) from the holy commandment passed on to them (2:21). Often ὑποστρέφω is used of one's returning to a certain location (e.g., Gal 1:17; Luke 4:1; Acts 8:25; Josephus, *J.W.* 1.229), but here it involves a returning to one's former state or pattern of beliefs, similar to the metaphoric meaning of ἐπιστρέφω (e.g., Gal 4:9; Mark 4:12; Matt 13:15; cf. 2 Pet 2:21; Jas 5:20).[66] The thought presupposes one of two plausible options: 1) this turning might suggest the notion of one's walking away from the path of righteousness to follow the road to error and destruction, as did Balaam (2:15); 2) the thought is similar to Jesus' parable of the seven unclean spirits who, after being cast out, return back (ὑποστρέφω) to their former human host to make that individual seven times worse (Luke 11:24-26; cf. Matt 12:43-45). In favor of the latter, 2 Pet 2:20 clearly echoes this parable when saying "the last state has become worse for them than the first."[67] *For 2 Peter, believers who fall away are in a worse predicament than their original pre-converted status.*

The reason for the worsened state seems to be twofold: first, if the author has Jesus' story in mind, there is an amplification of wickedness in which the apostate becomes more obdurate to God than before;[68] second, given the context of 2 Peter 2, they are worse off than before because they will have no excuse when they stand

---

65. Cf. BDAG, 324. Green, *Jude and 2 Peter*, 302, relates the term to moral entanglement and apostasy (cf. Prov 28:18; Epictetus, *Discourses* 3.22.69; Polybius 24.11.3; Plato, *Laws* 814E).

66. See further BDAG, 1041 (ὑποστρέφω); cf. 382 (ἐπιστρέφω). Passages in the main text use the latter word.

67. Similar references include *Herm. Sim* 9.17.5-18.2; *Herm. Vis.* 4.2; *Apoc. Pet.* 3; 1 *Clem* 46.8; John 5:41; *Acts. Thom.* 46; Irenaeus, *Haer.* 1.16.3.

68. Unlike Matthew's larger context, however, there is no indication that such a person has committed the unpardonable sin. Apostates, it seems, still have a chance to repent and return to the Lord (cf. 2 Pet 3:8-9; Jude 22-23).

before the Lord on judgment day: "it would have been better for them never to have known the way of righteousness than to have known it and then turn back" (2:21). This pattern bears similarities with a *Tobspruch*, a form of Hebrew wisdom following "better to . . . than to . . ."[69] They possessed conversion knowledge of Christ and the relationship that ensues because of it (cf. ἐπιγινώσκω: 1:2, 8), but afterwards they rejected it.[70] The author may be influenced here by the Jesus saying that the one who knows the Lord's will and does not do it will be judged more severely than the one who did not know the Lord's will (Luke 12:47–48).[71] Hence, Jesus' prophecies of end-time defectors as well as some of his teachings against apostasy provide a significant backdrop for 2 Peter 2.

The apostates turn back from "the holy commandment" (2:21b), which is probably understood as the ethical precepts of Christ as taught by the apostles (cf. 2 Pet 3:2; 1 John 3:23; 5:2; 2 John 6; John 13:34; Gal 6:2; 1 Cor 7:19; 1 Tim 6:14).[72] This would also seem to include acceptance of Christ's lordship and the necessity of following him.[73] Significant parallels may be found in the "commandments" of 2 Clement (though in this source the plural is used). The commandments are given in a context in which the recipients are called to repent and warned against apostasy and the final condemnation it brings (2 Clem. 17). These commandments are ethically based and associated with sayings of Jesus, such as loving God with all one's heart and mind,[74] doing the will of God or Christ,[75] and being faithful.[76] In 2 Peter the holy commandment most likely refers to Jesus' main teachings that bring about a person's sanctification if obeyed. *For the Petrine author, turning back from the holy commandment is tantamount to turning away from Jesus and his ethical teachings.*

Christian defection is then graphically depicted in the imagery of a dog returning to its vomit and a washed pig returning back to its wallowing in the mud (2:22).

---

69. Cf. Snyder, "*Tobspruch*," 117–120. See also *Barn.* 5.4; *Herm. Sim.* 9.17.5; *Herm. Mand.* 5.2.7; 12.5.4.

70. *Contra* NET Bible (notes on 2 Pet 2:20; cf. 1:2), which creates a dichotomy between saving-relational knowledge and merely being outwardly part of a circle of Christ-followers. Judas is provided as an example, but as we have examined, Judas is an authentic disciple in the Synoptic Gospels; he is only inauthentic in John's portrayal of him.

71. Alternatively the "better . . . than" language echoes Jesus' words about apostasy and final judgment in Mark 9:42–48 and 14:21.

72. Bigg, *Peter and Jude*, 286, would associate it with teachings found in the Sermon on the Mount; whereas in Senior and Harrington, *1 Peter, Jude and 2 Peter*, 278, it is more generally the Christian faith (cf. Jude 3; 1 Cor 15:3) similar to the "way of truth" (2:2) and the "way of righteousness" (2:21).

73. Cf. Davids, *2 Peter and Jude*, 251.

74. *2 Clem.* 3.4/Matt 22:36–41 cf. 15:8.

75. *2 Clem.* 4:1–5; 6:7; 8:4/Matt 7:21–23.

76. *2 Clem.* 8:4–6/Matt 25:21, 23; Luke 16:10.

Both dogs and pigs were considered unclean animals by ancient Jews (Matt 15:26–27; Mark 5:11–16; 7:27–28; cf. Ps 21[22]:16–20). For the early Christians, dogs were often associated with false teachers and apostates (Matt 7:6; Phil 3:2; Rev 22:15; *Did.* 9.5; Ign. *Eph.* 7.1).[77] The Petrine author associates beasts with the false teachers (2 Pet 2:12, 16 cf. Jude 10; *Gospel of Truth* 33.15–16). The dog returning to its vomit is derived from Prov 26:11,[78] and it is quite possible that our author has been informed by this book already in 2 Pet 2:10b (cf. 3:3) where Prov 21:24 contrasts the haughty scoffers and the righteous, lending to the authors' two-ways motif.[79]

Nothing in Prov 26 mentions pigs, however. John Elliott claims that in certain circles Epicureans were charged with being hedonistic pigs "wallowing in their self-serving passions."[80] A more plausible subtext for 2 Peter is the story of Ahiqar. In the narrative Nadin, the nephew and adopted son of Ahiqar, betrays him, and this treachery is described by Ahiqar as such: "My son, thou hast been to me like the swine that had been to the baths, and when it saw a muddy ditch, went down and washed in it."[81] Both 2 Peter and Ahiqar relate the pig's going into the mud to the phenomenon of defection; that which is cleansed has become unclean again. For the author of 2 Peter, *the apostate's conversion and washing related to water baptism is reversed by a metaphorical baptism in mud.*

One counter argument that is sometimes brought forth in relation to 2:22 focuses on the nature of the dog and pig, which has never changed. These animals may have been cleaned up outwardly, but inwardly they remain unclean; hence, the proverb allegedly suggests these apostates were never genuine believers.[82] But this meaning stretches the proverb further than what the author likely intended. It was

---

77. See further sources in Nanos, "Paul's Reversal"; LSJ, 1015.

78. On dogs eating vomit see also *Syr. Menander* 2.58.

79. Witherington, *Hellenized Christians*, 2.362, connects 2 Pet 2:20–22 with wisdom sources such as Prov 1:17; 15:17; 21:16 LXX; Eccl 7:2, 5.

80. Elliott, "Peter," 5.285. Elliott does not reference a primary source for this thought. Neyrey, *2 Peter, Jude*, 127–28, does not make the connection with Epicureans here, but in close proximity to this verse he suggests the Hebrew word for "scoffer" (3:4), may be related to the Greek word for "Epicurean."

81. Based on 8.18 of the Syriac version of *Ahiqar*: see OTP 2.487. For other references to pigs wallowing in mud, see Aubineau, "La thème du <<bourbier>>," 201–4.

82. See, e.g., Carson, "2 Peter," 1057–58; Peterson, "Apostasy," 19–20. Similarly Schreiner, *1, 2 Peter, Jude*, 365 writes: "In the final analysis, those who fell away never really changed their nature. They remained dogs and pigs inside. They may have washed up on the outside and appeared to be different, but fundamentally they were dogs and pigs. In other words, they were always unclean; they only seemed to have changed." Dunham, "Exegetical Study of 2 Peter 2:18–22," proposes that sin is at stake rather than apostasy in 2:20–22 (40–54). This view can only be entertained at the great expense of contextual meanings of words and phrases such as ἡττάομαι, ὑποστρέφω, "last state worse than the first," etc., let alone the prominent theme of apostasy that runs throughout 2 Peter. Schreiner (360n117) exposes further weaknesses in Dunham's view.

commonly understood among early Christians that human dispositions and sinful habits could be changed (e.g., 1 Cor 6:9–10; 1 Thess 1:9; Eph 2:1–6), unlike animals, which act only in the way God and nature intended for them (e.g., Luke 9:58; Matt 6:26; 9:36; 10:16; Jas 3:3; cf. Gen 1:20–25). The Petrine author seems to share this view. For him, animals behave the way they do by nature, instinctively (cf. φυσικός: 2 Pet 2:12). Their nature is not expected to change. *The point of the analogy, then, is not that the dog or pig's nature was expected to change, but that after purging and washing they have reversed this cleansing.*[83] More importantly, it should be stressed that the animal analogies primarily show in a graphic way how the apostates had originally escaped sinful defilement (i.e., the metaphors of "vomit" and "mud") and were cleansed from these defilements as Christian converts, only to fall away and return again to their previous state of defilement.

There is no reason to insist that the author's language of God's salvific work among the faithful in 1:1–5 precludes genuine apostasy in 2:20–22.[84] Both divine initiative and human responsibility are assumed in the letter (e.g., 1:5–10), and in all likelihood the Petrine author saw no contradiction in both affirming God's gracious benefits to the Christians in 1:1–5 while at the same time maintaining that Christians are susceptible to falling away and sometimes actually *do* fall away, as in 2:1, 20–22.

---

83. Moreover, in the proverb the dog has not been washed on the *outside*, only the pig. The dog's vomit comes from his stomach, and so his cleansing took place on the *inside* before he returns to consume it. It is possible that this implies that the apostates were once cleansed on the inside (like the dog), perhaps involving inner change and repentance from sin, and washed on the outside (like the pig), involving water baptism (cf. 2 Pet 1:9; 1 Pet 3:21). Problematic with this comparison is that it runs the risk of stretching the analogy further than what the author intended.

84. Contrast Schreiner, *1, 2 Peter, Jude*, 331, 364, who denies genuine apostasy in 2 Peter despite the ramification of the salvific aspect of the word "escape" (ἀποφεύγω) when one compares 1:3–5 with 2:20–22. He explains that "the language used in 2 Peter is phenomenological. In other words, Peter used the language of 'Christians' to describe those who fell away because they gave every appearance of being Christians" (365; cf. 331). But no explanation is given for why we should accept passages such as 2:1, 20–22 as phenomenological while passages such as 1 John 2:19 (used by Schreiner to support that apostates were never genuine believers; cf. 365) should *not* be interpreted along the same phenomenological lines. The original recipients in 2 Peter probably would not have made such an intricate distinction between the phenomenon of apostasy and an allegedly different reality behind it. Both the recipients and their author were unfettered by modernistic theological debates on this issue, and they seem to have no *a priori* reason to deny the false teachers were once genuinely converted and then fell away. Moreover, there is no reason for us to assume that the author of 2 Peter would view apostasy the same way as the Johannine author. They are almost certainly not the same person, and they are responding to different situations, opponents, and false teachings.

THE HOPE OF REPENTANCE FOR ALL (3:9)

In the context of the author's claim that the Day of the Lord will involve judgment against the ungodly and destruction of the fallen world (3:1–13), he encourages his audience that delay of the *parousia* is for their benefit. "The Lord is patient toward you, not wanting any to be destroyed but all to reach repentance" (3:9).[85] The text suggests that human beliefs and actions can contradict God's desires (βούλομαι).[86] The plural "you" in this verse refers to the readers of the letter (cf. 3:1, 8, 14). Thus "all" (πάντας) may be limited to "you." In other words God is being patient with the Christians the Petrine author is addressing (cf. *1 Clem.* 8.5).[87] In early Christian circles the need to repent oftentimes relates to conversion.[88] Sometimes Christians who are already converted are nonetheless commanded to repent of sin and wrongdoing (cf. 2 Cor 7:9–10; *1 Clem.* 8:1–5; *2 Clem.* 17.1; *Herm. Mand.* 4.3.3; *Herm. Vis.* 2.2.5). In some cases apostates are likewise encouraged to repent (2 Tim 2:25; *Herm. Vis* 4.1.3; cf. Jude 22–23). A warning to repent seems relevant, then, at least for the unstable believers and new converts among the recipients who might be influenced by the false teachers (2 Pet 2:14, 18; 3:15–17).

The need for the Christians to repent is confirmed for several reasons. First, the "some" in 3:9a might include congregation members who deny the *parousia* or otherwise hold to false notions about the eschaton. They have been influenced by the false teachers and need to repent. Second, in 3:11–12 the believers are able to speed up, as it were, the *parousia* if they exemplify holiness and godliness. This passage assumes that God would no longer need to delay the end in that case because the recipients have repented or at least live in a way that requires no repentance (cf. 3:9).[89] Third, they must strive to be found blameless (ἀμώμητος) before the Lord on judgment day (2 Pet 3:14; cf. Jude 24; Phil 2:15; Col 1:22), presumably because

---

85. Cf. Rom 2:4; Rev 2:21; *1 En.* 60.5; *2 Bar.* 21.20–21; Justin, *Apology* 1.28. The Majority text has "toward us" rather than "toward you," and other manuscripts have "on account of (διά) you" (e.g., ℵ, A). The better manuscript traditions have "toward (εἰς) you" (p⁷², B, C, cop, etc.; cf. Metzger, *Textual Commentary*, 636).

86. This may be similar to the false prophets who are held responsible for not doing God's will in Matthew 7:21–23; albeit, in Matthew's case θέλημα is used instead of βούλομαι. Differently, Schreiner, *1, 2 Peter, Jude*, suggests two wills in God, a desired and decreed will, and 3:9 points to the former (cf. Ezek 18:32). He holds to this view, in part, by interpreting other texts (e.g., John 6:37; Acts 13:48; Rom 8:29–30) to mean that God ordains only some to be saved (381–82). The view allows for some of God's desires to be frustrated or otherwise not come to pass. Highly questionable in 2 Peter is the idea of God selecting only some individuals to be saved, a view that is not clearly supported in this letter.

87. Cf. Kraftchick, *Jude, 2 Peter*, 162: all cannot be saved (e.g., 3:6–7) and so the "all" refers to the audience "who have repented or will soon repent."

88. E.g., Luke 5:32; Acts 11:18; 26:20; Ign. *Eph.* 10.1; *Herm. Sim.* 8.11.1.

89. On 2 Pet 3:12 see further, Witherington, *Hellenistic Christians*, 2.378–79.

they might be rejected if they do not repent. Fourth, they are to consider the Lord's delay as salvation (2 Pet 3:15a), which seems to echo the thought in 3:9, making repentance a prerequisite for their final salvation. We could infer from this pericope that unrepentant Christians whose beliefs and actions have been influenced by the false teachers will not be saved. The Lord is delaying his coming because their very salvation is at stake (3:15a). The author does not want them to be judged and punished along with the ungodly (3:7). Interestingly, these would seem to be the very Christians he affirms as "called," "beloved," and sharing in the same gracious faith of the author (1:1, 3: 3:1, 8, 14).

Then again, the author might have in mind the scoffers when mentioning in 3:9 that "some" think the Lord is delaying his promise. If so, then it would seem that they too are able to repent and avoid perishing.[90] Certain scholars interpret the emphatic "all" (πάντας) in this verse to mean *all people*.[91] In short, the "all" may be a call for everyone to repent—those who are Christians, those who are apostates, and those who have never been converted. It is also evident from other Christian traditions that God desires all humanity to be saved (e.g., 1 Tim 2:4–6; 4:10; Titus 2:11). In any case, it is not likely that 2 Peter is presenting absolute universalism here if the author affirms divine judgment against the unrighteous at the *parousia* (3:6–7; cf. 2:4–9). Possibly God's desire is fulfilled in a corporate sense, having all nations come to repentance but not necessarily every individual (cf. Matt 24:14; John 12:32; Rev 7:9–14; Rom 11:32).[92] The "all" would seem to include a possibility for the apostates to be restored. Karl Kuhn claims that "even vermin such as the false teachers may be called to repentance [and this] challenges the neat dichotomy characteristic of apocalyptic thought that otherwise pervades the letter . . . God's mercy subverts rigid categories and confident expectations of who will and will not be counted among the faithful."[93] In the end, even though the addressees seem to be primarily in view in this pericope, *the "all" in 3:9 is vague enough to include not only the Christians but also the unbelieving world and even the apostates.*

FALLING FROM STEADFASTNESS (3:17)

The letter closes not only with a charge for the recipients to grow in grace and knowledge, but it also warns them against committing apostasy (3:17–18). The beloved are

---

90. E.g., Davids, *2 Peter and Jude*, 281.
91. E.g., Fuchs and Reymond, *Saint Pierre, Saint Jude*, 116.
92. See further examples in Str.B. 3.774.
93. Kuhn, "2 Peter 3:1–13," 311–13, quote from 312. See also Richards, *Reading 1 Peter, Jude, and 2 Peter*, 380–81.

to take heed against the error of lawless individuals and guard themselves against falling from their own steadfastness (3:17). This statement, in fact, may encapsulate the purpose of the book: it is a "wake-up call" for the Christians to be on guard. Peter Davids, who maintains this view, says of the letter's purpose: "It is a pointing out of the error of the lawless men and women so that, seeing the error and its danger, the addressees will recoil from it and remain secure."[94] The Christians must not be "carried away" by the false teachers. Συναπάγω refers to being led astray (cf. Gal 2:13), and here the nuance may be similar to the root verb ἀπάγω, pointing again to two ways. They must stay on the righteous path; the wrong way leads (ἀπάγω) to destruction and is hosted by false teachers and prophets who seduce followers with their deceptive teachings and immoral lifestyle (cf. Matt 7:13–15). If the recipients of the letter are not careful they could lose their "steadfastness" (στηριγμός: 3:17), which probably suggests that their stability in the truth of the Christian message could be lost, much the same way that the unstable fall prey to the false teachers (cf. ἀστήρικτος: 2:14; 3:16).[95] The notion of steadfastness in this case is not much different than perseverance.[96] *To "fall" from steadfastness, then, is to fall away from the truth of the Christian message* (cf. ἐκπίπτω: Gal 5:4). The believers who have been called and allotted faith by God are still susceptible to the errors of the false teachers, and like these teachers, they are vulnerable to committing apostasy at the present time and so be destroyed at the eschaton.

CONCLUSION

The letter of 2 Peter reflects a community of recipients acculturated with Hellenistic thought and language as well as having some knowledge of Jewish traditions. They are probably Gentile Christians who belong to churches previously influenced by Paul (cf. 2 Pet 3:15). The Petrine author warns them against false teachers inside the church, who have brought with them an eclectic blend of worldly philosophies and corrupt ethics. The passage 2:1—3:4 borrows from Jude, but it is not clear that they face the same opponent. The author of 2 Peter reconfigures information from Jude to address the specific situation of his recipients. It is possible that the opponents are a dissident Pauline group who have distorted the teachings of Paul's gospel of

---

94. Davids, *2 Peter and Jude*, 312.

95. The term ἀστήρικτος in these verses may be contrasted with the related στηριγμός in 3:17. Likewise, the more positive στηρίζω in 2 Pet 1:12 is related to στηριγμός. On the word relationships, see Kraus, *Sprache*, 328, 356.

96. We notice that Harder, "στηρίζω," 7.657, in fact denotes στηριγμός as "perseverance" and compares its meaning with 2 Pet 1:12 and 2 John 9.

grace and delayed *parousia* and use such teachings as a license for immoral living (3:15–16). The author considers the opponents to be false teachers and apostate Christians (2:1, 20–22), and assimilation to immoral ways of Hellenistic outsiders seems to be a major threat they pose. Unless entirely stereotyped by the author's vituperative language, vices such as greed and sexual excesses seem to be practiced by the opponents (2:3, 14, 18). From our author's perspective, the false teachers were once redeemed by Christ but are now apostates. They deny his lordship by means of their immoral lifestyle and denial of the *parousia* (2:1, 20–22; 3:3–7). They are said to teach "heresies," (2:1), false teachings that stray from the centrality of the apostolic message, belief in Jesus as Lord, and obedience to Christ's ethical precepts.

Their apostasy is also described in terms of two ways: they turn from the way of righteous to the way of Balaam, which triggers for the recipients thoughts about Balaam as a false prophet who leads astray the Israelites and instigates them to commit fornication with outsiders, Moabite women in this case (2 Pet 2:15; cf. Num 25). They reject Christ's ethical precepts and have become all the worse for it, similar to Jesus' story of the man who is cleansed of one wicked spirit and then becomes worse when seven spirits possess him. Their apostasy reverts their conversion and cleansing from sin, and it is depicted as a dog returning to his vomit and a washed pig returning to the mud (2 Pet 2:20–22). They were once authentic believers who are now apostates and will suffer eschatological destruction (3:10–12; cf. 2:1, 3–6, 9; 3:16). Unstable Christians and new converts are especially susceptible to the false teachers, and all Christians need to practice virtues with faith as the foundation so that they do not fall away, whether as gradual defectors (1:5–13), precipitate defectors (2:18), or intellectual doubters (cf. 2:1; 3:1–4). They must also beware that they do not apostatize from the stability they enjoy through the truth of the Christian message (3:17–18). The *parousia* has been delayed so that all people, both Christians and non-Christians, would repent and be saved (3:8–9). This repentance is presumably open for the apostate teachers as well. Those who do not repent will be destroyed at the eschaton.

In suggesting the possibility of restoration 2 Peter may have been influenced by Jude. The latter epistle addresses apostate teachers that are infiltrating the congregations, in this case a Jewish Christian community or communities are being threatened (cf. Jude 4–6, 11–13), and it stresses more clearly than 2 Peter the possibility of the apostates' restoration, even false teachers who bring about the apostasy of other Christ-followers (Jude 22–23). Both 2 Peter and Jude may be set in contrast with the communities in Matthew and John, which consider false teachers to have never been authentic believers. More clearly than most New Testament writings, 2 Peter emphasizes the apostates as once genuine believers who were redeemed and delivered from the defilements of the fallen world, much the same way he speaks of his recipients whom he identifies as "called" and "beloved" (1:3–4; 3:17). As apostates they are now set on a course for divine destruction. If the opponent in 2 Peter is a Paulinist libertine group, this evinces one more time that various communities in the New Testament confessed Christ but served him rather differently. What is not supported in 2 Peter is the idea that the Petrine and authentic Pauline communities were set at odds. The author calls Paul "our beloved brother" (3:15).

5

Jude

Antinomianism and the Vilification of Apostate Church Intruders

The epistle of Jude purports to be written by the brother of James and is traditionally attributed to the half-brother (or step-brother) of Jesus.[1] Scholarship today is divided over the identity of the author; a number favor the letter as pseudonymous.[2] Both sides posit various support for their positions.[3] If the letter is pseudonymous it is odd that the author would choose to call himself "Judas," a name permanently etched in early Christian memory with someone who betrayed Jesus. And even though he specifies himself as a different Judas, the brother of James, we

---

1. Mark 6:3; Matt 13:55; 1 Cor 9:5; Acts 1:14; Eusebius, *Hist. eccl.* 1.7.14; 3.19.1–20.6. Supporters of Jude as the author include e.g., Bauckham, *Relatives of Jesus*, 171–78; Charles, *Literary Strategy*, 65–90; Knoch, *Petrusbrief, Judasbrief*, 159–62; Hiebert, *Second Peter and Jude*, 185–95.

2. E.g., Heiligenthal, *Zwischen Henoch und Paulus*, 24; Rowston, "Most Neglected Book," 559–61; Vögtle, *Judasbriefe, 2 Petrusbrief*, 4–11; Horrell, *Peter and Jude*, 103.

3. Those who favor a pseudonym notice, e.g.: 1) the problem of false teachers and the polemic stereotypes against them as a later development beyond the first generation of Christ-followers; 2) the mention of the "faith" as delineating the content of apostolic teaching rather than personal faith (Jude 3); 3) the author's reference to the apostles as though they lived in an earlier time (Jude 17–18); 4) no mention of Jesus as the author's brother; and 5) a Greek style that betrays a Greek writer, not a Galilean Jew whose early business may have been carpentry. Those maintaining Jude as the author respond that: 1) the document need not be a late work on the basis of its polemical style; 2) "faith" in Jude 3 refers to the early gospel message, not a rule of faith (cf. Gal 3:23; 1 Cor 16:13); 3) Jude 17–18 only suggests that some apostles previously visited and instructed the recipients, not that they had all already died; 4) Jude's omission of Jesus as his brother is an argument from silence, particularly if he considers him to be "Lord" (Jude 4); and 5) Galilee was influenced by Hellenism, quite possibly to the extent that Jude would have known Greek, especially if he did missionary work among Gentile converts (cf. 1 Cor 9:5).

wonder why he would not choose a better-known leader. It seems more plausible for us to accept the writing as authentically from Jude or at least conveying one of his messages. We will approach the letter as originating from a Galilean Jew who was the brother of James and Jesus.[4] Jude seems to write as though James is still alive (Jude 1), which causes us to lean towards a date for this letter before James' martyrdom (c. 62 CE).[5] Speculations abound on the recipients' location,[6] and one view suggests it was an encyclical covering many areas.[7] We will leave the location unknown.[8] The author cites Jewish sources and apocalyptic traditions that are no doubt familiar to the recipients, and so perhaps the best option for their identity would be Jewish Christians.[9] Jude may be writing to one or more Jewish Christian communities.

THE OPPONENTS AS APOSTATE CHRISTIAN INTRUDERS (3-4; CF. 5-10)

In the last few decades a growing number of exegetes have abandoned libertine or emergent Gnostics as the teachers denounced by Jude, an older view that was once widely held.[10] Other scholars identify the opponents as liberated *pneumatikoi* similar to extremists in 1 Corinthians,[11] or Pauline antinomianists indulging in ecstatic experiences and scorning angelic powers (Rom 3:8; 6:1; Col 2:18),[12] or itinerant charismatics infiltrating the congregation, rejecting authority (Jude 4, 8-10), living

---

4. For further study, see Bauckham, *Relatives of Jesus*; idem, *Jude, 2 Peter*, 3-17; and on the letter's Palestinian matrix see e.g., Gerdmar, *Rethinking the Judaism-Hellenism Dichotomy*. For early church allusions or references to the letter, see Bigg, *St. Peter and St. Jude*, 307-8; Fuchs and Reymond, *Saint Pierre, Saint Jude*, 149-50.

5. Bauckham, *Jude, 2 Peter*, 15, notices Jude does not include an epithet such as "blessed" or "just" for James (cf. Eusebius, *Hist. eccl.* 2.23.4; *Gos. Thom.* 21), descriptors one might expect if he were already dead.

6. E.g., Gerdmar, *Rethinking the Judaism-Hellenism Dichotomy*, 30-63, 278-323 (Palestine); Paulsen, *Zweite Petrusbrief und der Judasbrief*, 45 (Alexandria); Grundmann, *Judasbrief*, 15 (Syria); Davids, *2 Peter, Jude*, 22 (Galilee-Syria); Schnelle, *Einleitung*, 418 (Asia Minor).

7. E.g., Joubert, "Persuasion in the Letter of Jude," 78.

8. With Fuchs and Reymond, *Saint Pierre, Saint Jude*, 144.

9. See Harrington, *Jude and 2 Peter*, 187; Witherington, *Jewish Christians*, 577-79.

10. For the Gnostic or proto-Gnostic positions see e.g., Frankemölle, *1 Petrusbrief, 2 Petrusbrief, Judasbrief*, 124-25; Kelly, *2 Peter, Jude*, 231; Werdermann, *Irrlehrer des Judas*. The proto-Gnostic tendency is still supported by, e.g., Viljoen, "Faithful Christian Living amidst Scoffers," 514. The opponents as Essenes, a view presented by Daniel, "La mention des Esséniens," 503-21, has not won a strong following. For discussion on the various views related to the opponents, see Bauckham, *Jude and the Relatives*, 162-68.

11. E.g., Senior and Harrington, *1 Peter, Jude and 2 Peter*, 181-82.

12. E.g., Sellin, "Häretkier des Judasbriefes," 206-25.

immorally (6–8, 10), speaking against angels (8–10), and spreading their doctrine to the recipients at common meals (11–13).[13] It is certainly possible for the opponents to have misconstrued Pauline teachings to the extent of celebrating charismatic excesses or antinomianism or both, but such a view seems to go beyond what the text actually says. If 2 Peter condemns such a rival (cf. 2 Pet 3:16–17), this should not be used as a reliable guide for determining that Jude does likewise, despite verbal similarities between the two letters.

One rather difficult question to determine is the extent to which Jude's polemics accurately portray the opponents' practices once we consider exaggerations and conventionalities in his message. The opponents are no doubt a real threat to the community (4, 22–23),[14] but this should not make us assume the complete accuracy of Jude's description of them, especially when he is discouraging his audience against following them. The "beloved" (3, 17, 20) are set in contrast to "these" (οὗτοι) ungodly individuals (8–16), so as to foster an attitude of us-versus-them. The author portrays them as ungodly intruders from another space outside the community (4). In this manner, as Robert Webb rightly affirms, Jude presents them as the "other," and so drives a wedge between his opponents and the audience who are encouraged to view them as having a maligned character or "negative *ēthos*."[15] William Brosend distills twenty-five charges against the opponents in this brief letter and rightly concludes the letter as an exercise in "rhetorical overkill."[16] Once the author's words are stripped away of denunciations and negative stereotypes, little is left to ascertain about the situation behind the letter or the aberrant doctrines promulgated by the opponents.[17] Jerome Neyrey perceptively says, "We have only Jude's labeling of the situation, and we do not know how his rivals would describe it."[18]

Even so, unique to the opponents is their speaking against angels and feasting at church dinners (8–10, 12), which may go beyond the author's typical rhetoric to convey their actual practices. The situation centers on outsiders who infiltrate the church and are influencing congregation members (3–4). If they share in the *agape*

---

13. E.g., Bauckham, *Jude, 2 Peter*, 11–12.

14. And not merely a general one, as maintained by Wisse, "Jude in the History of Heresiology," 133–43, who interprets the letter as an "eschatological tract" generally against end-time false prophets as "heretics."

15. Webb, "Rhetorical Function of Visual Imagery," 128.

16. Brosend, "Letter of Jude," 292–305, quote from 304. On one end the accusations may be boiled down to a traditional list of "seven deadly sins" (sloth, lust, anger, pride, envy, gluttony, greed), and on the other they may be relegated to twenty-five *ad hominem* insults. Brosend opts for a *via media* position.

17. An approach that attempts to derhetoricize this letter is in Thurén, "Hey Jude!," 451–65.

18. Neyrey, *2 Peter, Jude*, 53.

dinners, they probably claim to be followers of Christ. As we will observe through text, *the author clearly thinks they live immorally and considers them apostates, former Christians who now threaten the faithful community* (cf. 5–8, 11–16). The fact that Jude encourages the saints to win back those who embrace such a view (see on vv. 22–23 below) suggests that we are not *merely* dealing with vilifications when it comes to the opponents' adverse behavior and infiltration in the congregation.[19] This position nonetheless can only be determined from the author's perspective, and so his point of view is what we must pursue. It is doubtful that the opponents would consider themselves apostates and accept Jude's associating them with reprobates from Israel's tradition-history and bad flukes of nature.

DENYING CHRIST THROUGH IMMORAL LIVING (3–4)

Jude's writing is structured as a letter, but a large portion of its inner content reads as a miniature homily denouncing the false teachers by appealing to the Hebrew scriptures and early Jewish traditions. Rhetorically speaking, it is deliberative in attempting to persuade the audience to take positive action in contending for the faith (3, 20–23), but it is epideictic in placing blame on the opponents in the present.[20] The author wants the recipients to affirm with him that the intruders are ungodly and will be judged by God at the eschaton.[21] Jude 3 begins with conventional language of the author "having all eagerness" to write to them about their common salvation or well-being.[22] The author builds rapport with the audience before stating the purpose of the writing: they must contend earnestly for the gospel faith once delivered to the saints. It is not entirely clear that anything significant can be deciphered about the situation on the basis of whether Jude was already writing a letter to them, or was intending to do so, before allegedly hearing bad news about false teachers in their congregation.[23] Possibly, this thought made it expedient for him to write them urgently

19. Contrast Thurén, "Hey Jude!," 459.

20. Joubert, "Persuasion in the Letter of Jude," 79, considers Jude as epideictic. If the thesis stands in Jude 3, however, this would seem to suggest a deliberative emphasis as Watson, *Invention, Arrangement, and Style*, 32–34, stresses. The letter's arrangement includes the exordium and thesis (*propositio*) in verse 3, exposition on the nature of the case in dispute (*narratio*) in v. 4, and vv. 5–19 are the supporting proofs (*probatio*). The concluding unit (*peroratio*) in vv. 20–23 gives final exhortations in which the central thesis in v. 3 is reiterated and amplified: the believers are to build up and contend for the faith.

21. See Webb, "Eschatology of the Epistle of Jude," 148–50. Yet paradoxically, Jude seems to hold out a hope for their restoration (22–23).

22. Cf. 2 Pet 1:5, 10; *Barn.* 4.9; Richard, *Reading 1 Peter, Jude, and 2Peter*, 250.

23. For the debate on whether Jude was already writing them or intended to, see especially Vögtle, *Judasbrief, 2 Petrusbrief*, 21–23. On the Greek manuscripts of this verse see Wasserman, *Text and Transmission*, 248.

about the threat. Then again, the noun ἀνάγκην may be conventional for epistolary openings so that Jude is not stressing a sudden hazard but is politely apologizing for not writing to them sooner. He now finds it "suitable" (ἀνάγκην) to inform them about contending for the faith.[24]

The opponents are not necessarily teaching a set of false doctrines or distorted Christology. Based on the numerous charges against them, *their error revolves around a lifestyle that is so immoral and out of sync with the authentic gospel message that Jude considers their behavior and works to be a denial of Christ* (4d). An early hallmark of apostasy centered on denial as a believer's public repudiation of Christ in the face of persecution (Matt 10:33; 26:70–72; Luke 12:9; 2 Tim 2:12; Rev 2:13; *Diognetus* 10.7). For Jude the opponents' denial of Christ does not result from persecution or false teachings about the nature of Christ but from their ungodly deeds. Their actions demonstrate their essential repudiation of righteousness and holiness brought about through Christ and the message of faith (cf. ἀρνέομαι in 2 Pet 2:1; Titus 1:16; *Herm. Sim.* 8.1–3[74]).[25] From the author's perspective they do not submit to Christ as their master; therefore, he is not lord of their lives. In this sense they embrace antinomianism, though not necessarily as Pauline libertines. No doubt *the opponents would see things differently; they confess Christ rather than deny him, and this is how they gained entrance into the community of the faithful*.[26]

Jude 4 also claims the intruders pervert God's grace in order to engage in sensual practices. The word ἀσέλγεια frequently appears in vice lists in the New Testament and conveys sexual excess.[27] Given the high content of sexual innuendos in Jude, sexual license is likely the predominant thought here (cf. Jude 6–8; 2 Cor 12:21; Gal 5:19; Eph 4:19).[28] Μετατίθημι can mean "to turn away" or "to desert" and finds audience in sources depicting a change of loyalties or desertion from ancestral traditions and ideology (2 Macc 7:24; Diog. Laër. *Lives* 7.37, 166; Polybius, *Histories* 5.111.8; 24.9.6).[29] Paul uses it to describe the Galatians turning away from God to

---

24. Cf. Thurén, "Hey Jude!," 456, who argues that both σωτηρία and ἀνάγκη are commonly used in Greek for conventional letters. See also Koskenniemi, *Studien zur Idee*, 67–87.

25. Reese, *2 Peter and Jude*, 78, understands the denial in terms of Christology and soteriology: "One way to deny Jesus Christ is to fail to acknowledge that he is the master, the one who brings both salvation and destruction."

26. If the recipients knew the individuals whom Jude warns them against, his words may have even came as a shock to them. Along these lines is Webb, "Rhetorical Function of Visual Imagery," 127–28, who rightly sees that Jude's words about their denying Christ do not reflect the opponents' language, especially given that they were allowed into the community and may have even been teachers (cf. Jude 12).

27. See Goldstein, "ἀσέλγεια," 1.169; Bauernfeind, "ἀσέλγεια," 1.490.

28. The word ἀσέλγεια often leans toward sexual license (cf. Goldstein, 1.169).

29. Cf. Neyrey *2 Peter, Jude*, 55–56.

follow a different gospel (cf. Gal 1:6). On this view the word in Jude suggests the opponents have deserted God's grace for an immoral lifestyle. However, μετατίθημι often takes on this meaning in the middle voice,[30] but in Jude 4 the verb is active and so it perhaps means "to change," "transfer," or "pervert." In either case, from Jude's perspective the opponents reject God's grace. They distort the unmerited favor of God into cheap grace and a license to sin (cf. Rom 6:1). Arichea and Hatton may be on track here regarding the perverting of grace: "They seem to think that, since God loves people so much that he forgives them of their sins, people can commit as many sins as they like, for the more they sin the more God loves them."[31]

The author continues that the intruders' punishment was written down long ago (Jude 4b; cf. Rom 15:4). This does not mean that God predestined them as rebels to be condemned forever, nor does it refer to their deeds being written on heavenly tablets that will be opened on judgment day to show their condemnation is well deserved.[32] Rather, their self-induced immoral lifestyle finds its antiquarian "type" in prophetic divine judgments against the ungodly. In this case the author probably has Enoch in mind, whom he believes prophesied about the coming judgment against the ungodly back at the beginning of Israel's tradition history (Jude 14-15/1 En. 1.9; cf. Gen 5:18-24).[33] Their condemnation is not fixed, however. If Jude believes they still have a chance to be restored (Jude 22-23), then they are not locked into fulfilling the typology. Their future judgment is best understood as hypothetically prefigured through the ancient predictions.

Several times in the letter Jude stresses the intruders as "ungodly" (ἀσεβής, ἀσέβεια, ἀσεβεῖν: 4c, 15-16, 18), perhaps another indication from verse 4 that he already has the prophecy of Enoch in mind, which uses the word repetitively (14-15). To this end the intruders are said to deny the only Master and Lord Jesus Christ, similar to the ungodly in Enoch denying the "name of the Lord of the Spirits" (1 En. 38:2; 41:2; 45:2; 46:6; 48:10).[34] The ungodly are contrasted with elect and holy

30. Cf. BDAG, 642.

31. Arichea and Hatton, *Jude*, 18.

32. The former is supported in *1 En.* 108.7, but this appendix to Enoch would probably not be known to Jude (so Bauckham, *Jude, 2 Peter*, 35). The latter is affirmed by Charles, *Literary Strategy*, 100-101, and *1 En.* 89.61-64; 90.14-22; 1QS 7.2; 10:6-8; *Jub.* 5.13; *2 Bar.* 24.1; Exod 32:32-33; Rev 20:12. In some cases the entire human history may be written down in advance (e.g., *1 En.* 81.12; 93.1-3; *T. Ash.* 7.5), but as Bauckham, *2 Peter*, 35, rightly questions, how would Jude have known what was written on the tablets?

33. Hence "this" condemnation (τοῦτο τὸ κρίμα) looks forward to the judgments the author presents starting with Jude 5 and culminating with vv. 14-15. Jude seems to use both oral and written sources. The Enoch text resembles Aramaic and Greek versions, and when our author alludes to Israel's scriptures, a Hebrew version rather than the LXX seems to be used. See Bauckham, *Jude, 2 Peter*, 6-7.

34. Cf. Charles, *Literary Strategy*, 191.

ones and will suffer divine judgment on God's day of visitation (*1 En.* 1:1, 9; cf. 2 Pet 2:5–6; 3:7; Rom 1:18; *1 Clem.* 14.5; *Barn.* 15.5). In Jude they are ungodly because they are immoral. Francois Viljoen says it well when he writes that although the words conveying ἀσεβής "in general refer to disrespect of God or gods, in Jewish context they had a strong ethical connotation. A disrespectful attitude towards God results in conduct, which has no respect for the will of God."[35]

DENOUNCING APOSTATES, PAST AND PRESENT (5–10)

Jude 5–19 is devoted to denouncing the intruders. Our author uses a number of Jewish Second Temple writings in this section.[36] In several of these sources a pattern of divine judgment against the wilderness generation, fallen angels, and/or Sodom (5–7) is found (Sir 16:6–14; 3 Macc 2:4–7; *T. Naph.* 3.4–5; *Jub.* 20.2–7; CD 2.17–3.12; cf. 2 Pet 2:4–8).[37] Among those who have no portion in the world to come, for example, *m. Sanhedrin* 10.2–3 includes the flood generation, the men of Sodom, the wilderness generation, Balaam, and Korah. All are mentioned in Jude.

The wilderness generation was saved from Egypt by the "Lord" or "Jesus" (Jude 5).[38] Despite the effectiveness of this deliverance, the Lord eventually acted a "second time" (δεύτερον), this time in judgment, destroying the wilderness generation because of their unbelief.[39] Jude's Jewish audience, steeped in traditions rich with examples of apostasy, would have understood this verse as one of many accounts of God saving his people and afterward destroying them on account of their rebellion against him. The audience was already fully informed about such things (5a), and so Jude reminds them of what they had been previously taught. Likewise, in early

---

35. Viljoen, "Faithful Christian Living amidst Scoffers," 515.

36. See Schlosser, "Les jours de Noé," 13–36; Wolthuis, "Jude and Jewish Traditions," 21–41; Charles, *Literary Strategy*, 91–166.

37. Cf. Bauckham, *Jude, Peter*, 46–47; Watson, *Jude*, 189.

38. For the former designation see Wasserman, *Text and Transmission*, 262–66. For the latter, see P^{72} [God Christ], A, B, 33, 81, vg.; Osburn, "Text of Judas 5," 107–15. Also compare 1 Cor 10:4, 9; Heb 11:26; and the son of man who sits in judgment (*1 En.* 69.26–29). It is possible, perhaps even likely, that if Jude did not originally include "Jesus" in Jude 5, he still understood Jesus as the "Lord" of v. 5 (cf. v. 4). In either case it cannot be derived sufficiently from the acceptance of Christological preexistence in Jude that the opponents denied this, *pace* Osburn, 113.

39. Kraftchick, *Jude, 2 Peter*, 37, writes that ἅπαξ refers to "a quality of God's liberation of Israel. God's action was 'once for all' and should have been sufficient for Israel's full deliverance into the promised land, but Israel's disobedience rendered it ineffective." However, the original placement of ἅπαξ after ὅτι is found only in some of the important manuscripts (e.g., ℵ, C). It may have stood originally behind εἰδότας, as in P^{72}, B, A, *TR*, etc. (see Metzger, *Textual Commentary*, 657). If so, then "once for all" refers to the audience's previous knowledge of the exodus story, not the deliverance of the exodus people.

Christian circles the wilderness generation is portrayed as a prime case of apostasy to stir Christians away from following this negative example (1 Cor 10:1-12; Heb 3-4). Jude implies that Christians are the antitype of the Israelites.

The source in verse 5 is probably oral or simply ad hoc, but Israel's rebellion in the wilderness is lucidly portrayed in Num 11-25, in which many of the people did not make it to Canaan because of their unbelief (cf. Jude 5),[40] grumbling against God (cf. 16), rebelling against Moses and Aaron during the Korah incident (cf. 11), and committing sexual immorality with the Moabite women (at the instigation of Balaam according to later traditions; cf. 11). Many were destroyed in the wilderness (ἀπόλλυμι: Jude 5; cf. vv. 10c, 11d; John 3:14-16). *By way of this hypothetical type, the author anticipates the fate of the intruders who will be eschatological destroyed* (cf. Jude 14-15).[41] The wilderness generation's apostasy in Jude 5 centered on unbelief, and perhaps the point of comparison is intended to convey the intruders' unfaithfulness to Christ.[42]

Several arguments have been presented against our understanding of this passage as an authentic case of apostasy: 1) a comparative analogy between Israel and the church does not relate to every aspect; 2) not all the Israelites genuinely belonged to God; those who apparently fall away demonstrate they are not truly God's people; 3) responses to biblical warnings determine retrospectively who is an authentic believer;[43] and 4) Jude 1, 24-25 promises that God (or Christ) will preserve for final salvation those whom he had called.[44] Five points make this counter position unreliable:

First, although typology between Israel and the church often breaks down at intricate levels, the point on apostasy is not one of them. This phenomenon is

---

40. Cf. Num 14:11.

41. See further 2 Pet 2:1, 12; 3:9; 1 Cor 1:18; 8:11; Rom 14:15; Oepke, "ἀπόλλυμι," 1.395-96.

42. Similarly, Perkins, *Peter, James, and Jude*, 149.

43. E.g., Schreiner, *1, 2 Peter, Jude*, 447: "We ought not necessarily to conclude ... that the Israelites liberated from Egypt were truly circumcised in heart, that they truly belonged to the people of God. Indeed, those who sinned in the wilderness and were then judged demonstrated that they did not truly belong to the Lord at all, that they did not have circumcised hearts in the first place ... Those who 'apostatize' reveal that they were not truly members of God's people (cf. 1 John 2:19). Responses to warnings reveal, retrospectively, who really belongs to the people of God."

44. In Jude 1 the dative phrase Ἰησοῦ Χριστῷ τετηρημένοις could mean "kept for Jesus Christ" with God as the implied agent (most versions); or "kept by Jesus Christ" (NIV); or ambiguous enough to retain both meanings (NET footnote); or "kept through union with Jesus Christ (Goodspeed), assuming a relational model similar to Pauline literature. The preservation of those who are called, in any event, is for the eschaton (cf. 1 Pet 1:4-5; 1 Thess 5:23; *1 En.* 100.5; Kratz, "τηρέω," 3.354-55). The threefold expression of *called*, *loved*, and *kept* seems influenced by the Isaianic tradition, in which Israel is divinely called (Isa 41:9; 42:6; 48:12), loved (42:1; 43:4), and kept (42:6; 49:8). See Arichea and Hatton, *Jude*, 7. The recipients of Jude's letter are clearly identified as God's people.

supported elsewhere in Jude 4, 6, 11, 12, 22–23 as well as comparative accounts in Israel's scriptures and Second Temple literature (as we noticed above) and similar early Christian sources that compare aspects of the wilderness generation with the church (e.g., 2 Pet 2; 1 Cor 10:1–12; Heb 3–4).

Second, examples of inauthentic individuals who are only outwardly God's people, such as in 1 John 2:19, involve different situations than what we find in Jude and should not be used as a panacea to explain other accounts of apostasy.

Third, the idea that biblical warnings only reveal who genuinely belongs to God is not something Jude himself teaches. The argument introduces theological ideas foreign to our text, often with the circular presupposition that all those who fall away are not genuine.

Fourth, the promises of perseverance in Jude 1, 24–25 are informed, in part, by conventional language typical of opening pericopes and closing comments of blessing in ancient Christian letters (e.g., 2 Pet 1:1–11; 1 Cor 1:1–9; Phil 1:1–6; 1 Thess 5:23–24; *1 Clem.* 64). Such sayings generally are intended to foster good will and encouragement to the readers. Nowhere in the actual heart of Jude's letter, which has a distinct thesis and supporting proofs, is the promise of perseverance mentioned. Rather, in the body of the message apostasy is affirmed as a reality (e.g., Jude 5, 11) and perseverance includes the recipients' responsibility to keep *themselves* in God's love (21).[45] Jude assumes that God graciously works with, through, and in his people, and these people as individuals are able to reject God's grace. The sad irony of the wilderness generation is that, in Israel's traditions, the faithful God did in fact "keep" the people of Israel throughout their wanderings in the wilderness, but only a remnant; the rest were punished by death on account of their various sins and apostasies. A similar tragedy will result in final destruction for the opponents who are former Christians. One plausible inference that can be drawn from this is that the beloved recipients who are presently kept by God might also fall away if they do not keep themselves in the love of God (cf. 21).[46] The "love of God" could mean that they are to persevere in their love for God or that they must continue in God's love for them (Jude 1; cf. John 15:9). In either case, their perseverance requires an action or appropriate response on their part. Bauckham, who opts for the latter nuance, rightly says in relation to ἑαυτοὺς ἐν ἀγάπῃ θεοῦ τηρήσατε: "Without obedience to God's will, fellowship with God can be forfeited, and this is the danger with which the anti-

---

45. Vögtle, *Judasbrief, 2 Petrusbrief*, 18, rightly sees that the sense of keeping in Jude 1, in light of vv. 20f, is not referring to absolute predestination.

46. On "beloved" as a term related to election, see Rom 1:7; 2 Thess 2:13; Deut 32:15; Fuchs and Reymond, *Saint Pierre, Saint Jude*, 155.

nomian doctrine of the false teachers threatens the church."[47] Clearly, if God's people are kept until the *parousia* this does not necessarily mean that every individual who belongs to the people is immune from apostasy and divine judgment.

Fifth and finally, a perspective that rejects apostasy in Jude 5 simply does not reflect the way most first-century Jewish and Jewish Christian audiences would have interpreted this example of the wilderness generation. Their familiarity with their own traditions makes it very likely that they would think of the people in the wilderness as *their own elect people*. These are fellow Israelites whom God favored and delivered from Egypt, but they suffered divine judgment because of their apostasies in the wilderness (e.g., Exod 32; Num 11–16, 20–21, 25; Deut 8:19–20; Pss 78:11–55; 95:7–11; 106:24–25; Wis 18:20–25; *1 En.* 89.28–40; Josephus, *Ant.* 3.15.1–2[310–315]; Philo, *Spec.* 4.126–31).[48] Jude simply affirmed and amplified what they already knew and had been repeatedly taught (Jude 5a). Israel fell away through unbelief and was divinely judged in the wilderness, and *Jude wants his community of believers to compare the opponents with the wilderness generation. The intruders are apostates who will be punished by God. A further implication that may be adduced from the letter is that the recipients must not be influenced by the opponents' immorality lest the same thing happen to them.*

The fall of the angels in Jude 6 provides a second example of defection, this one from the heavenly realm instead of earth. In the words of J. Daryl Charles, it shows that "apostasy in the Christian community has both earthly and heavenly antecedents."[49] The angels did not "keep" (τηρήσαντας) but deserted their first place, and now they are reserved for eternal punishment. Jude 6 assumes a narrative about angels who, as sons of God, engaged in illicit sex with women from the earth (cf. Gen 6:1–4), a story often repeated in ancient Jewish sources, including the Enoch tradition (*1 En.* 1.5; 6.2; 10.7–15; 14.3; 16.2; 86; 91.15; 106.5–12).[50] According to perhaps the most popular version of the legend, these angels lusted after human females and cohabited with them, producing a race of giants.[51]

Our author insinuates in Jude 6 that the intruders did something similar—they fell away to sexual vice and will also be eternally punished. The play on the word

---

47. Bauckham, *Jude, 2 Peter*, 113. Bauckham also affirms from the parallel in John 15:9 that the disciples remain in divine love by keeping Christ's commandments (cf. John 15:10).

48. On divine judgment in ancient Jewish wilderness traditions, see further Oropeza, *Paul and Apostasy*, 124–26.

49. Charles, *Literary Strategy*, 116.

50. See further Nickelsburg and Baltzer, *1 Enoch*, 140–41; and Dan 4:10–20; CD 2.17–19; *2 Bar.* 6.10–14; *Jub.* 4.15, 22; *T. Reub.* 5.6–7; 2 Pet 2:4.

51. For elaboration on the story, see Mayor, *Jude and II Peter*, clviii–clxvi. On sex as an issue in Jude 6, see Bauckham, *Jude, 2 Peter*, 51; Schreiner, *1, 2 Peter, Jude*, 447–48.

"keep" (τηρέω) contrasts the called and beloved Jewish Christian recipients who are kept by Jesus Christ (1, 24) and are to keep themselves in God's love (21). The angels did not "keep" themselves but turned away from God, and so did the intruders.[52] The point of connection between the fallen angels (6) and Sodom (7) is not merely that both the angels and Sodomites experienced divine judgment but that both stories involve illegitimate sexual relationships between humans and angels (cf. Gen 19). In the case of Sodom, however, wrongful sex was advanced by the men who lusted after Lot's angelic guests.[53]

The intruders are likewise denounced as committing a similar vice in Jude 6–8, and they slander the "glories," which probably refers to some type of speaking against angels (Jude 8–10; cf. 2 Pet 2:10–12).[54] The angels they slander do not seem to administer Mosaic Law or moral order,[55] neither of which is mentioned in Jude. Nor are these angels demonic since "glory" is not typically used to identify evil spirits.[56] The angels in Jude 8 are probably the "holy ones" who will assist the Lord when he executes judgment on the ungodly (14–15). Jude's opponents despise these angels, either indirectly by denying a final judgment in which angels participate, or more directly, by the opponents denying their own final punishment for living immorally. From Jude's perspective their punishment will be meted out by Christ and his angels at the second coming (Jude 18; cf. 2 Pet 3:3–7). Michael's refusal to rebuke Satan suggests a *qal wahomer*—if Michael the chief angel refused to revile a wicked angel like Satan, how much more is it presumptuous for these human intruders to revile good angels? Their instinctual desires will lead to their being eternally destroyed (φθείρω: Jude 10; cf. 1 Cor 3:17; Ign. *Poly.* 5.2).[57]

---

52. Jones, "Apostate Angels," 23, notices that these angels are also "kept" under "bonds" and "chains" and writes that God's punishment for apostasy here is "both severe and permanent." But unlike the angels, the intruders' apostasy is not necessarily permanent if they still have a chance to be restored (Jude 22–23).

53. Differently in Gen 19, Morschauser, "Hospitality, Hostiles, and Hostages," 461–85, argues that by the residents of Sodom wanting to "know" the angels, they wanted to interrogate them as potential spies, and Lot offers his daughters as a hostage exchange. However, Carson, "Jude," 1072–74, rightly responds that the sexual sense of Gen 19:8 cannot be easily dismissed, and a comparison between this verse and 19:5 suggests that both verses are referring to sexual relations.

54. See further Zech 3:2; 2 *En.* 22.7; *Ascen. Isa.* 9.32; 1QH 10.8; Philo, *Spec.* 1.8.45; Neyrey, *2 Peter, Jude*, 69.

55. Contrast Chaine, *Les épîtres catholiques*, 307–8; Bauckham, *Jude, 2 Peter*, 58–59.

56. Contrast Werdermann, *Irrlehrer des Judas*, 33. For further viewpoints see Vögtle, *Judasbriefe, 2 Petrusbrief*, 49–59.

57. Cf. BDAG, 1054; Davids, *2 Peter and Jude*, 64.

EXAMPLES OF UNGODLINESS: CAIN, BALAAM, AND KORAH (11, 16)

Jude's "woe" in verse 11 is perhaps derived from *1 Enoch*, which contains a goldmine of woe sayings in the *Epistle of Enoch* (*1 En.* 92–105).⁵⁸ This section heaps woes against those who are obstinate, wealthy, drink excessively, and commit unrighteous deeds (94.6–8; 95.4–7; 96.4–8; 97.7–8; 98.9–16; 99.1–2, 11–15; 100.7–9; 103.5–8). Consistent with Jude's labeling of the intruders as ungodly, the unrighteous in *1 Enoch* are godless and characterized by sin, and they are contrasted with the pious who do righteous deeds.⁵⁹ As with other early traditions, the woes in *1 Enoch* are a prelude to the coming day of reckoning against sinners. On judgment day they will suffer destruction, darkness, and burning fire (cf. 94.9; 95.6; 96.8; 97.10; 98.10–16; 99.11–16; 100.8–9; 103.7–8).⁶⁰ If Jude's thoughts here are derived from 1 Enoch, then it seems that *Jude's woe is thus prophetic and heralds the impending doom of the ungodly intruders when Christ returns on judgment day.*

Our author's verbal attack on the intruders may have also been influenced by Isa 56:10–12, which portrays spiritual leaders as greedy, immoral shepherds who turn aside from the path of righteousness, have no understanding, and are dreamers because they remain fast asleep in drunken stupor (cf. Jude 8, 10–12).⁶¹

The opponents are then compared with three ungodly characters in Israel's tradition-history: Cain, Balaam, and Korah (11). We have here in seminal form a teaching on two ways: the path that leads to destruction, which is the "way" (ὁδός) of Cain, Balaam, and Korah; and the path that leads to eternal life, which is the way of the Spirit and love (20–22). By associating the opponents with infamous characters of Israel's past, the author once again distances his audience from them. *The opponents' behavior or "walk" ultimately leads to divine destruction.*⁶²

In the Genesis story it may be said that Cain was originally pious by having fellowship with God. His jealousy over Abel caused him to murder his brother (Gen 4). In this sense Cain may be considered an apostate, and to follow in his footsteps or go "in the way" of Cain would thus be to commit sin and apostasy. This may

---

58. The dating of these chapters generally goes back to the second century BCE; cf. Nickelsburg and Baltzer, *1 Enoch*, 8; Charlesworth, *OTP* 1.7.

59. Cf. Nickelsburg and Baltzer, 423. The translation of Charles, *APOT*, uses terms related to godlessness in *1 En.* 93.8; 94.11; 98.15; 99.1, 8–10; 100.9; 104.9.

60. On the "woe" sayings in this section, see Nickelsburg and Baltzer, 416.

61. The idea of drunkenness is conveyed in the MT but not LXX. Alternatively, the aspect of dreaming might refer back to Balaam's soothsaying abilities as a dreamer (e.g., Ps.-Philo 18.2 in *OTP*, 2.325).

62. Webb, "Rhetorical Function of Visual Imagery," 132, perceptively writes regarding Jude 11 that "the order of the verbs involved indicates an intensifying progression from behaving in a particular way ('they walk') to passionate commitment ('they abandon themselves') to total destruction ('they perish')."

be similar to Israel's kings forsaking the LORD and following "in the way" of their fathers by committing evil deeds (e.g., 1 Kgs 15:26, 34; 16:2; 2 Kgs 8:18, 27; 16:3). Nevertheless, later traditions associate Cain with vices such as hatred, murder, and greed (Josephus, *Ant.* 1.52-56; *T. Benj.* 7.5; 1 John 3:11). Neyrey would add from Philo and certain Targums of Gen 4:8 Cain's godlessness and atheism: the primeval murderer denies "divine judgment, afterlife, and postmortem retribution."[63] Even so, perhaps one of the main assumptions behind Jude's connection of this character with the intruders is that Cain is viewed as a type of "teacher" of ungodliness (cf. Philo, *Post.* 35, 38-39).[64] The intruders likewise are ungodly teachers by being selfish shepherds (ἑαυτοὺς ποιμαίνοντες: Jude 12), and *like Cain they could lead astray members of Christ's beloved community.*

Balaam is a frequently mentioned with a negative reputation in ancient Hebrew, Jewish, and Christians traditions (Num 22–24; 31:8, 16).[65] In quite a few of these traditions he instigates the Israelites to eat food sacrificed to idols and commit fornication with Moabite women (e.g., Josephus, *Ant.* 4.126-30; Philo, *Moses* 1.292-99; cf. Num 25:1-18; Ps 105[106]:28-31; Hos 9:10; 1 Cor 10:7-8). Later traditions associate him with sexual perversions, including sexual relations with his donkey, a cow, and performing enchantments with his penis (*b. Sanhedrin* 105-6[11.1D,2C, 8D,H,J, 9K-L]; *Tg. Ps.-J.*). In Num 22–24 Balaam knows the God of the Israelites and yet comes against God's people when Balak, king of Moab, offers him a fee for divination so that he would curse the Israelites. The main point of connection between the story of Balaam and Jude 11 is that the intruders have dedicated themselves to follow Balaam's error of greed (Jude 11; cf. v. 16d). He is likewise mentioned in 2 Peter: and the false teachers of that letter have abandoned the way of righteous and follow instead the way of Balaam, the mad prophet who loved unrighteous financial gain (2 Pet 2:15-16; cf. v. 1). In both Jude and 2 Peter, then, Balaam's primary flaw involves greed.

It is not clear that he is mentioned in Jude because he was once faithful to God and then turned apostate. Balaam was always an outsider and soothsayer, unattached to God's elect people.[66] Nevertheless, some traditions consider him a genuine prophet (Josephus, *Ant.* 4.6.1-13§100-158; *Num. Rabbah* 20.7; *b. Sanhedrin* 106a).[67]

63. Neyrey, *2 Peter, Jude*, 72-73, 124-25, quote from 125.

64. Cf. Charles, *Literary Strategy*, 122.

65. See further Josh 13:22 LXX; 24:9; Deut 23:4-5; Judg 1:27 LXX; Mic 6:5; Neh 13:2; Rev 2:14; 4Q339; Josephus, *Ant.* 4.6.3 [107-11]; Philo, *Moses* 268 [45]; 281[51]; 300[55]; *Unchangeable* 181[37]; *Worse* 71[20]; *Migr.* 113-15[20]; *L.A.B.* 18; *Pirkē Aboth* 5.19[22]; *m. Sanhedrin* 10.2; and Greene, "Balaam: Prophet," 57-106; idem, "Balaam as Figure," 82-147.

66. On Balaam's origin see Hackett, "Balaam," 1.571.

67. Cf. Bauckham, *Jude, 2 Peter*, 81.

Did he pervert his gift of communicating with God so that Jude considers him a backslidden prophet led astray by greed? More clearly, he led the men of Israel astray through their affairs with Moabite women. There may be a hint of that seduction shining through by Jude's use of πλάνη in verse 11, which often connotes deception and leading astray people from the path of righteousness to venture on the wrong path (e.g., Prov 14:8; Tob 5:14; Wis 12:24; *Ascen. Isa.* 2.10; 2 Thess 2:11; Eph 4:14; Jas 5:20). Possibly both Balaam and the people's seduction are in view. *Balaam has been seduced by greed and he seduces others to sexual immorality* (cf. 2 Tim 3:13). In any case, Balaam, not the Israelites, is seen as the main "type" pointing to the intruders in Jude 11.

Korah, the third character mentioned in verse 11, is punished for his rebellion (ἀντιλογία) against the authorities God had appointed (Num 16).[68] Korah was a prominent Levite within Israel's community during its wilderness travels (Num 16:1–2; cf. 26:58; 2 Chr 20:19). Together with 250 leaders in the community, he came against the leadership of Aaron and Moses. *Korah's rebellion implicates him as an apostate teacher among God's people, similar to the intruders in Jude.*[69] God made the earth swallow up Korah and his leaders alive into *Sheol*, together with their possessions, and other rebels were consumed with divine fire (Num 16). Jude emphasizes this judgment as Korah being "destroyed" (ἀπώλοντο), which not only looks back to his punishment in the wilderness but also looks forward to the eschatological judgment of the intruders (cf. Jude 5, 10, 13, 15). The opponents are denounced as grumblers, and this probably has in mind Korah's grumbling in the wilderness (Jude 16; cf. 1 Cor 10:10). In early Jewish and Hebrew writings, the notion of grumbling is viewed as rebellion and carries with it severe consequences, especially when tied to Israel's wilderness incidents. As George Coats maintains, "The act of murmuring poses a challenge to the object of the murmuring which, if unresolved, demands loss of office, due punishment, and perhaps death."[70] Our author mentions the intruders as grumblers in order to denounce them again as apostate rebels who will be punished by God, similar to the party of Korah and the wilderness generation.

---

68. Cf. Wis 18:20–25; Sir 45:18–19; 4Q423 5; Philo, *Flight* 26[145–46].

69. Marshall, *Kept by the Power*, 163, correctly adds Korah as another example of those who have lapsed from righteousness in Jude. He also includes in this category Balaam, the fallen angels, and wilderness generation. It is not clear, however, that Balaam was ever righteous.

70. Coats, *Rebellion in the Wilderness*, 249.

TREES, ROCKS, STARS, AND APOSTASY (12–13)

The concept of being "twice dead" (δὶς ἀποθανόντα) describes the opponents in the metaphor of trees that are both barren and uprooted (Jude 12). Some scholars suggest the intruders are morally dead and suffer a "second death" when Christ returns (cf. Rev 2:11; 20:14; 21:8; *Tg. Isa.* 65:15; *Tg. Onq. Deut.* 33:6; Philo, *Rewards* 70).[71] Problematic with this view is that the text may suggest they are already dead and yet the final judgment at the coming of Christ is still futuristic (Jude 6, 14–15, 21, 24).[72] Bauckham compares verse 12 with 11 to portray the second death "as though already accomplished."[73] However, an eschatological "second death" presupposes a prior physical death, and neither of these has taken place in reference to Jude's opponents at the time of the letter. Hence, this interpretation of the phrase is awkward to say the least.

A second option is for us to interpret "twice dead" as "totally dead."[74] This explanation needs corroborative support elsewhere in Jude and is weakened by the fact that numeration plays an important role in this letter (e.g., "second," v. 5; "seventh," v. 14). Regardless of how emphatically it is stated, Jude 12 seems to convey two distinct deaths.

A third interpretation considers the opponents to be externally unproductive and internally dead.[75] This interpretation stays faithful to the tree metaphor, and may assume something similar to dead works coming from spiritually dead persons.

A fourth alternative is for us to consider "twice dead" as another reference to the intruders' apostasy.[76] They were at one time spiritually dead[77] and then became

71. E.g., Vögtle, *Judasbrief, 2 Petrusbrief*, 68; Bauckham, *Jude, 2 Peter*, 88; Kelly, *Peter and Jude*, 273.

72. Although a proleptic aorist is not impossible here, the aorist participle ἀποθανόντα in Jude 12 is probably best translated "having died twice" (NET note), matching the sense of the following aorist participle ἐκριζωθέντα ("uprooted"). Most translations simply render it "twice dead" (e.g., ESV) or "doubly dead" (e.g., NASB).

73. Bauckham, *Jude, 2 Peter*, 88.

74. Schreiner, *1, 2 Peter, Jude*, 467.

75. Kraftchick, *Jude, 2 Peter*, 51.

76. On this view see Green, *2 Peter and Jude*, 136; Bigg, *Peter and Jude*, 335; Frankemölle, *1, 2 Petrusbrief, Judasbrief*, 138 ("... die Irrlehrer als Entwurzelte nicht mehr zur Gemeinde gehören").

77. Cf. Eph. 2:1, 5; Col 2:13; Matt 8:22; Luke 9:60; 15:24; 1 John 3:14. We notice that Matthew 8:22, written in the matrix of a Jewish-Christian community and together with Luke 9:60 evinces this source as a saying of Jesus (Q) that he spoke originally to Jews, makes the thought of being spiritually dead relevant for Jews prior to becoming followers of Christ. In other words, the thought in the NT is not always referring to Gentiles prior to their conversion to emergent Christian faith. See also the first common plurals "we" and "us" in Eph 2:1–3 suggesting that the Pauline author, presumably Jewish, includes himself among those who were once spiritually dead. The upshot of these observations is that it is quite plausible for Jude's recipients to understand that prior to first becoming Christ-followers, both they and the intruders were spiritual dead even though Jewish.

spiritually alive as believers, but because of immoral living they have died again spiritually, becoming lifeless tress rooted out from any union with Christ (cf. Heb 6:4–8; John 15:1–6; Rom 11:17–24; Col 2:6–7). This view has several advantages. First, the intruders are repeatedly viewed or implied as apostates in the letter (Jude 5, 6, 11, 13, 23). Second, it makes both deaths a phenomenon of the past, complementary with their being uprooted (12). The notion of being uprooted is a further description of the tree's death that is perhaps itself understood as apostasy (cf. ἐκριζόω in *Herm. Mand.* 9.9). Third, it fits well with a stress on their worthlessness in Jude 12: they are not only waterless clouds but lifeless trees. Finally, their present state of being "dead" would anticipate their being void of God's Spirit, mentioned in Jude 19. *The intruders are "twice dead" because they originally had no spiritual life, then were made alive in the Spirit through Christ, but afterward became apostate and once again void of spiritual life.* As useless, dried-up trees, the only thing remaining is for them to be destroyed in fire at the final judgment (cf. 7, 11, 23).[78] Ultimately any view we select must be somewhat tentative because Jude simply does not give us enough information to be more certain about the phrase "twice dead." The third or fourth options, however, are the most plausible, and the thought is ambiguous enough to suggest the possibility of both meanings.

It appears that Jude 12 not only conveys the intruders as apostates but also the congregation members who would follow them. The opponents are imagined as dangerous reefs or "rocks" (σπιλάδες) of the sea that can cause a boat to be shipwrecked if it sails too closely. The term σπιλάς has been variously interpreted as spots or blemishes, "dirty persons," or stumbling blocks that can cause people to fall.[79] The word, however, frequently means a rock on the sea or seashore (e.g., Josephus, *J.W.* 3.420) and it can be used to depict shipwrecks (Polybius, *Histories* 1.37.2).[80] The nautical aspects of wind, sea, waves, and foam in Jude 12–13 lend to this meaning. But what would a rock be doing at a love feast? This is perplexing imagery to say the least.[81] *Perhaps the thought of a ship's close encounter with the dangerous rocks is being compared to the believers' close contact with the intruders at congregational*

---

78. Naturally an eschatological judgment by fire may be compared with the "second death" of other Jewish and Christian literature (e.g., Rev 20:6, 14), but this is not how Jude articulates the coming judgment in his letter.

79. The first option is based on the similar word σπίλος in 2 Pet 1:23 (cf. Eph 5:27), the second comes from BDF, 26§45, and for the third see Isa 8:14–15; Matt 16:23. See further options in Neyrey, *2 Peter, Jude*, 74–75.

80. See further LSJ, 1628; BDAG, 938; and Witherington, *Jewish Christians*, 620–21.

81. Which lends to Neyrey, *2 Peter, Jude*, 75, rejecting this option. Charles, *1–2 Peter, Jude*, 300, suggests a double meaning of spots (pollution)/rocks.

love feasts[82]—*a spiritual shipwreck can occur by getting too close.* The metaphorical shipwreck of the believers would, no doubt, mean the destruction of their faith as followers of the intruders (cf. 1 Tim 1:19; *Barn.* 3.6).

Moreover, as wayward stars the opponents are seen as causing ships that rely on their navigation at night to be lost at sea (Jude 13 NET). In the ancient world it was sometimes believed that the planets are kept on their course by angels (cf. *1 En.* 82); planets with irregular patterns, and falling stars, were often associated with disobedient celestial beings. Addressing this phenomenon, Bauckham draws our attention to the watchers that fell from heaven (*1 En.* 18.13–16, 21.3–6) and suggests the stars in Jude 13 may be another reference to the fallen angels (cf. 6).[83] The imagery in Jude 13 assumes at any rate that these luminaries have wandered off their proper orbital course. *The intruders, like wayward stars, have strayed from the way of godliness into apostasy, and they lead astray navigators who rely on them for direction* (Jude 13; cf. *1 En.* 80.6–8). Divine judgment awaits the unrepentant apostates, as Jude 13–15 makes clear. Jude has the Lord Jesus Christ in mind when citing *1 En.* 1.9 (Jude 14–15): the Lord will execute judgment upon all the ungodly at his *parousia*, including the intruders.

RESTORING THE APOSTATES AND THEIR FOLLOWERS (20–23)

In the final section of this letter the *propositio* is recapitulated and amplified: the Jewish Christians whom Jude addresses again must contend for the faith: 1) they are to build themselves in the apostolic faith they have received (Jude 20a); 2) unlike the intruders who are void of the Spirit, the beloved saints are to pray under the Spirit's guidance and control (20b; cf. 19); 3) they must keep themselves in God's love as they await divine mercy and eternal life at the second coming of Christ (21); and finally, 4) they are to have mercy on some and save others (22–23).[84]

Who are these people they are supposed to reach? Peter Spitaler makes the case that διακρινομένους in Jude 22 refers to disputers rather than doubters. He bases this meaning on its normal classical/Hellenistic sense, on the verb's parallel meaning in Jude 9, and the parallel structuring of "these are they" (16, 19) and "but

---

82. So Bauckham, *2 Peter, Jude*, 85–86. In the NET's notes on Jude 12 it is suggested that the rocks could have been mistaken as pillars of the church (cf. Gal 2:9; Matt 16:18) by the congregation members. These rocks need not be hidden but visible, as were the false teachers. Conversely, Witherington, *Jewish Christians*, 620, thinks the proper meaning is a *hidden* rock (cf. Plutarch, *Moralia* 2.101B[12]).

83. Bauckham, *Jude, 2 Peter*, 89.

84. A number of textual variants occur in the closing verses, but we accept the three-clause pattern in Jude 22–23, against P[72] and similar variants. For discussion see Wasserman, *Text and Transmission*, 126, 320–31.

you" (17, 20–21) to suggest that the querulous grumblers and separatists are the same individuals as the disputers whom Jude's audience is supposed to reach.[85] His arguments support in a convincing way that the intruders are the disputers in Jude 22. Hence, their restoration from apostasy is still possible; they are not hopelessly condemned to eternal judgment. Even so, we must question whether the intruders alone are in mind in verses 22–23. Given that they have infiltrated the church, they may have influenced some of the congregation members, and this is why some of the author's descriptions of them include their followers (e.g., navigational dangers 12–13). Apparently *Jude's faithful readers are to reach both the intruders and those influenced by them.*[86]

Jude 22–23 seems to echo a blend of Amos 4:11 and Zech 3:2–4. The former text refers to Israel as a piece of burning wood snatched out of the fire, which is compared with Lot's family escaping God's judgment in Sodom. In Jude 7 Sodom and Gomorrah were destroyed by "eternal fire" because of sexual immorality. Jude reconfigures the allusion from Amos to affirm that believers who win back an apostate save that person from a fiery condemnation at the eschaton (23; cf. 14–15). The passage from Zechariah refers to Joshua the high priest as a representative of the remnant of Israel escaping destruction related to exile (a firebrand rescued from the fire). Joshua is wearing clothes soiled with excrement (צוֹאִים), which would disqualify him from priestly service. The filthy garments, metaphorically referring to iniquity, were then removed from him and he was given splendid vestments.[87] There may be an assumption in Jude that a clean garment alludes to the new nature of a baptized convert to the Christian faith (cf. Eph 4:22–24).[88] If so, then a garment stained with excrement might imply that the apostates' new nature has been ruined by sin (cf. Jude 8; Rev 3:4).

---

85. See further Spitaler, "Doubt or Dispute," 201–22. It seems best to translate οὓς simply as "some" or "some . . . others . . ." (see Porter, *Idioms*, 133; Zerwick, *Grammatical Analysis*, 741).

86. Here Viljoen, "Faithful Christian Living amidst Scoffers," 521, correctly includes both groups. Contrast Kraftchick, *Jude, 2 Peter*, 65–66, who thinks the verses do not refer to opponents but to two groups in the congregation: 1) those vacillating between the teaching of the truth and that of the intruders—they are on the "brink of destruction"; and 2) those who doubt and merely need to be forgiven and reasoned back to confidence. Witherington, *Jewish Christians*, 632, suggests a threefold progression from doubters to those presently falling away to those who have already fallen away. If Spitaler, "Doubt or Dispute," 201–22, is correct, however, the doubters are a non-existent group.

87. Cf. Clark and Hatton, *Zechariah*, 120–21; NET Bible. On fleshly stains, Davids, *2 Peter and Jude*, 104–5, has an interesting discussion. Vögtle, *Judasbrief, 2 Petrusbrief*, 106–7, suggests excommunication through Jude 22–23. But the verses have more to do with the recipients avoiding sin rather than the sinner.

88. See further, Neyrey, *2 Peter, Jude*, 92.

Whereas the Jewish Christians are to attempt winning back the intruders and their followers, they are also cautioned to fear God (Jude 23). They too could be susceptible to the intruders' sins, apostatize, and then face God's fiery judgment. This potential danger is perhaps one reason why Jude provides a counterbalance to verse 23 in verse 24. A fear of being judged by God is not the final word. He gives conventional words of assurance in the form of a closing doxology to the auditors: God is able to keep them safe (24–25). Here perseverance is seen not as human effort, as in verse 21, but as God's gracious activity among the faithful. God is able to keep them safe until they appear in his presence without blemish, presumably on judgment day. And *provided that* they do not follow the ways of the opponents, he certainly *will* keep them for final salvation. In the end they are given a responsibility to be aware of their susceptibility to the errors of the false teachers (21, 23), and yet they can be assured in the closing doxology that God is able to keep them safe (24–25). Jude assumes a reciprocal relationship between the divine and human—*God will keep those who keep the faith.* Conventional characteristics aside, the author is not giving the believer an absolute guarantee of final salvation in the present moment; he is assuring the congregation members that they do not have to be filled with anxiety or intimidated by the intruders when confronting them with the truth of the gospel. God is on their side.

CONCLUSION

The letter of Jude was written to a Jewish Christian audience familiar with the many sources to which the author alludes. The situation centers on the danger of intruders who participate in the community's love feasts (3–4, 12). The manner in which they are denounced as intruders, ungodly, and Christ-deniers, among other things, and the way they are compared with infamous people from Israel's past, suggest vilification and conventional stereotyping by Jude. The only perspective of their apostasy we can determine from the letter, however, is the author's point of view. Based on what Jude writes, we find that these opponents deny Christ as their master by means of their immoral lifestyle. By this lifestyle they reject God's grace and the message of the gospel faith related to Christ. It is evident that the opponents profess Jesus as Christ, however, and this is how they gained entrance into the Christian community.

It can be suggested through the barrage of the author's condemnations of them that their practices include some form of sexual sin and a haughty denial of the role of angelic powers in divine judgment (8–10, 14–15). They are also accused of greed (11, 16). The author considers them to be apostates comparable to the wilderness generation in exodus stories and fallen angels in Enoch traditions (5–6). They follow the path of Cain, who abandoned his original piety to follow the path of ungodliness; they follow Balaam, who was led astray by greed and caused Israel to commit apostasy; and they are apostate rebels like Korah, who came against divine authority and was destroyed (11). Their apostasy and negative influence in the church is also confirmed by Jude's metaphors depicting them as trees that were dead, came to spiritual life, and now are dead again; as dangerous rocks in the sea upon which vessels become shipwrecked; and as rogue stars that have strayed off their orbital paths and mislead ship navigators who depend on them for guidance (12–13). The beloved followers of Christ must persevere by keeping themselves in the love of God, who is also at work in them and keeping them safe (1, 21, 24). The letter anticipates the opponents' future divine punishment—a fiery destruction at the *parousia* (e.g., 7, 11, 13–15). Even though their judgment was predicted long ago by Enoch, the author still holds out a hope for restoration for both them and those who follow them (22–23). He encourages the faithful Christ-followers to win back the apostates and their pupils.

The problem of apostate Christians espousing antinomianism, in the sense of immoral living that encumbers the faithful community, is a problem in both Jude and 2 Peter. The audience in 2 Peter is primarily Gentile, and the author borrows the message of vituperation from Jude but omits many allusions to Jewish sources, most notably the writings of Enoch. The Christians in Jude are Jewish, and whereas 2 Peter encounters a group who have distorted Pauline teachings on grace, Jude's opponent are presumably Jewish Christians, with no evidence that they are libertine Paulinists. Both letters compare the opponent with Balaam, in particular his vice of greed and leading God's people astray (Jude 11; 2 Pet 2:15).

Jude's recollection of Israel's rebellion in the wilderness resembles the words of Paul in 1 Cor 10 and the author in Heb 3–4. These sources, however, use the story to warn their congregations against apostasy. This reason only partially motivates Jude, who is more interested in comparing the *opponents'* apostasy and impending judgment with the wilderness generation's conduct and fate. Our author's both/and combination of God keeping the congregation safe *and* the members keeping themselves in the love of God is similar to Paul's delicate balance when he stresses both divine and human agency at work in the process of salvation (e.g., Phil 1:12–13; 1 Cor 10:12–13; 2 Thess 2:13–15). In this manner the reality of individual believers committing apostasy is affirmed without denying God's gracious work within the community. Unlike the Matthean churches, another Jewish Christian community facing antinomian opponents, the intruders in Jude are considered apostate Christians who seem to have genuinely experienced spiritual life at one time. Matthew, on the other hand, views false prophets in the community as imposters who were never genuinely believers in Christ. On a different note, and similar to the Jewish Christian community in James, Jude ends his letter with a challenge for his recipients to seek the restoration of those who have fallen away. In Jude's case, though, it is clear that those who are to be reached are still attending the group's fellowship meetings or at least their *agape* dinners.

6

Revelation

Overcoming Assimilation and the Imperial Cult in Asia Minor

Revelation is attributed to John (Rev 1:1, 9), but his precise identity cannot be determined. Justin Martyr believed the author to be the son of Zebedee, one of the twelve apostles, who was said to be banished on the isle of Patmos (*Dial.* 81.4).[1] But this identity sits awkwardly with Rev 21:14, where John mentions the Twelve without any indication that he belongs to this number.[2] One plausible suggestion is that this author had contact with the Johannine community in Asia Minor (e.g., 1:11; 2:1) or perhaps belonged to this group at an earlier or later stage than when the Johannine writings were produced.[3] The profuse amount of allusions to Israel's scriptures and familiarity with apocalyptic lends credibility to the supposition that the author is Jewish.[4] The author in any case does not claim to be an apostle or elder; he appears to be a prophet within a group of prophets (22:6, 9; cf. 1:10; 10:11; 11:10, 18; 16:6; 18:24; 22:16a).[5]

---

1. Cf. Irenaeus, *Her* 4.20.11; Eusebius, *H.E.* 3.18.1; 3.23.5; 4.26.2. On the authorship of Revelation see further Aune, *Revelation*, 1.xlvii–lvi; Brown, *Introduction*, 802–05.

2. Connections have been made to show language and thematic similarities between Revelation and the Johannine writings, but in the end the evidence is not very favorable for our suggesting the same author wrote both these works. For comparisons, see, e.g., Prigent, *Apocalypse*, 36–50; Traeger, *Johannesapocalypse*, 11–20. For differences, see, e.g., Roloff, *Revelation*, 11–12; Charles, *Revelation*, 1.cxvii–clix.

3. On the discussion see further Schnelle, *Einleitung*, 436–37, 537–38.

4. See, e.g., Hirschberg, "Jewish Believers in Asia Minor," 217–30, 238.

5. See Aune, "Prophetic Circle of John," 103–16; Bauckham, *Climax of Prophecy*, 84.

Churches under Siege of Persecution and Assimilation

The interpretation of Revelation has long been a matter of fascination, debate, and abuse.[6] In the opening verse the word ἀποκάλυψις appears, but it is not clear whether John intended the term to mean simply "revelation" or indicate a literary form similar to Jewish contemporaries and predecessors such as *1 Enoch*, *4 Ezra*, *2 and 3 Baruch*, and Daniel.[7] This book is nevertheless recognized by the majority of scholars as primarily apocalyptic literature.[8] Even so, the book opens as a letter addressed to seven churches; it is not purely apocalyptic but is mixed in genre.[9] David Hellholm adds an important aspect to our understanding of apocalyptic by writing that the genre is "intended for a group in crisis with the purpose of exhortation and/or consolation by means of divine authority."[10] This would involve using otherworldly concepts and images to modify the group's thoughts and behavior in positive ways to help it see its temporal situation in light of the heavenly world and so encourage the members to endure hardships related to their situation. In this manner apocalyptic involves both paraenesis and persuasion. Perception and behavioral modifications are necessary for the well-being of the group and to discourage apostasy and judgments that would ensue from this.[11]

Revelation employs what may be understood as the rhetoric of fear,[12] encouraging proper behavior through words and depictions highlighting the consequences of both the righteous and unrighteous.[13] The consequences are eternal—in the end the righteous are blessed with the divine glory in New Jerusalem, and the wicked are fated with destruction in the Lake of Fire (Rev 20–22). Revelation 1–3 takes on the form of a letter with a rhetorical aim of dissuading the churches from the negative issues addressed, and the risen Christ is the person who speaks to the seven churches, lending to the writing's authoritative nature (1:1, 12–18; 2:1).

---

6. For histories of interpretation, see, e.g., Prigent, "L'interpretation de l'Apocalypse," 189–210; Koester, "Recent Studies of the Book of Revelation," 109–122; Osborne, "Recent Trends," 473–504.

7. See Collins, *Apocalyptic Imagination*, 3.

8. Collins, "Morphology of a Genre," 9, gives a standard definition for apocalypse as "a genre of revelatory literature with a narrative framework, in which a revelation is mediated by an otherworldly being to a human recipient, disclosing a transcendent reality which is both temporal, in so far as it envisages eschatological salvation, and spatial in so far as it involves another, supernatural world."

9. See further Linton, "Reading the Apocalypse," 9–41; deSilva, *Seeing Things John's Way*, 9–14.

10. Hellholm. "The Problem of Apocalyptic Genre and the Apocalypse of John," 27.

11. Aune, "Problem of Genre," 91, writes along these lines: "A central purpose of the author was to motivate the audience to pursue a life of faithfulness and purity in order to avoid the punishments awaiting those who follow the wrong path."

12. Cf. Rev 11:18; 14:7; 15:4; 19:5.

13. See on fear and *pathos*, deSilva, "Emotions in the Apocalypse," 90–114; idem, "Emotions in John's Visions," 1–34.

SITUATIONS OF THE COMMUNITIES IN REVELATION (REV 1–3, 13, 17–18)

Revelation was written anywhere from the time of Emperor Nero to Domitian (c. 64–96 CE). Beale claims the consensus of scholars places it towards the end of Domitian's reign (c. 95–96 CE) and a minority places it immediately before the temple's destruction in 70 CE.[14] Eusebius mentions that during the reign of Domitian (c. 81–96 CE) John the apostle was banished to Patmos. When Nerva came to power (c. 96–98 CE) John was released and returned to Ephesus where he lived until the time of Trajan (Eusebius *Hist. eccl.* 3.17–23 [20.11-11; 23.1]). This record from Eusebius is not entirely clear. Clement of Alexandria mentions that John's banishment ended "after the tyrant's death," which could either refer to Nero or Domitian (Clement, *Salvation;* Eusebius, *Hist. eccl.* 3.23.5).[15]

Perhaps Aune is correct by suggesting, on the ground of source criticism, that Revelation was written in stages, with 1:7–12a and 4:1—22:5 written in the first "edition," and the title, doxology, letters to the seven churches, conclusion, and epilogue added in a second. The first stage collects visions and prophetic narratives possibly as early as the 50s and 60s CE, which were then compiled in a first edition around 70 CE; then the second edition was completed either in the late 90s or during Trajan's reign (98–117 CE).[16] If this is correct then Revelation does not reflect the time of Domitian alone but a time dating back to Nero or earlier and extending all the way to at least the later years of Domitian. Our problem is determining which portions of text fit *where* in the two editions. Nero's name may reflect the number 666 when we translate his title and name from Greek to Hebrew (Rev 13),[17] and he may represent the sixth ruler in Rome *if* the numeration is not entirely symbolic and we begin our count with Julius (cf. 17:9–11).[18] The temple in Rev 11 may presuppose a date close to the temple's destruction in Jerusalem (70 CE). Such portions can date back to the time of Nero or Vespasian.

Many other sections of Revelation, however, seem to fit better with the time of Domitian. The visions in 6:9–11 and 7:9–14, for example, depict many saints and

---

14. Beale, *Revelation*, 4.

15. Why John would be banished rather than executed is not known. See discussion in Collins, *Crisis and Catharsis*, 102–03.

16. Aune, *Revelation*, 1.lvi–lxx, cv–cxxxiv.

17. Other significant options are that the Greek word "beast" (θηρίον) in Hebrew (תריו) is 666, and "Jesus" is 888 (cf. *Sib Or* 1.324–31), a parody of the beast. For more options, see Aune, *Revelation* 2.769–73.

18. Of course the numbers in 17:9–11 may be symbolic depicting the short time left for the Beast or Rome given that 5 of its 7 heads have already fallen: e.g., Mounce, *Revelation*, 315–16. Prigent, *Apocalypse*, 68–71, however, aptly defends the numbers here are historically focused.

martyrs who have been dead for a presumably long time. Revelation 6:6 may be hinting at Domitian's edict restricting the cultivation of grapes (c. 92–93 CE), and 13:3 implies the death of Nero. Laodicea's wealth despite a devastating earthquake in 61 CE, Smyrna's late beginnings as a church (c. 61–64 CE), and Ephesus's loss of "first love" all fit better with a later time comparable with Domitian's era. The imperial cult and persecution in Asia Minor also fits better with Domitian's time.[19] Nero's persecution of Christians was in Rome, not Asia, and there is no evidence that he demanded Christians to worship him or have any image dedicated to him.[20]

Apart from church fathers who say that Nero and Domitian persecuted the early Christians,[21] Pliny reports to Trajan in the early second century that some Christians in Asia Minor renounced their faith twenty years earlier (Pliny, *Letters* 10.96.6). This apostasy probably happened mainly as a result of persecution during the time of Domitian. Clement of Rome also appears to be referring to persecution during the time of Domitian (c. 96 CE; *1 Clem.* 7.1; cf. 5.1).[22]

Then again, sometimes misperceptions about Domitian's reign color one's interpretation of Revelation. John places on a cosmic level the social conflicts his community in Asia Minor has experienced by rejecting Rome's power, and this has been interpreted by some as an empire-wide persecution of Christians decreed by the emperor. The impression we are sometimes left with is that Domitian reigned as a wild-eyed, merciless tyrant who ordered his soldiers to hunt down Christians systematically throughout his empire and feed them to hungry lions if they failed to worship him as god.[23] The persecution of Christians by imperial edict on a mass scale resembles more the later reigns of Decius and Diocletian. Although ancient historians speak profusely of Domitian's savage and immoral behavior, Leonard Thompson has argued that such claims (e.g., from Suetonius, Pliny, and Tacitus) represent biased reporting attempting to make emperor Trajan look good and Domitian look evil. Other writers such as Quintilian, Martial, Statius, Frontinus,

---

19. On Domitian's designation as "Lord and God" (*dominus et deus noster*) and images of him, see Martial, *Epigrams* 10.72; Statius, *Silv* 1.6.84; Suetonius, *Domitian* 8.13; 13.1–2; Pliny, *Panegyricus* 33.4; 52.6; Cassius Dio 67.4.7; further, Friesen, *Imperial Cults*, 43–55, 60–62, 148–50; Price, *Rituals and Power*, esp. 157, 197–98.

20. On Nero and the Imperial cult, see Friesen, *Imperial Cults*, 85–86, 90–91, 148–49, 174; Jones, "Roman Imperial Cult," 5.807.

21. e.g., Tertullian, *Apol.* 5; Melito of Sardis in Eusebius (*H.E.* 4.26.9); Eusebius, *H.E.* 3.17–20.

22. Cassius Dio mentions the execution of Cassius and banishment of Domitilla, but unlike Eusebius (*H.E.* 3.18.5) the charge is atheism and keeping Jewish customs, which nonetheless could be understood as Christian: cf. Court, *Revelation*, 99–100.

23. Contesting negative portrayals of Domitian are, e.g., Thompson, *Apocalypse and Empire*; Collins, *Crisis and Catharsis*, 84–110.

and Silius Italicus portray him in a more positive light.[24] However, this evidence can cut both ways, and it should be questioned how "objective" the latter authors would have been, especially if any were attempting to flatter the emperor.[25] First-century Roman persecution of Christians, in any case, does not seem to arise from a direct command by Nero or Domitian to be worshipped as "lord and god."[26]

In Rev 2–3 the conflict is viewed by some scholars as internal. It involves factions related to Christian groups against other Christian groups, especially the churches in Asia Minor against the followers of the "false apostles," "Nicolaitans," and those who adhere to the doctrines of "Balaam" and "Jezebel."[27] But the conflict is also external, and this is definitely the emphasis throughout the rest of the book (e.g., 2:9, 13; 3:9; cf. chs. 12–13). Oppression, harassment, discrimination, and the physical persecution of Christians mostly seem to occur as a result of conflicts between the churches and outsiders, that is, their non-Christian neighbors. These struggles were local, and the outsiders from time to time perhaps requested Roman officials to step in and give unfavorable verdicts against Christians, whom they frequently perceived as social deviants, enemies of local deities, and disloyal to the empire.[28] *What we have in Revelation, then, are both internal and external situations, with the churches experiencing different and overlapping problems including assimilation, apathy, and social, economic, and religious clashes.*[29] We will observe these conflicts below through the seven churches.

There remain some valid reasons to suggest that some of the church communities in Asia Minor were experiencing local mistreatment because of their refusal to participate in the local imperial cult. Revelation often connects persecution with the saints' refusal to participate in what appears to be imperial worship that is tied into the socioeconomic system (13:1–18; 14:9; 15:2; 16:2;17:6; 19:20; 20:4; cf. 12:6, 14–17). First-century cities in Asia Minor such as Pergamum established an impe-

---

24. See further Thompson, *Apocalypse and Empire*, 95–115.

25. See Slater, "Social Setting of the Revelation," 236–38. For one thing Quintilian gives divine honor to Domitian (*Inst.* 4, prefaces 2, 5).

26. Collins, *Crisis and Catharsis*, 77, says that Domitian did not persecute Christians "as Christians." The problems arise from social unrest and conflicts with Jews, wealth, and antipathy with Gentile neighbors; none of which were Roman-initiated but local in character (98). My view is that the imperial cult is nonetheless a problem for the Christian communities in Asia Minor and they were in fact harassed for being Christians (see main text).

27. Internal conflicts are stressed by, e.g., Duff, *Who Rides the Beast?*, 3–16; Royalty, *Ideology of Wealth*.

28. E.g., 1 Pet 4:14; Matt 10:17–23; Luke 21:12; Acts 5:41; John 15:21; Tacitus, *Annals* 15.44. See further on the issue in Slater, "Social Setting of Revelation," 242–56.

29. Similarly, Friesen, "Satan's Throne," 352–56, argues for several social settings, mostly conflicts with outsiders. See also deSilva, "Honor Discourse," 82–87; Collins, *Crisis and Catharsis*, 4–7.

rial cult with the offices of high priest and a *neokoros*, who underwrote expenses for temple maintenance. The religious leaders of the imperial cult seem to be portrayed by the False Prophet who causes Roman society to worship the image of the Beast (13:11–17). The Beast refers to Caesar and veneration of him as deity. Smyrna, Ephesus, and other cities in Asia Minor also became centers for the imperial cult.[30] The citizens of these communities would seem to be patriotic and zealous for the imperial cult. It is easy to imagine how harassment and persecution could take place in such cities when Christians refused to participate in events promoting imperial worship and societal traditions. On a local level the Christians probably experienced social and economic discrimination, and they may have suffered from physical violence on sporadic occasions (cf. Rev 1:9; 2:9–10, 13; 6:9–11). Beale orchestrates a plausible conflict related to trade guilds:

> [Christians] were expected to pay their "dues" to trade guilds by attending annual dinners held in honor of the guilds' patron deities. Homage to the emperor as divine was included along with worship of such local deities. For the culture in general these expressions of loyalty were part of being patriotic. After all, the patron gods of the guilds together with the imperial god of Rome were purportedly responsible for the social and economic blessings that the culture had enjoyed. Refusal to show gratefulness to these gods was bad citizenship. The occasional economic deprivation and official governmental persecution still would have tempted Christians to compromise with local trade guild cults and emperor worship.[31]

This does not mean, however, that Revelation was written for the express purpose of comforting church members who were presently being persecuted. *The main purpose of the book is to combat assimilation and apostasy.* The visions, images, and exhortations are geared towards encouraging the recipients to worship God rather than idols and persevere in their faithfulness to Christ. *Perseverance comes by way of their resisting idolatry and pressures from the socioeconomic system related to it, and it also includes their remaining loyal to Christ when sporadic persecutions of church members take place.* The latter is strongly implied by the depictions of martyrs (e.g., 2:13; 6:9–11) and chapters 11–13. The sense of urgency and severe judgments against the imperial cult and its economic system that we find in the later portions of Revelation make better sense if the suffering of the saints includes physical persecution and martyrdom that perhaps starts during the reign of Nero and takes place

---

30. See Friesen, *Imperial Cults*, 29–31, 47–50, 55–59, 150; idem, *Twice Neokoros*, 49–53. Further examples of early imperial cults, some dating back to BCE, may be seen in Winter, *After Paul Left Corinth*, 270–301.

31. Beale, *Revelation*, 30.

from time to time afterward. It is expected to increase as the end approaches; hence, the pressing nature of the book comes more from John's visions than the audience's perception of things. Despite the augment of tribulation brought about by outsiders, John and his audience could trust that vengeance belongs to God and he will repay the Roman system according to its works. He will do violence to this system because it has done violence to the church. Depictions of divine wrath against the enemies of the church probably helped congregants deal with aggressive feelings in a nonviolent way.[32]

The Christians in Revelation could respond to the imperial cult in several ways.[33] First, they could peacefully resist it and face various consequences from outsiders whether ridicule, insults, discrimination, exclusion, slander, incrimination, imprisonment, fines, confiscations, physical harm, torture, or death. Second, they could compromise through minimal participation in civil responsibilities that perhaps fall short of actual emperor worship. The book's denunciation of the Balaamites and followers of Jezebel (ch. 2), along with its general call for the saints to be separate from Roman "Babylon" (e.g., 18:4), would militate against this option. Third, they could attempt to change the civil duties and laws pertaining to it. This is an unlikely option given that local and imperial government did not function like a modern democracy. Fourth, they could form a Christian resistance movement and fight against the Roman system and its military. This, too, would be an unlikely option given the peacemaking teachings of Jesus and the historical example of Zealots in Palestine that attempted such resistance a few decades earlier with disastrous consequences. In Revelation a hope is placed on the second coming of Christ to take vengeance on society for its wrongdoings (ch. 19). Fifth, they could abandon Roman society and move to a place untainted by the imperial cult, a difficult but possible option. Sixth, they could be deceptive, outwardly worshipping Caesar but inwardly worshipping God. This practice might have been justified on the grounds of a "higher" ethic or "lesser of two evils" in order to preserve one's family and self.[34] Revelation 21:8, 27 and 22:15, however, condemn all liars. Finally, they could decide to deny Christ, commit apostasy, and worship Caesar. Among the seven options, the first one seems to be the closest to the message conveyed Revelation. The churches are encouraged

---

32. Historically speaking, however, sometimes such depictions have had a reverse effect on the readers. Collins, *Crisis and Catharsis*, 171, addresses this point and is no doubt correct about the reversal of violence apocalyptic may have. For similar examples of violence in relation to modern prophecies, see Oropeza, *99 Reasons*, 82, 114, 122–23, 172–73.

33. See Boring, *Revelation*, 21–23, for a similar list of options.

34. Beale, *Revelation*, 32, 265, using a similar paradigm, brings up an example of compromise by Christians outwardly participating in pagan worship but praying *for* Caesar instead of *to* Caesar. They perhaps knew but misunderstood Jesus' words to render to Caesar what is Caesar's (Mark 12:17).

to persevere despite potential persecutions. They must neither compromise with the Roman system nor commit apostasy.

THE SEVEN CHURCHES IN ASIA MINOR (2:1—3:22)

We recognize a major distinction between the addresses to the seven churches (Rev 1–3) and the visions that follow (Rev 4–22). A pattern of interlocking sevens also permeates the structure of the book.[35] The recipients of Revelation are called "servants" (1:1), a term sometimes referring to Israelites, but here the people of God are servants of Christ Jesus (Rev 2:20; 7:3; 19:2, 5; 22:3, 6; 1 Cor 7:22; Gal 1:10; Eph 6:6; Col 4:12).[36] This term in Revelation suggests God's ownership and sealing of his people with an ethical implication that God's people must serve him and not the Beast.[37] More prominent is the term "saints" (ἅγιος), which appears thirteen times in the book and refers to God's people. It applies to all Christians[38] and is frequently linked with suffering or persecution perhaps echoing the trials of God's people in Daniel (Rev 13:7; 16:6; 17:6; 18:20, 24; 20:9/Dan 7:18–27).[39] Due to certain congregants' participation in compromised practices (e.g., Rev 2:14, 20), and John's desire for them to be separated from the Roman system (18:4), one of his goals in this work is to get the recipients to see themselves as a holy people and servants set apart for God alone.[40] In this manner he wishes to build up their identity in Christ and deter them from identifying and assimilating with Roman culture and its economic system. Interestingly the word "saint" does not appear in the seven letters section but later on in the book (5:8; 8:3, 4; 11:18; 13:7, 10; 14:12; 16:6; 17:6; 18:20, 24; 19:8; 20:9). The word reflects John's special use of the term rather than the readers' own designation.

The book is addressed to and circulated among seven churches in seven cities of Asia Minor (1:11). Ephesus is mentioned first, and if the ethnicity of the members did not change significantly over the decades, then many of the Christians in this city are Gentiles (e.g., Acts 19–20; 1 Tim 1:3; 3 John 1, 9, 12). Likewise, other congregations in Asia Minor seem to be composed of primarily Gentiles (Eph 2:11; Col 3:1; 1 Pet 1:1; 4:3–4). We assume that many members of the seven churches are

---

35. See, e.g., Schüssler Fiorenza, *Judgment and Justice*, 174. For a survey of prominent structures, see Osborne, "Recent Trends," 495–504. Critical of chiastic structures in Revelation is DeSilva, "Critique of the Use of Chiasm," 343–71.

36. So Aune, *Revelation*, 1.12–13.

37. Cf. Trebilco, "Issue of Self-Designation," 67 (cf. 61–65); Pattemore, *People of God*, 131–32.

38. Rev 13:10; 14:12; 19:7–8.

39. See Pattemore, *People of God*, 118–24.

40. Cf. Trebilco, "Issue of Self-Designation," 70.

also Gentiles. Concerns related to idolatry, idol meats, and fornication that appear in various sections of the book betray a Gentile audience (Rev 2:14, 20, 24; 9:21; 14:8; 21:8; 22:15). Even so, the genre of Jewish apocalyptic, the faithful 144,000 (7:4-8), temple imagery (11:1-3), heavenly Jerusalem (21:10-27), and possible conflicts with local synagogues (e.g., 2:9), among other things, suggest that at least some of John's audience may be Jewish Christians.[41]

The literary pattern of the messages addressed to the churches in chapters 2-3 may be distilled as follows:[42] 1) the destination of the recipient (*adscriptio*); 2) command to write (γράψον); 3) description of the sender beginning with τάδε λέγει; 4) diagnosis of the church situation (*narratio*) often beginning with a commendation and opening with I know (οἶδα); 5) diagnosis of the church situation in which accusations (*accusatio*) are presented against the church (for five of the seven churches—Smyrna and Philadelphia are not accused);[43] 6) exhortation in imperatival language for the church (*exhortatio*); 7) consequence or declaration of penalty (*sanctio*) for unethical behavior (in five of the seven churches); four penalties are hypothetical, but for Thyatira the consequences are inevitable;[44] 8) promise of reward (*remuneratio*) for the overcomer; and 9) concluding proclamation: the one who has an ear, let him hear what the Spirit says to the churches (Ὁ ἔχων οὖς ἀκουσάτω τί τὸ πνεῦμα λέγει ταῖς ἐκκλησίαις). The messages are relevant to the particular church under examination, but in a secondary sense they may also pertain to "the churches" (cf. Rev 2:7 et al; 2:23; 10:10-11), and the reason why seven churches are mentioned instead of more in Asia Minor (e.g., Colossae, Hierapolis) probably implies a symbolic understanding of the number seven as conveying a sense of universality applicable for all churches in every region.

The letters are addressed to the messenger (τῷ ἀγγέλῳ) of the church primarily in the second-person singular. This messenger could be an angel, a human leader (cf. 19:10; 22:9), or even some sort of personification of the spirit in the church.[45] The word normally refers to heavenly beings, and most likely this is the sense here (e.g., 5:2, 11; 8:2; 14:2, 10, 18; 16:1; 18:21). These angels may be viewed as patrons, guardians, or representatives over the churches (19:10; 22:9).[46] If so, then a strong sense of

---

41. Hirschberg, "Jewish Believers in Asia Minor," 223, suggests that Jewish believers have a "central significance" in Smyrna and Philadelphia, and they would take comfort in the message of Rev 3:7-13.

42. For structural formations of Rev 2-3, see esp. Aune, *Revelation*, 1.119-29.

43. This too would be considered part of the *narratio* but, because we will be focusing on accusations, I am making a distinction here.

44. Both numbers 6 and 7 would be considered the central section or *dispositio* according to Aune, *Revelation*, 1.122.

45. For options see, e.g., Müller, *Offenbarung*, 87-89.

46. See further, Dan 10:13, 21; 12:1; Deut 32:8 LXX; *Ascen. Isa.* 3:15; 1QM 12:1-10; *1 En.* 20.5;

corporate identity is assumed between these beings and their churches because they are commended and rebuked on behalf of the congregations' conduct.[47] The alternation between second-person singulars and second-person plurals throughout the oracles also keeps the congregations' members in view as John's target audience.[48] Many words and phrases directed to the seven churches are especially relevant to the recipients' perseverance and apostasy.[49] Such language attests to the purpose of the book in general and this section of it in particular. As we shall observe below through the prophetic voice of John, *the Christ of Revelation is primarily concerned that the churches and their members not commit apostasy as a result of assimilation, suffering persecution, or being lulled into indifference and complacency via materialism.*

LOSING THEIR FIRST LOVE: THE EPHESIANS, FALSE APOSTLES, AND NICOLAITANS (2:1-6)

The first *adscriptio* is to the church in Ephesus, which is perhaps the most prominent church in the region. In earliest Christian writings it is mentioned most often of the seven congregations (2:1-6).[50] If the message to the seven churches is written

---

Aune, *Revelation*, 1.110; Str.B. 1.781-83; 2.707-8; 3.437-40.

47. These angels are placed in Christ's hand and are sometimes rebuked perhaps as a way of demonstrating Christ's superiority and authority over them as well as the churches (cf. 1:20). This depiction would be one way to subvert angel veneration that was prominent in the region (cf. Rev 19:10; 22:8-9). On angels see further Stuckenbruck, *Angel Veneration and Christology*.

48. Special thanks to David DeSilva for this insight.

49. I.e., perseverance, endurance (ὑπομονή): 2:2, 3, 19; 3:10 (cf. 1:9; 13:7-10; 14:9-12); To become/not become weary, toil (κοπιάω): 2:2-3; To bear (βαστάζω): 2:3; To leave, forsake, abandon (ἀφίημι): 2:4; To remember (μνημονεύω) the former ways: 2:5; 3:3; To fall (πίπτω): 2:5 (cf. 9:1; 12:4); To repent (μετανοέω): 2:5, 16, 21-22; 3:3, 19 (cf. 9:20-21; 16:9, 11); "If not . . ." (εἰ δὲ μή), implying failure to comply with command/exhortation (2:5, 16, 22; 3:3; cf. also 2:21: "I gave her time to repent"); To overcome, conquer (νικάω): 2:7, 11, 17, 26; 3:5, 12, 21; To hear (ἀκούω), implying obedience: 2:7, 11, 17, 29; 3:6, 13, 22; To suffer, endure (πάσχω): 2:10; To not fear (φοβέω): 2:10; To be faithful (γίνομαι + πιστός): 2:10 (cf. 2:13; 2:24: the remnant; i.e., those remaining faithful); Tribulation, suffering (θλῖψις): 2:9-10, 22 (cf. 1:9; 7:14); To test, tempt/ trial, temptation: 2:10 (πειράζω); 3:10 (πειρασμός); To hold fast (κρατέω): 2:13, 25; 3:11; To not deny (ἀρνέομαι): 2:13 (Christ's faith); 3:8 (Christ's name) (cf. 1:3, 9; 13:7-10; 14:12); To cast a stumbling block (σκάνδαλον): 2:14; To lead astray (πλανάω): 2:20; To keep (τηρέω): 2:26 (until the end); 3:3 (the first works); 3:8, 10 (Christ's word); 3:10 (reciprocates Christ keeping them) (cf. 14:9-12); Dead and about to die: 3:1-2 (contrast 2:11); To strengthen, confirm (στηρίζω): 3:2; To be watchful, wake up (γρηγορέω): 3:2-3; To not stain, defile (μολύνω) one's garment: 3:4; To not erase, blot out (ἐξαλείφω) one's name from the book of life: 3:5 (contrast 13:8; 22:18-19); To not go out of God's temple: 3:12 (contrast removal 2:5; vomiting out: 3:16; and implications of 2:16, 22-23; 3:3); Blind (τυφλός): 3:17-18; To be earnest, zealous (ζηλεύω): 3:19.

50. Cf. Acts 18:19-20:28; 21:29; 1 Cor 15:32; 16:8; Eph 1:1; 1 Tim 1:3; 2 Tim 1:18; 4:12; Ign. *Eph.* 1; cf. Johannine community (volume one). In the NT, see Thyatira in Acts 16:14. On Laodicea see Col 2:1; 4:13-16.

Revelation

at the close of the first century, the church in Ephesus had been founded over forty years earlier, with perhaps only a few elderly members remaining from the original congregation. A Pauline church existed in Ephesus from the time of Paul's evangelism in that area in about 55 CE (Acts 19). Even prior to this time, however, a church or group of Jewish believers in Jesus as the Christ may have existed.[51] By the time the church is addressed in Revelation, many of those belonging to the Pauline community would have been born and raised in the Christian community. And the Johannine community, if they had not merged with the Pauline believers, had now been in Ephesus for a couple of decades.[52] Evidently the vision of Christ in Revelation addresses all Christian groups in Ephesus.

In the *narratio* Christ commends the church by acknowledging the congregation's works (2:2; cf. ἔργον: 2:5, 19; 3:1, 8, 15). Works stand out prominently in Revelation because on the day of judgment the Lord will render to everyone as their deeds deserve (2:23c; 14:13; 20:12–13). This view was held in common with other emerging Christian groups (e.g., Matt 25:31–46; Rom 2:6; 2 Cor 5:10; 2 Tim 4:14; 1 Pet 1:17). The white throne judgment in Rev 20:11–15 depicts a day of reckoning in which both non-Christians and Christians who were not martyred in 20:4 will be judged. Works, it seems, are to be associated with the manifestation of righteous behavior, and the thought in Revelation may echo the Johannine Jesus in which both the righteous and unrighteous are known by their deeds (John 3:20–21; 7:7; 1 John 3:12).

In Rev 2:2–3 we uncover a hint of Jesus' parable of the Laborers in the Vineyard who toil and bear the burden of the day working for the landowner (Matt 20:1–12). Unlike the first laborers in the parable, however, the Ephesians do not complain about the last workers getting paid the same amount as they do; rather, they are commended for not growing weary in their labors for the kingdom of God. They have persevered through troubles bearing them patiently for the sake of Christ's name and proved themselves faithful (Rev 2:2–3; cf. 2:19; 3:10). In essence they live in a way Christ would want them to live as a people dwelling in the midst of an environment that is hostile to all that he represents. The thought of their patience for Christ's name includes putting up with harassment and discrimination for being identified as "Christian" (cf. 1 Pet 4:16). *Their faithfulness through hardships has demonstrated the authenticity of their Christian confession.* The local outsiders probably interpreted

---

51. See, e.g., Acts 18:19–21. Trebilco, *Early Christians in Ephesus*, 107–9, 153, suggests that some Jews may have adhered to the Christ message as early as Pentecost in Acts 2:5, 9 (c. 33 CE). If so, then there is no reason for us to assume that all the Christians in Ephesus during the 50s and 60s CE were Paulinists.

52. See further my treatment of the Johannine writings in volume 1.

a person who claims to be "Christian" as someone who refuses to participate in societal activities that promote cultural cohesiveness and patriotism, such as the worship of Artemis and devoted loyalty to Caesar. The Christians would be seen as peculiar and antisocial, shunning the very things their compatriots take pride in as a famous religious center and the provincial temple warden.

The Ephesians are commended also for their intolerance of evil and their discernment in detecting false apostles. The counterfeit leaders should not be confused with the "super apostles" and agents of Satan that Paul warned against forty years earlier (cf. 2 Cor 11:1–14). That generation had probably passed away. More relevant for the Ephesians are earlier records about leaders from among their own ranks who during the last days would exploit for financial gain and cause members to go astray, whether by denying the resurrection or teaching Jewish myths and dietary regulations (Acts 20:28–32; 1 Tim 4:1–5; 2 Tim 3:1–6). In addition to deceivers in the Pauline church, others from the Johannine community held to false beliefs about the nature of Christ (cf. 1 John 4:1–6; 2 John 8–11). Perhaps the Christians in Ephesus at the end of the first century had taken seriously these earlier warnings against false teachers and contested them accordingly. They tested and exposed as fraudulent the crooked shepherds of God's flock and itinerant preachers who perhaps claimed to be the successors of first-generation apostles or claimed to possess apostolic authority. Throughout the church's extended history the believers in Ephesus had challenged those who would lead them astray from the gospel message into apostasy.[53]

It does not appear to be the case that the false apostles are associated with the Nicolaitans (Rev 2:6).[54] The Nicolaitans seem to be another group the Ephesians encountered (2:6 cf. 2:15). Among various options scholars have associated them with the Balaamites (cf. 2:14), "Jezebel" (2:20), a Gnostic-like sect, fallen Hellenistic Jews, and post-Paulinists turned antinomian and unconcerned about eating meat sacrificed to idols (cf. 1 Cor 8; 2 Pet 3:16–17).[55] The name "Nicolaos" may be a Greek play

---

53. False teachers again attempt to visit this church in the early second century, according Ign. *Eph.* 7–9.

54. Contrast, e.g., Roloff, *Revelation*, 44. Correctly, Trebilco, *Early Christians in Ephesus*, 302, says the apostles are mentioned as a past threat (aorist tenses), but the Nicolaitans are mentioned as an ongoing conflict (present tenses). Likewise, the adversative ἀλλά in 2:6 starts a new thought separating the two groups.

55. On the Gnostic view see, e.g., Schüssler Fiorenza, *Justice and Judgment*, 114–32; on Hellenistic Jews, e.g., Lupieri, *Apocalypse*, 116; on Paulinists, e.g., Hemer, *Seven Churches*, 87–94. See discussions in Giesen, *Offenbarung*, 100–103. Another possibility associates Nicolaos's bodily abuse with ascetic practices (cf. 1 Tim 4:1–6). If this is the original error of the Nicolaitans, then the Ephesians are not coming against a sect that is morally lax regarding the physical body but one that is too strict. One weakness with this view is that the church in 2:14–15 would then be rebuked for having adherents who are too morally loose (Balaamites) and others who are ascetic (Nicolaitans). This is not impossible

on the words "conqueror" and "people," which brings it into orbit with "Balaam," meaning in Hebrew "lord of the people" or "he has destroyed the people."[56] Apart from similarity in word meanings, a connection between what the Balaamites practice in 2:14 (fornication and consumption of idol meats) and the Nicolaitans in 2:15 is made by the use of οὕτως ("so," "in this manner," "in this way") plus ὁμοίως ("likewise," "similarly," "in the same way"). The words perhaps suggest that the latter group practices the same things as the former. However, if the point of comparison rests squarely on their casting a stumbling block before "Israel," then the content of their teachings and practices are not necessarily the same. Rather, both the Balaamites and Nicolaitans lead God's people into apostasy, causing them to go astray from the way God intends for them.[57] In the end it is not clear that the Nicolaitans eat idol meats and commit fornication as do the Balaamites.

Some early accounts of the Nicolaitans' origin purport that Nicolaos, one of the seven Jewish-Hellenistic ministers in Jerusalem mentioned in Acts 6:5, was the founder. He apostatized, and his followers adhered to Corinthian Gnosticism and were known for unrestrained, indulgent behavior related to fornication and idol foods (Irenaeus, *Haer.* 1.26.3; Hippolytus, *Haer.* 7.24). Others assert that the Nicolaitans were given over to sexual pleasures by perverting Nicolaos's words that one ought to abuse the flesh (Clement of Alexandria, *Miscellanies* 2.20; Eusebius, *Hist. eccl.* 3.29.1–3). The thought according to Eusebius arises from the matrix of Nicolaos being accused of jealousy by the apostles on account of his beautiful wife. In response the deacon reportedly gave consent to anyone who wished to marry her. The longer version of Ignatius, *Trallians* 11B claims the Nicolaitans were lovers of pleasure and malicious speeches, but this version does not make a connection between this group and the minister from Acts 6. Whether this group actually stemmed from Nicolaos or not, the early sources tend to agree that the Christian sect practiced immoral behavior. But it is always possible that this belief about their unethical behavior is due to church fathers associating the Nicolaitans with the Balaamites. The Ephesians, in any case, are commended for not following the deeds of the Nicolaitans.

The *accusatio* in this pericope centers on the Ephesians abandoning their "first love" (Rev 2:4). These Christians seem to have fallen into some sort of indifference

---

given diverse behaviors within early congregations (e.g., 1 Cor 5:1–5; 6:12–20; and yet see 7:1), but it is nonetheless odd from the vantage point that both groups are mentioned in practically the same breath.

56. Cf. Watson, "Nicolaitans," 4.1107. On the other hand, a distinction between the two names is made by Aune, *Revelation*, 1.149, who argues that Balaam is a pejorative name whereas Nicolaos is one of honor.

57. Notice also the adverb οὕτως could be translated "as follows" without highlighting a comparison. If translated "so," Vincent, *Word Studies*, 2.449, provides an interesting interpretation: "Even as Balak had Balaam for a false teacher, hast thou the Nicolaitan teachers."

towards the things of God. Today, earliest remains of the Christian district in Ephesus suggest this community was not at all impoverished.[58] They had become a thriving merchant class that had to be warned against extravagance in dress and setting their hopes in riches (cf. 1 Tim 2:8–10; 6:6–10, 17). Perhaps their preoccupation with gaining wealth led to some of them losing their love for the things of Christ. The thought may come close to the Matthean Jesus' prediction about an apostasy and increase in lawlessness whereby the love of many would grow cold (Matt 24:10). But lawlessness, at least, does not appear to be a problem for the Ephesians—the church does not tolerate evil persons (Rev 2:2). We find another relevant comparison by observing the Johannine Jesus' exhortations for his followers to love the Father, the Son, and one another (e.g., John 13:34–35; 14:15, 21–24; 15:12–13), which are variations of the great commandment to love God and their neighbors as themselves (Mark 12:29–31; Matt 22:37–39; Luke 10:27).[59] If in fact love was stressed to the Christ-followers in Ephesus by the elder of the Johannine community so that their not helping needy believers was considered sin,[60] and if this group in Rev 2 has any of the same members, then such an accusation by the glorified Christ would be especially poignant to them. It seems that *despite prior teachings, the Ephesians had allowed their love for God, Christ, and fellow believers to grow cold.*

Next, the Ephesians are exhorted (*exhortatio*) to remember how far they have fallen, repent, and do the first works (Rev 2:5). These works are presumably their previous deeds that originated from the motivation of love.[61] How this would look different than their present works is not known. Perhaps their current works were being done with a wrong attitude, more for duty's sake than love. More plausible is that their lack of love evolved into a preoccupation with business pursuits, neglecting prayer, fellowship, helping out fellow believers, and being a witness to outsiders. Christ calls them back to a more fervent love that exemplifies itself in their unified fellowship, devotion to God, and unselfish giving of themselves to others. They must repent,[62] but unlike the non-believers whose repentance is bound up with conversion,[63] the Ephesian congregants are already believers who had been converted years earlier. Their repentance involves something similar to confession

---

58. On the socioeconomic level of Christians in Western Asia Minor, see Duff, *Who Rides the Beast?*, 24–29; cf. 37.

59. There is no need to decide on which end of this equation the Ephesians lacked; loving God and Christ spills over to loving one's neighbor.

60. 1 John 2:10; 3:10–11, 16–23; 4:7–12; 5:1; 2 John 5; cf. 1 John 3:17–18.

61. So Witherington, *Revelation*, 96.

62. μετανοέω: 2:5; cf. 2:16, 21–22; 3:3, 19.

63. Cf. 9:20–21; 16:9, 11.

and forgiveness (cf. 1 John 1:9; Matt 6:9-11; Luke 11:4). The Ephesians must ask God to forgive them for their lack of love, and they must go back to doing their former works.

A call to remember is often used in paraenetic contexts[64] and frequently challenges the early believers to walk according to appropriate Christian standards both morally and spiritually (cf. Rom 15:15; 1 Cor 15:1; 1 Thess 1:5-10; 4:1-2; Heb 10:32-35; 2 Pet 1:12-13).[65] This idea is certainly present in 2:5. Further it is possible that the aspect of remembrance would evoke God's warning to Israel not to forget God and fall away during times of prosperity: they were to remember God's commandments and what God had done for them by delivering them from Egypt and leading them through the wilderness as he taught them to depend on him (e.g., Deut 6:12; 8:2-20; 9:7; 32:18; cf. 4:9-26; 26:13). Similarly, the Ephesians must recall their earlier years of fervency as new believers who were grateful for their deliverance from sin and demonstrated that gratitude by their earnest love for God and others. Beyond Deuteronomic allusions, however, the Ephesians had to consider how backslidden they had already become in comparison to those earlier times of fervent love. The word for fallen (πίπτω: 2:5) is sometimes used to convey apostasy (cf. 1 Cor 10:12; Rom 11:11, 22; Heb 4:11). The Ephesians had not yet rejected their faith (cf. Rev 2:2-3), but *if they remain on the course of loveless behavior, then they might end up forgetting about God and their Christian commitment altogether.*

The conditional εἰ δὲ μή ("if not . . .") introduces negative consequences that will take place if the *exhortatio* is not followed. Should the church fail to comply with Christ's exhortation to repent, they will be punished (*sanctio*). Christ will come and remove the lampstand from the unrepentant church's place (2:5b). These words recall priestly narratives in which Israel's great lampstand is placed before the Holy of Holies, the meeting place between God and Israel's representatives (e.g., Lev 24:2-4; 1 Kgs 7:49; Zech 4:1-14).[66] If Christ's presence is in the midst of the seven lampstands, and these lampstands represent the seven churches (Rev 1:12-13, 20; 2:1), then the threat of removal is nothing less than his banishing the church from his presence. This punishment suggests either that the congregation would be destroyed or no longer be recognized as belonging to Christ or both.

Christ's coming to the church represents a visitation in judgment, but when? His *parousia* is imminent (1:3, 7) and such intimations about his second coming

---

64. E.g., 1 Thess 2:9; Eph 2:11; 2 Pet 3:1; Jude 5.

65. Cf. Aune, *Revelation*, 1.147: "In the OT and early Judaism, the motif of 'remembering' was sometimes used in contexts where people were summoned to repentance (Isa 44:21; 46:8-9; Mic 6:5; Sir 7:28; 23:14; 28:6-7; 38:22)."

66. See, e.g., Prigent, *Apocalypse*, 160.

should not be excluded from 2:5. *When Christ returns to defeat his enemies and fully establish his kingdom, the unrepentant Ephesians would be excluded from his presence.*[67] When we compare this consequence with other New Testament writings, it is virtually indistinguishable to what happens to apostates on judgment day. Unlike the churches of Pergamum and Thyatira, however, the corporate identity of the Ephesian church is stressed without specifying individuals or sectors of the congregation that are doing right or wrong things. Even though it is not stated, Christ's eschatological punishment no doubt pertains only to the members of the church who do not repent. In other words, even if this church as a whole will not repent, this does not preclude that some individuals from within the church could not repent and escape future judgment. The same would appear to be true for all the churches, especially Pergamum, Thyatira, and Sardis where righteous members of the group who have not participated in the accusation leveled against the respective churches are acknowledged.

OVERCOMERS AND COWARDS (2:7; CF. 21:7-8, 11; 22:15)

The exhortation to the seven churches to hear what the Spirit says (2:7, 11, 17, 29; 3:6, 13, 22) recalls Jesus' words in the gospels, which in turn points to the prophetic texts in which God sends the prophet to a spiritually obdurate people (Mark 4:9, 23–25; Matt 11:15; Luke 8:8; cf. Isa 6:9–10; Ezek 3:27; 12:2).[68] The requirement in Revelation to "hear" should be understood in terms of obedience. Although the auditors are expected to repent, these words leave open the possibility that some members in Ephesus and the church at large (i.e., "to the churches") may not respond to the exhortations.[69]

---

67. Contrast Beale, *Revelation*, 231–32, who understands the judgment here to mean that their light would no longer be a witness to anyone (cf. Isa 42:6–7; 49:6; Matt 5:13–14; Mark 4:23; Luke 8:8). He argues that the coming of Christ in this passage is not the second coming but a general visitation (cf. Dan 7:13; Mark 10:45; Luke 7:34; 19:10; Matt 10:23; Mark 13:26; 14:62). Otherwise the punishment would be irrelevant, for the church could only be a witness before the *parousia*. This view comes up deficient in light of Osborne, *Revelation*, 118, who maintains that ἔρχομαι in the early chapters always refers to the *parousia* (1:4, 7–8; 2:16; 3:10–11). Osborne does not consider this an either/or issue but one in which present and future interplay: "Christ's coming in judgment in the present is a harbinger of his final coming. In the context Christ's displeasure will be felt both in the present and at the final judgment."

68. See esp. Beale, *Revelation*, 236–38. The message of obduracy, especially in Isa 6, is often repeated in early church communities as an apologetic to explain why many Jews rejected Jesus as the Christ—their apostasy and spiritual blindness was predicted long ago in Isaiah (see on Mark 4:10–12 in volume 1; cf. Rom 11:7–8; *Barn.* 9.5; Justin, *Dial.* 12.2; Tertullian, *Modesty* 8.5; *Marc.* 3.6).

69. Even so, Prigent, *Apocalypse*, 161, writes that prophetic writing elicited by God's Spirit can be understood by those who have encountered God's Spirit. A more puzzling passage that may also in-

Revelation

The overcomer or one who conquers (τῷ νικῶντι/ὁ νικῶν: 2:7; 2:11, 17, 26; 3:5, 12, 21) relates to the metaphor of war; in Revelation a spiritual battle is waged against the saints by the Dragon and Beast (cf. Rev 12:7, 11; 13:7).[70] The overcomer does not commit apostasy but remains faithful through the struggle; among the believers in Ephesus he or she is the one who takes heed to Christ's warnings and repents. Such individuals gain a heavenly reward (*remuneratio*) and inheritance (cf. 2:26; 21:7). The notion of overcoming reflects the words of the Johannine Jesus, who taught his followers to endure tribulation in the world and yet be joyful and at peace knowing that Jesus has overcome the world (John 16:33; 1 John 5:4–5). In Revelation Christ overcomes as the "Lamb" and "Lion of the tribe of Judah," whose death redeems humankind (Rev 5:5–10)—he is viewed as conqueror over sin, death, and the satanically inspired kingdom of the Beast (1:18; 3:21; 17:14; 19:11–21).

Those who overcome the Dragon and the Beast are able to do so through their redemption in Christ as well as their witness and confession before outsiders, even if this requires being put to death (12:11; 15:2 cf. 1:9; 6:9; 12:17; 19:10; 20:4). The mar-

---

teract with spiritual obduracy is Rev 22:11, where not only are the righteous/holy charged to practice righteousness/holiness, but the unrighteous/filthy are to do unrighteousness/filthiness (cf. Dan 12:10). One way of interpreting the negative side of this verse is to compare it with Israel's scriptures where obduracy leads to divine judgment or is itself viewed as such judgment (cf. Isa 6:9–10; 29:9–10; Jer 44:25; Ezek 3:27; 20:39). God's people frequently become hardened, spiritually blind, or dull of hearing because of their own stubbornness and rebellion against God (Exod 32:9; 33:3–5; 34:9; Lev 26:41; Deut 9:6–27; 10:16; 29:3; 31:27; Ezek 3:7, 20; 18:5–32; Jer 5:19–23; Zech 7:8–13. See further Judg 2:19; 1 Sam 15:23; 2 Kgs 17:24; Neh 9:16–29; Sir 15:11–20; Schenker, "Gerichtsverkündigung und Verblendung," 563–75; Räisänen, *Divine Hardening*, 45–66; Evans, *To See and Not Perceive*, 47–52; McLaughlin, "Their Hearts Were Hardened," 8; Beale, *Revelation*, 236–38; 1132–33). Oftentimes the remedy for those who are hardened is repentance and a renewed heart (Deut 30:6; Josh 24:23; Jer 31:33; Ezek 11:19; 36:26; 1QS 5:4–5; Philo, *Spec.* 1.304–307; cf. Isa 63:17–18; 1 Kgs 8:58; Ps 119:36; 1QH 18.17–21). The people are held responsible for their spiritual blindness—they must keep God's covenant if they wish to prosper; rejecting it incurs divine punishment (cf. Josh 24:15; Deut 30:1–6, 19). If Rev 22:11 follows such thoughts, we would suspect the verse marshals a rhetorical strategy to shock the hearer to repentance (cf. Rev 2:5, 16, 21; 3:1, 19). A second option for this verse is that there is an element of prophetic call to John similar to Rev 2:7 and passages in Isaiah, Ezekiel, and Daniel. He is sent to a rebellious people with this message of revelation from Christ, and some will accept it while others will reject it. Osborne, *Revelation*, 787, writes that John and his leaders' "task is not to act as moral policemen but simply to proclaim the prophecies (22:10) and let God do his work." A third explanation is that 22:11 anticipates the sudden coming of Christ in 22:12, and when that event takes place it will be too late to alter one's character (e.g., Sweet, *Apocalypse*, 305). Differently, Prigent, *Apocalypse*, 638, suggests that the last days will expose the true character of people. Ultimately, however, Prigent suspects that "a foreign element has been forcefully integrated without being harmonized with the context." The passage, in any case, seems to have as its rhetorical aim the auditors' repentance. Hence, unless no one among the audience needs to repent, the first option of God hardening the unrighteous/filthy would seem to be counterproductive to the rhetorical aim.

70. Friedrich, "Socio-Political Reading of Revelation," 207, adds that "to conquer" may be used in Revelation to counter the theme of "victory" espoused by imperial propaganda.

tyrs would rather lose their mortal life and so gain eternal life than save the former at the price of the latter (cf. John 12:25; Mark 8:35; Matt 16:25; Luke 9:24). Spiritual victory comes at the high cost of their being willing to die for the cause of remaining faithful to Christ, resisting vices, performing righteous deeds, and resisting satanic powers (Rev 21:7–8; cf. 2:10–11, 26; 3:4–5, 11–12; 12:11; 14:12; 15:2; 17:14).[71]

In contrast to the overcomers in 21:7, *the "cowardly," "faithless," and "liars" who suffer the second death in 21:8 include former believers who turned apostates for fear of being persecuted.* The faithless probably includes those who renounce their faith, and liars include those who deny Christ as Lord. Especially relevant to the cowardly (δειλός) is the second-century tradition of a Phrygian Christian named Quintus, who, under the proconsul of Statius Quadratus in Asia Minor, committed apostasy by turning coward (δειλιάω) and offering a sacrifice to Caesar (*Mart. Pol.* 4; cf. 8.2; 9.2–3).[72] The conduct of the cowardly in Revelation most likely assumes a similar backdrop—they are Christians who turn apostate by succumbing to the imperial cult. Similarly, Hermas mentions the double-minded who "whenever they hear of tribulation commit idolatry because of their cowardice [δειλία], and they are ashamed of the name of their Lord" (*Sim.* 9.21.3). Such apostates are mentioned among the vicedoers in Rev 21:8. Kenneth Strand suggests the "categories of non-inheritors" here reflect the characteristics of those creating problems in the seven churches.[73] Indeed some vicedoers in 21:8, such as fornicators and idolaters, are found in the churches (i.e., Pergamum, Thyatira), but others such as murderers are not clearly seen. Other vice lists in Revelation seem to focus primarily on the practices of outsiders (cf. 9:20–21; 22:15) and are somewhat conventional regarding "pagan" practices. The term "dogs" in 22:15, however, may be identifying Christian apostates and false teachers (cf. 2 Pet 2:22; Matt 7:6; *Did.* 9.5; Ign. *Eph.* 7.1).[74] At any event some of the terms in 21:8 refer to apostates, the antithesis of Christians who overcome by persevering until Christ returns.

The specific reward for those who overcome in 2:7 is that they will eat of the tree of life in the paradise of God (cf. Gen 2:9), an indication that they will partici-

---

71. Strand, "'Overcomer,'" 250–51, rightly affirms the theme of overcoming to be integral for Revelation and that the saints' reward and release for overcoming is "deserved." On the concept see further Wis 4:2; *4 Ezra* 7.127–28; *2 Clem.* 16.2; Bauckham, *Revelation*, 88–94.

72. Contrast Polycarp who refuses to deny Christ and thus suffers martyrdom; unlike the cowardly, he adheres to a heavenly voice that charges him to be strong (ἰσχύω) and act like a man (ἀνδρίζω) in *Mart. Pol.* 9.1. Other aspects of apostasy in this text include a denial of faith (2.4) and reviling Christ (9.3). Eternal fire is the consequential punishment for falling away (2.3).

73. Strand, "Overcomer," 151.

74. An alternative interpretation of "dogs" relates the term to the cult of Hecate: cf. Strelan, "Outside Are the Dogs," 148–57.

pate in the blessings of the heavenly Jerusalem (Rev 22:1–5).[75] The reversal of the curse of Eden takes place at the end of Revelation (cf. 21:4; 22:1–3), and a number of particulars in chapters 21–22 are seen in the rewards to the overcomers among the seven churches (chs. 2–3). Colin Hemer, for example, associates the cross with the tree of life (2:7); the reversal of the curse is made possible through salvation provided by Christ's redemptive act on the cross.[76] Matthijs den Dulk traces a salvation-historical framework related to the overcomer's promises in Rev 2–3 to uncover a progression from the creation story to the exaltation of Christ. The creation tale is implied by the tree of life in Rev 2:7 (cf. Gen 2:9), and then the storyline progresses to the subject of death in 2:11 (cf. Gen 2:17), manna and ephod stones related to the holy place in 2:17 (cf. Exod 16:32–34; 28:9–10; 28f), the star prophecy of Balaam in 2:26–28 (cf. Num 24:17), the book of life and garments related to Sinai in 3:5 (cf. Exod 32:32–34), the pillars of the temple in Jerusalem in 3:12 (cf. 1 Kgs 7:21), and Christ's ministry and exaltation in 3:21.[77] The progression in the text implies a relationship with God and the original couple in paradise through the promise given to the first of the seven churches (Rev 2:7), then a disturbance through death (2:11), a restoration in part by service in the tabernacle (2:17), the predicted reign of Messiah (2:26–28), a weak union at Sinai (3:5), and intimations of a partially glorious temple (3:12) before reaching the promise of the Messiah's reign via the promise to seventh church (3:21).[78]

Portions of at least some of the promises made to each church are well supported by den Dulk, but other promises are less clear.[79] The gist of his argument is nevertheless sustained. The combined promises of Rev 2–3 recapitulate a delicate subnarrative of *Heilsgeschichte* from paradise to paradise lost, and then from partial restoration to paradise restored through the Messiah. To this we would add that the promises find their fulfillment in the climactic ending in Rev 20–22 when the overcomers are rewarded and experience God's presence. Even so, if the promises of reward are eternal and anticipate the culmination of all things,[80] then it follows that the sanctions given to the seven churches, at least those pertaining to Christ's coming, point to eternal punishment (2:5, 16; 3:3; cf. 11:18; 21:8). *The church members in Asia Minor will experience either the reality of eternal reward or eternal punishment*

---

75. Cf. *4 Ezra* 2:12; 8:52; *Pss. Sol.* 14:2–3; *T. Lev* .18.10–11; 1QH 6.14–19; 7.4.

76. Hemer, *Seven Churches*, 44. The tree of life likewise stands as a polemic against the fertility cult of Artemis in Ephesus (44–47).

77. Dulk, "Promises to the Conquerors," 516–22.

78. Ibid., 521.

79. E.g., see Dulk's interpretation of the stone in 2:17 and white garment in 3:5.

80. 2:7, 11, 17, 26; 3:5, 12, 21; cf. 11:18; 21:7; 22:12.

depending on their deeds. If we nullify the reality of apostasy in these texts then we also cheapen the value of those who overcome.

SMYRNA AND THE SYNAGOGUE OF SATAN (2:8–11)

The next *adscriptio* is to the church in Smyrna (2:8–11), which experiences poverty, tribulation, and blasphemy from the "synagogue of Satan." Possibly their poverty came about through local persecutions in the form of property confiscation, imprisonment, and economic discrimination (cf. Heb 10:32–34). At very least their unwillingness to compromise with idolatry and assimilation, especially in separating themselves from various trade guilds, has contributed to their economic condition. Although the congregation is poor, they are considered spiritually rich (Rev 2:9 cf. 2 Cor 6:10; 8:9; Philo, *Good Person* 17). Christ himself is their source of wealth,[81] and their anticipated eschatological prize for faithfulness is a "crown of life" (2:10). In a general way the church of Smyrna's circumstances reminisce Jesus' saying, "Blessed are you poor, for yours is the kingdom of God" (Luke 6:20).

Their opponents are the "synagogue of Satan" who are accused of "blasphemy" (βλασφημία). This could mean that they curse the name of Christ (Rev 2:9 cf. Acts 13:45; 18:5–6; 26:11; 1 Cor 12:3) or slander the church (Mark 7:22; Ign. *Eph.* 10.2). The latter would seem to affect the Smyrnan Christians more directly than the former, but it is always possible that both aspects are in view. If the opponents' blasphemy includes their attributing the works of the congregation to Satan, this would be similar to the religious leaders blaspheming God's Spirit by claiming Jesus' miracles were done by the prince of demons (cf. Mark 3:20–30; Matt 12:22–32; Luke 11:14–23). Perhaps the opponents' accusation is thrown back at them by calling them the synagogue of Satan.

The identity of this synagogue and the "Jews" in 2:9 and 3:9 has sparked endless discussions.[82] We concur with many scholars that there are certain Jews in Smyrna who are perceived as persecuting the local church.[83] They are perhaps called the "synagogue of Satan" not merely because they attend a local synagogue but also as a counter-accusation for their reproaching Christ and his church as demonic. As well, they might be given this label because Satan is perceived as influencing them

---

81. Cf. Royalty, *Ideology of Wealth*, 160, who among other things adds that Christ wears gold and has golden lampstands (Rev 1).

82. For samplers see, e.g., Mayo, *Those Who Call Themselves Jews*; Lohse, *Synagogue des Satana*; Frankfurter, "Jews or Not?," 403–25; Borgen, "Polemic in the Book of Revelation," 199–211; Collins, "Insiders and Outsiders," 187–210.

83. Contrast Frankfurter, "Jews or Not?," 403–25, who thinks they are Gentiles of Pauline persuasion, and Wilson, "Gentile Judaizers," 613–14, who considers them to be Gentile Judaizers.

to persecute the church (12:3–4, 10–17; 20:7–10; cf. 2:13). If so, it would seem that they are unwittingly used by Satan who is viewed as a deceiver (20:8, 10; cf. 2:26). The accusation is similar to that of the Johannine Jesus in John 8:44, "you are of your father the devil," which is motivated in the narrative by Jesus' response to a crowd seeking to kill him and claiming that he is demon-possessed (John 8:40, 48). In the gospel passage the opponents are clearly apostate Jewish Christians. It is possible that the main opponents in Smyrna were once Christ-followers who defected and then turned hostile toward the local church. They may have influenced others in the synagogue to do likewise. But this tantalizing view lacks appropriate support.

In any case sporadic persecutions of the Christ-followers by Jewish sects are evident from Josephus and early Christian literature, though the latter sources are biased (Joshephus, *Ant.* 20.9.1; Acts 7–9, 13–14; 17:5–10; 1 Thess 2:14–16; Justin, *Dial.* 16; 17.1; 47.4; 93.4; 108.3; 137.2; Eusebius, *Hist. eccl.* 5.16.12).[84] This information steers us away from the idea that John's community is not addressing an actual conflict in Smyrna or Philadelphia but is attempting only to foster enmity between the churches and the local synagogues for the purpose of safeguarding against church members defecting to these synagogues.[85] To be sure, Christian vilification of Jews helped confirm the boundaries between churches and synagogues,[86] but harassment and persecution in Revelation still reflects a live crisis.

After the Judean war with Rome, Jewish communities from the Diaspora had to pay taxes to the Roman temple of Jupiter Capitolinus and felt pressured to demonstrate civil loyalties. The number of God-fearers in Asian synagogues perhaps played a factor in helping assuage societal alienation of the Jews, but if any of these Gentiles changed their loyalty to local Christian congregations, this may have caused a loss of social prestige for certain Jewish communities.[87] Moreover, as Peter Hirschberg suggests, because the early Christians were often associated with emergent Judaism, this association had a tendency to discredit local Jewish communities before the eyes of their Hellenistic-Roman neighbors who considered the Christian way as superstitious and politically dangerous. Such factors may have been incentives for expelling Christ-followers from the synagogues, a phenomenon seen in John 9:22; 12:42; and 16:2. As such, Christians would no longer be under the legal protection and exemptions of the Jewish religion (*religio lecita*). They would be left "at the mercy of the Romans."[88]

84. See further Charles, *Revelation*, 1.56–57.
85. Contrast Duff, "Crisis Mongering," 148, 168.
86. See Collins, "Vilification and Self-Definition," 308–20.
87. Cf. Hirschberg, "Jewish Believers," 221.
88. Hirschberg, "Jewish Believers," 222.

Churches under Siege of Persecution and Assimilation

A plausible scenario in Smyrna is that the local synagogue ostracized the Christ-followers, presumably a large amount being Jewish, from attending the synagogue. This left them vulnerable to harassment by Gentile outsiders. To make matters worse, some of the synagogue members possibly brought forth accusations against church members before local Roman officials.[89]

Revelation 2:9 and 3:9 nonetheless are not blanket statements against all Jews but typical of the kind of harsh language a minority group would use against a religious majority. No doubt, both the Christian community in Smyrna and their opponents from the synagogue made claims of being perpetrators of Israel's traditions.[90] This predicament would be similar to the Jews from the Qumran sect considering other religious Jews to be the congregation of traitors and the assembly of Belial (CD 1.12; cf. 1QH 2.22; 1QHa 10.22). Criticisms and denunciation like these also ring true within early Christian circles: as we have observed already, the author of 2 Peter does not hesitate to use vituperative language against apostate Christians (2 Pet 2), nor does Paul when it comes to calling his Christian opponents "servants of Satan" (cf. 2 Cor 11:1–14).

Church members in Smyrna receive no accusation from Christ. They must remain faithful and not be afraid of the persecution they will encounter (Rev 2:10). The devil will soon cast some of them into prison and they will be tried for "ten days," which could be understood either as literal days or symbolic for a complete period of testing (cf. Gen 24:55; Dan 1:12–15; Jer 42:7). If the devil and Satan in Rev 2:9–10 are used interchangeably (cf. 12:9), the implication may be that Satan will influence the synagogue to help bring about this imprisonment. If prisons at this time were normally used as holding places before a sentence was carried out, then either pardon or punishment would await the Christians after the period of testing. Regardless of the outcome they are to remain faithful until death (2:10; cf. 12:11). Some faint words of Jesus in the relation to the persecutions of his followers may be heard in the background—the person who endures to the end will be saved (Mark 13:13; Matt 10:22; 24:13).

The promise of a "crown of life" (Rev 2:10; cf. 3:11) may allude to Zech 6:14 LXX, in which "the Branch" will build God's house, and a priestly or royal crown will be given to those who endure (ὁ δὲ στέφανος ἔσται τοῖς ὑπομένουσιν). The crown is

---

89. See support for this view in, e.g., Acts 18:12–17; *Mart. Pol.*, 12.2–3; 13.1; 17.2; 18.1 Justin, *Dial.* 17.1; 108.2; 117.3; *Apology* 1.26.7; 2.12; Origen, *Cels.* 6.27.

90. Cf. Borgen, "Polemic in the Book of Revelation," 199–211. On the Christian's minority status, Lambrecht, "Synagogues of Satan," 291, estimates out of a population of 60 million in the Roman Empire at the end of the first century, 50,000 were Christians and 4–5 million were Jews. On the evidence for Jews in Asia Minor and Smyrna, see Trebilco, *Jewish Communities in Asia Minor*.

a reward for perseverance,[91] and in this case there are hints of the saints functioning as a royal priesthood (cf. Rev 1:6; 5:10; 20:6). Yet the idea of receiving a crown could just as easily be derived from an athletic metaphor that stresses the prize of a garland (στέφανος) for victory after the contest is over (1 Cor 9:25; 2 Tim 4:8; Jas 1:10; cf. 1 Pet 5:4). Paul associates a wreath of victory to finishing his metaphorical footrace in the course of life. Apostasy would amount to his disqualification from the race (cf. 1 Cor 9:24–27). In biblical contexts the metaphor suggests the endurance of hardship or death in order to receive honor and a glorious prize at the end of the ages. A crown for martyrdom already seems to be known in Jewish tradition by the time of Revelation (cf. 4 Macc 17:15; cf. 6:10; 11:20; 13:15).[92] A promise of reward for those who overcome assures them that they will not be hurt by the "second death" (Rev 2:11; cf. 20:6). *The faithful and fearless attitude expected of the Smynans in 2:10 may be contrasted with the faithless and cowardly apostates who are harmed by the "second death" in 21:8.* In the Targums the thought refers to death in the world to come[93] and the second death essentially has this same meaning in Revelation, though here it more specifically related to the Lake of Fire, where the Beast, False Prophet, Satan, vicedoers, and apostates are finally punished (20:14; 21:8 cf. 19:20).

THE "THRONE OF SATAN" AND "BALAAM" IN PERGAMUM (2:12–17)

The church in Pergamum is commended for holding fast to Christ's name and not denying faith even when a saint named Antipas was slain among them (2:13). The words echo Jesus who claims that those who confess him before others he will confess before his heavenly Father at the *parousia*, and those who deny him before others he will deny and exclude from his kingdom (Matt 10:32–33; Luke 12:8–9; cf. Mark 8:38; Luke 9:26; 2 Tim 2:12). The faithful in Pergamum show their endurance through their willingness to suffer for and "hold fast" to his name (κρατέω: cf. Col 2:19; 2 Tim 2:15). They do not deny "my faith," which here may be referring to the embodiment of teachings about Jesus, or more likely, the genitive in ὁ πιστός μου has an objective meaning: "faith in me."[94] The martyr named Antipas is not known in other early sources. A later tradition from Andrew of Caesarea (fifth century)

---

91. This allusion is addressed in Jauhiainen, *Zechariah in Revelation*, 97–99, who recognizes that such thoughts were already "in the air" in early Christian writings.

92. In early Christian traditions, see *1 Clem.* 5.1 which may have been written before Revelation. Further on the crown motif, see in *Ascen. Isa.* 9.10f; *T. Ben.* 4.1; 1 QH 9.25; 1QS 4.7; *Apoc. Ezra.* 6.17.

93. Cf. *Tg. Isa.* 22:14; 65:6, 15; *Tg. Onq. Deut.* 33:6.

94. Cf. Bratcher and Hatton, *Revelation*, 52. "My name" probably refers to the idea of suffering for Christ's namesake, a thought essentially meaning that these Christians were not ashamed of identifying themselves as Christians, even if this meant persecution (cf. 2:3).

Churches under Siege of Persecution and Assimilation

claims Antipas as the bishop of Pergamum who was killed in the days of Domitian for refusing to renounce Christ and commit idolatry. He was imprisoned in a statue of a bronze bull and died when it became overheated. The validity of this story is almost impossible to determine.[95] His death no doubt would have been known in the memory of the audience, and the phrase "in the days" implies that this event happened years or perhaps even decades before Revelation was written. His death seems associated with the "throne of Satan" and "where Satan dwells," and it is possible that he was brought in from some other city to be executed in Pergamum.[96]

The city's connection with Satan is probably not meant to single out Jewish opponents, as in Smyrna. Persecution in Pergamum comes from "Satan's throne" not the "synagogue of Satan." Several better options for the former include: 1) the alter of Zeus Soter; 2) the temple of Asklepios Soter; 3) the imperial cult represented by the temple of Augustus and Roma ("Sebastion"); 4) the βῆμα or judge's tribunal (proconsul); 5) Pergamum as a great religious center; or 6) Pergamum as a center for persecuting God's people.[97]

In favor of options 1 and 2 are that both are associated with the symbol of a serpent, and Satan is called a serpent in Rev 12. In favor of number 3 is that the social situation in Revelation seems to be primarily against imperial worship, and Pergamum was the first center for the imperial cult in the region.[98] In favor of number 4 is that Pergamum had become a senatorial headquarter for Rome after 27 BCE, and Antipas may have been tried and executed by the tribunal. In favor of number 5 is the eclectic way this explanation combines numbers 1–3. Number 6 is weak on historical ground but fits well with Satan's role in Revelation, which is primarily to persecute the saints (2:9; 12:3–4, 10–17; 20:7–10).[99] When used in a negative sense, "throne" (θρόνος) connotes the kingdom of the Beast (13:2; 16:10) who represents Rome and the imperial cult. The Beast is given power by Satan (the Dragon) and persecutes the saints (ch. 13). In this light the "throne of Satan" comes closest to a combined meaning of numbers 3, 4, and 6. Satan works through the power of Rome

---

95. Prigent, *Apocalypse*, 174, mentions this account as possibly a legend.

96. Referring to παρ' ὑμῖν ("near /beside you") in 2:13, Hemer, *Seven Churches*, 86, suggests this possibility and designates the area as "Satan's headquarters." Alternatively the phrase may be understood as, "in that place of yours": cf. Smalley, *Revelation*, 69.

97. See more options in Aune, *Revelation*, 1.182–83; and for historical background see, e.g., Friesen, "Satan's Throne," 356–67; Ramsey, *Letters to the Seven Churches*, 281–315.

98. See, e.g., Aune, *Revelation*, 1.182.

99. Friesen, "Satan's Throne," opts for this view, showing that Asia Minor did not have one imperial headquarters but a few, and so Pergamum would not be unique in this regard. He further maintains that no reference can be found for the imperial cult in Rev 2–3 (363, 365–66). Granted, Smyrna and Ephesus were other great centers for the imperial cult, but Pergamum was the first, and the "throne of Satan" does not need to be reduced to one meaning in Revelation.

and the imperial cult to oppose God's people. Perhaps Antipas was the first martyr in the area to be killed in defiance of the cult. Nevertheless early Christian witnesses may have evangelized their neighbors aggressively and denounced idolatry. It is rather likely, then, that a number of the locals, whether devotees to Zeus, Asklepios, or other deities, would have turned hostile toward members of the church from time to time.

Despite their faithfulness amidst adverse circumstances, the glorified Christ has a matter against the church in Pergamum. Some of its members adhere to the doctrine of Balaam and the Nicolaitans (2:14-15; cf. 2:6). Whereas it is not clear what the latter group believed (see Ephesus above), the former participates in eating idol meats (εἰδωλόθυτος) and committing fornication. Their practice alludes to the Balaam tradition at Baal-Peor where Balak, king of Moab, causes Israel to sin by getting Moabite women to commit fornication and idolatry with the Israelite men. In ancient Jewish literature Balaam is the one who instigates Balak to cause Israel to be unfaithful to God by getting them to commit fornication and sacrifice to foreign deities at Baal-Peor (Philo, *Mos.* 1.294-305; Ps.-Philo 18:13; Josephus, *Ant.* 4.6-12[126-155]; *y. Sanhedrin* 28CD; cf. Num 25). Balaam also becomes associated with greed, vice, and false teachings (see further in Jude 11; 2 Pet 2:15). As a result of Balaam's influence, a "stumbling block," that is, an object that causes one to fall and commit apostasy (σκάνδαλον), was cast before the Israelites (Rev 2:14). *A Christian party within the church of Pergamum likewise leads God's people astray by eating idol meats and committing fornication, and so in this sense they are associated with Balaam.* These individuals probably do not associate themselves directly with Balaam or his teachings; rather, "Balaam" is a name attributed to them that disqualifies them from being approved by God.[100]

If an earlier saying of Jesus is present here, what immediately comes to our mind is his warning that his disciples should not cause fellow believers to stumble (σκανδαλίζω), that is, fall away from Christ (Matt 18:6-9; Mark 9:42-47; Luke 17:2). Interestingly enough, Paul uses σκανδαλίζω to describe how the stronger members' consumption of idol meats in Corinth might cause weaker members to apostatize (1 Cor 8:13). What precisely is being condemned about idol meats? The spectrum extends anywhere from Christians buying food sacrificed to idols that is sold in the marketplace to Christians offering such foods in cultic precincts during religious ceremonies and thus almost indistinguishable from idolatry. The latter end of the spectrum is probably more in view than the former.[101] Strong boundaries against idol meats in Revelation are understandable given a context in which emperor wor-

---

100. Along these lines is Schnelle, *Einleitung*, 533.
101. So Trebilco, *Early Christians in Ephesus*, 312-14.

Churches under Siege of Persecution and Assimilation

ship was becoming more pronounced, and some Christians had perhaps already been convicted as criminals for refusing to pay homage to idols. With this emerging trend in view, *some of the food may have been dedicated to Caesar as deity*.[102]

Although veneration of Caesar may have been evident earlier in Corinth, neither Paul nor the Corinthians faced conflicts related to persecution for refusing such veneration forty years earlier. Paul's leniency on idol meats in 1 Cor 8–10 seems to be a thing of the past, and later Christian sources draw clearer boundaries against the practice.[103] Some of the church members in Pergamum apparently thought much along the lines of the strong/*gnosis* Corinthians. Since Paul and his colleagues influenced churches in western Asia Minor,[104] it is quite possible that congregation members in Pergamum maintained loose boundaries on foods similar to the Corinthians. If so, then perhaps they justified eating idol foods even in temple precincts on the ground that there is only one God and no other deities exist, including the spirit of Caesar. In addition, perhaps they were motivated by a reaction against previous religious influences in the region that had been too legalistic on external matters such as food and sex (cf. 1 Tim 4:1–5; Col 2:20–23).

In early Jewish and Christian sources idolatry and fornication often are linked together as a conventional way of describing the vices "pagans" practiced,[105] and they are among the vices prohibited by the emerging Christians at the Jerusalem Council (Acts 15). Although early Christian communities condemn sexual immorality,[106] the committing of fornication (πορνεύω) in Revelation may be metaphoric rather than literal in meaning.[107] The Christians in Pergamum and Thyatira are sexually immoral in the sense of being unfaithful to God by comingling with the Roman economic system and compromising with the imperial cult (cf. Rev 2:20). They, like the kings of the earth, commit spiritual fornication with the Whore of Babylon (cf. 17:2; 18:3, 9; 19:2). The prostitution of the Whore is to be interpreted in light of Rome's economic trade with other countries, which presumably leads to the exchange of religious practices (cf. Isa 23:17; Mic 1:7; Nah 3:4; 2 Kgs 9:22).

---

102. On this possibility see Hemer, *Seven Churches*, 95, 240n72.

103. E.g., *Did.* 6:3; Aristides, *Apology* 15:5; Justin, *Dial.* 35; Tertullian, *Apology* 9; Clement of Alexandria, *Strom.* 4.16; *Paed.* 2.1; Origen, *Cels.* 8.28; cf. *Sib. Or.* 2.96.

104. E.g., Colossians; Ephesians; Acts 20.

105. E.g., Wis 12–14; Rom 1:18–32; cf. Rev 9:20–21.

106. E.g., Mark 7:21; 1 Thess 4:3–8; 1 Cor 6:12–20; Heb 12:16; Jude 7.

107. On fornication as metaphoric for marital unfaithfulness see, e.g., Hos 1–2; Erlandsson, "זָנָה," 4.101–4. Contrast Witherington, *Revelation*, 103, who suggests the fornication in Pergamum is referring to either sex with temple prostitutes or the "sexual dalliance that went on at dinner parties held in the temple precincts."

Aune seems correct to suggest that the prostitute is a descriptive parody of Dea Roma, the goddess personifying Rome who appears on coins during that era. On the sestertius (c. 71 CE, minted in Roman Asia) Roma, wearing military garb, sits on the seven hills of Rome, similar to the seven-headed Beast in Rev 17. Below her, the twins, Remus and Romulus (founders of Rome), suckle beneath a she-wolf. By Roma's feet is the river god Tiber. The mystery name (Rev 17:5: Mystery Babylon—Mother of Harlots and Abominations on the Earth) parodies the label ROMA on the sestertius coin. The problem with "Babylon" in Revelation 18 involves trade and political alliances that Rome has with the kings of the earth. Trade and economy are related to idolatry and the mark of the Beast (Rev 13). On the sestertius, Roma is holding a parazonium sword, an appropriate instrument for slaughtering Christians and Jews.[108]

Beyond this, the intermarriage between Christians and non-Christians might be implied in the idea of fornication and adds a literal aspect to the term in Revelation (cf. Tob 4:17; *T. Levi* 14.6; *Jub.* 25.1; 30.1–17).[109] Paul and the Petrine author are aware of such intermarriages but do not consider them to be fornication or apostasy (1 Cor 7:12–16; 1 Pet 3:1–6), but Paul does seem to discourage the idea of single Christians marrying unbelievers (1 Cor 7:39; cf. 2 Cor 6:14).[110] In Revelation, it seems that *some of the churches in Asia were compromising their witness through assimilation with non-believers*. Perhaps desiring to climb up the socioeconomic ladder, these churches associate with the practices of outsiders.

As is the case with the other churches with which Christ has an accusation, Pergamum is called to repent. If the church does not alter its compromised behavior, he will come against this congregation and fight against those who hold to the doctrine of Balaam and the Nicolaitans with the sword of his mouth (Rev 2:16; cf. 1:16; 2:12; 19:15, 21). This imagery is sometimes associated with the word of God that is able to metaphorically pierce hearts (Heb 4:12; cf. Eph 6:17; Ps 52:2; Wis 18:15–16). Similar to Revelation, the Qumran community threatens apostates and covenant breakers with a judgment by the sword when messiah comes (CD 1.17; 3.11; 7.13; 8.1; 19.10, 13).[111] More specifically the imagery recalls the messianic servant of the

---

108. Aune, *Revelation*, 3.919–28.

109. Duff, *Who Rides the Beast?*, 56, 59, addresses the option of intermarriage, along with a "simple toleration" of pagans (59) and a "metaphorical reiteration" of eating idol meats (56). On intermarriage as sin/apostasy, see, e.g., Deut 7:1–4; 1 Kgs 11:1–13; Ezra 9–10; Neh 13:23–27; 4QMMT 75–82; Philo, *Spec.* 3.29; Josephus, *Ant.* 8.190–98; Hauck and Schulz, "πόρνη," 6.589; Cohen, *Beginning of Jewishness*, 241–62; Hayes, "Intermarriage and Impurity," 3–36; Gaca, *Making of Fornication*.

110. On later intermarriages between Christians and unbelievers being discouraged, see Tertullian, *Ux.* 2.3–8; Cyprian, *Lapsed* 6; cf. Wilson, *Leaving the Fold*, 127.

111. See Fekkes, *Isaiah and Prophetic Traditions*, 121n52.

Churches under Siege of Persecution and Assimilation

LORD who has a sharp sword or weapon coming out of his mouth (Isa 11:4; 49:2). Jan Fekkes distills similar metaphors in early Jewish and Christians sources[112] and classifies them according the agent (Messiah/prince), the action (smite/destroy), the sphere (earth/people/wicked), the instrument (rod/breath/sword), and a genitive phrase ("of his mouth"). He compares these sources with Isa 11:4 to show a common motif about the Messiah's power as judge in the eschaton, a motif that is found also in Rev 19:15, 21 when Christ returns as the Word of God and slays his enemies with the sword that comes out of his mouth. The Messiah's sword contrasts the executive authority of earth's rulers (cf. 6:3–4; 13:10; 20:4) to show Christ as the "universal judicial authority."[113] In 2:16 *Christ functions as the agent of God's judgment and his sword pertains to his judicial authority to destroy the unrepentant Balaamites and Nicolaitan Christians, along with the nations that fight against him, at his second coming.*[114] They along with other idolaters, fornicators, and apostates will be judged and sentenced to the second death (21:8). Interestingly, in Israel's scriptures Balaam is first threatened by the "sword" and then eventually killed by it (Num 22:23, 31; Josh 13:22), and in later traditions he is excluded from the "world to come" (cf. *b. Sanhedrin* 90a; 105a; *Abot R. Nat.* 31b–32a).[115]

The rest of the church in Pergamum has a responsibility to repent; they have permitted these false teachings of the Balaamites and Nicolaitans to influence some of their members, and true repentance would involve confronting followers of these doctrines, much the same way the Ephesians contend against the false apostles and hate the deeds of the Nicolaitans. The text is not clear if the rest of the congregation will also face judgment. Christ will come to the church of Pergamum *suddenly* (ταχὺ) and this may recall the manner in which Christ's *parousia* takes place when he punishes the wicked and those who remain unprepared for his return, as intimated by the Parables of the Thief in the Night and Ten Virgins (Matt 24:42–25:13).[116] His contention nonetheless is specifically against "them" (Rev 2:16: πολεμήσω μετ' αὐτῶν), i.e., those who adhere to the doctrines of the Balaamites and Nicolaitans.

The one who overcomes in Pergamum will be given "hidden manna" and a white stone with a new name written on it (Rev 2:17). Manna recalls the miraculous

---

112. E.g., *4 Ezra* 13.9–11, 37–38; *1 En.* 62.2; *Pss. Sol.* 17.24, 35; 4QpIsa^a 8–10; 1QSb 5 24–25; 2 Thess 2:8.

113. Fekkes, *Isaiah and Prophetic Traditions*, 117–122, quote from 120.

114. Rev 2:16 and 19:11–21 are rightly seen by ibid., 121, as depicting the same general event.

115. Cf. Beale and McDonough, "Revelation," 1094.

116. On connections between Revelation and the *parousia* in Jesus' parables, see especially Bauckham, *Climax of Prophecy*, 92–117.

heavenly food given to the Israelites on their wilderness journey (Exod 16:15).[117] It was hidden by being placed in a jar before the Lord (Exod 16:32-35) or reserved for the messianic world to come (cf. 2 Macc 2:4-6). The thought may also allude to the Passover meal when a piece of the unleavened bread is broken off and wrapped in a cloth. This piece, known as the *afikoman*, is hidden until the end of the *seder* (cf. *m. Pesahim* 10.8). David Daube argues that the broken piece originally referred to the coming Messiah.[118] Whether the audience of Pergamum would have connected the Messiah and manna with the thought of unleavened bread being hidden at the Passover meal cannot be determined. The Johannine Jesus, in any case, associates himself with manna in the wilderness when he claims to be the "bread of life" (John 6:31-35). Hence, it is certainly possible that as one's eating from the tree of life relates to communion with the cross (Rev 2:7), so one's consumption of the hidden manna relates to communion with Christ and perhaps anticipates the messianic banquet (2:17; cf. 19:7-9). The reward for abstaining from idol foods is eating manna in the presence of Christ.

No scholarly consensus can be presently reached regarding the meaning of the white stone and new name.[119] Terminology for the latter is borrowed apparently from Isa 62:2 and 65:15 and involves a future reward for God's afflicted.[120] *Targum Isa.* 65:15b is perhaps closer to the meaning in Revelation: "and the Lord YHWH will slay you with the second death (cf. Rev 2:17), but his servants, the righteous, he will call by a different name."[121] Perhaps the reward of a new name in Rev 2:17 (and 3:12) is connected with the Semitic concept of reputation (cf. Isa 56:4-5; Job 30:8).[122] More than this it probably refers to faithful individuals who leave behind their literal, earthly names for new, heavenly ones that are comparable with their character and deeds, similar to Jesus calling Simon "Peter," the Rock (Matt 16:18), and John and James "Boanerges," the Sons of Thunder (Mark 3:17). With their new identities the overcomers in Revelation inherit the full realization of God's kingdom

---

117. Cf. Ps 78:25; 105:40; Neh 9:15; Wis 16:20; *4 Ezra* 1.19; *2 Bar.* 29.8; *Sib. Or.* 7.148-49.

118. Carmichael, "Eucharist and the Passover," 45-67; Daube, *He That Cometh*. From this perspective the notion of "*afikoman*" is derived from the Greek for "the coming one" or "he that has come" (*afikomenos*).

119. For options see Hemer, *Seven Churches*, 94-103.

120. Cf. Fekkes, *Isaiah and Prophetic Traditions*, 128-30. On this reading the new name in 2:17 does not share the same meaning with 3:12 (cf. 19:12).

121. Translation in Aune, *Revelation*, 1.190. The name is probably intended to be secretive, and so perhaps it is useless to speculate on the exact designation.

122. See, e.g., Fuller, "I Will Not Erase His Name," 302-6, who on the concept of "name" in Rev 2-3 writes that good works produce a good, heavenly reputation that results in an "honorable eternal identity" (304, 306).

and what the Johannine Jesus meant in terms of being "born anew" and "born from above" (John 3:3, 5).

The stone may refer to the ephod stones if Dulk is correct (Exod 28:9–29).[123] But another option is for us to associate the stones with black and white pebbles (ψῆφος) thrown into an urn to determine a person's guilt or innocence. The white stone is used for acquittal (Ovid, *Metamorphoses* 15.41–42; cf. Plutarch, *Moralia* 186F; *Alcibiades* 22.2[202D]).[124] This second option makes good sense given that Pergamum was a judicial center. The risen Christ through John may have been declaring his authority as judge over the imperfect and unrighteous tribunals of the *Pax Romana*. His verdict for the overcomers is "not guilty."

"JEZEBEL" IN THYATIRA (2:18–29)

The church in Thyatira is commended for its works, love, faithfulness, service, and endurance. The members also are commended for improving their works over the years (2:19). Conditions such as these might mark a vibrant, healthy church under normal circumstances, but its faithfulness and virtuous qualities did not make its members exempt from the need to repent. Christ's *accusatio* against them centers on their admittance of "Jezebel," a self-proclaimed prophet, to teach and lead astray Christ's servants by committing fornication and eating idol meats. The name is undoubtedly adopted from the wife of King Ahab and daughter of the non-Israelite priest from Tyre. She persecuted the prophets of God and encouraged Israel to worship Canaanite deities (cf. 1 Kgs 16:31; 18–21; 2 Kgs 9; Josephus, *Ant.* 8.13.1–13.8[316–356]; 9.4.2[47]; *Ag. Ap.* 1.18). The woman in the Thyatiran church is code-named "Jezebel" as a way to discredit her ministry by associating her with a name of an enemy of the true prophets of God. She gained her authority, it seems, through prophesying, and her following must have been quite considerable if she is able to influence both her "children" and others who commit "adultery" with her (2:22–23).

Paul Duff considers this woman to be the main rival of John. The prophets in this region face an internal struggle in which the majority of church members stand between the two poles: one "conservative" (John) and the other "liberal" (Jezebel). Jezebel tolerates idol meats and fornication. These practices are said to have been conducive to the Christian's social and economic advancement in the non-Christian

---

123. Dulk, "Promises to Conquerors," 518.

124. Cf. BDAG, 1098; Hemer *Seven Churches*, 97. A similar aspect may rest behind 1 Sam 25:29 which involves the registration of sheep and goats by pebbles. See further, Oppenheim, "Operational Device," 121–28; Eissfeldt, *Beutel der Lebendigen*, 25.

society.¹²⁵ In Revelation she is the virtual equivalent of the Whore of Babylon (Rev 17–18), and John's description of the two is comparable and functions as innuendo to malign Jezebel by condemning the woman from Babylon. The former is portrayed through the latter as an "undisciplined woman unfit to lead."¹²⁶ Duff's perspective highlights how Jezebel mimics the Whore of Babylon—both, for instance, are associated with fornication and vice (cf. 14:8; 17:2; 18:3; 19:2).

This view assumes, however, a primarily internal conflict within the seven churches, while virtually nothing is said about congregational divisions in Rev 4–22. Moreover Jezebel, the main culprit behind the faction, is never mentioned again after 2:20.¹²⁷ The idol foods and fornication associated with Jezebel resemble the influence of Balaam in Pergamum, but in this case the prophet is a woman and, unlike the Balaamites, she is directly involved in teaching (διδάσκω) these things to congregation members, not merely tolerating them (cf. 2:20). Nevertheless, Duff's comparison between Jezebel and the Whore of Babylon speak to the seriousness of the problem in the church. From the perspective of our author, the woman of Thyatira leads astray the saints (πλανάω: 2:20). This thought may convey the use of deception¹²⁸ or a wandering away from the path of righteousness.¹²⁹ These nuances probably overlap in 2:20–23—*Jezebel is viewed as a false prophet leading congregants away from the path of the overcomers onto a route that leads to apostasy and destruction. This is what presumably happened to her disciples; they were once vibrant church members who were led astray by her teachings. As a result they will face divine punishment* (2:23).

Elsewhere in Revelation the Whore of Babylon (18:23), the False Prophet (13:14; 19:20), and Satan (12:9; 20:3, 8, 10) all lead astray their clients, but the customers in these instances seem to be non-Christians. More relevant to Jezebel's practice in 2:20 is Jesus' warning to his followers not to be led astray (πλανάω) by false prophets during the upcoming crisis that will take place before his second coming (Matt 24:4–5, 11, 24; Mark 13:5–6; Luke 21:8). In both the churches of Asia Minor and the gospels, those who are in danger of being deceived by false teachers are Christ's servants.

The exhortation to the fourth church, Thyatira, rests at the center of the message to the seven churches. The wordiest discourse of the seven is directed at this church (Rev 2:18–29), which may suggest its importance among the seven. It is the only

---

125. Duff, *Who Rides the Beast?:*, 57–59, 127.
126. Ibid., 112; cf. 89–92.
127. This is an important criticism raised by Sullivan, Review of *Who Rides the Beast?*, 569–70.
128. Cf. John 7:12; 1 John 2:26; 3:7; *T. Levi* 10.2; *T. Jud.* 15.5; Ign. *Magn.* 3.2; Origen, *Cels.* 5.5.29.
129. Deut 11:28; Wis 5:6; 2 Pet 2:15, 25; Jas 5:19–20; *Did.* 6.1; *Herm. Vis.* 3.7.1; cf. πλάνη in Jude 11; 1 John 4:6. See further references in Braun, "πλανάω," 6.228–53.

church in which divine punishment is inevitable. Jezebel will suffer an imminent judgment before Christ's *parousia* takes place. Unlike the threat of judgment given to the other churches, there is no indication in the message to Thyatira that Jezebel's punishment will take place at the *parousia*. She has been given ample time to repent of her immorality and has refused (2:21–22a). Hence, no further warning will be given to her; Christ will punish Jezebel and news of this will spread to all the other churches. Using imagery appropriate to her fornication, the passage asserts that Jezebel will be cast into a "bed" (κλίνη), which probably relates to a Hebrew idiom for "bed of illness" (cf. Exod 21:8; 1 Macc 21:18; Jdt 8:3).[130] Divine judgment through sickness calls to mind the Corinthian situation related to socioeconomic disparity, irreverence, and drunkenness at the Lord's Supper. The congregation members were punished so that they would not be condemned along with "the world" (cf. 1 Cor 11:29–32). *The final destiny of Jezebel is not mentioned. Once bedridden it is possible that she will be granted another opportunity to repent.*

Her adulterous clients will be cast into "great tribulation" (Rev 2:22; cf. 7:14; Matt 24:21) either to face the same kind of plagues the unbelievers face in Revelation 6–16 or some other horrible affliction. Unlike Jezebel, however, they can avoid this judgment if they repent of following her deeds.[131] This group, then, does not appear to belong to her inner circle of followers.[132] Her "children" or disciples will face a severer judgment—they will be killed by plagues or some other means (2:23).[133] Unlike the first group, it is not clear that they will be given a chance to repent and so deter divine punishment. Christ will not tolerate another generation of these apostates in the church. Their final destination is not stated, but their death seems to resemble the type of destructive calamities that come upon the unbelievers in Rev 6–19. Moreover, if apostates are assigned to the Lake of Fire as we have argued (cf. 21:8), then it is quite possible, even plausible, that the final end of Jezebel's disciples is assumed to be the second death.

As a result of their death, all the churches will know that Christ searches the hearts and minds of his people to render to everyone according to their works (2:22–23). Again if the churches see or hear of this judgment, we are probably not

---

130. Cf. Aune, *Revelation*, 1.205.

131. Some manuscripts (e.g., A, Arm, Eth, TR) use "their" (αὐτῶν) instead of "her" (αὐτῆς) deeds, but the latter is correct being the more difficult and better supported reading. Jezebel's clients must repent of exercising the deeds that Jezebel promotes, i.e., eating idol meats and committing fornication.

132. Osborne, *Revelation*, 159, suggests they may not have been "full members" as were Jezebel's "children." Alternatively, the adulterous group refers to those participating in her sinful behavior, and the "children" refer to those adhering to her teachings; cf. Beasley-Murray, *Revelation*, 91.

133. Interestingly, the children of the original Jezebel were likewise killed because of her sins (cf. 1 Kgs 21:17–29; 2 Kgs 9:30–37; 10).

dealing with the *parousia* in this case. The punishment visited upon Jezebel and her followers is intended to get other churches to fear and thus purify themselves from false and assimilating influences. Verse 2:23 resembles Jer 17:9-18, in which the LORD searches the heart and minds of his people and renders to them according to their deeds. Those who forsake him will be put to shame on the day of disaster. The glorified Christ likewise searches the hearts of his followers, and his purifying and penetrating eyes of "fire" are aware of all the good and bad works his churches do (Rev 2:18; cf. 1:14-15; 2:1, 5:6; John 2:25; 16:30; 21:17; Matt 9:4). He will judge all people accordingly, even those who attend his churches, with rewards for the righteous and retribution for the unrighteous (Rev 18:6; 20:12-13; 22:12).[134]

Not everyone in the church of Thyatira is threatened with judgment, however. A remnant of the assembly has not been influenced by Jezebel and "the deep things of Satan" (2:24). The "deep things of Satan" (τὰ βαθέα τοῦ σατανᾶ) may be something that was said by Jezebel and her followers, but more likely the phrase is a parody for the "deep things of God" (cf. 1 Cor 2:10; Rom 11:33). What Jezebel calls the "deep things of God" in reference to her teachings are really the "deep things of Satan" because her teachings are deceptive and lead believers astray (cf. Rev 12:9; 13:14; 18:23; 20:3, 8, 10). No other "burden" (βάρος) will be placed on the remnant except that they persevere in patience. The notion of βάρος probably alludes to the Jerusalem meeting's decision that Christian Gentiles should not be given any other burden related to the Law of Moses except to abstain from idol foods, fornication, blood, and things strangled (Acts 15:28-29). The followers of Jezebel reject even these minimal requirements.[135] Perhaps the words "as they say" (ὡς λέγουσιν: Rev 2:24) involve their criticism that the meeting in Jerusalem's decision to abstain from idol foods and fornication is a needless burden. The remnant in Thyatira who do not adhere to Jezebel's teachings are encouraged to "hold fast" (κρατέω), that is, remain faithful and cling to Christ until he returns; the overcomer is to keep working for Christ until the "end" in order to be saved (2:25-26; cf. 2:13; 3:11).[136] In the upcoming age the overcomer will be given the "morning star" and authority over the nations (2:26-29).[137] The promise is one in which the Christ-followers participate

---

134. Cf. Ps 27:4; Prov 24:12; Sir 16:12; 35:19; *Jos. Asen.* 28.3; *Pss. Sol.* 2.16-35; Rom 2:6; 2 Cor 5:10; 11:15; 2 Tim 4:14; 1 Pet 1:17; *1 Clem.* 34:3; Ign. *Magn.* 11.3. In Rev 2:23 Christ's judgment on Jezebel may be seen as a prelude or paradigm for final judgment; see Giesen, *Offenbarung*, 121.

135. Cf. Schnelle, *Einleitung*, 533.

136. In 2:26 τὰ ἔργα μου ("my works") as Bratcher and Hatton, *Handbook on Revelation*, 63, rightly affirm, "does not mean the things that Christ does but the things he orders his followers to do."

137. As in 22:16 where the morning star is predicated on Christ, the term in 2:28 probably relates to the messianic rule (cf. Num 24:17-24; cf. *T. Levi* 18.3; *T. Jud.* 24.1; CD 7.18-8.19; 1QM 11.6-7; 4QTest 91-3).

Churches under Siege of Persecution and Assimilation

in the authority and reign of Christ and mete out justice and punishment (Rev 1:6; 3:21; cf. Ps 2:8–9; 45:7; 110:2; Isa 11:4; 30:37; 1 Cor 6:3).

SARDIS AND ITS DEATH AND DYING MEMBERS (3:1–6)

The church in Sardis has a "name" of being alive that suggests a renown reputation from a human perspective, but from the exalted Christ's point of view they are spiritually dead and incomplete, not finishing what they have started.[138] The congregation, in other words, is asleep and unprepared for the events that will soon take place. The city was famous for being impenetrable because of its steep acropolis,[139] but in its early history it was taken by Cyrus of Persia due to its protectors' lack of vigilance (c. 549–546 BCE). The city was taken again by Antiochus III as a result of the protectors' negligence (c. 214 BCE).[140] The locals no doubt grew up knowing these stories so that the reputation and vigilance mentioned in 3:1–3 would strike deep chords within the Sardian hearers.

The city's background helps color our text, but since the church is primarily in view instead of the city, the concepts of fame and vigilance require further unpacking. The congregation must "watch" (γρηγορέω) and strengthen the rest of its members, or else Christ will return to them as a "thief in the night" and they will not be prepared, unless they repent (3:2–3). The warning clearly alludes to the Thief in the Night sayings of Jesus (cf. 2:16; 16:15). The church needs to be spiritually vigilant and prepared for the second coming. This day will catch unbelievers and immoral Christ-followers by surprise, and they will be punished with destruction (Luke 12:37–39; Matt 24:42–43; 25:1–10; Mark 13:34–37).[141]

On a deeper level the imperative for the church in Sardis to be watchful (γίνου γρηγορῶν) also may recall the scene at Gethsemane where Jesus warns his sleepy disciples to watch and pray or else they will enter into temptation (cf. Matthew 26:38–40; Mark 14:38). Peter's denial of Christ that same night stands as a perpetual reminder for Christians lacking vigilance. The command for the church in Sardis to strengthen (στηρίζω) or renew their inward commitment sounds similar to Jesus telling Peter to strengthen the other wayward disciples after he repents from his denial (Luke 22:32). Christ warns the church in Sardis that he is coming as a thief and its members are not ready to meet him. *If the believers do not repent and renew their commitment to him, when he returns he will bring judgment on them that will*

---

138. The Moffat translation is more emphatic: "Nothing you have done is complete."
139. Cf. Lucian, *Merc. cond.* 13.
140. See further Hemer, *Seven Churches*, 131–33.
141. Cf. 1 Thess 5:1–9; 2 Pet 3:10; *Gos. Thom.* 103; *Did.* 16.1; *Mart. Pol.* 1.3.

be similar to the destruction the negligent protectors of the city experienced centuries earlier.

Their status of being alive probably extends beyond the city's great name to the actual reputation of the church. In times past they were fervent for the things of Christ, perhaps as strong witnesses to their unbelieving neighbors, vigilant in prayer, and exercising spiritual gifts. At very least they exemplified what it meant to have spiritual life in Christ. A touch of irony is present by the fact that Christ now considers them "dead" (3:1). We can interpret this to mean they lack spiritual life, but in what sense? It is possible that this meaning anticipates the inevitable outcome in the future if the congregants do not repent—they will be dead in the sense of being separated from God. This kind of death would cause them to be alienated from Christ and eternal life with the ramification of being destroyed by the second death (cf. 20:10; 21:8).[142] Another possibility is that the notion of being dead in 3:1 is a hyperbolic reference to their lack of zeal that has now become a spiritual crisis. More specifically in 3:2, the congregation members in Sardis are at the point of spiritual death—they are "about to die."[143] That they are "about to die" almost certainly means they are still spiritually alive. The best explanation of 3:2, however, is to interpret "the things that remain which are about to die" (τὰ λοιπὰ ἃ ἔμελλον ἀποθανεῖν) as referring to the *remaining church members* who still survive but are on the verge of death.[144] In other words, as a corporate entity the church had already become apostate from Christ's perspective. It had become spiritually dead (3:1). Some of its congregation members, however, are still alive but are soon going to die as well (3:2). *They are believers whose spiritual life is ebbing away so that they are now on the brink of apostasy and spiritual death,*[145] *and they will experience the second death as their final destiny if they continue on this track.*

142. Contrast Beale, *Revelation*, 279–82, who considers the danger in Sardis not in terms of apostasy but inauthenticity: "the *so-called* Christians of Sardis are living in such a way as to call into question whether or not they possess true, living faith in Christ" (273). But this viewpoint is undermined if some of the congregation members are still spiritually alive in Rev 3:2. These are authentic Christians who have spiritual life but are on the verge of death, and if so, then the contextual meaning seems straightforward enough: many of the church members once had spiritual life but already died spiritually (3:1), and now those who still possess life are about to die also if they are not strengthened (3:2). Contrast also Fuller, "I Will Not Erase His Name," 305, who thinks a loss of heavenly reputation rather than loss of eternal life is at stake. However, reputation and identity (and not just "privileged" ones) both can be lost. This context suggests "life" = eternal life (cf. book of life: 3:5) rather than merely loss of reward, honor, or privileged status in the world to come. The imagery of death/life in 3:5 is also present in 3:1. Spiritual life and death overlap with eternal life and death.

143. See Collins, *Apocalypse*, 24, who nevertheless addresses this church as lapsed and "fallen away" (23).

144. Cf. Osborne, *Revelation*, 174–75.

145. Here ἔμελλον is imperfect and may be understood as a progressive perfect: cf. Burton, *Syntax*,

Churches under Siege of Persecution and Assimilation

Apparently, through loss of fervency and apathy, the church fell into this backslidden state. No particular vice is attached to the congregation, but given the commendation related to those who have kept their garments unsoiled (3:4), a problem related to purity or sanctification can be surmised. A more specific issue, such as their committing fornication or consuming idol meats, runs us off into indefensible conjecture. More generally, perhaps we could surmise that their ethics and attitudes were slowly being compromised and their values now resembled those of outsiders. A slow process of assimilation, then, might be the problem. The church must return to earlier instructions; its members are called to remember and hold fast to the traditions they previously heard and received (3:3; cf. 1 Thess 2:13; Phil 4:9; 1 Cor 15:1–3).[146] There is no indication, however, that they now embrace a set of false religious teachings. Rather, it seems that they have become sluggish and indifferent towards their reception of Christian teachings. We are reminded of the similar predicament of the Christian recipients in Hebrews (Heb 2:1–4; 5:11—6:6). *The church in Sardis has been undermined by gradual defection.*

Another group in Sardis is the smallest. They are the "few" (ὀλίγος) members who remain faithful and have not soiled their garments.[147] They are considered worthy of Christ and will walk with him in "white" (Rev 3:4). Their state of purity suggests a spiritual and morally sanctified condition (cf. Rev 7:13–14; 14:4; 22:14; cf. Zech 3:1–10).[148] The other church members, it seems, lack these conditions, and so are unprepared for the second coming. The image of a white garment also points to righteousness and heavenly reward related to eternal life (Rev 6:11; 7:9, 13; 16:15; 19:13; cf. *b. Sabbat* 114a; *Herm. Sim.* 8.2.3; *Acts of Paul* 38; *5 Ezra* 2.39). One final image that may be relevant for the Sardinians is that Roman citizens wore white togas when celebrating victory (e.g., Juvenal, *Satires* 10.45). Given the city's famous military history, for the locals this thought may have called to mind conquerors wearing white and walking in a triumphal procession.[149] Such imagery would be similar to John's vision of the final battle scene when Christ returns with his heavenly army dressed in white (Rev 19, esp. vv. 11, 14). Those who remain faithful to Christ are viewed as conquerors from the Lord's perspective.

---

13. For Osborne, *Revelation*, 175, the imperfect may indicate they have been in the "process of dying" for a while and now are reaching its final point.

146. Prigent, *Apocalypse*, 195, associates this verse with the miraculous character of their conversion that allows them to receive and hear the gospel.

147. These persons are identified as "names" in 3:4 probably because their names are listed in the Book of Life in 3:5: cf. Giesen, *Offenbarung*, 128.

148. See Jauhiainen, *Zechariah in Revelation*, 81–82.

149. See further Hemer, *Seven Churches*, 147.

OVERCOMERS, APOSTATES, AND THE BOOK OF LIFE
(3:5; 13:8; 17:8; 20:12-15)

In 3:5 the overcomer will be clothed in white garments and that person's name will not be erased from the Book of Life. Christ will confess the overcomer's name before his Father and the angels. In parallel passages those who confess Christ in the midst of hostile societies he also will confess before God, and those who deny him will be denied access to his kingdom (e.g., Luke 12:8-9; Matt 10:32-33; 2 Tim 2:14-15; 2 Clem. 3.2). In short, such passages along with Revelation promise that those who faithfully wear Christ's name in the present age will be granted access to Christ's heavenly kingdom in the age to come.

The thought behind the Book of Life in 3:5 relates to God's remembrance of the faithful and their good works (cf. Mal 3:16).[150] This book does not actually provide eternal life for those whose names are found in it; rather, it simply identifies those who have life in the age to come and are enrolled for citizenship in God's fully realized kingdom (Rev 20:15-20).[151] The overcomers receive their rewards at the *parousia*. Hence, the promise of not being blotted out of the Book of Life is a future assurance for them in the present. As they continue to persevere in the present age, they can be confident that they will eventually be rewarded with life in the age to come and a place in the New Jerusalem (21:27 cf. 21:23).

Some scholars imply or suggest the possibility that individuals whose names appear in Book of Life can be erased/blotted out (ἐξαλείφω) of it if they do not persevere.[152] Thus, "I will certainly not erase his name from the Book of Life" in 3:5 implies the possibility that a person's name *can* be removed from the book. This would mean that such a person is no longer recognized as belonging to Christ; he or she has been removed from citizenship in God's kingdom. It is unlikely that the phrase merely functions as a *litotes* so that an affirmative is meant by the negative or contrary expression, "I will not erase . . .": i.e., that the overcomer's name will *definitely be* listed in the Book of Life. The Sardian church experienced spiritual life and then spiritual death (3:1-2), the thought of which would be quite similar to once being registered in the Book of Life and then removed from it. In 3:5, then, *the overcomers are assured that, unlike the "dead" members in Sardis who fell away and have had their names erased from the Book of Life, Christ will not blot out the overcomers' names from the book.*

---

150. So Fuller, "I Will Not Erase His Name," 300. Even so, this does not exhaust the Book of Life's meaning. The notion of eternal life is also present.

151. See further Isa 4:3; Ps 69[68]:27-28; *1 En.* 108.3; *Jub.* 30.20-22; *Jos. Asen.* 15.3-4; Phil 4:3; cf. Dan 7:9-10; 12:1-2; *1 En.* 47.3; 90.20; *T. Levi* 18.59-60; *Odes Sol.* 9.11; Heb 12:23; Luke 10:20.

152. E.g. Harrington, *Revelation*, 69; Prigent, *Apocalypse*, 198; Roloff, *Revelation*, 59.

Churches under Siege of Persecution and Assimilation

Revelation 22:18–19 from the Textus Receptus is sometimes used as proof that names could be blotted out of the Book of Life because the "book of life" rather than "tree of life" appears in this text (cf. KJV). But the former phrase is a mistake made by Erasmus when translating the final six verses in Revelation from the Vulgate into Greek.[153] The most reliable manuscripts of this text omit "book of life" and thus cannot be used as supporting evidence for 3:5 except in the more general sense of confirming that disobedient Christians can in fact be removed from God's eternal kingdom. It is sometimes suggested that the Eighteen Benedictions expunge apostates and *minim* by claiming that they have been erased from the Book of Life.[154] If the "Nazarenes" are included among these apostates, and *if* the Sardian Christians had been alienated from a local synagogue (similar to churches in Smyrna and Philadelphia), they may have heard a similar condemnation raised against them and would thus take great comfort in the promise that Christ would not erase their names from the Book of Life. This polemical reading of 3:5 tends to mitigate implication related to apostasy, and the condemnation of the opponents against the Christians is being thrown aside as false. Problematic with this view is that there is no implication, unless here, that the Christians in Sardis experienced conflicts with the synagogue.

Perhaps more relevant to the thought in 3:5 are passages derived from Israel's scriptures that support the reality of having one's name erased from a divine book of enrollment (Exod 32:32–33; Ps 69[68]:27–28; cf. Isa 48:19; 56:5; 1 Clem. 53.4–5). That a name is blotted out from under heaven generally suggests a removal of that person or nation from the memory of God's people.[155] In Greco-Roman tradition Athenian criminals would be blotted out of the roll of citizens before execution.[156] These sources tend to support the idea that John's audience, who seem to be familiar with both early Jewish and Hellenistic traditions, would have understood the possibility of a name being once included in God's heavenly roll book but later erased from it.

---

153. Cf. Metzger, *Textual Commentary*, 690: "The corruption of 'tree' into 'book' had occurred earlier in the transmission of the Latin text when a scribe accidentally miscopied the correct word *ligno* ('tree') as *libro* ('book')."

154. Cf. 12th Benediction of the *Shemoneh Esreh*, and see, e.g., Osborne, *Revelation*, 180n15; Beale, *Revelation*, 282. Evidence supports an ancient Jewish community in Sardis with their own synagogue; see Hemer, *Seven Churches*, 134–38.

155. e.g., Exod 17:14; Deut 7:24; 9:14; 25:19; 29:19–20; 2 Kings 14:27; Ps 9:5–6; Sir 47:22; 1 Macc 12:53; 2 Esdr 2:7; *Jub* 30.19–23.

156. Dio Chrysostom, *Rhod.* 84; Xenophon, *Hellenica* 2.3.51; cf. Hemer, *Seven Churches*, 148; Aune, *Revelation*, 1.225.

Another passage in Revelation on the Book of Life reveals that a number of people whose names do not appear in the book will be cast into the Lake of Fire (20:15). The scene of judgment day in 20:10–15, however, reveals that more than one book is opened. Other apocalyptic writings from the Second Temple era likewise mention a plurality of scrolls that are opened (e.g., Dan 7:10; *4 Ezra* 6.20; *1 En.* 47.3; 90.20; *2 Bar.* 24.1). A compilation of various Jewish and early Christian traditions generally disclose three books that are relevant to the coming judgment in Revelation: 1) the Book of Life, a record of those who are righteous and worthy; 2) the book of deeds, a record of all good and bad deeds of people; and 3) the book of destiny, a record involving the events of the world, or destinies of all peoples, or both.[157] Revelation 20:12 may suggest all three books or at least the first two. Ultimately what matters most is whether one's name appears in the Book of Life. Perhaps the other scrolls, then, provide justification for the names appearing or not appearing in the Book of Life.

In 17:8 the earth dwellers' names have not been written in the Book of Life "from the foundation of world." Another interpretation of this verse, however, is that due to solecism, ellipsis, or something dropping out of the original text, either the Beast or the Book of Life was the original referent for that which was from "the foundation of the world." If so, then it could be argued that the Book of Life starts with either a clean slate or includes everyone's name at the beginning of creation. The assumption might be that God or angels then record human deeds and include or exclude names based on those deeds. This explanation would be compatible with other passages on the Book of Life from Jewish tradition. Problematic with this perspective is the lack of ancient textual variants to support the Beast or Book of Life as the proper referent for "from the foundation of the world." In the most reliable manuscripts of 17:8, the earth dwellers seem to be the appropriate referent. They are always categorized as unbelievers in Revelation (cf. 6:10; 8:13; 11:10; 13:14; 17:2), and 17:8 seems to mean either that this group was predestined as unbelievers who would finally be condemned or that God knew their deeds beforehand and could thus record them as excluded from the Book of Life from the very beginning of time (cf. *T. Mos.* 1:14; 12.4–5, 13).

---

157. On the first see *1 En.* 108.3; *Jub.* 30.22; *T. Jac.* 7.27-28; Luke 10:20; Phil 4:3; Rev 3:5; 13:8; 17;8; 21:27; *1 Clem.* 53.4; *Herm. Vis.* 1.3.2; *Herm. Mand.* 8.6; *Sim.* 2.9; *Apoc. Pet.* 17; Rabbinic *Benediction* 12. One the second see Ps 56:8; Isa 65:6; Jer 22:30; Mal 3:16; Dan 7:10; *1 En.* 81.4; 89.61-77; 98.7; 104.7; *4 Ezra* 6.20; *Jub.* 24.1; 30.22; 36.10; *Ascen. Isa.* 9.22; *Lev. Rabbah* 26; *Gen. Rabbah* 81. On the third see Ps 56:8; 139:16; *Jub.* 5.12-19; 16.9; 23.32; *1 En.* 81.2; 106.19; 107.1; *2 En.* 22.12; 53.2; *T. Ash.* 2.10; 7.5; *T. Levi* 5:4; 4Q537 1.3-4; *Herm. Vis.* 1.3.3-4; Eusebius, *Hist. eccl.* 6.38. See further, Paul, "Heavenly Tablets," 345–53; Str.B. 2:169–70.

Churches under Siege of Persecution and Assimilation

Revelation 13:8 also mentions the Book of Life, affirming that either the Beast or its worshippers are not written in the Book of Life of the Lamb that was slain "from the foundation of the world."[158] Here the phrase may refer to the Lamb's redemptive act of being slain "from the foundation of the world," perhaps suggesting that the plan of salvation through Christ has been established from pre-historic times (cf. 1 Pet 1:18–20; *T. Mos.* 1.14). Alternatively, when we compare this verse with 17:8, the phrase could refer to the worshippers of the Beast. A third option is that the Beast's name has not been written in the Book of Life from the foundation of the world.[159] With this third option we have a unique individual (or role) that is either predestined or foreknown in pretemporal history. In this manner the Beast functions as a parody of the preexistent Christ who is the Alpha and Omega.[160] Unlike Christ, however, the Beast who "was, and is not, and is to come" (cf. 17:8) is neither eternal nor preeminent but is destined instead for destruction instead of permanent dominion over creation (Rev 19:20; 20:10; cf. 2 Thess 2:3, 8). Nothing is mentioned about the Beast's freedom to thwart his satanic role and repent—this is not the point of the visions. He functions as Christ's nemesis in the book, and the readers are assured that God knew all along that this enemy of the church would not ultimately prevail; despite his success and power over earth dwellers, his fate has been sealed from the foundation of the world.

Even if we accept this third interpretation as correct, and 13:8 does not refer to an entire multitude of people who have never been included in the Book of Life, there remains a tension between the possibility of removing names from the Book of Life in 3:5 and the non-possibility of including names in 17:8.[161] The context of 17:8, as well as 13:8, true to apocalyptic genre, presents spatially enriched language and images in which destinies are often viewed as fixed or seen from the heavenly vantage point from beginning to end. We are invited to see the destinies of the righteous and wicked from this point of view. Revelation 3:5, on the other hand, is more epistolary in form. The language is temporally enriched and not fixed but verbally stresses a need for the churches to change their current behavior and repent. If the destinies of the righteous and wicked in chapters 4–22 seem to be more fixed than in the admonitions to the seven churches in chapters 1–3, this has much to do with

---

158. Another possible option is to translate the phrase as referencing believers: "All the people in the world will worship him [the Beast], except those whose names had been written . . .": cf. TEV; Bratcher and Hatton, *Handbook on Revelation*, 198.

159. Cf. Michaels, *Interpreting the Book of Revelation*, 92–94.

160. On christological parody in Revelation see Bauckham, *Climax of Prophecy*, 431–41.

161. Mounce, *Revelation*, 114, and Klein, *New Chosen People*, 153, emphasize the tension between the verses.

the apocalyptic form the book adopts in the later chapters. Chapters 1–3 function more as a letter with prophetic discourse. David Aune determines that prophecy and apocalyptic differ importantly on a sociological level. Prophecy is not as dichotomous between wicked and righteous; it hopes the former would repent and the latter persevere in faithfulness. Apocalypticism is adopted by an oppressed community, a minority group anticipating an "eschatological denouement, in which they would be rewarded and the wicked punished."[162] The impasse we seem to face when comparing 3:5 and 17:8 turns on genre differences, and so a thorough synthesis between the passages is not, and perhaps cannot, be entirely satisfactory.

If these verses do not contradict one another, then any prior divine knowledge or ordination of names that are included or excluded from the Book of Life should not rule out human repentance and the ability to change one's course from spiritual death to life. Christ's invitation to any human individual in 3:20 strongly attests to this.[163] Equally one's course can change from spiritual life to death, as in Sardis. The dangers of apostasy in the churches of Asia Minor are real enough, and the stakes are no less than eternal. If we must use theological categories to affirm consistency between 3:5 and 17:8, then at least on an individualistic level some sort of non-coercive foreknowledge may be entertained.[164] More appropriately, however, we should allow for the tension to remain and respect genre differences. Ancient readers were obviously more comfortable with such paradoxes than we are today.

With this qualification established, we can now venture into some uncharted territory with the goal of raising new possibilities and perhaps relieving some older tensions. One major distinction between 3:5 and 17:8 is that the former has in view individual Christians in the present rather than an entire multitude of unbelieving people in a vision portraying the future, as is the case with the latter. Whatever else we might discover by comparing the two verses, we probably should not assume automatically that because the flat characters of a corporate group of unbelievers have always been excluded from the Book of Life, then this means that believers as individuals have always been *included* in the Book of Life and can never be erased from it. There remains a strong possibility that even though the earth dwellers as a corporate entity are foreknown or predestined to destruction, individual earthlings may still have opportunities to repent and escape the coming judgment. This assumption seems to be one of the main reasons why even in the final phases of eschatological calamities the gospel is still preached and, incidentally, certain unbelievers turn to

162. Aune, "Apocalypse Renewed," 70.
163. On Rev 3:20, Osborne, *Revelation*, 212, is instructive.
164. Or along synthetic lines another option is to concede with Caird *Revelation*, 49, that Revelation exemplifies "conditional predestination."

Churches under Siege of Persecution and Assimilation

God (10:11; 11:3, 13; 14:6–7). This phenomenon happens despite the counter images of unbelievers who refuse to repent after experiencing certain plagues (9:20–21; 16:9, 11). In a similar manner, even if we assume that the community of saints has been included in the heavenly registrar from the beginning of time, this does not preclude that individual names and churches from among this community could be erased if they turn away from God.

At least one text from the Talmud has a variant that is perhaps compatible with both 3:5 and 17:8. It states that on the special day of Rosh Hashanah, three books are opened—one for the righteous, one for the wicked, and one for the intermediate: "The thoroughly righteous are immediately inscribed and sealed for life. The thoroughly wicked are immediately inscribed and sealed for death. The fate of the intermediate is suspended until the Day of Atonement: if they are found deserving, they are inscribed for life; if not found deserving, they are inscribed for death" (TB *Rosh Hashanah* 16b).[165] In a somewhat similar way the concept of election in Israel's scriptures may be categorized in terms of the elect (God's beloved), anti-elect (God's enemies such as the Canaanites), and non-elect (the majority of other people in the world).[166] We could surmise that a meaning akin with this one rests behind Revelation with the Lamb as elect, the Beast as anti-elect, and the rest of humanity either elect or non-elect on the basis of which one of these two they follow.

PERSEVERANCE IN PHILADELPHIA (3:7–13)

The church in Philadelphia is promised an open door because even though they have "little power" or authority in their city, they have kept Christ's teachings and commands and have not denied his name (Rev 3:7–8).[167] They apparently experienced suffering and persecution in the past and have proven themselves faithful by not denying Christ. The thought is reiterated differently in 3:10: they have kept "the word of my patience" (τὸν λόγον τῆς ὑπομονῆς μου), i.e., Christ's exhortation for them to persevere.[168] An allusion to the teaching of Christ on perseverance probably suggests Jesus' warnings in the gospels for his followers to persevere (ὑπομένω)

---

165. ET in Paul, "Heavenly Tablets," 350.

166. See Kaminsky, *Yet Jacob I Loved*, for many passages from the Hebrew scriptures that support this reading.

167. The church's little power probably indicates their smallness or insignificance in relation to their non-Christian neighbors. Duff, *Who Rides the Beast?*, 45–46, thinks they are similar to the Smyrnans in being disenfranchised socially and economically. But unlike Smyrna, there is no mention of poverty in this city.

168. Differently Prigent, *Apocalypse*, 205, believes Christ's message is referring to Christ's own perseverance of suffering and thus alludes to the Passion.

through the coming eschatological crisis (cf. Matt 24:13; Mark 13:13; Luke 21:17). In Luke 21:12–17, before the end takes place, Christ-followers would be persecuted, handed over to synagogues and prisons, and stand before officials. Jesus assures them that he would bestow them with words of wisdom before their accusers, and in their perseverance (ὑπομονή) they would gain their souls. In a similar manner the Philadelphians have persevered through local conflicts and are now promised rewards for their endurance.

Similar to the situation in the Smyrna, the opponents in Philadelphia come from the "synagogue of Satan," presumably people from the local synagogue who oppose the church (3:9 cf. 2:9). The presence of a thriving Jewish community in first-century Philadelphia, however, lacks proper evidence.[169] Be that as it may, the glorified Christ in Revelation claims that those from the "synagogue of Satan" will bow down before the congregants' feet and confess that "I have loved you" (3:9 cf. Isa 49:23; 60:14; 1QM 12.14–15; 19.6). Similar phrases are echoed in Isaiah and other prophetic traditions, but Rev 3:9 provides an ironic twist: in the Jewish traditions, Gentiles are the ones who bow down before the Jews,[170] but in 3:9 the opponents from the synagogue will bow down before Philadelphian believers.[171] The opponents will know that Christ has "loved" or elected the Philadelphians (cf. 1:5).[172] This view is in keeping with John's association of the saints with elect Israel (e.g., 21:7)

The open door in 3:9 may refer to missionary opportunities,[173] but more likely from the context it is referring to guaranteed access into the Davidic kingdom with Christ as the one who possesses the "key of David" (cf. Isa 22:22–23; Isa 45:1–7) as the chosen official over the New Jerusalem.[174] He has the authority to open and close the city's doors in order to let in those who seek him and shut out those who rebel against him. The church in Philadelphia is promised access into the heavenly city, and the overcomer will become a permanent pillar in the city's temple (Rev 3:12–13; cf. Gal 2:9; 1 Tim 3:15; *1 Clem.* 5:2; 1QS 8.7–9).[175]

This open door is also related to Rev 3:10: because they have kept (τηρέω) Christ's word to persevere, they will be kept from the "hour of testing" that will come upon the whole world to try the earth dwellers. This sort of testing frequently

---

169. So Hemer, *Seven Churches*, 175.

170. Isa 49:23; 60:14; Zech 8:20–23; *1 En.* 10.21; *Sib. Or.* 3.716–35.

171. On irony in this passage, see Friesen, "Sarcasm in Revelation," 140–41.

172. Cf. John 13:1; Gal 2:20; Deut 4:37; 10:15; Isa 41:8; *4 Ezra* 3.13–14.

173. E.g., 1 Cor 16:9; Acts 14:27.

174. See further Fekkes, *Isaiah and Prophetic Traditions*, 130–32; Beale and McDonough, "Revelation," 1096–97.

175. See Friesen, "Sarcasm in Revelation," 139–40.

refers to an eschatological time a distress,[176] but the exact words in 3:10 (πειρασμός/ πειράζω) are used only here and in 2:2, 10. The time of suffering and tribulation, it seems, has already been set in motion and Christians are now enduring these things at the present moment (cf. 1:9; 2:9). The "whole earth" primarily includes the nations belonging to the Roman Empire (12:9; 16:14),[177] and the earth dwellers refer to unbelievers (6:10; 8:13; 11:10; 12:12; 13:8; 17:2, 8).[178] It is likely that 3:10 is a promise that the Philadelphians will be kept from harm when God brings judgment and plagues on his enemies (chs. 6–16). They will be protected supernaturally much like the 144,000 that have God's seal on them (Rev 7:1–3; 9:1–4; cf. John 17:15). This is not to say that the Christians in general or Philadelphians in particular would not suffer persecution in the future (cf. Rev. 4:1 with ch. 13), but that persecution from the Beast and Satan should not be equated with the coming wrath of God. The Philadelphians will not experience God's wrath. They will be like Israel protected from the plagues that God sent on Egypt during the exodus era.

The Philadelphian congregation, like the Smyrnans, receives no accusation from Christ, but the members are told that Christ will come suddenly, and they must hold fast to that which they possess in order that "no one takes your crown" (3:11; cf. 2:10). The point is that they must continue in perseverance until Christ returns if they are to inherit their eternal reward for overcoming (cf. 1:3; 2:11, 16). *Whatever promise of assurance 3:10 provides, it does not mean that the church does not have to endure hardships in the present age. Moreover, it does not preclude the possibility that congregants within the church of Philadelphia could still fall away; otherwise, there would be no compelling reason to exhort them to hold fast (κρατέω) lest someone take away their victory crown.*

The overcomers will become a pillar in God's house and the name of God (22:4; cf. Exod 28:36), the name of God's city (New Jerusalem), and the new name of Christ (19:12) will be written on them, suggesting God's ownership of them and their permanent residence in God's city (3:12).[179] After Christ returns, the overcomers will belong to the heavenly temple and New Jerusalem (cf. 21:2), and as fixtures in the Lord's house they will never be cast out of it (cf. John 6:37; *1 En.* 90.28–29). This promise is set for the *parousia* after their present struggle and endurance is over.

176. Cf. Dan 12:1; *T. Mos.* 8.1; *Jub.* 23.11–21; *2 Bar.* 27.1–15; Matt 24:15–31; Rev 7:14.

177. *1 En.* 37; 2 Esd 2:2; *2 Bar.* 70; CD[a] 10.9; Josephus, *Ant.* 11.3; Philo, *Gaius* 16; cf. Dan 12:1–2; Acts 11:28; 17:6; Luke 2:1; BDAG, 561.

178. Cf. Brown, "Hour of Trial," 308–14.

179. Interestingly, the pillars of Solomon's temple have names in 1 Kgs 7:21; 2 Chr 3:17. On the new name of the overcomer, see Rev 2:17; 3:1, 5. In early Judaism, three are called by the name of the Holy One: the righteous, the Messiah, and Jerusalem (*b. Baba Batra* 75b; cf. Str.B. 3.795–96).

APOSTASY THROUGH WEALTH:
THE CHURCH IN LAODICEA (3:14-22)

The final *adscriptio* is to the church in Laodicea that resides by the Lycus River near Hierapolis and Colossae (cf. Col 2:1; 4:13, 15-16). Various aspects about the ancient city have been conducive for the interpretation of Rev 3:14-21, including evidence of the city as a bank center ("rich"), the prominence of wool (clothing), its medical school ("eye salve"), and a double pipeline that may have caused the cold water from Colossae (eleven miles away from Laodicea) to warm up and the hot water from Hierapolis (six miles away) to cool down (hence, "lukewarm"). It is also likely that the local water contained high mineral deposits that made people sick when they drank it ("vomit"). After the city suffered a major earthquake in the early 60s CE, it refused assistance from Rome and built itself up to be an affluent center ("I have need of nothing").[180]

The spiritual barometer in the Laodicean church, like the churches in Sardis and Ephesus, had dropped significantly due to a state of indifference towards the things of God. They are described as neither cold nor hot but lukewarm, and so the Christ is about to vomit them out of his mouth (3:15-16). The inhabitants of the city would benefit from both hot water for bathing and cold for drinking; lukewarm water is neither of these. The notion of vomiting in Israel's scriptures cluster around several motifs, including: 1) drunkenness;[181] 2) overeating/bad digestion;[182] 3) vomiting as a metaphor related to riches;[183] 4) bad company;[184] 5) analogy for apostasy/returning to one's folly;[185] and 6) metaphorical descriptions of the expulsion of wicked or disobedient inhabitants from their land.[186]

The description of vomiting in 3:16 shares affinities with option 3, but ultimately 6 comes closest to the meaning: God's people Israel are to obey God by keeping his laws so that their promised land does not vomit them out of it (Lev 20:22). The idea of expulsion in this case conveys divine judgment and curse. *The imagery in Rev 3:16 connotes that the Laodiceans are about to be expelled from the mouth of Christ and thus cut off from the person of Christ. In essence they will cease to be recognized as his*

---

180. See ancient sources and evidence in, e.g., Wood, "Local Knowledge," 263-64; Ramsey, *Letters to the Seven Churches*, 413-30.

181. Isa 19:14; 28:7-8; Jer 25:27; cf. Philo, *Drunkenness* 221.

182. Prov 25:16; Sir 31:21; Jon 2:10; cf. *m. Miqvaot* 10.8.

183. Job 20:15, 18-19.

184. Prov 23:6-8.

185. Prov 26:11; cf. 2 Pet 2:22; *Syr. Menander* 2.52-58; *Gospel of Truth* 33.15.

186. Lev 18:25-28; 20:22. On the concept of vomiting the LXX mostly uses ἐμέω/ ἐξεμέω; Hebrew uses קִיא (see lexical references in LEH *ad loc*; BDB, 883). Proverbs 26:11 uses ἔμετος.

church. Similar to the church in Ephesus, this judgment would be corporate involving the church as a whole (cf. 2:5). The judgment involves a removal from Christ's presence, no doubt with eternal consequences. These thoughts enter into the orbit of the words of the Johannine Jesus who describes himself in the imagery of a vine and his followers the branches (John 15:1–6). His saints are to abide in him to have eternal life, and the person who does not remain in him is cast away as a branch to wither and be burned.

If this congregation's problem is complacency, then *the way they fell into this error seems to be a result of their wealth* (Rev 3:17). The church members in Laodicea have been lulled to spiritual slumber through prosperity, comfort, and self-sufficiency. This is not idolatry per se, and yet the Johannine author considers wealth to be bound up with idolatry (e.g., 13:16–17); both venues lead to assimilation and apostasy. Even so, unlike the Christians for Pergamum and Thyatira who want to advance socially and economically and thus compromise in the area of religious practices with outsiders, *the Laodiceans have already reached a high status*. As Adela Yarbro Collins suggests, "they were under much less pressure to conform to pagan customs. Without such pressure, without a crisis, they became complacent."[187] In a sense this church resembles the Whore of Babylon who lives in luxury, claiming she is not a widow and will experience no mourning even though she will become desolate and naked (18:7; cf. 17:16). *Like the Whore, the Laodiceans love the world by reveling in "the arrogance of life"* (cf. 1 John 2:15–16).

Descriptions of the church's affluence evoke vestiges of Jesus' teachings against covetousness and materialism. In the Parable of the Rich Fool (Luke 12:15–21) the wealthy man becomes self-absorbed and stingy, storing up treasure for himself instead of the kingdom of God. This character exemplifies why it is difficult for the rich to enter God's heavenly reign (cf. Luke 16:19–31;18:24–25; Mark 10:24–25; Matt 19:23–24). The Laodicean congregants also may be compared with the third seed in the Parable of the Sower, which receives the word of God but is choked by the deceitfulness of riches so that it bears no fruit (Luke 8:7, 14; cf. Mark 4:7; Matt 13:7). Such individuals trust in their wealth rather than God; as such, they are often excluded from God's kingdom (e.g., Luke 16:19–31; 18:18–25). The words of Jesus in the gospels continue to ring true for the Laodiceans: "You cannot serve God and mammon" (Luke 16:13; Matt 6:24).

The church's true condition from the heavenly perspective is one of misery, pity, shame, spiritual poverty, and blindness (Rev 3:17; contrast 2:9).[188] The most

---

187. Collins, *Apocalypse*, 30.
188. On the terms see Osborne, *Revelation*, 208.

serious charge that relates to apostasy is blindness,[189] which might echo remotely the reversal of conditions between the man whom Jesus healed of blindness and those who expelled the man from the synagogue. They claim to see but are spiritually blind and remain in sin (John 9:39–41). The church's wealth and self-sufficiency has drawn its members away from a right standing with Christ into a backslidden condition. The only possible cure for them is to repent; otherwise divine judgment against the congregation will be inevitable.

They are counseled to buy gold tried in the fire, intimating a refinement that fosters purity and quality. A few encounters with suffering and hardship, then, would do them well (Rev 3:18–19 cf. 1 Pet 1:7; Isa 1:25; Zech 13:9; Ps 66:10). They should likewise purchase and wear garments of purity and righteous deeds instead of being shamefully naked before the Lord's eyes (cf. Rev 3:4; 19:8). This exhortation perhaps suggests they were soiled with assimilation. It is quite possible that they gained their wealth be compromising with the economic structures and trade guilds of their culture, a cooperation that probably required them to participate in non-Christian worship.[190] Next, they should anoint themselves with eye salve so that they may no longer be spiritually blind. This may suggest that the Laodiceans need to return to Christ in faith and humility for the healing of their spiritual ailment. Robert Royalty perceptively draws attention to the sarcasm here: the Laodiceans are to buy products *from Christ* instead of commerce, which then draws "an implicit comparison between the commercially derived wealth of the Laodicean church and the true wealth of heaven to which the Christians of Asia gain access by endurance and suffering (2:9)."[191] Despite his severe rebuke the glorified Christ still loves the church in Laodicea (3:19a).[192] As long as he does not "vomit" this congregation out of his mouth, it still belongs to him.

In the final *remuneratio* we arrive at a conclusion relevant to both the Laodiceans and all the churches (3:20–21). The person who overcomes will be allowed to sit with Christ on his throne, even as Christ has overcome and is set on his Father's throne (3:21), which pictures the reign of the faithful with Christ in the coming kingdom (Luke 22:30; Matt 19:28).[193] Jesus stands at the door and knocks. If anyone hears him and opens the door, he will sup with that person and the person will sup with

---

189. Even so, "shame" in 3:17 may also indirectly relate to apostasy if Bultmann, "αἰσχύνω," 1.189 is correct in claiming that αἰσχύνη primarily refers to shame brought on by "divine judgment."

190. See Trebilco, *Early Christians in Ephesus*, 437.

191. Royalty, *Ideology of Wealth*, 171.

192. Cf. Heb 12:6–8; *1 Clem.* 56:4; Prov. 3:12; Philo, *Prelim.* 177

193. Cf. Rev 1:6; 5:10; 20:4, 6; 22:5; 2 Tim 2:12; Dan 7:18, 27; Ps 110:1; 4Q521; *1 En.* 45.3; 51.3; 55.4; *T. Levi* 13.9.

Jesus (Rev 3:20). The invitation in this context, strange enough, is given to Christians rather than non-believers, and Jesus is pictured standing outside a house where he waits to be invited in by the believer! One perspective highlights that Jesus is being portrayed as a wealthy patron who eats with clients at a supper party. Hence, to eat with Jesus is a status-raising event for his "clients," the members of the church, and thus points to the believer's heavenly wealth.[194] Another view is that the passage shares affinities with the words of Jesus about his unexpected return (Luke 12:35–38).[195] Each believer is viewed as a doorkeeper and servant who must keep watch until Christ returns. In this case the supper may refer to the Messianic banquet (Rev 19:7–9). Richard Bauckham compares the Jesus *logion* in Luke 22:28–30 (cf. 22:37) and Matt 19:28 with Rev 3:20–21 to capture the idea of Jesus as the master rather than the guest of the watchful servants. He condescends to eat with them in his own house.[196] If Bauckham is correct then the message of Revelation ends with a final allusion for congregation members to be spiritually prepared for the *parousia*. This is stressed to every individual believer rather than to the church as a corporate entity or to the angel of the churches. *It could be implied that if a believer is not prepared to answer when Christ knocks, that believer will be excluded from the messianic banquet.*

The danger of apostasy through riches seems to be a repetitive temptation for the Christian communities in Asia Minor. Within the Johannine community in Ephesus the hospitality of its members assumes they possess homes large enough to accommodate itinerant guests (2 John 10–11; 3 John 5–8). The Johannine author exhorts his readers to be detached from the world (1 John 2:15–17) and exemplify love through material generosity towards poor brothers and sisters (1 John 3:16–18).[197] Timothy must instruct his congregation in Ephesus about deception and the love of money which leads people to spiritual destruction (1 Tim 6:9–10). The wealthy in the church are to be generous and not haughty (6:17–19), and wealthy women are not to dress extravagantly (2:9). The Pauline communities in Asia Minor are warned against the vice of greed (Eph 5:5; Col 3:5), and the Lukan Paul must claim to the elders in Ephesus that he has not coveted silver, gold, or clothes (Acts 20:33). Moreover, as we have argued, the community in Hebrews is probably situated somewhere in Asia Minor. They too appear to be an affluent church (e.g., Heb 13:2, 16) and they are warned against coveting money (13:5).

194. Cf. Royalty, *Ideology of Wealth*, 174.

195. Cf. Roloff, "Siehe, ich stehe vor der Tür," 452–66; idem, *Revelations*, 65.

196. Bauckham, *Climax of Prophecy*, 107–8. Here the house and door are simply included in the saying to emphasize the point of being ready for Christ's coming. There is no allegorical meaning behind the word "door" so as to interpret it as the servant's heart.

197. For further elaboration on Johannine and Pastoral passages in relation to wealth, see Trebilco, *Early Christians in Ephesus*, 404–34.

Among quite a few first-century churches in Asia Minor, then, the Christians are tempted to compromise their faith by the lure of wealth. *In Revelation in particular, wealth is seen as an acute danger that leads to apostasy because the Roman system has blurred economic and religious boundaries* (Rev 13, 17–18). The churches of Laodicea, Sardis, and Ephesus are all called to repent of their indifferences that have led them to a condition of loveless character, compromise, and assimilation. It is not clear that these and the other churches would have perceived their shortcomings the same way John does.[198] But since the glorified Christ speaks through John to these churches in chapters 2–3, this adds to the authoritative nature of John's discourse. After hearing the seven messages, if the churches come against any of its content, they come against Christ and the Spirit of prophecy.

APOSTASY AND COMMUNITY IN REV 4–22 AND THE PRESERVATION OF THE 144,000 (REV 7; CF. 14)

Beginning in 4:1 the revelation of what will come in the future is disclosed to John. Perhaps more appropriately the visions convey the temporal poles of events now and not yet (cf. 1:19), and they repeatedly allude to traditions, myths, ideas, and events of the past such as the Exodus, Maccabean Revolt, Leviathan mythology, and the Jewish War with Rome so that a pastiche of past, present, and future elements may be discovered throughout the rest of the book. In this section we are dealing with polyvalent meaning in an emphatic way. The apocalyptic genre here may be seen as art, requiring readers and auditors to look at the word paintings in a way that requires them to fill in some of the blanks, and many readers will do this differently. In a sense the apocalyptic visions in the book function together as though they were an interactive comic book or graphic novel. The artist and writer portray the story through drawings and panels, and they fill in some of the captions and balloons but then hand it over to the readers to fill in the rest.

A so-called scientific meaning for these passages in Revelation is virtually impossible and perhaps disrespects the original aim of these texts, which, from the original readers' perspective, were intended to be futuristic, hence not fully known. Moreover, from the contemporary readers' perspective looking backward, these texts have not been "fulfilled" in a consistent and clearly conceivable way. The observations of our study on apostasy in this section must therefore remain tentative as one of many ways to view the texts.

---

198. In Ephesus, Trebilco, *Early Christians in Ephesus*, 346–47 says they may not have agreed with his views, at least before hearing Revelation.

Churches under Siege of Persecution and Assimilation

Even so, we should ask how the churches in Asia Minor may have interpreted Rev 4–22. If the warnings they were given pertained to the immediate future and the second coming with eternal judgment marked out against them if they did not repent, and if their promised rewards pertained to the eternal kingdom, then it is reasonable to assume that such readers and auditors of the visions would have understood the coming judgments of God as pertaining to *them* and not simply outsiders and God's enemies. The call to come out of "Babylon" and the warning of judgment by eternal torment against those who take the mark of the Beast pertains to them and requires their perseverance and keeping God's commands (14: 9–12; 18:4; cf. 13:9–10). Bauckham rightly claims, in reference to the judgments in Revelation, "the portals of judgment were there precisely to shock and even to scare such readers into an understanding of where they stood in the spiritual crisis of their time," and this makes vivid the sobering alternatives we find between insiders and outsiders in 22:14–15.[199] Certainly the idolaters, fornicators, and liars in this passage, as well as the cowards in 21:7–8, would have been read by many congregants in Asia Minor as indictments against their compromising practices and potential to deny Christ and worship the Beast.

We have already addressed the matter of the Beast referring to Caesar and the imperial cult, the False Prophet as the *neokoros* or high priest of the cult, and the Whore of Babylon as the Roman system and economic trade, and so these figures will not detain us further except to reiterate that the threat these images pose for Christians pertains to apostasy. Through economic sanctions and persecution the Beast and Whore lure the saints into idolatrous worship and assimilation with a system opposed to God (e.g., 11:7; 13:7, 13–17; 17:6; 18:3–5). Equally, names that appear or do not appear in the Book of Life (13:8; 17:8; 20:11–15) and the conception of vice lists relevant to overcomers and cowards (e.g., 21:8) will not be repeated here. At least two other images in the later chapters of Revelation, however, are still relevant for our discussion: the 144,000 (chs. 7, 14) and the Dragon's conflict with the Woman (ch. 12).

Various identities for the 144,000 have been suggested including Jews, Jewish Christians, a Jewish remnant, Gentile Christians, all Christians, and Christian martyrs.[200] Their identity is best connected with Israel. Not only are the 144,000 comprised of the twelve tribes of Israel (7:4–8),[201] but this passage may be depict-

---

199. Bauckham, "Judgment in the Book of Revelation," 14 cf. 21.

200. See options in e.g., Beale, *Revelation*, 416–23.

201. Joseph has replaced the name of Ephraim, and Dan is not mentioned perhaps because of a negative reputation or apostasy (cf. Gen 49:17; Judg 18:30; Jer 8:16; *Liv. Pro.* 3.17–20; *T. Dan* 5:4–8 [but see the tribe's restoration beginning in *T. Dan* 5.9]). Then again, this tribe may be missing by mistake,

ing the fulfillment of the hope of Israel's restoration, a theme prominent in Israel's scriptures and early Jewish and Christian sources.[202] Jewish particularity cannot be erased from 7:4-8, and their association with the great multitude in 7:9-17 may be that salvation history has prioritized the Jews before Gentiles so that the true Israel in Christ began with the Jews and later added the Gentiles.[203] The 144,000 represent the remnant of Israel in Christ (cf. 14:1-5), and the great multitude beginning in 7:9 are Gentile Christians and martyrs.[204] In 14:4 the remnant are purchased not "from within" or "from among" men, but "away from" (ἀπό) "men." The final meaning is no indication that their identity is not Jewish.[205] The 12,000 from each tribe are "out of" or "out from" (ἐκ) the tribes of Israel (7:4), suggesting a special group that was part of a larger group. This idea finds parallels in Ezek 9:4-8, which describes a segment of Israel (remnant) rather than the whole. Compatible with this view is the distinction between Jewish and Gentile Christians in the last days mentioned by Paul, who claims that all Israel will be saved before the culmination of the eschaton takes place (cf. Rom 9-11).[206] If something similar is being portrayed in Rev 7, the idea may be related to the concept of Jew first, then Gentile (cf. Rom 1:16). In Rev 14:4 the 144,000 are called the "firstfruits" or first Christians.

The sealing of the 144,000 has often been understood in terms of divine protection, but this may be deciphered further to determine whether the protection is physical or non-physical. The latter opens up the possibility that final perseverance is assured to those who are sealed.[207] Their sealing, it seems, functions both as a

gloss, or simply to keep the number at twelve. Later Christians have speculated that the Beast comes from Dan, but the Beast is associated with Caesar who is obviously not an Israelite!

202. See Deut 30:3-5; Isa 11:11-16; 27:12-13; 49:5-6; Jer 31:7-14; Ezek 37:15-23; Hos 11:10-11; Ps 106:47; 147:2; 2 Macc 2:7; Sir 36:11; Tob 13:13; *1 En.* 57; *4 Ezra.* 13.12-47; *2 Bar.* 78.5-7; 1QM 2-3; *T. Jos.* 19.4; *Pss. Sol.* 11.2-7; Matt 19:28; Luke 22:30; 24:21; Acts 1:6; Rom 11.

203. In this respect my view is similar to Hirschberg, *Das eschatologische Israel*; idem, "Jewish Believers in Asia Minor," 224-30. Feuillet, "144,000 Israélites," 191-224, believes the text refers to the remnant of Christian Jews and associates this community as arising from the tragedy of 70 CE.

204. The 144,000 might appear to be alive at the same time the "great multitude" is already receiving rewards if the multitude is spatially in heaven or regarded from the vantage point of the eschaton's culmination (i.e., they stand before the throne and the Lamb: Rev 7:9). A couple of other distinctive nuances between the two groups are that, whereas the great multitude is innumerable, the 144,000 are counted and require sealing. Secondly, martyrs are included in the great multitude; their victory (palm symbol) is that they have overcome tribulation and are given access to the Lamb's eschatological kingdom. In the Lamb's kingdom, they will no longer thirst or hunger and all their sorrow will disappear (21:4-6; 22:1, 17).

205. Contrast Mayo, *Those Who Call Themselves Jews*, 96-98, and see the response of Sanders, Review of *Those Who Call Themselves Jews*.

206. Hirschberg, "Believing Jews in Asia Minor," 228, is more cautious, suggesting that John is more discrete than Paul of Rom 11:25-27.

207. On the first option see Aune, *Revelation*, 2.443, who thinks the safeguarding is from plagues

marker identifying them as belonging to God (cf. Isa 44:5) and as protection from the coming wrath of God that takes place in chapters 8–16.[208] The angels hold the four winds that provide an interlude from calamities that come upon the earth during the previous judgment of the sixth seal (7:1–3; cf. 6:12–17).[209] In this sense, the sealing of the 144,000 protects them from the unsealing of the scrolls that depict the various judgments. When the calamities ensue again, the 144,000 are kept from the dangerous "locusts" that attack only those who do not have the mark of God on them (cf. 9:4). This protection is reminiscent of the exodus story where Israel is shielded by God via the blood of the lamb on their doorposts during the first Passover. The Egyptians, on the other hand, suffer the death of their firstborn as a punishment from God (Exod 12). Ezekiel 9:4–5 provides another parallel. Only Israelites who grieve over the abominations taking place in their respective community are given a mark or "taw" on their forehead. The rest are killed. The divine protection that is meant for the 144,000 is primarily physical; they are guarded from plagues and catastrophes coming upon the earth.

Nevertheless, the passage does seem to affirm something more than physical safety. It is quite possible that the final salvation of the 144,000 is also meant if they are pictured as being present with the Lamb in Rev 14:1–5. This scene is in keeping with the nature of apocalyptic to observe images from the heavenly perspective of beginning to end. Israel's protection may have been understood by the original auditors as something similar to Paul's claim that all Israel will be saved (cf. Rom 11:26). If so, then the seal seems to function as a salvific guarantee for the corporate remnant of Israel. The number identifying this group is symbolic (12 x 12,000) suggesting the number of tribes in Israel and totality of Jewish followers of the Lamb.[210] Hence, the vision is not guaranteeing that every individual Christian will finally persevere, nor is it denying that individual Christians can fall away.[211] *The promise is to the corporate body of Jewish believers, who as a community will survive the plagues*

---

and persecution. Against this view Collins, *Apocalypse*, 52, writes that the sealing "does not symbolize divine protection from physical harm and death. Rather, it symbolizes divine protection within and in spite of suffering and death." For the second option in relation to perseverance, see especially Beale, *Revelation*, 409–15.

208. Similarly is Pattemore, *People of God*, 129, who adds that the seal conveys God's ownership and security.

209. On protection against catastrophes, see further Schüssler Fiorenza, *Judgment and Justice*, 66.

210. Interestingly, Luke (post-70 CE), via James, speaks of tens of thousands of Jews (μυριάς) believing in Jesus as Messiah in Acts 21:20; albeit, the context intends to portray the number of Jewish believers at the time of Paul's arrest (c. 58–60 CE).

211. Differently, Marshall, *Kept by the Power*, 178, associates the identity of the 144,000 with the great multitude but nevertheless arrives at a similar conclusion to my own: "since the number [144,000] is a symbolic one it does not necessarily follow that all who have been sealed will certainly persevere."

and be with Christ. The first-century Jewish Christians among the auditors in Asia Minor could take comfort in God's protection and final salvation, *assuming that* they remain blameless and do not deny Christ (cf. 14:5).

THE DRAGON AND A THIRD OF THE STARS FROM HEAVEN: APOSTATE SAINTS? (REV 12)

The center of the book rests on the people of God and their witnesses to the nations and Israel. The content in this section highlights the martyrdom of the faithful witnesses by the Beast (Rev 11), persecution of the newborn male child and his mother by Satan (Rev 12), and a general persecution via economic sanctions (Rev 13). This section is consistent with the idea that in Revelation the saints are called to persevere when suffering tribulations. A vision interacting with perseverance and apostasy is in 12:3–4, where the Dragon (Satan) attempts to devour the child (the Messiah) of the woman who is crowned with twelve stars; in our view she represents the remnant of faithful Israel.[212] In the portent, the Dragon's tail drags away a third of the stars and casts them to the earth (12:4). This does not seem to indicate that a third of the angels rebelled with Satan, even though an apostate angel might represent the star falling to earth and opening up the bottomless pit (cf. 9:1, 11)[213] and stars sometimes represent angels in similar literature (e.g., *1 En.* 18.14; 21.3–6; 86.1–3; 88.3; Isa 24:21–22). The Dragon casts down to *earth* these stars, the identity of which seems different than the rebellious angels who fight along with the Dragon (Satan) against Michael and his hosts in *heaven*. The Dragon is finally cast down to the earth with these angels only after they lose the battle in 12:7–9. The combat, it seems, takes place at the time of Christ's crucifixion; the next scene refers to the redemption that the Lamb has provided (12:10–11).

A comparison with Dan 8:10 seems close to the meaning of Rev 12:4 and may suggest the fallen stars refer to humans or saints (cf. Dan 12:1, 3).[214] We also notice that the stars may represent churches (Rev 1:20).[215] On this reading the tail of the Dragon drags down the people of God through persecution, and there may also be a secondary meaning related to deception and apostasy (Dan 8:10, 22–25; 11:29–39;

---

212. The woman's crying in birth may indicate the sufferings of the Jewish people in view of their long awaited Messiah. For options on the woman's identity, see recently Mayo, *Those Who Call Themselves Jews*, 145–58; Sumney, "Dragon Has Been Defeated," 105.

213. On this star as a fallen angel see Beale, *Revelation*, 491–93.

214. See also Isa 60:19–20; Matt 13:43; 2 Macc 9:10; *As. Mos.* 10.8–10; *1 En.* 43.1–4; 46.7–8; 1QH 7.22–25.

215. On the connection between stars and humans, see further Beale and McDonough, "Revelation," 1123–24; Beale, *Revelation*, 218–19, 636–37.

Rev 12:9). In Revelation persecution and apostasy go hand in hand, requiring perseverance among the saints (12:11, 13, 17; 13:7, 10; 14:9–12; cf. 6:9–11; 11:2–7; 17:6; 18:24; 20:4). Those whom the Dragon persecutes or causes to fall away may be either Israelites or Christians, but *since the messianic child is not yet born when the Dragon casts down the stars (12:4–5), this image might be pointing to a persecution and apostasy in Israel's past,* such as the sufferings they experienced under King Antiochus Epiphanes IV (cf. 1–2 Macc; Dan 8:10; 11:29–39; 12:1–3). On the other hand, a number of similar combat myths were known in the ancient world, and some in fact depict stars being knocked down.[216] *It may be the case that the falling stars in 12:4 are merely intended to demonstrate the Dragon's ferocious power.*

The woman is then transported to the wilderness where she is protected from the Serpent (Satan) for three-and-a-half times, and so Satan wars with her children (12:14–17). If the remnant of Israel identifies this woman, then the picture of her escape may allude to Christian Jews from Jerusalem who escaped to Pella in order to avoid the Jewish War with Rome (67–70 CE).[217] The three-and-a-half times in the wilderness would then be representative for the general period of the Jewish War. Here their protection resembles that of the 144,000 in chapter 7, but in this case the woman's protection is from a destruction or persecution brought on by Satan.[218] The woman, in any event, precedes the Messiah in time by giving birth to him. On a different level the three-and-a-half times may reconfigure the time mentioned in Dan 7:25; 9:27; 12:7 and refer to the entire messianic era until the *parousia*. If so, then the image of the woman being protected in the wilderness again evinces God's physical and spiritual protection of the corporate community of messianic Jews who will never cease to be his elect people. God will see to it that this body of believers perseveres until the *parousia* without being physically destroyed or abandoning Christ as a corporate community. Even on this alternative reading, nothing is said about individualistic final perseverance. The woman's other "children" would seem to be Gentile Christians, here perhaps viewed in terms of fulfilling second exodus-wilderness prophecies, a number of which portray the nations joining the remnant of Israel on a final journey to Zion.[219]

Does the Serpent/Dragon prevail against these children? They are certainly persecuted, but it would seem that they too, like the woman, are preserved as a cor-

216. For examples, see Collins, *Combat Myth*, 59–100; Collins, *Daniel*, 332–33. The latter, however, writes that a reference to humans as stars would be "highly exceptional."

217. Cf. Eusebius, *Hist. eccl.* 3.5.

218. We notice also a protection of God's inner sanctuary in Rev 11:1–2. This seems to be likewise the case for the two witnesses in 11:5 at least until the Beast from the abyss kills them in 11:7.

219. E.g., Isa 11; 35; 40–55; Hos 11:8–11; 12:9–13; 13:4–15; Amos 2:10–3:2; Mic 4:1–8; 7:11–15; Hab 3:1–7; Hag 2:4–5; Zech 10:8–12; 12:8; 14:8–9; cf. Exod 15:12; 19:4; Deut 1:31–33; 32:10–15.

porate group—the "great multitude" that stand before Christ in 7:9–17 seems to portray Gentile saints and martyrs. The preservation of Jewish-Christians is stressed, however, probably because they are now clearly the minority of believers ever since 70 CE, and the Lord wished to assure this community that they have a special place in his kingdom. Likewise, their election brings into sharper contrast the "synagogue of Satan," which opposes the churches of Smyrna and Philadelphia. It is quite plausible that if the members of these churches once attended local synagogues then a good number of them may be Jewish Christians who are among the audiences in Asia Minor hearing these prophecies as they were originally read.

A FINAL WARNING TO THE CHRISTIAN AUDIENCE (22:18-19)

The closing words of Revelation declare curses on those who would tamper with the book: "I myself testify to everyone who hears the words belonging to the prophecy contained in this book, if anyone adds to these things, God will add to him the plagues which are written in this book; and if anyone takes away from the words of the book of this prophecy, God will take away his share from the tree of life and out of the holy city, which are written in this book" (Rev 22:18–19; cf. Deut 4:2; 12:32; *1 En.* 104.11; Josephus, *Ag. Ap.* 1.42–43; *Did.* 4.13).[220] The passage functions as a protection formula used on important and sacred texts that guarantees the integrity of its content as well as guarding that integrity from being tampered with in the future. It functions as sort of a copyright.[221] In the words of Aune, "John's use of this formula, combined in a unique and rhetorically skillful way with two conditional curses, indicates that the author viewed his composition as both *complete* and *inspired*."[222]

The final warning would be read and heard by audiences of Christian communities wherever this book was publically circulated, beginning in Asia Minor. The curse presupposes the possibility of eternal judgment on those who would violate the book's content. If anyone would distort the content of this authentic prophecy to render it false or misleading then such a person would be doing a work tantamount to that of a false prophet. Beale opts for the position that 22:19 is not addressing the loss of salvation, but "a denial of final salvific reward for those who have claimed outwardly to be Christians but have never had true faith."[223] But this explanation

---

220. The Textus Receptus replaces "tree of life" with "Book of life," but this is an error (see main text above). Contrary to some popular opinions, 22:18–19 is not referring to the close of the canon of the New Testament. Neither John nor his audience would have understood such a meaning. The book/scroll only refers to Revelation.

221. See examples and discussion in Aune, *Revelation*, 3.1208–16.

222. Aune, *Revelation*, 3.1237; emphasis original.

223. Beale, *Revelation*, 1153.

does not do justice to the universal scope of the verse. The warning of curse is for "*everyone* who hears," which would pertain both to Christians who have true faith as well as those who do not (22:18: παντὶ τῷ ἀκούοντι... ἐάν τις...). Our author is indiscriminate about who might tamper with the book. *That such a believer would be excluded from the New Jerusalem and suffer the plagues of God's wrath surely means that God will disown that Christian.* This act would seem to be synonymous with committing apostasy. The severity of the warning is nevertheless intended foremost to discourage anyone from attempting to tamper with the book's content.

CONCLUSION

The main purpose of Revelation is to motivate the churches in Asia Minor, comprised of Gentiles and Jews, to perseverance in view of the short time before Christ's return. They are to avoid assimilation with the Roman system that would compel them to adopt its socioeconomic values and participate in the imperial cult. For the author, assimilation leads to apostasy. Through John's prophetic use of the voice of the glorified Christ and depictions of graphic visions portraying the fates of the righteous and wicked, the audience is encouraged to proper behavior and godly fear, and warned of the eternal consequences that will plague them if they do not repent of spiritual negligence and various practices that Christ detests. The Christian communities in this region struggle with internal dangers of apathy and the promotion of lax boundaries between the church and the Roman world. They face external pressures and harassments to conform to the religious and economic mores of a society that paid homage to wealth, social status, and Caesar as Lord. The Christians must be overcomers persevering until Christ's *parousia*, and thus they will be rewarded on the last day. If they apostatize by succumbing to the Roman system, they will be numbered among the vicedoers as cowards, idolaters, fornicators, and liars for denying Christ, and their eternal place will be excluded from the beloved city (21:7–8; 22:14–15).

The church in Ephesus stands fast against the Nicolaitans and Christian leaders who claim apostolic authority but teach false doctrines and exploit congregations, akin with the false teachers mentioned in the earlier Pastoral and Johannine letters (2:1–7). But these believers have failed to maintain their original fervency, which exemplified itself in the motivation to do works for the sake of loving one another as well as their neighbors and God. Similar to the church in Laodicea, their condition may have developed from a preoccupation or acquisition of wealth, and in this sense these churches have compromised with the Roman economic system (3:14–22). However the Ephesians may have lost it, they now lack love. Likewise, the church of

Sardis struggles with some type of spiritual apathy even though it was once a vibrant congregation (3:1–6). Some of its members are already considered apostates being spiritually dead to Christ. A second group is about to fall away, and only a small remnant has remained spiritually faithful to Christ, uncompromised when it comes to assimilation. All three congregations suffer from gradual defection; through lack of zeal and negligence their members have been lulled to a spiritual slumber and are now in a backslidden condition.

They are also in danger of divine judgment, and so the Christ of Revelation calls them to repentance. The consequence of not repenting would be that the Ephesian and Laodicean congregations will be removed from Christ's presence and no longer belong to him. The church in Sardis will be unprepared for Christ's *parousia* and members erased from the Book of Life. In essence, if these churches remain unrepentant they will be excluded from the New Jerusalem when Christ returns, and on judgment day they will face the second death, the Lake of Fire. Divine judgment, however, is conveyed on a corporate level for these communities; repentant individuals within these churches would seem to escape the punishment determined for the church as a whole. Restoration after punishment is not mentioned probably because the letters are viewed in light of the imminent return of Christ—*now* is the time to repent.

The churches in Pergamum and Thyatira have compromised by eating food sacrificed to idols and committing fornication, practices that are associated with the doctrine of "Balaam" (2:12–29). The latter vice, however, is shorthand for their comingling with Roman society; it may not be literally denoting sexual immorality unless the term includes intermarriage with non-believers. These churches desire upward mobility in the socioeconomic order at the expense of compromising Christian commitments. A prophet in Thyatira code-named Jezebel has influenced the congregation and functions as a prelude to the Whore of Babylon by seducing her clients to eat idol meats and commit fornication. Christ has been patient with her but now her judgment is inevitable because she refuses to repent. The judgment that she and her colleagues and disciples will face is primarily temporal, taking place before the *parousia* so as to warn other churches not to follow her ways. Although her immediate disciples will be "killed," the possibility of restoration may be left open for Jezebel and her other constituents. Unrepentant members in Pergamum, however, would seem to face divine judgment when Christ returns.

Only the churches in Smryna and Philadelphia escape accusations and the threat of judgment (2:8–11; 3:7–13). The former has suffered poverty, perhaps as a result of socioeconomic discriminations from outsiders, and both churches seem to face conflicts with local synagogues. These churches have remained faithful despite local harassment; Philadelphia will escape future tribulation, but members of the congregation in Smyrna will soon suffer imprisonment. Both churches are encouraged to continue in faithfulness and not fall away.

The Beast, the False Prophet, and the Whore of Babylon are viewed as persecuting the churches, and these images primarily represent the imperial cult and the economic system of Rome (Rev 13, 17–18). The Christians must overcome them to participate in the New Jerusalem. A special protection is given to the 144,000 and the woman who bears the male child (Rev 7, 12). Both these images depict the prophetic restoration of the remnant of Israel. These apocalyptic images suggest that God will not allow the extinction of Jewish-Christians; this community will be persevered until the end despite persecutions. Even though the Dragon's mission is to destroy the saints (Rev 12) he will not succeed in destroying the woman (Jewish Christians) or her children (Gentile Christians).

The book of Revelation ends with a warning that Christians must not distort the content of the book's prophecies. To do so would incur divine judgment upon them whereby they would be excluded from the beloved community and suffer the same destruction as unbelievers and apostates (22:18–19).

We find in Revelation a group of Christian communities in Asia Minor that face temptations similar to the churches in this region in other New Testament writings. The danger of apostasy related to wealth, prominent in Laodicea and Ephesus, is especially a temptation in the Pauline church of Ephesus, where Timothy is instructed against the love of money and encouraged to have his congregation members dress modestly and be generous with their wealth (1 Tim 2:9; 6:9–10, 17–19). The churches in the area are also warned specifically against greed (Eph 5:5; Col 3:5). Likewise the Christians in the homily of Hebrews, another community that may be in Asia Minor, are warned against wealth (Heb 13:5). These examples suggest that early Christian communities in Asia Minor struggled to find a proper balance between spiritual purity and socioeconomic status. In Revelation, Rome offers them a way to economic security via the imperial cult: they could continue buying and selling as long as they take the mark of the Beast.

Some of the church members in Thyatira and Pergamum maintain a similar attitude regarding idol meats as do the "strong" in 1 Corinthians, without realizing that the times had changed and the leniency Paul once communicated to his church on this issue had now given way to more serious threats from the imperial cult and economic compromise. Needless to say, the voice of Paul on this issue did not win the day with many Christians at the dawn of the second century. On the other hand, the voice of Jesus in the gospels is repeated and perpetuated behind the prophetic warnings to the seven churches in Revelation. The warning that they not deny but confess his name sounds similar to Jesus' warnings that those who deny him in the present age will be denied by him in the age to come (Rev 2:13; 3:5, 8; cf. Matt 10:32–33; Luke 12:8–9; Mark 8:34–38). And the church in Ephesus was losing its first love (Rev 2:4), which seems to be the reverse of Jesus' command to love God and one another, the hallmark of Christian identity (e.g., John 13:35; Mark 12:28–31). Moreover, Jesus predicted a similar apostasy of Christians losing their love in the end times (cf. Matt 24:10–12). No doubt the Christians in Asia Minor at the end of the first century still believed in the imminence of the second coming, and from their perspective Jesus' sayings related to perseverance and apostasy in the end times had special relevance for their situation.

Conclusion

We will now revisit our four-fold endeavor of the three volumes to identify the communities from which the warnings and defections arise, the nature of apostasy that is committed in the respective communities, the consequences related to apostasy, and compare the various New Testament communities' views of apostasy and its consequences. We have already examined these venues in diverse locations within the chapters of each of the volumes, especially in their conclusions, but a more thorough-going *mise en scène* will now be explored that has the fourth point in mind by comparing the views of the New Testament authors. This comparison will help shed further light on the subject and may raise more questions for future studies. In this grand finale, along with the General Epistles and Revelation, we will interact with the all three volumes of *Apostasy in the New Testament Communities* including the Gospels, Acts, Johannine writings, and Pauline writings.

THE NEW TESTAMENT COMMUNITIES

The emerging Christian communities represent a variety of backgrounds and situations. Many of the communities are predominantly Gentiles who are Christ-followers, as deciphered from Mark, Luke-Acts, most Pauline letters, and 1–2 Peter. A mixture of Jews and Gentiles may be seen, however, in the communities of the Johannine writings, Romans, Hebrews, and Revelation. The communities in Matthew, James, and Jude appear to be primarily Jewish Christ-followers. Preponderance on the issue of keeping the Law is found especially in Matthew and James. In terms of authorship, if the undisputed letters of Paul are our paradigm, then a significant portion of the New Testament has been influenced by Hellenistic Jewish minds.

The locations of these communities cluster around several major areas: Palestine-Syria and by extension the communities of the Diaspora (Matthew, James, Jude, and narratives in the Gospels, Acts, and Galatians 2), western Asia Minor (Johannine writings, Ephesians, Colossians, Pastoral Letters, Revelation, and possibly Hebrews),

Galatia and northern Asia Minor (Galatians, 1 Peter), Macedonia-Achaia (1–2 Thessalonians, 1–2 Corinthians, Philippians), and Rome (Mark, Romans). Several of the sources from western Asia Minor address a problem with false teachings infiltrating the congregations. The Pastoral Letters, Acts 20, and Revelation 2:2 might be referring to the same group of false leaders in Ephesus, but we failed to find other plausible connections between sources from this area that are addressing the same deceptions, except in a general sort of way. In terms of moral conduct it may be significant that a number of Asian communities are warned against greed or the misuse of wealth (Pastoral Letters, Revelation 3; Ephesians 5:3, Colossians 3:5), and in the Johannine community the command to love one another must be authenticated, among other things, by helping needy brothers and sisters (1 John 3:17).

The New Testament communities each face unique challenges. Their opponents are identified variously as immoral or antinomian apostate Christian teachers (2 Peter, Jude), apostate ascetic Christian teachers (Pastoral Letters), false prophets (Matthew), Christ-deniers who have defected from the beloved community (Johannine writings), zealous Jewish-Christian teachers and adherents of the Law (e.g., Galatians, Philippians 3), Jewish "super apostles" (2 Corinthians), an Essene-like sect (Colossians), hostile non-believing Gentiles (e.g., Acts, 1-2 Thessalonians, Philippians 1, Hebrews, 1 Peter), and Nero or the Roman imperial cult (Mark, Revelation). The opponents are frequently outsiders (e.g., hostile Gentiles, Rome, Essene-like sect), but they are sometimes intruders or insiders who influence the churches (e.g., Matthew, Galatians, Jude, 2 Peter), and sometimes insiders become outsiders (e.g., Matt 18; 1 Cor 5; 1 Tim 1; Johannine writings). Some sources may address more than one set of opponents relevant to the community (e.g., the Johannine writings, Philippians, Ephesians). The opponents and apostates in these writings, then, are as diverse as the respective authors and Christ-communities they are perceived as threatening.

Dangers include the potential apostasy of entire church communities (e.g., Galatians, 2 Corinthians, Revelation, Hebrews), while other writings focus on apostate individuals, factions, or secessionists (e.g., Mark, 1 Corinthians, Johannine writings). Some sources discuss the apostasy of a third party (e.g., Rom 9–11, 2 Thess 2), and some communities are not perceived by the authors as being in great danger of apostasy; hence, the subject is discussed primarily by way of preventative maintenance or general exhortations (e.g., Philippians, Ephesians).

The sprawling amount of communities, opponents, and situations among the early Christ-communities to a certain extent mirrors the ancient Greco-Roman world and its plethora of religious, philosophical, and ideological options. Jewish beliefs of time also betray a set of diverse alternatives, as Josephus' discussions on determinism and human actions in relation to Pharisees, Sadducees, and Essenes exemplify (e.g., Jos. *Ant.* 13.172.73). If such diversity is evident in the cultures of the first-century world of the New Testament, it would seem to be self-evident that similar diversity of beliefs holds true for communities of the emerging Christian faith. In this study we have observed that such a perspective reflects the authors and communities' understanding of apostasy and restoration.

THE NATURE OF APOSTASY IN THE NEW TESTAMENT

We have defined in the Introduction of volume one that apostasy is "the phenomenon that occurs when a religious follower or group of followers turn away from or otherwise repudiate the central beliefs and practices they once embraced in a respective religious community." If this definition is given a Christian context as we find in the New Testament, then apostasy may be understood as the phenomenon that occurs when a Christ-follower or group of followers turn away from or otherwise repudiate the central claims they once embraced as a member of a respective community in Christ. Faith and obedience towards Jesus Christ would seem to be central. With this view in mind, what makes a member or group belonging to the community in Christ turn away from Christ, God, or the community in Christ? In the New Testament we have uncovered several factors that result in apostasy. Some of the categories below overlap, and we have read that certain communities are susceptible to more than one of these.

First, *unbelief* is a major form of apostasy. The author of Hebrews associates unbelief with the disobedient wilderness generation and warns his listeners not to fall away in the same manner (Heb 3–4). Pride, arrogance, and disobedience towards God, in fact, interact with unbelief and spiritual obduracy. Along these lines, the Christ-followers in Rome are warned against conceit and racism that could lead to their being cut off from Christ (Rom 11:20–22). Doubt can also be seen as leading to apostasy and judgment (cf. Rom 14:23). The opponents in 2 Peter may have become apostates because of intellectual doubts—they no longer believe in an imminent return of Christ. Unbelief is the antipode to faith, and ultimately a number of forms that lead to apostasy (persecution, suffering, malaise, complacency) might be seen as variations of it. Related to Christian defection, Israel's apostasy is described in the Gospels, Acts, and Romans 9–11 and centers on Jewish unbelief towards the gospel message of Jesus as the Christ, which is generally perceived by the authors of the New Testament as a rejection of God's prophetic plan for God's people. In these sources Israel's failure to find faith and repentance comes about through obduracy towards God's messages spoken through appointed messengers, whether through

Jesus, his followers, or the ancient prophets who predicted the new era ushered in by the advent of the Christ. This obduracy is understood differently by the sources even though most recall corporate Israel's spiritual blindness as conveyed in Isaiah 6. Mark claims that Israel's hardness of heart, a condition that plagues even Jesus' closest disciples and family members, has been caused by God who has hardened them as a form of divine judgment (Mark 4). Matthew, on the other hand, suggests that the Israelites harden their own hearts (Matthew 13). Differently, the Johannine author highlights among the many unbelievers a large group of "Jews" who once believed in Jesus but then reject him (John 6, 8). This perhaps suggests that the Johannine community interprets certain Jewish-Christ followers of its own day to be apostates.

Second, it is assumed or mentioned by the authors that falling away is caused by *persecution* (e.g., Mark, Matthew, Hebrews, Revelation). Prominent in the Gospels are the sayings of Jesus that predict an end-time apostasy related to persecution, and his disciples are warned against publically denying him or losing eternal life in order to save their physical life (e.g., Mark 8:34–38; 13:12; Matt 10:24–39; 24:9–13; Luke 9:23–26). Likewise the exemplary Parable of the Sower has the second "seed" falling away on account of persecution (Mark 4; Matt 13). We have maintained that the afflictions experienced by Mark's community reflect Emperor Nero's persecution of the early Christians. Beyond the Gospels, marginalization and harassment has brought about a state of malaise in the community of Hebrews, and in Revelation sporadic persecution has been experienced by some of the churches in Asia Minor, and it is anticipated that things will get much worse on account of Rome's economic system and the imperial cult. The community in 1 Peter faces alienation caused by local outsiders, and one of the strategies of the author is to suppress the audience's thoughts about falling away by stressing their identity as "Christian." Paul's letters and Luke-Acts tend to mitigate the fear of failing or renouncing Christ on account of persecution. They both admit it happens (e.g., Luke 9:24; 1 Thess 3:5), but the general "play-down" seems motivated in part by Paul's refusal to deny Christ and his calling on account of his own afflictions experienced as a missionary (e.g., Rom 1:16; 2 Cor. 11). Luke may be motivated by his idealistic portrayal of Paul and other apostles in Acts.

A third area relates apostasy to *general suffering and hardships*. The letter of James is exemplary here. The sufferings mentioned in this source do not seem to arise in particular from persecution as such, but illness, struggles against temptations, strife among members of the community, and economic exploitation brought about by the wealthy and those in power. The author challenges them to endure hardships as they continue on the path of life until the *parousia* takes place. If they fail to persevere through various testings, they would end up on the path of apostasy and death (1:13–16; cf. 5:19–20). Although Paul often equates suffering with things related to persecution, he does mention on his lists of hardships some general sufferings not necessarily related to mistreatment caused by outsiders (e.g., Rom 8:35; 2 Cor 11:25–29). One of the general hardships he experiences as a worker for God, interestingly enough, is the defection of congregation members (2 Cor 11:29). Even so, Paul interprets such sufferings as beneficial and marks of authentic election and apostleship. The Petrine author also views sufferings in a similar way, and even though such difficulties are mostly interpreted in light of persecution and marginalization (e.g., 1 Pet 4:12–19), domestic abuse also seems to be a form of suffering (e.g., 1 Pet 2:18–21; 3:1; cf. v. 13).

A fourth category of apostasy involves *false teachings and factions*. Matthew warns its community against falling away through lawless false prophets, and the end-times will see an increase of false teachers and messiahs who will cause many to apostatize from faith in Christ (Matt 24; cf. 7:15–23). Significant in regard to false teachers is that Matthew condemns those who fail to keep the Law, whereas Paul in essence condemns those who do (Galatians). More pointedly, the community in 2 Peter is warned against Paul's teachings that have been used and distorted by the false teachers and their followers (2 Pet 3:15–17). The Johannine writings imagine a situation in which a group of members defected from the community over the community's teachings related to the nature of Christ (e.g., 1 John 2:18–24; 2 John 7–9; cf. John 6, 8; 1 John 5:20). Those who broke away perhaps still confess to be Christ-followers. Apparently they claim that Jesus is the Christ, but they do not believe that he is God, and so from the Johannine point of view, they deny Jesus as Christ. Another leader in the community named Diotrephes rejects the elder's authority (3 John). Paul encounters conflicts with Jewish-Christian missionaries who teach the "works of the Law," and Gentile congregants in Galatia are warned that they will fall from grace and be cut off from Christ if they follow these teachings (Galatians). Other Pauline communities face the threat of defection by adhering to similar or other false teachings (e.g., Pastoral Letters, Colossians, Ephesians). The false teachers in 2 Peter are thought to be apostate Christ-followers who deny teachings related to the *parousia*.

Factional behavior is interpreted as a vice by Paul (e. g., Gal 5:19–21; 2 Cor. 12:20). Divisions of a more general sort are found in the Corinthian congregation (strong vs. weak) and among the Thessalonians (unruly idlers). Disputes over table fellowship may bring about defections among congregation members in both 1 Corinthians 8–10 (idol foods) and Romans 14 (Jewish dietary rules). Jesus in a similar way warns his leaders that if they cause "little ones" who believe in him to fall away, they will suffer condemnation (Mark 9; Matt 18; Luke 17). The Corinthians who listen to other Christian leaders that come against Paul's authority are also warned of apostasy (2 Corinthians).

A fifth category of apostasy distills what perhaps might be best described as *malaise*. The community in Hebrews is the prime example of this. Their potential to fall away comes about through discouragement, reluctant hearing, and neglecting to attend fellowship meetings (e.g., Heb 2:1–4; 5:11–6:12; 10:25). Other factors also seem to play into their condition, including marginalization (persecution), unbelief, and a lack of zeal. The author seems to think that reluctance towards hearing the spoken messages of leaders and accepting exhortations given by fellow believers are signs of a condition leading to apostasy. Such falling away seems gradual, and the end result may be that congregants arrive at a point of rejecting all devotion to God or Christ and refuse to fellowship with God's people anymore. This category may share in common with the next an attitude of indifference.

A sixth area is similar to the previous category and might be described as *indifference and negligence towards the things of God*. The churches of Ephesus, Sardis, and Laodicea in Revelation exemplify this condition: the first church lost its original love for God and others, the second church had fallen into a state of spiritual slumber, and the third had become complacent as a result of a comfortable lifestyle, self-sufficiency, wealth, and pride. The church in Ephesus had become indifferent towards Jesus' commands to love God and love one another. The church in Laodicea had become lukewarm. Whereas malaise is a negative condition that relates to a lack of zeal, complacency might be considered a positive condition by those who experience it, but it manifests itself through spiritual apathy and negligence. No doubt, Laodicea had compromised with the economic, anti-god system of Rome. Perhaps the end result of indifference might lead to the churches forgetting altogether about Christ and his community. Their backslidden condition is serious enough for the Christ of Revelation to demand their immediate repentance or else face the threat of being disowned by him. A condition of negligence is also seen in the parables of the Talents and Minas (Matt 25:14–30; Luke 19), and failure to perform works of love is fatal in the story of the Sheep and Goats (Matt 25:31–46). To violate the love command, in fact, would be seen as a violation of the Law in Matthew and defection in James 2. The apostates in 2 Peter 2 are also accused of violating this command. For the Johannine community, abiding in Christ's command to love one another plays a central part of one's abiding in Christ; the alternative is to abide in death and apostasy (John 15; 1 John 3–4). Hence, in the New Testament it might be said that negligence towards the things of God is manifest in a significant way by *neglecting the command to love one's neighbor.* No doubt, *neglecting one's love for God* also plays a major factor in this.

A seventh and final factor is that the Christ-followers commit apostasy through committing *vice or being assimilated with the non-Christ society.* Many of the New Testament warnings fall into this category. The Gentile congregations in particular are often warned that sin and vices can lead to falling away, that is, their reversion back to their pre-converted status as idolaters (1 Cor 10; Rev 2), fornicators (1 Thess 4; 1 Cor 5–6; cf. Heb 13:4), or practitioners of other vices (e.g., Gal 5:19–21; 1 Cor 6:9–10; Eph 5:3–5; 1 Pet 2:11; 4:2–6; Rev 21:8; cf. Rom 1:18–32).

Idolatry and fornication aside, the vice of greed appears in certain texts and often evinces a social problem related to wealthy members of the communities. They are warned that greed and misuse of wealth can lead to apostasy in Luke-Acts and 1 Timothy. The audience of Luke-Acts and Timothy's congregation in Ephesus may have included some people from the upper echelons of society. Likewise in Jude and 2 Peter the opponents are stereotyped as greedy. Paul says similar things about his opponents in 2 Corinthians, and Judas' betrayal and apostasy in the Gospels is brought about by greed. Related to this vice is the misuse of wealth or conditions developing from one's wealth. The church in Laodicea of Revelation 3 appears to be thriving in the merchant class, and they are rebuked for their complacency related to materialism, and so they must repent. The congregation in Corinth houses a mixture of poor and moderately wealthy Greeks. The socially prominent members who eat idol meats in this community may be among the same individuals who selfishly consume the best food at the love feasts and shame the poor. Both James and the Johannine community stress the importance of exemplifying the command to love one's neighbor by helping the poor.

In the Jewish-Christian communities false teachers that lead the congregation astray are stereotyped with immoral behavior (Jude; cf. 2 Pet), and violators of Jesus' interpretation of the Torah are considered lawless and unrighteous (Matthew). The Matthean Jesus warns his disciples to be morally prepared for his *parousia* or face divine retribution (Matt 24–25), and James recognizes wrong desires as the culprit to sin, apostasy, and friendship with the world (James 1:13–15; cf. 4:1–5). An emphasis on discouraging assimilation with Greco-Roman culture and false teachings pervades certain texts (e.g., Revelation; Eph 4–5; Col 3; 1 Pet 4:1–5; 1 John 2:15–17). Paul is more lenient with the strong/*gnosis* Corinthians on assimilation (e.g., 1 Cor 8–10) than other leaders might have been comfortable with (e. g. Acts 15:19–29; Rev. 2).

Conclusion

In sum, unbelief, persecution, suffering, false teachings, divisions, malaise, indifference, negligence towards the love command, and assimilation and vice-doing are all seen in the New Testament communities as factors that result in apostasy. Most of the categories may find counterparts among the Jewish Diaspora, but at least one difference is that the early Christ communities do not uniformly attach apostasy with eating foods prohibited by the Law (e.g., 2 Macc 7; cf. Lev 11; Deut 14), as the disputes between Pauline churches and other emerging Christians clearly attest (Gal 2; Acts 15; Rom 14; Col 2; 1 Tim 4; cf. Mark 7). Perhaps another difference is that marriages between Jews and foreigners were often interpreted as apostasy (e.g. Jos. *Ant*. 8.190-98; cf. Deut 7:1-4; 1 Kings 11:1-13). Marriages between emergent Christians and unbelievers do not see to play a part in the New Testament warnings, except perhaps innuendo as one of the forms of fornication in Revelation 2. Although new marriages between Christians and non-Christians seem discouraged by Paul (1 Cor 7:39; cf. 2 Cor 6:14), he, as well as the Petrine writer, do not seem to interpret such marriages as a form of apostasy or necessarily leading to apostasy (cf. 1 Cor 7; 1 Pet 3).

THE CONSEQUENCES OF APOSTASY IN THE NEW TESTAMENT

The consequences of apostasy often center on or anticipate a final judgment when Christ returns (e.g. Mark, Matthew, Johannine writings, Pauline letters, Hebrews, Jude, 2 Peter; Revelation). This judgment will confirm that the apostate is disowned or not recognized by Christ (e.g., Mark 8:35-39; Matt 10:33-39; 1 John 2:28; Rev 2-3). He or she is denied entrance into the heavenly kingdom (e.g. Gal 5:19-21; 1 Cor 6:9-10; Heb 12) and is condemned in the imagery of final destruction (1 Cor 8, 10; Rom 14; Phil 3:19f; Heb 10:38-39; Jude 7, 11, 13-15), or burning and *Gehenna* (e.g., Mark 9:42-48; Matt 13, 25; John 15:6; Heb 6:9-10; James 3:1-6; 2 Pet 3; Rev 20-21). However, 1 Corinthians 3 presents two kinds of judgments: the one who is building amiss on the foundation of Christ will still be saved even though suffering some undisclosed loss at the eschaton, and yet those believers who destroy the community of Christ through their factional behavior will be eschatologically destroyed. Differently, Luke's Gospel speaks of a greater judgment awaiting Christ's followers who know God's will, and a lesser judgment for other people who do not know God's will (Luke 12:41-48; cf. James 3:1). For Paul, if righteousness is by faithfulness, then judgment is by works—according to this author and others, the Christ-followers will be judged according to their works (e.g., Rom 2:1-16; 14:10; 1 Cor 4:4-5; 2 Cor 5:10; 11:15; Col 3:24f; cf. James 5:9-12; Matt 25; Rev 2-3).

Sometimes the Christ-community expels the apostate from the congregation as a form of punishment (Matthew 18, 1 Corinthians 5; 1 Tim 1:19–20; Titus 3:10; Gal. 4:30; 2 Cor 13:1–2; cf. 2 Thess 3:6–15). However, the punishment is intended to be remedial—a hope seems to be that the person would repent or ask forgiveness (e.g., 1 Cor 5:5; Matt. 18). Frequently the Christ-followers attempt to restore defectors and sinners (James 5:19–20; Jude 22–23; Matt 18:15; Gal 6:1; 2 Cor 2:5–8; 2 Tim 2:24–26). Both Jude and 2 Timothy even attempt to restore false teachers, and Paul anticipates the full restoration of apostate Israel at the end of the eschaton (Rom 9–11). In the Gospels, Peter is the prime example of a person who denies Christ but is fully restored. The authors seem to hold to a perspective much different than the author of Hebrews who considers it impossible to restore apostates (Heb 6:4–6; 10:26; 12:15–17). The Johannine community is somewhat similar. Its elder considers apostasy to be a sin leading to death, but unlike the author of Hebrews, he simply does not encourage praying for the apostate's restoration (1 John 5:16). Luke's version of the unpardonable sin, unlike the Synoptic parallels that attribute it only to the scribes and Pharisees (Mark 3; Matt 12), seems to be associated with Christian apostasy related to upcoming persecutions (Luke 12:4–12). However, we have argued that it could only be committed in unique circumstances when the Spirit is manifest (Luke 12:10), and Luke also presents counter-examples of restoration for defectors and deniers of Christ (Luke 12:9; 15:11–32; 22:54–62). The audience that read Acts seems to be encouraged to pray for the restoration of people like Simon Magus (Acts 8). In Hebrews, there are no exceptions for defectors. The person who commits apostasy cannot be restored, *unlike* the views of Paul, James, Jude, and others in the New Testament.

Among the New Testament communities, we are left with two very different views of restoration from apostasy. In the second and later centuries the two perspectives clash again. Hermas attempts to reconcile the tension (e.g., *Vis.* 2.2.1–5; *Sim.* 9.26.5–6; *Mand.* 4.1.8; 4.3.1–7), but the phenomenon of apostasy brought about by Rome's persecutions make it expedient for Christian leaders to ask whether defectors could be restored to the church (e.g., Donatists vs. Novatians). This conflict over restoration shows once again diversity of viewpoints related to apostasy both in the early centuries of the Church and in the New Testament.

COMPARATIVE APOSTASY IN THE NEW TESTAMENT

Throughout the three volumes and in this conclusion we have compared various New Testament authors and their communities in relation to apostasy and have observed a repetitive pattern which suggests that these authors interpreted apostasy differently. The two competing views of restoration among New Testament communities is just one example. Some other tensions include the following.

The Gospels provide us with different reports concerning Judas Iscariot's betrayal and its consequences. In Mark he is a disciple that falls away and remains a hardened individual who will be divinely condemned (Mark 14:21). In Luke–Acts, he is a genuine disciple that apostatizes, meets a gruesome death in a field, and his office must be replaced by another because he is excluded from God's kingdom. In Matthew, however, Judas repents of his betrayal and, unlike his end in Luke-Acts, he hangs himself. We are left with the paradox of repentance and suicide as the last acts of Judas, possibly suggesting that his heavenly fate will be more lenient than Mark and Luke imagined. The Judas of John's Gospel presents yet another portrait. Judas is a representative defector whose condemnation is sealed as the "son of destruction." In keeping with the Johannine emphasis that those who departed from the community were never genuine believers (1 John 2:19), Judas was always a wolf among sheep—the very first time he appears in the Fourth Gospel, Judas does not believe, and Jesus already calls him a devil (John 6:64–72). We are thus presented with very different portraits of Judas: he was a genuine follower of Christ who betrayed Christ and fell away (Synoptic Gospels), but in John he was never truly a believer in the first place. In the end, he is a hardened traitor who will be condemned (Mark, Luke-Acts, John), but in Matthew he repents. Finally, he dies two different deaths (Matthew, Luke-Acts). Once again we notice the same phenomenon when comparing New Testament authors. They seem to interpret apostasy, and this time the *same* apostasy, quite differently.

To a certain extent the differences are understandable. Apart from the authors' various agendas in these Gospels, the possible traditions they received, the situations of the communities to which they write, and the cultural, ethnic, and socio-economic differences among these communities, it seems that few would care to remember accurate details about an apostate among Jesus' closest disciples. We could suspect that great shame was attached to such an act. When it comes to a subject as negative as apostasy, perhaps we are noticing something similar among the other early communities in the New Testament. Few of these authors would seem to care about portraying their opponents' beliefs accurately. And the subject of falling away is normally raised by way of warning, a type of language that is rhetorically motivated. Among other languages, throughout our study we have noticed that our authors employ status degradation (e.g., Johannine writings), stereotyping (e.g., Jude), frank speech (e.g., Paul), suppression (e.g., 1 Peter), suspense (e.g., Luke-Acts), fear (e.g., Hebrews), and of course, vilification (e.g., Colossians, 2 Peter, *et al*). Beyond this, their use of earlier traditions related to apostasy help them formulate ideas interacting with their arguments and presentations, including Isaianic obduracy (e.g., Gospels), exodus-wilderness themes (e.g., Galatians, 1 Corinthians, Hebrews, Luke-Acts, *et al*), covenantal blessings and curses (e.g., Paul, Hebrews), two-ways motifs (e.g., Matthew, James, Jude, *et al*), and apocalyptic judgments (e.g., Thessalonians, Revelation).

Beyond Judas, some emerging Christian communities considered other Christians and their communities to be apostates. We have mentioned and discussed this point repetitively throughout our chapters. These opponents include those whom we find in the Johannine writings, Galatians, 2 Corinthians, Philippians, the Pastoral letters, 2 Peter, Jude, and portions of Acts. Similarly, the false prophets in Matthew and those called Balaamites and Nicolaitans in Revelation also seem to come from Christian sects. We have no copies of the opponents' materials, and so we must rely on the New Testament authors' perspectives. We could only surmise whether the opponents felt the same way about our authors and their communities. It is quite likely that in many cases the opponents would have considered themselves to be right with God and Christ, and perhaps they considered those whom we now find in the New Testament canon to be apostates and false teachers. What would the post-Paulinists, condemned by the author in 2 Peter, have to say about this author if they were given a voice? How would Matthew's opponents view their own exorcisms and works that were done in the name of Christ? Is it possible that those whom Paul calls "super apostles" and "servants of Satan" in 2 Corinthians actually had a legitimate reason to question Paul's authority and his methods of operation? If they are definitely Christ-followers and Paul does not fault them with false teachings, how would other ancient Christ-communities perceive them? Or for that matter, how would James perceive the Jewish-Christian missionaries whom Paul condemns in Galatians?

Not only do the New Testament authors interpret third parties as apostates who remain anonymous to us, but at times we read that these authors might belong to communities that consider other New Testament authors to be apostates or at least off course in their beliefs. The communities following James and Paul are a classic case of this. In Acts 21 we read that Paul is warned by James in Jerusalem that thousands of Jewish Christ-followers of the Diaspora believe that Paul teaches apostasy from the Law. As we have surmised, might not it be the case that James 2, which seems written to this same group of people as in Acts 21, intends to clarify the position of James on the Law, faith, and works as distinguishable from Paul's? The problem in Antioch reveals Jewish Christ-followers, including James and Peter, maintaining Jewish customs related to the Law that Paul vehemently denounces and will use as a springboard to warn the Galatians against falling away by adhering to comparable behavior and practices (Galatians). We have observed that Paul does not adhere to the dietary prohibitions related to Mosaic Law that James regulates for Gentile Christ-followers (Acts 15; cf. 1 Cor 8–10). Paul could allow for the eating of idol meats, whereas it is highly doubtful that James, Peter, Matthew, and John in Revelation, would allow their members, even if Gentiles, that same privilege. Such differences introduce a complex web of interrelated issues concerning Law, Jewish purity customs, Jew-Gentile relationships, assimilation, and apostasy. The primary issue at stake for idol meats in Paul and Acts centers on church unity, but then again, without such unity apostasy becomes a danger because, for Paul, factionalism leads to apostasy. In Revelation the consumption of idol meats leads directly to assimilation and apostasy, but the times and circumstances had changed from the Christian movement's earlier days.

In light of the various perspectives on apostasy and tensions pertaining to them in the New Testament, we can repeat some valuable insights we have learned, and perhaps advance a few more.

First, what we have in the New Testament may be understood as *perceived apostasy*. This view takes into consideration the diverse perspectives of the authors and communities on defectors, restoration, Judas, Christian opponents, and warnings against falling away. The many different communities and their authors did not always believe the same things, and their perceptions of what constitutes an apostate depend much on *who* is identifying the other as apostate. John Barclay comes to a similar perspective regarding ancient Jews of the Diaspora.

Second, despite diversity in the New Testament, we have uncovered ideas that are quite *universal about apostasy* that seem to be held in common among the authors and communities to which they write. All these authors teach or assume the idea that *if a person repudiates Jesus Christ, that person is an apostate*. Such falling away occurs most clearly through the modes of persecution and unbelief (e.g., Gospels, Hebrews), and perhaps most objectively by a person's public renunciation of Christ and departing from anything resembling the Christ community. The nuance of "Christ" might mean different things depending on whether the one who heard the name was Christian, non-Christian Jew, non-Christian Gentile, or Roman. It no doubt meant for the believers that Jesus was the risen Lord. Essentially, if a Christian stopped being a Christian and demonstrated this in tangible ways, whether through public denial, renouncing Jesus as Messiah, lighting incense to Caesar, returning to the devotion of local deities, betraying Christian friends to their persecutors, or a combination of these, then such things would suffice to say that a defection had taken place. That person would be "out" of the community in Christ. Presumably such a person or group would choose to leave the community as did the Johannine defectors (though in this case the Johannine community's definition of Messiah may have been narrower than other Christian communities of the time). Next, the authors seem to be in unison on the idea that *a Christian's behavior or vice doing could become so heinous that such a person is considered an apostate even if he or she does not otherwise renounce Christ.* Certainly, the deeds of the Christ-followers would need to be compatible with Jesus' commands to love God and one another. A lifestyle of committing acts that contradict these central teachings of Jesus would be interpreted as apostasy. In fact, we have noticed in New Testament sources that even one's *neglect* of doing works related to love, let alone acts that contradict it, constitutes apostasy for some of these authors. Beyond the royal commands of Christ, certain vices such as idolatry, fornication, and greed are condemned wherever they appear, and such a lifestyle of immorality would constitute a falling away. However, there are many shades of gray; for example, when does the consumption of idol meat become idolatry? And exactly which vices or how many may be committed before a person is identified as "apostate" or expelled from a congregation? Whereas, immoral and unethical behavior may constitute apostasy for all the New Testament authors, such behavior is interpreted and shaped differently by them.

Third, our study on apostasy in the New Testament provides further insights and may raise further questions related to other *theological issues.* Various kinds of apostasies and consequences related to them are conveyed in the New Testament with quite a few tensions. Hence, the time is ripe to question the task of theologians who compile together various passages across the vast horizon of diverse authors and communities in the New Testament, such as is commonly done when "prooftexting" to support particular systematic-theological positions such as Calvinism or Arminianism. We must seriously ask whether these endeavors should be abandoned. Such an approach to the subject of apostasy can be misleading and quite often distorts proper biblical interpretation of the respective books and passages. To be sure, we cannot escape our social locations and the presuppositions that come with it, but if we already aim to "defend" a theological position when interpreting a text, our outcomes will be very predictable, sometimes to the point of getting the New Testament authors to say what *we* want them to say even if they are saying something quite different. The attempt to get *all* the various New Testament passages to communicate the same theological truths about apostates often distorts and oversimplifies biblical studies. We should not make grand statements about New Testament apostates as is typically done by certain theologians who claim that all apostates have lost their salvation and cannot be restored, or they all will be restored at a future time, or they all were never truly saved in the first place, or they all lose heavenly rewards rather than salvation. As we have demonstrated through this study, apostasy in the New

Testament is more complex than such grand statements will allow. We should not be reinterpreting every relevant verse in the New Testament in light of the apostates in Hebrews 6:4–8, or the defectors in 1 John 2:19, or the mitigated punishment in 1 Corinthians 3:10–15. Nor should we assume that because the false prophets in Matthew 7:15–23 never belonged to Christ, this means that the false teachers in 2 Peter 2:1–22 also never belonged to Christ.

For some interpreters, ministers, laity, institutes, and Christian denominations the thought of diverse viewpoints on apostasy in the New Testament raises questions about their understanding of biblical authority. Some points I raised earlier in Hebrews are worth expanding on here. First, in whichever way we attempt to define biblical and church authority, our pursuit of this subject should be governed by humility, integrity, and if necessary, the courage to admit that we might be wrong or that the traditions and heritage handed to us might need readjustments. Without this admittance, further discussion on the subject, I think, is virtually useless. Second, perhaps one's definition of biblical authority should take into consideration the inherent diversity of viewpoints we find in the writings, not only in reference to apostasy and restoration, but also in reference to the Law, identity in Christ, Jewish and Gentile relationships, and so on. Is it possible that New Testament authority itself must rest on God's authority, and this is one exploration worth further scholarly pursuits? Third, despite diversity in the New Testament, we have addressed some universally held beliefs mentioned earlier: the repudiation of Jesus Christ and his commands is viewed by the authors of the New Testament as apostasy. Likewise related to the rejection of Christ's commands is the practice of heinous immoral conduct, which the New Testament authors also identify as apostasy. Thus, what we have in the New Testament is unity and diversity, and the confirmation that certain beliefs and practices in the emerging Christian communities are more central than others. Hopefully such thoughts might build bridges to further discussions in scholarly, theological, and denominational circles.

Fourth and finally, on sociological, practical and ethical levels, our understanding of the various ways one could fall away helps provide insight for those who examine contemporary social patterns attempting to discern what leads to individuals abandoning their religious commitments. As we discussed earlier (see in volume one, Gospel of Mark), Stephen Wilson examines ancient and contemporary religious apostasy in view of sociology, and Wilson presents three categories that he finds relevant for early Jewish and Christian sources: gradual defectors, precipitate defectors, and antagonistic apostates. If we wish to add to his study, the communities in Hebrews, Revelation, James, and the third "seed" of the Parable of the Sower (especially Luke's version) may be considered in danger of gradual defection. We find perhaps some antagonistic apostates through the false teachers in the Pastoral letters, the defiant apostates in Hebrews 10, and Judas. Those in danger of a precipitate defection may include the Galatians (esp. 1:6), the Thessalonians (1 Thess 3:5), the new believers whom the false teachers attempt to seduce in 2 Peter 2–3, and the second "seed" of the Parable of the Sower. Further connections between contemporary and ancient studies on apostasy may generate more fully developed probings along these and other lines in the future.

This study has also inadvertently refuted a notion that is popularly construed today by misguided teachers and laity: one's deeds and lifestyle does not really matter "so long as you have faith and believe." The New Testament pattern of apostasy shows repeatedly that belief alone does not "secure" an individual so that he or she possesses a fixed, one-way ticket to heaven, especially if that belief stands independent of moral behavior. The communities addressed in the New Testament already believe, but they are still warned against falling away, and this danger may result in their final destruction in the age to come. The authors rhetorically endorse the idea of fearing God rather than promoting a "God is my buddy" attitude. Something similar to the kind of view we are criticizing may in fact be the false security warned *against* in passages such as 1 Corinthians 10:1–12, Romans 6:1, and Revelation 3:14–19. If anything else, on a practical level, this study should spark an incentive for good moral conduct. In the New Testament, we wish to confirm with Paul that, not only is election by grace and righteousness by fidelity, but also judgment is by works.

Finally this study interrelates with ethical perspectives on how different religions and cultures view each other. Reflecting on thoughts from Miroslav Volf (see Introduction, volume one), how does a willingness to embrace the "other" reflect on the notion of apostasy in the New Testament? While the NT authors do not frequently attempt to empathize with their opponents, there is the notion of reconciliation and restoration in a number of these writings. Paul, Jude, and others believe that even those who oppose them can be restored to God. Whereas the sharp dichotomy between the Johannine community and its apostates seems to run counter to this notion, vestiges of God's love for the world may be seen even in this community's literature. In Matthew, final judgment is based on how one treats others and puts to practice the teaching of Jesus to love one's neighbor as oneself. In this Gospel, *both* Christians and non-Christians are held responsible to such love. A key to embracing the "other" might be for us to continue developing the principles of love and reconciliation.

Bibliography

Achtemeier, Paul J. *1 Peter: A Commentary on First Peter*. Hermenia. Minneapolis: Fortress, 1996.
Adamson, James B. *The Epistle of James*. NICNT. Grand Rapids: Eerdmans, 1976.
Allen, David M. *Deuteronomy and Exhortation in Hebrews*. WUNT 2/238. Tübingen: Mohr/Siebeck, 2008.
Arichea, Daniel C., and Eugene Albert Nida. *A Handbook on the First Letter from Peter*. UBSHB. New York: United Bible Societies, 1980.
Arichea, Daniel C., and Hatton, H. A. *A Handbook on the Letter from Jude and the Second Letter from Peter*. UBSHB. New York: United Bible Societies, 1993.
Attridge, Harold W. *The Epistle to the Hebrews*. Hermeneia. Philadelphia: Fortress, 1989.
———. "The Psalms in Hebrews." In *The Psalms in the New Testament*, edited by Maartin J. J. Menken and Steve Moyise, 197–212. New York: Continuum, 2003.
Aubineau, M. "La thème du <<bourbier>> dans la littérature grecque profane et chrétienne." *RSR* 33 (1959) 201–4.
Aune, David Edward. "Apocalypse Renewed: An Intertextual Reading of the Apocalypse of John." In *Reality of the Apocalypse: Rhetoric and Politics in the Book of Revelation*, edited by David L. Barr, 43–70. SBLSymS 39. Atlanta: SBL, 2006.
———. "The Apocalypse of John and the Problem of Genre," *Semeia* 36 (1986) 65–96.
———. "The Prophetic Circle of John of Patmos and the Exegesis of Revelation." *JSNT* 37 (1989) 103–16.
———. *Revelation*. 3 vols. WBC 52A–C. Dallas: Word, 1997–1998.
Baker, William R. "Who's Your Daddy? Gendered Birth Images in the Soteriology of the Epistle of James (1:14–15, 18, 21)." *EvQ* 79 (2007) 195–207.
Balch, David. "Hellenization/Acculturation in 1 Peter." In *Perspectives on 1 Peter*, edited by Charles H. Talbert, 79–102. NABPRSS 9. Macon, GA: Mercer University Press, 1986.
Baltzer, Klaus. *The Covenant Formulary*. Philadelphia: Fortress, 1971.
Baltzer, Klaus, and Peter Machinist. *Deutero-Isaiah: A Commentary on Isaiah 40–55*. Hermeneia. Minneapolis: Fortress, 2001.
Balz, Horst. "παρρησία, ας, ἡ." In *EDNT* 3.45–47.
Bateman, Herbert W., editor. *Four Views on the Warning Passages in Hebrews*. Grand Rapids: Kregel, 2007.
Bauckham, Richard J. *The Climax of Prophecy: Studies on the Book of Revelation*. Edinburgh: T. & T. Clark, 1993.
———. "For What Offense Was James Put to Death?" In *James the Just and Christian Origins*, edited by Bruce Chilton and Craig A. Evans, 199–232. NovTSup 98. Leiden: Brill, 1999.

Bibliography

———. "James and the Jerusalem Community." In *Jewish Believers in Jesus: The Early Centuries*, edited by Oskar Skarsaune and Reidar Hvalvik, 55–95. Peabody, MA: Hendrickson, 2007.

———. *James: Wisdom of James, Disciple of Jesus the Sage*. London: Routledge, 1999.

———. *Jude and the Relatives of Jesus in the Early Church*. Edinburgh: T. & T. Clark, 1990.

———. *Jude, 2 Peter*. WBC 50. Waco, TX: Word, 1983

———. "Judgment in the Book of Revelation." *Ex Auditu* 20 (2004) 1–24.

———. "The Martyrdom of Peter in Early Christian Literature." In *ANRW* II.26.1, edited by Wolfgang Haase, 539–95. Berlin: de Gruyter, 1992.

———. "Pseudo-Apostolic Letters." *JBL* 107 (1988) 469–494.

———. "Scripture and Authority." *Transformation* 15 (1998) 5–11.

———. "2 Peter: An Account of Research." In *ANRW* II.25.5, edited by Wolfgang Haase, 3713–52. Berlin: de Gruyter, 1988.

———. *The Theology of the Book of Revelation*. NTTh. Cambridge: Cambridge University Press, 1993.

———. "Tradition in Relation to Scripture and Reason." In *Scripture Tradition and Reason: A Study in the Criteria of Christian Doctrine. Festschrift for R. P. C. Hanson*, edited by B. Drewery and Richard Bauckham, 7–32. Edinburgh: T. & T. Clark, 1988.

Bauder, Wolfgang. "Fall, Fall Away." In *NIDNTT* 1.606–08.

Bauernfeind, Otto. "ἀσέλγεια." In *TDNT* 1.490.

Beale, G. K. *The Book of Revelation: A Commentary on the Greek Text*. NIGTC. Grand Rapids: Eerdmans, 1999.

Beale, G. K., and S. M. McDonough. "Revelation." In *CNTOT*, 1081–61.

Beare, Francis Wright. *The First Epistle of Peter: The Greek Text with Introduction and Notes*. Oxford: Blackwell, 1947.

Beasley-Murray, G. R. *The Book of Revelation*. NCB. London: Oliphants, 1974.

Bechtler, Steven Richard. *Following in His Steps: Suffering, Community, and Christology in First Peter*. SBLDS 162. Atlanta: Scholars, 1998.

Becker, Jürgen. *Untersuchungen zur Entstehungsgeschichte der Testamente der zwölf Patriarchen*. AGJU 8. Leiden: Brill, 1970.

Bénétreau, Samuel. *L'Epître aux Hébreux*. CEB 10, 12. Vaux-sur-Seine: Editions de la Faculté Libre de Théologie Evangélique, 1989, 1990.

———. *Le Premiere Epître de Pierre*. CEB 1. Vaux-sur-Seine: Editions de la Faculté Libre de Théologie Evangélique, 1984.

Benko, Stephen. "Pagan Criticism of Christianity during the First Two Centuries A.D." *ANRW* II.23.2, edited by Wolfgang Haase, 1055–1118. Berlin: de Gruyter, 1980.

Bernheim, P. A. *James, Brother of Jesus*. London: SCM, 1997.

Best, Ernest. *1 Peter*. NCB. Grand Rapids: Eerdmans, 1971.

Bigg, C. *The Epistles of St. Peter and St. Jude*. ICC. Edinburgh: T. & T. Clark, 1901.

Block, D. I. *Judges, Ruth*. NAC. Nashville: Broadman, 1999.

Bolling, R. G. "Judges." In *ABD* 3.1107–14.

Borchert, Gerald L. *Assurance and Warning*. Nashville: Broadman, 1987.

Borgen, Peder. "Polemic in the Book of Revelation." In *Anti-Semitism and Early Christianity: Issues of Polemic and Faith*, edited by Craig A. Evans and D. A. Hagner, 199–211. Minneapolis: Fortress, 1993.

Boring, M. Eugene. *1 Peter*. ANTC. Nashville: Abingdon, 1999.

———. *Revelation*. Interpretation. Louisville: John Knox, 1989.

Bratcher, Robert G., and Howard Hatton. *A Handbook on the Revelation to John*. UBSHB. New York: United Bible Societies, 1993.
Braun, Herbert. "πλανάω, πλανάομαι, ἀποπλανάω, ἀποπλανάομαι, πλάνη, πλάνος, πλανήτης, πλάνης." In *TDNT* 6.228–53.
Brosend, William F. *James and Jude*. NCBC. Cambridge: Cambridge University Press, 2004.
———. "The Letter of Jude: A Rhetoric of Excess or an Excess of Rhetoric?" *Interpretation* 60 (2006) 292–305.
Brown, Jennifer K. "Just a Busybody? A Look at the Greco-Romans Topos of Meddling for Defining ἀλλοτριεπίσκοπος in 1 Peter 4:15." *JBL* 125 (2006) 549–68.
Brown, Nobel B. "The Concept of Apostasy in Jewish and Christian Apocalyptic." PhD diss., Southern Baptist Theological Seminary, 1963.
Brown, Raymond E. *The Churches the Apostles Left Behind*. New York: Paulist, 1984.
———. *An Introduction to the New Testament*. New York: Doubleday, 1997.
Brown, Schuyler. "The Hour of Trial, Rev. 3.10." *JBL* 85 (1966) 308–14.
Brox, Norbert. *Der erste Petrusbrief*. EKKNT 21. Zürich: Benziger, 1979.
Bruce, F. F. *The Epistle to the Hebrews*. NICNT. Grand Rapids: Eerdmans, 1990.
Buchanan, George Wesley. *To the Hebrews*. AB 36. Garden City, NY: Doubleday, 1972.
Bultmann, Rudolf. "αἰσχύνω, ἐπαισχύνω, καταισχύνω, αἰσχύνη, αἰσχρός, αἰσχρότης." In *TDNT* 1.188–90.
Burchard, Christoph. *Der Jakobusbrief*. HNT 15, 1. Tübingen: Mohr/Siebeck, 2000.
Burton, Ernest De Witt. *Syntax of the Moods and Tenses in the New Testament*. Rev. ed. Grand Rapids: Kregel, 1976.
Caird, G. B. *The Revelation of St. John*. BNTC 19. Peabody, MA: Hendrickson, 1993.
Callan, Terrance. "Use of the Letter of Jude by the Second Letter of Peter." *Biblica* 85 (2004) 42–64.
Campbell, Barth. *Honor, Shame, and the Rhetoric of First Peter*. SBLDS 160. Atlanta: Scholars, 1998.
Cargal, Timothy B. *Restoring the Diaspora. Discursive Structure and Purpose in the Epistle of James*. Atlanta: Scholars, 1993.
Carmichael, D. B. "David Daube on the Eucharist and the Passover Seder." *JSNT* 42 (1991) 45–67.
Carson, D. A. "1 Peter." In *CNTOT*, 1015–45.
———. "2 Peter." In *CNTOT*, 1047–61.
———. *Exegetical Fallacies*. 2nd ed. Carlisle: Paternoster; Grand Rapids: Baker, 1996.
———. "Jude." In *CNTOT*, 1069–79.
Caulley, Thomas S. "The False Teachers in Second Peter." *SBibTh* 12 (1982) 27–42.
———. "'They Promise Them Freedom': Once Again the ψευδοδιδάσκαλοι in 2 Peter." *ZNW* 99 (2008) 129–38.
Chaine, Joseph. *Les épîtres catholiques: La seconde épître de saint Pierre, les épîtres de saint Jean, l'épître de saint Jude*. EBib. Paris: Gabalda, 1939.
Charles, J. Daryl. *Literary Strategy in the Epistle of Jude*. Scranton, PA: University Scranton Press, 1993.
———. *Virtue amidst Vice: The Catalog of Virtues in 2 Peter 1*. JSNTSup 150. Sheffield: Sheffield Academic, 1997.
Charles, J. Daryl, and Erland Waltner. *1–2 Peter, Jude*. BCBC. Scottdale, PA: Herald, 1999.
Charles, R. H. *A Critical and Exegetical Commentary on the Revelation of St. John*. ICC 44. Edinburgh: T. & T. Clark, 1920.

Bibliography

Chester, Andrew, and Ralph P. Martin. *The Theology of the Letters of James, Peter, and Jude.* NTTh. Cambridge: Cambridge University Press, 1994.

Christensen, Duane L. *Deuteronomy 21:10—34:12.* WBC 6B. Dallas: Word, 2002.

Clark, David J., and Howard Hatton. *A Handbook on Haggai, Zechariah, and Malachi.* UBSHB. New York: United Bible Societies, 2002.

Coats, George W. *Rebellion in the Wilderness: The Murmuring Motif in the Wilderness Traditions of the Old Testament.* Nashville: Abingdon, 1968.

Cockerill, Gareth L. "A Wesleyan Arminian View." In *Four Views on the Warning Passages in Hebrews*, edited by Herbert W. Bateman, 257–92. Grand Rapids: Kregel, 2007.

Cohen, Shaye J. D. *The Beginning of Jewishness: Boundaries, Varieties, Uncertainties.* HCS 31. Berkeley: University of California Press, 1999.

Collins, Adela Yarbro. *The Apocalypse.* 2nd ed. NTM. Collegeville, MN: Liturgical, 1990.

———. *The Combat Myth in the Book of Revelation.* Missoula, MT: Scholars, 1975.

———. *Crisis and Catharsis: The Power of the Apocalypse.* Philadelphia: Westminster, 1984.

———. "The Function of Excommunication in Paul." *HTR* 73 (1980) 251–63.

———. "Insiders and Outsiders in the Book of Revelation and Its Social Context." In *"To See Ourselves as Others See Us": Christians, Jews, and "Others" in Late Antiquity*, edited by Jacob Neusner and Ernest S. Frerichs, 187–210. SPSH. Chico, CA: Scholars, 1985.

———. "Vilification and Self-Definition in the Book of Revelation." *HTR* 79 (1986) 308–20.

Collins, John J. *The Apocalyptic Imagination: An Introduction to Jewish Apocalyptic Literature.* BRS. Grand Rapids: Eerdmans, 1998.

———. *Daniel.* Hermeneia. Minneapolis: Fortress, 1993.

———. "Introduction: Towards the Morphology of a Genre." *Semeia* 14 (1979) 1–20.

———. "The Testamentary Literature in Recent Scholarship." In *Early Judaism and Its Modern Interpreters*, edited by Robert A. Kraft and George W. E. Nickelsburg, 268–85. The Bible and Its Modern Interpreters 2. Atlanta: Scholars, 1986.

Court, John M. *Revelation.* NTG. Sheffield: JSOT Press, 1994.

Croy, N. Clayton. *Endurance in Suffering: Hebrews 12:1–13 in Its Rhetorical, Religious, and Philosophical Context.* SNTSMS 98. Cambridge: Cambridge University Press, 1998.

Daniel, C. "La mention des Esséniens dans la texte grec de l'Épître de S. Jude." *Mus* 81 (1968) 503–21.

Daube, David. *He That Cometh.* London: Council for Christian-Jewish Understanding, 1966.

Davids, Peter H. *The Epistle of James: A Commentary on the Greek Text.* NIGTC. Grand Rapids: Eerdmans, 1982.

———. *The First Epistle of Peter.* NICNT. Grand Rapids: Eerdmans, 1990.

———. *The Letters of 2 Peter and Jude.* PNTC. Grand Rapids: Eerdmans, 2006.

———. "The Meaning of ἀπείραστος in James i.13." *NTS* 24 (1978) 386–92.

———. "Palestinian Traditions in the Epistle of James." In *James the Just and Christian Origins*, edited by Bruce Chilton and Craig A. Evans, 33–57. NovTSup 98. Leiden: Brill, 1999.

———. "Why Do We Suffer? Suffering in James and Paul." In *The Missions of James, Peter, and Paul: Tensions in Early Christianity*, edited by Bruce Chilton and Craig Evans, 435–66. NovTSup 115. Leiden: Brill, 2005.

De Jonge, Marinus. *The Testament of the Twelve Patriarchs: A Study of Their Text, Composition and Origin.* Assen: Van Gorcum, 1953.

deSilva, David A. *Despising Shame: Honor Discourse and Community Maintenance in the Epistle of Hebrews.* SBLDS 152. Atlanta: Scholars, 1995.

———. "Honor Discourse and the Rhetorical Strategy of the Apocalypse of John." *JSNT* 71 (1998) 79–110.

———. *An Introduction to the New Testament: Contexts, Methods & Ministry Formation.* Downers Grove, IL: InterVarsity, 2004.

———. *Perseverance in Gratitude: A Socio-Rhetorical Commentary on the Epistle "to the Hebrews."* Grand Rapids: Eerdmans, 2000.

———. *Seeing Things John's Way: The Rhetoric of Revelation.* Louisville: Westminster John Knox, 2009.

———. "The Strategic Arousal of Emotions in John's Visions of Roman Imperialism: A Rhetorical-Critical Investigation of Revelation 4–22." *Neotestamentica* 42 (2008) 1–34.

———. "The Strategic Arousal of Emotions in the Apocalypse of John: A Rhetorical-critical Investigation of the Oracles to the Seven Churches." *NTS* 54 (2008) 90–114.

———. "X Marks the Spot? A Critique of the Use of Chiasm in Macro-Structural Analyses of Revelation to John." *JSNT* 30 (2008) 343–71.

Deterding, Paul E. "Exodus Motifs in First Peter." *ConJ* 7 (1981) 58–65.

Dibelius, Martin, and Heinrich Greeven. *James*. Hermeneia. Philadelphia: Fortress, 1976.

Dillard, Raymond B. *2 Chronicles*. WBC 15. Dallas: Word, 1987.

Dov, Noy. "Apostasy." In *Encyclopaedia Judaica*, edited by Cecil Roth and Geoffrey Wigoder, 3.201–16. Jerusalem: Keter, 1972.

Dryden, J. de Waal. *Theology and Ethics in 1 Peter: Paraenetic Strategies for Christian Character Formation.* WUNT 2/209. Tübingen: Mohr/Siebeck, 2006.

Dschulnigg, Peter. "Der theologische Ort des Zweiten Petrusbriefes." *BZ* 33 (1989) 161–77.

Dubis, Mark. *Messianic Woes in 1 Peter: Suffering and Eschatology in 1 Peter 4:12–19.* SBL 33. New York: P. Lang, 2002.

———. "Research on 1 Peter: A Survey of Scholarly Literature since 1985." *CBR* 4 (2006) 199–239.

Duff, Paul B. "'The Synagogue of Satan': Crisis Mongering, and the Apocalypse of John." In *Reality of the Apocalypse: Rhetoric and Politics in the Book of Revelation*, edited by David L. Barr, 147–68. SBLSymS 39. Atlanta: SBL, 2006.

———. *Who Rides the Beast?: Prophetic Rivalry and the Rhetoric of Crisis in the Churches of the Apocalypse.* Oxford: Oxford University Press, 2001.

Dulk, Matthijs den. "The Promises to the Conquerors in the Book of Revelation." *Biblica* 87.4 (2006) 516–22.

Dunham, Duane A. "An Exegetical Study of 2 Peter 2:18–22." *BSac* 140 (1983) 40–54.

Dunn, James D. G. *The Theology of Paul the Apostle.* Grand Rapids: Eerdmans, 1998.

———. *Unity and Diversity in the New Testament: An Inquiry into the Character of Earliest Christianity.* 2nd ed. London: SCM, 1990.

Dunnill, John. *Covenant and Sacrifice in the Letter to the Hebrews.* SNTSMS 75. Cambridge: Cambridge University Press, 1992.

Eisenbaum, Pamela M. *The Jewish Heroes of Christian History: Hebrews 11 in Literary Context.* Atlanta: Scholars, 1997.

Eissfeldt, Otto. *Der Beutel der Lebendigen:* Altestamentliche Erzählungs- und Dichtungsmotive im Lichte neuer Nuzi-Texte. Berlin: Akademie Verlag, 1960.

Elgvin, Torleif. "Jewish Christian Editing of the Old Testament Pseudepigrapha." In *Jewish Believers in Jesus: The Early Centuries*, edited by Oskar Skarsaune and Reidar Hvalvik, 278–304. Peabody, MA: Hendrickson, 2007.

Bibliography

Ellingworth, Paul. *The Epistle to the Hebrews: A Commentary on the Greek Text.* NIGTC. Grand Rapids: Eerdmans, 1993.

Ellingworth, Paul, and Eugene Albert Nida. *A Handbook on the Letter to the Hebrews.* UBSHS. New York: United Bible Societies, 1994.

Elliott, J. K. "Is Post-Baptismal Sin Forgivable?" *BT* 28 (1977) 330–32.

Elliott, John H. *The Elect and the Holy: An Exegetical Examination of I Peter 2:4–10 and the Phrase βασίλειον Ἱεράτευμα."* NovTSup 12. Leiden: Brill, 1966.

———. *1 Peter: A New Translation with Introduction and Commentary.* AB 37B. Garden City, NY: Doubleday, 2000.

———. "1 Peter, Its Situation and Strategy: A Discussion with David Balch." In *Perspectives on 1 Peter*, edited by Charles H. Talbert, 61–78. NABPRSS 9. Macon, GA: Mercer University Press, 1986.

———. *A Home for the Homeless: A Sociological Exegesis of 1 Peter, Its Situation and Strategy.* Philadelphia: Fortress, 1981.

———. "Peter, Second Epistle of." In *ABD* 5.282–87.

———. "The Rehabilitation of an Exegetical Step-Child: 1 Peter in Recent Research." *JBL* 95 (1976) 243–54.

Endo, Shusaku. *Silence.* Translated by W. Johnston. New York: Taplinger, 1969.

Erlandsson, S. "זָנָה." In *TDOT* 4.99–104.

Evans, Craig A. *To See and Not Perceive: Isaiah 6.9–10 in Early Jewish and Christian Interpretation.* JSOT 64. Sheffield: JSOT Press, 1989.

Fanning, Buice, M. "A Classical Reformed View." In *Four Views on the Warning Passages in Hebrews*, edited by Herbert W. Bateman, 172–219. Grand Rapids: Kregel, 2007.

Fekkes, Jan. *Isaiah and Prophetic Traditions in the Book of Revelation: Visionary Antecedents and Their Developments.* JSNTSup 93. Sheffield: Sheffield Academic, 1994.

Feld, Helmut. *Der Hebräerbrief.* ErFor 228. Darmstadt: Wissenschaftliche Buchgesellschaft, 1985.

Feldman, Louis H. *Jew and Gentile in the Ancient World: Attitudes and Interactions from Alexander to Justinian.* Princeton: Princeton University Press, 1993.

Feldmeier, Reinhard. *Die Christen als Fremde: Die Metapher der Fremde in der antiken Welt, im Urchristentum und im 1. Petrusbrief.* WUNT 64. Tübingen: Mohr, 1992.

———. *Der erste Brief des Petrus.* THKNT 15/1. Leipzig: Evangelische Verlagsanstalt, 2005.

Feuillet, A. "Les 144,000 Israélites marqués d'un sceau." *NovT* 9 (1967) 191–224.

Fitzmyer, Joseph A. "Habakkuk 2:3–4 and the New Testament." In *To Advance the Gospel: New Testament Studies*, 236–46. New York: Crossroad, 1981.

Ford, J. Massyngberde. "The Mother of Jesus and the Authorship of the Epistle of Hebrews." *University of Dayton Review* 11 (1975) 49–56.

———. *Revelation: Introduction, Translation, and Commentary.* AB 38. Garden City, NY: Doubleday, 1975.

Forkman, Göran. *The Limits of the Religious Community: Expulsion from the Religious Community within the Qumran Sect, within Rabbinic Judaism, and within Primitive Christianity.* ConBNT 5. Lund: Gleerup, 1972.

Fornberg, Tord. *An Early Church in a Pluralistic Society: A Study of 2 Peter.* ConBNT 9. Lund: Gleerup, 1977.

Frankemölle, Hubert. *Der Brief des Jakobus.* ÖTKNT 17. Gütersloh: Gütersloher Verlagshaus, 1994. 2 Volumes.

———. *1. Petrusbrief; 2. Petrusbrief; Judasbrief.* NEchtB 18, 20. Würzburg: Echter, 1987.

———. "Das semantische Netz des Jakobusbriefes. Zur Einheit eines umstrittenen Briefes." *BZ* 34 (1990) 161–97.

Frankfurter, David. "Jews or Not? Reconstructing the 'Other.'" *HTR* 94 (2001) 403–25.

Friedrich, Nestor Paulo. "Adapt or Resist? A Socio-Political Reading of Revelation 2.18–29." *JSNT* 25.2 (2002) 185–211.

Friesen, Steven J. *Imperial Cults and the Apocalypse of John: Reading Revelation in the Ruins*. Oxford: Oxford University Press, 2001.

———. "Sarcasm in Revelation 2–3: Churches, Christians, True Jews, and Satanic Synagogues." In *Reality of the Apocalypse: Rhetoric and Politics in the Book of Revelation*, edited by David L. Barr, 127–144. SBLSymS 39. Atlanta: SBL, 2006.

———. "Satan's Throne, Imperial Cults, and the Social Setting of Revelation." *JSNT* 27.3 (2005) 351–73.

———. *Twice Neokoros: Ephesos, Asia and the Cults of the Flavian Imperial Family*. Leiden: Brill, 1993.

Fuchs, Eric, and Pierre Reymond. *La deuxième épître de saint Pierre ; L'épître de saint Jude*. 2nd ed. CNT 13b. Geneva: Labor et Fides, 1988.

Fuller, J. William. "'I Will Not Erase His Name from the Book of Life' (Revelation 3:5)." *JETS* 25.3 (1983) 297–306.

Gaca, Kathy L. *The Making of Fornication: Eros, Ethics, and Political Reform in Greek Philosophy and Early Christianity*. Berkeley: University of California Press, 2003.

Gerdmar, Anders. *Rethinking the Judaism-Hellenism Dichotomy: A Historiographical Case Study of Second Peter and Jude*. ConBNT 36. Stockholm: Almqvist & Wiksell, 2001.

Geyser, A. S. "The Letter of James and the Social Condition of His Addressees." *Neotestamentica* 9 (1975) 25–33.

Gheorghita, Radu. *The Role of the Septuagint in Hebrews: An Investigation of Its Influence with Special Consideration to the Use of Hab 2:3–4 in Heb 10:37–38*. WUNT 2/160. Tübingen: Mohr/Siebeck, 2003.

Giesen, Heinz. *Die Offenbarung des Johannes*. RNT. Regensburg: F. Pustet, 1997.

Gileadi, Avraham, editor. *Israel's Apostasy and Restoration: Essays in Honor of Roland K. Harrison*. Grand Rapids: Baker, 1988.

Gilmour, Michael J. *The Significance of Parallels between 2 Peter and Other Early Christian Literature*. AcBib 10. Atlanta: SBL, 2002.

Gleason, Randall C. "The Eschatology of the Warning in Hebrews 10:26–31." *TynBul* 53 (2002) 97–120.

———. "A Moderate Reformed View" and "A Moderate Reformed Response." In *Four Views on the Warning Passages in Hebrews*, edited by Herbert W. Bateman, 157–71, 246–56, 322–35, 336–77. Grand Rapids: Kregel, 2007.

Goldstein, H. "ἀσέλγεια, ας, ἡ *aselgeia* licentiousness, debauchery." In *EDNT* 1.169–70.

Goppelt, Leonhard. *A Commentary on 1 Peter*. Edited by Ferdinand Hahn, translated and augmented by John E. Alsup. Grand Rapids: Eerdmans, 1993.

Gray, Patrick. *Godly Fear: The Epistle to the Hebrews and Greco-Roman Critiques of Superstition*. AcBib 16. Atlanta: SBL, 2003.

Gräßer, Erich. *Der Glaube im Hebräerbrief*. Marburg: Elwert, 1965.

———. *An die Hebräer*. 3 vols. EKKNT 17. Zürich: Benziger, 1990, 1993, 1997.

Green, Joel B. *1 Peter*. THNTC. Grand Rapids: Eerdmans, 2007.

Green, Michael. *2 Peter and Jude*. TNTC. Leicester: InterVarsity; Grand Rapids: Eerdmans, 1968.

Bibliography

———. *2 Peter Reconsidered*. London: Tyndale, 1961.
Greene, John T. "Balaam: Prophet, Diviner, and Priest in Selected Ancient Israelite and Hellenistic Jewish Sources." In *SBL Seminar Papers 1990*, edited by David J. Lull, 57–106. Atlanta: Scholars, 1989.
———. "Balaam as Figure and Type in Ancient Semitic Literature to the First Century BCE, with a Survey of Selected Post-Philo Applications of the Balaam Figure and Type." In *SBL Seminar Papers 1989*, edited by David J. Lull, 82–147. Atlanta: Scholars, 1990.
Grudem, Wayne A. "Perseverance of the Saint: A Case Study from Hebrews 6:4–6 and the Other Warning Passages." In *The Grace of God, the Bondage of the Will*, edited by Thomas R. Schreiner, 1.209–25. Grand Rapids: Baker, 1995.
Grundmann, Walter, Paul Althaus, and Erich Fascher. *Der Brief des Judas und der zweite Brief des Petrus*. THKNT 15. Leipzig: Deichert, 1974.
Guthrie, Donald. *Hebrews: An Introduction and Commentary*. TNTC 15. Downers Grove, IL: InterVarsity, 2007.
Guthrie, George H. "Hebrews." In *CNTOT*, 919–95.
———. "Hebrews in Its First-Century Contexts: Recent Research." In *The Face of New Testament Studies: A Survey of Recent Research*, edited by Scot McKnight and Grant R. Osborne, 414–43. Leicester: Apollos; Grand Rapids: Baker Academic, 2004.
———. *The Structure of Hebrews: A Text-Linguistic Analysis*. Leiden: Brill, 1994.
Hackenberg, W. "ἐπιγινώσκω." In *EDNT* 2.24–25.
Hackett, J. A. "Balaam." In *ABD* 1.569–72.
Hagner, Donald Alfred. *Hebrews*. NIBC 14. Peabody, MA: Hendrickson, 1990.
Hanse, Hermann. "λαγχάνω." In *TDNT* 4.1–2.
Harder, Günther. "στηρίζω, ἐπιστηρίζω, στηριγμός, ἀστήρικτος." In *TDNT* 7.653–57.
Harrington, Daniel J. *What Are They Saying about the Letter to the Hebrews?* New York: Paulist, 2005.
Harrington, Daniel J., and Donald P. Senior. *1 Peter, Jude, and 2 Peter*. SP 15. Collegeville, MN: Liturgical, 2003.
Harrington, Wilfrid J. *Revelation*. SP 16. Collegeville, MN: Liturgical, 1993.
Hartin, Patrick. J. *James*. SP 14. Collegeville, MN: Liturgical, 2003.
———. *James and the Sayings of Jesus*. JSNTSup 47. Sheffield: JSOT, 1991.
———. *A Spirituality of Perfection: Faith in Action in the Letter of James*. Collegeville, MN: Liturgical, 1999.
Hartley, John E. *Leviticus*. WBC 4. Dallas: Word, 1992.
Hasel, G. F. *The Remnant: the History and Theology of the Remnant Idea from Genesis to Isaiah*. Berrien Springs, MI: Andrews University Press, 1972.
Hauck, Friedrich, and Seigfried Schulz. "πόρνη, πόρνος, πορνεία, πορνεύω, ἐκπορνεύω." In *TDNT* 6.579–95.
Hayes, Christine. "Intermarriage and Impurity in Ancient Jewish Sources." *HTR* 92 (1999) 3–36.
Heen, Erik M., Philip D. Krey, and Thomas C. Oden. *Hebrews*. ACCS 10. Downers Grove, IL: InterVarsity, 2005.
Heiligenthal, Roman. *Zwischen Henoch und Paulus: Studien zum theologiegeschichtlichen Ort des Judasbreifes*. TANZ 6. Tübingen: Francke, 1992.
Hemer, Colin J. *The Letters to the Seven Churches of Asia in Their Local Setting*. BRS. Grand Rapids: Eerdmans, 1989.

Hengel, Martin. "Der Jakobusbrief als antipaulinische Polemik." In *Tradition and Interpretation*, edited Gerald F. Hawthorne and Otto Betz, 248–78. Tübingen: Mohr/Siebeck, 1987.

———. *Judaism and Hellenism: Studies in their Encounter in Palestine during the Early Hellenistic Period*. 2 vols. London: SCM, 1974.

Hewitt, Thomas. *The Epistle to the Hebrews: An Introduction and Commentary*. TNTC. Grand Rapids: Eerdmans, 1960.

Hiebert, D. Edmond. *Second Peter and Jude: An Expositional Commentary*. Greenville, SC: Unusual Pub., 1989.

Hirschberg, Peter. "Jewish Believers in Asia Minor According to the Book of Revelation and the Gospel of John." In *Jewish Believers in Jesus: The Early Centuries*, edited by Oskar Skarsaune and Reidar Hvalvik, 217–40. Peabody, MA: Hendrickson, 2007.

———. *Das eschatologische Israel: Untersuchungen zum Gottesvolkverständnis der Johannesoffenbarung*. WMANT 84. Neukirchen-Vluyn: Neukirchener, 1999.

Hofius, Otfried. *Katapausis: Die Vorstellung vom endzeitlichen Ruheort im Hebräerbrief*. WUNT 11. Tübingen: Mohr/Siebeck, 1970.

Holladay, William L. *The Root Sûbh in the Old Testament: With Particular Reference to Its Usages in Covenantal Contexts*. Leiden: Brill, 1958.

Hollander, H. W., and Marinus De Jonge. *The Testament of the Twelve Patriarchs: A Commentary*. SVTP 8. Leiden: Brill, 1985.

Hoppin, Ruth. *Priscilla's Letter: Finding the Author of the Epistle to the Hebrews*. San Francisco: Christian University Press, 1997.

Horrell, David G. *The Epistles of Peter and Jude*. EpC. Peterborough: Epworth, 1998.

———. "The Label Χριστιανός: 1 Pet. 4:16 and the Formation of Christian Identity." *JBL* 126 (2007) 361–81.

Hossfeld, Frank-Lothar, Erich Zenger, Linda M. Maloney, and Klaus Baltzer. *Psalms 2: A Commentary on Psalms 51–100*. Hermeneia. Minneapolis: Fortress, 2005.

Howe, Bonnie. *Because You Bear This Name: Conceptual Metaphor and the Moral Meaning of 1 Peter*. BIS 81. Leiden: Brill, 2006.

Hübner, Hans. "πληροφορία, ας, ἡ." In *EDNT* 3.107.

Hughes, Philip Edgcumbe. *A Commentary on the Epistle to the Hebrews*. Grand Rapids: Eerdmans, 1977.

Hurst, L. D. *The Epistle to the Hebrews: Its Background of Thought*. SNTSMS 65. Cambridge: Cambridge University Press, 1990.

Hvalvik, Reider. "Jewish Believers and Jewish Influence in the Roman Church." In *Jewish Believers in Jesus: The Early Centuries*, edited by Oskar Skarsaune and Reidar Hvalvik, 179–216. Peabody, MA: Hendrickson, 2007.

Isaacs, Marie E. *Reading Hebrews and James: A Literary and Theological Commentary*. Reading the New Testament Series. Macon, GA: Smyth & Helwys, 2002.

Jauhiainen, Marko. *The Use of Zechariah in Revelation*. WUNT 2/199. Tübingen: Mohr/Siebeck, 2005.

Jeremias, Joiachim. "Paul and James." *ExpTim* 66 (1955) 368–71.

Jobes, Karen H. "The Syntax of 1 Peter: Just How Good is the Greek?" *BBR* 13 (2003) 159–73.

Jobes, Karen H. *1 Peter*. BECNT. Grand Rapids: Baker Academic, 2005.

Johnson, Luke Timothy. *Hebrews*. NTL. Louisville: Westminster John Knox, 2006.

———. *The Letter of James*. AB 37A. New York: Doubleday, 1995.

———. "The Use of Leviticus in the Letter of James." *JBL* 101 (1982) 391–401.

Johnson, Richard W. *Going outside the Camp: The Sociological of the Levitical Critique in the Epistle of Hebrews.* JSNTSup 209. London: Sheffield Academic, 2001.

Jones, David W. "The Apostate Angels of 2 Pet. 2:4 and Jude 6." *F&M* 23 (2006) 19–30.

Jones, Donald L. "Roman Imperial Cult." In *ABD* 5.806–9.

Joslin, Barry C. "Can Hebrews Be Structured?: An Assessment of Eight Approaches." *CBR* 6 (2007) 99–129.

Joubert, Stephan J. "Persuasion in the Letter of Jude." *JSNT* 58 (1995) 75–87.

Kaminsky, Joel S. *Yet Jacob I Loved: Reclaiming the Biblical Concept of Election.* Nashville: Abingdon, 2007.

Käsemann, Ernst. "An Apologia for Primitive Christian Eschatology." In *Essays on New Testament Themes*, translated by W. J. Montague, 169–95. SBT 41. London: SCM, 1964.

———. *The Wandering People of God: An Investigation of the Letter to the Hebrews.* Minneapolis: Augsburg, 1984.

Katz, P. "The Quotations from Deuteronomy in Hebrews." *ZNW* 49 (1958) 213–23.

Kaufmann, Kuhler, and Gottheil, Richard. "Apostasy and Apostates from Judaism." In *The Jewish Encyclopedia*, edited by Isidore Singer, 2.12–18. New York: KTAV, 1901.

Kelly, J. N. D. *The Epistles of Peter and Jude.* BNTC. Peabody, MA: Hendrickson, 1969.

Kessler, John. *The Book of Haggai: Prophecy and Society in Early Persian Yahud.* Leiden: Brill, 2002.

Kilpatrick, George Dunbar. "Übertreter des Gesetzes, Jak 2,11." *TZ* 23 (1967) 433.

Kistemaker, Simon J. *Peter and Jude.* NTC. Grand Rapids: Baker, 1987.

Klauck, Hans-Josef. "Moving in and Moving Out: Ethics and Ethos in Hebrews." In *Identity, Ethics, and Ethos in the New Testament*, edited by Jan G. van der Watt, 417–43. BZNW 141. Berlin: de Gruyter, 2006.

Klein, William W. *The New Chosen People: A Corporate View of Election.* Grand Rapids: Zondervan, 1990.

Kloppenborg, John S. "The Emulation of the Jesus Tradition in the Letter of James." In *Reading James with New Eyes*, edited by Robert L. Webb and John S. Kloppenborg, 121–50. LNTS 342. London: T. & T. Clark, 2007.

Knoch, Otto. *Der Erste und Zweite Petrusbrief; Der Judasbrief.* RNT. Regensburg: F. Pustet, 1990.

Koch, Dietrich-Alex. "Der Text von Hab 2_{4b} in der Septuaginta und im Neuen Testament." *ZNW* 76 (1985) 68–85.

Koester, Craig R. *The Epistle to the Hebrews: A New Translation with Introduction and Commentary.* AB 36. New York: Doubleday, 2001.

———. "Recent Studies of the Book of Revelation." *LQ* 14.1 (2000) 109–22.

Koskenniemi, Heikki. *Studien zur Idee und Phraseologie des Griechischen Briefes bis 400 n.Chr.* Suomalaisen Tiedeakatemian toimituksia B 102/2. Helsinki: Suomalainen Tiedeakatemia, 1956.

Kraft, Heinrich. *Die Offenbarung des Johannes.* HNT 16a. Tübingen: Mohr, 1974.

Kraftchick, Steven John. *Jude, 2 Peter.* ATNC. Nashville: Abingdon, 2002.

Kratz, R. "τηρέω *tēreō* guard, preserve; hold fast to, keep, follow." In *EDNT* 3.354–55.

Kraus, Thomas J. *Sprache, Stil und historischer Ort des zweiten Petrusbriefes.* WUNT 2/136. Tübingen: Mohr/Siebeck, 2001.

Kruger, Michael J. "The Authenticity of 2 Peter." *JETS* 42 (1999) 645–71.

Kuhn, Karl A. "2 Peter 3:1–13." *Interpretation* 60.3 (2006) 311–13.

Kümmel, Werner Georg. *Introduction to the New Testament.* London: SCM, 1977.

Laansma, Jon. '*I Will Give You Rest*': *The 'Rest' Motif in the New Testament with Special Reference to Mt 11 an Heb 3-4*. WUNT 2/98. Tübingen: Mohr/Siebeck, 1997.

Lambrecht, Jan. "'Synagogues of Satan' (Rev. 2:9 and 3:9) Anti-Judaism in the Book of Revelation." In *Anti-Judaism and the Fourth Gospel*, edited by Reimand Bieringer et al., 279-92. Louisville: Westminster John Knox, 2001.

Lane, William L. *Hebrews*. 2 vols. WBC 47A, B. Dallas: Word, 1991.

Lapham, F. *Peter: The Myth, the Man, and the Writings: A Study of Early Petrine Text and Tradition*. Sheffield: Sheffield Academic, 2003.

Laws, Sophie. *The Epistle of James*. BNTC. Peabody, MA: Hendrickson, 1993.

———. "James, Epistle of." In *ABD* 3.621-28.

Leschert, Dale F. *Hermeneutical Foundations of Hebrews: A Study in the Validity of the Epistle's Interpretation of Some Core Citations from the Psalms*. NABPRDS 10. Lewiston E. Mellen, 1994.

Lewis, Thomas W. "And If He Shrinks Back (Heb 10:38b)." *NTS* 22 (1975) 88-94.

Lichtenberger, Herman. "πῦρ, ός, τό *pyr* fire." In *EDNT* 3.197-200.

Lindars, Barnabas. *The Theology of the Letter to the Hebrews*. NTTh. Cambridge: Cambridge University Press, 1991.

Linton, Gregory L. "Reading the Apocalypse as Apocalypse: The Limits of Genre." In *The Reality of the Apocalypse: Rhetoric and Politics in the Book of Revelation*, edited by David L. Barr, 9-41. SBLSymS 39. Atlanta: SBL, 2006.

Lockett, Darian. *Purity and Worldview in the Epistle of James*. LNTS 366. London: T. & T. Clark, 2008.

Löhr, Hermut. *Umkehr und Sünde im Herbräerbrief*. BZNW 73. Berlin: de Gruyter, 1994.

Lohse, Eduard. *Synagoge des Satans und Gemeinde Gottes: Zum Verhältnis von Juden und Christen nach der Offenbarung des Johannes*. Münster: Institutum Judaicum Delitzschianum, 1992.

Louw, Johannes P., and Eugene Albert Nida, editors. *Greek-English Lexicon of the New Testament: Based on Semantic Domains*. 2 vols. 2nd ed. New York: United Bible Societies, 1989.

Lünemann, Gottlieb, and Maurice J. Evans. *Critical and Exegetical Handbook to the Epistle to the Hebrews*. Edinburgh: T. & T. Clark, 1882.

Lupieri, Edmondo. *A Commentary on the Apocalypse of John*. Grand Rapids: Eerdmans, 2006.

Mackie, Scott D. *Eschatological and Exhortation in the Epistle of Hebrews*. WUNT 2/223. Tübingen: Mohr/Siebeck, 2007.

Malina, Bruce J., and John J. Pilch. *Social-Science Commentary on the Book of Revelations*. Minneapolis: Fortress, 2000.

Manson, T. W. "The Problem of the Epistle to the Hebrews." *BJRL* 32 (1949) 1-17.

Manson, William. *The Epistle to the Hebrews: An Historical and Theological Reconsideration*. London: Hodder and Stoughton, 1951.

Marcus, Joel. "The Evil Inclination in the Epistle of James." *CBQ* 44 (1982) 606-21.

Marshall, I. Howard. *1 Peter*. IVPNTC. Downers Grove, IL: InterVarsity, 1991.

———. *Kept by the Power of God: A Study of Perseverance and Falling Away*. 3rd ed. LES. Carlisle: Paternoster, 1995.

Martin, Ralph P. *James*. WBC 48. Waco, TX: Word, 1988.

Martin, Troy W. *Metaphor and Composition in 1 Peter*. SBLDS 131. Atlanta: Scholars, 1992.

Mathewson, Dave. "Reading Heb 6:4-6 in Light of the Old Testament." *WTJ* 61 (1999) 209-25.

Bibliography

Mayes, A. D. H. *Deuteronomy*. NCB London: Oliphants, 1979.

Mayo, Philip L. *"Those Who Call Themselves Jews": The Church and Judaism in the Apocalypse of John*. PTMS 60. Eugene, OR: Pickwick, 2006.

Mayor, Joseph B. *The Epistle of St. James: The Greek text, with Introduction, Notes, and Comments*. 2nd ed. London: Macmillan, 1897.

———. *The Epistle of St. Jude and the Second Epistle of St. Peter: The Greek Text with Introduction, Notes, and Comments*. London: Macmillan, 1907.

Mays, James Luther. *Hosea*. OTL. London: SCM, 1969.

McCullough, John Cecil. "The Impossibility of a Second Repentance in Hebrews." *BTB* 20 (1974) 1–7.

———. "Isaiah in Hebrews." In *Isaiah in the New Testament*, edited by Steve Moyise and Maarten J. J. Menken, 159–73. London: T. & T. Clark, 2005.

McKnight, Scot. *1 Peter*. NIVAC. Grand Rapids: Zondervan, 1996.

McLaughlin, John L. "Their Hearts Were Hardened: The Use of Isaiah 6,9–10 in the Book of Isaiah." *Biblica* 75 (1994) 1–25.

Metzger, Bruce M. *A Textual Commentary on the Greek New Testament*. 2nd ed. Stuttgart: Deutsche Bibelgesellschaft/United Bible Societies, 1994.

Meyer, L. V. "Remnant." In *ABD* 5.699–71.

Michaels, J. Ramsey. *1 Peter*. WBC 49. Waco, TX: Word, 1998.

———. "1 Peter." In *DLNT*, 921.

———. *Interpreting the Book of Revelation*. GNTE 7. Grand Rapids: Baker, 1992.

Michel, Otto. *Der Brief an die Hebräer*. Göttingen: Vandenhoeck & Ruprecht, 1984.

Miller, Donald G. *On This Rock: A Commentary on First Peter*. PTMS 34. Allison Park, PA: Pickwick, 1993.

Mitchell, Alan C. *Hebrews*. SP 13. Collegeville, MN: Liturgical, 2007.

Mitchell, Margaret M. "The Letter of James as a Document of Paulinism?" In *Reading James with New Eyes*, edited by Robert L. Webb and John S. Kloppenborg, 75–98. LNTS 342. London: T. & T. Clark, 2007.

Moffat, James. *A Critical and Exegetical Commentary on the Epistle to the Hebrews*. ICC. Edinburgh: T. & T. Clark, 1948.

Montefiore, Hugh. *A Commentary on the Epistle to the Hebrews*. BNTC 15. London: A. & C. Black, 1964.

Moo, Douglas J. *The Letter of James*. PNTC. Grand Rapids: Eerdmans, 2000.

———. *2 Peter, and Jude*. NIVAC. Grand Rapids: Zondervan, 1996.

Moore, G, E. *Judges*. ICC. Edinburgh: T. & T. Clark, 1895.

Morschauser, S. "'Hospitality,' Hostiles, and Hostages: On the Legal Background to Genesis 19.1–19." *JSOT* 27 (2003) 461–85.

Mounce, Robert H. *The Book of Revelation*. NICNT. Grand Rapids: Eerdmans, 1977.

Moyise, Steve. "Isaiah in 1 Peter." In *Isaiah in the New Testament*, edited by Steve Moyise and Maarten J. J. Menken, 175–188. London: T. & T. Clark, 2005.

Müller, Ulrich B. *Die Offenbarung Des Johannes*. ÖTKNT 19. Gütersloh: Gütersloher, 1984.

Myllykoski, Matti. "James the Just in History and Tradition: Perspectives of Past and Present Scholarship (Part 1)." *CBR* 5 (2006) 73–122.

Nanos, Mark D. "Paul's *Reversal* of Jews Calling Gentiles 'Dogs' (Philippians 3:2): 1600 Years of an Ideological Tale Wagging an Exegetical Dog?" *BibInt* 17 (2009) 448–82.

Newman, Barclay Moon, and Eugene Albert Nida. *A Handbook on the Acts of the Apostles*. UBSHB. New York: United Bible Societies, 1993.

Neyrey, Jerome H. "The Form and Background of the Polemic in 2 Peter." *JBL* 99 (1980) 407–31.

———. *2 Peter, Jude: A New Translation with Introduction and Commentary*. AB 37A. New York: Doubleday, 1995.

Nickelsburg, George W. E., and Klaus Baltzer. *1 Enoch*. Hermenia. Minneapolis: Fortress, 2001.

Niederwimmer, Kurt. *The Didache: A Commentary*. Hermeneia. Minneapolis: Fortress, 1998.

Nixon, R, e. *The Exodus in the New Testament*. TNTL 1962. London: Tyndale, 1963.

Nongbri. Brent. "A Touch of Condemnation in a Word of Exhortation: Apocalyptic Language and Graeco-Roman Rhetoric in Hebrews 6:4–12." *NovT* 45 (2003) 265–79.

Noth, Martin. *A History of Pentateuchal Traditions*. Chico, CA: Scholars, 1981.

Noth, Martin. *The Deuteronomic History*. Sheffield: JSOT Press, 1971.

Oberholtzer, Thomas Kem. "The Failure to Heed His Speaking in Hebrews 12:25–29." *BSac* 146 (1989) 67–75.

———. "The Thorn-Infested Ground in Hebrews 6:4–12." *BSac* 145 (1988) 319–28.

Oepke, Albrecht. "ἀπόλλυμι, ἀπώλεια, Ἀπολλύων." In *TDNT* 1.394–97.

Oppenheim, A. L. "On an Operational Device in Mesopotamian Bureaucracy." *JNES* 18 (1959) 121–28.

Oropeza, B. J. "Laying to Rest the Midrash: Paul's Message on Meat Sacrificed to Idols in Light of the Deuteronomic Tradition," *Biblica* 79 (1998) 57–68.

———. *99 Reasons Why No One Knows When Christ Will Return*. Downers Grove, IL: InterVarsity, 1994.

———. *Paul and Apostasy: Eschatology, Perseverance, and Falling Away in the Corinthian Congregation*. WUNT 2/115. Tübingen: Mohr/Siebeck, 2000.

———. "The Warning Passages in Hebrews: Revised Theologies and New Methods of Interpretation." *CBR* 10, forthcoming.

Osborne, Grant R. "The Christ of Hebrews and Other Religions." *JETS* 46 (2003) 249–67.

———. "A Classical Arminian View." In *Four Views on the Warning Passages in Hebrews*, edited by Herbert W. Bateman, 86–128. Grand Rapids: Kregel, 2007.

———. "Recent Trends in the Study of the Apocalypse." In *The Face of New Testament Studies: A Survey of Recent Research*, edited by Scot McKnight and Grant R. Osborne, 473–504. Leicester: Apollos; Grand Rapids: Baker Academic, 2004.

———. *Revelation*. BECNT. Grand Rapids: Baker Academic, 2002.

Osburn, Carroll D. "The Text of Judas 5." *Biblica* 62 (1981) 107–15.

Painter, John. *Just James: The Brother of Jesus in History and Tradition*. Edinburgh: T. & T. Clark, 1999.

Panning, Armin J. "Exegetical Brief: What Has Been Determined (ἐτέθησαν) in 1 Peter 2:8?" *Wisconsin Lutheran Journal* 98.1 (2001) 48–52.

Paschke, Boris A. "The Roman *ad bestias* Execution as a Possible Historical Background for 1 Peter 5.8." *JSNT* 28.4 (2006) 489–500.

Pattemore, Stephen. *The People of God in the Apocalypse: Discourse, Structure, and Exegesis*. SNTSMS 128. Cambridge: Cambridge University Press, 2004.

Paul, Shalom M. "Heavenly Tablets and the Book of Life." *Journal of the Ancient Near Eastern Society of Columbia University* 5 (1973) 345–53.

Paulsen, Henning. *Der Zweite Petrusbrief und der Judasbrief*. KEK 12/2. Göttingen: Vandenhoeck & Ruprecht, 1992.

Bibliography

Pearson, Sharon Clark. *The Christological and Rhetorical Properties of 1 Peter.* SBEC 45. Lewiston: E. Mellen, 2001.

Penner, Todd C. *The Epistle of James and Eschatology: Re-Reading an Ancient Christian Letter.* JSNTSup 121. Sheffield: Sheffield Academic, 1996.

Perkins, Pheme. *First and Second Peter, James, and Jude.* Interpretation. Louisville: John Knox, 1995.

Peterson, David G. *Hebrews and Perfection: An Examination of the Concept of Perfection in the 'Epistle of Hebrews.'* SNTSMS 47. Cambridge: Cambridge University Press, 1982.

Peterson, Robert A. "Apostasy." *Presbyterion* 19 (1993) 17–31.

Pfitzner, V. C. *Hebrews.* ANTC. Nashville: Abingdon, 1997.

Picirelli, Robert. "The Meaning of 'Epignosis.'" *EvQ* 47 (1975) 85–93.

Piper, John. *'Love Your Enemies': Jesus' Love Command in the Synoptic Gospels and in the Early Christian Paraenesis.* SNTSMS 38. Cambridge: Cambridge University Press, 1979.

Popkes, Wiard. *Der Brief des Jakobus.* THKNT 14. Leipzig: Evangelische Verlagsanstalt, 2001.

Porter, Stanley E. *Idioms of the Greek New Testament.* Sheffield: Sheffield Academic, 1999.

———. *Verbal Aspect in the Greek of the New Testament with Reference to Tense and Mood.* SBG. New York: P. Lang, 1989.

Prasad, Jacob. *Foundations of the Christian Way of Life According to 1 Peter 1, 13–25: An Exegetico-Theological Study.* AnBib 146. Rome: Pontifical Biblical Institute, 2000.

Preisker, Herbert. "νωθρός." In *TDNT* 4.1126.

Price, S. R. F. *Rituals and Power: The Roman Imperial Cult in Asia Minor.* Cambridge: Cambridge University Press, 1984.

Prigent, Pierre. *L'Apocalypse de saint Jean.* CNT 14. Geneva: Labor et Fides, 2000.

———. "L'interpretation de l'Apocalypse en debat." *ETR* 75 (2000) 189–210.

Proctor, John. "Judgment or Vindication? Deuteronomy 32 in Hebrews 10:30." *TynBul* 55 (2004) 65–80.

Proulx, P. and L. Alonso Schökel. "Heb 6,4–6: εἰς μετάνοιαν ἀνασταυροῦντας" *Biblica* 56 (1975) 193–209.

Räisänen, Heiki. *The Idea of Divine Hardening: A Comparative Study of the Notion of Divine Hardening, Leading Astray, and Inciting to Evil the Bible and the Qur'an.* PFES 25. Helsinki: Finnish Exegetical Society, 1976.

Ramsey, William M. *The Letters to the Seven Churches.* Reprint. Grand Rapids: Baker, 1979.

Rappaport, U. "Alcimus." In *ABD* 1.145.

Raymond Brown. *The Message of Hebrews: Christ above All.* BST. Leicester: InterVarsity, 1988.

Reese, Ruth Anne. *2 Peter and Jude.* Grand Rapids: Eerdmans, 2007.

Reicke, Bo. *The Epistles of James, Peter, and Jude.* AB 37. Garden City, NY: Doubleday, 1964.

Rengstorf, Karl Heinrich. "ὑποστέλλω." In *TDNT* 7.597–98.

Rhee, Victor (Sung-Yul). *Faith in Hebrews: Analysis within the Context of Christology, Eschatology, and Ethics.* SBibL 19. New York: P. Lang, 2001.

Rice, George E. "Apostasy as a Motif and Its Effect on the Structure of Hebrews." *Andrews University Seminary Studies* 23 (1985) 29–35.

Richard, E. J. *Reading 1 Peter, Jude, and 2 Peter: A Literary and Theological Commentary.* RNT. Macon, GA: Smith & Helwys, 2000.

Richards, E. Randolph. "Silvanus Was Not Peter's Secretary: Theological Bias in Interpreting διὰ Σιλουανοῦ . . . ἔγραψα." *JETS* 43 (2000) 417–32.

Rissi, M. *Die Theologie des Hebräerbriefs: Ihre Verankerung in der Situation des Verfassers und seiner Leser* Tübingen: Mohr/Siebeck, 1987.

Roloff, Jürgen. *The Revelation of John*. Translated by John E. Alsup. CC. Minneapolis: Fortress, 1993.

———. "'Siehe, ich stehe vor der Tür und klopfe an': Beobachtungen zur Überlieferungsgeschichte von Offb. 3, 20." In *Vom Urchristentum zu Jesus: Festschrift für J. Gnilka*, edited by H. Frankenmölle and K. Kertelge, 452–66. Freiburg: Herder, 1989.

Ropes, James Hardy. *A Critical and Exegetical Commentary on the Epistle of St. James*. ICC. Edinburgh: T. & T. Clark, 1978.

Rowland, Christopher. *Revelation*. EpC. London: Epworth, 1993.

Rowston, Douglas J. "The Most Neglected Book in the New Testament." *NTS* 21 (1975) 554–63.

Royalty, Robert M. *The Streets of Heaven: The Ideology of Wealth in the Apocalypse of John*. Macon, GA: Mercer University, 1998.

Sabourin, Leopold. "Crucifying Afresh for One's Repentance." *BTB* 6 (1976) 264–71.

Salevao, Iutisone. *Legitimation in the Letter to the Hebrews: The Construction and Maintenance of a Symbolic Universe*. JSNTSup 219. Sheffield: Sheffield Academic, 2002.

Sanders, Jack T. Review of *"Those Who Call Themselves Jews": The Church and Judaism in the Apocalypse of John*, by Philip L. Mayo. *RBL* 4 (2008) n.p. Online: http://www.bookreviews.org/bookdetail.asp?TitleId=5405&CodePage=5405.

Sandt, Huub van de, editor. *Matthew and the Didache: Two Documents from the Sam Jewish-Christian Milieu?* Minneapolis: Fortress, 2005.

Schechter, Solomon. *Aspects of Rabbinic Theology: Major Concepts of the Talmud*. Reprint. Peabody, MA: Hendrickson, 1998.

Schelke, K. H. *Der Petrusbriefe—Der Judasbrief*. HTKNT. Freiburg: Herder, 1980.

Schenck, Kenneth L. "Philo and the Epistle to the Hebrews: Ronald Williamson's Study after Thirty Years." *SPhiloA* 14 (2002) 112–35.

Schenker, A. "Gerichtsverkündigung und Verblendung bei den vorexilischen Propheten." *RB* 93 (1986) 563–75.

Schlier, Heinrich. "ἀφίστημι, ἀποστασία, διχοστασία." In *TDNT* 1.512–14.

Schlosser, J. "Les jours de Noé et de Lot: A propos de Luc, XVII, 26–30." *RB* 80 (1973) 13–36.

Schnelle, Udo. *Einleitung in das Neue Testament*. Göttingen: Vandenhoeck & Ruprecht, 1994. ET: *The History and Theology of the New Testament Writings*. Translated by M. Eugene Boring. Minneapolis: Fortress, 1998.

Schnider, Franz. *Der Jakobusbrief*. RNT 20. Regensburg: F. Pustet, 1987.

Schrage, Wolfgang. "συναγωγή, ἐπισυναγωγή, ἀρχισυνάγωγος, ἀποσυνάγωγος." In *TDNt* 7.798–852.

Schreiner, Thomas R. *1, 2 Peter, Jude*. Nashville: Broadman & Holman, 2003.

Schüssler Fiorenza, Elizabeth. *The Book of Revelation: Judgment and Justice*. Philadelphia: Fortress, 1985.

Schutter, W. L. *Hermeneutic and Composition in 1 Peter*. WUNT 2/30. Tübingen: Mohr/Siebeck, 1989.

Seitz, Christopher R. "The Patience of Job in the Epistle of James." In *Konsequente Traditionsgeschichte: Festschrift für Klaus Baltzer zum 65. Geburtstag*, edited by Rüdinger Bartelmus, Thomas Krüger, and Helmut Utzschneider, 373–83. OBO 126. Göttingen: Vandenhoeck & Ruprecht, 1993.

Seitz, Oscar Jacob Frank. "Antecedents and Significance of the Term *Dipsychos*." *JBL* 66 (1947) 211–19.

Bibliography

Seland, Torrey. "παροίκους καὶ παρεπιδήμους: Proselyte Characterizations in 1 Peter?" *BBR* 11 (2001) 239–68.
Sellin, Gerhard. "Die Häretiker des Judasbriefes." *ZNW* 77 (1986) 206–25.
Selwyn, E. G. *The First Epistle of St. Peter*. 2nd ed. Grand Rapids: Baker, 1981.
Senior, Donald, P., and Daniel J. Harrington. *1 Peter, Jude, and 2 Peter*. SP 15. Collegeville, MN: Liturgical, 2003.
Sevenster, J. N. *Do You Know Greek:? How Much Greek Could the First Jewish Christians Have Known?* NovTSup 19. Leiden: Brill, 1968.
Sidebottom, E. M. *James, Jude, and 2 Peter*. NCB. Greenwood, SC: Attic, 1967.
Simon, Marcel. "From Greek Hairesis to Christian Heresy." In *Early Christian Literature and the Classical Intellectual Tradition: In Honorem Robert M. Grant*, edited by William R. Schoedel and Robert L. Wilken, 101–16. ThHist 54. Paris: Éditions Beauchesne, 1979.
Skaggs, Rebecca. *The Pentecostal Commentary on 1 Peter, 2 Peter, Jude*. Cleveland: Pilgrim, 2004.
Slater, Thomas B. "On the Social Setting of the Revelation of John." *NTS* 44 (1998) 232–56.
Smalley, Stephen S. *The Revelation to John: A Commentary on the Greek Text of the Apocalypse*. Downers Grove, IL: InterVarsity, 2005.
Smith, Terence V. *Petrine Controversies in Early Christianity: Attitudes towards Peter in Christian Writings of the First Two Centuries*. WUNT 2/15. Tübingen: Mohr/Siebeck, 1985.
Snaith, Norman H. *The Distinctive Ideas of the Old Testament*. London: Epworth, 1945.
Snyder, G. F. "The *Tobspruch* in the New Testament." *NTS* 23 (1977) 117–20.
Spicq, Ceslas. *L'Épître aux Hébreux*. Paris: J. Gabalda, 1977.
———. *Les Épîtres de Saint Pierre*. SB. Paris: Gabalda, 1966.
Spitaler, Peter. "Doubt or Dispute (Jude 9 and 22–23): Rereading a Special New Testament Meaning through the Lens of Internal Evidence." *Biblica* 87 (2006) 201–22.
Starr, James M. *Sharers in the Divine Nature: 2 Peter 1:4 in Its Hellenistic Context*. ConBNT 33. Stockholm: Almqvist & Wiksell, 2000.
Stewart-Sykes, A. "The Function of 'Peter' in 1 Peter." *ScrBul* 27 (1997) 8–21.
Strand, Kenneth A. "'Overcomer': A Study in the Macrodynamic of Theme Development in the Book of Revelation." *AUSS* 28 (1990) 237–54.
Strelan, Rick. "'Outside Are the Dogs and Sorcerers . . .' (Revelation 22:15)." *BTB* 33 (2003) 148–57.
Stuart, Douglas K. *Hosea-Jonah*. WBC 31. Waco, TX: Word, 2002.
Sullivan, K. Review of *Who Rides the Beast?* by Paul Duff. *CBQ* 64 (2002) 569–70.
Sumney, Jerry L. "The Dragon Has Been Defeated—Revelation 12." *RevExp* 98 (2001) 103–15.
Sweet, J. P. M. *Revelation*. WPC. Philadelphia: Westminster, 1979.
Talbert, Charles H. "Once Again: The Plan of 1 Peter." In *Perspectives on 1 Peter*, 141–51. NABPRSS 9. Macon, GA: Mercer University Press, 1986.
Thiel, W. "Zum Bundbrechen im AT." *VT* 20 (1970) 214–29.
Thomas, C. Adrian. *A Case for Mixed-Audience with Reference to the Warning Passages in the Book of Hebrews*. New York: P. Lang, 2008.
Thompson, James W. *Hebrews*. Paideia. Grand Rapids: Baker, 2008.
———. "The Rhetoric of 1 Peter." *ResQ* 36 (1994) 237–50.
Thompson, Leonard L. *The Book of Revelation: Apocalypse and Empire*. Oxford: Oxford University Press, 1990.

Thurén, Lauri. *Argument and Theology in 1 Peter: The Origins of Christian Paraenesis.* JSNTSup 114. Sheffield: Sheffield Academic, 1995.

———. "Hey Jude! Asking for the Original Situation and Message of a Catholic Epistle." *NTS* 43 (1997) 451–65.

———. *The Rhetorical Strategy of 1 Peter, with Special Regard to Ambiguous Expressions.* Åbo, Finland: Åbo Academy Press, 1990.

Thyen, Hartwig. *Der Stil des jüdisch-hellenistischen Homilie.* FRLANT 47. Göttingen: Vandenhoeck & Ruprecht, 1955.

Tongue, D. H. "The Concept of Apostasy in the Epistle to the Hebrews." *TynBul* 5.6 (1960) 19–27.

Townsend, M. J. "James 4:1–14: A Warning Against Zealotry?" *ExpTim* (1976) 211–13.

Trebilco, Paul. "What Shall We Call Each Other? Part Two: The Issue of Self-Designation in the Johannine Letters and Revelation." *TynBul* 54 (2003) 51–73.

Truex, Jerry. "God's Spiritual House: A Study of 1 Peter 2:4–5." *Direction* 33.2 (2004) 185–93.

Tsuji, Manabu. *Glaube zwischen Vollkommenheit und Verweltlichung: Eine Untersuchung zur literarischen Gestalt und zur inhaltlichen Kohärenz des Jakobusbriefes.* WUNT 2/93. Tübingen: Mohr/Siebeck, 1997.

Ulrichsen, Jarl H. *Die Grundschrift der Testament der zwölf Patriarchen: Eine Untersuchung zu Umfang, Inhalt und Eigenart der ursprünglichen Schrift.* Acta Universitatis Upsaliensis, Historia religionum 10. Uppsala: Almqvist & Wiksell, 1991.

Urbrock, W. J. "Blessings and Curses." In *ABD* 1.755–61.

Verbrugge, Verlyn D. "Towards a New Interpretation of Hebrews 6:4–6." *CTJ* 15 (1980) 61–73.

Viljoen, Fracois P. "Faithful Christian Living amidst Scoffers of the Judgment Day: Ethics and Ethos in Jude and 2 Peter." In *Identity, Ethics, and Ethos in the New Testament*, edited by Jan G. van der Watt, 511–33. BZNW 141. Berlin: de Gruyter, 2006.

Vögtle, Anton. *Der Judasbrief, der 2. Petrusbrief.* EKKNT 22. Düsseldorf: Benziger, 1994.

Volf, Miroslav. "Soft Difference: Theological Reflections on the Relation between Church and Culture in 1 Peter." *Ex Auditu* 10 (1994) 15–30.

Vouga, François. *L'Epître de saint Jacques.* CNT 13a. Geneva: Labor et Fides, 1984.

Wall, Robert W. *Community of the Wise: The Letter of James.* The New Testament in Context. Valley Forge, PA: Trinity, 1997.

Wallace, Daniel B. *Greek Grammar beyond the Basics: An Exegetical Syntax of the New Testament with Scripture, Subject, and Greek Word Indexes.* Grand Rapids: Zondervan, 1996.

Wand, J. W. C. *The General Epistles of St. Peter and St. Jude.* WC. London: Methuen, 1934.

Ward, Roy Bowen. "Partiality in the Assembly: James 2:2–4." *HTR* 62 (1969) 87–97.

Wasserman, Tommy. *The Epistle of Jude: Its Text and Transmission.* ConBNT 43. Stockholm: Almqvist & Wiksell International, 2006.

Watson, Duane F. *Invention, Arrangement, and Style: Rhetorical Criticism of Jude and 2 Peter.* SBLDS 104. Atlanta: Scholars, 1988.

———. "Nicolaitans." In *ABD* 4.1106–7.

———. Review of *Restoring the Diaspora*, by Timothy B. Cargal. *JBL* 114 (1995) 348–51.

Webb, Robert L. "The Eschatology of the Epistle of Jude and Its Rhetorical and Social Functions." *BTB* 6 (1996) 139–51.

———. "Intertexture and Rhetorical Strategy in First Peter's Apocalyptic Discourse: A Study in Socio-Rhetorical Interpretation." In *Reading First Peter with New Eyes: Methodological*

      Reassessments of the Letter of First Peter, edited by Robert L. Webb and Betsy Bauman-Martin, 72–110. LNTS 364. London: T. & T. Clark, 2007.

———. "The Rhetorical Function of Visual Imagery in Jude: A Socio-Rhetorical Experiment in Rhetography." In *Reading Jude with New Eyes*, edited by Robert L. Webb and Peter H. Davids, 109–35. LNTS 383. London: T. & T. Clark, 2008.

Weinfeld, M. "בְּרִית." In *TDOT* 2.253–79.

Weiss, Hans-Friedrich. *Der Brief an die Hebräer: Übersetzt und erklärt*. KEKNT 13. Göttingen: Vandenhoeck & Ruprecht, 1991.

Werdermann, Hermann. *Die Irrlehrer des Judas und des 2 Petrusbriefes*. BFCT 17.6. Gütersloh: Bertelsmann, 1913.

Wiedermann, T. *Emperors and Gladiators*. London: Routledge, 1992.

Wilken, Robert L. *The Christians as the Romans Saw Them*. New Haven, CT: Yale, 2003.

Williamson, Ronald. "The Eucharist and the Epistle to the Hebrews." *NTS* 21 (1974–75) 300–312.

———. *Philo and the Epistle to the Hebrews*. ALGHJ. Leiden: Brill, 1970.

Wilson, Stephen G. "Gentile Judaizers." *NTS* 38 (1992) 605–16.

———. *Leaving the Fold: Apostates and Defectors in Antiquity*. Minneapolis: Fortress, 2004.

Wilson, Walter T. "Sin as Sex and Sex with Sin: The Anthropology of James 1:12–15." *HTR* 95 (2002) 147–68.

Winter, Bruce W. *After Paul Left Corinth: The Influence of Secular Ethics and Social Change*. Grand Rapids: Eerdmans, 2001.

———. "The Public Honouring of Christian Benefactors: Romans 13:3–4 and 1 Peter 2:14–15." *JSNT* 34 (1988) 87–103.

———. "'Seek the Welfare of the City': Social Ethics according to 1 Peter." *Themelios* 13 (1988) 91–94.

Wisse, Frederik. "The Epistle of Jude in the History of Heresiology." In *Essays on the Nag Hammadi Texts in Honour of Alexander Böhlig*, edited by Martin Krause, 133–43. NHS 3. Leiden: Brill, 1972.

Witherington, Ben. *Letters and Homilies for Jewish Christians: A Socio-Rhetorical Commentary on Hebrews, James and Jude*. Downers Grove, IL: IVP Academic, 2007.

———. *Revelation*. NCBC. Cambridge: Cambridge University Press, 2003.

———. *A Social-Rhetorical Commentary on 1–2 Peter*. Vol. 2 of *Letters and Homilies for Hellenized Christians*. Downers Grove: IVP Academic, 2007.

Wolff, H. W. *Hosea*. Hermenia. Philadelphia: Fortress, 1974.

Wolthius, Thomas. "Jude and Jewish Traditions." *CTJ* 22 (1987) 21–41.

Wood, P. "Local Knowledge in the Letters of the Apocalypse." *ExpTim* 73 (1961–62) 263–64.

Wray, Judith Hoch. *Rest as a Theological Metaphor in the Epistle to the Hebrews and the Gospel of Truth: Early Christian Homilectics of Rest*. SBLDS 166. Atlanta: Scholars, 1998.

Wright, N. T. "How Can the Bible be Authoritative?" *Vox Evangelica* 21 (1991) 7–32.

———. *The Last Word: Beyond the Bible Wars to a New Understanding of the Authority of Scripture*. San Francisco: HarperSanFrancisco, 2005.

Zerwick, Max, and Mary Grosvenor. *A Grammatical Analysis of the Greek New Testament*. Unabridged 3rd rev. ed. Rome: Pontifical Biblical Institute, 1988.

Ancient Sources Index

HEBREW SCRIPTURES/ SEPTUAGINT

Genesis

1:20–25	148
2:2–3	28
2:9	192, 193
2:17	193
3:17	28
4	165
4:1–8	82, 142, 166
5:18–24	159
5:22–24	86
6–9	101
6:1 4	163
6:9	86
12	93
15:6	71, 93
17	93
19	101, 164
21:10	59
22	79, 93
23:4	108
24:35	90
24:55	196
25:5–6	59
25:29–34	63
25:32–33	62
26:34–35	63
27	62
27:30–40	63
27:34	62, 63
27:36	62
27:38	63, 64
37–50	101, 102
49:17	224

Exodus

3:5	50
3:17	28
3:18	28
4:1,9	28
4:22–23	20, 62
6:5–6	112
10:21–22	65
12	226
12:5	78
12:5–7	112
12:11	112, 119
13:13	62
13:21	34
15:12	228
16:2–3	112
16:4, 15	35, 203
16:32–34	193, 203
17:2	20
17:7	20
17:14	212
19:3–8	115, 120
19:6	112, 117
19:12–19	65, 66, 120
20:11	28
20:13–14	71, 83
20:18	16
21:8	206
21:29–34	16
22:21	109
28:9–10	193
28:9–29	204
28:28f	193
28:36	218
29:45	20
32	163

Ancient Sources Index

Exodus (*continued*)

32:1–4	112
32:9	20, 191
32:32	62
32:32–33	159, 193, 212
32:32–34	193
33:3–5	191
33:5	20
34:9	20, 191
34:16	23
40:38	34

Leviticus

4:2	9, 49
5:18	49
10:10	62
11	241
11:44	118, 120
13	9
18:21	62
18:25–28	219
19:2	118
19:12	112
19:18	71, 86, 89, 90
19:34	108, 109
20:22	219
22	9
24:2–4	189
24:10–23	74
25:23	109
26:1–13	98
26:15	101
26:14–39	98
26:27–30	27
26:40–44	98, 101
26:41	191
27	9

Numbers

9:13	21
11–25	161, 163
13–14	29, 68
13–20	121
14	10, 22, 49
14:2	26
14:5	26
14:7	26
14:9	20, 23
14:10	26
14:11	20, 23, 26, 161
14:16	27
14:21–23	20, 22, 26
14:21–35	41
14:23–40	101
14:29–33	23, 26
14:40	23
15:22–31	49
15:24–29	9, 16
15:26–31	41, 69
15:28–35	22
15:30–36	9
16	167
16:1–2	167
18:15	62
20:2–13	10
22–24	166
22:23	202
22:31	202
24:17	193
24:17–24	207
25	135, 143, 152, 199
25:1–18	166
26:58	167
27:17	123
31:8	166
31:16	143, 166

Deuteronomy

1:9	19
1:17	55
1:31	19
1:31–33	228
4:2	229
4:9	14
4:9–26	189
4:11–12	65
4:20–31	99
4:23–24	67
4:23–31	98, 101
4:26	28
4:30–36	28
4:34	20
4:37	217
4:39f	28
5:17–18	71
5:20–26	28
5:22–25	65

5:26	22	19:4	49
5:32–33	97	19:11–13	52, 98
6:6	28	19:21	52
6:12	189	22:1	94
6:16	20, 80	23:4–5	166
6:24	28	25:12	52
7:1–4	201, 241	25:19	212
7:4	21	26:17	20
7:8	112	27:11	28
7:6–9	20, 101	28–30	62
7:24	212	28–32	10
7:25	137	28:1	28
8:2	20	28:9	20
8:2–5	59	28:20–24	101
8:2–20	189	28:26	27
8:11	28	28:36–37	101
8:15	19	28:66–67	53
8:19–20	163	28:68	99, 101
8:20	28	29:14–21	61
9:3	67	29:17	98
9:6	20	29:18	61
9:6–27	191	29:18–20	41, 69, 212
9:7	189	29:19b–21	62
9:13	20	29:20	62
9:14	212	29:24–25	101
9:19	120	30:1	45
9:22	20	30:1–6	191
9:23	28	30:2	97
10:12–13	20	30:3–5	225
10:16	20	30:4	112
10:17	53	30:6	191
10:19	109	30:15	31, 86, 142
11	62	30:16	20
11:11	45	30:18–19	28, 45, 142, 191
11:16–17	98	30:20	28
11:26–28	45	31:6	10, 98
11:28	95, 205	31:6–16	101
12:32	229	31:8	10, 98
13:1–5	138	31:16–17	98, 101
13:1–8	98	31:19–22	98
13:3	20	31:27	20
13:6	20	32:4	20
13:6–8	74	32:8	16, 183
13:5–11	52	32:10	19
14	241	32:15	21, 162
17:2	101	32:18	189
17:2–6	52, 53	32:22	45
17:12	9, 98	32:35	50, 53
18:20–22	138	32:36	53

Ancient Sources Index

Deuteronomy (continued)
32:41–43	53
32:46	14, 16, 28
33:6	168, 191
33:8	20

Joshua
3:10	22
7:11–15	101
13:22	166, 202
22:22–23	21
22:29	21
23:13	145
23:16	101
24:15	86, 191
24:33	191

Judges
1:27	166
2	101
2–6	101
2:1	101
2:3	145
2:10–23	98
2:11	98
2:14	98
2:17	98
2:19	98, 191
2:20	101
3:7–11	98
3:8	98
3:12	98
4:1	98
4:2	98
4:3	98
5:2–31	66
6:1	98
6:6–7	98
8:13	98
10:6–16	98
10:7	98
13:1	98
17	98
17:6	99
18:1	99
18:30	224
19:1	99
21:25	99

1 Samuel
2:17	98
2:27–36	101
2:29	98
2:34–35	98
12:9	98
15:23	191
21:4f	62
25:29	204

2 Samuel
2:23	21
23:6	45

1 Kings
11:1–13	241

2 Kings
14:27	212

1 Chronicles
22:9	28
22:18	28
23:25–26	28
29:15	109

2 Chronicles
3:17	218
6:36–39	99
12:5	10
20:19	167
28:6	101
28:22	21
33:10–13	99
36:1–23	99

Ezra
9–10	201

Nehemiah
4:14	53
9:12	34
9:15	35, 203
9:16–29	191
9:19	34

9:21	34
9:27	98
9:34–36	14
13:2	166
13:23–27	201

Job

1:7 (RSV)	128
5:11	90
5:16f	90
15:29f	90
18–19	219
20:15	219
29:11–12	90
30:8	203
31:16–25	90
42:10–17	90

Psalms (MT/ LXX [MT])

2:8–9	208
8:4–6	17
8:5–7	16
9:5–6	212
21[22]:1	17
21[22]:5	17
21[22]:6–18	17
21[22]:14–15	127
21[22]:16–20	147
21[22]:22–23	16, 17
23[24]:4	85
27:4	207
32:1	97
33 [34]	121
33[34]:9	35
33[34]:13–15	121
33[34]:13–17	122
36:10	22
37:2	89
38[39]:12	109
39[40]:6	56
45:7	208
46[47]:3	53
51:9	97
52:2	201
56:8	213
66:10	221
69[68]:27–28	211, 212
77[78]	19
77[78]:24	35
78:25	203
80[81]	19
86:11	86
93–100	27
94[95]	10, 19, 20, 27, 28, 29, 68
94[95]:7–11	19, 20, 27, 45
94[95]:8	20
94[95]:9	20
94[95]:10	20, 34
94[95]:11	28, 41
104[105]:40	35
105[106]	19
105[106]:28–31	166
105:[146]	20
105:39	34
106:41	98
106:47	225
106[107]:40	19
109[110]:1	6
110:1	74, 221
110:2	208
117[118]:6f	11
117[118]:22	117, 118
118:20	74
118:30 (LXX)	142
118[119]:15	20
118[119]:19	109
118[119]:33	20
118[119]:151	20
119:36	191
139:16	213
146:2	112
146:10	56
146:49	56
147:2	225
151:5	56

Proverbs

1:17	147
2:16	83
3:7	14
3:11–12	14, 59
3:12	221
3:20	14
3:21 LXX	14
3:25	14
3:34	71
4:10–27	86

Proverbs (continued)

4:26	60
7:6–27	83
7:18	58
7:25–27	82
10:12	97
11:31	126
14:8	167
14:12	86
15:17	147
16:18	22
16:25	86
18:12	22
21:16 LXX	147
21:24	147
22:29 LXX	30
23:6–8	219
24:12	207
25:16	219
26	147
26:11	147, 219
27:1	90
27:14	21
28:18	145
28:24 LXX	55
30:20	83

Ecclesiastes

7:2	147
7:5	147

Isaiah

1:4–9	100
1:9	100
1:25	221
1:28	100
2:3	65
4:2–3	100
4:2–6	45
4:3	211
5:1–7	45
5:24	100
6	190
6:1–10	100
6:8	18
6:9–10	18, 190, 191
6:9–11	30
6:10	97, 122
7:3	18
7:9	32
7:14	18
8:3	18
8:11–15	120
8:11–18	18
8:12–13	54, 118
8:14	115, 117, 118
8:14–15	169
8:17	10, 16, 18
8:18	18, 65, 118
10:20–23	100
11	124, 228
11:1–2	116
11:1–10	106
11:2–3	124
11:4	202, 208
11:11–16	225
11:12	115
12:2	114
13:13	66
13:14	123
13:21–22	19
15	115
19:14	219
22:22–23	217
23	115
23:17	200
24:5	101
24:21–22	227
25	114
25:6–11	123
26:1	52
26:7–10	123
26:11	52
26:20	52, 55, 56
27:12–13	225
28:7–8	219
28:16	65, 115, 117
29:9–10	191
29:18–19	100
30:37	208
31:5	114
32:14–15	124
33:12	45
33:14	67
33:20	66
33:22	114
35	100, 228

35:2	124	50:1	100
35:4	114	50:9	108
35:5	100	51	100
35:8–10	101, 106	51:11	123
35:10	123	51:11–16	65
37:4	22	52:1	124
37:17	22	52:3	100, 112
40–44	100	52:5	140
40–55	228	52:7–12	123
40:1–5	116	52:12	114
40:1–11	101, 106	53	115, 122, 123
40:6	89	53:3	100
40:6–8	116	53:5–6	122
41:8	217	54:6–7	100
41:9	20, 161	56:4–5	203
42:1	115	56:5	212
42:6	161	56:8	106
42:6–7	190	56:10–12	165
43:1–7	114	57:3	83
43:5–7	101, 106	57:17–18	100
43:14–44:5	115	58:8	114
43:20–21	115, 117	59:3	66
43:22	115	59:13	100
43:23	115	59:21	124
44:1–2	115	60:1–13	124
44:2–3	124	60:14	217
44:3	116	60:19–20	227
44:4	14	61:7	123
44:5	226	62:2	203
44:24–45:7	116	62:4	100
44:21	189	63	100
44:28	116	63:7–14	19
45:1	116	63:17–18	191
45:4	116	63:18	50
45:1–7	217	65:6	213
45:13	100	65:9	115
45:17	15, 114	65:11	100
46:3	100	65:15	203
46:8–9	189	66:8–18	65
46:13	65	66:16	67
48	15	66:24	27, 45, 67
48:12	161		
48:19	212	**Jeremiah**	
49:2	202	1:16	100
49:5–6	225	1:17	119
49:6	101, 106, 112, 190	2:5	21, 87
49:8	114	2:11	100
49:14–15	100	2:13	22, 47
49:23	217	2:13–19	100

273

Ancient Sources Index

Jeremiah (continued)

2:19	56, 100
3:6–12	100
3:14	21, 100
3:19	83
3:21–22	100
4:1	100
5:1–6	100
5:7	100
5:10	101
5:18	101
5:19	100
5:19–23	191
6:13	138
6:30	63
7:12–16	41
7:24–29	100, 101
7:29	63
8:16	224
8:19	87
9:12–14	100
10:3	87
10:10	22, 66
11:10	101
12:7–13	100
13:25	100
14:10–12	56
14:19	63
14:21	101
15:6	66, 100
16:11	100
17:13	22
17:9–18	207
17:23	20, 100
18:15	100
19:4–6	100
21:8	31, 142
21:8–14	86
22:9	100f
22:24	101
22:30	213
23:27	100
23:33–40	100
25:27	219
25 [32]:29	126
27:6 LXX	123
29:4–23	112
31:7–14	225
31:32	15, 101
31:33	191
31:33–34	9
31:36–37	100, 101
33:24–26	100
33[26]:7–16 LXX	138
33–40	100
33:24–26	100
32:38	20
39–45	100
39:40	21
42:7	196
44:25	191
51:5	100

Lamentations

1–5	100

Ezekiel

3:7	191
3:18–20	66
3:20	191
3:21	94
3:27	190, 191
4:14	62
7:7	48
8–10	100
9:4–8	225
9:6	126
11:9–11	126
11:19	191
12:2	190
14:13	36
15:8	36
16:38	83
17:15–19	101
18:5–9	101
18:5–32	191
18:21–32	97, 101
18:24	36, 97
18:30	97
18:32	149
20:1–22	19
20:4–31	101
20:8	21
20:27	36
20:30–32	100
20:33–34	100
20:35–38	100f

Ancient Sources Index

20:38	21	**Hosea**	
20:39	191	1–2	99, 200
22:25	127	1–5	101
22:26	62	1:5	99
23:3	100	2:8–10	99
23:8	100	2:9–12	99
23:45	83	2:13	65
33:11	97	2:14–23	99
33:31	144	2:15	99
34	74, 123	2:23–25	100, 115
34:4	94, 122	3:1	83
34:16	122	3:5	100
36:25	32	4:3	99
36:26	191	4:4–5	99
37:15–23	225	4:6–19	99
39:20	66	4:10–13	99
39:26	101	5:4	99
40–48	101	5:4–7	99
45:20	9	6:1	99f
46:11	65	6:7	99, 101
		6:11	100
Daniel		7:2	99
1:12–15	196	7:10	99
4:10–20	163	8:3	66
6:16–27	128	8:4–6	99
7:9–10	211	8:6	20
7:10	213	8:13	99
7:13	190	8:14	99
7:18	221	9:10	99, 166
7:18–27	182	9:13–17	99
7:25	228	10:1–8	99
7:27	221	10:14–15	99
8:10	227, 228	11:5	99
8:13	50	11:8–11	228
9:9	21	11:10–11	100, 225
9:11	45	12:9–13	228
9:27	228	13:1–3	99
10:13	183	13:4–15	228
10:21	183	13:6	99
11:29–39	227, 228	14:2–3	99
12:1	183, 218, 227	14:1–7	100
12:1–2	211, 216		
12:1–3	228	**Joel**	
12:3	227	1:15	48
12:7	228	2:10–11	66
12:10	191	3:16	66
22–25	227	4:14	48

275

Ancient Sources Index

Amos
2:4	20
2:10–3:2	228
3:1–2	101
3:2	126, 128
4:11	171
5:21	65
5:21–27	19

Jonah
2:10	219

Micah
1:7	200
3:4	10
4:1–8	228
6:8	86
2:12	100
6:5	166, 189
7:11–15	228
7:18–20	101

Habakkuk
2:4	32, 55
3:1–7	228

Zephaniah
1:18	52, 67

Haggai
2:4–5	228
2:6–7	66
2:6–9	66

Zechariah
3	101
3:1–10	210
3:2	164
3:2–4	171
4:1–14	189
6:14 LXX	196
7:8–13	191
7:12	20
8:20–23	217
10:8–12	228
12:3	50
12:8	228
12:10	51
13:7	123
13:9	221
13:12	138
14:8–9	228

Malachi
2:6	86, 97
2:10–12	101
3:1–6	126
3:16	211, 213
4:5–6	101

APOCRYPHA

Tobit
1:3	142
4:17	201
5:14	167
13:13	225
14:4–6	101

Judith
5:9–19	112
8:3	206
11:19	123
13:16	144
16:17	67

Wisdom
1–6	142
2:24	82
3:1	65
3:1–12	59
3:4	65
3:10	14, 21
4:2	192
4:3	59
5:6	142, 205
5:6–7	95
6:7	55
6:9	36
6:17–20	137

12–14	200
12:2	36
12:10	63
12:20–26	126
12:24	95, 167
14:11	145
14:12	20
15:5	31
15:17	31
16:20	203
18:15–16	201
18:20–25	19, 163, 167

Sirach

1:28	84
1:30	22
2:1–11	80
4:29	30
7:28	189
7:34	61
13:8	14
15:11–17	86
15:11–20	79, 191
15:17	80
16:6–14	160
16:12	207
19–21	93
23:14	189
25:4	80
28:6–7	189
28:22–26	22
28:23	142
31:21	219
34:19	56
35:3	21
35:19	207
36:11	225
36:13–14	74
38:22	189
45:18–19	56, 167
47:22	212

1 Maccabees

2:19–20	21
2:52	93
3:45	50
3:51	50
7:5–25	49
9:54–57	49
12:53	212
13:50	144
21:18	206

2 Maccabees

1:24	53
1:27	112
2:3	21
2:4–6	203
2:7	225
3:17	67
4:14	15
5:16	62
6:12–16	126
7	241
7:24	158
8:2	62
8:33	120
9:10	227
12:22	67
14:3	49
14:42	51

3 Maccabees

2:2	63
2:4–7	160
2:14	62, 63
2:18	50
3:9	51
4:16	63

4 Maccabees

5:8	58
6–7	69
6:7	46
6:9	47, 58
6:10	197
6:27–29	47
7:1–3	47
7:16	47
8:28	58
10:10	59
11:20	59, 197
12:12	67
13:1	58
13:15	197
14:1	47

Ancient Sources Index

4 Maccabees (*continued*)

15:30	81
17:15	197

2 Esdras

2:2	218
2:7	212

NEW TESTAMENT

Matthew

3:7	32
3:8	31
3:11	31
4:1–11	129
4:4	43
4:17	31, 48
5:3	89
5:7	90
5:8	60
5:11–16	147
5:12–13	60
5:13	50
5:13–14	190
5:17–20	76
5:19	90
5:21–26	82, 83
5:27	83
5:29	88
5:34	75
5:34–37	89
5:39–44	60
6:1–18	87
6:9–11	189
6:13	79, 141
6:24	220
6:26	148
7:1	75
7:1–5	89
7:6	50, 147, 192
7:11	86
7:12	45, 76
7:12–19	142
7:13	141
7:13–14	86
7:13–15	151
7:15	14, 138
7:16–26	45
7:21–23	36, 138, 146
7:24–27	75
8:22	168
9:4	207
9:36	148
10:16	148
10:17–23	179
10:22	26, 196
10:24–39	237
10:23	190
10:28	54, 89, 120, 126
10:32	197, 233
10:32–33	197, 211, 233
10:33	124, 158
10:33–39	241
11	20
11:15	190
12	242
12–15	30
12:22–32	194
12:31–32	103
12:36–37	88
12:43–45	145
12:46–50	89
13	237, 241
13:7	220
13:15	145
13:19	30
13:30	45
13:31–32	45
13:36–43	45
13:43	227
13:55	71, 154
15:26–27	147
16:18	170, 203
16:23	169
16:25	192
16:28	35
18	103, 235, 239, 242
18:6–9	199
18:9	88
18:10–14	97
18:12	9
18:15	97, 103, 242
19:23–24	220
19:28	221, 225

20:1–12	185	3:20–21	73
21:31	40	3:20–30	194
21:42	115	3:28–30	103
21:42–44	117	3:29	40
22:5	15	4	237
22:6	51	4:7	220
22:36–41	146	4:9	30, 190
22:37–39	188	4:10–12	86, 190
22:37–41	86	4:12	97, 145
23:13	87	4:23	143, 190
23:23–27	87	4:23–25	30, 190
24	20, 238	5:11–16	147
24–25	119, 240	6:3	71, 154
24:4	20, 21, 142	6:5	32
24:4–5	205	7	241
24:4–11	95	7:1–23	73
24:8–13	119, 142	7:4	32
24:9–13	237	7:8	32
24:10–12	233	7:21	63, 200
24:10	188	7:22	194
24:11	138	7:27–28	147
24:13	26, 79, 119, 217	8:34–38	233, 237
24:14	150	8:35	192
24:15–31	218	8:35–39	241
24:21	206	8:38	17, 57, 124, 197
24:22	126	9	239
24:24	95, 138, 142	9:42–47	199
24:42	128	9:42–48	146, 241
24:42–43	208	9:47	88
24:42–25:13	202	10:16	32
24:45–51	134	10:24–25	220
25	241	10:27	38
25:1–10	208	10:45	190
25:13	128, 196	10:50	55
25:14–30	239	11:30	32
25:21	146	12:10	115
25:31–46	32, 92, 185, 239	12:10–12	117
25:41	88	12:17	181
26:41	77	12:27	22
26:70–72	158	12:28–31	233
27:18	82	12:29–31	188
		12:40	87
Mark		13:5	21, 142
1:4	31	13:5–6	205
1:4–5	31	13:12	237
1:12–13	129	13:13	26, 196, 217
1:12–14	19	13:20	126
3	242	13:22	138
3:17	203	13:26	190

Ancient Sources Index

Mark (continued)

13:34–37	208
13:35–37	128
14:21	146, 243
14:27–29	122
14:38	77, 208
14:50	122
14:55–62	74
14:61–64	6
14:62	190

Luke

2:1	218
2:34	118
3:3	31
4:1	145
4:1–13	129
4:13	77
5:32	149
6:20	89, 194
6:22–23	122
6:27–28	122
6:36	90
6:47–49	75
7:34	190
8:4–10	30
8:5	50
8:7	220
8:8	190
8:13	21, 77
8:14	220
8:15	25, 55, 78
8:29	19
9:23–26	237
9:24	192, 237
9:26	17, 124, 197
9:58	148
9:60	168
10:20	62, 211, 213
10:27	188
11:4	79, 189
11:13	35
11:14–23	194
11:24–26	145
12:1	50
12:4–5	54
12:4–12	242
12:8–9	197, 211, 233
12:9	40, 158, 242
12:10	40, 70, 103, 242
12:15–21	220
12:35	119
12:35–38	222
12:37–39	208
12:41–46	134
12:41–48	241
12:47–48	146
12:48	87
14:23	30
15:1–17	97
15:11–32	40, 242
15:24	168
16:10	146
16:13	220
16:19–31	220
17	239
17:2	199
18:18–25	220
18:24–25	220
19	239
19:10	190
20:17	115
20:17–19	117
20:48	87
21:8	20, 205
21:12	179
21:12–17	217
21:17	217
21:19	55, 78
21:24	50
21:34	14
21:36	16
22:28	77
22:28–30	222
22:30	221, 225
22:31–32	103
22:32	97, 208
22:54–62	40, 242
23:40	87
24:47	31

John

1	182
1:10–12	73
1:12	143
2:25	207
3:3–7	35
3:3	204

3:5	51, 204
3:14–16	161
3:20–21	185
4:1–6	40
4:10	35
4:23	35
5:28–29	32
5:41	145
6	237
6:31–35	203
6:31–58	35
6:37	149, 218
6:64–72	243
7:2–5	73
7:7	185
7:12	205
7:37–39	35
8	237
8:14	63
8:32	49
8:40	195
8:44	195
8:48	195
9	182
9:22	195
9:39–41	221
10:35	43
12	182
12:25	192
12:32	150
12:40	97
12:42	195
13:1	217
13:34	146
13:34–35	188
13:35	233
14:15	188
14:21–24	188
15	239
15:1–6	169, 220
15:6	45, 241
15:9	162, 163
15:10	163
15:12–13	188
15:21	179
16:30	207
16:33	191
17:3	49
17:5	115
17:12	56, 95
17:15	218
17:24	115
19:11	87
19:34–37	51
21	41, 131
21:17	207

Acts

1:6	225
1:7	63
1:14	154
1:15–16	73
1:22	32
2	36
2:4	51
2:5	185
2:9	106, 185
2:14	73
2:19	15
2:22	15
2:23	114
2:32–36	74
2:38	34, 35
2:38–39	51
2:43	15
3:1	73
3:11	73
3:19	31
4:1	73
4:11	115
4:13	73, 105
4:23	73
4:31	36
5:1–11	36
5:3–5	73
5:17	82, 138
5:31	31
5:41	179
6	72, 187
6:5	187
6:6	32
6:7	7
7	7
7–9	195
7:6	108
7:30	16
7:35	16
7:38	16

281

Acts (*continued*)

Reference	Page
7:38–42	19
7:39	66
7:51–57	74
7:52	60
7:53	16
7:55–60	6
8	242
8:14	73
8:17–19	32
8:20	35
8:25	145
9:17–18	32
10:34	120
10:45	35
11:15–18	35, 51
11:18	31, 149
11:26	116
11:28	72, 218
12:1	108
12:1–5	108
12:17	73
13–14	195
13:3	32
13:5	72
13:14f	72
13:15	8
13:24	31
13:40–41	21
13:43	72
13:45	82, 194
13:48	149
13:50	108
14:5	51
14:5–6	108
14:15	22, 31, 87, 123
14:19	7, 108
14:27	217
15	76, 91, 200, 241, 245
15:13–21	73
15:19	123
15:19–29	75
15:19–39	45
15:20	63
15:28–29	207
15:29	63
15:36–39	91
16:14	184
16:19–24	108
17:5–10	195
17:6	218
17:30	31
18	3
18:2	4
18:5–6	194
18:7	47
18:10	108
18:12–17	196
18:19–21	185
18:19–20:28	184
18:26	72
19	185
19–20	182
19:4	31
19:6	32
19:8	72
19:23–34	7
19:29–31	108
20	132, 200, 235
20:20	31, 56
20:21	32
20:27	56
20:28	14
20:28–32	138, 186
20:29	77
20:31	128
20:33	222
21	76, 91, 244
21:17–18	71, 73
21:18–24	73
21:20	226
21:20–21	43, 94
21:20–24	91, 139
21:28	50
21:29	184
22:16	136
22:19	72
24:5	138
24:6	62
24:17	72
26:5	138
26:11	72, 194
26:18	34, 123
26:20	32
26:28	116
26:29	123
27:16	4
28:14	4

Romans

1	122
1:5	114
1:7	162
1:16	124, 225, 237
1:17	55, 92
1:18	160
1:18–32	200, 240
2:1–16	241
2:3	16
2:4	149
2:6	92, 120, 185, 207
2:11	120
3:1–2	43
3:8	155
3:28	93
4:2–3	93
4:3	93
4:6	93
5	80, 122
5:3	55, 124
5:3–5	78, 104
5:12–20	80
5:15	35
6:1	155, 159
6:12–19	145
6:16	83, 139
6:16–23	134
6:20–23	139
6:23	31
7:14–25	81
7:23	121
8:4–13	121
8:9	51
8:9–14	35
8:18–39	104
8:29–30	149
8:35	238
9–11	103, 225, 235, 242
9:22	56, 141
9:32–33	117
9:33	115
10:3	9
10:17	15, 25
11	41, 225
11:7–8	190
11:11	87, 189
11:16	82
11:17–24	169
11:20–22	236
11:22	25, 189
11:25–27	225
11:26	226
11:32	150
11:33	207
12:2	120
12:3	135
12:12	124
12:14	60
12:17–21	126
13:12	48, 55
14	241
14:4	22, 46, 89
14:10	120, 241
14:12	120
14:14	92
14:15	161
14:23	46, 236
15:3	54
15:4	159
15:4–5	78
15:6	124
15:15	189
15:19	15
15:26	72

1 Corinthians

1:1–9	113, 162
1:8–9	126
1:8	79
1:9	46
1:12	131
1:18	161
1:23	117
2:10	207
2:16	78
3:1–3	31
3:5–7	63
3:16	83
3:10–15	45
3:10–17	120
3:17	164
4:4	120
4:4–5	241
5	103, 235
5–6	240
5:1–5	187
5:5	41, 70, 242

283

1 Corinthians (continued)

5:6	83
6:2–19	83
6:3	208
6:9–10	148, 240, 241
6:9–20	63
6:11	136
6:12–20	187, 200
6:20	139
7	241
7:1	187
7:12–16	201
7:19	146
7:22	182
7:23	139
7:39	201, 241
8	186, 241
8–10	45, 91, 200, 240, 245
8:9	21
8:11	161
8:13	199
9:1–2	73
9:5	131, 154
9:13–24	83
9:24–27	57, 104, 197
9:25	197
9:27	45, 88
10	173, 240, 241
10:1–11	19
10:1–12	12, 161, 162
10:2	34
10:4	160
10:5	56
10:7–8	166
10:9	160
10:10	167
10:12	21, 66, 189
10:12–13	173
10:13	46, 126
11:19	138
11:29–32	206
12:3	194
12:4–11	36
12:8–13	124
12:9	135
12:13	35, 51
15	32, 65
15:1	189
15:1–3	210
15:2	25
15:3	146
15:7	73
15:25–26	81
15:32	184
16:9	217
16:13	154

2 Corinthians

1:3–7	104
1:18	46
2:5–7	41
2:5–8	103, 242
2:11	128
4:4–6	34
5:10	92, 120, 185, 207, 241
5:17	25
6:10	194
6:14	201, 241
7:9–10	149
8:9	194
9:13	124
9:14f	35
11	237
11:1–14	186, 196
11:15	207, 241
11:25–26	108
11:25–29	238
11:26	19
11:29	238
12:2	116
12:20	238
12:21	158
13:1–2	242
13:13–14	35

Galatians

1:6	159
1:10	182
1:11–12	3
1:13	60
1:17	145
1:18–19	71
1:19	73
2	75, 76, 91, 241
2:1	73
2:1–9	75
2:1–15	75

2:1–16	43, 73, 91
2:4	59, 138
2:6	93
2:9	71, 73, 170, 217
2:10	72, 91
2:12	55, 73
2:13	151
2:16	92
2:20	217
3:5	15
3:10	45
3:11	55
3:13	139
3:19	16
3:23	154
3:27–28	25
4:9	97, 145
4:30	59, 242
5:4	61, 151
5:6	92
5:10	46
5:11	117
5:15	21, 103
5:17	121
5:19	158
5:19–21	238, 240, 241
5:20	138
6:1	42, 70, 242
6:1–5	91, 103
6:1–6	96
6:2	146

Ephesians

1:1	184
1:1–14	115
1:4	115
1:13–14	35
1:17	136
2:1	168
2:1–6	148
2:1–3	168
2:5	31, 168
2:11	182, 189
2:12	109
2:19	109
2:20	115
3:7	35
4–5	240
4:1	142
4:7	35
4:13	78
4:14	167
4:19	158
4:20–24	58
4:22–24	171
4:27	128
5:3–5	240
5:5	222, 232
5:8	34
5:26	136
5:27	169
6:6	182
6:8	120
6:9	120
6:17	201

Philippians

1:1–6	162
1:1–11	113
1:10	79
1:12–13	173
1:28	56
2:1	35
2:15	149
3:2	147
3:6	60
3:10	123
3:18–19	56
3:19	141, 241
3:20	62, 109
4:3	211, 213
4:9	210

Colossians

1:13	34
1:15–18	4
1:22	149
1:22–23	25
2	241
2:1	184, 219
2:2	46
2:6–7	169
2:8–10	4
2:12	32
2:13	168
2:13–23	8
2:16–23	4

Ancient Sources Index

Colossians (*continued*)

2:18	155
2:19	197
2:20–23	200
3	240
3:1	182
3:5	222, 232
3:5–7	63
3:8–10	58
3:24f	241
3:25	120
4:12	182
4:13	219
4:13–16	184
4:15–16	219

1 Thessalonians

1:3	92
1:5	46
1:5–10	189
1:9	22, 31, 123, 148
2:2	51
2:9	189
2:13	43, 210
2:14	104
2:14–16	195
2:19	63
3:3	83
3:4	83
3:5	124, 128
4:1	142
4:1–2	189
4:1–8	63
4:2	83
4:3–8	200
4:5	142
5:1–9	134, 208
5:3	16
5:6–8	128
5:19	97
5:23	78, 161
5:23–24	162
5:24	46

2 Thessalonians

1:4	55
1:4–10	126
2	235
2:1–3	134
2:3	56, 134, 141, 214
2:6	83
2:8	134, 202, 214
2:11	167
2:13	35, 162
2:13–15	173
3:3	46

1 Timothy

1:1	235
1:3	182, 184
1:9	62
1:13	9
1:19	14, 170
1:19–20	242
2:4	49, 136
2:4–6	150
2:8–10	188
2:9	222
3:15	217
4	241
4:1	21, 138
4:1–4	138
4:1–5	8, 186, 200
4:1–6	186
4:3	49
4:7	62
4:10	150
4:14	32
4:16	94
6:6–10	6, 188
6:9	77
6:9–10	222, 232
6:14	146
6:17	188
6:17–19	232
6:20	63

2 Timothy

1:8	124
1:12	124
1:15	66
1:16	124
1:18	184
2:4	145
2:12	158, 197, 221
2:14–15	211

2:15	124, 197	2:1–4	6, 12, 13, 18, 19, 30, 53, 66, 67, 210, 239
2:16	63	2:2	12, 16
2:24–26	41, 103, 242	2:2–4	12, 36
2:25	49, 149	2:3	13–16, 36
2:26	145	2:3–4	3, 36
3:1–3	135	2:3–5	12
3:1–5	138	2:4	6, 15, 18, 51
3:1–6	186	2:5	15, 16
3:4	83	2:5–8	12, 17
3:7	49	2:5–9	15, 17
3:8	45	2:5–13	13, 16, 68
3:13	95, 142, 167	2:5–18	8
3:16	43	2:5–4:13	11
4:8	197	2:9	15, 18, 35, 61
4:10	47	2:9–10	58
4:12	184	2:9–13	62
4:14	185, 207	2:10	17, 24, 27
4:17	127	2:10–13	17, 18
4:21	133	2:11	15, 18
		2:11–12	5, 17

Titus

1:1	136	2:11–13	18, 25
1:15	61	2:11–17	25
1:16	45, 158	2:12	6, 17
2:11	150	2:13	6, 18, 59, 60
3:3	9	2:14	58
3:5	35, 136	2:14–15	15
3:10	138, 242	2:14–17	28
		2:14–18	25
		2:17	5, 9, 15, 64
		2:18	17

Philemon

2	47	3–4	4, 18, 23, 26, 29, 33, 37, 38, 49, 57, 64, 68, 161, 162, 173, 236, 259
		3:1	5, 8, 18, 25, 35, 47, 59, 60

Hebrews

1	3, 5, 50	3:1–5	25
1:1	17	3:2–6	18
1:1–14	8	3:6	10, 13, 14, 23, 25, 26, 55, 60
1:1–2:4	11		
1:2	12, 47	3:7	19, 23, 26
1:3	15, 36	3:7–11	6, 19, 21
1:5	12	3:7–4:11	12
1:5–13	6	3:7–4:13	6, 19
1:6	16, 62	3:8	20, 29, 62
1:13	6, 39, 50	3:10	20, 24, 29, 34, 142
1:14	12, 15, 17, 47, 64, 59, 122	3:11	21, 22, 27, 38, 41
2:1	8, 10, 12, 13, 14, 23, 26, 29, 33, 49	3:12	5, 10, 19, 21, 22, 23, 25, 26, 61, 66
2:1–3	6, 12, 14, 48		

Hebrews (continued)

Reference	Pages
3:12–14	10, 19
3:13	24, 26, 39, 48, 50, 57, 68
3:13–14	23
3:14	13, 14, 24–26, 35, 48, 68
3:15	19, 23, 26, 62
3:15–16	29
3:16	62
3:16–19	12, 33
3:17	23, 24, 29, 34
3:17–19	23
3:18	27
3:19	26
4–6	262
4:1	6, 10, 13, 14, 18, 26, 27, 36, 53, 61, 67, 142
4:1–11	10
4:2	15, 23, 31, 201
4:2–3	23, 26, 68
4:3	19, 22, 24, 27, 41
4:3–10	28
4:3–11	27
4:4	5, 28
4:5	27, 41
4:6	23
4:7	19, 23, 26
4:7–11	52
4:8–11	27
4:9	20
4:10	28, 39
4:10–11	24
4:11	10, 13, 21, 23, 26, 28, 189
4:12	15, 22
4:13	13
4:14	13, 47
4:14–16	8, 24, 58
4:14–5:10	8
4:14–10:39	11
4:15	9
4:16	10, 13, 23, 25
5:2	8, 9, 49
5:7	54, 67
5:7–10	58
5:8–9	23
5:9	17, 36
5:11	31, 46, 48, 67
5:11–12	6, 26
5:11–14	30
5:11–6:6	210
5:11–6:12	6, 13, 30, 239
5:12	31, 32, 67
5:12–14	31
5:12–6:3	5
5:12–6:12	68
6	40, 262
6:1	8, 13, 31
6:1–2	32–34
6:1–3	31, 33
6:1–4	37
6:1–5	37
6:2	32, 35
6:3	33
6:4	25, 33–35, 51, 54
6:4–5	12
6:4–6	33, 34, 36, 37, 39–42, 68, 103, 242, 259, 262
6:4–8	12, 16, 18, 68, 169
6:5	15, 36
6:6	22, 29, 31, 33, 38, 64
6:7	12
6:7–8	29, 32, 45, 62, 69
6:7–12	45
6:8	39, 45, 48, 63
6:9	5, 15
6:9–10	241
6:9–11	56
6:9–12	46
6:10	47
6:10–12	12
6:11	25, 46, 48
6:11–12	6
6:12	36, 48, 59, 64, 67, 122
6:13–10:18	8
6:17	12
6:18	38
6:18–19	8
6:18–20	10
6:19	10, 14
7–10	58
7:3	5
7:11	12
7:12	66
7:16	26
7:16–28	9
7:19	12, 65
7:20	26
7:22	10

Ancient Sources Index

7:23–25	10	10:24	47
7:25	8, 10, 15	10:24–25	39, 47, 48
7:27	38	10:24–26	24
7:28	17	10:25	6, 17, 23, 25, 41, 46, 47, 52, 67, 239
8–9	4		
8–10	5	10:25–30	18
8:1–5	18	10:26	22, 38, 39, 41, 48–50, 56, 57, 64, 136, 242
8:5	15		
8:7–13	6, 12	10:26–29	38, 42, 51, 56, 57, 69
8:9	15	10:26–31	10, 12, 48
8:12	8, 9	10:27	15, 49, 52, 53, 67
8:17–18	18	10:27–31	48, 52
9:7	9, 34, 49	10:28	52
9:9	38, 49	10:28–29	52
9:10	32	10:29	10, 15, 35–37, 39, 40, 50–53, 61
9:11	12, 17		
9:11–10:18	12, 32	10:29–30	49
9:12	38, 50	10:30–31	45, 53
9:13	49	10:31	22, 53, 67
9:13–14	50	10:32	33, 34
9:14	9, 22	10:32–34	53, 67
9:15	35, 59, 64	10:32–35	189
9:20	50	10:32–34	4–6, 8, 47, 48, 54, 57, 59, 194
9:26	9, 12, 38, 58		
9:26–28	15, 39, 55	10:32–39	54, 67
9:26–29	34	10:35	8, 10, 11, 16, 46, 48, 50, 54
9:28	9, 12, 38		
10:1	12, 15	10:35–36	12, 55, 57
10:2	34, 38, 49	10:35–39	42, 56, 57, 69
10:4	38	10:36	78, 120
10:5–8	6	10:36–39	48, 68, 79
10:6	56	10:37	52
10:7–10	55	10:37–38	25, 55, 255
10:8	56	10:38	56, 65
10:10	9, 15, 38, 65	10:38b	259
10:11	38	10:38–39	33, 46, 48, 50, 241
10:13	50	10:39	53, 62, 141
10:14	15, 17, 38, 65	11	4, 8, 55, 57
10:14–17	8, 10	11:1	24, 46
10:16	10	11:1–12:29	11
10:16–17	9	11:4–12:2	24
10:19	5, 8, 25, 50	11:6	24, 31, 38, 46, 56
10:19–22	23, 46	11:7	67
10:19–23	24, 46	11:7–8	64
10:19–31	40	11:7–38	6
10:19–39	6, 69	11:8	4, 15, 23, 59
10:22	10, 49	11:9	4
10:22–24	13	11:10	12, 65
10:23	25, 46, 47	11:13–16	4

289

Ancient Sources Index

Hebrews (continued)

11:15	66
11:15–16	57
11:16	12, 17, 57
11:20	15, 64
11:23–28	54
11:24–27	48
11:25	58, 63
11:25–26	64
11:26	4, 12, 16, 160
11:31	23
11:32	3
11:35	65
11:34–40	46
11:36–38	5
11:38	4, 15
11:39–40	65
11:40	17
12	6, 18, 59, 66, 241
12:1	8, 13, 57, 58, 78, 145
12:1–2	11, 27, 28
12:1–3	55
12:1–13	57
12:1–28	69
12:1–29	6
12:2	24, 47
12:2–3	17
12:2–4	48, 58, 67
12:3	4
12:4	28
12:5–6	14
12:5–11	59
12:6–8	221
12:8	26, 59
12:10	15
12:10–11	59
12:12	29
12:12–13	60
12:14	60
12:14–16	58
12:14–17	60
12:15	21, 23, 28, 61, 62, 68
12:15–17	16, 26, 242
12:16	58, 62, 63, 68, 200
12:16–17	33, 38, 60, 61
12:17	22, 31, 38, 39, 41, 56, 63, 64, 70, 122
12:14–21	65
12:18–29	64
12:20–21	14, 120
12:21	53, 67
12:22	45, 57, 65
12:22–24	10, 60, 66
12:22–28	29
12:23	60, 62, 64, 211
12:24	32
12:25	13, 14, 21, 66
12:25–26	66
12:25–29	12, 45, 68
12:26	6, 34
12:26–28	12
12:27	66
12:28	13–15, 54, 61, 64, 67
12:28–29	18, 29
12:29	6, 45, 66
13:2	6, 222
13:3	4, 6, 8, 48, 67
13:4–5	60
13:4	62, 63, 70, 240
13:5	6–10, 46, 232
13:6	6, 54
13:7	4, 6, 15, 65
13:9	29
13:9–10	7
13:11–14	4
13:12	9
13:13	6, 8, 13, 18, 48, 67
13:14	12, 15, 29, 48, 65
13:15	13
13:16	6
13:17	23
13:19	3, 24
13:20–21	9
13:21	55
13:22	5, 24
13:23	5, 6, 8, 14
13:24	5

James

1:1	71–75, 94f, 103
1:2	79
1:2–4	77–80, 95f, 103f
1:2–11	77
1:3	92
1:4–8	86
1:5	79
1:5–8	77, 84–89
1:5–11	79

1:6	92	2:22	78, 92
1:8	84	2:23	71, 93
1:9–11	72, 77, 79, 86f, 89f, 96	2:24	93
1:10	197	2:26	92
1:11	75	3:1	72, 77, 88, 96
1:12	72, 77, 79, 89	3:1–2	72, 78, 88, 104
1:12–15	77, 79f, 86. 104	3:1–6	104
1:12–19	79, 81	3:1–18	84–89
1:13	84	3:2	87
1:13–16	80–84, 95, 103	3:3	148
1:14	80, 140	3:3–6	88
1:15	80, 82, 89	3:6	75, 82f, 85, 88
1:15–18	86, 104	3:7–12	88
1:16	89, 95, 104	3:9	88
1:17	78, 84, 96	3:11–12	71
1:17–19	81f	3:12	75
1:18	82f, 86, 93, 96	3:13	71, 75, 89
1:19–21	86	3:13–17	83f, 86, 96, 103
1:19–27	84–89	3:14–18	77, 84, 86, 96
1:20	86	3:14–4:6	104
1:21–22	82, 86, 93	3:15	83
1:22–25	75, 77, 86, 89	4:1	21, 71, 82, 121
1:25	75, 77f, 86f	4:1–2	84
1:26–27	72, 83, 85–87, 89, 92	4:1–4	75, 81
2:1	72, 75, 92	4:1–5	79–84
2:1–13	72, 86, 89–91	4:1–10	77, 86, 103
2:1–14	72	4:2	82, 90
2:2–3	72, 75, 89	4:4	71, 77, 83–85
2:4–7	71	4:4–5	71
2:5	89, 92, 96	4:4–10	83, 85, 88
2:6–7	77, 89, 104	4:5	80
2:8	71	4:5–7	80
2:8–12	75, 86, 93, 103	4:6	71, 90
2:9–11	104	4:6–10	84
2:10	87	4:7	80, 83
2:10–13	90	4:7–10	81, 88, 104
2:11	71, 83, 90	4:8	84–89
2:12	72, 82f, 90, 92	4:11	75, 86, 103
2:13	77, 89f	4:11–12	84–90
2:14	71, 92	4:11–17	84, 95, 104
2:14–26	75f, 86, 91–94	4:12	82, 87, 89, 104
2:15–16	75, 89	4:13–17	89f
2:16	71	4:14	71
2:17–20	92	4:15	89
2:18	94	4:15–17	90
2:19	92	4:17	89
2:20	71, 94	5:1	87
2:21	93	5:1–6	72, 77, 86, 89f, 104
2:21–25	75, 93	5:3	72

Ancient Sources Index

James (continued)

5:4	75
5:5	72
5:6	71, 81f
5:7–9	72, 75, 78, 83
5:7–11	86, 96, 103
5:9	78, 87, 89
5:10	78
5:11	75, 78f, 90
5:12	75, 84–89, 104
5:12–16	94
5:13–14	71, 78
5:13–19	72, 96
5:14	72, 75, 78, 96
5:15–16	78, 89, 92, 94f
5:15–20	82
5:16	78, 95
5:17	75
5:19–20	9, 20, 41f, 70, 78–80, 82f, 85f, 94–97, 103f, 145, 167, 205

1 Peter

1:1	4, 74, 105–110, 113–119, 130, 133, 182
1:1–5	112f, 117, 119, 129
1:2	114, 118
1:2–3	116
1:3	110, 114, 125
1:3–12	113
1:4	112, 122, 125
1:4–5	161
1:5	113f, 119, 125f
1:5–9	116
1:6–7	77, 110–13, 123–27, 221
1:6–9	130
1:7–9	125
1:8	125
1:9	113f, 120, 121
1:10–12	112, 118
1:10–19	112–18
1:11	115, 123–27
1:13	125, 128
1:13–19	130
1:13–21	112–14, 118–22
1:14	107, 112, 118–21, 136
1:15	111, 119
1:15–16	111f, 118, 120
1:17	107, 111f, 119f, 126, 130, 185, 207
1:18	107, 112f, 119, 127, 136
1:18–19	115
1:18–21	120, 214
1:19	112, 118
1:20	114f
1:21	113, 118f, 125
1:22	118, 121
1:22–2:3	120
1:23	107, 110, 114, 116
1:23–25	116, 120
2:1	113, 120–22
2:1–9	129
2:2	109, 110, 113f
2:2–3	35, 116, 120
2:4	115
2:4–9	116
2:4–10	117, 118
2:5	107, 117f
2:5–9	107, 112f
2:6	114f, 118f
2:7	118f
2:8	116–18, 120
2:8–9	115
2:9	115, 118, 120
2:9–10	107, 115, 116
2:9–11	110–12
2:9–12	34, 111
2:11	4, 107–10, 114, 118–23, 130, 240
2:11–12	119, 121
2:12	115, 118, 119, 121
2:12–18	129
2:12–3:6	130
2:13–14	110
2:14–15	118
2:16	122
2:17	130
2:17–18	110, 117, 120
2:18–20	110
2:18–21	129, 238
2:19–20	108, 123
2:20	118, 123–27
2:21	123
2:21–25	115, 130
2:22–25	122f
2:23	123

2:24	105
2:25	9, 95, 117, 121–123, 238
3	241
3:1	111, 118f, 121, 129
3:1–2	119
3:1–6	201
3:1–9	110
3:3	110
3:5	118
3:6	107, 111, 118, 125
3:7	112, 114, 122
3:9–12	114, 118–22
3:11	111
3:10–12	122
3:13	129
3:14	123
3:14–15	54, 111, 118
3:15	118, 125
3:16	119
3:16–17	107–110, 114–118, 121, 123–27
3:17	118, 123, 125, 130
3:18	123
3:18–20	122
3:21	34, 148
4:1	113, 123
4:1–2	124
4:1–4	121
4:1–5	240
4:1–6	129
4:2–4	107–112
4:2–6	240
4:3–4	110, 131, 182
4:4	121
4:4–6	128
4:5	113, 120, 126
4:6	122
4:7	112f, 125
4:8	97
4:10–11	124
4:12	77, 110–13
4:12–13	123
4:12–14	123
4:12–16	130
4:12–19	123–27, 238
4:13	114, 123, 125
4:14	114–18, 124, 179
4:14–16	121
4:14–19	129
4:15	108, 109, 121, 123, 124
4:16	114–119, 124, 129, 185
4:17	117, 119, 126, 128
4:17–18	130
4:17–19	119f, 126
4:18	120, 126
4:19	118f, 121, 123, 126
5	109
5:1	123, 125
5:2	117, 128
5:4	123
5:4–6	112–14, 120, 197
5:6	113, 125
5:8	113f, 119, 124, 127, 128
5:8–10	111, 113, 119, 123, 127–129, 130
5:9	108, 113, 117, 119, 128
5:9–10	130
5:10	112f, 115f, 125, 128
5:12	106, 110–13, 125, 130, 133
5:13	106, 114–18, 116
5:14	110, 115, 117, 129

2 Peter

1	136, 142
1:1	133, 135, 150
1:1–5	144, 148
1:1–10	135
1:1–11	162
1:2–3	136
1:3	150
1:3–4	139, 144, 152
1:4	144
1:5	136, 157
1:5–10	135, 140, 148
1:5–13	152
1:8	136
1:9	136, 148
1:10	22, 137, 157
1:11	137
1:12	151
1:12–13	136, 189
1:13	142
1:15–19	138
1:16	78
1:16–18	133
1:16–19	137
1:16–21	134

Ancient Sources Index

2 Peter (*continued*)

Reference	Pages
1:20–21	137
1:23	169
2	134, 136, 137, 162, 196
2:1	134, 137–39, 141–44, 148, 152, 158, 161
2:2	139
2:1–3	56, 132, 137
2:1–3:4	132, 151
2:1–22	138
2:2	135, 140, 142
2:3	139–41, 152
2:3–6	152
2:3–10	134
2:4	132, 163
2:4–6	141
2:4–7	141
2:4–8	160
2:4–9	150
2:4–10	141
2:5	142
2:5–6	135, 160
2:5–8	135
2:6	132, 139
2:7	142
2:7–8	136, 142
2:8	142
2:9	137, 139, 141, 152
2:10	147
2:10–11	134
2:10–12	132, 164
2:11–19	142
2:12	144, 147, 148, 161
2:12–13	139, 141
2:13	120, 132, 151,
2:14	45, 136, 139, 140, 143, 149, 151, 152
2:15	20, 132, 139, 142, 144, 145, 152, 173, 199, 205
2:15–16	166
2:16	135, 147
2:17	132, 141
2:18	132, 135, 136, 139, 140, 143, 144, 149, 152
2:18–19	144
2:18–20	144
2:18–22	137
2:19	134, 135, 139, 144
2:19–22	135
2:20	143–45, 146
2:20–21	136. 144
2:20–22	135, 137, 143, 144, 147, 148, 152
2:21	134, 135, 141, 142, 145, 146
2:22	50, 146, 147, 192, 219
2:24	97
2:25	205
3	134
3:1	108, 132, 133, 136, 149, 150, 189
3:1–3	132
3:1–4	134, 138, 140, 152
3:1–9	138
3:1–13	139, 149
3:2	43, 132, 133, 146
3:3	135, 147
3:3–4	133
3:3–7	152, 164
3:5–7	66
3:6–7	150
3:7	56, 135, 141, 150, 160
3:8	149, 150
3:8–9	145, 152
3:9	31, 134, 141, 149, 150, 161
3:10	208
3:10–11	134
3:10–12	152
3:10–13	141
3:10–15	137
3:11–12	149
3:12	149
3:13–14	134
3:14	149, 150
3:15	131, 133, 134, 150, 151, 153
3:15–16	76, 94, 132, 152
3:15–17	149, 238
3:16	56, 136, 140, 141, 151, 152
3:16–17	156, 186
3:17	135, 137, 144, 150, 151, 153
3:17–18	150, 152
3:18	135, 140

1 John

1:8	142
1:9	189
2:10	188
2:15	83
2:15–16	220
2:15–17	222, 240
2:18–24	40, 238
2:19	148, 161, 162, 243, 247
2:21	49
2:26	20, 95, 205
2:28	241
3–4	239
3:2	60
3:7	95, 205
3:10–11	188
3:11	166
3:12	185
3:14	168
3:15–16	132
3:16–18	222
3:16–23	188
3:17	235
3:17–18	188
3:23	146
4:1–6	186
4:6	205
4:7–12	188
5:1	188
5:2	146
5:4–5	191
5:16	96, 103, 242
5:16–18	40
5:20	238

2 John

1	49
5	188
6	146
7	171
7–9	238
8	21
8–11	186
9	151
10–11	222

3 John

5–8	222

Jude

1	73, 161, 162, 164, 173
3	146, 154, 156, 157
3–4	155–57, 172
4	132, 138–40, 154, 155, 156, 158, 159, 162
4–6	152
5	139, 141, 154, 159, 160–63, 167–69, 189
5–8	157
5–10	155, 160
5–19	160
6	162–164, 168–170
6–7	132, 141
6–8	156, 158, 164
7	164, 169, 173, 200, 241
8	61, 164, 165, 171
8–10	132, 155, 156, 164, 172
8–16	156
9	170
10	147, 156, 164, 167
10–12	165
11	142, 161, 162, 165, 166, 169, 172, 173, 199, 205, 241
11–13	132, 152, 156
11–16	157
12	156, 158, 162, 166, 168–70, 172
12–13	168, 169, 171, 173
13	167, 169, 170
13–15	170, 173, 241
14	168
14–15	159, 161, 164, 168, 170–172
15	167
15–16	159
16	132, 165, 167, 170, 172
17	156, 171
17–18	132, 154
18	159, 164
19	169, 170
20	156, 170
20–21	171
20–22	165
20–23	170

Ancient Sources Index

Jude (continued)

21	162, 164, 168, 170, 172, 173
21–22	70
21–23	103, 171
22	170, 171
22–23	41, 42, 96, 103, 149, 152, 156, 157, 159, 162, 164, 170, 171, 173, 242
23	169, 171–73
24	137, 141, 149, 164, 168, 172, 173
24–25	161, 162, 172

Revelation

1	194
1–3	176, 182, 214, 215
1:1	175, 176,
1:3	189, 218
1:5	46, 217
1:6	197, 208, 221
1:7	51, 189
1:7–12	177
1:9	175, 180, 191, 218
1:10	175
1:11	175,
1:12–13	189
1:12–18	176
1:14–15	207
1:16	201
1:18	191
1:19	223
1:20	189, 227
2	181, 188, 240
2–3	4, 16, 70, 179, 183, 193, 198, 203, 223, 241
2:1	175, 176, 189, 207
2:1–6	184
2:1–7	230
2:2	78, 185, 188, 218
2:2–3	185, 189
2:3	78
2:4	187, 233
2:4–5	6, 42, 136
2:5	185, 188, 189, 190, 191, 193, 220
2:6	186, 199
2:7	183, 190, 191–93, 202, 203
2:8–11	194, 231
2:9	179, 183, 194, 198, 217, 218, 220
2:9–10	180, 196
2:10	194, 196, 197, 218
2:10–11	192
2:11	168, 190, 191, 193, 197, 218
2:12	201
2:12–17	197
2:12–29	231
2:13	158, 179, 180, 193, 197, 207
2:14	166, 182, 183, 186, 187, 199
2:14–15	199
2:15	186, 187, 191, 201
2:16	193, 202, 208, 218
2:17	191, 193, 202, 203, 218
2:18	207
2:18–29	205
2:19	78, 185
2:20	20, 95, 142, 182, 183, 186, 200, 205
2:20–23	205
2:21	63, 149, 191
2:21–22	206
2:22	206
2:22–23	206
2:23	183, 185, 205, 207
2:24	183, 207
2:25–26	207
2:26	191, 195
2:26–28	193
2:26–29	207
2:29	190
3:1	185, 191, 192, 209, 218
3:1–2	136, 211
3:1–3	42, 208
3:1–6	208, 231
3:2	209
3:2–3	208
3:3	193, 210
3:4	171, 210, 221
3:4–5	192
3:5	62, 191, 193, 211, 212, 214–16, 218

Ancient Sources Index

3:6	190	7:9	210, 225
3:7–8	216	7:9–14	150, 177
3:7–13	183, 216, 213	7:9–17	225, 229
3:8	185	7:13	210
3:9	179, 194, 217	7:13–14	210
3:10	55, 185, 216, 218	7:14	126, 206
3:11	196, 207, 218	8:2	183
3:11–12	192	8:3	182
3:12	191, 193, 218	8:4	182
3:12–13	217	8:13	213, 218
3:13	190	9:1	227
3:14–15	136	9:1–4	218
3:14–21	219	9:4	226
3:14–22	219, 230	9:4–8	225
3:15	185	9:11	227
3:15–16	219	9:20–21	192, 216
3:16	219	9:21	183
3:16–19	6, 42	10:10–11	183
3:17	220f	10:11	175, 216
3:18–19	221	11	177, 227
3:19	191, 221	11–13	180
3:20	215, 222	11:1–2	228
3:20–21	221, 222	11:1–3	183
3:21	191, 193, 208, 221	11:2	50
3:22	190	11:2–7	228
4–22	182, 205, 214, 223, 224	11:3	216
4:1	218, 223	11:7	224
4:1–22:5	177	11:10	175, 213, 218
5:2	183	11:13	216
5:5–10	191	11:18	175, 176, 182, 193
5:6	207	12	198, 224, 227, 232
5:8	182	12–13	179
5:9	139	12:3–4	195, 198, 227
5:10	197, 221	12:4	227, 228
5:11	183	12:4–5	228
6–16	125, 218	12:6	179
6–19	206	12:7	191
6:3–4	202	12:7–9	227
6:9	191	12:9	196, 205, 207, 218, 228
6:9–11	65, 177, 180, 228	12:10–11	227
6:10	213, 218	12:10–17	195, 198
6:11	210	12:11	191, 192, 196, 228
6:12–14	66	12:12	218
6:12–17	226	12:13	228
7	223–225, 232	12:13–17	129
7:1–3	218, 226	12:14–17	179, 228
7:3	182	12:17	190, 191, 228
7:4	225	13	177, 198, 201, 218, 223, 227, 232
7:4–8	183, 224, 225		

Ancient Sources Index

Reference	Pages	Reference	Pages
13:1–18	179, 228	17:14	137, 191, 192, 218
13:2	198	17:16	220
13:7	182, 191, 224, 228	18:3	200, 205
13:8	211, 213, 214, 218, 224	18:3–5	224
13:9–10	224	18:4	181, 182, 224
13:10	182, 202, 228	18:6	207, 224
13:11–17	180	18:7	220
13:13–17	224	18:9	300
13:14	142, 205, 207, 213	18:20	182
13:16–17	220	18:21	183
14	223, 224	18:23	94, 207
14–17	179	18:24	175, 182, 228
14:1	65	19	181, 200, 210
14:1–5	225, 226	19:2	182, 200, 205
14:2	183	19:5	176, 182
14:3–4	139	19:7–9	203, 222
14:4	82, 210, 225	19:8	221
14:5	227	19:10	183, 191
14:6–7	216	19:11–12	202
14:7	176	19:11–21	191
14:8	106, 183, 205	19:12	218
14:9	179	19:13	210
14:9–12	224, 228	19:15	201, 202
14:10	183	19:20	179, 197, 205, 214
14:12	182, 192	19:20–21	200
14:13	185	19:21	201, 202
14:18	183	20	45
15:2	179, 191, 192	20–21	241
15:4	176	20–22	176, 193
16:1	183	20:3	205, 207
16:2	179	20:4	179, 191, 202, 221, 228
16:3	138	20:6	169, 197, 221
16:6	175, 182	20:7–10	195, 198
16:9	106, 216	20:8	195, 205, 207
16:10	198, 218	20:9	182
16:11	216	20:10	67, 88, 195, 205, 207, 209, 214
16:14	218	20:10–15	213
16:15	208, 210	20:11–15	185, 224
16:18–21	66	20:12	159, 213
17	201	20:12–13	32, 92, 185, 207
17–18	205, 223, 232	20:12–15	211
17:2	200, 205, 213, 218	20:14	168, 169, 197
17:3	106	20:15–20	211, 213
17:5	106, 201	21:1–2	65, 66
17:6	179, 182, 224, 228	21:2	218
17:8	56, 211, 213–16, 218, 224	21:4	193
17:9	106, 225	21:7	191, 192, 217
17:9–11	177	21:7–8	190, 192, 193, 224, 230
17:11	56		

… *Ancient Sources Index*

21:8	168, 181, 183, 192, 193, 197, 206, 209, 224, 240
21:10–27	183
21:11	190
21:14	175
21:17	50
21:23	211
21:27	181, 211, 213
22:1–3	193
22:1–5	193
22:3	182
22:4	60, 218
22:5	221
22:6	175, 182
22:8–9	183
22:9	175, 183
22:11	39, 191
22:12	120, 207
22:14	210
22:14–15	224, 230
22:15	147, 181, 183, 190, 192
22:16	175
22:18	230
22:18–19	43, 212, 229, 232
22:19	229

PSEUDEPIGRAPHIC SOURCES

Apocalypse of Elijah
4.2	126

Apocalypse of Ezra
6.17	197

Aristeas, Letter of
166	61

Assumption of Moses
10.8–10	227

2 Baruch
3.20	65
4.2	65
4.8	20
6.10–14	163
9.2	126
11.1	106
13.8–11	126
13.9–11	126
21.20–21	149
24.1	159, 213
27.1–15	218
28.3	126
29.8	203
44.15	67
48.30–41	125
48.42–43	80
67.2	50
70	218
75.5	126
78.5–7	225
78–86	132
78.1–7	112
84–85	112
85.1–9	101
85.12	39, 63

1 Enoch
1.1	160
1.5	163
1.9	159, 160, 170
5.4	21
6.2	163
10.4	19
10.7–15	163
10.21	217
10.22	144
14.3	163
16.2	163
18.13–16	170
18.14	227
20.5	183
21.3–6	170, 227
22.3–9	65
37	218
38.2	126, 159
43.1–4	227
45.3	221
46.7–8	227

Ancient Sources Index

1 Enoch (continued)

47.3	211, 213
48.2–7	6
51.3	221
55.4	221
57	225
60.5	149
62.2	202
69.26–29	160
80.6–8	170
81.2	213
81.4	213
81.12	159
82	170
86	163
86.1–3	227
88.3	227
89.28–40	163
89.61–64	159
90.20	211, 213
90.28–29	218
91–105	142
91.9	67
91.15	163
92–105	165
93.1–3	159
93.8	165
94.6–8	165
94.9	165
94.11	165
95.4–7	165
95.6	165
96.4–8	165
96.8	165
97.7–8	165
97.10	165
98.9–16	165
98.10–16	165
98.15	165
99.1	165
99.1–2	165
99.8–10	165
99.11–15	165
99.11–16	165
100.5	161
100.7	92, 120
100.7–9	165
100.8–9	165
100.9	165
102.1	45
103.5–8	165
103.7–8	165
104.9	165
104.11	229
106.5–12	163
108.3	211, 213
108.7	159

2 Enoch

22.7	164
22.12	213
30.15	86
62.2–3	41

3 Enoch

10.3–6	7
12.5	7
16.1	7

4 Ezra

1.19	203
2.12	193
3–5	106
3.13–14	217
5:41	126
6:20	213
6:25	126
6.26	125
7.26	65
7:27	126
7.38	67
7.99	65
7.116–31	80
7.127–28	192
8.33	92
8.50–9.13	125
8.52	193
9.10–12	45, 63
10.19–48	106
10.44	65
13	74
13.9–11	202
13.12–47	225
13.16–23	126
13.35–39	65, 202
13:48–50	126
15.43–16.34	106

16.78	45

5 Ezra
2.39	210

Jubilees
1.5–25	101
1.27–29	16
4.15	163
4.22	163
5.1–13	16
5.12–19	213
5.13	159
15.34	45
16.5	67
16.9	213
17.15–18	93
20.2–7	160
21.4–5	22
23	126
23.11–21	218
23.32	213
24.1	213
25.1	201
25.1–8	63
30.1–17	201
30.20–22	211
30.22	213
33.13–16	45
35.14	69

Martyrdom and Ascension of Isaiah
2.10	167
3.2	135
3.15	183
9.10	197
9.22	213
9.32	164

Orphica
5–8	142

Sibylline Oracles
1.165–70	39
2.286–95	67
2.96	200
3.601–615	126
3.716–35	217
7.148–49	203
8.399–400	86
8.399–401	142

Hellenistic Synagogal Prayers
11.2–3	86

Joseph and Aseneth
8.9–10	34
12.9–11	127
15.3–4	211
28.3	207

Lives of the Prophets
3.17–20	224

Odes of Solomon
7.29	21
9.11	211

Pseudo-Philo
(Liber antiquitatum biblicarum)
12.4	101
18	166
18.2	165
18.13	199

Psalms of Solomon
1.9	21
2.4	56
2.16–35	207
3.9–12	22
3.10–12	56
8.12	50
8.28–30	112
9.2	112
11.2–7	225
14.2–3	193
17	74
17.24	202
17.35	202
35	202

Ancient Sources Index

Syriac Menander (Sentences)

2.52–58	147, 219

Testament of Jacob

7.27–28	213

Testament of Job

9–15	90

Testament of Moses

1.14	213, 214
8–9	126
8.1	218
9.1–7	126
12.4–5	213
12.13	213

Testament of the Twelve Patriarchs

Testament of Asher

1.5–9	85
1–4	80
2.10	213
3.1	85
3.1–7	85
4.1	85
5	102
6.2	85
7	102
7.5	159, 213

Testament of Benjamin

6	102
7.5	166
10.8–9	126

Testament of Dan

5	102
5.4–8	224
5.9	102, 224
6.16	134

Testament of Gad

8	102

Testament of Issachar

4	102
6	102
6.1	102
6.3	102

Testament of Joseph

1.3	86
2.6–7	81
3.8	81
5.2	58
17.2	97
19.4	225

Testament of Judah

15.5	205
23.5	102
24.1	207

Testament of Levi

4.1	126
5.4	213
10.2	102, 205
13.9	221
14.1	102
14.6	201
15	102
16.5	102
18.3	207
18.59–60	211

Testament of Naphtali

3.4–5	160
4–7	102
4.3	102
4.4–5	102

Testament of Rueben

5.6–7	163

Testament of Simeon

3.2	82

Testament of Zebulun

9	102
9.5	102
9.7	102
10.3	67

JOSEPHUS AND PHILO

Josephus

Against Apion

1.42–43	229

Jewish Antiquities

Reference	Page
1.14	21
1.52–56	166
2.45	65
3.15.1–2[310–315]	163
4.6.1–13§100–158	166
4.6.3[107–11]	166
4.6–12[126–155]	199
4.67	15
4.126–30	166
4.140–49	135, 143
6.86	55
7.4.1[75]	137
8.2.2	21
8.13.1–13.8[316–356]	204
8.190–98	201
9.4.2[47]	204
11.131–33	106
11.3	218
15.136	16
15.14	106
15.39	106
18.5.2	32
18.310–73	106
20.9.1[199–203]	73
20.100	140

Jewish War

Reference	Page
1.229	145
2.17.10[455]	144
3.420	169
4.311	61
14.171	50

Philo

On the Sacrifices of Cain and Abel

Reference	Page
63	57
81	63
120	63
135	63

On the Life of Abraham

Reference	Page
34	78
47	78

Allegorical Interpretation

Reference	Page
1.62	63
3.213	41

On the Cherubim

Reference	Page
71	81

On the Embassy to Gaius

Reference	Page
3.80	58
282	106

On Flight and Finding

Reference	Page
26[145–46]	167
84	41

That Every Good Person Is Free

Reference	Page
17	194

On the Migration of Abraham

Reference	Page
90–92	47

On the Life of Moses

Reference	Page
1.[14].83	55
1.294–304	143
1.294–305	199

On the Posterity of Cain

Reference	Page
35	166
38–39	166

On the Preliminary Studies

Reference	Page
177	221

On Rewards and Punishments

Reference	Page
70	168
152–63	101
172	101

On the Special Laws

Reference	Page
1.304–307	191
1.8.45	164
1.102	62
3.29	201
4.80–82	81
4.126–31	163

On the Virtues

Reference	Page
212–20	109

That the Worse Attacks the Better

Reference	Page
50	142
103	142
119	142

Ancient Sources Index

QUMRAN LITERATURE

1QS
2.8	67
4.2	142
4.13	67
3.13–4.26	126
3.18–4.26	142
3.25–4.26	80
4.7	197
5.4–5	191
6.27–7.2	41, 69
7.2	159
7.16–24	41
7.18–23	21
8.7–9	217
10.6–8	159

1QSb
5 24–25	202

1QM
2–3	225
11.6–7	207
12.1–10	183
12.14–15	217
19.6	217

1QH
2.22	196
6.14–19	193
7.4	193
7.22–25	227
10.8	164
11.3–18	126
17.13	67
18.17–21	191

1QHa
10.22	196

4Q339
	166

4Q393
.3	101

4Q423
5	167

4Q504
3	59
4.7	101

4Q521
	221

4Q537
1.3–4	213

4QpIsa^a
	202

4QMMT
75–82	210

4QTest
91–93	207

CD
1.12	196
1.17	201
2.14–16	80
2.17–19	163
2.17–3.12	201
3.11	160
3.15	142
5.18	16
7.13	201
8.1	201
19.10	201
19.13	201
20.1–8	101

LATER JEWISH/RABBINIC SOURCES

m. Abot
2.4	47
5.3	93
5.18	41

Abot of Rabbi Nathan

20	80
31–32	202

b. Bekhorot

31A	101

b. Berakot

5a	80

t. Demai

2.9	101

Gen. Rabbah

9.7	80
65	63
81	213

Lev. Rabbah

26	213

Mekilta Exod.

20.18	16

m. Miqvaot

10.8	219

Num. Rabbah

20.7	166

Pirke Aboth

5.19[22]	166

Pesiq Rabbati

21	16

b. Sabbat

114a	210

b. Sanhedrin

106a	166
110b	27

m. Sanhedrin

10.3	27

t. Sanhedrin

13.5	41

Shemoneh Esreh Benediction

12	41, 212–213

Targum Isaiah

22:14	197
65:6	197
65:15	168, 197

Targum Neofiti

Gen 4:8	142

Targum Onqelos

Deut 33:6	168, 197

Targum Pseudo-Jonathan

Gen 4:8	142

b. Yoma

69b	80

GRECO-ROMAN SOURCES

Aristophanes

Birds

1649–50	59

Aristotle

Parts of Animals

3.3	14

Politics

1291A	31

Ancient Sources Index

Aristotle (continued)

Rhetoric

2.5.1	46
2.5.5	52
2.5.16	46

Aulus Gellius

Attic Nights

5.14.7–11	127

Cassius Dio

67.4.7	178

Cicero

Laws

2.7.19–27	109

Pro Sexto Roscio Amerino

27.75	135

Dio Chrysostom

Orations (Discourses)

32.11	46
34–39	55
59.10.3	127
60.13.4	127

Demosthenes

Against Macartatus

51	59

1 Olynthiac

1.16	55

1 Philippic

4.51	55

Diodorus Siculus

13.70.3	55
15.33.1	137

Diogenes Laertius

Lives and Opinions of Eminent Philosophers

4.6	56
7.37	158
7.166	158

Epictetus

Discourses

1.7.30	30
2.16.39	31
2.23.38	67
3.22.69	145

Euripides

Orestes

362	13–14
607	55

Herodotus

Histories

1.2	13
3.48	13
2.150	14
2.182	13
4.115	67
9.99	13
9.101	137

Homer

Iliad

4.157	50

Horace

Odes

3.6.5–8	109

Isocrates

De Pace

41	55

Panegyricus

43	65
46	65

Juvenal

Satires

10.45	210

Maximus of Tyre

16.3b	135

Ovid

Metamorphoses

15.41–42	204

Lucian

Salaried Posts in Great Houses

13	208

Martial

Epigrams

10.72	178

Liber spectaculorum

5	127
7	127
8	127
21	127

Plato

Euthyphro

12B–C	67

Laws

814E	145
869E–870A	82

Protagoras

358D	67

Republic

433A	31

Statesman

299C	21

Pliny

Letters

10.96	110
10.96.2f	63, 116
10.96.6	178
10.96.1–10	108

Panegyricus

33.4	178
52.6	178

Plutarch

Alcibiades

22.2[202D]	204

Agesilaus

3.1–5	59

Dialogues on Love

756 A–B, D	109

Cato the Younger

1.6	30

Moralia

754a	14
186F	204

Pericles

37.2–5	59

Polybius

Histories

1.37.2	169
3.63.7	30
4.8.5	30
4.60.2	30
5.111.8	158
6.40.14	56
10.32.3	56
12.12.2	36
24.11.3	145
24.9.6	158

Ancient Sources Index

Quintilian

Institutio Oratoria
Preface
179
4 179

Rhetorica ad Herennium
4.37.49–50 46

Seneca

De Clementia
1.25.1 127

Epistulae Morales
85.2 135
88.20 31

De Providentia 59

Suetonius

Gaius Caligula
27.3 127

Nero
16 108
39 108
29.1 127

Domitian
8.13 178
10.1 127
13.1–2 178

Statius

Silv
1.6.84 178

Strabo

Geography
9.2.31 14

Tacitus

Annals
15.44 108, 116, 127, 179

Xenophon

Hellenica
2.3.51 212

EARLY CHURCH FATHERS, NT APOCRYPHA, GNOSTIC WRITINGS

Acts of Paul and Thecla
38 210

Acts of Thomas
46 145

Second Apocalypse of James
44.13–17 72

Ambrose

Penance
2.2 39, 42

Apocalypse of Peter
1.1 138
3 145
15.30 15
17 213

Aristides

Apology
15.5 200

Barnabas (Epistle of)
1 35
3.6 170
4.1 145
4.9 157
4.10 47
4.13 13
4.14 10
5.4 146

5.11	60	16.2	192
9.5	190	16.4	97
11.2	47	17	146
15.5	134, 160	17.1	149
18	86		
18–20	142		
19.2	47		

Clement of Alexandria

Miscellanies
2.20	187

Paed.
2.1	200

Salvation — 177

Stromata
4.16	200

1 Clement

4.9	60
4.13	60
5.1	178, 197
5.2	60, 217
6.2	60
7.1	178
7.4–5	63
8.1–5	149
8.5	149
11.1	11
11.2	85
14.5	160
16.6	20
23.3	84
34.3	207
35.5	142
45:4	60
46.2	47
46.8	145
49.5	97
53.4	212
53.4–5	212
56.4	221
59.2	136
64	162

Pseudo-Clementine

Recognitions
1.66–71	74

Cyprian

Epistles
50–52[47–48]	42

On the Lapsed — 42
6	201

Didache

1–6	142
4.13	47, 229
6	86, 95
6.1	205
6.3	200
9.5	147, 192
11.5–10	138
12.5	116
16.1	208
16.2	47
16.3	138

2 Clement

3.2	211
3.4	146
4.1–5	146
4.5	55
5.5–6	137
6.7	146
8.4	146
8.4–6	146
10.1	145
10.3	58
13.1	128
15.1	66

Diognetus

Epistle
5.1–7	110

Ancient Sources Index

Diognetus (*continued*)

Epistle (continued)

5.5	110
10.7	158

Epiphanius

Refutation of all Heresies

59.1.1–59.3.5	42

Eusebius

Ecclesiastical History

1.7.14	154
2.1.2–4	73
2.14.6	106
2.15.2	106
2.23.1–3	73, 74
2.23.3–20	6
2.23.4	155
2.25.1–8	106, 108
3.1.1–2	107
3.3.5	3
3.4	133
3.5	228
3.13	133
3.19.1–20.6	154
3.19.1–3.20.7	73
3.21	133
3.23.5	177
3.25.3–4	133
3.29.1–3	187
3.31	133
3.39.15	106
4.6.2	140
4.7.11	108
4.23.11	106
5.1–2	42
5.1.14–26	108
5.2.8	42
5.6.1	133
5.16.12	195
6.14.2–4	3
6.19.9	140
6.20.3	3
6.25.11	133
6.25.11–14	3
6.38	213
6.43	42
8.17.6–9	109
9.1–3	109
9.5.2	108
9.9.1	109

Gospel of Phillip

101	58

Gospel of Thomas

12	73
21	155
37	58
54	89
103	203

Gospel of Truth

33.15–16	147, 219

Hermas, the Shepherd of

Mandates

4.3.3	149
5.2.7	146
8.6	213
9.1–11	84
9.9	169
10.2.2	85
11.9	72
11.13	72
11.14	72
12.5.4	146

Similitudes

6.2.6–7	145
8.1–3[74]	158
8.2.3	210
8.8.2	21
8.8.5	21
8.9.1	21
8.11.1	149
9.17.5	146
9.18.3–4	55
9.21.3	85
9.26.3	47

Visions

1.3.2	213
	1.3.3–4
2.2.5	149

2.32	21
3.6.2	47
3.7.1	20, 205
3.7.2	21
4.2	145
4.2.6	84

Hippolytus

The Apostolic Tradition	58

Refutation of All Heresies
7.24	187

Ignatius

To the Ephesians
1	184
5.3	47
6.2	138
7–9	186
7.1	147, 192
10.1	149
10.2	194
11.2	116

To the Magnesians
3.2	205
11.3	207

To the Philadelphians
11.2	106

To Polycarp
2.1–3	119
4.2	72
5.2	164
7.3	116
8.1	106

To the Romans
3.2	116
4.3	106

To the Smyrnaeans
12.1	106

To the Trallians
3	72
6.1	138
12.3	45

Ireneaus

Against Heresies
1.16.3	145
1.26.3	187
3.1.5	106
3.3.3	133

Jerome

De Viris Illustribus	72

Letters
120.11	133

Justin Martyr

Apology
1.26.7	196
1.28	149
1.31.6	140
1.26	108
1.36	138
1.62.12	34
1. 65.1	34
2.12	196

Dialogue with Trypho
12.2	190
16	195
17.1	195f
22.5	34
35	200
35.3	135
47.4	195
51.2	135
81.4	175
93.4	195
108.2	196
108.3	195
117.3	196
137.2	195

Hortatory Address to the Greeks
32	35

Origen

Against Celsus
2.3	109

Ancient Sources Index

Origen (*continued*)

Against Celsus (*continued*)

5.5.29	205
5.35	109
6.27	196
8.28	200
8.69	109

Polycarp

Martyrdom of Polycarp

1.3	208
4	192
8.2	192
9.1	192
9.2–3	192
14.1	136
17.2	142

Philippians

5.3	121
7.2	128
14.1	106

Tertullian

Apology

2.6–7	108
4.2	109
5	178
9	200

Against Marcion

3.6	190

On Modesty

8.5	190

To His Wife

2.3–8	201

Author Index

Achtemeier, Paul J., 105, 107, 109, 114–18, 120, 125, 126, 249
Adamson, James B., 94, 97, 249
Allen, David M., 10, 16, 45, 53, 61, 62–64, 249
Arichea, Daniel C., and Eugene Nida, 128, 249
Arichea, Daniel C., and Hatton, 135, 136, 143, 159, 162, 249
Attridge, Harold W., 7, 9, 16, 21, 24, 28, 30, 32, 35, 38, 40, 46, 62, 63, 249
Aubineau, M., 147, 249
Aune, David Edward, 50, 175–77, 182–84, 187, 189, 198, 201, 203, 206, 212, 215, 225, 229, 249

Baker, William R., xi, 82, 249
Balch, David, 110, 249, 254
Baltzer, Klaus, 102, 249
Baltzer, Klaus, and Peter Machinist, 115, 249, 257, 261, 263
Balz, Horst, xii, 46, 249
Bateman, Herbert W., 14, 15, 30, 249, 252, 254, 255, 261
Bauckham, Richard J., 7, 43, 74, 75, 77, 84, 89, 105, 106, 132–35, 137, 138, 142, 144, 154–56, 159, 160, 162–64, 166, 168, 170, 175, 192, 202, 214, 222, 224, 249, 250
Bauder, Wolfgang, 21, 250
Bauernfeind, Otto, 158, 250
Beale, G. K., xii, 177, 180, 181, 190, 191, 209, 212, 224, 226, 227, 229, 250
Beale, G. K., and S. M. McDonough, 202, 217, 227, 250
Beare, Francis Wright, 250
Beasley-Murray, G.R., 206, 250
Bechtler, Steven Richard, 106, 113, 250
Becker, Jürgen, 102, 150

Bénétreau, Samuel, 7, 112, 128, 250
Benko, Stephen, 108, 250
Bernheim, P. A., 73, 250
Best, Ernest, 250
Bigg, C., 106, 132, 140, 146, 155, 168, 250
Block, D. I., 99, 250
Bolling, R. G., 99, 250
Borchert, Gerald L., 9, 250
Borgen, Peder, 194, 196, 250
Boring, M. Eugene, 181, 250
Bratcher, Robert G., and Howard Hatton, 197, 207, 214, 251
Braun, Herbert, 20, 205, 251
Brosend, William F., 71, 88, 156, 251
Brown, Jennifer K., 111, 251
Brown, Nobel B., 97, 251
Brown, Raymond E., 107, 251
Brown, Schuyler, 218, 251
Brox, Norbert, 106, 112, 124, 251
Bruce, F. F., 35, 36, 251
Buchanan, George Wesley, 22, 40, 42, 62, 251
Bultmann, Rudolf, 221, 251
Burchard, Christoph, 82, 251
Burton, Ernest De Witt, 209, 251

Caird, G. B., 215, 251
Callan, Terrance, 132, 251
Campbell, Barth, 112, 251
Cargal, Timothy B., 80, 95, 96, 251, 265
Carmichael, D. B., 203, 251
Carson, D. A., xii, 25, 115, 147, 164, 251
Caulley, Thomas S., ix, x, 134, 135, 137, 142, 143, 251
Chaine, Joseph, 164, 251
Charles, J. Daryl, 135, 154, 159, 160, 163, 166, 251

Author Index

Charles, J. Daryl, and Erland Waltner, 136, 169, 251
Charles, R. H., xv, 165, 175, 195, 251
Chester, Andrew, and Ralph P. Martin, 3, 92, 133, 252
Christensen, Duane L., 98, 252
Clark, David J., and Howard Hatton, 171, 252
Coats, George W., 167, 252
Cockerill, Gareth L., 10, 36, 252
Cohen, Shaye J. D., 201, 252
Collins, Adela Yarbro, 177-79, 181, 194, 195, 209, 220, 226, 228
Collins, John J., 102, 176, 228
Court, John M., 178, 252
Croy, N. Clayton, 59, 252

Daniel, C., 155, 252
Daube, David, 203, 252
Davids, Peter H., xii, 71, 75, 77, 78, 80, 81, 83, 87, 106, 123, 132, 135, 137, 144, 146, 150, 151, 155, 164, 171, 252, 266
De Jonge, Marinus, 102, 252, 257
DeSilva, David A., ix, 5, 12, 17, 24, 31, 45, 52, 58, 59, 67, 83, 105, 176, 179, 182, 184, 252
Deterding, Paul E., 112, 253
Dibelius, Martin, and Heinrich Greeven, 88, 253
Dillard, Raymond B., 99, 253
Dov, Noy, 97, 253
Dryden, J. de Waal, 111, 114, 117, 119, 121, 253
Dschulnigg, Peter, 142, 253
Dubis, Mark, 110, 111, 115, 124-26, 253
Duff, Paul B, 179, 188, 195, 201, 204, 205, 216, 253, 264
Dulk, Matthijs den, 193, 204, 253
Dunham, Duane A., 147, 253
Dunn, James D. G., 44, 93, 253
Dunnill, John, 4, 253

Eisenbaum, Pamela M., 4, 253
Eissfeldt, Otto, 204, 253
Elgvin, Torleif, 102, 253
Ellingworth, Paul, 13, 15, 25, 26, 34, 36, 47, 49, 51, 59, 63, 254
Ellingworth, Paul, and Eugene Albert Nida, 21, 27, 254
Elliott, J. K., 138, 254
Elliott, John H., 105-10, 115, 117, 118, 123, 133, 147, 254

Endo, Shusaku, 50, 254
Erlandsson, S., 200, 254
Evans, Craig A., 1991, 249, 250, 252, 254

Fanning, Buice M., 26, 38, 254
Fekkes, Jan, 201-3, 217, 254
Feld, Helmut, 5, 254
Feldman, Louis H., 71, 254
Feldmeier, Reinhard, 105, 109, 110, 111, 127, 254
Feuillet, A., 225, 254
Fitzmyer, Joseph A., 55, 254
Ford, J. Massyngberde, 3, 254
Forkman, Göran, 49, 97, 254
Fornberg, Tord, 133, 144, 254
Frankemölle, Hubert, 72, 83, 155, 168, 154
Frankfurter, David, 194, 255
Friedrich, Nestor Paulo, xiv, 191, 255, 256, 266
Friesen, Steven J., 178-80, 198, 217, 255
Fuchs, Eric, and Pierre Reymond, 132, 150, 155, 162, 255
Fuller, J. William, 203, 209, 211, 255

Gaca, Kathy L., 201, 255
Gerdmar, Anders, 155, 255
Geyser, A. S., 72, 255
Gheorghita, Radu, 255
Giesen, Heinz, 186, 207, 210, 255
Gileadi, Avraham, 97, 255
Gilmour, Michael J., 132, 255
Gleason, Randall C., 4, 64, 255
Goldstein, H., 158, 255
Goppelt, Leonhard, 119, 126, 255
Gray, Patrick, 50, 52, 54, 56, 67, 246, 255
Gräβer, Erich, 4, 15, 22, 34, 49, 54, 55, 62, 255
Green, Joel B., 117, 122, 133, 255,
Green, Michael, 132, 139, 144, 145, 168
Greene, John T., 166, 256
Grudem, Wayne A., 34, 36, 256
Grundmann, Walter, Paul Althaus, and Erich Fascher, 155, 256
Guthrie, Donald, 256
Guthrie, George H., 5, 8, 17, 37, 51

Hackenberg, W., 49, 256
Hackett, J. A., 166, 256
Hagner, Donald Alfred, 64, 250, 256
Hanse, Hermann, 135, 256
Harder, Günther, 151, 256
Harrington, Daniel J., 6, 256

Author Index

Harrington, Daniel J., and Donald P. Senior, 133, 146, 155, 256, 264
Harrington, Wilfrid J., 211, 256
Hartin, Patrick. J., 71, 75, 78, 84, 86–88, 94, 96, 256
Hartley, John E., 98, 256
Hasel, G. F., 97, 256
Hauck, Friedrich, and Seigfried Schulz, 201, 256
Hayes, Christine, 201, 256
Heen, Erik M., Philip D. Krey, and Thomas C. Oden, 36, 256
Heiligenthal, Roman, 154, 256
Hemer, Colin J., 186, 193, 198, 200, 203, 204, 208, 210, 212, 217, 256
Hengel, Martin, 71, 76, 105, 257
Hewitt, Thomas, 36, 257
Hiebert, D. Edmond, 154, 257
Hirschberg, Peter, 175, 183, 195, 225, 257
Hofius, Otfried, 25, 257
Holladay, William L., 97, 257
Hollander, H. W., and Marinus De Jonge, 102, 257
Hoppin, Ruth, 3, 257
Horrell, David G., ix, 109, 114, 116, 124, 125, 128, 154, 257
Hossfeld, Frank-Lothar, Erich Zenger, Linda M. Maloney, and Klaus Baltzer, 27, 28, 257
Howe, Bonnie, 116, 257
Hübner, Hans, 46, 257
Hughes, Philip Edgcumbe, 13, 14, 35, 36, 257
Hurst, L. D., 4, 257
Hvalvik, Reider, 5, 250, 253, 257

Isaacs, Marie E., 22, 26, 257

Jauhiainen, Marko, 197, 210, 257
Jeremias, Joiachim, 92, 257
Jobes, Karen H., 105, 107, 118, 120, 121, 126, 127, 257
Johnson, Luke Timothy, 71, 78, 82, 85, 87, 90, 91, 97, 257
Johnson, Richard W., 6, 20, 25, 30, 31, 36, 38, 50, 52, 258
Jones, David W., 164, 258
Jones, Donald L., 178, 258
Joslin, Barry C., 26, 258
Joubert, Stephan J., 155, 157, 258

Kaminsky, Joel S., 216, 258

Käsemann, Ernst, 57, 133, 258
Katz, P., 61, 258
Kaufmann, Kuhler, and Gottheil, Richard, 97, 258
Kelly, J. N. D., 117, 121, 134, 144, 155, 168, 258
Kessler, John, 66, 258
Kilpatrick, George Dunbar, 90, 258
Kistemaker, Simon J., 258
Klauck, Hans-Josef, 29, 38, 258
Klein, William W., 117, 214, 258
Kloppenborg, John S., 75, 258, 260
Knoch, Otto, 154, 258
Koch, Dietrich-Alex, 55, 258
Koester, Craig R., 5, 8, 10, 12, 16, 20, 24, 30, 39, 40, 47, 54, 58, 59, 63, 65, 66, 176, 258
Koskenniemi, Heikki, 158, 258
Kraft, Heinrich, 152, 158
Kraftchick, Steven John, 134, 149, 160, 168, 171, 258
Kratz, R., 161, 258
Kraus, Thomas J., 132, 134, 138, 151, 258
Kruger, Michael J., 133, 258
Kuhn, Karl A., 150, 258
Kümmel, Werner Georg, 133, 258

Laansma, Jon, 29, 259
Lambrecht, Jan, 196, 259
Lane, William L., 7, 14, 24, 25, 31, 33, 51, 52, 59, 259
Lapham, F., 107, 132, 259
Laws, Sophie, 75, 83, 109, 259
Leschert, Dale F., 17, 259
Lewis, Thomas W., 56, 259
Lichtenberger, Herman, x, 67, 259
Lindars, Barnabas, 7, 24, 39, 52, 259
Linton, Gregory L., 176, 259
Lockett, Darian, 86, 259
Löhr, Hermut, 9, 23, 24, 26, 29, 31, 32, 39, 52, 63, 259
Lohse, Eduard, 194, 259
Louw, Johannes P., and Eugene Albert Nida, 138, 259
Lünemann, Gottlieb, and Maurice J. Evans, 3, 4, 259
Lupieri, Edmondo, 186, 259

Mackie, Scott D., 4, 8, 12, 13, 15, 24, 28, 53, 259
Malina, Bruce J., and John J. Pilch, 259
Manson, T. W., 4, 259
Manson, William, 7, 259

315

Author Index

Marcus, Joel, 80, 259
Marshall, I. Howard, 33, 36, 51, 95, 97, 117, 167, 226, 259
Martin, Ralph P., x, xii, 76, 82, 92, 94, 133, 252, 259
Martin, Troy W., 106, 113, 114, 121, 125, 259
Mathewson, Dave, 34, 35, 259
Mayes, A. D. H., 101, 260
Mayo, Philip L., 195, 225, 227, 260
Mayor, Joseph B., 90, 94, 163, 260
Mays, James Luther, 99, 260
McCullough, John Cecil, 18, 38, 45, 260
McKnight, Scot, 24, 120, 126, 256, 260, 261
McLaughlin, John L., 191, 260
Metzger, Bruce M., 3, 23, 55, 94, 118, 124, 127, 140, 149, 160, 212, 260
Meyer, L. V., 101, 260
Michaels, J. Ramsey, 107, 113, 118, 122, 126, 214, 260
Michel, Otto, 49, 60, 260
Miller, Donald G., 105, 260
Mitchell, Alan C., 4, 16, 38, 39, 49, 60, 260
Mitchell, Margaret M., 76, 260
Moffat, James, 13, 50, 58, 63, 208, 260
Montefiore, Hugh, 260
Moo, Douglas J., 78, 79, 133, 260
Moore, G, E., 99, 260
Morschauser, S., 164, 260
Mounce, Robert H., 177, 214, 260
Moyise, Steve, 122, 124, 249, 260
Müller, Ulrich B., 183, 260
Myllykoski, Matti, 75, 260

Nanos, Mark D., ix, 147, 260
Newman, Barclay Moon, and Eugene Albert Nida, 105, 260
Neyrey, Jerome H., 134, 139, 142, 147, 156, 158, 164, 166, 169, 171, 261
Nickelsburg, George W. E., and Klaus Baltzer, 163, 165, 252, 261
Niederwimmer, Kurt, 142, 261
Nixon, R, E., 112, 261
Nongbri, Brent, 45, 46, 261
Noth, Martin, 98, 261
Noth, Martin, 99, 261

Oberholtzer, Thomas Kem, 38, 67, 261
Oepke, Albrecht, 161, 261
Oppenheim, A. L., 204, 261

Oropeza, B. J., 9, 19, 34, 42, 53, 98, 163, 181, 261
Osborne, Grant R., 8, 42, 176, 182, 190, 191, 206, 209, 210, 12, 215, 220, 256, 261
Osburn, Carroll D., 160, 261

Painter, John, 71, 74, 76, 261
Panning, Armin J., 117, 118, 261
Paschke, Boris A., 127, 261
Pattemore, Stephen, 182, 226, 261
Paul, Shalom M., 213, 216, 261
Paulsen, Henning, 132, 155, 261
Pearson, Sharon Clark, 115, 262
Penner, Todd C., 71, 72, 79, 85, 262
Perkins, Pheme, 161, 262
Peterson, David G., 6, 262
Peterson, Robert A., 147, 262
Pfitzner, V. C., 29, 60, 262
Picirelli, Robert, 136, 262
Piper, John, 122, 262
Popkes, Wiard, 76, 78, 83, 89, 94, 262
Porter, Stanley E., 25, 143, 171, 262
Prasad, Jacob, 113, 119, 120, 262
Preisker, Herbert, 30, 262
Price, S. R. F., 178, 262
Prigent, Pierre, 175–77, 189, 190, 191, 198, 210, 211, 216, 262
Proctor, John, 53, 262
Proulx, P. and L. Alonso Schökel, 29, 37, 262

Räisänen, Heiki, 191, 262
Ramsey, William M., 107, 198, 219, 260, 262
Raymond, Brown, 251, 253, 262
Reese, Ruth Anne, 158, 262
Reicke, Bo, 262
Rengstorf, Karl Heinrich, 55, 262
Rhee, Victor, 6, 262
Rice, George E., 12, 262
Richard, E. J., 150, 157, 262
Richards, E. Randolph, 106, 262
Rissi, M., 7, 262
Roloff, Jürgen, 175, 186, 211, 222, 263
Ropes, James Hardy, 71, 78, 86, 90, 263
Rowland, Christopher, 263
Rowston, Douglas J., 154, 263
Royalty, Robert M., 179, 194, 221, 222, 263

Sabourin, Leopold, 37, 263
Salevao, Iutisone, 5, 6, 34, 263

Author Index

Sanders, Jack T., 225, 263
Sandt, Huub van de, 76, 263
Schechter, Solomon, 80, 263
Schelke, K. H., 263
Schenck, Kenneth L., ix, 66, 263
Schenker, A., 191, 263
Schlier, Heinrich, 21, 263
Schlosser, J., 160, 263
Schnelle, Udo, 5, 155, 175, 199, 207, 263
Schnider, Franz, 263
Schrage, Wolfgang, 72, 263
Schreiner, Thomas R., 105, 112, 117, 121, 125, 128, 133, 144, 147–49, 161, 163, 168, 263
Schüssler Fiorenza, Elizabeth, 182, 186, 226, 263
Schutter, W. L., 105, 117, 263
Seitz, Christopher R., 263
Seitz, Oscar Jacob Frank, 85, 263
Seland, Torrey, 109, 264
Sellin, Gerhard, 155, 264
Selwyn, E. G., 118, 226, 264
Senior, Donald, P., and Daniel J. Harrington, 133, 146, 155, 256, 264
Sevenster, J. N., 71, 264
Sidebottom, E. M., 264
Simon, Marcel, 138, 264
Skaggs, Rebecca, 105, 137, 264
Slater, Thomas B., 179, 264
Smalley, Stephen S., 198, 264
Smith, Terence V., 132, 134, 264
Snaith, Norman H., 97, 264
Snyder, G. F., 146, 264
Spicq, Ceslas, 3, 14, 38, 51, 133, 264
Spitaler, Peter, 170, 171, 264
Starr, James M., 135, 264
Stewart-Sykes, A., 107, 264
Strand, Kenneth A., 192, 264
Strelan, Rick, 192, 264
Stuart, Douglas K., 99, 264
Sullivan, K., 205, 264
Sumney, Jerry L., 227, 264
Sweet, J. P. M., 264

Talbert, Charles H., 109–11, 249, 254, 264
Thiel, W., 97, 264
Thomas, C. Adrian, 13, 26, 51, 264
Thompson, James W., 25, 112, 264
Thompson, Leonard L., 178, 179, 264
Thurén, Lauri, 112, 114, 156–58, 265
Thyen, Hartwig, 8, 265

Tongue, D. H., 7, 265
Townsend, M. J., 82, 265
Trebilco, Paul, 182, 185, 186, 196, 199, 221, 222, 223, 265
Truex, Jerry, 117, 265
Tsuji, Manabu, 76, 265

Ulrichsen, Jarl H., 102, 265
Urbrock, W. J., 97, 265

Verbrugge, Verlyn D., 26, 265
Viljoen, Fracois P., 155, 160, 171, 265
Vögtle, Anton, 133, 144, 154, 157, 162, 164, 168, 171, 265
Volf, Miroslav, 111, 248, 265
Vouga, François, 87, 265

Wall, Robert W., 88, 265
Wallace, Daniel B., 13, 25, 36, 58, 265
Wand, J. W. C., 265
Ward, Roy Bowen, 72, 265
Wasserman, Tommy, 157, 160, 170, 265
Watson, Duane F., 95, 135, 144, 157, 160, 187, 265
Webb, Robert L., 123, 125, 156–58, 165, 258, 260, 265, 266
Weinfeld, M., 101, 266
Weiss, Hans-Friedrich, 5, 22, 35, 51, 66, 266
Werdermann, Hermann, 155, 164, 266
Wiedermann, T., 128, 266
Wilken, Robert L., 108, 264, 266
Williamson, Ronald, 35, 38, 266
Wilson, Stephen G., 51, 97, 140, 194, 201, 247, 266
Wilson, Walter T., 81, 266
Winter, Bruce W., 110, 111, 180, 266
Wisse, Frederik, 156, 266
Witherington, Ben, 5, 39, 62, 72, 89, 90, 120, 121, 133, 141, 147, 149, 155, 169–71, 188, 200, 266
Wolff, H. W., 99, 266
Wolthius, Thomas, 266
Wood, P., 219, 266
Wray, Judith Hoch, 27–29, 266
Wright, N. T., 43, 266

Zerwick, Max, 23, 37, 171, 266

Subject Index

Acculturation, 84, 104, 110-11, 249
Affliction (see Suffer), 54, 78, 123-24, 130, 206, 237
Aliens (see Resident...)
Antinomian(ism) (see also Law) vii, ch. 5, 94, 134, 154-58, 173, 186, 234
Antioch (Syrian), 75-77, 208, 228, 244
Antithetical, 86, 92
Antichrist (see also the Beast), 40
Apathy (see also Complacency, Indifference, Spiritual Dullness), 179, 210, 230f, 239
Apollos, 3, 256, 261
Apostasy (see also Unbelief, Persecution, Suffering, Vices),
    antagonistic, 51, 95, 247-48
    (in) communities, (see Communities)
    consequences of (see Judgment), 1, 176, 241-42
    definition, 1
    diversity/unity of, 43, 70, 236, 242-48
    gradual, 16, 32, 61, 72, 131, 136, 152, 210, 231, 239, 247f
        nature of, 234, 236-41
        perceived, 1, 235, 245
        precipitate, 32, 140, 152, 247, 248
        rhetorical suppression of, 113, 130f, 237, 243
Arena, 127-29
Ashamed, 10, 11, 17, 19, 25, 57, 68, 85, 124, 192, 197
Asia Minor, ch. 6, 179-83, 188-93, 196, 198, 200, 205, 215, 222-37, 257, 262,
Assimilation, vii, ch. 6, 1, 49, 60, 111, 112, 129, 134, 135, 143, 152, 175, 179, 180, 184, 194, 201, 210, 220-24, 230, 231, 240, 241, 245

Assurance (see also Confidence), 8-11, 39, 46, 113, 114, 126, 130, 131, 137, 172, 211, 218, 250
Authority (of James, Peter, etc.), 3, 77, 131, 155, 173, 176, 184, 186, 202, 204, 207f, 216f, 230, 238f, 244
Authority of Scripture, 43, 247

Balaam(ites), 135, 138, 142f, 145, 152, 160f, 165-67, 173, 179, 181, 186f, 193, 197, 199-202, 205, 231, 244
Baptism, 32, 34, 38, 39, 42, 49, 51, 58, 147, 148, 254
Beast (the), 147, 177, 179, 182, 191, 197f, 201, 213f, 216, 218, 224f, 227f, 232
Beasts, Wild (lions, *ad bestias*), 27, 127-29
Behavior (see Moral Behavior), 20, 31, 44, 45, 69, 81, 84, 85, 93, 98, 103, 110, 116, 119, 121, 122, 128, 129, 134, 135, 138, 157, 158, 165, 176, 178, 183, 185, 187, 189, 201, 206, 214, 230, 238, 240, 241, 245, 246, 248
Believe, Belief (see Faith; Unbelief), 1, 7, 21, 23, 24, 31, 33, 37, 39, 44, 48, 70, 73, 76, 96, 108-10, 118, 120, 138-41, 145, 149, 150, 152, 159, 160, 161, 163, 170, 175, 186, 187, 199, 216, 225, 233, 235-39, 241, 243-45, 247-48
Birthright, 60-64, 68f
Blasphemy, 6, 7, 50, 74, 194f
Blessings (see also Curse), 37, 53, 64, 65, 78, 97, 98, 100, 116, 180, 193, 244, 265

Subject Index

Blindness, spiritual (see also Obduracy), 73, 100, 136, 190, 191, 220, 221, 237
Book of Life, 184, 193, 209–16, 224, 229, 231
Boundaries (see also Outsider), 83, 88, 110, 195, 199, 200, 223, 230, 252

Caesar (see also Imperial Cult, Nero), 44, 50, 180f, 186, 192, 197, 200, 224f, 230, 245
Cain, 142, 165–67, 173
Calling, 93, 112, 130, 135, 137, 194, 196, 203, 237, 260
Chosen (see Elect), 20, 89, 106, 112, 115, 117, 214, 217, 258
Christ (see Messiah), xv, 1, 4–19, 22, 24–30, 32, 33f, 35, 37, 38f, 40–42, 44–47, 50–53, 55, 56, 59, 60, 62, 64, 67–70, 72, 73f, 75, 77, 79–85, 87, 89f, 92–95, 103f, 111–20, 122, 127, 130, 133–40, 143–44, 146, 152–54, 157–61, 164, 165, 168–70, 172–74, 176, 180–82, 184–86, 188–204, 206–12, 214, 216–219, 221–225, 227–231, 234–247, 261, 262
Christian(s), Christianity (see Communities), vii, xi, 4, 5, 7, 10–12, 16, 18–37, 42–55, 58, 62–76, 84–88, 91–96, 102–4, 107–125, 130, 132, 133, 135–44, 146, 148–55, 160–64, 168, 169, 171–74, 178–81, 184–89, 192, 195–200, 204, 207, 210, 213, 216, 221–240, 242, 244–247, 249, 250–257
Christology, 4–6, 11, 72, 158, 184, 250, 262
Church, (see Communities, Corporate), 46–48, 65, 67, 69, 71–75, 91, 103, 106, 107, 121, 133f, 138f, 144, 151, 154–56, 161–63, 170, 171, 173, 178–222, 230–33, 235, 239, 240, 242, 245, 247, 250, 254, 257, 260, 263, 265
   Mixed Church, vii, xi, 133, 144, 154, 196, 242, 250, 254, 257, 258, 260, 263, 265
Circumcision, (Uncircumcision), 75, 92, 93
Communities, 1, 196, 234–36
   Antioch (see Antioch, Syrian)
   Asia Minor (see Asia Minor)
   Ephesus (see Ephesus, Ephesian)
   In Hebrews, 3–70
   In James, 71–104
   Jerusalem (see Jerusalem)
   In Jude, 152–72
   Laodicea, 219–23
   Markan, 42
   Matthean, 77, 173, 188, 240
   Johannine, ix, 1, 40, 42–44, 131, 148, 175f, 184–86, 188, 191, 195, 203, 204, 220, 222, 230, 234–48, 265
   Pauline, ix, 3–5, 7, 14, 25, 74, 76, 87, 93, 94, 130, 131, 133, 134, 151, 153, 155–58, 161, 168, 173, 185, 186, 194, 222, 232, 234, 238, 241
   Pergamum, 197–204
   Petrine, 105–51
   Philadelphia, 216–18
   Sardis, 208–210
   Smyrna, 194–97
   Thyatira, 204–8

Complacency (see also Indifference), 131, 136, 184, 220, 236, 239f
Condemn(ation), 45, 46, 87, 89, 103, 111, 139, 141f, 146, 159, 171, 212, 239, 243, 261
Confess, Confession (see also Deny), 10, 11, 17, 32, 34, 44, 46–48, 50, 51, 56, 62, 69, 70, 82, 95, 108, 109, 124, 139, 158, 185, 188, 191, 197, 211f, 217, 233, 238
Confidence, 6, 8–10, 23–26, 30, 46, 48, 54–57, 69, 106, 108, 171
Convert, Conversion, 8, 9, 31–35, 37, 38, 49, 51, 58, 68, 96, 97, 108–10, 112, 114, 121–23, 136f, 143, 144, 146, 147, 149, 152, 168, 171, 210
Corporate/Collective body, people, groups, nations, 1, 5, 9, 10, 12, 13, 15, 19, 20–22, 26–29, 33–37, 41, 47, 49, 53, 57, 58, 61, 63–66, 74, 77, 83, 84, 88, 90, 94, 96–130, 134, 138, 142, 145, 150, 152, 159, 160–63, 166–72, 173, 179, 182, 185–191, 198, 199, 202, 206, 207, 212–19, 222, 227, 236, 239, 240–42, 244, 225, 228, 258
Covenant, 4, 6, 9–12, 14, 16, 27, 28, 38, 45, 49, 50–53, 61, 65–67, 69, 83, 97–102, 114, 191, 201

319

Subject Index

Covenant Pattern (Ancient Israelite Traditions), 97–103
Covetousness (see Greed) 77, 220
Coward(s), 85, 190, 197, 224, 230
Cross, Crucifixion, 10, 38, 51, 58, 139, 193, 203, 246, 254
Curse(s), 10, 17, 27, 45, 52, 58, 62, 68, 95, 97, 98, 166, 193, 194, 219, 227, 229, 230

Dark(ness), 34, 116, 165
Death, 6, 9, 10, 12, 15, 16, 24, 27, 28, 31, 35, 40, 47, 50–52, 58, 64, 69, 72–74, 76–90, 93–97, 103, 104, 109, 116, 121, 127, 128, 136, 139, 141, 144, 162, 167–69, 177, 178, 181, 191–93, 196–98, 202, 203, 206, 209f, 211, 215, 216, 226, 231, 238, 239, 242, 243
Deception (see False Teachings, Led Astray, Seduction), 14, 20, 21, 24, 95, 142, 167, 222, 227
Deeds (see Works), 30, 41, 80, 102, 115, 158, 159, 165, 166, 185, 187, 188, 192, 194, 202, 203, 206, 207, 213f, 221, 246, 248
Deliverance (see Salvation), 12, 15, 20, 102, 121, 123, 128, 160f, 189
Demon(s), Demon-possession (see also Satan), 92, 194, 195
Deny, Denial of Christ (see also Renunciation), vii, 40–44, 51, 71, 73, 114, 124f, 126, 132, 134f, 138, 139, 142, 148, 149, 152, 157–159, 164, 172, 173, 181, 184, 186, 192, 197f, 208, 211, 216, 224, 226, 227, 229, 230, 233, 237, 238, 245
Desire (wrongful, lust), 79–84, 120, 138, 140, 156, 163f
Despair, Discouragement (see Malaise)
Destruction, Eternal destruction, 29f, 45, 52, 53, 56, 62, 66, 67, 69, 82, 95, 97, 100, 104, 117, 137, 138, 141–45, 149–53, 158, 162, 165f, 170, 171, 173, 176, 177, 205, 208, 209, 214, 215, 222, 228, 232, 241, 243, 248
Determinism, Arbitrary Choice of God (see also Predestination, Freedom) 236,
Devil (see Satan), 15, 77, 85, 88, 103, 123, 127–30, 195, 196, 243

Diaspora, 74, 78, 80, 94–96, 103, 109, 113, 116, 129, 130, 195, 234, 241, 244, 245, 251, 265
Discipline, 57–60
Disobedience (see Obedience), 10, 16, 21, 23f, 24, 29, 37, 40, 41, 57, 68, 101, 117, 118, 160, 236
Dogs, 127, 147f, 192
Double-Mindedness, 84–86, 96, 103, 192
Dragon (see also Satan, Devil), 191, 198, 224, 227–29, 232
Draw back (Shrine back)
Drunk(enness), 99, 165, 206, 219

Economy, Socio-economic system, 89, 109f, 129–31, 179f, 182, 188, 194, 200f, 204, 206, 216, 220f, 223f, 227, 230f, 227, 230–32, 237, 239, 243
Elect, Election, 20, 101, 114–17, 119, 130, 137, 144, 162, 216, 229, 238, 248, 254
End Times (see Eschaton), 51, 70, 140, 233, 238
Endurance (see also Perseverance), 54, 57, 81, 103, 184, 197, 204, 217, 218, 221
Ephesus, Ephesian, 1, 7, 16, 56, 177, 180, 182, 184–94, 198, 199, 219–23, 230, 232, 233, 235, 239, 240
Epicureans, 134, 142, 147
Esau, 33, 59–64, 68–70
Eschaton, Eschatology (see also second coming), 4, 8, 15, 24, 28, 53, 71, 72, 79, 85, 133, 157, 253, 255, 258, 261, 262, 265
Essenes, 155, 236
Eternal Life (see also Salvation), 67, 119, 125, 165, 170, 192, 209–11, 220, 237
Eternal Security (see Assurance, Security)
Ethics (see also Immorality), 104, 136, 151, 210
Eucharist (see Lord's Supper), 35f, 203, 251, 266
Exodus, New Exodus, 100, 106, 112f, 115–20, 124, 129, 130, 160, 173, 218, 223, 226, 228, 244, 253, 261
Expulsion (see also Excommunication), 28, 98, 103, 219, 254

Subject Index

Excommunication (see also Expulsion), 171, 252
Exhortation (see also Warning), 6, 8, 13, 19, 21, 23–27, 41, 48, 60f, 66, 68, 85f, 112, 119, 121, 135, 157, 176, 180, 183f, 188–90, 205, 216, 221, 235, 239

Faction(s), 108, 111, 138, 179, 205, 235, 237, 241
Faith, Faithfulness, xii, 1, 4–6, 9–18, 23–25, 27, 29, 31, 32f, 34, 46–59, 64f, 65, 68–70, 73, 75, 76, 78f, 79, 83–93, 96, 98, 101, 104, 108, 109, 111, 113, 114f, 118–21, 124–30, 135–37, 140–62, 166–73, 176, 178, 180, 183–86, 189–200, 203, 204, 207, 209–11, 215, 216, 221, 223, 227, 229–32, 236f, 238, 241, 244, 248, 250, 256, 262, 265
False teachings, false prophets/teachers, 16, 36, 41, 43, 50, 104, 130, 131, 134f, 136–58, 163, 166, 170, 172, 174, 186, 192, 199, 202, 205, 230, 235, 238f, 240–42, 244, 247, 248, 251
False Prophet (the... from Revelation), 180, 197, 205, 224, 232
Fear (of God, Judgment), 11, 14, 17, 19–21, 23, 27, 39, 45f, 52–56, 65–67, 69f, 75, 109, 120, 130, 172, 176, 195, 207, 230, 237, 243, 248
Food, food laws (see also Idol, Idol Meats), 5, 7f, 31, 47, 58, 92, 166, 187, 199, 200f, 203, 205, 207, 231, 238, 240, 241
Foreknowledge, 114, 115, 215
Foreigner (see Outsider/Insider), 101, 107, 109, 110, 241
Forget (...God, Christ, teachings, etc.), 9, 14, 33, 97–101, 136, 189, 239
Forgive(n), Forgiveness, 35, 38, 42, 48–50, 61, 69, 74, 82, 97, 159, 171, 189, 242
Fornication, Sexual vice, 23, 63, 91, 143, 152, 163, 166, 183, 187, 199–201, 204–7, 210, 231, 240, 241, 246, 255
Forsake, 10f, 11, 98–101, 142, 184, 207
Freedom (human), (see also Responsibility), 15, 78, 134, 135, 137, 142, 143, 214, 251

Fruit, fruit of the Spirit, 45, 82, 84, 137, 142, 220, 225

Gehenna (see also Hell), 75, 88, 241
Gentile(s), 5, 7, 22, 31, 32, 43, 44, 52, 63, 67, 71, 72, 74–76, 91–93, 96, 102, 103, 107, 109, 116–18, 121–23, 129–31, 133, 135, 151, 154, 168, 173, 179, 182, 183, 194–96, 207, 217, 224, 225, 228, 229, 230, 232, 234, 235, 238, 240, 245, 247, 254, 260, 266
  Mission, 91
Genuine (belief/believer), ungenuine, inauthentic, 13, 25, 26, 37, 87, 51, 92, 147, 147, 153, 162, 166, 243
Giants, 163
Gnostic(ism), 72, 134, 155, 186, 187
God-fearer(see also Gentiles), 75, 195
Grace, Gift, Favor, 11, 18, 21, 35–37, 40, 50, 51, 53, 60, 61, 67, 68, 80, 106, 111, 112, 117, 119, 120, 125, 134, 150, 152, 158, 159, 162, 172, 173, 238, 248, 256
Greed, Covetousness, 6, 77, 131, 134, 140, 152, 156, 166, 167, 172, 173, 199, 220, 222, 232, 235, 240, 246

Hardened heart (see Obduracy, Blindness)
Heaven(ly) (see also Kingdom of God), 10–12, 14, 17, 18, 29, 35, 45, 57, 60–62, 64–70, 74, 86, 114, 122, 125, 159, 163, 170, 176, 183, 191–93, 197, 203, 209–22, 225–27, 241, 243, 246, 248, 261, 263
Hell, Hades (see also Gehenna, Judgment, Lake of Fire), 88, 120
Hellenism, Hellenize, 49, 63, 71, 105, 120, 121, 133, 141, 147, 154, 155, 255, 257, 266
Heretics, heresy (see also False teachings/beliefs), 138, 139, 156, 264
Holiness (see Sanctify)
Holy Spirit (see also Blasphemy of), 35, 36, 40, 51
Honor, Dishonor (see also Ashamed), 58, 59, 107, 112, 179, 180, 187, 197, 209, 251–53, 255
Household, 25, 107, 110, 117, 121, 125, 129, 139

Subject Index

Humble, Humility, 84, 86, 99, 221, 247
Hypocrite, Hypocrisy, 140

Idol(atry), Idol meats, 16, 22, 31, 44, 61, 85, 87, 91, 98–102, 109, 166, 180, 183, 186, 187, 192, 194, 198–207, 210, 220, 224, 230–32, 238, 240, 245, 246, 261
Immorality, moral failure (see also Moral; Ethics), 23, 41, 63, 83, 95, 134, 136, 138, 144, 157, 161, 163, 167, 171, 200, 206, 231, 246
Imperial (cult), 22, 127, 130f, 175, 178–81, 191f, 198–200, 224, 230, 232, 235, 237
"In Christ," 11, 25, 93, 115–17
Indifference (see also Spiritual Dullness), 8, 15, 184, 187, 210, 219, 223, 239, 241
Individualism (see also Corporate), 9f, 25, 56f, 61, 78–80, 88, 96, 104, 115, 117–19, 124, 141, 149f, 162f, 173, 190f, 214–16, 222, 226, 228, 231, 235, 247
Intertextual(-ity), 22, 83, 249
Intruders, ch. 5

James (brother of Jesus), 6, 41, 42, 44, 71–97, 101, 103, 104, 107, 133, 154, 155, 161, 174, 203, 226, 234, 237, 239, 240–42, 244, 245, 247
  as apostate, 73–74
Jerusalem (see also New Jerusalem), 3, 4, 7, 10, 11, 14, 28, 45, 50, 57, 65, 66, 69, 71–76, 88, 91, 99, 100, 102, 103, 112, 176, 177, 183, 187, 193, 200, 207, 211, 217, 218, 228, 230–32, 244, 250
Jew, Jewish, Judaism (see also Diaspora), 4–7, 16, 19–22, 27, 31, 32, 34, 39, 40, 43–47, 50, 52, 62, 63, 67, 69, 71–82, 84, 85, 87–97, 101–5, 107, 109, 113, 117, 125, 131, 133, 135, 140, 142, 147, 151, 152, 154, 155, 157, 160, 163, 164, 166–76, 178, 179, 183, 185–87, 189, 190, 194–202, 212, 213, 217, 218, 223–38, 240, 241, 244, 245, 247
Jewish Christian(s), 5, 7, 22, 39, 43, 52, 62, 71–79, 84, 88–96, 102–104, 107, 152, 155, 163, 164, 168–74, 183, 195, 224, 227, 229, 232, 235, 238, 240, 244
Jewish custom(s), 73, 92, 178, 244
Jezebel, 179, 181, 186, 204–8, 231
Judgment (Divine Judgment, Final Judgment, Judgment Day), 1, 13, 32, 45, 48, 53, 54, 62, 64, 66, 68, 79, 82, 87–90, 92, 93, 100, 103, 104, 112, 118, 125, 126, 128, 130, 137, 139, 141, 146, 149, 150, 159, 160, 163–66, 168–70, 172, 190, 191, 206, 207, 213, 219, 221, 231, 232, 237, 241, 248, 265
Justification (see also Righteousness), 76, 213

Kingdom, Kingdom of God, 34, 61, 66, 67, 89, 99, 137, 185, 190, 191, 194, 197, 198, 203, 211, 212, 217, 220, 221, 224, 225, 229, 241, 243
Knowledge (spiritual), Wisdom, Insight, 4, 5, 14, 16, 18, 20, 36, 48, 49, 75, 77, 79, 83–86, 99, 103, 104, 114, 115, 129, 133, 135–37, 140, 143, 144, 146, 147, 150, 151, 158, 160, 184, 190, 215, 217, 219, 245–247
Korah, 56, 59, 160f, 165–67, 173

Lake of Fire, 176, 197, 206, 213, 231
Law, Torah, works of the, 16, 21, 43, 47, 52, 73, 75, 76, 78, 80, 81, 83, 84, 86, 87, 90–96, 104, 109, 135, 164, 207, 234, 235, 238–41, 244, 245, 247
Lawless(ness), 45, 95, 99, 134, 138, 142, 151, 188, 238, 240
Led astray, 41, 79, 82, 95, 151, 167, 173, 205
Libertine (see also Antinomian), 94, 153, 155, 158, 173
Life (see Eternal Life), 6, 16, 22, 30, 31, 33–36, 42, 47, 51, 55–58, 61, 64, 67, 79–83, 86, 88, 90, 93, 96, 101, 103, 104, 114, 118–21, 125, 127, 128, 130, 165, 169, 170, 173, 174, 176, 184, 192–94, 196, 197, 203, 209–16, 220, 224, 229, 231, 237
Light, 34, 123, 190
Lions (see Beasts; Satan)
Lord's Supper (see also Love/Love Feast), 35, 206
Loss of Reward, 209

Subject Index

Love, 16, 28, 44, 47, 76, 85f, 90, 92, 94, 96, 99, 103, 109, 115, 121f, 130, 135f, 142, 159, 161-65, 169f, 177, 184-89, 204, 217, 220-23, 230, 235, 239-41, 246, 248
    First Love (lost), 178, 184-90, 233
    Law of Love, 76, 86, 89-91, 104
    Love Feast, 169f, 172, 240
Loyalty (see Faith, Faithfulness; Betrayal), 180, 186, 195
Lust (see Desire, Covetousness)

Malaise, 8, 40, 42, 67-69, 236f, 239, 241
Marginalize(d), 7, 8, 11, 53, 105, 107, 122
Mark of the Beast (see Beast, Six-hundred and sixty-six)
Marriage, Intermarriage, 62, 63, 201, 231, 241, 256
Martyr, Martyrdom, 46, 48, 58, 65, 69, 73, 74, 77, 103, 106, 133, 155, 175, 178, 180, 185, 192, 197, 199, 224, 225, 227, 229, 250
Messiah, messianic, 16, 17, 30, 44, 55, 74, 115, 123-26, 193, 201-3, 207, 218, 222, 226-28, 238, 245, 246, 253
Monotheism, 109
Moral Behavior (see Immorality, Ethics; Virtue(s), Vice(s), Obedience, Righteous), 93, 103, 248
Moses, 10, 16, 20, 53, 58, 65, 68, 69, 98, 108, 120, 132, 135, 161, 166, 167, 207
Murmuring, 23, 121, 167, 252
Mystery, 41, 201

Neokoros, 180, 224
Nero, 33, 37, 41, 69, 107, 127, 177-80, 222, 232, 235, 237
New Exodus (see also Exodus), 100, 112, 118, 129
New Jerusalem (see also Zion), 10f, 14, 57, 65, 176, 183, 193, 211, 217f, 230-32
Nicolaitans, 179, 184-87, 199, 201f, 230, 244

Obduracy, 20, 122, 136, 190, 191, 236, 237, 244
Obedience, Disobedience, 10, 11, 16, 18, 21, 23, 24, 29, 30, 37, 40, 41, 57, 58, 68, 78, 84, 86, 92-94, 101, 104, 114, 117-20, 125, 139, 152, 160, 162, 184, 190, 236
One-hundred and forty-four thousand (the 144,000), 183, 218, 223-27, 232
Opponents, 1, 6, 7, 43, 44, 50, 53, 74, 87, 92, 103, 130, 134, 137-40, 142, 148, 151, 152, 155, 156-160, 162-73, 194-96, 198, 212, 217, 235, 236, 240, 243, 244, 245, 248
Outsider/Insider, 4-11, 17, 18, 44, 45, 48, 54, 60, 67, 69, 73, 83, 84, 89, 107, 108, 111, 116, 118, 120, 123, 124, 126, 129-31, 138, 140, 141, 152, 156, 166, 179, 181, 185, 188, 191, 192, 194, 196, 201, 210, 220, 224, 231, 235, 237, 238, 252
Overcomer(s), 183, 190-93, 203-5, 207, 211, 219f, 224, 230

Pagan(s), 107, 108, 111, 113, 131, 135, 181, 191, 192, 200, 201, 220, 250
Parousia (see also Second Coming, Eschaton), 28, 48, 78, 79, 83, 89, 93, 103, 128, 132-34, 137-41, 149, 150, 152, 163, 170, 173, 189, 190, 197, 202, 206, 207, 211, 218, 222, 228, 230, 231, 237, 238, 240
Patriarch(al), 81, 102
Patron, 180, 183, 223
Penance (see Repent), 39, 42
Persecution, 1, 4-8, 15, 17, 33, 37, 40-42, 46-50, 54, 56, 57, 67, 69, 70, 73, 77, 78, 104, 105, 107-9, 119, 123-31, 158, 178-80, 182, 184, 194, 195-98, 200, 216, 218, 224, 226-28, 232, 236-39, 241, 242, 245
Perseverance (see also Endurance, Preservation), vii, 5, 6, 9, 11, 12, 17, 23-25, 27, 29, 31, 34, 36, 45, 52, 55, 59, 63, 67, 71, 77-81, 92, 103-5, 118, 124, 125, 135, 151, 162, 172, 180, 184, 197, 216-18, 224-28, 230, 233, 253, 256, 259, 261
Preservation/Kept, 56, 61, 80, 101, 114f, 127, 161-64, 170, 181, 210, 216-18, 223-29
Peter, vii, ix, xv, 1, 4, 6, 41, 42, 44, 73, 92, 105-73, 195, 196, 203, 208, 234-48
Pharisee, 40, 74, 116, 236, 242

323

Subject Index

Pigs, 50, 143, 147
Poor, the, 75, 76, 79, 89–91, 240
Prayer, xv, xvi, 3, 9, 10, 23, 77–79, 84, 85, 87, 95, 122, 188, 209
Predestination (see also Determinism), 118, 162, 215
Preexistence, 44, 160
Preventatives (against apostasy, etc.), 23–27, 29, 33, 68, 80, 120, 235
Pride, 156, 186, 236, 239
Priest(hood), 5–9, 11, 15, 17, 25, 28, 30f, 39, 49–51, 66, 73, 98f, 112, 117, 171, 180, 189, 196f, 204, 224
Prison, imprisonment, 3f, 6, 48, 54, 67, 108, 181, 194, 196, 198, 217, 232
Pseudonym, 72, 105, 133, 154
Punishment, Divine (see Judgment) 46, 59, 82, 99, 102, 120, 173, 191, 205, 206
Purpose of God, divine necessity, 56

Qal Wahomer, 16, 52, 64, 164
Qumran, Qumran community (see also Essenes), 41, 196, 201, 254

Racism (Prejudice), 236
Reciprocation, 17, 101, 172, 184
Reconciliation, 38, 97, 248
Redeem, Redemption, 82, 112, 119, 139, 140, 152, 153, 191, 227
Religious authorities/leaders, 180, 194
Reluctant Listening, 30–33
Remnant, 10, 24, 26, 82, 97, 99–101, 106, 112, 114, 116, 127, 162, 171, 184, 207, 224–28, 231, 232, 256, 260
Renunciation (see also Deny), 44, 129, 178, 192, 198, 245f
Repent, Repentance, 9, 19, 31, 32, 34, 36–42, 49, 63, 64, 68, 70, 98, 101, 102, 131, 141, 145, 146, 148–50, 152, 170, 184, 188–91, 201, 202, 204, 206, 208, 209, 214–16, 221, 223, 224, 230, 231, 236, 239, 240, 242, 243, 260, 263
Resident Aliens, 4, 107–112, 119, 129
Rest (enter into; see also Sabbath), 27–29
Restore, Restoration, 1, 3, 9, 10, 22, 37–44, 52, 68–71, 74, 82, 85, 96–104, 116, 122–24, 130, 150, 152, 157, 159, 164, 171, 173, 174, 193, 224, 225, 231, 232, 236, 242–48, 255

Resurrection, 32, 65, 93, 186
Responsibility (human), 10, 79, 112, 125, 135, 148, 162, 172, 202
Reversal, 50, 124, 147, 181, 193, 221, 260
Rhetoric, 27, 46, 52, 88, 91, 112, 135, 156, 176, 249, 251, 253, 255, 259, 261, 264
Rich, Riches (see also Greed), 77, 85, 86, 89, 90, 160, 188, 194, 219, 220, 222
Righteous/Righteousness, unrighteous, 11, 14, 21, 36, 55, 56, 59, 60, 65, 68, 74, 81, 83–86, 88, 93, 95, 104, 122, 126, 134–36, 139, 141–43, 145–47, 150–52, 158, 165–67, 176, 185, 190–92, 203–5, 207, 210, 213–16, 218, 221, 230, 240, 241, 248
Rome, 3, 4, 33, 42, 44, 63, 69, 75, 82, 106–108, 127, 128, 177, 178, 180, 195, 198, 200, 201, 223, 228, 232, 235–237, 239, 242

Sabbath, 5, 28
Salvation, xv, 3, 6, 9–12, 14–19, 22, 29, 30, 35–38, 46, 50, 55, 59, 61, 67, 82, 83, 86, 88, 89, 103, 104, 112, 113, 114, 116, 119–23, 125, 126, 130, 137, 141, 150, 157, 158, 161, 172, 173, 176, 177, 193, 214, 225–27, 229, 246
Sanctify, Sanctification, Holiness, 15, 17, 28, 35, 50f, 59–62, 69, 78, 98, 114, 116, 146, 149, 158, 191, 210
Sanhedrin, 27, 41, 74, 160, 166, 199, 202
Satan (the Devil, Evil one), 83, 88, 102, 125, 127–29, 164, 179, 186, 191, 192, 194–98, 205, 207, 214, 217, 218, 227–29, 244, 253, 255, 259
    Roaring Lion (as a), 127–29
    "Synagogue of," 194–97, 217
    Throne of, 197–204
Second Coming, 17, 29, 48, 78, 114, 119, 130, 133, 134, 164, 170, 181, 189, 190, 202, 205, 208, 210, 224, 233
Second Death, 168f, 192, 197, 202f, 206, 209, 231
Second Exodus (see New Exodus)
Sect, Sectarian, 7, 22, 62, 110, 138, 186, 187, 196, 235, 254
Security, 61, 111, 226, 232, 248

Subject Index

Seven Churches (of Asia Minor; see Community), 182–84
Sexual Immorality (see Fornication), 23, 41, 63, 83, 161, 167, 171, 200, 231
Shame (see Ashamed), 33, 38, 58, 59, 112, 124, 207, 220, 221, 240, 243, 251, 252
Shrink back, 54–57, 59, 67–69
Sin (see also Vices, Idolatry, Fornication, Greed), 9, 11, 21, 23, 24, 28, 38–43, 46, 49–51, 55–58, 69, 70, 77, 80–82, 86, 89, 90, 95–97, 102–104, 121, 122, 124, 137, 145, 147–49, 152, 159, 165, 171, 172, 188, 189, 191, 199, 201, 221, 240, 242, 254, 266
    Sinner(s), 69, 85, 94, 97, 171,
    Sinning, 9, 48, 49, 56, 141, 143
    Willful Sin, 48–52
Six-hundred and sixty-six (666), 177
Sluggishness, 30, 210
Spiritual Dullness, 30, 37, 40, 48, 67, 100, 136, 191
Standing firm, Steadfast, 10, 27, 79f, 85, 110–13, 125, 127, 150–52
Star(s), 170, 173, 193, 207f, 227f
Stephen, 6, 74
Stumbling block, 184, 187, 199
Suffer(ing), 11, 17, 29, 30, 42, 44, 46, 47, 58, 59, 68, 71, 77–82, 89, 90, 98, 100–102, 104, 107–9, 111, 113, 114, 119, 122–26, 128–31, 140, 152, 160, 165, 168, 180, 182, 184, 192, 197, 206, 216, 218, 221, 226, 227, 230, 231, 232, 236–39, 241, 250, 252
Synagogue, 7, 8, 72, 75, 89, 194–196, 198, 212, 217, 221, 229, 253

Tempt(ation), 7, 77, 79–82, 86, 89, 95, 103, 104, 111, 123, 129, 141, 184, 208, 222, 232
Testing, Trials, 19, 20, 41, 76–79, 84, 86, 93, 95, 103, 104, 108, 111, 113, 119, 123–25, 128, 129, 141, 182, 196, 217
Thief in the Night, 128, 134, 202, 208
Tongue (misuse of the), 87–89
Torture, 47, 108, 181
Triumph(al Procession), 121, 210
Two Ways, 60, 77, 84–86, 95, 96, 104, 142, 143, 147, 151, 152, 165, 244

Unbelief, 10, 21, 23, 24, 29, 37, 40, 41, 57, 68, 117, 118, 121, 160, 161, 163, 236, 239, 241, 245
Unfaithful (see Faith, Faithfulness), 10, 48, 83, 99, 199, 200
Ungodly, 126, 141f, 149f, 156–60, 164–66, 170, 172f

Vice(s), 63, 91, 119, 129, 135, 136, 143, 144, 158, 163, 164, 173, 192, 199, 205, 210, 222, 224, 231, 238, 240, 241, 246, 251
Vilification, 49, 63, 90, 111, 130, 157, 172, 195, 243
Virtues, 28, 34, 47, 84, 102, 111, 135–37, 152, 251
Vomit, 146–48, 152, 184, 219, 221

Warning (see also Exhortation), 1, 7–13, 15, 17–23, 26f, 29f, 33f, 36, 39, 46, 53f, 57, 66–68, 70, 82, 87, 97f, 119, 149, 161f, 186, 189, 191, 199, 203f, 208, 216, 224, 229f, 232–34, 240f, 243, 245
Watch Motif, 14, 37, 61, 128, 129, 208, 222
Wavering, 46–48, 69
Wealth (see also Rich, Riches), 6, 60, 77, 83, 84, 89, 90, 103, 104, 131, 178, 179, 188, 194, 219–23, 230, 232, 235, 239, 240, 263
Whore of Babylon, 200, 205, 220, 224, 231f
Wilderness (–Generation), 11f, 19–29, 33–35, 38, 41, 49, 56f, 62, 68f, 99–101, 106, 112, 115f, 118–21, 124, 127–30, 160–63, 167, 172f, 189, 203, 228, 236, 244
Will of God/Lord, 78, 84, 146, 160
Wisdom (see Knowledge, spiritual), 5, 14, 36, 75, 77, 79, 83–86, 103, 104, 136, 146, 147, 217, 250,
Woe, 165
Women, 63, 135, 143, 151, 152, 161, 163, 166, 167, 199, 222
Works, Deeds (see also Law, works of the), 22, 28, 30, 31, 41, 47, 55, 75, 76, 80, 86, 87, 89–94, 102, 104, 111, 112, 115, 158, 159, 165, 166, 168, 181, 185, 187–89, 192, 194, 202, 203, 204, 206, 207, 211, 213, 221, 230, 239, 241, 244, 246, 248

Subject Index

World, *cosmos*, 4, 12, 15, 27, 44, 50, 54, 80, 81, 83–88, 95, 103, 108, 109, 114, 118, 123, 138, 140, 141, 143–45, 149, 150, 153, 160, 170, 176, 191, 197, 202, 2503, 206, 209, 213, 214, 216, 217, 220, 222, 228, 230, 235, 236, 240, 248, 254

Zealot, 76
Zion (heavenly; see also New Jerusalem), 29, 45, 64–68, 114, 117, 123, 228

www.ingramcontent.com/pod-product-compliance
Lightning Source LLC
Chambersburg PA
CBHW080118020526
44112CB00037B/2770